Y0-ARX-142

Java™ CAPS Basics

Java™ CAPS Basics

Implementing Common EAI Patterns

Michael Czapski
Sebastian Krueger
Brendan Marry
Saurabh Sahai
Peter Vaneris
Andrew Walker

PRENTICE HALL

Upper Saddle River, NJ • Boston • Indianapolis • San Francisco
New York • Toronto • Montreal • London • Munich • Paris • Madrid
Capetown • Sydney • Tokyo • Singapore • Mexico City

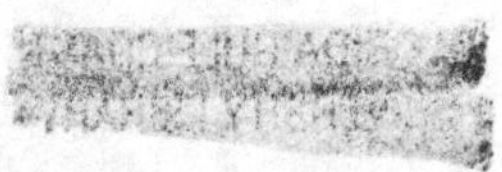

The publisher offers excellent discounts on this book when ordered in quantity for bulk purchases or special sales, which may include electronic versions and/or custom covers and content particular to your business, training goals, marketing focus, and branding interests. For more information, please contact: U.S. Corporate and Government Sales, (800) 382-3419, corpsales@pearsontechgroup.com.

For sales outside the United States, please contact: International Sales, international@pearsoned.com.

This Book Is Safari Enabled

The Safari® Enabled icon on the cover of your favorite technology book means the book is available through Safari Bookshelf. When you buy this book, you get free access to the online edition for 45 days.

Safari Bookshelf is an electronic reference library that lets you easily search thousands of technical books, find code samples, download chapters, and access technical information whenever and wherever you need it.

To gain 45-day Safari Enabled access to this book:

- Go to informit.com/onlineedition
- Complete the brief registration form
- Enter the coupon code RSGP-E1MF-1USJ-UKFG-MUS6

If you have difficulty registering on Safari Bookshelf or accessing the online edition, please e-mail customer-service@safaribooksonline.com.

Visit us on the Web: informit.com/ph

Library of Congress Cataloging-in-Publication Data

Java CAPS basics : implementing common EAI patterns / Michael Czapski ...
[et al.].
p. cm.
Includes bibliographical references and index.
ISBN-13: 978-0-13-713071-9 (hardcover : alk. paper)
ISBN-10: 0-13-713071-6 (hardcover : alk. paper)
1. Java (Computer program language) 2. Enterprise application integration (Computer systems) I. Czapski, Michael.
QA76.73.J38J3633 2008
005.13'3—dc22 2008007526

ISBN-13: 978-0-13-713071-9
ISBN-10: 0-13-713071-6
Text printed in the United States on recycled paper at Courier in Westford, Massachusetts.
First printing, April 2008

Contents

Preface

In their book *Enterprise Integration Patterns: Designing, Building, and Deploying Messaging Solutions* [EIP], Gregor Hohpe and Bobby Woolf elaborate on the subject of Enterprise Application Integration using messaging. They present, discuss, and illustrate over sixty EAI design patterns. These patterns, they believe, are key patterns most designers of EAI solutions will use when building enterprise integration solutions. Most examples in [EIP] use raw C# and raw Java to illustrate details of EAI patterns under discussion. Most of these patterns can be implemented succinctly, elegantly, and comprehensively using tools and technologies provided in the Sun Java Composite Application Platform Suite [Java CAPS].

This book is about implementing selected enterprise integration patterns, discussed in [EIP], using Java CAPS as the means to building practical enterprise integration solutions. It bridges the gap between the somewhat abstract pattern language and the practical implementation details. It is designed for integration architects, solution architects, and developers who wish to quickly implement enterprise solutions with Java CAPS. It discusses how enterprise integration patterns can be implemented quickly and efficiently by leveraging the Java CAPS tools and the authors' field experience.

While this book discusses Java CAPS implementation of [EIP] patterns, it does not discuss the patterns in depth. It is assumed that you are already familiar with the subject and need to apply the theoretical knowledge using Java CAPS.

This book is also about basics of the essential Java CAPS Suite components, based on the premise that you cannot apply patterns if you cannot effectively use the tools with which to do it. Since the complete Java CAPS offering has so many components, including ones that are not essential to integration, this book elaborates only on the basic integration tools: eGate, eInsight, eWays, and Java Message Service (JMS).

This book also provides information you may need to effectively use Java CAPS. A considerable amount of Java CAPS-related material, provided in the text, is not published anywhere else.

The accompanying CD-ROM provides over 60 detailed examples that illustrate concepts and patterns under discussion. Some examples are high level, illustrating specific points. Other examples follow a step-by-step approach.

Java CAPS projects discussed and developed as examples are available for import and perusal.

How This Book Is Organized

This book is divided into three sections. Section I, "Preliminaries," contains chapters that discuss integration and background Java CAPS topics, including enterprise integration styles, Java CAPS architecture, and project structure and deployment.

Section II, "Patterns Review and Application," covers most [EIP] patterns with discussion of Java CAPS approaches to implementing them. This section includes chapters dealing with message exchange patterns, message correlation, messaging infrastructure, message routing, message construction, message transformation, messaging endpoints, and system management patterns and concepts. While discussing Java CAPS implementation of specific patterns, relevant Java CAPS concepts and methods are also discussed. When discussing implementations of the Message Sequence pattern, for example, Java CAPS concepts of JMS serial mode concurrency, Sun SeeBeyond JMS Message Server FIFO modes, and serializing eInsight Business Processes via JMS and XA are also discussed.

Section III, "Specialized Java CAPS Topics," discusses non-pattern matters of importance like solution partitioning, subprocess and Web Services implementation, management, reusability, scalability and resilience options, and others that are not covered elsewhere. This section also covers security features of Java CAPS.

The accompanying CD-ROM contains over 60 detailed examples implementing most of the patterns and concepts under discussion as well as two complete example solutions using many of the patterns discussed and illustrated in this book. The CD-ROM also contains a detailed practical walkthrough of generation and use of cryptographic objects such as X.509 Certificates, PKCS#12 and JKS Keystores, and related matters.

About the Examples

Conventions

Java CAPS Enterprise Designer (eDesigner) is a NetBeans-based Integrated Development Environment (IDE), which developers use to design and build Java CAPS integration solutions. The vast majority of tasks can be accomplished in eDesigner by means of manipulating components represented by graphical objects, connecting graphical objects with lines, filling information in dialog boxes and property sheets, and choosing components in drop-down menus. The intention was to make development of integration solutions easy for business analysts and similar persons whose coding skills might not be up to the task in nongraphical environments. Since development of Java CAPS solutions results in production of J2EE Enterprise Applications, this graphical orientation might come as a bit of a surprise to hardcore J2EE developers used to writing raw Java and the fine-grained control they exercise through deployment descriptors and other J2EE artifacts. Be that as it may, you will find most Java Collaboration examples shown using Java source code rather than its graphical equivalent. This is principally to make the samples concise, clearly showing essential parts of each solution, and to minimize wasting space on graphics that add no particular value to the discussion. Every one of the Java Collaborations could have been shown in "Standard mode," but that would have required numerous pictures, pretty much one for each Java statement, to illustrate what just a few lines of Java code can show in just a few lines. Figure P-1 shows an example of a Java Collaboration in Standard mode.

Evident are several lines of pseudocode in the Business Rules pane and just one mapping in the Business Rules Designer pane.

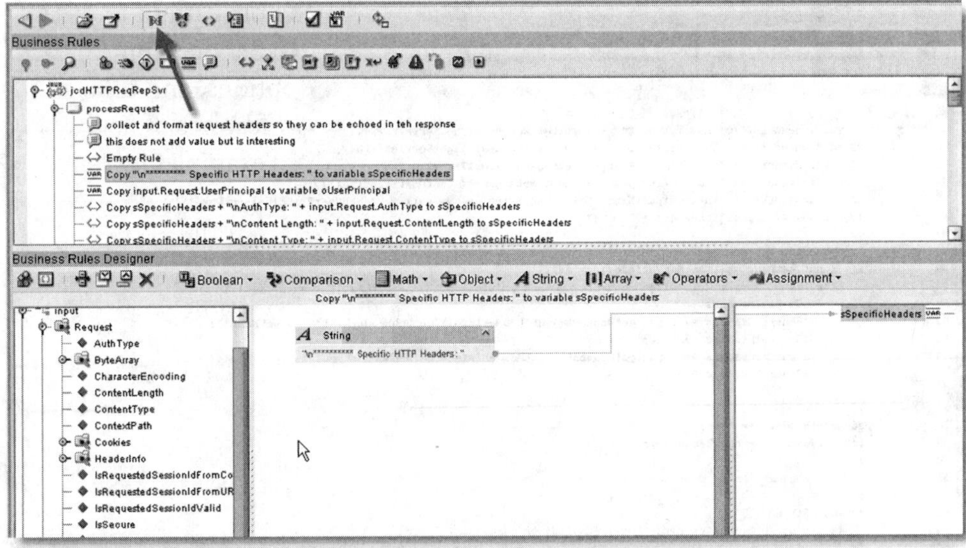

FIGURE P-1: Java Collaboration in Standard mode

In contrast, the same Java Collaboration in Source Code mode is much more illuminating, as seen in Figure P-2, as it shows all there is to know about 30 or so lines of code all at once.

Since switching between Standard mode and Source Code mode is a button-click away, we chose to use Source Code mode for Java Collaboration examples.

eInsight Business Processes are much easier to understand when presented in the graphical view, appearing similar to what is shown in Figure P-3. Object icons, taken from the Business Process Modeling Notation, are quite pleasant to look at, in this author's opinion.

In contrast, working directly with BPEL4WS XML source, an example of which is shown in Figure P-4, which is possible, is in this author's opinion bordering on cruel and unusual punishment, just as working directly with any other XML-based procedural language would be.

So, Java Collaborations are mostly shown in the Source Code mode, and eInsight Business Processes are mostly shown with the Business Rules Designer.

How you work with the tool is still up to you.

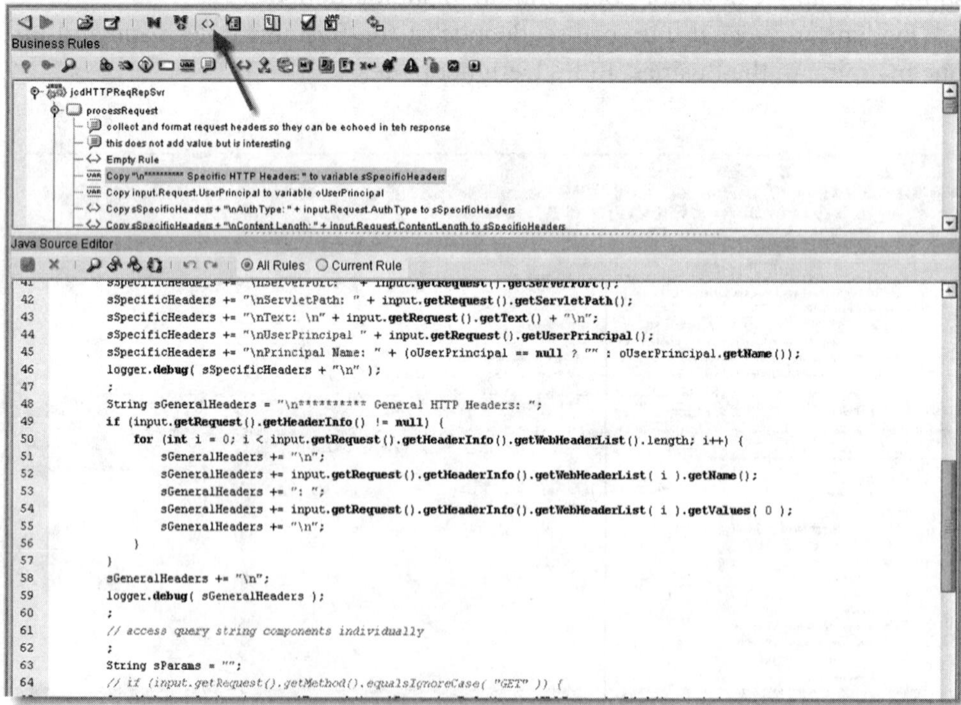

FIGURE P-2: Java Collaboration in Source Code mode

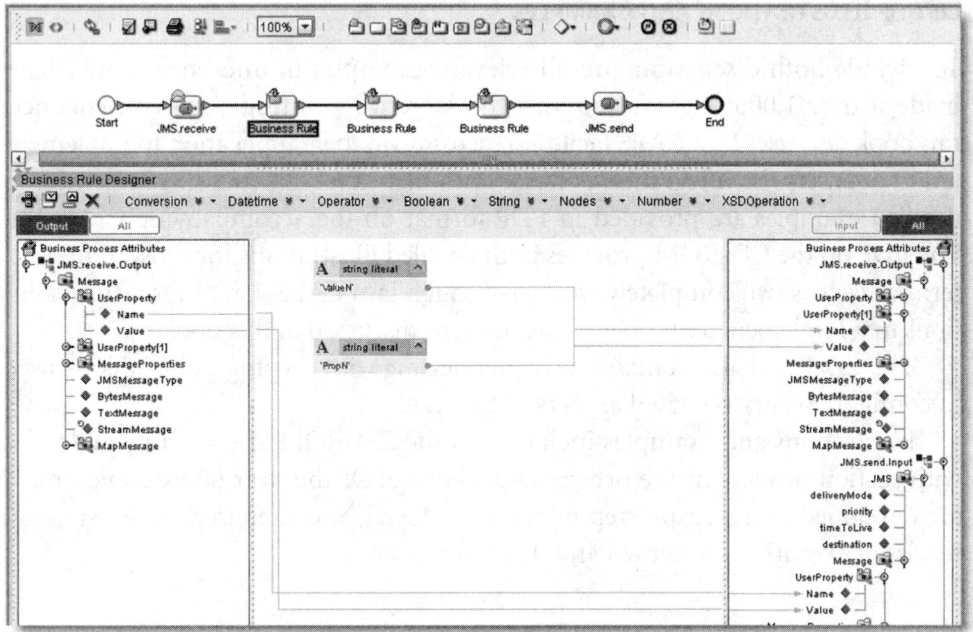

FIGURE P-3: eInsight Business Processes in the graphical view

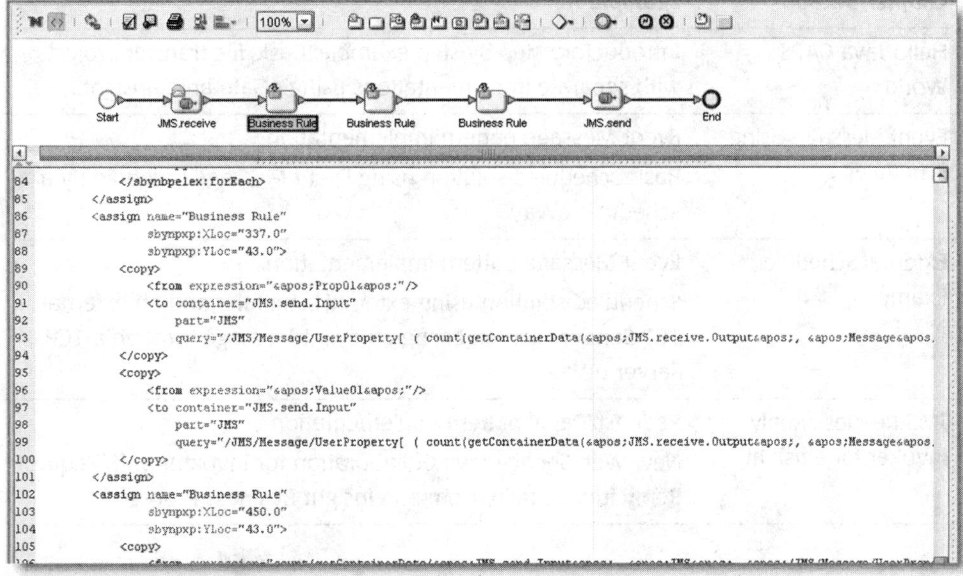

FIGURE P-4: BPEL4WS XML source

List of Illustrations and Examples

To include both discussion and all relevant examples in one book would have made it over 1,000 pages in length—too large for printing. As a consequence, this book discusses Java CAPS facilities, focusing on their application to implementation of enterprise integration patterns with high-level illustrations. References to detailed examples are provided in PDF format on the accompanying CD-ROM. The PDF on the CD-ROM provides both detailed illustrations for most of the patterns as well as two completely worked-through Java CAPS–based case study solutions that implement a number of the patterns discussed in this book.

The CD-ROM also contains a chapter dealing with cryptographic objects used to configure security-related aspects of the suite.

Illustrations and examples included on the CD-ROM are listed in Table P-1, with section headers in the order of appearance. Of the over 60 examples, most are developed in a step-by-step manner, deployed, and exercised. In most cases, results of execution are shown and discussed.

Table P-1: Illustrations and Examples in Part II

Chapter/Section	*Example Topic*
Hello Java CAPS World	Introductory step-by-step example. Basic file transfer projects with separate implementations using eGate and eInsight.
Event Message Using Scheduler	Event Message pattern implementation. Basic scheduled solution using Event Message triggered by a Scheduler eWay.
External Scheduler Example	Event Message pattern implementation. Scheduled solution using external scheduler and an external TCP Sender client injecting an Event Message through a TCP Server eWay.
JMS Request/Reply Invoker for eInsight	Request/Reply pattern implementation. New Web Service Java Collaboration for invoking JMS Request/Reply functionality from an eInsight Business Process.

TABLE P-1: Illustrations and Examples in Part II *(continued)*

Chapter/Section	*Example Topic*
JMS Request/ Response Auction Pattern	Request/Reply pattern implementation. Java Collaboration and JMS Request/Reply–based implementation of an Auction pattern where the fastest responder wins.
HTTP Request/ Response	Request/Reply pattern implementation. A series of HTTP requestor and HTTP responder implementations using both HTML and XML payloads, prefaced by a recap of HTTP principles and mechanics.
SOAP Request/ Response	Request/Reply pattern implementation. Specialization of a HTTP request/response implementation using explicitly constructed and parsed SOAP XML messages as requests and responses.
Web Service Request/ Reply	Request/Reply pattern implementation. Web Service request/response implementation as an example of a Request/Response pattern using both eInsight Business Processes and Java Collaborations.
JMS Serial Mode Concurrency	Message Sequence pattern. Using Sun SeeBeyond JMS Message Server facilities for implementation of message sequence preserving solutions.
Sun SeeBeyond JMS FIFO Modes	Using Sun SeeBeyond JMS Message Server facilities for implementation of message sequence preserving solutions. Series of examples demonstrates the impact of different Sun SeeBeyond JMS Message Server FIFO modes on message sequence.
Serializing Business Processes with XA	Message Sequence pattern. Examples illustrating the impact of imposing XA transactionality on eInsight Business Processes and how it affects message sequence preservation (new in v. 5.1)
Message Expiration	Java Collaboration and JMS-based example illustrating Message Expiration.

(continues)

TABLE P-1: Illustrations and Examples in Part II *(continued)*

Chapter/Section	***Example Topic***
Batch Local File Streaming	Data streaming examples using Batch Local File eWay with discussion of buffering and its impact on message throughput.
eTL Streaming	Very basic eTL example streaming data from a flat file to a database table and a functionally equivalent Java Collaboration example.
Temporary JMS Destinations	Anti-example illustrating the use of an explicitly created JMS temporary destination.
Static Selector	Example illustrating the use of static JMS selectors.
Dynamic Selector	Example illustrating the use of dynamic JMS selectors, constructed at runtime and used in a Java Collaboration to explicitly choose messages to receive.
Resilient JMS with JMS Grid	Example of a simple JMS Grid-based automatic JMS Client failover.
JMS Message Body Formats	Example collaboration that inspects JMS header properties to determine JMS message body format and branch.
Dead Letter Channel in 5.1.2	Example exercising JMS Redelivery Handling functionality with undeliverable message being delivered to a Dead Letter Queue.
eInsight XA Transactionality	Example inducing success and failure outcomes that demonstrate XA transactionality of an eInsight Business Process with side effects in non-XA-capable resources.
eInsight Persistence	Illustration of eInsight persistence, eInsight monitoring, and eInsight restart-recovery of in-flight process instances.
Resequencer: Basic Version	Simple resequencer with memory-based message buffer.
Resequencer: Persisted Version	More sophisticated resequencer with RDBMS-based message buffer and message sequence persistence.
Routing Slip	Routing slip-based message routing solution using JSM and Java Collaborations.
JMS User Properties Envelope Wrappers	Series of examples demonstrating Envelope Wrapper pattern implemented using JMS message header properties in Java Collaborations and eInsight Business Processes.

TABLE P-1: Illustrations and Examples in Part II *(continued)*

Chapter/Section	*Example Topic*
Content Enricher	Content Enricher implementation using eInsight and Oracle eWay to receive a Purchase Order, enrich it with pricing information for an Oracle database, and produce an Invoice.
Polling File System	Series of examples polling local file system using Scheduler eWay–driven and Batch Inbound–driven Batch Local File eWay to implement polling solutions.
Polling JMS Destination	Try-wait-retry FTP delivery solution implementing JMS Destination polling for retry scheduling.
Durable Subscriber	Example illustrating the concept of a JMS topic durable subscriber and behavioral differences between nondurable and durable subscribers.
Idempotent Receiver	Example illustrating message duplication detection–based Idempotent receiver solution.
Multi-Input Service Activator	Example using the OpenTravel Alliances XML Schema documents to implement a Service Activator solution that allows the business service to be activated through a file submission, JMS message submission, and Web Services invocation.
Monitoring eInsight-based Solutions	Example illustrating eInsight persistence, persistence for reporting, and runtime monitoring of eInsight Business Process instances.
Simple Alert Processor for a JMS Channel	Example implementing a simple solution that receives and processes Alert Agent alerts delivered through the JMS Alert Channel.
Catching "Uncatchable" Exceptions	Example using Alert Agent infrastructure to catch and process exceptions that occur outside the Java Collaborations and Business Processes and therefore cannot be caught and processed in JCDs or BPs. Catching and processing a database connectivity exception is the subject of this example.
Programmatic Management	Example Java Collaboration that uses the JMX instrumentation to programmatically start and stop a specified Java CAPS component, such as another Java Collaboration or a Business Process service.

(continues)

TABLE P-1: Illustrations and Examples in Part II *(continued)*

Chapter/Section	*Example Topic*
JMS Latency	Java Collaboration and eInsight Business Process examples illustrating calculation of JMS message delivery latency.
eInsight Correlation Processor: First Cut	Example of an incorrect, naïve implementation of eInsight correlation.
eInsight Correlation Processor: Second Cut	Example of correct implementation of a simple eInsight correlation with a simple correlation key.
Derived Correlation Identifiers	Example of a more complex eInsight correlation with a structured, message-derived correlation key based on a subprocess-based correlation key derivation solution.
Derived Correlation Identifiers: Alternative	Alternative example of a more complex eInsight correlation with a structured, message-derived correlation key based on Java Collaboration correlation key derivation preprocessor.
Message Relationship Patterns	Series of examples of using eInsight correlation facilities to implement Message Relationship patterns: Header-Items-Trailer Correlation, Any Order Two Items Correlation, Any Order Two Items Correlation with Timeout, Items-Trailer Correlation, Header Counted Items Correlation, Counted and Timed Items Correlation, Timed Items Correlation, Scatter-Gather Correlation.
Items-Trailer Correlation	Reimplementation of the Items-Trailer Correlation using a Java Collaboration, JMS, and dynamic JMS selectors—no eInsight.
Using New Web Service Collaborations	Example of using New Web Service Java Collaborations to implement reusable modules for use as activities in eInsight Business Processes.
Using eInsight Subprocesses for Reusability	Series of examples of using eInsight subprocesses as reusable components for use as activities in eInsight Business Processes: Request/Response, OneWay Operation, and Notification Subprocess implementations.
Using eInsight Web Services for Reusability	Series of examples of using Web Services as reusable components for use as activities in eInsight Business Processes: Request/Response, OneWay Operation, and Notification Web Service implementations.
JMS-Triggered Java Collaborations	Example of exception and JMS redelivery handling in a JMS message–triggered Java Collaboration.

TABLE P-1: Illustrations and Examples in Part II *(continued)*

Chapter/Section	***Example Topic***
Other Java Collaborations	Example of exception processing in a non-JMS message–triggered Java Collaboration.
JMS-Triggered Business Processes	Example of exception handling in a JMS message–triggered eInsight Business Process demonstrating behavior differences between XA and non-XA processes.
Fault Handlers	Example of using Fault Handlers in eInsight Business Processes.
Secure Sockets Layer (SSL, TLS)	Series of examples illustrating the use of SSL in Java CAPS solutions, both HTTP eWay- and Web Services-based. Covers server-side and mutual authentication for both server and client endpoints.
Web Service, Stored Procedures, and XA	Complete case study implementing an Employee Database Maintenance process with a multi-database update, Web Services, Oracle Stored Procedures, and an XA Business Process. This example implements and exercises a large number of patterns and suite features.
Example Travel Reservation	Complete Travel Reservation case study using Web Services orchestration and eInsight exception handling and compensation. This example implements and exercises a large number of patterns and suite features.
Handling Repeating Nodes in BPEL	Example of handling repeating nodes from XSD-based OTD in eInsight.
XML Deep Parse vs. Shallow Parse	Example implementing lazy XMLparse.
Using Multi-Operation WSDL	Example of implementing a multi-operation Web Service using WSDL and eInsight.
Cryptographic Objects	Step-by-step discussion of cryptographic objects required to configure PKI-related aspects of Java CAPS, with tools, commands, and scripts necessary to create certificate signing requests, convert between various certificate formats, and create various keystore types.

Acknowledgments

First and foremost, I would like to acknowledge my family, Lorraine, Natalie, and Daniel, who graciously tolerated the long hours I put into this project, encouraged me through the process, and rejoiced with me as I reached each significant milestone. Without their support, this project would not be possible.

Sun's announcement of the Red October program in November 2005, under which all Sun Software was going to be made available for download and use, was met with mixed reaction among some of the former SeeBeyond folk. Java CAPS is a complex enterprise application integration platform, not a lone-developer IDE or a data center technologist–configured infrastructure package. Some felt that making the Java CAPS suite freely downloadable would be unhelpful. This was particularly so as a major gap was perceived to exist between material in product documentation and the product and context knowledge an enterprise architect and integration developer would need to effectively use Java CAPS. I felt that a book bridging this gap, and showing examples of Java CAPS solutions implementing enterprise integration patterns, would be appropriate and timely.

Although the manuscript took three times as long to write as I originally anticipated, I made some of the material available to individuals both inside and outside Sun well before it was completed. This was to validate the original intent, to help answer specific questions, and to get early feedback on the content and coverage of various topics. I wish to acknowledge these individuals, particularly Jason Baragry, who took time to review most of the chapters and provided valuable feedback that helped shape the manuscript. I also wish to acknowledge other members of the seebeyond-l community at the ITtoolbox, who took time to provide feedback and who encouraged me to continue.

While this project is largely my own and was almost exclusively undertaken in my own time, there were occasions when I worked on it during my regular hours. Ray Gear at SeeBeyond and subsequently at Sun, and Angelo Joseph at Sun, are due credit for encouraging me to finish the project and tolerating the occasional diversion.

I wish to thank my collaborators, Sebastian Krueger, Brendan Marry, Saurabh Sahai, Peter Vaneris, and Andrew Walker, all talented Java CAPS field practitioners, for providing material for various chapters and for reviewing the manuscript. In particular, the topics Brendan and Peter addressed would likely not have been covered if they had not provided the material. I would also like to thank Dean Hansen, who provided notes on some of the material in early chapters and reviewed parts of the material.

Special thanks go to Jason Fordham and Peter C. Berkman, my colleagues at Sun, for trying to make a virtual image of the Solaris 10-based Java CAPS installation available in time for inclusion on the CD-ROM accompanying the book. Although through no fault of theirs this did not happen, I am grateful to them for the effort.

Last, but not least, I would like to thank Carol J. Lallier, who made sure the text is in English, however American it may be; Kim Arney, who laid out the book; Diane Freed and Richard Evans, who proofed and indexed the book; Elizabeth C. Ryan, who managed the publication process; Myrna Rivera, Gabriele De Celis, and Laurie Wong, my colleagues at Sun Microsystem, who handled the promotion of this book inside and outside Sun; and Greg Doench, who took a punt and walked me through the process of writing and publishing a book.

Michael Czapski
Sydney, December 2007

About the Authors

Michael Czapski has 25 years of experience in the IT industry, the last 10 in the field of enterprise application integration. He provides Java CAPS expertise and leverages Java CAPS capabilities in solutions spanning the spectrum of Sun Microsystems software offerings.

Michael has written a number of technical whitepapers on various topics for ICAN and Java CAPS, addressing, among others, Java CAPS security configuration, WS-Security implementation in Java CAPS, and application of EAI patterns to Java CAPS solutions. He is a Java CAPS Apostle, an active contributor to Java CAPS communities and forums, and a presenter at various industry conferences.

Sebastian Krueger started working on EAI software with SeeBeyond ICAN 5.0.5 in late 2005 and has since worked on all Sun Java CAPS eGate, eInsight, and eXchange product components, as well as on JMS Grid.

Initially providing Java CAPS consulting services to the New Zealand market, he now works for the Inland Revenue Department of New Zealand, where he is a senior analyst programmer.

Sebastian is a Sun-Certified Java Programmer and an LPI-Certified Linux Professional.

Brendan Marry has over 10 years of experience in IT and is currently an integration solutions architect for Sun Microsystems in Auckland, New Zealand, responsible for the design and delivery of enterprise integration architectures using Java CAPS.

He has over 4 years of experience at Sun, specifically around the Sun Java CAPS. Brendan worked in the Java Mobile space and Java Enterprise space in Europe before immigrating to New Zealand and joining Sun. He enjoys providing project management and solution architectural advice, vision, and guidance to his clients using the Java CAPS products.

Saurabh Sahai has over 13 years of experience in IT, developing enterprise-class middleware software and commercial solutions for major software vendors. Over the past 4 years, he has worked as an integration architect within the Sun SOA/EAI professional service practice, where he is responsible for the architecture and delivery of advanced Sun Java CAPS–based solutions to major commercial and government clients within Australia and New Zealand.

Prior to Sun Microsystems, he worked for about 9 years as a J2EE/middleware architect for Fujitsu Australia Software Technologies, developing Java/J2EE/C++–based middleware software for Fujitsu's INTERSTAGE enterprise product set. He has extensive experience developing commercial J2EE applications using major application servers and open-source frameworks.

Saurabh is based in Sydney, Australia, and loves listening to jazz in his spare time.

Peter Vaneris has 19 years of experience in the IT industry, the last 2 in the field of Java CAPS support. Prior to working with Java CAPS, Peter specialized in system administration, monitoring, automation, and enterprise management.

Andrew Walker has 18 years of experience in IT and originally joined SeeBeyond in January 1999, where he started working with one of the early EAI software products, then known as DataGate. Subsequently, he has worked with all the EAI software products released by SeeBeyond and now Sun Microsystems. Andrew has broad experience in architecting and implementing EAI and SOA solutions for customers in the Asia–Pacific region. He is currently based in Singapore and provides Java CAPS consulting services throughout the Asia–Pacific region as part of his job role in Sun Microsystems Professional Services.

SECTION I

Preliminaries

CHAPTER ONE

Enterprise Integration Styles

With contributions from Dean Hansen

1.1 Introduction

Java CAPS is a toolbox that supports many Enterprise Application Integration (EAI) styles. Its core components deliver message-based application-to-application integration. Java CAPS also enables other styles of integration, including composite applications, Web Services orchestration, single-customer view, and service-oriented architectures.

The fundamental premise of application integration is that it should be non-invasive. This philosophical approach minimizes application changes and costs associated with integration. To that end, it leverages application capabilities rather than requiring applications to adapt to it. Because applications' integration capabilities vary, so too do integration styles that can be applied to them. In this spirit, an integration solution may use many different integration styles, driven by the capabilities of the applications being integrated. The following sections discuss the major integration styles and identify some of the Java CAPS components that can assist in their implementation.

This chapter also discusses issues of scalability and resilience and Java CAPS facilities that can assist in solution factoring for distribution and replication. These topics are discussed in greater detail in Chapter 13, "Scalability and Resilience."

1.2 File Transfer

File transfer is the most basic integration style. On the inbound side (inbound to the integration solution), it relies on the applications' ability to write data to files in a file system. On the outbound side (outbound from the integration solution), it relies on the applications' ability to read and process data from files in the file system. Applications would already be capable of interfacing with the file system or would be extended to produce/consume files. This is a rudimentary, non–real-time, batch-based, point-to-point approach that nevertheless is valid and appropriate in appropriate circumstances. A file transfer–based solution is not, by its nature, very scalable or very robust.

Java CAPS supports the file transfer integration style with a collection of Batch eWay Adapter variants. The Batch Local File eWay is appropriate for reading and writing files in the local file system.

The Batch FTP eWay is appropriate for pulling and pushing files to or from remote FTP servers. It includes support for Secure FTP variants such as FTP over SSL, SFTP (Secure FTP, a subprotocol of SSH), SCP (secure file copy, a subprotocol of SSH), and security infrastructure traversal variants with support for SOCKS and SSH tunneling.

The Batch Record eWay enables payload, delivered through one of the Batch eWay variants, to be broken up into fixed-length or delimited records, as well as assembly of messages into fixed-length or delimited records for writing to a file. The Batch Record eWay can be used in conjunction with the other Batch eWays to implement data streaming solutions that minimize memory consumption when processing large file payloads.

Finally, the Batch Inbound eWay, with its built-in interval times and the unique name feature, facilitates implementation of polling solutions that rename files as they find them and deliver unique filenames and paths to other inbound Batch eWays for processing.

Batch eWays can be used in conjunction with other Java CAPS components to implement file transfer–based solutions.

1.3 Database Sharing

[EIP] briefly discusses issues with multiple applications sharing a database and concludes that it is not the most appropriate method of application integration. While having multiple applications share one database might be difficult, because of the difficulty in developing a database schema that satisfies requirements of multiple disparate applications, it is no easier to share data between applications each with its own database. Whereas a solution with a single database shared by multiple applications does not require integration, a solution with multiple databases, or with a mix of a database and other external systems, does.

The major advantage of using database-based integration is that applications that already use databases do not need to be modified to enable the integration. Care must be taken, however, when updating data bypassing application logic, to avoid destroying referential integrity, some of which may be enforced by the databases and some of which may be provided by application logic.

The Java CAPS suite includes a series of eWay Adapters developed specifically to natively interoperate with all major relational databases and, through JDBC, with all JDBC-compliant databases. These adapters encapsulate all common database interaction functionality, including insert, update, delete and select operations on tables, views, prepared statements, and stored procedures. Each database-specific adapter provides a wizard that enables creation of Object Type Definitions corresponding to database objects, using schema metadata directly from the database. Solutions that select data from one or more databases and/or populate or update one or more other databases can be readily developed. Using Java-based database triggers, where a particular database supports this feature, a Java CAPS–based solution can be triggered to process inserted or updated data or to synchronize deletion with some other external system or data store, as close to real time as possible. Where not possible, a Java CAPS solution can poll database tables or views or schedule invocation of stored procedures.

For a database data structure to be accessed, an integration solution must embed the knowledge of this structure. This makes the solution tightly coupled to database structures and therefore potentially brittle. To offset this, a message transformation component may serve as a wrapper for the underlying database object, providing indirection and isolating the rest of the integration solution from the database structure.

Because of the heavy overhead of accessing and manipulating database resources, solutions that access databases may not be as scalable or perform as well as solutions that do not. If database schema contains binary large objects (BLOBs) or character large objects (CLOBs), the solutions will require special handling and will be more complex to implement and more resource intensive.

1.4 Remote Procedure Invocation

Distribution of functionality among multiple independent processes or hosts is what differentiates a monolithic application from a distributed application. Remote procedure call (RPC) [EIP] is the mechanism through which an application can remotely invoke specific functionality ("procedure") exposed by another application. This implies that the procedure encapsulates some functionality of interest, that the interface is published, and that both applications use the same wire protocol and data representation and semantics.

Of the common RPC technologies, Java CAPS, being Java-based, naturally supports Java Remote Method Invocation (RMI) and Common Object Request Broker Architecture (CORBA), though low-level Java programming is required. Through its ability to consume and publish Web Services, it also naturally supports that technology, though it does not support the RPC/Encoded style, as RCP/Encoded style is not WS-Interoperability compliant. In addition to these built-in capabilities, Java CAPS provides a COM/DCOM eWay Adapter that allows incorporation of COM/DCOM resources, such as Microsoft Excel spreadsheets, into enterprise integration solutions.

When necessary and appropriate, RPC can be used to orchestrate remote resources or expose a Java CAPS solution as a remotely invocable resource. Use of RPC-based technologies typically results in tightly coupled solutions, so care must be taken to minimize the amount of remote application knowledge that is built into a Java CAPS solution. Also note that most of the RPC technologies are platform-specific (COM/DCOM, Java RMI), thus making solutions nonportable and difficult to deploy and test. Care must be taken to isolate the use of such technologies into small, independently deployable components.

1.5 Messaging

[EIP] discusses shortcomings of file transfer, database sharing, and RPC and concludes that asynchronous messaging is the most appropriate pragmatic approach to EAI. [EIP] elaborates on the advantages and disadvantages, and contrasts this style with other integration styles.

Java CAPS is an excellent candidate to build a messaging system. It is, fundamentally, a many-to-many middleware messaging system, suitable for implementing both event-driven and service-oriented architectures. As a backbone messaging infrastructure, Java CAPS supports a number of Java Message Service (JMS) implementations from both Sun Microsystems and third parties. Both point-to-point and publish/subscribe messaging are supported. JMS API Kit is available to interface external applications directly to the JMS infrastructure. Message transformation logic can be implemented both in Java (Java Collaborations), Extensible Style Language (XSLT Collaborations), and Business Process Execution Language (BPEL).

Message routing can be implemented in Java and BPEL. Over 80 eWay Adapters are available to receive messages from external sources and deliver messages to external destinations. An eWay Development Kit facilitates development of custom adapters, if required. For these reasons, and because of its distributed nature, the product provides an enterprise architect with the flexibility to design the most appropriate solution to a given integration problem.

1.6 Service Orchestration

The notion of building services, with published interfaces and using standard wire protocols to encapsulate and expose specific application functionality, is gaining increasing popularity among enterprise architects. The idea that services can be combined in different ways to rapidly deliver differing business functionality has led to a great deal of activity aimed at the development of service-oriented architectures. Web Services, an implementation of the service concept using HTTP as the wire protocol to facilitate remote invocation across corporate firewalls, adopted XML for data representation and are generally invoked synchronously.

Business functionality is delivered, in this approach, through sequential invocation of appropriate services, also called service orchestration. Java CAPS eInsight is a business process manager and service orchestration engine. It can invoke Web Services, access non–Web Services external resources through eWay Adapters, implement transformation and routing logic, and so become the technology foundation of the enterprise service–oriented architecture. eInsight Business Processes and Java Collaborations can be exposed as Web Services invocable from other eInsight Business Processes, Java Collaborations, or external clients.

It is worth pointing out that Web Services—Simple Object Access Protocol (SOAP) over HTTP—largely suffers from the same problems as the RPC, most notably reliability, availability, scalability, latency, transactional integrity, ownership and control, and tight coupling between the client and the service. Deployment of Web Services intended to operate over untrusted networks, like the Internet, adds the issue of security and exacerbates the problems of latency, ownership and control, availability, and trust. These problems resulted in an explosion of standardization activities aimed at providing, for Web Services, the qualities of service taken for granted in traditional monolithic applications and which the original designers of SOAP never built into their design.

A complementary notion, that of building end-user applications providing a Web-based interface over orchestrations of enterprise resources, is the notion of

Composite Applications. It is argued that 80 percent of functionality required by a given end-user application would already be available as services or external system interfaces that can be exposed as services. The user interface and a small amount of "integration glue" would be required to deliver a new composite application that leverages the existing investment. Java CAPS provides all the tools necessary to build composite applications. The very name of the product embeds the notion of composite applications. eVision, a part of the Java CAPS suite, is the tool used to develop Web pages and Web page flows that orchestrate arbitrary resources in the same manner as a regular business process would.

Java CAPS allows the enterprise architect the flexibility to use all of the architectural styles in the same solution if requirements of the business dictate it.

1.7 Centralized versus Distributed

A typical integration solution connects multiple external systems to each other, performing enrichment, transformation, auditing, and other activities as messages are processed. The complexity of work that the integration solution must perform, and the architecture of the EAI toolset to be used, largely dictates the number of discrete components involved. The number of components, in turn, dictates both the scalability and the resiliency options available to the solution architect. Scalability and resiliency are both important, nonfunctional goals of the EAI architecture.

The fundamental component of the Java CAPS EAI solution is the Integration Server. Out of the box, Java CAPS 5.1.x Integration Server is the Sun Application Server 8.0 Platform Edition. Because they are Java EE compliant, Java CAPS Enterprise Applications can be deployed to a number of other Application Servers, including the Sun Application Server 8.2 Enterprise Edition and BEA WebLogic 9.1.

Java CAPS integration solutions are collections of Java EE applications, externally manifested as Enterprise Application Archive (EAR) files—self-contained units of functionality. Each Java EE application, the EAR file, is deployed to an Integration Server in its totality: no Java EE application can span multiple servers. The same EAR file can be deployed to multiple Integration Servers concurrently if it makes sense and if potential external resource conflicts are avoided or resolved. Thus the EAR file is the smallest unit that can be distributed among physical resources.

In Java CAPS, an EAR files is generated as a result of a developer creating a deployment profile, assigning components to logical host containers, and building the resulting integration solution project.

Decisions as to how many Java CAPS logical hosts and deployment profiles to use in an EAI solution and what components to assign to each deployment profile in each logical host are the most critical decisions affecting granularity of distribution and therefore scalability and, potentially, resilience.

Note

In Java CAPS, an EAR file is generated as a result of a developer creating a deployment profile, assigning components to logical containers, and building the resulting Enterprise Application. A deployment profile maps logical components to external system containers within a Java CAPS environment. An environment is a collection of external systems, Integration Servers, and, optionally, Message Servers. What Java CAPS components can be mapped in a single deployment profile is determined by what components are configured in one or more connectivity maps. A single deployment profile can use components form one or more connectivity maps, as long as all the connectivity maps are in the same project or subproject as the deployment profile. A single deployment profile can map components to multiple logical hosts, each with its own Integration Server and/or Message Server.

Note

Java CAPS EAI solutions are generally event driven. An external event triggers a component to receive a message from an external system or poll for a message in the external environment. The JCA Adapters, or eWays, as well as other endpoints like JMS Clients, are used by Java Collaborations or eInsight Business Processes. The eWays cannot be separated from the Java Collaboration Definitions (JCDs) or Business Processes that use them. Logical break points for dividing Java CAPS EAI solutions into separate deployments are JMS Destinations. Since each JMS Destination name is global to the JMS Message Server to which it is deployed, a connectivity map that contains a JMS Destination called queueA will be referring to the same JMS Destination as another connectivity map that contains a JMS Destination object called queueA, so long as both are deployed to the same Message Server.

By deciding to deploy all components of the EAI solution through a single deployment profile to a single logical host, the solution architect creates a centralized EAI infrastructure—a hub-and-spokes model of old. If the solution is small and there are no resilience considerations to address, this model is perfectly valid. Thanks to the inherent multithreading of the J2EE environment, this solution is much more scalable, within the single Integration Server, than the traditional hub-and-spokes solutions were.

If the ability to distribute components over multiple platforms for load-balancing, resilience, or scalability is desired, the solution must be architected to consist of multiple Enterprise Applications (in separate EAR files), each implementing a specific part of the overall solution. Solution components would exchange messages using JMS infrastructure or other distributed communication models like Web Services.

In strictly eGate-based solutions, where business functionality is implemented exclusively using Java Collaborations, breaking up the solution into deployable components is relatively easy. The enterprise architect merely picks a series of components that communicate with some other series of components using common JMS Destinations, and assigns them through one or more connectivity maps and one or more deployment profiles to multiple Integration Servers and Message Servers.

In solutions where most of the business functionality is implemented using eInsight Business Processes the refactoring task is harder. Distributed architecture must be devised before or concurrently with the design of Business Processes. The reason is simple: each Business Process is a single, indivisible component, deployed in its totality in a single Integration Server. There is typically a conflict between dictates of solution distribution and dictates of business process completeness and visibility. The architect must carefully weigh the benefits of implementing complete, large business processes against the costs of component failure and performance implications. Conversely, breaking up processes for performance or fault-tolerance reasons will result in loss of overall complete process visibility.

Ultimately, a solution architect must consider all the tradeoffs and design a solution that best reflects the business and technical environment on a case-by-case basis.

Scalability is the ability of the system to process increasing amounts of work by replicating components. Resilience is the ability of the system to continue operating in the face of failures.

While inherent scalability and resilience features are present in the J2EE platform, the Application Server, JMS, and the hardware platforms, scalability and resilience of the solution must be architected into it from inception to take advantage of these inherent features and add explicit features where they are lacking.

One of the fundamental means to facilitate scalability and resilience is factoring of the solution into smaller units for distribution and replication. Scalability and resilience requirements of the solution will initially dictate decisions about factoring. These decisions must, however, be informed by the capabilities of the toolset and the physical environment.

Java CAPS solution factoring is dependent on the nature of the solution. Strictly eGate-based solutions would be typically broken up at JMS Destinations, which are the logical break points. Strictly eInsight-based solutions may not have many JMS Destinations, so large business processes may need to be explicitly broken up into multiple smaller processes to address resilience and scalability requirements.

Technical details of solution factoring are discussed at some length and illustrated with examples in Chapter 13.

Breaking up a large solution into components using JMS Destinations as logical break points creates an opportunity to leverage JMS for load-balancing and scalability. A JMS queue can have multiple Competing Consumers, components that receive messages from the same queue, each of which will get a message if there is one. A JMS Destination–based load-balancing configuration comes into being when components of the solution, which receive messages from a specific queue, are replicated and multiple copies are deployed to multiple Integration Servers. In this configuration, the JMS Message Server is a single point of failure, so while scalability requirement can be addressed this way, resilience cannot. To also address this resilience issue, the JMS Message Server would have to be deployed in a clustered configuration with JMS backing store deployed to cluster-shared storage, or else a JMS Grid–based fault-tolerant JMS solution would be needed. This topic is further discussed in Chapter 13, section 13.5.

1.8 Chapter Summary

This chapter discussed the major integration styles and identified some of the Java CAPS components that can assist in their implementation. Integration styles, including file transfer, database sharing, remote procedure invocation, messaging, and service orchestration, were briefly discussed.

This chapter also discussed issues of scalability and resilience and Java CAPS facilities that can assist in solution factoring for distribution and replication.

CHAPTER TWO

Java CAPS Architecture

2.1 Introduction

The term *architecture* is used in many contexts. In this chapter, it is used to describe the components of the Sun Java CAPS Suite and how they relate to each other and to the environment in which they operate. Java CAPS is placed in the context of enterprise systems. Its architecture and components are defined, and their roles and relationships are described. Finally, solution development stages are described and their outputs placed in the context of the Java CAPS development and runtime environment.

2.2 Historical Note

Early versions of Enterprise Application Integration (EAI) tools, including those from STC (SeeBeyond under its earlier name), implemented a hub-and-spokes EAI model. A central Message Broker provided all transformation and management capabilities. Such implementations, while reasonably easy to manage, deploy, and maintain, suffered from resiliency and scalability limitations. A single server was a single point of failure. The higher the throughput required, the bigger and more capable the hardware platform had to be. Multithreading was typically not supported, so the Message Broker was not able to leverage multiprocessing capability of the hardware platform, if such was available. If the requirements exceeded hardware capability, multiple deployments on separate hardware platforms were required, likely with some form of a messaging bridge between them. Each eWay Adapter and the Message Broker was deployed as individual processes.

Later versions of the SeeBeyond EAI suite were totally distributed. eWay Adapters had built-in transformation capabilities, and standalone transformation components (Business Object Brokers) were available. All these capabilities and components were tied together through the underlying queuing infrastructure and communicated with it, and with the management and control dashboard, using the Transmission Control Protocol (TCP). Each eWay Adapter and Business Object Broker (BOB) was a standalone process and thus could be deployed on any supported machine regardless of where all the other components were deployed. Solutions could scale by improving capabilities of high-end machines or adding multiple low-end machines, or both. With multiple independent processes on a single machine, hardware multiprocessing capability could be taken advantage of if available.

Having many independent processes as part of an EAI solution was not always an advantage. Each process had its own hardware resources allocation requirements. Creation and destruction of processes is more expensive in terms of machine resources than creation and destruction of threads within a single process. Context switching and paging, associated with execution of many concurrent processes, are also expensive.

The most recent releases of the SeeBeyond ICAN and the Sun SeeBeyond Java CAPS platforms are Java EE based. Both use Java EE Application Server Containers to deploy integration components, implemented as Enterprise Java Beans (EJBs), taking advantage of container services, resource pools, multithreading, and other optimizations not available in earlier products.

The architecture of the EAI product greatly influenced the kinds of integration styles that could be used and the way in which scalability and resiliency were implemented. The capabilities of the external applications to be integrated also greatly influenced the kinds of integration styles that could be used and the kinds of Java CAPS components required by the integration solution.

2.3 Context

An integration solution operates within the context of a wider enterprise infrastructure and interacts with its various components. This context is defined by the external systems that the solution connects and influences interactions and interfaces that can be implemented.

While all manner of activities might take place inside an integration solution, messages upon which it acts typically come from one or more external systems and are typically destined for one or more external systems. Figure 2-1 diagrammatically depicts the Java CAPS solution context showing various components a Java CAPS solution might include.

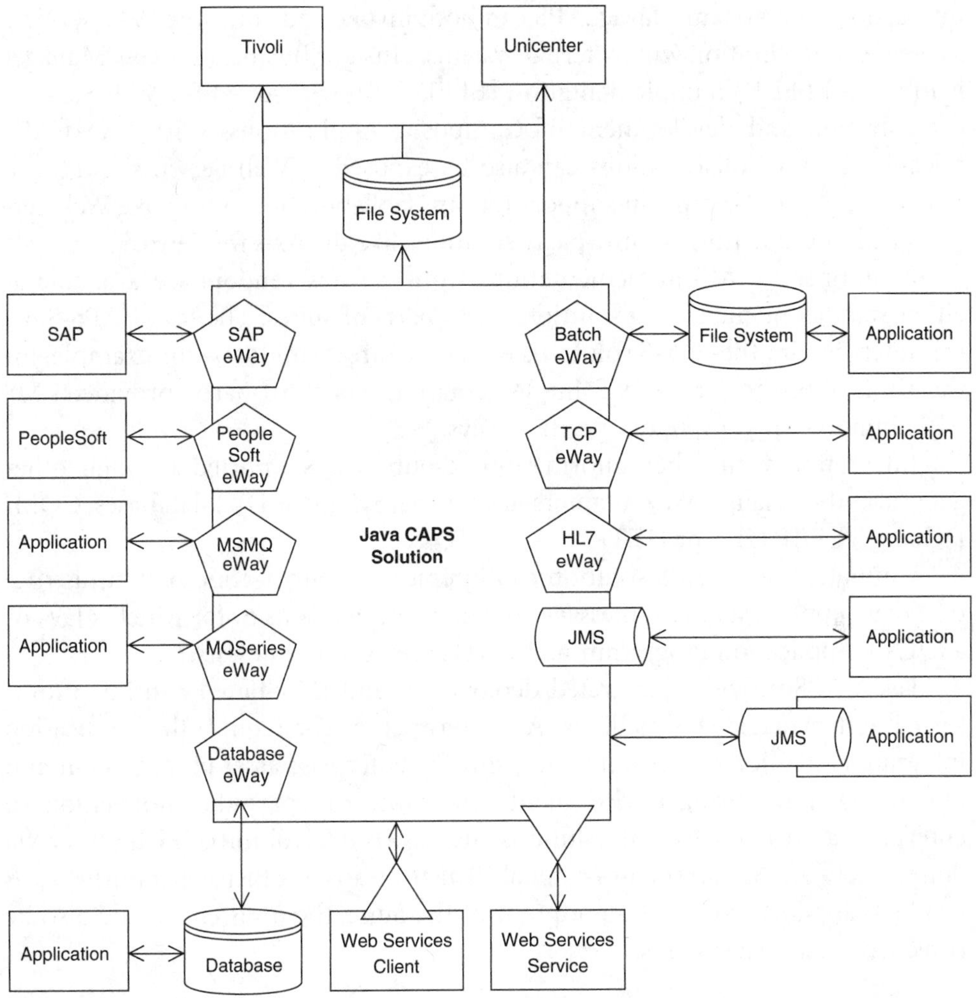

FIGURE 2-1: Java CAPS solution context

Java CAPS provides numerous JCA-compliant Adapters (eWays) for interaction with external systems, including both prepackaged adapters for major ERP systems, such as SAP or PeopleSoft, and generic adapters for interaction with technical infrastructure, such as a TCP/IP eWay or Batch eWays [Batch_eWay] with support for FTP, SFTP, and local file system access.

With increasing deployment of Web Services and Web Services enablement of applications, Web Services invocation is becoming one of the accepted means of interaction with systems. Java CAPS can both invoke and consume Web Services as means of integration with external systems. eInsight Business Process Manager is in fact a BPEL4WS implementation [BPEL4WS], well suited for Web Services orchestration and development of Composite Applications. With Java CAPS release 5.1, Java Collaborations can also be exposed as Web Services and, as of release 5.1.3, there is built-in support for Java Collaborations to invoke Web Services without resorting to third-party solutions like the Axis framework.

A number of JMS implementations from various vendors are available as either standalone messaging solutions or as parts of suites. The Java CAPS Suite can interact with these JMS solutions either via direct support—for example, for the IBM WebSphere MQ JMS implementation, via third-party–provided JMS API libraries—or via vendor-specific eWays.

Integration with other information resources is supported through other generic and specialist eWay Adapters like Oracle, Sybase or DB2 databases, COM/DCOM, TCP/IP HL7, or HTTP/S.

Ultimately, Java CAPS solution can interact with any technology infrastructure that supports standard message-exchange mechanisms or for which a Java or a C/C++ Application Programming Interface (API) library exists.

Java CAPS provides integrated deployment and JMX-based runtime monitoring and management facilities. An enterprise might require the application integration solution to also integrate with the enterprise asset management and operational monitoring environment. The Suite can provide information to enterprise asset management solutions such as IBM Tivoli or CA Unicenter via Simple Network Management Protocol (SNMP) traps or other mechanisms such products support. From the standpoint of the Suite, these systems could also be considered external systems.

2.4 Java CAPS Architecture

Java CAPS 5.1 completely separates the design time and the runtime environments. Figure 2-2 shows delineation between the design time and the runtime environments and various components each environment might include.

The design time environment consists of the Repository Server and the Enterprise Designer Integrated Development Environment (IDE).

The Repository stores all design time artifacts, both installed components and custom components, developed as part of integration solutions. The Reposi-

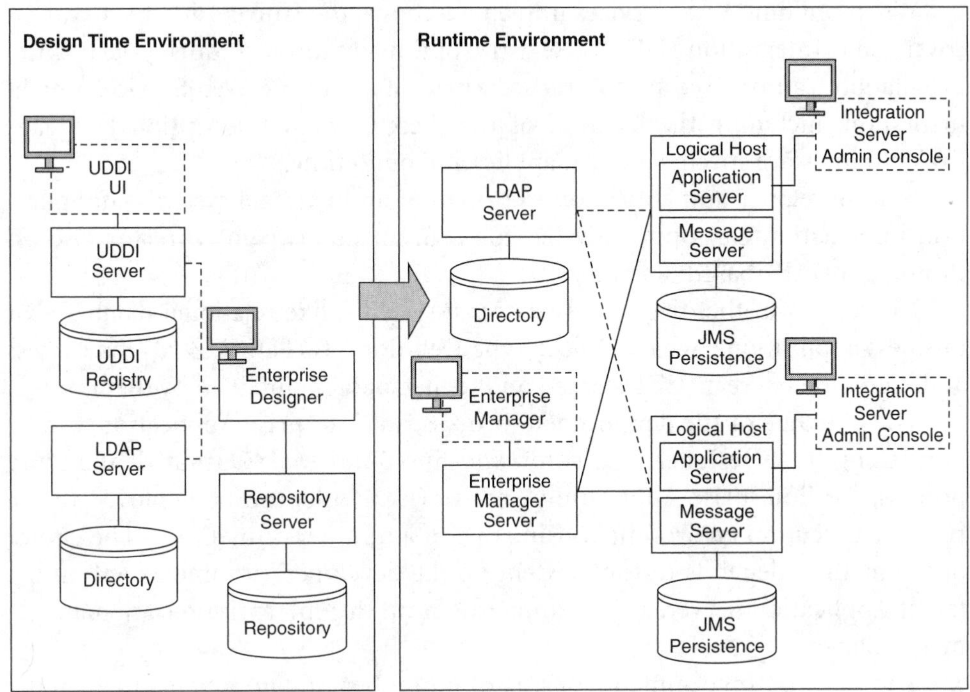

FIGURE 2-2: Java CAPS architecture

tory Server is supported on a number of operating systems, including Solaris, Windows, and Linux.

The Enterprise Designer, a NetBeans-based IDE, is the development tool containing integrated editors for all artifacts that may form a part of a Java CAPS solution. All Java Collaborations, eInsight Business Processes, connectivity maps, deployment profiles, environment components, and other objects supported by other elements of the Java CAPS suite are designed using the Enterprise Designer. The Enterprise Designer, through the Repository, supports a fully featured Version Control System that provides both branching and tagging, among other features.

Note
The Enterprise Designer (eDesigner), through Java CAPS version 5.1.3, is supported only on the Windows operating system platform.

When building Web Services implementations, the Universal Directory, Discovery, and Integration (UDDI) Registry, optionally installed during Java CAPS installation, can be used to publish information about the Web Services implementation, including the location of the Web Services Description Language (WSDL) interface specification, at application build time.

Both developer authentication information and external systems configuration information can optionally be stored in an Lightweight Directory Access Protocol (LDAP)-based directory.

Not shown in the diagram are external systems, like relational databases or business applications, which Object Type Definition (OTD) Wizards may access at design time to create OTDs based on the metadata maintained by them.

The outcome of the development process, an Enterprise Application, can be built using the eDesigner or a command-line build tool. Output of the build process, the Enterprise Application Archive (EAR) file, can be deployed to the runtime execution environment using one of a number of methods. The choice of the method depends to some extent on the developer, to some extent on the target Application Server, and to some extent on the enterprise release management policies.

The runtime environment consists of a number of components that can be deployed over a collection of physical machines.

Logical host, the name that is a holdover from the previous release of the product, roughly corresponds to the Application Server Instance. It consists of an Application Server instance and an optional JMS Message Server instance.

EAR files are deployed to the Application Server, which provides all the runtime services expected of a Java EE container. The JMS Message Server is the messaging infrastructure that Enterprise Applications can use to pass messages among themselves. As of Java CAPS 5.1.3, the Sun SeeBeyond Integration Server 5.1 (which is a version of the Sun Application Server 8.0 Platform Edition), the Sun Application Server 8.2 Enterprise Edition, and the BEA WebLogic Application Server 9.1 are supported as target application server containers for Java CAPS Enterprise Applications.

A number of JMS Message Server implementations can be used as messaging infrastructure. These include the default Sun SeeBeyond IQ Manager, the Sun Message Queue, the Sun JMS Grid 5.1.3, and the IBM WebSphere MQ 6.0.

Each supported Application Server comes with its own, typically Web-based, configuration application. The Sun SeeBeyond Integration Server provides an Integration Server Administration Console, loosely based on the Sun Application Server 8.0 Administration Console application. This console allows configuration of both the Sun SeeBeyond Integration Server and the Sun SeeBeyond IQ Manager (JMS Message Server).

Runtime configuration information can be provided to Enterprise Applications in one or both of two ways. At design time, eWay Adapters and other configurable components can be provided with fixed configuration information. Enterprise Archives will carry this information embedded in various descriptors and will use it at runtime. An LDAP-based directory server can also be used for storing configuration information. Rather then embedding configuration literals, the configured properties embed LDAP references to directory entries containing configuration values. At activation time, when the Application Server starts the application, LDAP references are resolved to actual values and are used for component configuration.

Note
While using LDAP for storing configuration information increases flexibility, bear in mind that, at least through Java CAPS 5.1.3, only string values are supported. Configuration properties, such as port numbers, that require numeric entries, cannot be referenced from LDAP. All configuration entries are stored in an LDAP directory in clear text.

Java CAPS and its Enterprise Applications support Java Management Extensions (JMX). Java CAPS provides monitoring and management of the runtime environment through the Enterprise Manager infrastructure. Unlike in its predecessor, Java CAPS Enterprise Manager is a standalone management agent that directly communicates with Application Servers, JMS Messages Servers, and runtime solution components. It does not access design time components, like Repository, to which ICAN 5.0 used to require access.

The Enterprise Manager's Web-based interface can be used to dynamically add Integration Servers and Application Servers to be monitored and managed. The Sun SeeBeyond IQ Manager can be managed and monitored through the Enterprise Manager. Other JMS Message Server implementations are also integrated into the monitoring and management interface, but some restrictions may exist.

The Sun JMS Grid, in addition to being integrated into the Enterprise Manager monitoring infrastructure, provides its own configuration, management, and monitoring infrastructure. The Sun Message Queue implementation is typically managed through the same interface as the Sun Application Server with which it is integrated.

2.5 Solution Development Stages

Because Java CAPS supports a number of Application Servers from different vendors, a single Enterprise Application can be, with some care, designed to be deployed to different Application Servers and to use different JMS Message Servers. To appreciate how that care can be exercised, it is helpful to understand the stages in which Java CAPS solutions are developed and what deployment decisions are made at each stage.

It is assumed that you have been exposed to Java CAPS and the development process. If not, "Hello Java CAPS World" in Part II (located on the CD-ROM that accompanies this book) may provide a starting point.

A typical Java CAPS solution consists of one or more eWay Adapters, what [EIP] calls endpoints, one or more message routers, translators, channels, consumers, and other components that vary from solution to solution in kind and in number.

The development process for a single deployable Java CAPS solution proceeds through three stages. In the first stage, OTDs, Collaborations, Business Processes, and other objects that vary with Java CAPS product are developed. These define data structures and processing logic in a manner that typically does not have dependencies on the physical environment in which the solution will ultimately run. In some cases, even the specific properties of Endpoints are not preset. The most notable examples of this are JMS Destinations. Java Collaborations and eInsight Business Processes do not embed the knowledge of what kind of JMS Destinations they will use, whether queues or topics.

Note
At the connectivity map design time, no decisions are made as to which Application Servers and which JMS Message Servers will provide the runtime environment for the solution. Different Application Servers and different Message Servers can be used for different parts of the same solution, and a solution described by a single connectivity map can be deployed to different Application and Message Servers.

In the second stage, one or more connectivity maps are created. These collect logical components, connect them to form message routes, name external systems connectors, and, in the case of JMS Destinations, specify the types of JMS Destination that will be used. Some other physical decisions are made at this stage and embedded in connectivity maps. Java classes used to implement specific functionality, bean pools sizes, names of directories and files, enveloping schemes, servlet names, and similar properties that, while related to the physical environment, do not predicate target Application Server or target Message Server environments are also configured in this stage.

Note
Certain eWay Adapters, which are platform specific, may restrict the choice of platforms to which a Java CAPS solution can be deployed. One of the most notable examples of this is the COM/DCOM eWay, which can be deployed only to a Microsoft Windows environment. The decision to use the COM/DCOM eWay immediately makes the solution that uses it platform specific.

In the third stage, Collaborations, Business Processes, JMS Destinations, and their relationships expressed through connectivity maps must be associated with physical resources and packaged into Enterprise Archives. In Java CAPS, physical resources are expressed as collections of Application Servers, Message Servers, and external systems containers in one or more environments. Application Servers, Message Servers, and external systems connectors are configured to be associated with physical machines by host names, port numbers, user credentials, contexts, paths and other attributes that vary from resource to resource.

Note
In Java CAPS, at most one Sun SeeBeyond IQ Manager JMS Message Server can be associated with a logical host even if the Enterprise Designer Environment allows configuration of more than one. This is because the Enterprise Manager can only interact with one and the Application Server Domain can only start one. It is possible to configure additional Sun SeeBeyond IQ Managers under the single logical host, but each such IQ Manager will have to be associated with a different Application Server Domain. This ability can be used to configure "Shadow IQ Managers" for the purpose of implementing a JMS Messaging Bridge between independent installations, for example, Java CAPS and SRE or Java CAPS and ICAN.

Given a collection of external resources in the environment, the deployment profile is the mechanism by which logical components of the solution are mapped to physical resources.

Note
Deployment profile is the configuration component that determines not merely which instance but also what kind of an Application Server or a JMS Message Server will be used at runtime.

Note
The same logical solution can be built for deployment to different physical environments merely by creating a deployment profile associated with the specific Java CAPS environment and building the solution.

Note
So long as care is taken to ensure that connectivity map configuration properties are appropriate across environments, the same solution can be built for deployment to development, testing, user acceptance testing (UAT), or production without the need to change any of the development artifacts.

Let's imagine that a solution was developed and deployed to an infrastructure that uses the Sun SeeBeyond Integration Server and the Sun SeeBeyond IQ Manager JMS Message Server. Some time later a need to improve resilience properties of the solution was identified. It was decided that the Sun Application Server 8.2 Enterprise Edition and the Sun JMS Grid, which provide the clustering support, would address that need. Both products were installed and configured. It is merely necessary to define a Java CAPS environment that includes the Sun Application Server 8.2 and the Sun JMS Grid, create a deployment profile associating the logical solution with the new physical environment, build the EAR file, and deploy. The original logical solution, without any changes, will operate in the new environment.

Note
If care was taken to ensure that no external systems configuration settings will clash, the same EAR file can be deployed to any number of Application and Message Servers of the kind for which the application was built. To elaborate, the same external Oracle database can be accessed concurrently by any number of instances of the Enterprise Application, but the same file in the same directory should not be.

Note
An Enterprise Application can only be deployed to the same kind of Application and Message Server as the ones for which it was built. To elaborate, an application whose components are associated, through the deployment profile, with the Sun SeeBeyond Application Server and the Sun JMS Grid Message Server cannot be deployed to the Sun Application Server 8.2 Enterprise Edition and the Sun Message Queue. To obtain an Enterprise Archive suitable for the new environment, simply create a new environment in the Enterprise Designer, create a new deployment profile, and build.

The final outcome of the three-stage development process is the Enterprise Archive, the deployment, and execution unit. It contains all components that the Enterprise Application will require at runtime.

2.6 Chapter Summary

This chapter described basic components of the Sun Java CAPS Suite required to implement application integration solutions, how they relate to each other and to the environment in which they operate. Java CAPS was placed in the context of an Enterprise IT infrastructure. Its architecture and components were defined, and their role and relationships were described. Solution development stages and their outputs were described and placed in the context of Java CAPS development and runtime environment.

CHAPTER THREE

Project Structure and Deployment

By Brendan Marry

3.1 Introduction

The Enterprise Designer Integrated Development Environment (IDE) is the Java CAPS development environment. It contains project and environment explorers and a series of editors, one or more for each of the products, the connectivity map editor and the deployment profile editor. Solutions under development are organized into projects. Projects are collections of subprojects, Collaborations, Business Processes, Object Type Definitions (OTDs), Connectors, and other development-time artifacts, which appear as subnodes to a project. Projects can be nested. Components from one or more projects can be used to build an Enterprise Application by creating a connectivity map that includes all required components, wherever they may be located within the Java CAPS Project hierarchy. Developers have a great deal of flexibility in organizing development artifacts into projects and project hierarchies. This chapter explores some of the options for managing projects in Java CAPS at design time, migration from environment to environment, and structure of environments. It also discusses selected deployment architectures suitable for small and large deployments and command-line build and deployment tools.

Many factors influence the project structures an organization might adopt. Some of the influencing factors are best practices that an organization may already have adopted for management of development processes, the size of the software development department, the nature of the application, and the preferences of the administration team responsible for the promotion process of a project through the testing, user acceptance testing (UAT), and production environments.

It is fair to assume that all environments fall somewhere in the spectrum from a single PC that is running under a desk to a highly available, clustered production environment with tightly controlled development, test, UAT, load testing, and production environments.

3.2 From Logical Solution to Physical Deployment

Chapter 2, section 2.5, discussed the stages in which Java CAPS solutions are developed.

The logical solution defines how project components process messages, how they receive and parse data into message structures, how they transform messages, and what protocols are used to pick up and deliver messages to end systems with which the solution will communicate. All development artifacts that jointly define the Enterprise Application are arranged and connected using the connectivity map. The connectivity map is a graphical view of the project's connectivity.

While some decisions on the physical aspects of Java CAPS solutions are made in connectivity maps, most physical aspects of Java CAPS solutions are made in the environment containers and associated with the logical solution through the deployment profile.

Physical aspects of the project, established through the deployment profile, include where the Enterprise Application is to be deployed and the connection properties its eWays use to make connections to the end systems. Java CAPS environments define the number and types of Integration, Application, and Message Servers and their properties, and the number, the kind, and the runtime configuration properties of external systems. The same logical solution can be deployed to different Java CAPS environments and therefore to different Integration, Application, and/or Message Servers as well as external systems with different configuration properties.

This separation between the logical solution and its physical environment allows Java CAPS solutions to be developed once and deployed to different environments, including solution testing and migration environments, from development to production.

3.3 Project Structure Considerations

Java CAPS projects are arranged in hierarchical, directory-like structures. These hierarchies contain collections of OTDs, Java Collaboration Definitions (JCDs), XSLT Collaboration Definitions (XCDs), XML Schema Definitions (XSDs), Web Services Description Language (WSDL) interface definitions, Business Processes, JMS Destinations, library jar files, and other artifacts that are used to create Java CAPS integration solutions. These components can be arranged in many ways, from a single project (a large bin approach) to many projects, possibly with subprojects, projects for common components, and projects for unique solution components.

This section describes one of the possible project structures, using a step-by-step definition approach, and discusses the reasoning that led to the development of this structure.

Note
The structure discussed below is only one of the possible project structures. This structure is tailored to large deployment environments. Other structures are possible and, depending on circumstances, may be more appropriate.

Let's start by creating a project folder under the eDesigner Project Explorer's root directory. Figure 3-1 shows an example of a root of project hierarchy.

Note
The name of the project influences the name of the resulting Enterprise Application Archive (EAR) file. In Java CAPS releases prior to release 5.1.3, it is not possible to change the name of the EAR file; hence it is important to consider the project directory name and directory hierarchy depth. Best practice is to adopt a standard naming convention, such as the four-layer naming convention corresponding to the four service-orientated architecture layers. Adding a prefix, for example, "bp" (business process) or "bs" (business service), followed by the name of the project, might be adopted as a practice to derive a name of a project directory. With such structure, the services created in each category will be listed one after the other under the root directory of the Enterprise Designer.

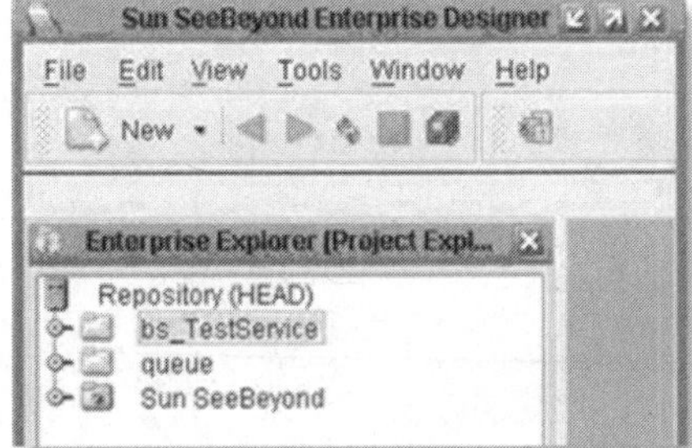

FIGURE 3-1: Project Explorer directory tree

Within each directory, a subdirectory will be created to contain the artifacts of the appropriate category. XSDs, WSDL interface definitions, OTDs, JCDs, XCDs, Business Processes, JMS Destinations, external library JARs, and external systems and connectors all would have a separate directory whose name would correspond to the category of objects it contains. Figure 3-2 shows a project hierarchy in which subprojects follow this sort of convention.

Once development of project components is complete, a connectivity map and a deployment profile for the project can be created.

3.3.1 Connectivity Map and Deployment Profile

Unlike other project components, which can be created in arbitrary locations within arbitrary project hierarchies, connectivity maps and their corresponding deployment profiles must exist in the same directory. Components defined through a connectivity map in one project directory are not visible to a deployment profile in another project directory.

Let's create a project's connectivity map(s) in the project's root directory; see Figure 3-3. An enterprise application may have more than one connectivity map. When a project is large, it is a good practice to break it up into logical groupings and create connectivity maps for each grouping, interconnecting connectivity map–based groups with JMS queues or topics.

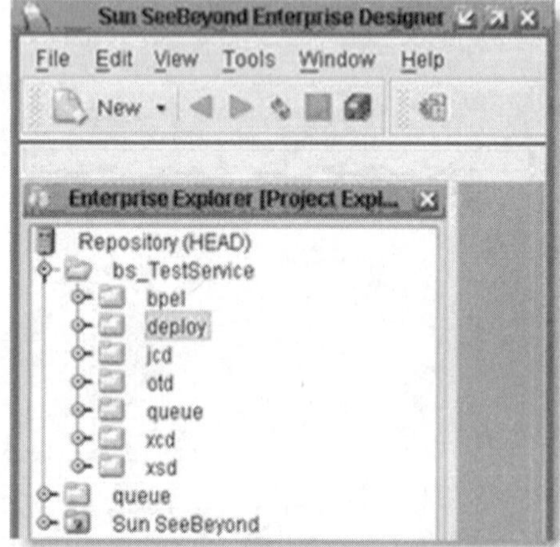

FIGURE 3-2: Sample Project folder structure

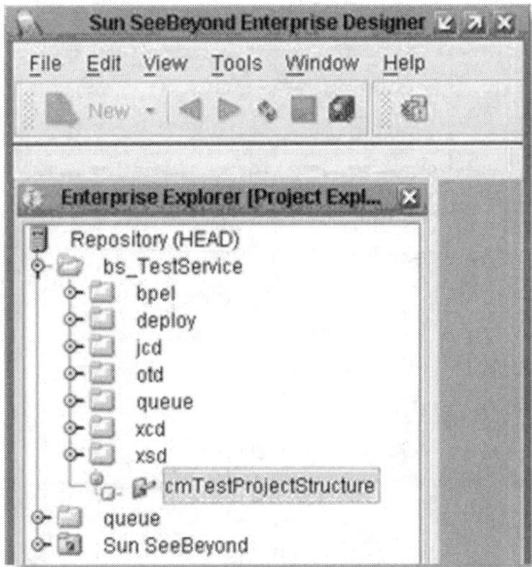

FIGURE 3-3: Connectivity Map placement

Processing components, JCDs, Business Processes, and XCDs, can be dragged and dropped onto the connectivity map directly from project directories in which they were created. Figure 3-4 shows a connectivity map constructed from components available in different project directories.

JMS Destinations, queues, and topics, as well as Web Services and HTTP connectors, can be explicitly created from the project context menu, so you can create them anywhere within the project hierarchy. Other connectivity map objects, most notably eWays but also eView applications and scheduler connectors, can only be created by selecting them from a drop-down menu in the Connectivity Map Editor. This causes them to be created in the same directory as the connectivity map. You can leave them there or use cut and paste to move them to the "deploy" directory to keep the root of the project tidy.

As will be discussed in Chapter 5, "Messaging Infrastructure," section 5.6.1, JMS Destinations with the same name, even if used in different connectivity maps, are, for the JMS Message Server, the same destinations. With multiple connectivity maps, intended to use the same JMS Destinations to interconnect project components, it is easy to accidentally misspell a destination name, unintentionally causing distinct destinations to be created and effectively disconnecting components. This is a consequence of automatic destination creation. This

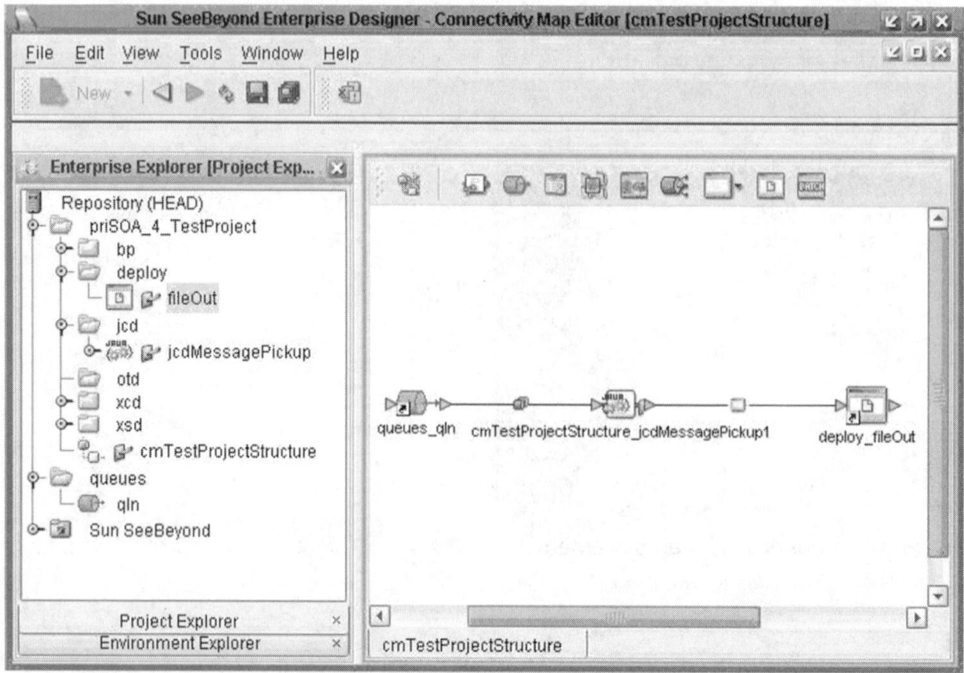

FIGURE 3-4: Constructing connectivity maps from components

kind of error is difficult to diagnose at development time. When working with enterprise systems that consist of components sharing JMS destinations across connectivity maps, it is advisable to create a queue directory, at the root level of the Repository or a related group of projects, for the global JMS Destinations and, possibly, create a per-project queue directory for local JMS destinations. In the example in Figure 3-5, a local project queue directory and a global queue directory were created.

Deployment profiles must be created in the directory that contains all the connectivity maps whose components are to be included in the resulting EAR. As the default name of the resulting EAR file is a combination of the project folder name and the deployment profile name, it is best to supplement the deployment profile name with a number. This number can double as a build number when new deployment profiles are created, incrementing the deployment profile number with each subsequent build. Figure 3-6 shows deployment profiles whose names follow this convention.

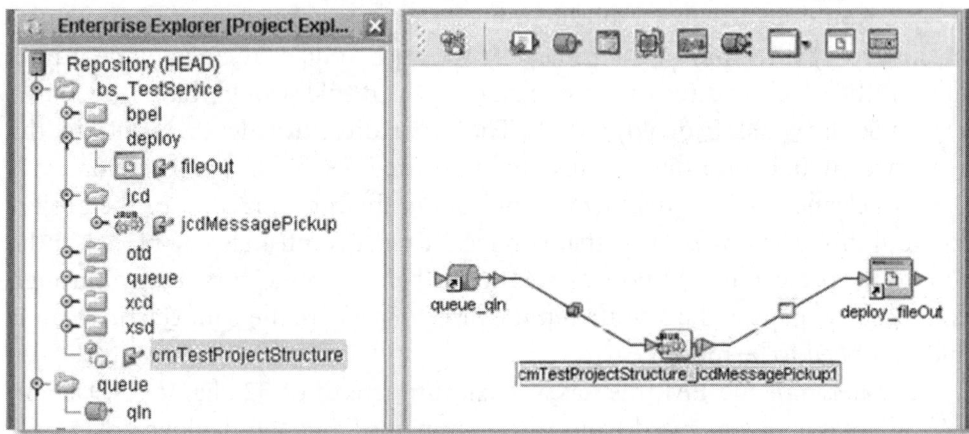

FIGURE 3-5: Using global and local queues

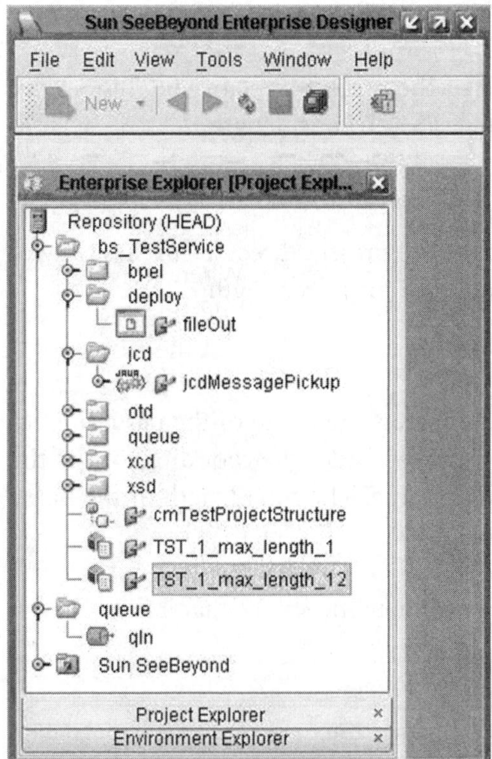

FIGURE 3-6: Numbered deployment profiles

We would expect to see both connectivity maps and deployment profiles in the deploy directory of the project. If we were to place the deployment profile in the deploy directory, the resulting EAR file would have the name bs_TestService_u002F_deployTST_1. The extra directory depth results in the sequence _u002F_ gratuitously inserted into the EAR file name. Therefore, it is perhaps cleaner to place deployment profiles in the root directory of the project to avoid this. The downside is that connectivity maps must also be placed in the root of the project. In addition, as mentioned before, connectors created through connectivity maps will be created in the directory where the connectivity map is and may need to be moved.

The name of the EAR file has a maximum length of 32 characters. Default EAR file name is generated from directory names and the deployment profile name. If the concatenated directory names and deployment profile name exceed the maximum length, the generated EAR file name embeds a part of the original path and a unique number. This may make the EAR file name difficult to relate to the original project. Default EAR file names are as follows:

32-character filename from the name of the project directory bs_TestService and the name of the deployment profile TST_1_max_length_1

```
bs_TestServiceTST_1_max_length_1.ear
```

33-character filename from the name of the project directory bs_TestService and the name of the deployment profile TST_1_max_length_12

```
bs_TestServiceTST _1_max_1294795462.ear
```

It is recommended to use the desired name as the name of the parent directory of the project, create the deployment profile under the root directory of the project, and include a build number in that name. The total length of the name should not exceed 32 characters.

Project directory name + deployment profile name <= 32 characters

Note

As of Java CAPS release 5.1.3, EAR file names can be explicitly set through the deployment profile properties.

3.3.2 Variables and Constants

As discussed in Chapter 2, section 2.5, most configuration settings related to the physical environment in which a solution will operate are associated with external system containers in the Java CAPS environment. These settings are inherited by the enterprise archive through the deployment profile and the build process. Each deployment profile can be created for a distinct Java CAPS environment, allowing different settings to be associated with different physical environments like development, test, staging, or production. Some settings, however, are configured through the connectivity map connectors. These will be inherited by all deployment profiles, which may not be desirable. Some settings may be used by multiple connectivity maps. Setting them individually in each connectivity map may be error-prone and burdensome if a change must be made. To facilitate externalization of such settings, Java CAPS project variables and project and environment constants can be used.

Environment constants must be created in the Java CAPS environment in which they are to be used. Project variables and project constants must be created in the same directory as the connectivity map in which they are to be used. Project constants are useful if the same fixed values are to be used in multiple connectivity maps in the same deployment. This could be a constant representing, for example, a name of a log file that all components must use. Changing the value of the constant will cause the new value to be used in all connectivity maps in which it is referenced.

Note
Project constants can be of type String or Password.

Project variables are useful if a property, which is set in the connectivity map, must vary from environment to environment.

Two project variables with names and types, one for an input file name and one for an output file name, are shown in Figure 3-7.

Once created, the variables are available to be used as values of any connectivity map connector properties. For example, let's select the "out" file connector in the connectivity map shown in Figure 3-8, then select the output file name parameter and select the outputFileName variable from the drop-down menu. This is illustrated in Figure 3-8.

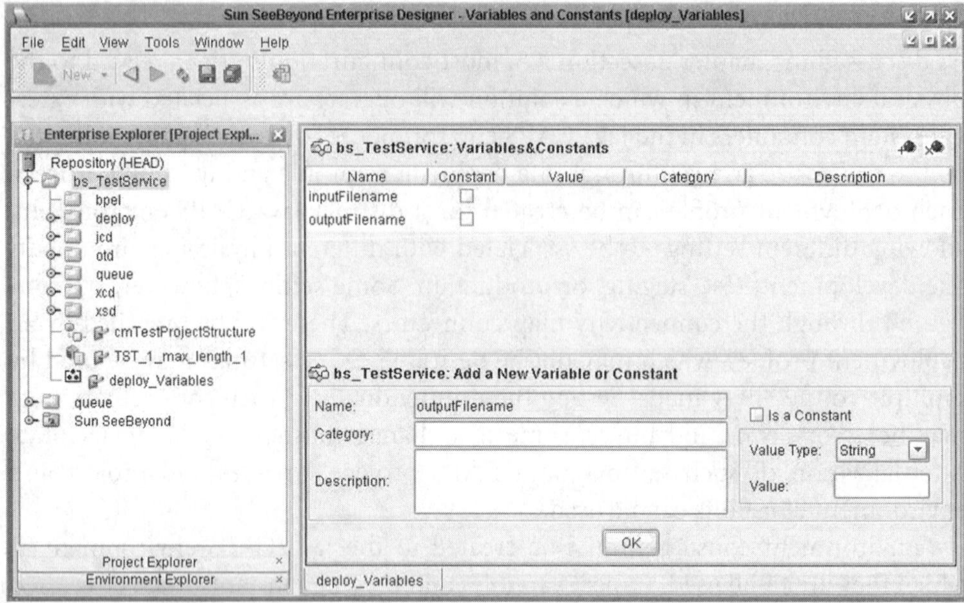

FIGURE 3-7: Variables and constants dialog

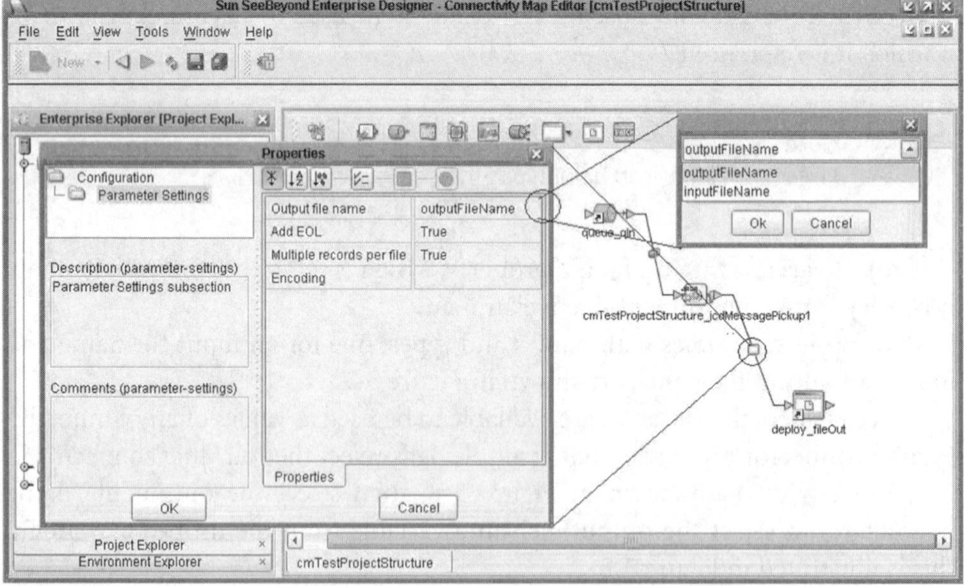

FIGURE 3-8: Using variable for component configuration

Before a project that uses project variables can be built, runtime values must be associated with the variables. Deployment Profile Editor's "Map Variables" button opens a dialog box that lists all project variables used in all connectivity maps for which the deployment profile is being constructed. The value of each variable can either be provided as a literal or substituted at build time through an environment constant. Providing a value as an explicit literal makes it deployment profile–specific; it is therefore recommended to use environment constants to provide build-time values for project variables.

To provide environment-dependent build-time values for project variables, it is necessary to define environment constants, using a dialog box similar to the one shown in Figure 3-9, for each of the Java CAPS environments for which the solution will be built.

Once constants are defined in the environment and the variables have been selected in the connectivity map, the deployment profile can be configured through mapping constants to variables, using controls in the dialog box similar to the one shown in Figure 3-10.

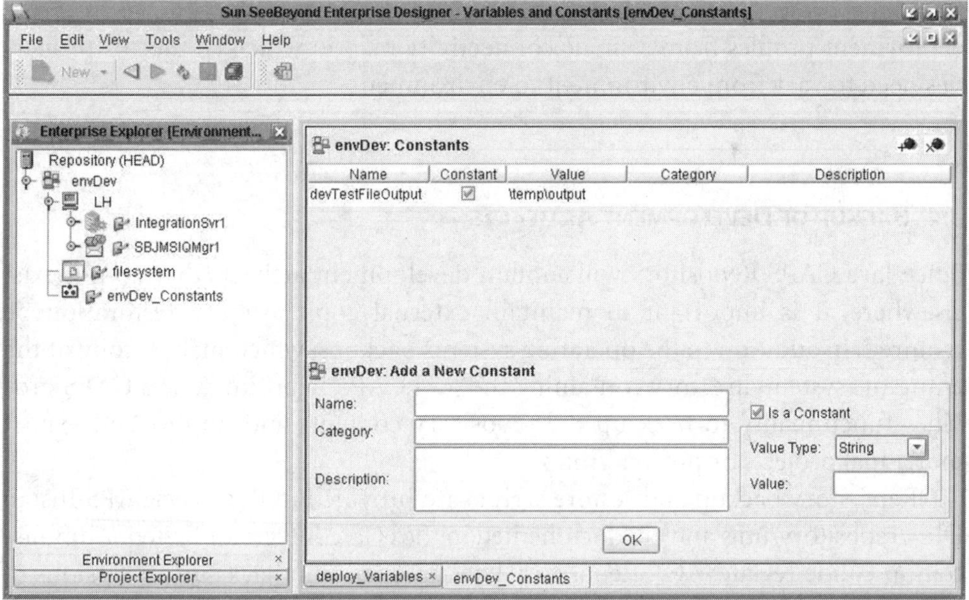

FIGURE 3-9: Defining environment constants

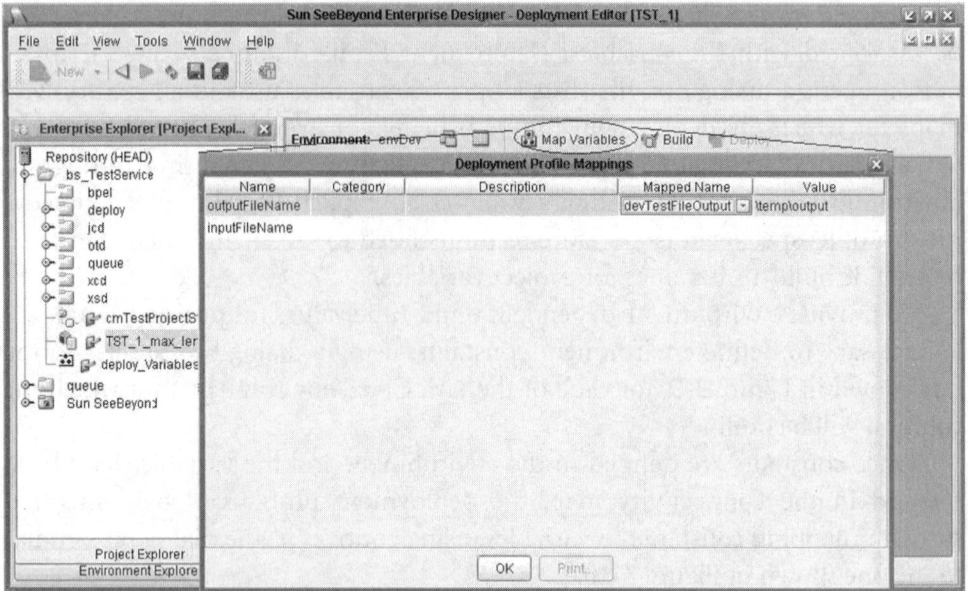

Figure 3-10: Mapping environment constant values to project variables

Using project variables and environment constants, it is possible to create deployment profiles from a single connectivity map in which connector properties need to vary from environment to environment.

3.4 Backup of Development Artifacts

Since Java CAPS Repository will contain development artifacts that do not exist elsewhere, it is important to maintain external copies should restoration be required. In addition to the operating systems backups, which make a copy of the entire file system directory containing the Java CAPS Repository, Java CAPS provides functionality to back up the repository contents and import and export individual projects or project groups.

Repository backup and restore scripts are provided in the <JavaCAPS Install Dir>/repository/utils and are documented in the eGate Integrator System Administration Guide [eGateSAG]. Repository backup operation backs up all versions of the projects objects.

Individual projects and project groups can be exported and imported using the Enterprise Designer or using export and import scripts provided in the <JavaCAPS Install Dir>repository/utils directory. Unlike repository backup, where all objects and all versions are backed up, project export only exports the current version of all objects in the selected projects.

To export a project using the eDesigner, right click on the project name and choose export, as shown in Figure 3-11.

It is possible to export not only a project by itself but also the project and any Java CAPS environments that may be the project's deployment targets. Figure 3-12 shows a list of projects that can be exported with one project chosen for export. Exporting Java CAPS environments will preserve a snapshot of environment settings at the time of export.

Having project exports include Java CAPS environment settings plays a key role in release management when an external source control system and a single repository are used for all environments.

When a project is exported, any dependent projects will be exported with it. A dependent project is any project that has any of its objects referenced by the project being exported.

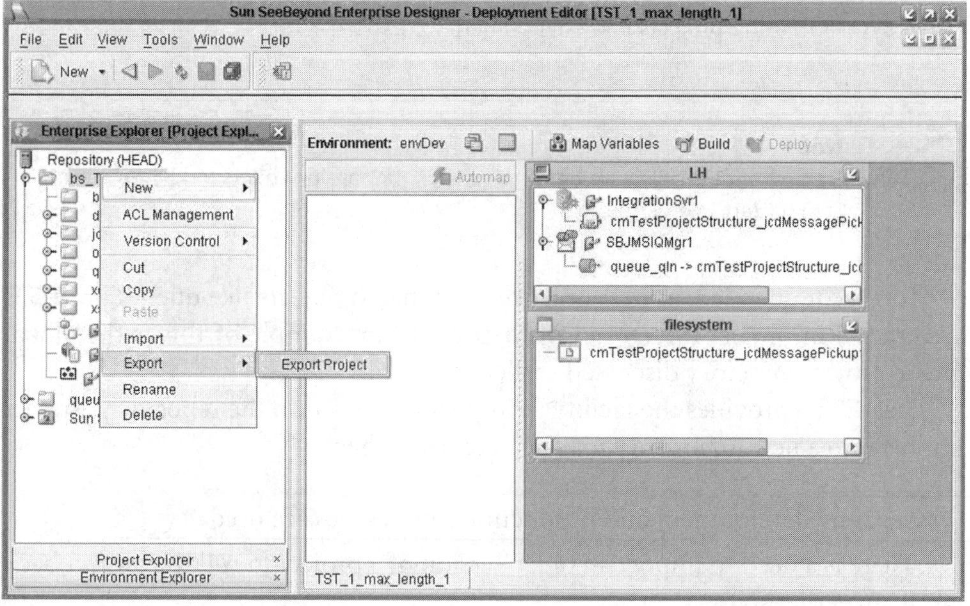

FIGURE 3-11: Initiating project export

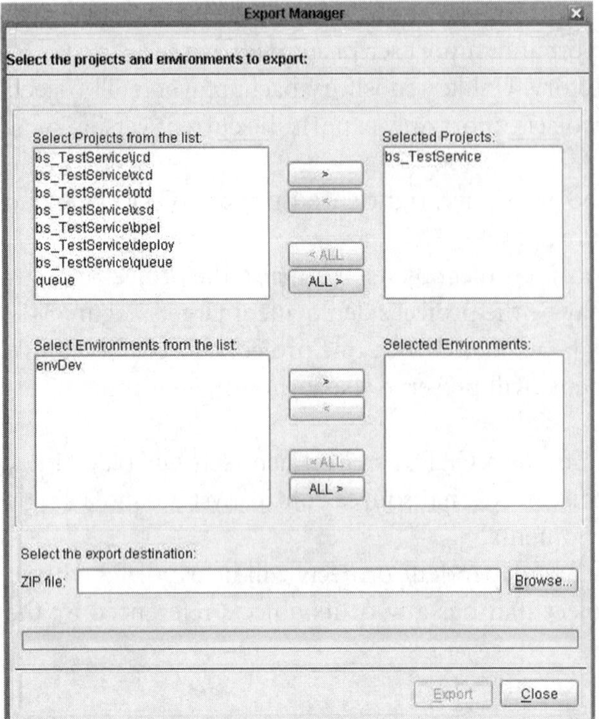

FIGURE 3-12: Choosing projects and environment for export

Note
Deployment profiles are the only objects that are not exported when a project is exported.

It is recommended, as best practice, that shared objects like queues or OTDs are created in project directories of their own. An example of this is the global queue project/directory discussed earlier.

Java CAPS provides the facility to import projects into the repository. Project import into a new Repository may be necessary when:

- Separate development and production repositories are used
- There is a need to import an older version of a project to roll the project back to an earlier state
- A project developed elsewhere is to be included in the solution

You import a project the same way you export a project, choosing an "import" option from the right-click menu in the Project Explorer (see Figure 3-13).

When importing a project, you must consider the following matters:

- Deployment profiles are not exported; hence it will be necessary to create them after importing a project.
- If the project already exists in the Repository, it is not possible to import the project without overwriting the current version of the project. This is desirable if there is a need to roll back to an earlier version of a project. Best practice is to rename the existing project <projectname>_latest and import the older version under the original project name.
- If the project has dependent projects that already exist in the Repository, import options will be given for the subprojects. Care must be taken not to import previous versions of dependent projects and thereby overwrite the current version. If the best practices are followed (where shared resources such as queues and OTDs are in global projects/directories), this issue can be minimized.

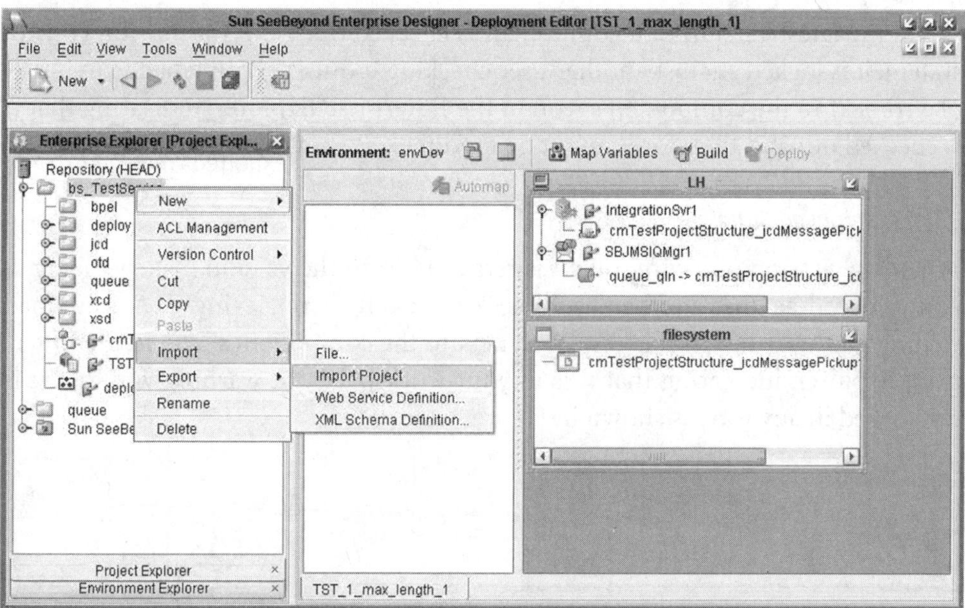

FIGURE 3-13: Initiating project import

3.5 Release Management

Let us examine options available to manage deployments in Java CAPS. We look at the built-in version control functionality, contained within the product, and how we can work with other source control/release management products.

3.5.1 Using Java CAPS Source Control System

Java CAPS has built-in functionality that allows management of versions of project components. We look at some of these features in this section. For a full description of these features, please refer to the Java CAPS eGate User Guide.

Let us start with the basics: check-in, check-out, and viewing the version history of components.

3.5.1.1 Checked-In State

When a component is checked in to the version control system, it is locked against modification until checked out, and a lock is displayed in the component's icon in the Enterprise Explorer, as shown in Figure 3-14.

3.5.1.2 Checked-Out State

When the latest version of a component is checked out from the version control system, it is locked against another user checking it out. A writing pad icon is displayed next to the component's icon in the Enterprise Explorer, indicating that it is checked out and therefore cannot be modified, as shown in Figure 3-15.

3.5.1.3 Retrieved State

When any version of a component is retrieved from the version history dialog, it is not locked against another user checking it out or retrieving it. A combined writing pad/warning icon is displayed next to the component's icon in the Enterprise Explorer, indicating that it is in your workspace but warning you that it is not locked in any way, as shown in Figure 3-16.

Figure 3-14: Checked-in state

Figure 3-15: Checked-out state

Figure 3-16: Retrieved state

You can access a component's version history through the Version Control menu, shown in Figure 3-17. Version Control History, similar to the one shown in Figure 3-18, allows viewing of version and tag history and retrieval of selected versions of objects to the workspace.

Version control allows you to maintain multiple versions of selected projects or environment components within a particular branch of the Repository. Version history of each component is recorded in a log file and can be viewed by means of a menu option.

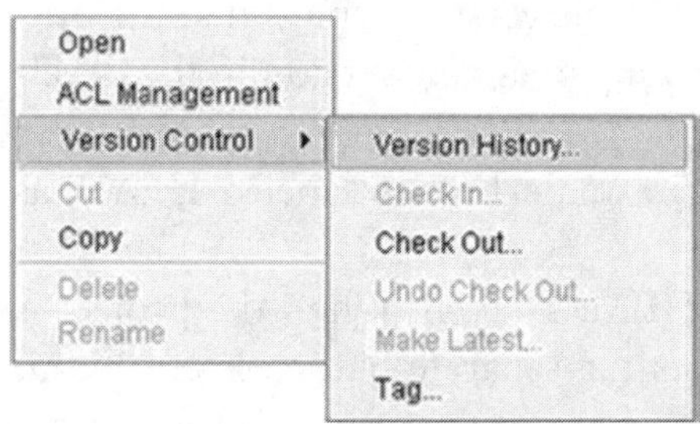

FIGURE 3-17: Navigating to Version History submenu

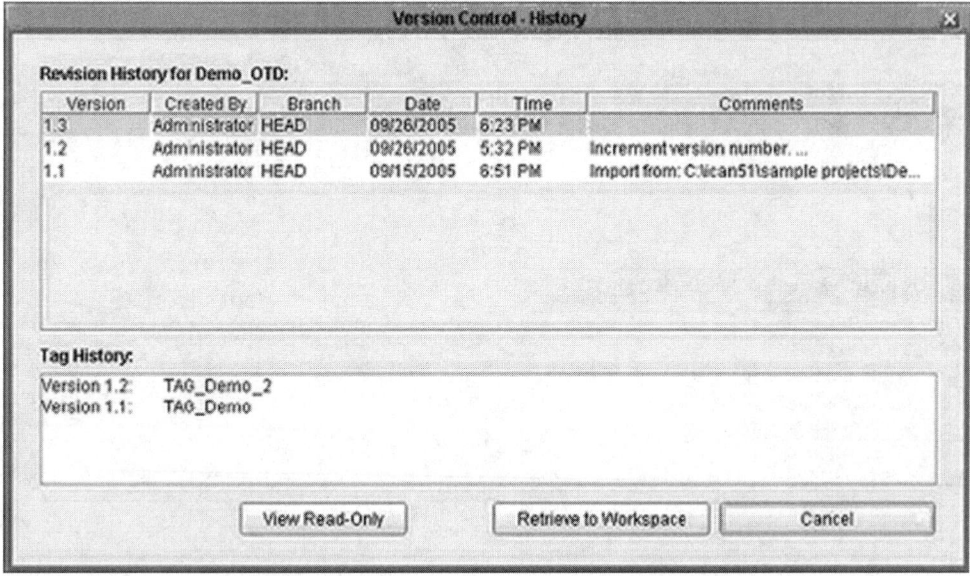

FIGURE 3-18: Viewing version history

Note
Note that more then one person logged into the Enterprise Designer using the same User ID will circumvent the version control system's check-in/check-out locking mechanism and may result in one person's work being overwritten by another's work. When multiple developers work with project components, each must have a unique Enterprise Designer User ID.

3.5.1.4 Branching

Repository branches enable you to isolate different versions of a specific project from each other. This allows maintenance of a stable version deployed to the production environment, for example, while working on a new version in the development environment.

At initial installation, the Repository has a main branch labeled HEAD, as shown in Figure 3-19.

Typically, a project is developed in the HEAD branch. When the project is ready to deploy to the production environment, a separate branch is created to contain that version of the project. The next version of the project is then developed in the HEAD branch.

When a project component is modified in a branch, the changes are confined to that branch; other branches are not affected.

Note
You cannot copy and paste components between branches.

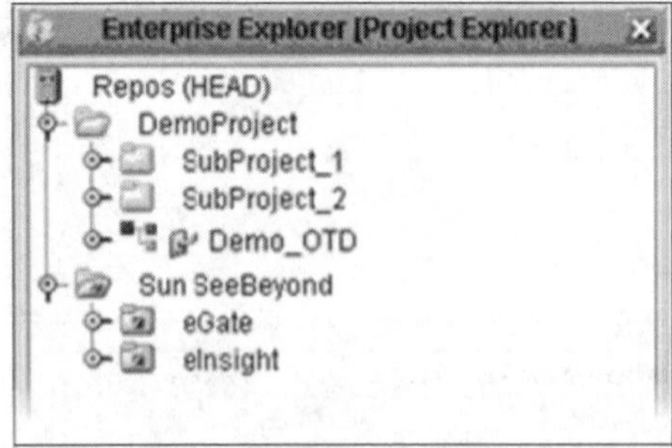

FIGURE 3-19: Project Explorer showing HEAD branch

3.5.1.5 Project Tagging

You can tag components either individually or as collections so that they can be retrieved for deployment by specifying the tag name. When a component, such as a project, is selected for tagging, all components contained in the project that are eligible for tagging are automatically included in a list, similar to the one shown in Figure 3-20. You can deselect individual components from the list if desired.

If a project contains subprojects, you can add the components contained in them to the list by checking the Recourse Project checkbox (subprojects themselves are not shown in the list). Only components that are checked in can be tagged; components that are checked out will be shown in the list but will be dimmed and deselected.

3.5.1.6 Deployment Profile Snapshot Version Control

The Deployment Profile Editor allows control over which version of the various project components get mapped in the deployment profile. The editor provides a spreadsheet-like view that displays project components and their versions. This view includes the component name, project path, current version in the users'

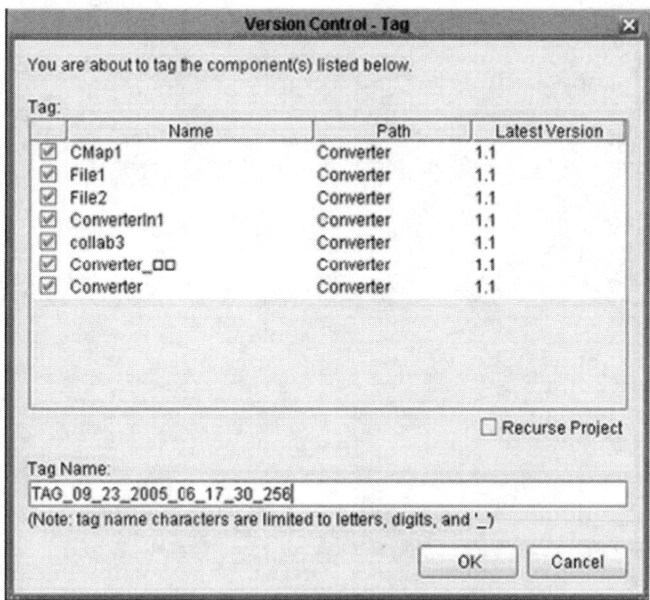

FIGURE 3-20: Project components eligible for tagging

workspace, tag on the version (if there is one), and to what external system the component is mapped.

This view is enabled by clicking the Spreadsheet View icon, like the one shown in Figure 3-21, in the Deployment Profile Editor toolbar.

The spreadsheet view has an option that is checked by default to show only those components that are eligible to be deployed, showing a component table similar to that shown in Figure 3-22. If not checked, components not ordinarily seen in the deployment profile (for example, the connectivity maps and OTDs) will be listed as well. Listing all components allows you to also specify the version of those components, whether they are deployable or not.

The spreadsheet view allows you to specify the version for each component by selecting a version or tag from a drop-down list. Selecting versions or tags does not affect your workspace but is only for setting up the versions to appear in a snapshot; only when the snapshot is retrieved will your workspace be modified.

FIGURE 3-21: Spreadsheet View icon

Environment: Environment1 Map Variables Build Deploy

Name	Path	Version	Tag	Deployed To
Collaboration_xslt	bpxslt_emp_503	1.1		LogicalHost1 -> IntegrationSvr1
BusinessProcess1	bpxslt_emp_503	1.1		LogicalHost1 -> IntegrationSvr1
emp_input_Employee	bpxslt_emp_503	1.1		
emp_output_Employee	bpxslt_emp_503	1.1		
FileIn_BusinessProcess11	bpxslt_emp_503	1.1		File1
BusinessProcess11_FileOut	bpxslt_emp_503	1.1		File2

Show deployable objects only Global Settings ... Snapshot...

Deployment1

FIGURE 3-22: List of components and their version

3.5.1.7 Creating Snapshots

The Deployment Profile Editor allows you to take a snapshot of the configuration currently in your workspace, as shown in the spreadsheet view. Clicking the "Snapshot" button presents a dialog, similar to the one shown in Figure 3-23, in which you enter a name for the snapshot.

3.5.1.8 Retrieving Snapshots

The Deployment Profile Editor gives you the option of deploying the latest component versions from the Repository or those versions recorded in a snapshot of your workspace at a previous time. Clicking the Global Settings button presents a dialog, similar to that shown in Figure 3-24, in which you can specify your choice and, if appropriate, name the desired snapshot.

In either case, if your chosen configuration is different from what is currently in your workspace, you will receive another dialog informing you that the action will modify what is in your workspace and offering you the opportunity to not perform the operation.

- If you select a specific snapshot that is different from what is currently in your workspace, the versions of those components used by the deployment profile that are part of the specified snapshot will be retrieved into your workspace as read-only versions.

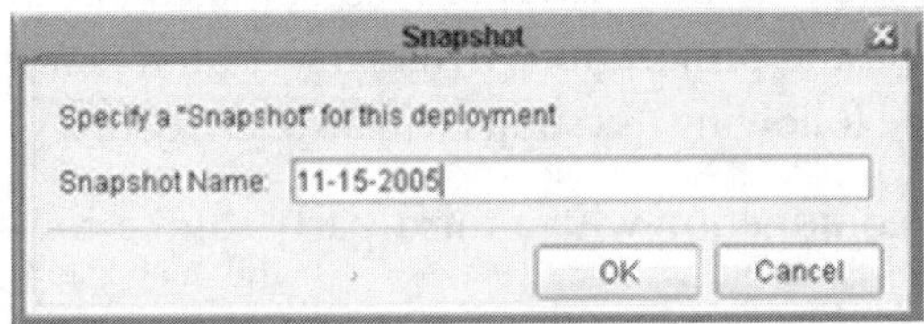

FIGURE 3-23: Naming snapshot

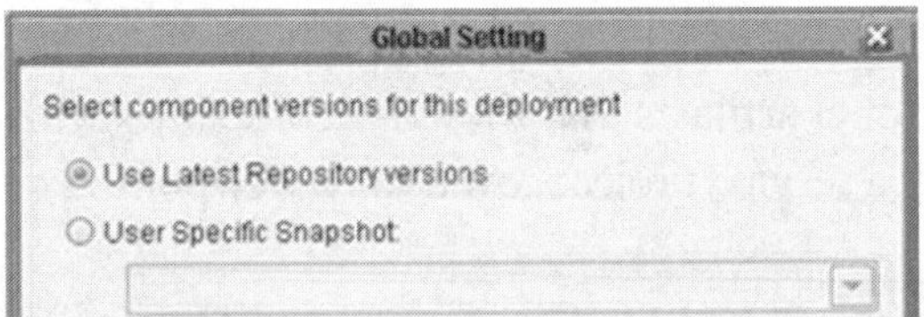

Global Setting
Select component versions for this deployment
Use Latest Repository versions
User Specific Snapshot
OK
Cancel

FIGURE 3-24: Specifying snapshot to retrieve

- If you select to use the latest Repository versions while another configuration is currently in your workspace, those components used by the deployment profile that are currently in your workspace will be removed and replaced by the latest versions from the Repository.

3.5.2 Using a Third-Party Source Control System

It is often found that an organization already uses a concurrent versioning system (CVS) or other source control system for release management of projects and services.

As we saw in the previous section, Java CAPS has its own source control functionality. Unfortunately, the Java CAPS repository file system does not allow its objects and files to easily be checked in and out by external version control systems.

This issue can be worked around by checking into the third-party version control system complete builds (the EAR files that are created) and the corresponding project exports. Exports contain the current version of project objects and code as well as the current environment settings and project configuration. This enables the organization to track changes and tag and redeploy earlier versions of services where necessary. This also enables monitoring and a single system control point for the testing and release process.

3.5.2.1 Migration and Rollback Process

When using a third-party source control system, the only Java CAPS objects that can reasonably be managed are project exports and project builds. In this section we look at the process in more detail. Specially, the following questions will be addressed:

- How do we manage our releases in conjunction with a third-party source control system?
- How do we roll back to an earlier release to fix a bug?
- How do we apply bug fixes to the current project code base?

Let us answer these questions, detailing the steps in releasing a project/service. We also look at best practices and the additional artifacts that should accompany such a release in the source control system from a service/project governance viewpoint.

3.5.2.2 General Release Process

The following discussion covers the general release process from service specification through implementation, deployment, and test.

At the start of a service development life cycle, the requirement and design documents for the project/service are checked in to the source control system. This results in the project's code and the supporting documentation being tagged at the same time, showing the release and modification history for the project. Figure 3-25 depicts the process.

Once the project has been built in Java CAPS, we

- Check in the EAR file and the project export zip file.
- Deploy the project EAR file (retrieved from the source control system) to the Java CAPS domain in the environment using the Enterprise Manager.
- Test the project and check in test results to the source control system.
- The iteration is complete.
- For the next iteration, we modify the code base to implement the new functionality specified in the next phase documentation.

3.5.2.3 The Rollback Release Process

In the event that an issue is discovered in a previously released version of a project, it is a requirement that we can revisit the code and settings of that release. This is achieved by the process depicted in Figure 3-26 and discussed below.

- Rename the project that we are currently working on <projectname>_latest before we import the earlier version.
- Make the changes to fix the bug to the imported project code.
- Build the project and check in the resulting EAR file to the source control system.
- Export the project form the Java CAPS Repository and check in to the source control system.
- Deploy the project and test bug fix.
- Update project documentation with test results in the source control system.
- Take note of the changes that were applied to fix the bug.
- Delete the imported project directory.
- Rename the <projectname>_latest project directory <projectname>.
- Apply the bug fix you have recorded to the code base.

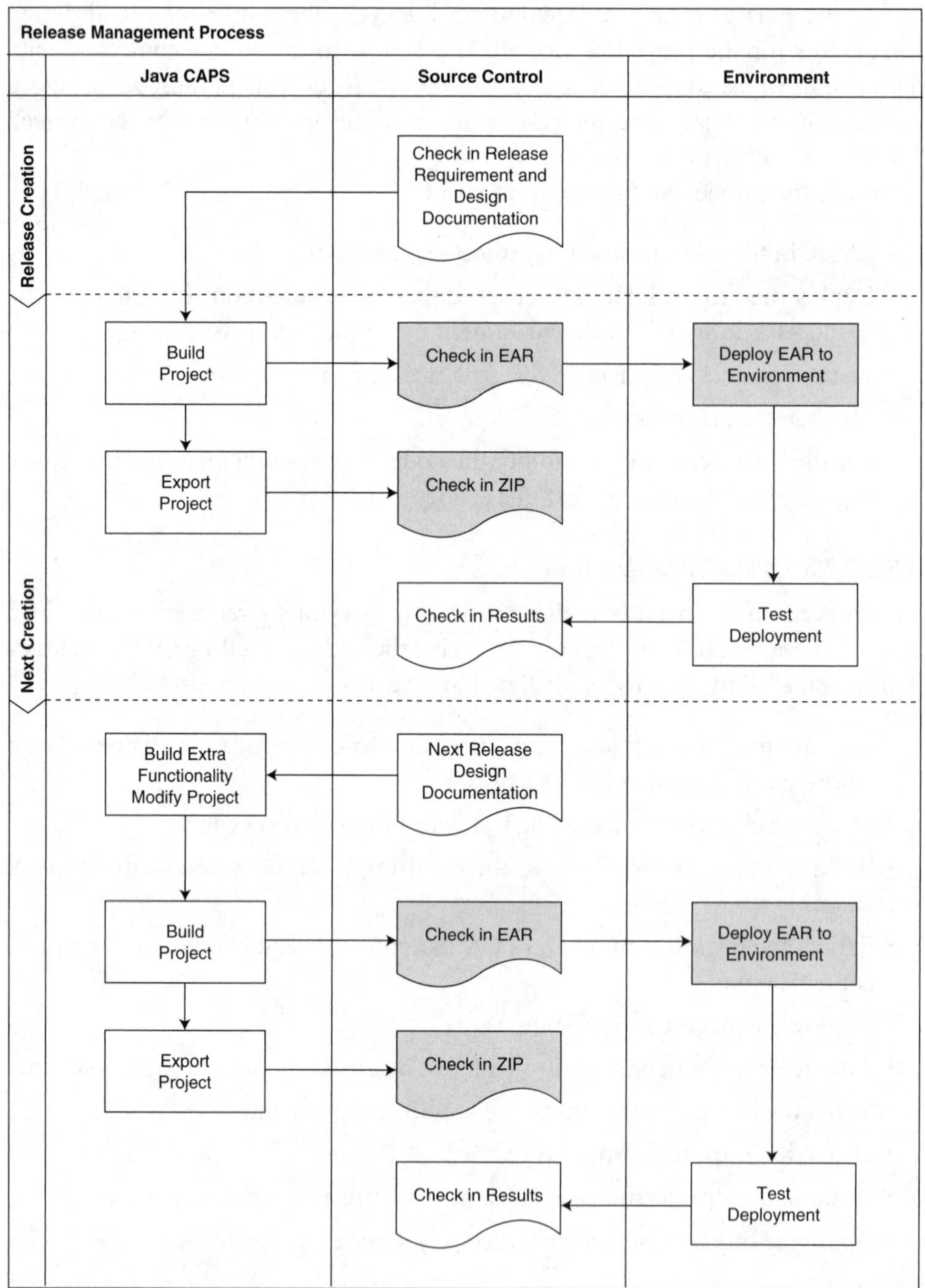

FIGURE 3-25: Release process

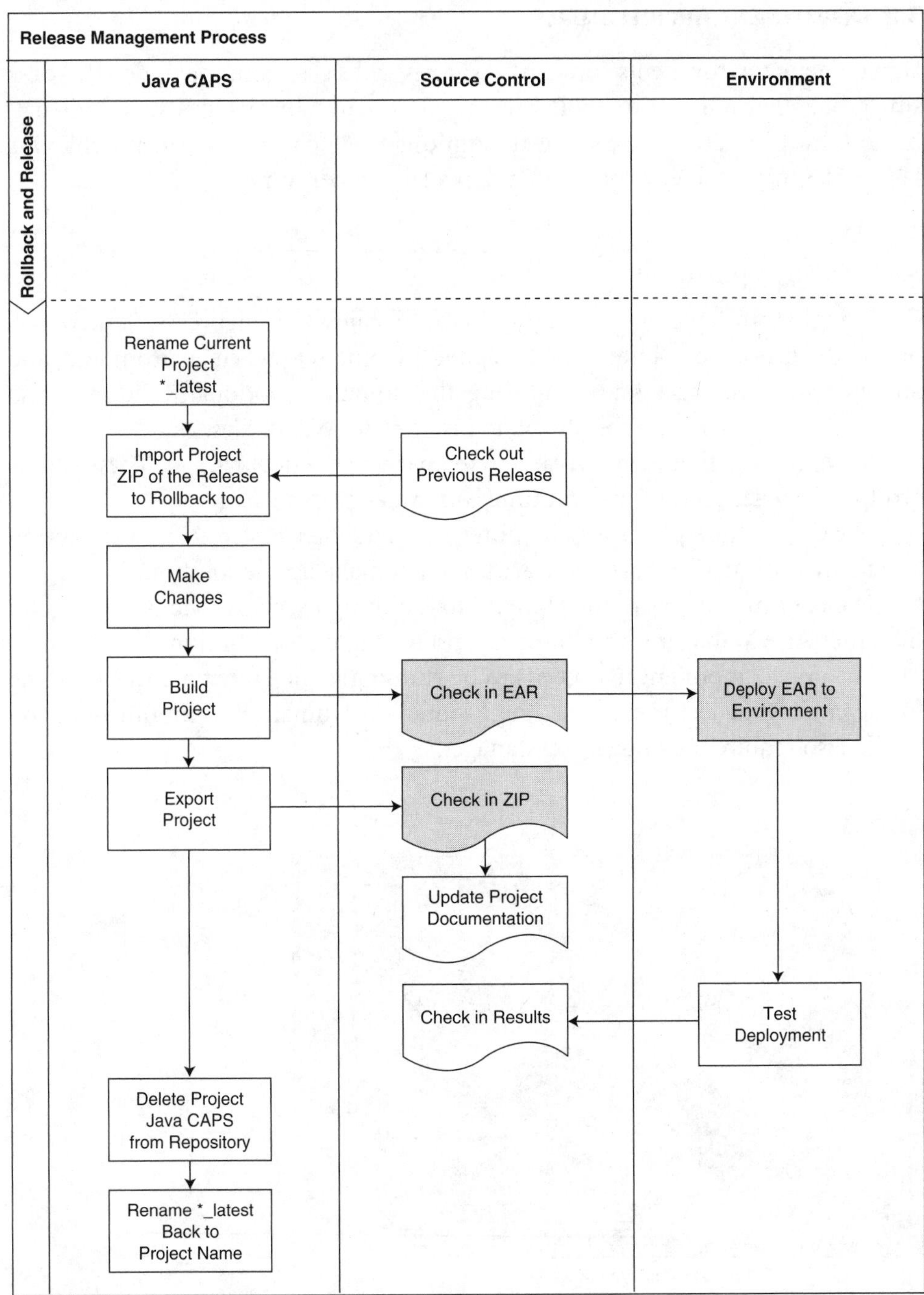

FIGURE 3-26: Rollback release process

3.6 Deployment Architectures

Deployment environments come in all shapes and sizes, from the under-the-desk single-box environment to cooled server room with clusters, grids, and virtualization. In this section we look at the options to be considered when deploying Java CAPS in a small environment and in a large environment.

3.6.1 Small Deployment

On a single-box deployment, diagrammatically shown in Figure 3-27, there will be one Repository, one Enterprise Designer, a Domain for each environment, and an Enterprise Manager for monitoring the domains. Optionally, we may also have a UDDI Server for publishing and discovering WSDL files.

As we can see, there are several moving parts in the deployment. These can be grouped into design time and runtime components, two each.

The design time pieces are the Enterprise Designer for creating the solution and the Repository for storing the artifacts that make up the solution.

The runtime pieces are the Domain for running/executing the processes and the Enterprise Manager for monitoring and managing the solution.

The only component that needs to be running is the Domain corresponding to the environment, for example, the Production Domain. For monitoring, you would also require the Enterprise Manager.

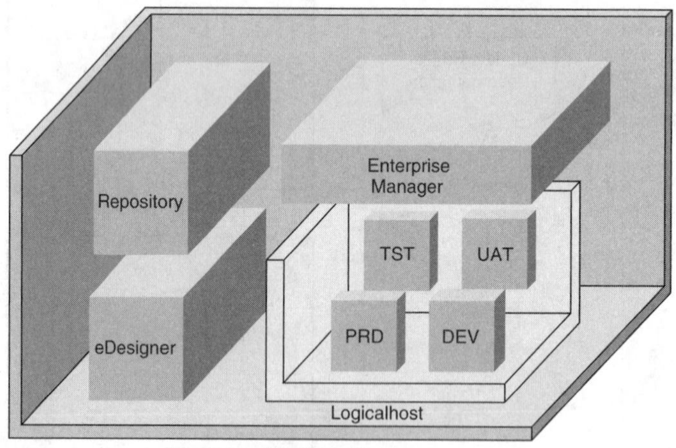

Figure 3-27: Single-box deployment

Using the Enterprise Designer's Environment Explorer tab, you would configure the settings of the end systems in each environment. Figure 3-28 shows a Java CAPS Environment Explorer with a number of separate environments, whose names are reminiscent of the purpose for which they were created.

In the example there are environments named DEV, TST, UAT, and PRD. In each of the environments the combination of the settings in each of the external systems (eWays), the Integration Server, Message Server, and environment constants shows the combination of logical and physical aspects of the project. Ideally, the only configuration changes required for a project to be deployed between DEV and TST, for example, should be contained in the environment settings.

Once the project is built, there are three options for deploying the Enterprise Archive to the runtime environment: using the Enterprise Designer's "Deploy" button, using the Enterprise Manager's Deployer, and using a deployment command-line utility (deplocli). In a single-machine environment, either method is appropriate; however, if there is separation of duties between the developer and

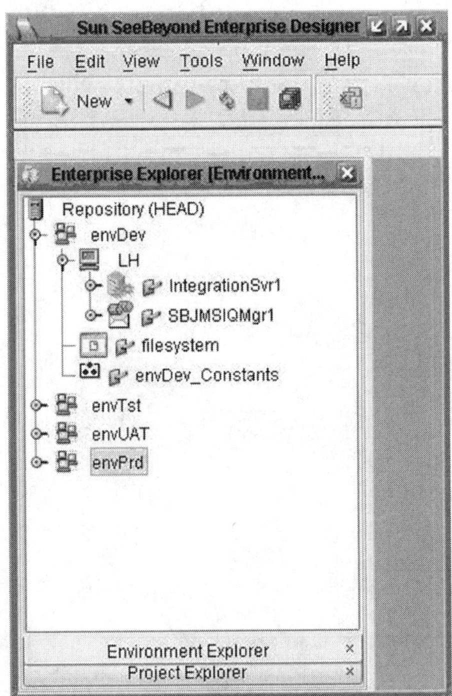

FIGURE 3-28: End system configuration

the administrator/deployer, it is recommended that the administrator/deployer use the Enterprise Manager or the command-line deployer tool.

3.6.2 Medium to Large Deployment

When we come to creating the structure for a clustered environment, we have an option to create one or two repositories. Let's discuss the pros and cons of both architecture deployment options.

Environment assumptions include the following:

- One machine for development, test, and UAT environments
- A production environment consisting of a clustered setup of two or more machines connected to shared storage, the storage area network (SAN)

If Java CAPS is deployed in a one-Repository configuration, as shown in Figure 3-29, all the environments are maintained in the one Repository. This makes maintenance of the platform and the environments easier.

When upgrades are required, they need only be applied to the one Repository. This eliminates issues around the levels of versions and patches (ESRs/hotfixes) between environments.

Some organizations maintain two totally separate environments with all components replicated, Repositories, logical hosts, queue managers, and so on. Figure 3-30 shows a two-Repository setup.

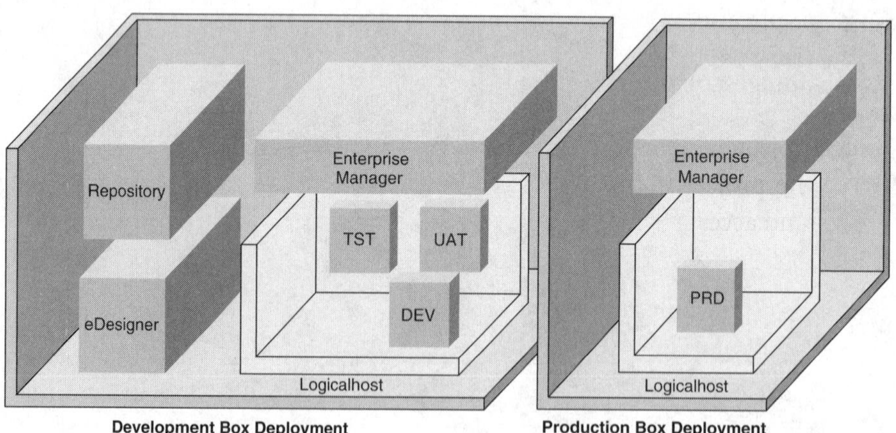

FIGURE 3-29: One-Repository setup

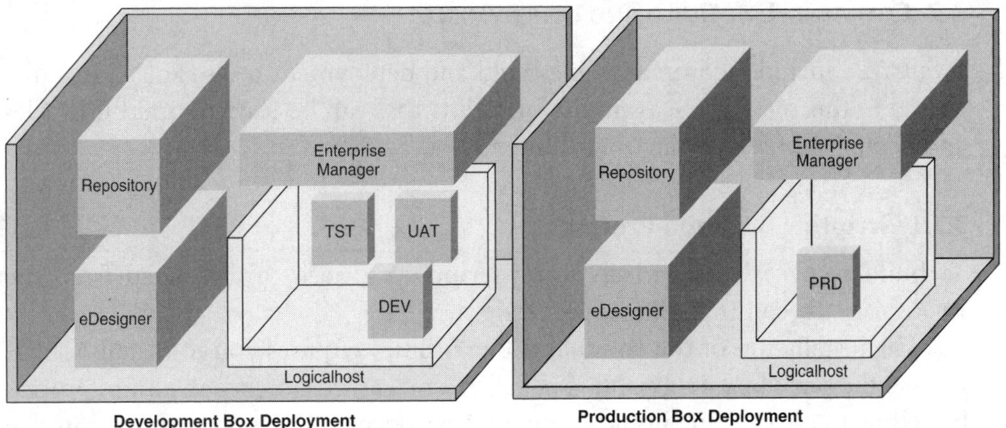

FIGURE 3-30: Two-Repository setup

In this architecture, each project needs to be exported from the development/test Repository and imported in to the production Repository. This raises the following disadvantages:

- When a project is exported, all components are in the export zip except the project's deployment profiles. Deployment profiles must be created again. Java CAPS Enterprise Designer knowledge is required.
- When automation of the deployments is required using the command-line tools, complications arise, as we see in section 3.7.

The advantages, on the other hand, are as follows:

- Once a project has been promoted to the production Repository, we have a version of the project that is under deployment control of a new environment. Control and access to this Repository can be restricted to one administrator.
- As the version of the project/interface is in the production Repository, it is isolated from development changes; so if a bug is discovered in the production code, it may be fixed without the risk of having to deploy untested changes to production from a development branch of the code.
- The versions of patches on the overall environment can be more tightly controlled by the production administrators.

3.7 Command-Line Build and Deployment

Java CAPS includes command-line build and deployment tools. The scripts discussed in this section are examples of scripts that can be used to build EAR files and deploy the files to their environments.

3.7.1 Scripting the Build Process

To build your services/projects using scripts, you need to download from the Repository the commandlinecodegen.zip file.

The installation of the command-line utilities requires you to install Apache Ant on the same box. Once Ant is installed, you can commence the build process by calling the ant.bat file in the commandlinecodegen directory with appropriate project settings. The eGate User Guide discusses this in some detail.

A more automated approach is to run these commands from an Ant script. A Java IDE, for example NetBeans, can be used to execute the Ant script. The following sample script builds an EAR file for a project. A slight amendment to remotebuild.xml file, in the commandcodegen directory, has been made to allow the script to work. The change is setting the settings for the Repository in the remotebuild.xml file in its init section.

3.7.2 Project Build Script

The sample build script is shown in Listing 3-1.

LISTING 3-1: Project Build Script

```
<?xml version="1.0" encoding="UTF-8"?>
<project name="Build Sample Service" default="all" basedir=".">
    <target depends="build_EAR, deploy_EAR_DEV" name="all">
    </target>
    <target name="build_EAR">
        <ant antfile="remotebuild.xml"
             dir="C:\JavaCaps5.1.2\commandlinecodegen\" >
          <property
             name="commandline.rep.projectName"
             value="bsSampleService" />
          <property
             name="commandline.rep.projectDeployName"
             value="DEV_1" />
        </ant>
    </target>
</project>
```

3.7.3 Project Deployment Script

A sample deployment script is shown in Listing 3-2.

LISTING 3-2: Project Deployment Script

```
<?xml version="1.0" encoding="UTF-8"?>
<project
name="Build Sample Service"
default="all"
basedir=".">
    <target
     depends="build_EAR"
     name="deploy_EAR_DEV"
    >
        <exec
         dir="C:/JavaCaps5.1.2/deploy/"
         executable="cmd"
        >
            <arg LINE="/c"/>
<!-
       deploycli.bat
          -host eaidev1
          -port 50100
            -u Administrator
            -pass homers list"/>
-->
            <arg value="deploycli.bat"/>
            <arg value="-host"/>
            <arg value="eaidev1"/>
            <arg value="-port"/>
            <arg value="50100"/>
            <arg value="-u"/>
            <arg value="Administrator"/>
            <arg value="-pass"/>
            <arg value="homers"/>
            <arg value="deploy"/>
            <arg value=
"C:\JavaCaps5.1.2\commandlinecodegen\localrepository\DEST\builds\bsSampleServiceDE
V_1\lh\IntegrationSvr1\bsSampleServiceDEV_1.ear"
            />
        </exec>
    </target>
</project>
```

Based on the experience of the author, best practice is to deploy a single Repository and adopt the release management strategy described earlier accompanied by an external source control system or a governance repository.

Develop the build and deployment scripts for each of your services that you create. This simplifies the release management process further down the line.

Deploy Java CAPS with one Repository and manage all your environments from this repository.

3.8 Chapter Summary

This chapter explored some of the options for organizing and managing projects in Java CAPS. Both design-time structure and organization, the use of variables for environment independence, and version control aspects of development were discussed. Issues of migration from environment to environment, structure of environments, deployment architectures suitable for small and large deployments, and command-line build and deployment tools were also discussed.

SECTION II

Patterns Review and Application

CHAPTER FOUR

Message Exchange Patterns

4.1 Introduction

This is the first in a series of chapters that specifically address [EIP] concepts and patterns. We address a number of [EIP] patterns and discuss how Java CAPS can be used to implement specific message-related patterns, which [EIP] groups together under the heading of Message Construction. In particular, the following patterns and specific Java CAPS concepts and solutions illustrations are discussed:

- Document Message
- Command Message
- Event Message
- Scheduler eWay and Job Scheduling
- Request/Reply
- JMS Request/Reply
- Auction Pattern
- HTTP Request/Reply
- HTTP eWay, Client, and Server
- eInsight Subprocess
- SOAP Request/Reply
- Web Service Implementation
- eInsight-based and Java Collaboration–based
- Return Address
- Correlation
- Message Sequence
- JMS Serial Mode Concurrency
- JMS FIFO Modes

- Serializing eInsight Using XA
- Message Expiration
- Java CAPS Configuration
- Message Journaling
- Format Indicator
- Data Streaming
- Message Security

4.2 Document Message

[EIP] discusses the subtle differences between a Command Message, a Document Message, and an Event Message, pointing out that the differences are semantic rather than structural or technological and that the semantics are solution-specific. From the Java CAPS perspective, any message is a Document Message in that it carries business data from component to component. Technologies used to create and manipulate the message are the same regardless of whether additional meaning is superimposed by the application.

It is implicitly assumed that a Document Message has some intrinsic business-specific structure. This structure can be parsed to obtain access to specific information of interest—HL7 Message, Database Table, and SAP IDOC. Chapter 7, "Message Construction," discusses Java CAPS facilities used for creation of messages and manipulation of their content.

4.3 Command Message

A Command Message [EIP] is a message whose role is to invoke a predefined activity, implemented by a component which is the destination of the message. In Java CAPS, every message would be a Command Message according to this definition. If a distinction is needed, then perhaps a message that causes the component to invoke logic different from the logic used to process ordinary messages should be considered a Command Message. All other messages, from the perspective of this component, would be Document Messages.

Java CAPS solutions, or solution fragments, like Java Collaborations or business processes, are always triggered by a message—a message delivered to an endpoint or a message delivered as a result of timer expiration.

The Scheduler Connector, which manages time schedules, could be considered a generator of Command Messages. The scheduler triggers invocation of the collaboration or the business process with which it is associated when a scheduled time is reached. It sends a message containing a fixed literal string to the component's listener. This message is a Command Message in that it causes the target collaboration or the business process to be activated and to perform its programmed activities. The component triggered this way typically operates on messages it collects by polling external systems, which is the reason it is designed to be triggered by a timer.

When not triggered by a scheduler, the Java CAPS component is triggered by a message, whose content typically contains business data to be processed. Unlike eWays, which operate on messages with eWay-specific and application-specific structure, JMS endpoints deliver messages regardless of their intrinsic structure. Further, JMS messages contain both the payload and a series of predefined properties, which can be supplemented by user-defined properties. A JMS message payload or properties could be used to construct a Command Message rather then a regular message with business payload.

4.4 Event Message

Event Message in a messaging system is a Document Message. As [EIP] states, "the difference . . . is a matter of timing and content." An Event Message typically carries very little or no content. Its purpose is to cause the receiver to begin its programmed activity. In this spirit, a Scheduler eWay, Java CAPS–provided timer-based trigger generates Event Messages whenever its timer expires or its schedule falls due. The Scheduler eWay delivers an Event Message, with a fixed body, to the component that uses it. Chapter 2, section 2.2, "The Event Message Using Scheduler," in Part II (located on the accompanying CD-ROM), illustrates the point with a simple Java CAPS project.

Note

The scheduler configuration is not particularly sophisticated, and the content on the input message is the literal string "StaticString." Note, too, that the schedule to which the eWay operates is configured through the connectivity map. A change to the schedule requires the solution to be rebuilt and redeployed.

When required to implement a solution where multiple events must take place according to different schedules, multiple Scheduler eWays must be configured. With only a few schedules, this is perhaps not too much of an issue. When the number of different schedules grows, the issue rapidly becomes a major inconvenience.

Cron, of the Unix world, is the typical yardstick used to measure scheduling solutions. Cron-like scheduling sophistication is what is sought. A reasonably sophisticated scheduling solution would support event triggering expressions like these:

- Simple time interval: every x minutes, every x hours, . . .
- Complex time intervals: every x minutes between xx:xx a.m. and yy:yy p.m., . . .
- Calendar-based interval: every day, every week, every month, every year, every x days, every x months, every x years, . . .
- Complex calendar-based interval: every weekday, every weekend, x weekday in a month, x weekday in month y, . . .
- Nested intervals, combination of intervals, . . .

It would also have the ability to supply job identifiers and job parameters so that correct jobs can be triggered and variable data provided to them.

When faced with a need for sophisticated scheduling, the first instinct is to build a sophisticated scheduler into the solution under construction. In Java CAPS, that would mean some form of a J2EE container–friendly schedule management mechanism. While a number of Java-based, Cron-like scheduling solutions have been developed, none have been integrated into Java CAPS.

A much simpler way to provide more sophisticated scheduling capability would be to use an external scheduler, perhaps Unix native Cron or Windows native Task Scheduler, to trigger a Java CAPS solution via an endpoint. The endpoint could be a JMS destination or a listener eWay—perhaps a TCP/IP eWay, a HTTP eWay, or even a Batch Local File eWay. The Java CAPS solution need not be aware of scheduling at all. All it needs to do is process a message when it comes—now. The external scheduling solution would decide when the "now" is. Chapter 2, section 2.2.1, "External Scheduler Example," in Part II, implements a simple project that illustrates this concept.

The obvious advantages of using external scheduler are:

- You can use the scheduling solution the platform provides or deploy another external scheduling solution of desired sophistication.
- You can maintain job schedule externally and modify it dynamically without changes to the Java CAPS solution.
- You can keep the Java CAPS solution free of scheduling concerns and complexities.

The obvious disadvantage is that the external scheduling solution is external to the Java CAPS solution.

If we consider replacing a number of Scheduler eWays with the same number of TCP/IP eWays to be an issue, we could consider introducing a single TCP/IP eWay that receives all scheduled event messages and uses a fixed or a dynamic router to route these messages to the parts of the solution they are to trigger.

Somewhere between the simplistic Scheduler eWay-based solution and the completely externalized solution is a "heartbeat"-based solution implemented using Java CAPS. One could design a solution that has a single Scheduler eWay that works to a repeated "heartbeat" schedule, say 1 minute. Every minute, a message is injected into the solution to trigger a "Schedule Keeper" collaboration. This collaboration, when it starts, prepares a list of minutes, with a list of jobs, possibly empty, associated with every minute, read from a file or a database. When triggered, the Schedule Keeper collaboration consults the list of minutes and, for the current minute, sends a JMS message for every job that is to be triggered at that time. The message contains job specifications for the job. Some downstream component receives the message and executes its programmed functionality. The Schedule Keeper collaboration would need to have sophistication necessary to parse job specifications, parse time intervals, parse execution windows and frequencies, parse job parameters, and assemble minute-by-minute job lists. This kind of sophistication calls for a reasonable amount of Java code, so it is not provided as an example.

4.5 Request/Reply

Some messaging solutions require that the recipient is active at the time of send, thereby guaranteeing to the sender that the message was received by the recipient. BEA MessageQ, a proprietary system from Oracle, is one such system. Other messaging solutions operate on a fire-and-forget or a store-and-forward basis, expecting the messaging infrastructure to deliver each message to the intended recipient whether that recipient is active at the time of send or not. JMS is one such system. The major difference, from the architectural perspective, is the timing. In the former case a message is delivered "immediately" or fails "immediately," so the sender can branch as appropriate upon sending the message. In the latter case, the message is delivered to the messaging system, which "immediately" acknowledges that it has assumed responsibility for delivery to the ultimate recipient. That delivery, however, may take some time if the recipient is not active for some time or may not take place at all if the recipient never appears. The sender will never know what the ultimate outcome was.

In some situations a solution may be architected such that major pieces of functionality are built as functions, modules, or services, accepting some input message, performing some processing, and producing some result. To implement such components, it is necessary that the invocation mechanism allows the invoker to invoke a component, provide the input data it needs, wait for the execution to complete, and receive the result. This interaction is what [EIP] calls the Request/Reply pattern.

In general, you could implement a Request/Reply pattern using any endpoints, with or without messaging infrastructure, as long as the requestor was engineered to make a request, wait for the reply, and receive it. Even file exchange can support the Request/Reply pattern. In fact, the Australian Energy Industry–developed Hokey-Pokey protocol uses the File Transfer Protocol (FTP) to implement a Request/Reply pattern for submitting aseXML (Australian Standard for Energy XML) documents. The sending component places a file containing an XML document in a "mailbox" of an Energy Hub, then polls the "outbox" at the Energy Hub for an Acknowledgment file. The exchange is not complete until the Acknowledgment file is received or a timeout occurs. This is a classic Request/Reply implementation.

Java CAPS provides a number of mechanisms to implement the Request/Reply pattern. Which of the different mechanisms is appropriate will depend on the problem that needs to be solved. While any endpoint type can be used to implement the Request/Reply pattern, we discuss only the more common, useful, and interesting mechanisms: JMS Request/Reply, HTTP Request/Reply, SOAP Request/Reply, and Web Services Invocation.

4.5.1 JMS Request/Reply

JMS is typically used to build store-and-forward messaging solutions. It also supports implementation of Request/Reply solutions using temporary JMS Destina-

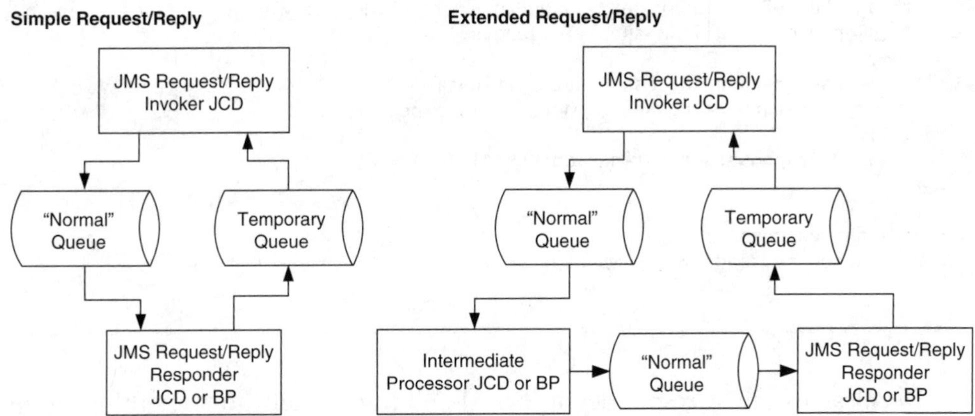

FIGURE 4-1: JMS Request/Reply models

tions. In Java CAPS, a Java Collaboration can be both a requester and a responder in a Request/Reply configuration. An eInsight Business Process can only be a responder, since no eInsight service exists that would allow an eInsight Business Process to invoke JMS Request/Reply functionality. All is not lost, however. Since an eInsight Business Process can invoke a "New Web Service" Java Collaboration as an activity, and a Java Collaboration can invoke JMS Request/Reply functionality, a JCD wrapper can be used to overcome this limitation. The models are illustrated in Figure 4-1.

The receive method of a Java Collaboration that serves as a responder in the simple Request/Reply model would look similar to that shown in Listing 4-1.

LISTING 4-1: __Book/MessageExchangePatterns/JMSRequestReply/jcdJMSReqResSrv

```
public void receive
    (com.stc.connectors.jms.Message input
    ,com.stc.connectors.jms.JMS W_JMSResponse )
        throws Throwable
{
    ;
    // extract request from input JMS message
    String sJMSRequest = input.getTextMessage();
    ;
    // process message content
    String sJMSResponse = sJMSRequest.toUpperCase();
    ;
    // determine whether to send response to a specific destination
    // or to the default Connectivity Map destination
```

```
    String sReplyTo = input.getMessageProperties().getReplyTo();
    if (sReplyTo != null && sReplyTo.length() > 0) {
        ;
        // have return address - set destination
        // to return response to where it is expected
        ;
        W_JMSResponse.setDestination( sReplyTo );
    }
    ;
    // send response
    W_JMSResponse.sendText( sJMSResponse );
    ;
}
```

Needless to say, a responder in a real solution would do something more interesting than convert the request string to uppercase.

Note that this particular collaboration could be used as both a Request/Reply responder and as a regular "pick from one JMS Destination and deliver to another JMS Destination" collaboration.

By obtaining the value of the JMS ReplyTo property in the input message, and setting it as a destination for the response message, we are turning this collaboration into a Request/Response processor. If the component that submitted a message did not set the ReplyTo property, the condition would be false and the response would go to the JMS Destination configured in the connectivity map.

Notice also that this collaboration does not need to be the one that directly interacts with the JMS Destinations set up by the requestor, as shown in the Extended Request/Reply model. There could be other Collaborations and Business Processes operating on the message, with multiple JMS destinations between the requestor and responder. As long as each component in the chain took care to propagate the value of the original ReplyTo property, the response would still get delivered to the original requestor. Propagation of the ReplyTo and other JMS message properties requires a bit more work, as much as two extra lines, as shown in Listing 4-2.

LISTING 4-2: _Book/MessageExchangePatterns/JMSRequestReply/jcdJMSReqResSrvPreserve

```
public void receive
    (com.stc.connectors.jms.Message input
    ,com.stc.connectors.jms.JMS W_JMSResponse )
        throws Throwable
{
    ;
    // extract request from input JMS message
```

```
    String sJMSRequest = input.getTextMessage();
    ;
    // process message content
    String sJMSResponse = sJMSRequest.toUpperCase();
    ;
    // create a JMS message to send out and populate it
    // with the payload and ReplyTo property value
    ;
    com.stc.connectors.jms.Message jmsResponse
        = W_JMSResponse.createTextMessage();
    jmsResponse.setTextMessage( sJMSResponse );
    jmsResponse.getMessageProperties().setReplyTo
        ( input.getMessageProperties().getReplyTo() );
    ;
    // send response
    W_JMSResponse.send( jmsResponse );
    ;
}
```

In the previous example, the sendText() method of the JMS Connector object was used to directly send the response string. In order to set properties, a message object is required. The payload and the properties of the object are set, and the message object is sent using the send() method. Needless to say, other properties, including user-defined properties, can be set before sending the message.

The JMS Request/Reply functionality relies on Java CAPS creating a temporary JMS destination, under the hood as it were, and transparently setting the ReplyTo property of the request message to the name of that destination. The requestReply() method puts the request message to a regular JMS destination, named in the connectivity map, and performs a blocking receive on the temporary destination. Once the message is received, or the time expires, the call returns to the collaboration.

The receive method of a basic Java Collaboration that invokes a JMS Request/Reply functionality might look like that shown in Listing 4-3.

LISTING 4-3: __Book/MessageExchangePatterns/JMSRequestReply/jcdJMSReqRespCli

```
public void receive
    (com.stc.connector.appconn.file.FileTextMessage input
    ,com.stc.connectors.jms.JMS JMSRRClient
    ,com.stc.connector.appconn.file.FileApplication W_toFile )
        throws Throwable
{
    String sRequestText = input.getText();
    ;
    final int _TIMEOUT_IN_MILLIS_ = 1000 * 30 * 1;
    ;
```

```
    // create a JMS Text Message and populate it using input data
    ;
    com.stc.connectors.jms.Message jmsRequest
        = JMSRRClient.createTextMessage();
    jmsRequest.setTextMessage( sRequestText );
    jmsRequest.storeUserProperty
        ( "MyPropertyName", "MyPropertyValue" );
    ;
    // invoke JMS Request/Reply functionality
    ;
    com.stc.connectors.jms.Message jmsResponse
        = JMSRRClient.requestReply
                ( _TIMEOUT_IN_MILLIS_, jmsRequest );
    ;
    // process response, including empty response
    // if request times out
    ;
    if (jmsResponse == null) {
        throw new javax.jms.JMSException
                    ( "Timed out waiting for Response" );
    }
    String sResponse = jmsResponse.getTextMessage();
    ;
    W_toFile.setText( sResponse );
    W_toFile.write();
    ;
}
```

This Collaboration is triggered by a File eWay and ultimately writes its output to a file using a File eWay. The content of the input file is set as the content of a request message. The JMS Request/Reply method is invoked with a timeout and a request message. The method will return a JMS message with the response or null if timeout occurs. The input message could be delivered by means other than a File eWay, and it could be preprocessed before being sent as a request. The response could be postprocessed and sent to some destination other than a File eWay. The point is that a JMS Request/Reply client is quite simple to implement in a Java Collaboration.

For the simple Request/Reply model, the connectivity map will look like Figure 4-2.

Note the final qDummyResponseNeverUsed JMS Destination. This destination is never used because the Collaboration explicitly sends the response message to the JMS Destination whose name is specified in the JMS ReplyTo property. In this case, it will be the name of the temporary destination created by the JMS Message Server for this requester. Note also that the connectivity map, which could otherwise be used as a good reflection of real connections, no longer accu-

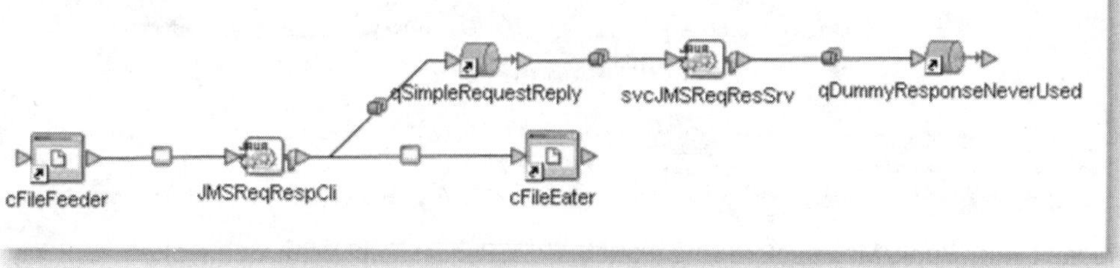

FIGURE 4-2: __Book/MessageExchangePatterns/JMSRequestReply/jcdJMSReqRespCli

rately depicts the interactions that take place. The literal "Dummy" is added to the name of the unused destination to give a strong hint that code may have to be inspected to discover what is actually happening.

We could have, without loss of functionality, produced a connectivity map where the output of the service svcJMSReqResSrv would be connected to the qSimpleRequestReply. This could, perhaps, be better for the simple case as it would suggest a Request/Response relationship, as shown in Figure 4-3.

For the extended Request/Reply mode, the connectivity map will look like that in Figure 4-4.

Here too we could have connected the output of svcJMSReqResSvc service to qPreservePropsQueue to suggest that the Request/Response pattern is used (Figure 4-5).

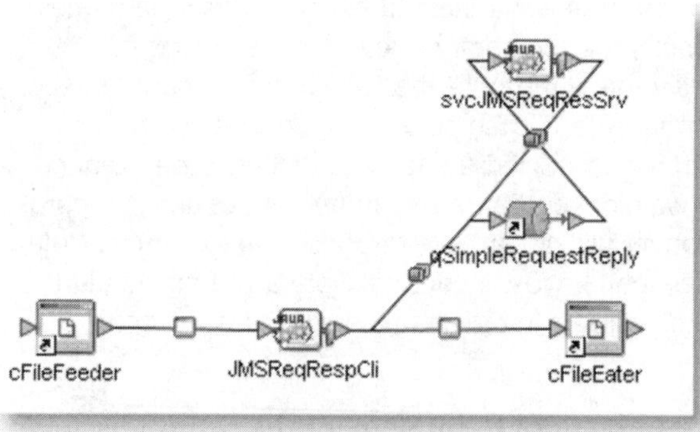

FIGURE 4-3: __Book/MessageExchangePatterns/JMSRequestReply/cmSimpleRequestReply01

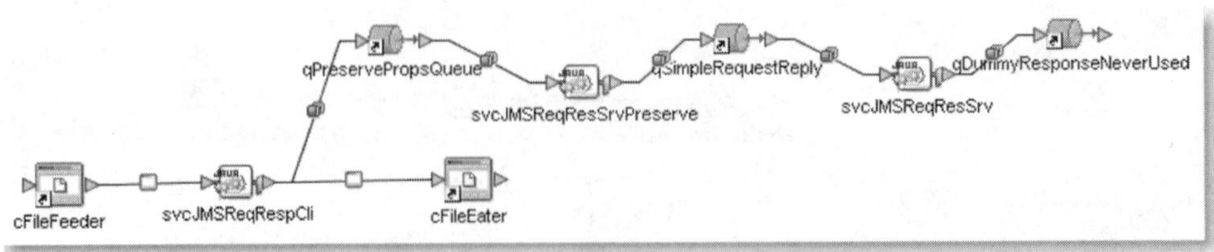

FIGURE 4-4: __Book/MessageExchangePatterns/JMSRequestReply/cmExtendedRequestReply

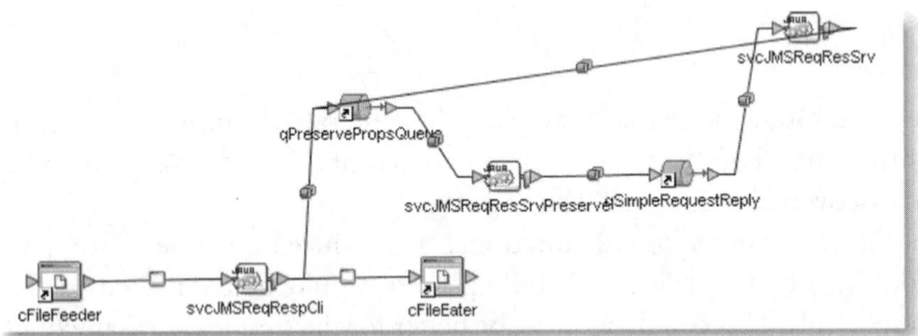

FIGURE 4-5: __Book/MessageExchangePatterns/JMSRequestReply/cmExtendedRequestReply01

Note

An important property of the temporary queue, created by the requestReply() method, is that it exists only as long as its creator exists. In this case, if the collaboration that invokes the requestReply() method exits, because the requestReply() timed out, for example, the temporary queue will be destroyed. If the responding service attempts to put a response message to the response queue, it will receive an exception because the temporary response queue no longer exists. This is a very desirable characteristic in Request/Response scenarios where a requestor will not wait longer than a certain amount of time. If appropriately designed, the responder will discard late responses on exception. Note, however, that the responses may be lost by design. Note also that should the system fail while request processing is in progress, message loss will occur.

Much as a Java Collaboration can be used to implement the responder logic, so too an eInsight Business Process can be used for this purpose, as shown in Figure 4-6. Similarly, and even more simply than in the case of a Java Collaboration, the ReplyTo property needs to be copied from the input JMS message to the des-

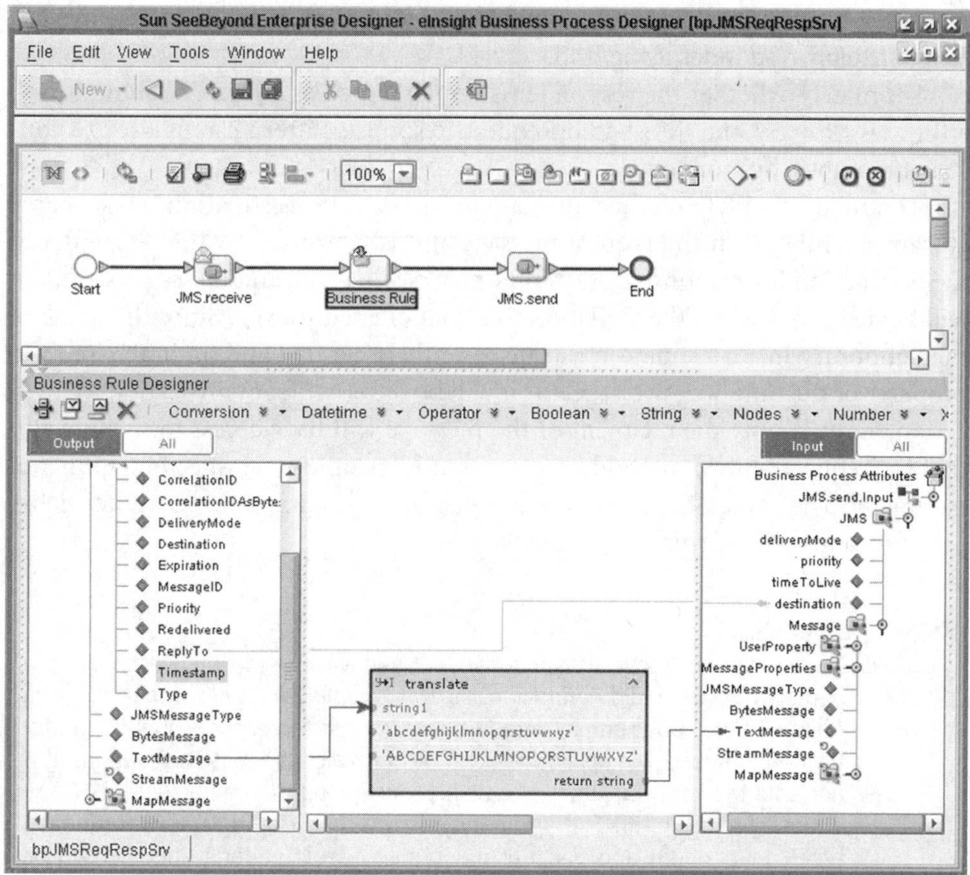

FIGURE 4-6: __Book/MessageExchangePatterns/JMSRequestReply/bpJMSReqRespSrv

tination property of the output JMS message. The infrastructure will take care of the rest.

Where building a JMS Request/Reply responder in eInsight is easy, building a JMS Request/Reply requestor is perhaps harder than it needs to be. It is necessary to write a Java Collaboration to wrap the call to the JMS requestResponse() method and invoke that collaboration as an activity in the Business Process. The collaboration will look almost exactly like the one presented earlier except it will be designed as a New Web Service collaboration, and the input and output will be message structures rather than connectors. Chapter 2, section 2.3.1, "JMS Request/Reply Invoker for eInsight," in Part II, illustrates the steps involved in creating a JMS invoker collaboration that can be used by an eInsight business process to invoke a Request/Reply responder using JMS.

Ultimately, whether the responder is implemented as a Java Collaboration or a Business Process, the JMS-based Request/Response pattern can be used to construct reusable components.

The requestReply() method uses a temporary JMS Destination whose name is transparently set in the request message and is later used by the responder as the destination for responses. The temporary destination, and messages within it, will be destroyed when the Collaboration that created it exits. Since the name of the temporary JMS Destination is transparently generated and set in the ReplyTo property of the outgoing message, (a) it will be different from invocation to invocation, and (b) only the recipient of the message will have access to it. Note also that the requestReply() method variant, used in sample code, specifies a timeout parameter. The value of that parameter must be large enough to guarantee delivery of responses in normal circumstances.

Note

The discussion above uses a somewhat awkward term, JMS Destination, to name what we would naturally call a JMS queue. This is because in the Java Collaboration code samples and Business Process screenshots, there is no distinction between queues and topics, both of which are JMS Destinations. It is not until the connectivity map is being constructed that the actual JMS Destination type is specified. This is handy as the code is generic and destination type–independent and because the same code, if general enough, can be used in solutions using queues and ones using topics.

A form of an Auction pattern, where the fastest responder wins, would be an interesting application of a JMS Request/Reply pattern, which uses topics rather than queues and has multiple responders configured in the connectivity map. Chapter 2, section 2.3.2, "JMS Request/Response Auction Pattern," in Part II, illustrates this concept with an example.

Note

An important point to note about the JMS requestReply() method is that, at least through version 5.1.3, both the requestor and the responder JMS Clients must be deployed to the same JMS Message Server. If the responder must be deployed to a different JMS Message Server, then other means of implementing a Request/Reply mechanism must be considered instead.

4.5.2 HTTP Request/Reply

The Hypertext Transfer Protocol (HTTP) is the embodiment of the Request/Reply pattern. An HTTP GET or an HTTP POST request is submitted to an HTTP Server, which returns a response. The term *HTTP Server* is used deliberately to describe a server that implements the HTTP Protocol. To use *Web Server* would be to invite confusion. Even in the early days of HTTP 0.9, an HTTP Server could return content other than text/html, which is what a "Web page," as implied in the term *Web server,* would be. With support for the Multipurpose Internet Mail Extensions (MIME) content-type specification and handling, the range of content types that can be returned by an HTTP Server is virtually limitless. These properties of HTTP are used to implement Request/Response solutions that deal with content other than the Hypertext Markup Language [HTML401]. HTTP makes provisions for PUT, DELETE, TRACE, CONNECT, and OPTIONS methods as well. Some of these, because of the inherent security concerns, are rarely implemented. Others are only implemented to support HTTP Proxies.

Before the advent of Web Services, a number of HTTP-based services were implemented by various parties. As predating Web Services standards, these services typically used HTTP POST to submit solution-specific requests and receive solution-specific HTTP Server responses as content of type text/plain, text/html, or text/xml. The most notable implementation of these is the HTTP Binding for the Electronic Business XML Business to Business Protocol Message Service [ebXMLMS] implementation, which is an HTTP POST Request/Reply–based implementation, and while it uses SOAP over HTTP, it is not a Web Services implementation. These kinds of services may now be rarely developed, but you may find yourself in need of integrating one into the solution you are building. Figure 4-7 depicts the HTTP Request/Response model.

Java CAPS includes, among others, the HTTP eWay—an Adapter that allows an integration solution to submit an HTTP POST or GET request, or to implement an HTTP Responder that processes HTTP GET or POST requests and returns content of the appropriate type.

Chapter 2, section 2.3.3, "HTTP Request/Response," in Part II, discusses details of the HTTP protocol, relevant to the examples, and shows a number of example HTTP Requestor Collaborations and an example HTTP Responder Collaboration using both GET and POST HTTP Methods, and returning both traditional HTML content and the XML content.

An HTTP Responder, the Java CAPS component that handles HTTP requests, can be implemented as either a Java Collaboration or an eInsight Business Process.

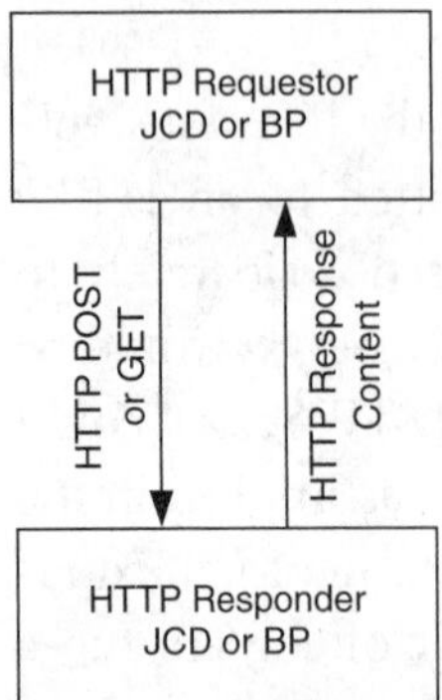

FIGURE 4-7: HTTP Request/Response model

However it is implemented, the responder ought to use information provided in request headers, request parameters, or the request body to perform whatever business function it has been designed to perform. It must then prepare the response body, populate the appropriate response headers, and return the response with the appropriate response status.

4.5.3 eInsight Subprocess

Chapter 12, "Reusability," section 12.4.1, discusses synchronous eInsight subprocesses and subprocess invocation. Invocation of synchronous subprocesses is another example of Java CAPS implementation of the Request/Reply pattern.

4.5.4 SOAP Request/Reply

With Sebastian Krueger

Java CAPS supports rapid implementation of Web Services through eInsight Business Processes and Java Collaborations using Web Services Description Language [WSDL] interface definitions, discussed in the next section. This section deals with the SOAP Request/Reply pattern as a specialization of the HTTP Request/Reply pattern and an example of a generic HTTP Request/Reply pattern that carries request data other than the traditional name/value pairs.

SOAP Request/Reply is a specialization of an HTTP Request/Reply, where the HTTP POST data block is a SOAP Message and the HTTP Response is a text/xml content carrying a SOAP Message. [SOAP1.2] also permits the use of the HTTP GET method, but the response must be a SOAP Message. ebXML Message Service [ebXMLMS], which is an HTTP POST Request/Reply–based implementation, uses SOAP. HTTP is one of the supported ebXML bindings. so an ebXML Message Service could be considered to be a SOAP over HTTP Request/Reply implementation that is not, strictly speaking, a Web Services implementation.

A SOAP Request/Reply could be implemented using the same tools and techniques as the HTTP Request/Reply. The only difference would be the content of the body text in both the request and the response. Chapter 2, section 2.3.4, "SOAP Request/Response," in Part II, illustrates building SOAP Request/Reply implementations from basic building blocks. This is both to provide an educational vehicle and to provide an example of how a Web Service can be implemented without the WSDL, or where special processing of SOAP Messages, not supported via the graphical user interface, is required.

Discussion in Chapter 2, section 2.3.4, "SOAP Request/Response," in Part II, presents a method of implementing a SOAP over HTTP Responder, effectively a Web Services implementation, using tools and techniques available in Java CAPS out of the box. While basic knowledge of SOAP and HTTP is required, the SOAP and HTTP handling implementation took much less time and effort to implement than it took to write about. The "service" is not exposed using the Universal Directory, Discovery and Integration [UDDI] infrastructure, available as part of the Java CAPS, nor is it built using a WSDL interface specification document. The next section discusses these matters.

The responder implementation, using SOAP Request/Reply, is a Web Service even though there is no WSDL interface definition for it and it is not registered with a UDDI Registry. It can still be invoked if an appropriate client is available.

With a WSDL interface definition [WSDL] in existence, and a tool such as Java CAPS, capable of generating a Web Services client implementation from a WSDL, we could build a Web Services client to exercise the SOAP Responder. We could also use other Sun tools, like the NetBeans IDE, or third-party tools like SoapUI, to build the Web Services client and exercise the Responder.

4.5.5 Web Services Implementation

Web Services invocation is a SOAP Request/Reply, as discussed in the previous section, overlaid with specific application semantics. A stock quote Web Services–based application will have SOAP requests and responses carry different information from an airline reservation Web Services–based application even though both will be using the SOAP Request/Response model.

Java CAPS directly supports generation of Web Services clients and providers from WSDL interface definition files [WSDL]. Chapter 12, section 12.5, discusses implementation and invocation of Web Services in Java CAPS at length. Chapter 2, section 2.3.5, "Web Service Request/Reply," in Part II, provides illustrations for the discussion of Java CAPS implementation of the Web Service Request/Reply pattern.

Java CAPS natively supports implementation and invocation of Web Services, whether with or without WSDL interface specifications. At one extreme it hides the complexities from a business analyst–level designer; at the other it facilitates the use of low-level technology infrastructure for fine-grained control by a hard-core Java developer.

Web Services invocation is one of the means of implementing the Request/Reply pattern, gaining in popularity as the technology underpinning service-oriented architectures now so much in vogue.

4.5.6 Request/Reply Summary

Java CAPS provides a variety of means through which a Request/Reply pattern can be implemented. JMS Request/Reply implementation, HTTP Request/Reply implementation, and its derivatives such as SOAP Request/Reply and Web Services invocation, as well as eInsight Subprocess invocation, were discussed in this section. Requirements of the endpoints largely dictate which method will be used in what circumstances.

4.6 Return Address

Section 4.5.1 discussed the use of JMS in Request/Reply scenarios. The requestor creates a temporary endpoint [EIP] and attaches its address to the message it sent. The downstream processing component, when finished with the message, uses that address as the destination to which to send the response. From the perspective of the requestor, the message exchange is synchronous. Rather than creating a temporary endpoint, a component could listen for messages on a regular endpoint. An upstream endpoint would attach the address to the message, and a downstream component would use that address to send the message to the correct destination. In the former case, the use of a temporary JMS destination is an example of dynamic routing [EIP]. In the latter case, it is an example of fixed routing [EIP] where the upstream component must have the knowledge of the existence of at least one other component in a solution, the listener with a fixed address, and the downstream component must have the knowledge of both the existence of the listener component and the means of extracting the address from the message. This results in tight coupling and interdependence between the three components. This also hides the routing architecture inside component logic and generally results in solutions that are harder to understand and harder to maintain.

Return Address is frequently used in asynchronous Request/Response solutions in which a response may not be ready for some time. It is usual, in these circumstances, to have the requestor submit a request and continue, without waiting for a response, and have a separate listener listen for the response and correlate it with the request.

Asynchronous Business-to-Business (B2B) exchanges are a special case of the Return Address pattern implementation, involving independent cooperating enterprises. The AS2 Protocol [AS2], for example, fairly widely used for secure message exchange in commercial environments, supports the asynchronous Message Disposition Notification (MDN) option—an asynchronous acknowledgment. By agreement between parties, a message sender specifies that asynchronous MDN is expected and provides the recipient with the URL to which to send the MDN. The sending of a message and the receipt of an acknowledgment are decoupled. The sender is responsible for receiving the acknowledgment and associating it with the message to which it applies.

4.7 Correlation

Correlation, the ability to collect related messages and process them together, is a sufficiently interesting matter to warrant an independent chapter. Chapter 11, "Message Correlation," contains a comprehensive discussion of Java CAPS correlation facilities using both the eInsight Business Process Manager Correlations and plain eGate-based facilities.

4.8 Message Sequence

[EIP] discusses requirements for message sequencing in the context of support for transfer of very large messages as a sequence of message chunks. Messages are broken up at the source, or at the entry into the messaging solution, and reassembled into a single message, or delivered to the ultimate destination, in order. It discusses the subject with a view of suggesting the means of attaching sequence numbers and message counts to messages as an aid to reassembling messages.

There are other circumstances when ensuring that message sequencing is preserved is critical to correct operation of the messaging solution. In healthcare environments, for example, where messaging solutions may be transferring laboratory results for patients, it is critical that a message carrying preliminary results or carrying partial results, typically sent first, arrives at the ultimate destination before a subsequent message that carries final results or updates, or supplements results carried by the original message. People's lives may depend on the preservation of message order.

In the case of fragmentation and reassembly of messages, as discussed extensively in [EIP], the Splitter is the component that breaks up large messages into clusters of smaller, related messages. It enriches each message fragment with the unique sequential identifier that identifies the cluster of related messages. It also enriches each message with the message sequence number identifying the position of the message within the cluster of messages and the "size" of the cluster. The Aggregator is the component that reassembles related fragments into a single message or that is responsible for submitting messages in order to some endpoint. It uses the cluster ID, the message sequence number, and the cluster size to collect related messages. It establishes the order of messages and detects when all the messages in the cluster have been received. Components that support this kind of functionality would implement some combination of the Correlation pattern, the Splitter pattern, the Aggregator pattern, and the Envelope Wrapper pattern. Correlation functionality would be required to allow the component to collect related messages. A Splitter might be required to break up a large message into smaller chunks. An Envelope Wrapper would be used to enrich each message with the metadata necessary for reassembly. Aggregator would be required to combine all related messages.

Note

As a general proposition, transferring very large messages through messaging systems is not a good idea. In many cases the messaging system must use an amount of memory many times the size of the largest message it is to process. This could lead to a memory shortage issue that could become particularly severe when dealing with large XML messages or contents of entire multimegabyte files. In general, the presence of very large messages in a messaging solution is an indication of poor solution architecture. The presence of large messages will always degrade performance and will likely lead to scalability and resilience issues. Where large XML documents may not be able to be broken up, content of large non-XML files may well be able to be processed using the Batch eWay in a streaming mode combined with the Batch Record eWay breaking data up into "records" and passing these on as soon as available. Depending on the relationship between records, implementation of a Message Sequence pattern may well be required to allow reassembly. The use of Batch eWay streaming is discussed in section 4.11.1.

Explicit message sequencing would use an Envelope Wrapper to carry sequencing metadata. It would use a Splitter and an Aggregator to break up and reassemble large messages, or ensure sequential processing of message fragments. Implementation of Aggregators in particular is reasonably complex. It requires the use of some form of Message Correlation and message store, in addition to the logic required to determine sequence commencement and completion. While such components could be made reasonably generic, or built as templates for reuse, they require a nontrivial development effort.

Java CAPS offers facilities that can be used to guarantee message sequence without explicit implementation of Message Sequencing components.

The Sun SeeBeyond JMS Message Server can be globally configured to support different FIFO processing modes. One of the modes is a fully serial first in, first out (FIFO) mode where receivers can only read a message after all previously read messages have been received and committed [JMSRef]. Serialization of message processing using JMS Message Server FIFO modes affects the behavior of Competing Consumers. This is discussed in the following sections.

4.8.1 JMS Serial Mode Concurrency

At the basic level, a JMS queue with a single Java Collaboration–based receiver can be configured to permit only one message to be collected and processed at a time. Since a JMS queue is a FIFO object, message order is preserved. The JMS Receiver Connector configuration properties, accessed through the connectivity map, allow JMS connectors to use Serial mode. This is the default. Unless this setting is changed, or multiple components are configured to receive from the JMS queue, the one component will always receive messages in the order in which they were deposited. This option is a per-JMS client connector configuration option.

Chapter 2, section 2.4.1, "JMS Serial Mode Concurrency," in Part II, illustrates the use of JMS Serial Mode Concurrency with specific Java CAPS examples.

To ensure messages are read from a JMS queue in the order in which they were written, use the JMS receiver client in the serial concurrency mode.

4.8.2 Sun SeeBeyond JMS Message Server FIFO Modes

The following discussion applies only to the Sun SeeBeyond JMS Message Server implementation.

In an ordinary course of events, when there is only a single receiver receiving from a JMS queue and it is configured to use the Serial Concurrency mode, messages will be received in the order in which they were queued. Two or more receivers configured to receive messages from the same JMS queue will compete for messages. If messages are arriving faster then a single receiver can process them, then when one receiver is busy another receiver will get a message to process. The receivers/consumers compete for messages. In the presence of Competing Consumers, processing behavior will vary with the JMS Message Server's global FIFO Delivery mode configuration. Each of the FIFO modes—Fully Concurrent Processing, Protected Concurrent, and Fully Serialized—has a different effect on concurrency of Competing Consumers and the ultimate order of messages processed by them.

Chapter 2, section 2.4.2, "Sun SeeBeyond JMS FIFO Modes," in Part II, illustrates behavior of Competing Consumers with different FIFO modes with a detailed example.

With the default global setting of Fully Concurrent Processing FIFO Delivery mode, all receivers will run in parallel and compete for messages. This will result in messages being processed in random order.

The Protected Concurrent FIFO mode ensures that order is preserved but allows parallel processing to still take place. This mode can be considered when designing solutions that can scale across multiple processors, for example.

The Fully Serialized FIFO mode causes message processing to be fully serialized. Message order is preserved, but there is no more parallelism in the solution.

Note

It is important to remember that the queue consumer concurrency setting is not graphically represented in the connectivity map, so a casual peruser may miss this important configuration setting. Also, it is important to remember that the special FIFO Delivery modes are not accessible through the connectivity map at all, but must be looked for through the Integration Server Administration console.

Note that message sequencing functionality provided by the JMS Concurrency and FIFO Delivery modes applies to all messages regardless of their relationships, if any. It could be that messages are somehow related. For example, a Patient Admission message, a Laboratory Request message, a Laboratory Results message, and a Patient Discharge message, all belonging to the same patient, might be expected to be processed in the order they were enumerated here. To process a Patient Discharge before Patient Admission, or Laboratory Results before Laboratory Request, may be incorrect, but processing a Patient Discharge message for one patient before a Patient Admission message for a totally unrelated patient may be perfectly valid. Support for this kind of message sequences requires the solution to explicitly recognize message relationships and to provide explicit message sequence–processing facilities. This issue was discussed in the opening part of this section.

4.8.3 Serializing Business Processes via JMS and XA

Ordinarily, the eInsight Business Process Engine will receive a JMS message and acknowledge its receipt to JMS as soon as it manages to create an instance of the process and deliver the message to its Receive activity. This is in contrast with the behavior of a Java Collaboration where the JMS message is not ordinarily acknowledged until the collaboration completes processing and returns. This implies that, in ordinary circumstances with many messages in a queue that feeds the process, there may be many Business Process instances concurrently processing messages. In effect, this is the same behavior as that exhibited by a Java Collaboration using the Connection Consumer Mode Concurrency and an unlimited pool. In the case of an eInsight Business Process, however, the setting of the Concurrency mode on the JMS receiver client makes no real difference. Since many eInsight Business Processes execute concurrently, it is very unlikely that messages will be processed in the order in which they were enqueued.

Java CAPS 5.1 extended the traditional Business Process Execution Language (BPEL) model to provide the capability to impose distributed transaction semantics on an eInsight Business Process. With no XA transaction, an eInsight Business Process would acknowledge the receipt of a JMS message as soon as it received the message. The process could then take any amount of time to process the message to completion. A new instance of a business process would be created as soon as another message became available in the JMS Destination from which the process was receiving messages. Both process instances could conceivably be executing concurrently, and the "younger" process could conceivably complete processing its message before the "older" process processed its message. This would cause the subsequent component to receive messages out of sequence, possibly necessitating resequencing. With a Serial Consumer mode and XA transaction semantics defined for the Business Process, a new instance will not be created until the first instance completes processing its message and commits. This will again guarantee that messages are delivered to the downstream component in the order in which they were received.

Chapter 2, section 2.4.3, "Serializing Business Processes with XA," in Part II, provides detailed examples illustrating this discussion. Business Process behavior both with and without XA is illustrated.

Note

Note that imposing XA semantics on eInsight Business Processes is not to be done lightly. Business Processes are intended to be long running, on the order of minutes, hours, days, or longer. Imposing XA semantics on long-running processes may lock resources that should not be locked for extended periods of time, databases for example. Keeping locks on such resources may result in increased resource contention, resource starvation, or deadlocks. This will affect both the stability and the performance of a solution. One should carefully consider implications of enabling XA on a process-by-process basis.

While Java CAPS provides facilities that can be used to ensure processing of messages in order, there will still be circumstances when these facilities will not provide the desired result. Ensuring break-up of messages and reassembly of fragments must be handled with solutions that implement Splitter, Aggregator, Envelope Wrapper, and Correlation patterns. Ensuring sequential processing of related messages requires similar solutions. Specific implementations of the Splitter, Aggregator, Envelope Wrapper, and Correlation patterns are discussed elsewhere in the book.

4.9 Message Expiration

The Sun SeeBeyond JMS Message Server supports message expiration. Expiration can be configured globally through the Integration Server Administration Console interface, as shown in Figure 4-8, and specified individually for each message by assigning appropriate values to the timeToLive property, as shown in Figure 4-9.

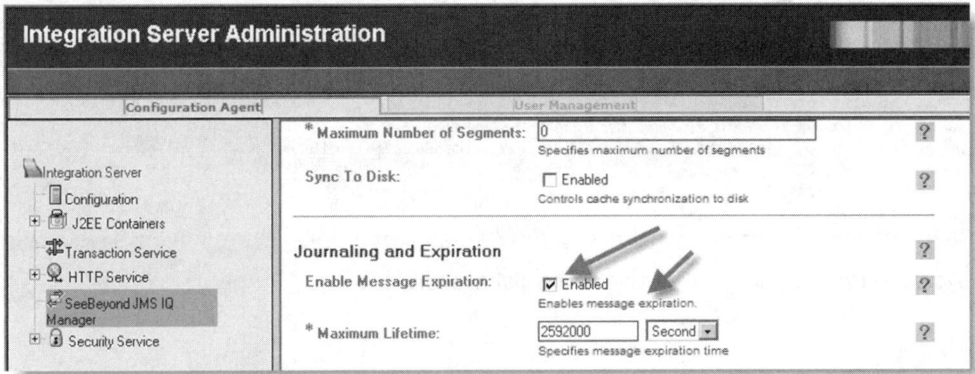

FIGURE 4-8: Assigning timeToLive value

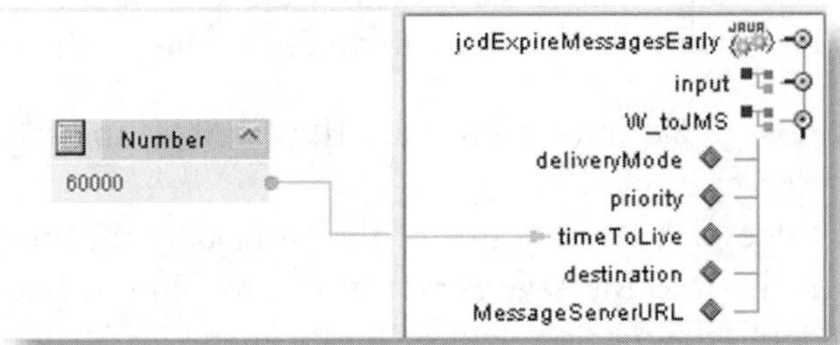

FIGURE 4-9: Assigning timeToLive value programmatically

By default, Maximum Lifetime is 30 days.

When message expiration is disabled, or the Maximum Lifetime is set to 0, messages that are not delivered to their destinations will be retained indefinitely in queues and in topics with durable subscribers.

Java Collaborations with outbound JMS connectors can be configured to assign the number of milliseconds, as a long integer, to the timeToLive property; see Figure 4-10. This allows the designer to explicitly specify message expiration. A variant with the explicit time-to-live parameter can also be used to specify explicit expiration when using one of the explicit JMS OTD send methods.

The message expiration property in the incoming JMS message specifies the Greenwich mean time (GMT) at which the message would have or has expired. While a message whose expiration time is in the past is supposed to be discarded

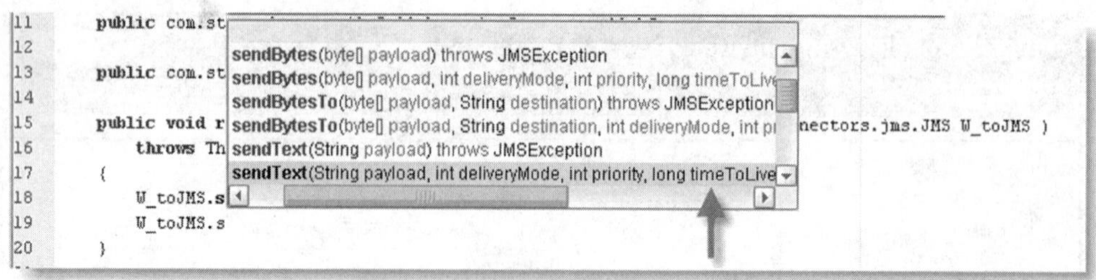

FIGURE 4-10: Assigning timeToLive in a collaboration

by the JMS Message Server implementation, the JMS 1.1 Specification [JMSSpec] suggests that this may not always be the case. The Specification states that:

> When a message is sent, its expiration time is calculated as the sum of the timetolive value specified on the send method and the current GMT value.

Chapter 2, Section 2.5, "Message Expiration," in Part II, illustrates message expiration with Java Collaboration examples.

If the receiving component does not set the value of timeToLive on the message it sends to the JMS queue, the JMS Message Server global Maximum Lifetime property will apply. By default, the message will sit in the queue for 30 days or until received by some component, whichever is sooner.

We can determine how long the message took to deliver from the sender to the receiver, if such knowledge is of interest, by setting a known timeToLive value in the sender and examining the expiration value in a receiver immediately downstream.

If Message Journaling was enabled, the message would have been journaled. Journaling takes place upon message delivery or message expiry.

Like Java Collaborations, eInsight Business Processes also have access to JMS timeToLive and expiration properties, as well as the current time in milliseconds; see Figure 4-11.

By using GMT, also known to the politically correct as the UTC (Universal Time Coordinated), we avoid issues that arise when messages cross time zones or when summer time/winter time crossovers occur while the message is in transit.

Solution designers can use the mechanism, in which a time offset or time-to-live is added to the time message that was created or sent, in GMT, to explicitly handle message expiration regardless of whether JMS is used. If expiration is needed,

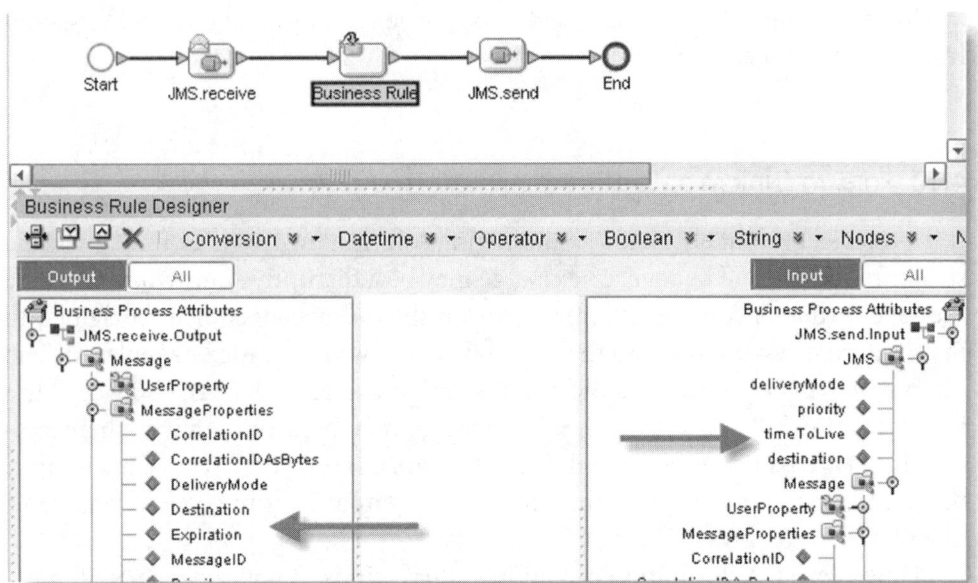

FIGURE 4-11: TimeToLive and Expiration properties in a Business Process

one or more Envelope Wrapper solutions can be used to carry the expiration time. Components can determine whether to discard or process messages after comparing expiry time to current time. In fact, using an explicit expiration time metadata item simplifies the solution by allowing any component downstream from the expiration setter to determine if the message expired, rather than having to reset the timeToLive parameter on each send, as is required when using JMS.

The Sun SeeBeyond JMS Message Server provides the Message Journaling service to allow copies of consumed or expired messages to be saved for inspection or reply at a later time. Journaling consumes resources; therefore, by default, Java CAPS JMS Message Server does not enable message Journaling. When enabled, through the Integration Server Administration Console interface, Journaling will apply to all messages carried through the JMS infrastructure. An Expiration Interval can be globally associated with messages held in the Journal. Unlike expired live messages, the expired journaled messages are not removed from the journal. Solution designers who use JMS Journaling must ensure that operational procedures are put in place to purge expired messages from the journal using command-line tools provided with the product.

Message Journaling is discussed at some length in Chapter 5, "Messaging Infrastructure," section 5.6.11.

4.10 Format Indicator

It is possible, even likely, that as a messaging solution evolves over time, message structures it uses will change. The change may be a disruptive one, where the new message format is completely different from the old message format originating in an external system, because the external system was upgraded or replaced. The old system will be retired, and the new system's messages will be the only ones the infrastructure will see at runtime. The change may be evolutionary, where new data fields are added or existing data fields change size or data type. Data in both the old format and the new format may be present at runtime concurrently and must be correctly processed.

How a Java CAPS solution can address these kinds of issues depends on message sources and the designer's ability to anticipate changes.

An eWay Endpoint may be format-specific to the point that it must be reconfigured or replaced to accommodate the change. A HL7 eWay, for example, can be configured to look for and validate certain fields in incoming HL7 messages. HL7 eWay's ability to validate data requires configuration of the HL7 version in use and sending and receiving application identifiers. If an external application starts sending HL7 messages of a different version, validation at the eWay may fail. To resolve this issue, the eWay would have to be reconfigured, and the solution that contains it would have to be rebuilt and redeployed. If it is expected that different HL7 versions will be processed by this eWay, validation may be disabled. Disabling validation at the eWay defers dealing with the issue of multiple versions to a component further downstream.

An endpoint may be message-format agnostic. A Batch Local File or a Batch FTP eWay, for example, deals with files. Neither deals with the structure of the files. Changing the format of messages in files will be transparent to both.

A JMS Client is message-format agnostic to a large degree. It differentiates between text messages, bytes messages, stream messages, and map messages, but within each it does not care whether the intrinsic format of the message, represented as a text message, for example, changed or not.

In most cases it is a Java Collaboration or an eInsight Business Process that has to account for changes in message format. Since in most cases messages are received as blobs, and are unmarshaled into OTDs for manipulation, the unmarshal step will fail if the message format does not agree with the format the OTD expects. Depending on the source of messages, and the way the solution designer deals with adversity, an unmarshal exception may result in message loss. When the message source is a JMS Client and the component that deals with the message is a Java Collaboration, for example, an unhandled unmarshal exception will cause the message to be rolled back to the JMS Destination from which it came. Since the same message will be resubmitted some time later, the cycle of unmarshal–rollback–resubmit will be entered and will only end when the message is removed, either manually or by a redelivery handling mechanism if configured. A designer could explicitly discard a message that fails to unmarshal by "handling" the exception in the Collaboration or the Business Process, causing it to return normally (i.e., consume the message). Neither of these solutions handles unexpected messages gracefully.

Since JMS messages contain both the payload and a series of properties, one of the solutions to the problem of recognizing different message formats would be to introduce a Format Indicator, a JMS user-defined property that carries an indication of what kind of message is being carried. This Format Indicator could allow Java Collaborations and Business Processes to choose, at runtime, which OTD to use to unmarshal the message. The Collaboration or the Business Process could be constructed to handle messages differently depending on the format.

Some component would need to determine what the format is in order to set the Format Indicator. One way to handle this would be to allow a component, early in the solution, to try to unmarshal the message to different OTDs and, depending on which succeeded, set the Format Indicator. Another, which is dependent on the nature of the message, would be to inspect some leading part of the message blob to attempt to deduce what kind of message is being carried.

It is possible that a message may need to traverse a Messaging Bridge, thus losing the metadata that could be carried in JMS user-defined properties. If the Message Format Indicator was carried as a JMS property, it too would be lost.

It would be best to design messages such that messages themselves carry a Format Indicator and are designed using techniques similar to those discussed in Chapter 7, "Message Construction," section 7.4, so that only a partial unmarshal is necessary to determine message format.

Format Indicator could also be used to handle multiple versions of a message interface. The indicator would be set to indicate to which version of the messaging interface the message conforms and would then be used by a content-based router to send the message to the component that implements the correct version of the interface. This would enable new versions to run alongside the old version while still using the same message infrastructure.

4.11 Data Streaming

As mentioned in section 4.8, handling of very large messages in a messaging solution may require memory resources many times greater than the size of the largest message to be handled. Frequently, the architect has no choice but to consume or produce a very large message, a file containing a batch or related transactions, for example, or a large and complex XML message generated by, or intended for, an external application. Handling such messages poses special challenges. Java CAPS can assist with Batch eWay support for data streaming when such messages are manifested as files in a file system. It is possible to break up large messages into components and process components individually, or collect components and assemble them into a large message. eTL, another of the products in the Java CAPS Suite, can assist in processing large volumes of data. While ETL (Extract, Transfer, and Load) is typically associated with one off-batch extraction and load of data, Java CAPS's eTL can be used both standalone and in-stream as part of a larger Java CAPS solution. We discuss eTL in this in-stream mode as a possible means of streaming data between a flat file and database table or between database tables and views.

4.11.1 Batch eWay Streaming

Java Collaborations that use Batch eWays are commonly implemented to read the entire content of the file into the Payload node of the Batch eWay OTD, then unmarshal it into some OTD that gives access to individual "records" or fields. If the file contains multiple records that will be processed individually downstream from the Batch eWay, it would be far more efficient to read the file a record at a time and release records for further processing as soon as available. Batch Record eWay provides the ability to stream file data into a parser that breaks it into records. The parser works with delimited, fixed-length, and "whole file is a single record" records through connectivity map–based configuration properties.

Batch eWay Streaming Adapter can be used for streaming data between an FTP Server and a local file, in either direction, without the need to use the Batch Record eWay. This is useful if a Java CAPS solution needs to obtain a large file from an FTP site for use locally or needs to send a local file to the remote FTP site as efficiently as possible. Chapter 9, "Messaging Endpoints," section 9.4.2, uses an example of local file-to-FTP Server streaming to illustrate polling JMS Destination as part of exception and retry handling.

Chapter 2, Section 2.6.1, "Batch Local File Streaming," in Part II, illustrates the concept of data streaming with several detailed examples, including the use of Batch Record, Java Buffered IO in conjunction with BatchLocalFile eWay's StreamAdapters, and eTL.

To stream a local file in, process its contents a piece at a time, and stream it back out again, you must use a BatchLocalFile and a BatchRecord for the inbound side as well as a BatchRecord and a BatchLocalFile for the outbound side. Because files are streamed, this collaboration can process files of arbitrarily large size without grossly inflating JVM memory use.

Note

For fixed record files, all records, including the last record, must be the same size. This means that you cannot use the batch record with an arbitrary-size record to emulate buffering unless it so happens that the last record is the same size as all other records. When it is not, the last read will fail and the bytes remaining to be read will not be accessible and will be lost. Exception will be thrown when that happens.

Streaming can be used to process files containing fixed-length records. Rather than specifying Record Type as Delimited, we specify it as Fixed and furnish the appropriate value for the Record Size.

Note

Specifying Record Type of Single Record is no different from not using the BatchRecord at all but instead using Batch eWay, in one of its variants, to load the entire file into memory as a single record.

If it is absolutely necessary to break a file into "buffer-sized" chunks without regard for delimiters or the size of the file, where the file is not guaranteed to have an even length that is a multiple of desired buffer size, it is still possible to stream the file. You would have to use a BatchRecord eWay with a fixed-length record of 1 byte on the input side and do your own buffering.

With Batch eWay, there are good, not so good, and downright bad ways of processing large volumes of data, as demonstrated in the examples. Which of the potential solutions for data streaming is best will very likely depend on the individual requirements.

4.11.2 eTL Streaming

eTL is the component of Java CAPS intended to be used for data extraction, transfer, and load. Typically used for bulk standalone extraction, conversion, and load of data, Sun SeeBeyond eTL tool can be also used inside an eInsight Business Process as part of a larger Java CAPS solution. Chapter 2, Section 2.6.2, "eTL Streaming," in Part II, provides a simple example of an eTL streaming solution and an "equivalent" Java Collaboration streaming solution.

4.12 Message Security

In some circumstances it may be necessary to ensure confidentiality and integrity of messages that travel through the messaging system. One or both of two methods are typically used to protect messages in transit.

More common and easier to relate to, because of its ubiquity, is the method that secures the point-to-point channel over which messages travel. Channel Security is typically provided by adding the Secure Sockets Layer (SSL) to the TCP/IP Protocol-based channels. SSL standard [SSL] specifies how encryption can be applied to all bytes traveling through a point-to-point channel. It also specifies how endpoints can authenticate each other, exchange cryptographic material, choose encryption algorithms, and negotiate protocol version. In essence, and this is trivializing the matter considerably, to complete establishment of a Secure Session, the two endpoints perform a Cryptographic Handshake, during which capabilities, cryptographic material, and credentials are negotiated and exchanged before any payload data is sent. If the SSL Handshake fails, no session is established and the endpoints do not exchange data. If the SSL Handshake succeeds, the endpoints cooperate, for the reminder of the session, in encrypting on send, and decrypting on receive, the byte stream that represents the payload data. Java CAPS provides the SSL-based Channel Security capability in the HTTP Client and the HTTP Server eWay, in the JMS Message Server implementation, and in the Web Services implementation framework. See Chapter 14, "Security Features," section 14.4, for a discussion on SSL configuration in Java CAPS for solutions using HTTP eWay and Web Services endpoints.

Less common is the method that individually secures each message. Since encryption and digital signature attributes are applied to the message itself, a secured message can traverse multiple channels and multiple components while preserving security. The Secure Messaging Extension eWay, available in ICAN 5.0.5, reappeared late in 2007 in conjunction with the release of the Sun B2B Suite 5.1 and the AS2 Protocol Manager, a successor to the eXchange Integrator of the 4.x and 5.0. It supports the Secure Multipurpose Mail Extensions (S/MIME) for encryption and digital signing, the XML Digital Signatures, and the XML Encryption functionality. The SME eWay provides an easy means of securing individual messages.

Chapter 14, section 14.5, discusses how data can be secured in transit using secure variants of the Batch eWay. These variants operate on files using different transfer security mechanisms.

4.13 Chapter Summary

This chapter discussed Java CAPS facilities and techniques used to implement specific message-related patterns that [EIP] groups together under the heading of Message Construction. The following patterns were discussed:

- Document Message
- Command Message
- Event Message
- Request/Reply
- Return Address
- Correlation
- Message Sequence
- Message Expiration
- Format Indicator
- Data Streaming
- Message Security

The chapter discussed a number of concepts and tools. In addition to regular Java Collaborations and eInsight Business Processes, the eTL tool was introduced, and its use in data streaming applications was discussed.

CHAPTER FIVE

Messaging Infrastructure

5.1 Introduction

This chapter deals specifically with Java CAPS messaging infrastructure in order to provide the background necessary to understand how [EIP] patterns that employ the messaging infrastructure are implemented in this chapter and elsewhere in the book.

This chapter discusses Java CAPS JMS infrastructure implementation specifics that have significant bearing on implementation of other patterns:

- Java Messaging Service
- JMS Implementation Interoperability
- Using JMS to Integrate Non-JMS Environment
- JMS Queues and Topics
- Temporary JMS Destinations
- Security
- Transactionality
- Concurrency
- Persistence
- Selectors
- FIFO Modes
- Throttling
- Redelivery Handling
- Message Journaling
- JMS Grid High-Availability JMS Implementation

This chapter then discusses specific [EIP] patterns that use the JMS or other Java CAPS infrastructure in their implementation:

- Competing Consumers
- Point-to-Point Channel
- Publish-Subscribe Channel
- Datatype Channel
- Invalid Message Channel
- Dead Letter Channel
- Guaranteed Delivery
- Channel Adapter
- Messaging Bridge
- Message Bus

Some of the patterns under discussion are presented in [EIP] in Messaging Channels, some in Message Construction, some in Messaging Endpoints.

5.2 Java Message Service (JMS)

The Sun JMS Specification defines a set of interfaces intended to unify client access to common services implemented in messaging infrastructures from disparate Message-Oriented Middleware (MOM) vendors [JMSSpec]. As a consequence, implementations from different vendors vary in their features and capabilities in the areas that the JMS Specification does not cover or explicitly leaves open to interpretation by implementers. In particular, JMS Specification does not address load-balancing and fault-tolerance functionality, asynchronous notification, administration, security, wire protocols, message type definitions, or message repository. Such nonstandard functionality is either provided by the implementation (e.g., administration), is built as part of an integration solution (e.g., load balancing, fault tolerance, security), or must be built into the integration solution explicitly.

JMS is an integral part of the Java CAPS. Sun SeeBeyond JMS implementation is the default mechanism through which messages are passed from component to component in a Java CAPS solution through release 5.1.3.

The various facilities of the JMS implementation are used to implement a number of patterns ranging from Content Router to Envelope Wrapper. Specific facilities used in these patterns are described in detail in the appropriate places.

Java CAPS 5.1.3 supports three JMS implementations from Sun as well as JMS implementations from other vendors, such as WebSphere MQ from IBM. The book discusses in detail the Sun SeeBeyond IQ Manager, the default Java CAPS JMS Message Server implementation, and briefly the Sun JMS Grid, the highly available JMS Message Server implementation that can be used to implement JMS clusters and other fault-tolerant solutions.

5.3 JMS Implementation Interoperability

The JMS Specification explicitly does not address physical implementation issues such as wire protocols or security. The most significant implication of this is that JMS implementations from different vendors are not interoperable. A solution that must use multiple JMS messaging implementations must provide one or more Messaging Bridges [EIP] to facilitate connecting the disparate messaging infrastructures.

Sun SeeBeyond JMS Message Server monitoring, message submission, message modification, message replay, and similar functionality are supported through the Enterprise Manager Web-based User Interface. Other JMS implementations may or may not have similar facilities. The administration and monitoring support for these other implementations may or may not be integrated with the Java CAPS environment, so the solution architecture should strive to minimize interactions with facilities outside the unified management domain to reduce complexity of operations support and runtime monitoring.

5.4 Using JMS to Integrate Non-Java Environments

Java CAPS is a J2EE-compliant environment. In general, to allow non-Java solutions, such as those based on .NET technologies or that use C or C++ language environments, to communicate with the Java CAPS–based integration solution, you would look at a higher-level Messaging Bridge that would transcend these low-level issues. You could, for example, use TCP-based Messaging Endpoints or use file system–based message exchange. The upside of this is the loose coupling. The downside is the increased overhead.

To allow non-Java CAPS–based solutions to readily exchange messages with the Java CAPS–based solutions, the Sun SeeBeyond JMS Message Server implementation provides a set of JMS application programming interfaces (APIs) and corresponding libraries for Java [JMSAPIJ], C/C++ [JMSAPIC], and COM+ [JMSAPICOM]. One or more of these API mechanisms can be used to allow an application to exchange messages with another application, whether Java CAPS–based or not, using the Sun SeeBeyond JMS Message Server. The APIs can also be used as the basis for higher-order wrapper APIs. For example, a C#-based simplified API, using the C/C++ API as the basis, has been developed and used in the field.

5.5 Queues versus Topics

JMS provides two kinds of managed objects: Connection Factories and Destinations. In a Java CAPS environment, Connection Factories, used to establish connections to JMS providers, are handled implicitly via deployment profiles and JMS Message Server containers. JMS objects that the developer deals with explicitly are JMS Destinations: queues and topics. A developer would use JMS queues to implement the point-to-point messaging style and JMS topics to implement the publish-subscribe messaging style. The distinction is not visible to a Java CAPS developer until a connectivity map needs to be constructed. At this point, the developer decides what kind of destination will be used and therefore what kind of messaging style will be implemented for the specific subset of integration solution to which the connectivity map applies. The developer is free to use both queues and topics in the same connectivity map to implement messaging that best addresses the business requirements of the solution.

A JMS queue is a Messaging Endpoint where only one receiver retrieves a particular message. If there is no current receiver, messages are retained in the queue until there is a receiver and messages are delivered, or until messages expire if finite message expiration is configured. Multiple receivers will compete for messages. A message delivered to one receiver will not be available to any other receiver.

A JMS topic is a Messaging Endpoint where all concurrent subscribers receive a copy of each message published to it. Effectively, each message is replicated as many times as there are active subscribers. In addition, if there are no active subscribers, and there are no durable subscriptions, messages will be discarded by the JMS Message Server. This behavior will change if there is a durable subscription. In this case, the JMS Message Server will keep messages until the there is a current subscription for that durable subscriber, in which case messages that were retained in the topic will be delivered to that subscriber.

The "if there are no current subscribers, and there are no durable subscriptions, messages will be discarded by the JMS Message Server" behavior can be put to good use. For example, a permanent Wire Tap [EIP] can be introduced such that as a message is processed by a component, a copy of it is published to the Wire Tap Topic. With no subscribers and no durable subscribers to the topic, the message will be discarded—a Dripping Wire Tap, if you like. At a later time, a component that processes messages from the Wire Tap could be implemented. This component only needs to subscribe to the Wire Tap Topic to start receiving messages that are published after that time. No changes to the publishing component are required.

If there is only one subscriber to a topic, messaging behavior is similar to that when there is only a single receiver from a queue. Rather than using a topic for the purpose of implementing a Dripping Wire Tap, you could send messages to a queue with a very short message lifetime and no receivers. The JMS Message Server would discard messages after they expired anyway. The net effect would be the same, but the resource consumption would not. After all, the Message Server would have to keep track of message expiration, however short, consuming resources to do so. With significant traffic, considerable resources could be wasted this way.

5.6 Sun SeeBeyond IQ Manager

5.6.1 JMS Destination Creation and Destruction

Unlike some other JMS implementations with which you might be familiar, where JMS Destinations have to be explicitly created and destroyed using some implementation-specific administration tools, the Sun SeeBeyond JMS Message Server, also known as the Sun SeeBeyond IQ Manager, does not require explicit creation or destruction of JMS Destinations. A JMS Destination is created automatically as soon as the first message intended for that destination is handed over to the JMS Message Server, or as soon as there is a subscriber to a topic or a receiver from a queue. JMS Destinations persist as long as the JMS Message Server is running or until explicitly deleted.

Note
If a JMS queue has no receivers, or a JMS topic has no subscribers, in any solution deployed to a logical host, the JMS Destination will not exist until there is a message to be delivered to it. This behavior is a consequence of automatic creation of JMS Destinations, but it may cause you some trepidation if you are checking to make sure all JMS Destinations exist when you start the solution.

Note
As a consequence of automatic creation and destruction of JMS topics, you may forget that a topic, with at least one durable subscriber registered, will be created each time the JMS Message Server starts, regardless of whether the subscriber ever actually subscribes. The durable subscription may have been registered during development iteration and, as a result of design change, may no longer be required. You must explicitly delete the JMS topic to remove the durable subscription.

Note
There is no visual indication in the connectivity map to advise whether the topic subscription is or is not durable.

5.6.2 Temporary JMS Destinations

Temporary JMS Destinations are created by a component and exist only so long as the component that created them exists. In ordinary circumstances, and I cannot think of other circumstances where this would not be the case, there is no good reason and no good way to explicitly create and use a temporary JMS Destination in a Java Collaboration within a Java CAPS solution. There is no way to create one in an eInsight Business Process at all, except by wrapping that kind of functionality in a Java Collaboration. For the purpose of JMS Request/Reply, the requestReply() method of the JMS Object Type Definition (OTD) will transparently create and use a temporary JMS Destination. Because a JMS requestReply() method implicitly creates a temporary destination, each time it is executed a new temporary destination will be created. Furthermore, both the publisher/sender and the subscriber/receiver must be deployed to the same Integration Server for the requestReply() method to work.

If it is absolutely necessary to create a temporary JMS Destination, it is possible to do so by obtaining a QueueConnectionFactory or a TopicConnectionFactory using the technique addressed in section 5.6.7.2, which discusses the means of implementing a dynamic selector in a Java Collaboration and using the JMS API calls to create and use all necessary objects.

Chapter 3, section 3.2.1 "Temporary JMS Destinations," in Part II (located on the accompanying CD-ROM), implements and discusses in detail a solution that uses an explicitly created JMS temporary queue.

Note

The solution discussed in the example is built to make a point that temporary JMS Destinations can be created and used in Java CAPS. It is not a solution that makes sense or that addresses requirements that cannot be addressed more simply and elegantly without going to the trouble of using low-level JMS APIs.

5.6.3 Security

The Sun SeeBeyond JMS Message Server can, optionally, ensure confidentiality of messages in transit and require client authentication. Since the JMS Specification explicitly does not address these issues, the functionality is implementation-specific and therefore nonportable. See [JMSREF] for specific details.

Note

The Sun SeeBeyond Integration Server uses global properties to reference keystores and truststores. See Chapter 14, "Security Features," section 14.4.3.1, for more detail on where and how to change default truststore and keystore. As a consequence, both JMS and HTTP over SSL must use the same keystore and truststore. Bear this in mind when configuring channel security for either component.

5.6.4 Transactionality

By Sebastian Krueger

A transaction is a unit of work, a sequence of operations that succeed or fail as a single unit. Transactions are essential to the successful and robust working of any enterprise application.

The behavior of any JMS server is such that when a message gets delivered to a JMS Destination and the acknowledgment is received by the message sender, the message can immediately be forwarded to the message consumer.

JMS transactions provide the capability to guarantee that all messages in a group of messages will get to the Message Server, or none of them will. Thus, messages delivered to the Message Server within a single transaction are not forwarded to the consumer until the producer has confirmed that the last message has been successfully sent (called a *commit*).

The scope of a JMS transaction can include any arbitrary number of messages.

Each transaction covers either the producer's session or the consumer's session, but not both. Thus, it is possible for transacted consumers/producers to interact with nontransacted producers/consumers.

Any messages that are not committed in a transaction will not be acknowledged and will be redelivered at a later point in time.

In distributed systems, a two-phased commit protocol allows multiple distributed resources to participate in a single transaction.

For example, we may want to produce messages to the Sun SeeBeyond IQ Manager, as well as update an Oracle database in a single global transaction. If the database update fails, we want to ensure that the JMS message is not sent as well. Thus, all tasks in the global transaction must either succeed together or fail together.

A resource (such as an Oracle database) can only take part in a global transaction if it supports the two-phased commit protocol. This protocol is usually implemented using the XA interface, which was developed by the Open Group and is the most popular standard for distributed transactions.

In Java CAPS each Java Collaboration is implemented as an Enterprise Java Bean (EJB) that employs container-managed transactions. This means that the EJB container that is part of the Sun SeeBeyond LogicalHost will handle transactions, which frees the developer (i.e., you) from having to deal with them.

Each time a message is sent, it is a separate transaction. By default, XA is selected in the connectivity map, as shown in Figure 5-1. Thus, each send operation participates in the overall container transaction to form one global transaction.

Note

The illustrations that follow make use of the Thread.sleep() construct. This construct, when used in a Java code running inside a J2EE container, violates the J2EE rules and should not be used. It is used here to "slow down" the collaboration to allow a human to inspect the related queue through the Enterprise Manager.

Rules are rules. It is okay to break the rules if the rule breaker is aware of and prepared to accept the consequences.

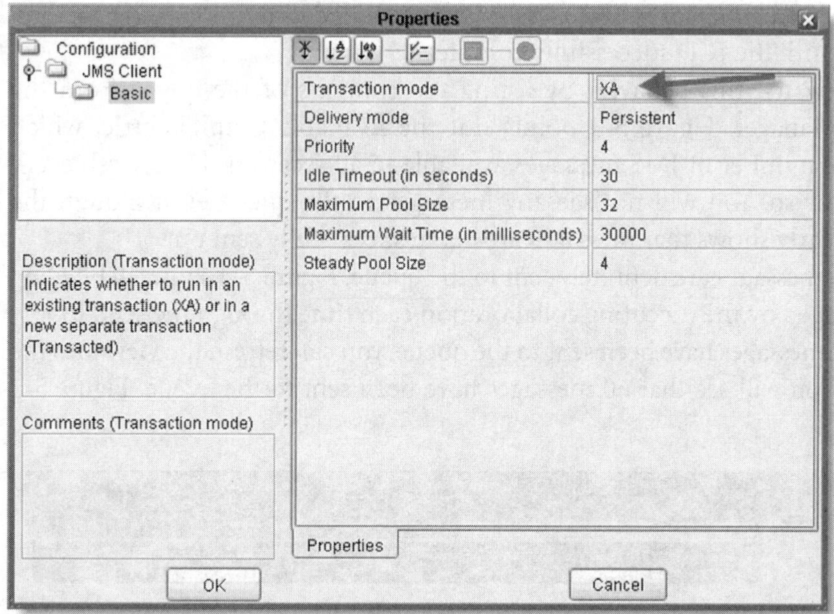

FIGURE 5-1: Default Transactionality setting

Thus, a transaction starts when the Java Collaboration Definition (JCD) is called and finishes when the JCD returns.

To demonstrate, consider the far-too-trivial example of having messages being sent out to a JMS destination by generating messages in a for-loop in the following manner in a single JCD. Figure 5-2 illustrates the points at which the XA transaction begins and ends.

```
public void start( com.stc.schedulerotd.appconn.scheduler.FileTextMessage input, com.stc.connectors.jms.JMS W_toJMS )
    throws Throwable
{        <-- Start of Transaction
    int iNumMessagesToSend = 60;
    for (int i = 0; i < iNumMessagesToSend; i++) {
        com.stc.connectors.jms.Message msg = W_toJMS.createTextMessage();
        msg.setTextMessage( "" + i );
        msg.getMessageProperties().setExpiration( 120000 );
        logger.debug( "\n--->>>Sending message: " + msg.getTextMessage() );
        W_toJMS.send( msg );
        Thread.sleep( 1000 );
    }
}        <-- End of Transaction
```

FIGURE 5-2: Transaction boundary in a collaboration

The expected behavior is that as messages are added to the queue, they are *not* committed until the JCD successfully completes.

We can watch this behavior by listing the contents of the queue from the Enterprise Manager. Figure 5-3 points out the Available Count metric, which indicates the number of JMS messages available to all receivers. Hit refresh every 10 seconds or so. You will not see any messages in the queue even though the server.log clearly shows that messages are being successfully sent out.

And yet, messages are definitely sent to the queue. Figure 5-4 shows debugging messages logged by the executing collaboration each time through the send loop!

Once all messages have been sent to the queue, you can refresh the view into the queue, and you will see that 60 messages have been sent to the queue. Figure 5-5

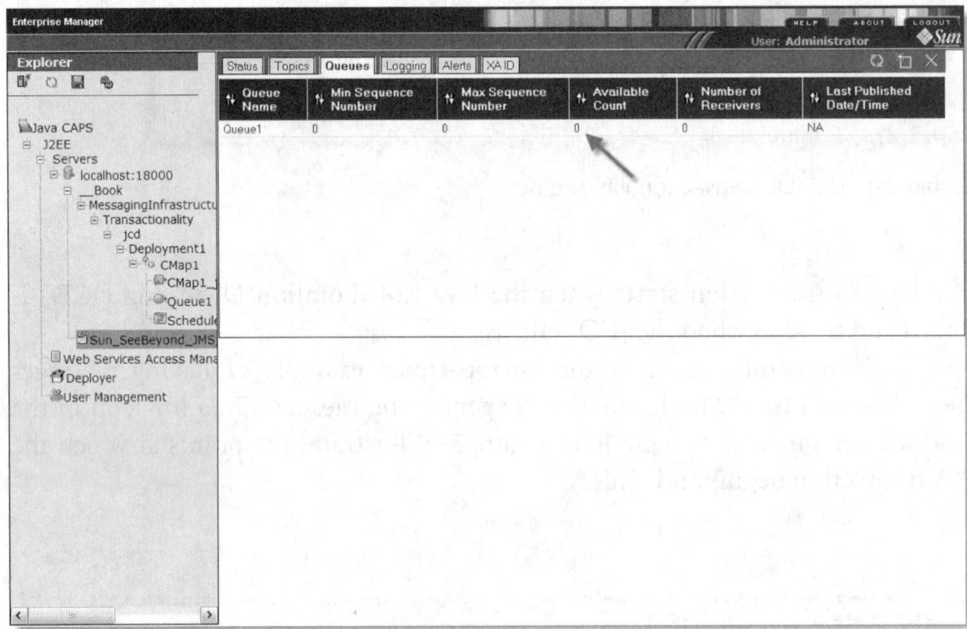

FIGURE 5-3: Confirming transactional behavior of a JCD using the Enterprise Manager

```
[#|2006-12-17T20:36:08.656+1300|FINE|IS5.1.2|STC.eGate.CMap.Collabs.jcd.CMap1_jcd
--->>>Sending message: 53|#]

[#|2006-12-17T20:36:09.656+1300|FINE|IS5.1.2|STC.eGate.CMap.Collabs.jcd.CMap1_jcd
--->>>Sending message: 54|#]
```

FIGURE 5-4: Collaboration execution trace

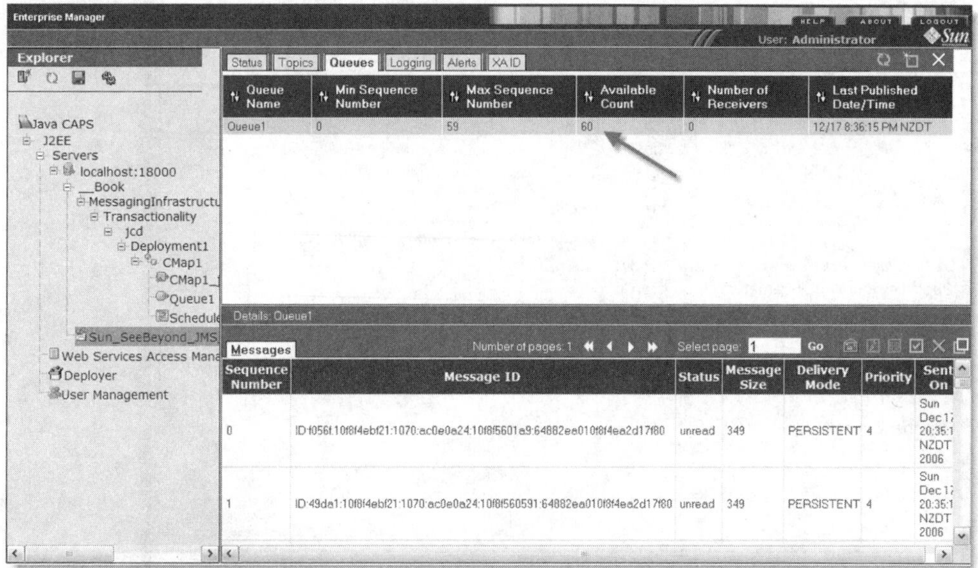

FIGURE 5-5: Committed JMS messages viewed through the Enterprise Manager

points out the Available Count metric, now indicating that 60 messages have been received by the JMS Message Server and are available to potential receivers.

If at any time during the sending of all those messages the server fails, the entire batch of 60 messages would be rolled back.

Now let's consider the Transacted setting shown in Figure 5-6.

Rebuild and redeploy the same project with the new setting selected in the connectivity map.

We can now watch every message arrive on the queue individually. That is, each message is committed as soon as the JCD receives an acknowledgment that it has arrived. Figure 5-7 indicates the commit point at which individual JMS messages are committed and are available to the potential receivers.

Note

In releases prior to 5.1, the default configuration for JMS Publisher's Transactionality property was Transacted. Each message was acknowledged as soon as it was received by the JMS Message Server. As of version 5.1.0, this default changed to XA. The behavior difference should be considered by developers used to the previous behavior or developers importing projects from release 5.0.

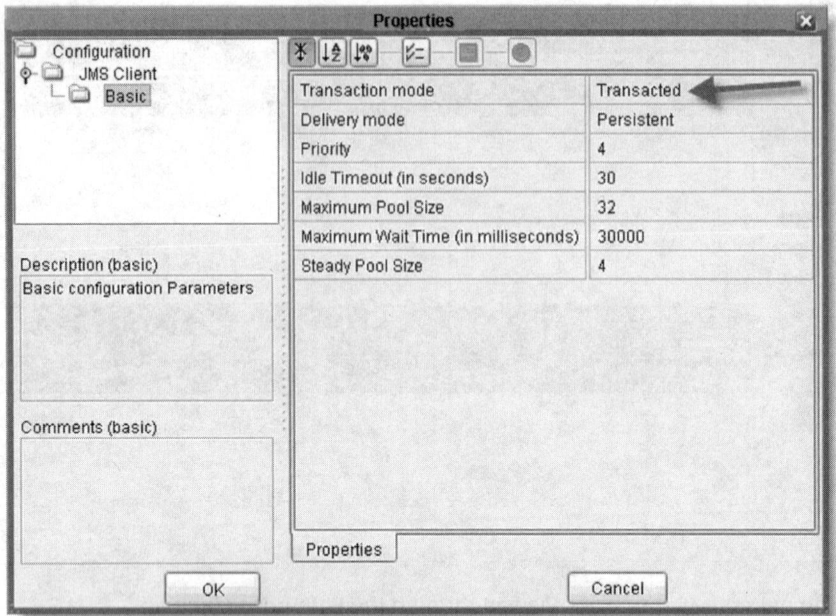

FIGURE 5-6: Transacted setting

```
public void start( com.stc.schedulerotd.appconn.scheduler.FileTextMessage input, com.stc.connectors.jms.JMS W_toJMS )
    throws Throwable
{
    int iNumMessagesToSend = 60;
    for (int i = 0; i < iNumMessagesToSend; i++) {
        com.stc.connectors.jms.Message msg = W_toJMS.createTextMessage();
        msg.setTextMessage( "" + i );
        msg.getMessageProperties().setExpiration( 120000 );
        logger.debug( "\n--->>>Sending message: " + msg.getTextMessage() );
        W_toJMS.send( msg );   <-- Individual Transaction
        Thread.sleep( 1000 );
    }
```

FIGURE 5-7: Transacted mode behavior

In an eInsight Business Process, this transaction behavior is the default. Unless we enforce XA over the entire Business Process, messages are immediately committed as they are acknowledged. For a detailed discussion of this topic, see Chapter 4, "Message Exchange Patterns," section 4.8.3, and in this chapter, section 5.14.5.1.

5.6.5 Concurrency

By Saurabh Sahai

Often the demands for performance and throughput require the ability to perform concurrent processing of incoming messages making optimum use of available resources. By default, when using the Sun SeeBeyond JMS server, messages in Java CAPS are delivered serially to the message consumers such as Java Collaborations or eInsight Business Processes. To enable concurrent processing of available messages, the default message delivery mode can be changed from Serial to Connection Consumer Mode. When using the Connection Consumer Mode, the Server Session Pool property should be set to a value equal to the maximum concurrent threads desired for concurrent processing of messages from the specified JMS Destination.

Note

The value specified for the Server Session Pool property must be less than or equal to the Message-Driven Bean (MDB) pool size configured for the integration server. The MDB pool size for each integration server is configured via the Enterprise Manager. Please refer to the eGate Integrator System Administration Guide for details regarding the setting of the MDB pool size.

Refer to Chapter 4, sections 4.8.1 and 4.8.2, for details on how to set up the concurrent consumer processing using the Sun SeeBeyond JMS Message Server. Section 5.8 also discusses an example of using eInsight processes to achieve concurrent message processing.The Sun SeeBeyond JMS server provides the ability to configure the order in which messages are processed by customizing the FIFO processing behavior for selected destinations. Using Connection Consumer Mode has implications for the order in which messages are processed.

5.6.6 Persistence

By Saurabh Sahai

The JMS Message Server is responsible for delivery of messages to registered consumers. Once the JMS Message Server receives the message from a producer, it keeps the message until it is successfully delivered to all consumers. The messages can be stored either in memory or in a persistent store. In the event of the Message Server crashing, all messages stored in memory by the Message Server will be lost forever and will not be delivered to the subscribers. Any messages that were stored in a persistent store, and not delivered to all registered consumers, will be available for delivery once the Message Server is up and running again.

For messages that need once and once only guaranteed delivery, as per the JMS Specifications, the Sun SeeBeyond JMS Server provides the facility to specify either the Persistent (which is the default) or Nonpersistent delivery mode to be used when sending messages. Using nonpersistent delivery mode has better performance characteristics and is suitable for cases where potential loss of messages is acceptable.

Note

It is important to keep in perspective the difference between the JMS delivery mode and subscription durability in the case of JMS topics. In case of a failure, a topic consumer that has been marked as being durable may still lose messages that were sent with a delivery mode of Nonpersistent. A durable consumer is only guaranteed to receive messages that are available in the Message Server for that particular consumer. If the Message Server crashes, all nonpersistent messages will be lost irrespective of whether the consumer is using durable subscription.

Configuring the desired delivery mode is done via the connectivity map in the Enterprise Designer. To bring up the dialog box containing the configurable JMS parameters, click on the property icon available on the center of the link connecting to the JMS Destination and select the desired delivery mode. Figure 5-8 illustrates the two possible delivery mode settings.

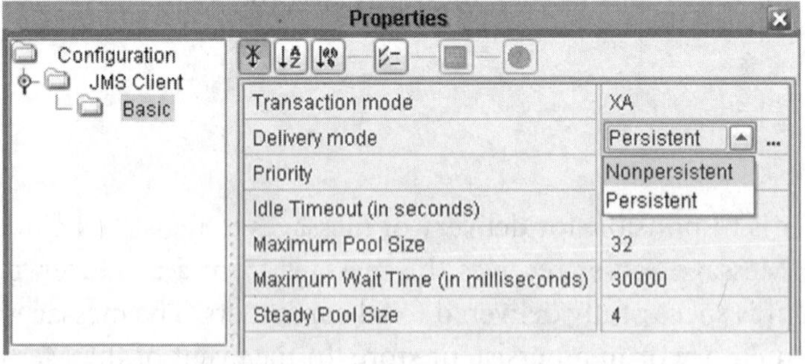

FIGURE 5-8: Setting Persistent and Nonpersistent modes

As with updating other connector properties, the project will need to be rebuilt and the resulting EAR file redeployed subsequent to any change in the properties.

The Sun SeeBeyond JMS Message Server stores persistent messages in disk files. Additional measures, such as the use of redundant disk configurations, should be taken in a production environment to ensure integrity and availability of disks used for the message store.

Section 5.14 further discusses topics related to guaranteed delivery for solutions using the Sun SeeBeyond JMS Message Server.

5.6.7 Selectors

JMS message selectors are a special case of a general Message Filter pattern [EIP] required to be provided by JMS implementations. The Java CAPS JMS Message Server supports static JMS selectors configured through the JMS Receiver/Subscriber properties. A programmatic method of implementing dynamic selectors using a JCD also exists for cases where static selectors are not appropriate or where only dynamically configurable selectors will do. The following sections discuss examples of implementations of both types of selectors.

To recapitulate, the JMS Specification [JMSSpec], section 3.8.1, states that a message selector is a string that uses a subset of SQL92 conditional expression syntax to specify an expression that will be evaluated at runtime using JMS message header fields. A message selector cannot reference JMS message body values. Message header field references are restricted to the following fields: JMSDeliveryMode, JMSPriority, JMSMessageID, JMSTimestamp, JMSCorrelationID, and JMSType. In addition to these predefined fields, selectors can also use arbitrary user properties. See [JMSSpec] for additional information concerning the structure and use of JMS selectors.

5.6.7.1 Static Selector

Java CAPS does not provide a nonprogrammatic way of setting JMS properties, whether JMS defined or user defined. Sun SeeBeyond JMS IQ Manager implementation can only use JMS header properties as part of a selector expression, as defined in the JMS Specification. In addition to JMS header properties, Sun JMS Grid implementation can also use XPATH expressions to select messages based on the content of message body, as long as the message body is XML. This facility is specific to JMS Grid and is not portable. According to the JMS Specification, JMS selectors can be arbitrarily complex SQL92 expressions. Multiple JMS header and user-defined properties can be used. In ordinary circumstances, JMS selector expressions are specified in Java CAPS at design time and cannot be changed without rebuilding and redeploying the project that uses them. Static selectors are configured through the JMS Receiver and Subscriber connector properties in the connectivity map. Figure 5-9 shows a Message selector property whose value is a static selector expression.

Here the selector expression is:

```
JMSCorrelationID = '12345' OR JMSCorrelationID = '12346'
```

Only messages whose Correlation ID contains one of the two values will get delivered to the service svc_jcdLogMessage. All other messages will remain in the queue until they expire or until some other, less discriminating component picks them up. You must be careful to use single quotation marks around literal values because double quotation marks have a special function in SQL92.

This topic is illustrated with an example in Chapter 3, section 3.2.1.1, "Static Selector," in Part II.

The presence of a static selector expression causes the JMS Message Server to deliver only selected messages to the collaboration downstream from the JMS Destination with the selector expression on the receiver/subscriber side.

Using static selectors, you can implement a Static Router pattern. For example, you can construct a connectivity map similar to that in Figure 5-10 to statically route messages to different services.

Here messages with different values are routed to different collaborations.

There are a couple of obvious drawbacks to implementing a static router this way, one of which is common to implementing a static router in general.

First, modifying a hardcoded static router, whether hardcoding is done within a component such as a Java Collaboration or a Business Process or is done within a connectivity map, requires that the component is modified and the deployment

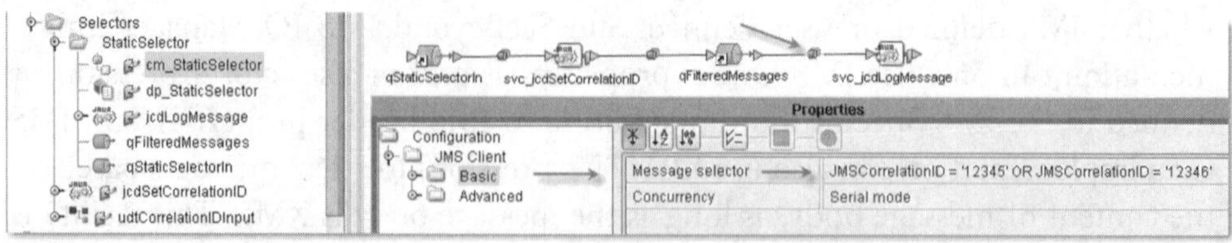

FIGURE 5-9: __Book/MessagingInfrastructure/Selectors/StaticSelector/cm_StaticSelector

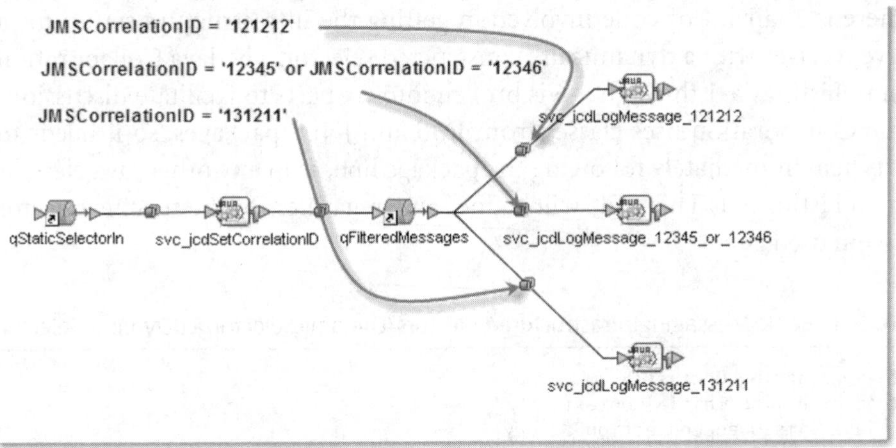

FIGURE 5-10: __Book/MessagingInfrastructure/Selectors/StaticSelector/cm_StaticRouter

profile–bound application is redeployed. If the static routes are not-so-static, then this can become a major maintenance issue.

Second, and specifically applicable to the JMS selector–based static router, there is no way to specify a "catch-all" selector except by inversing the conjunction of all other defined selectors. As soon as one selector needs to be added or modified, the catch-all selector would need to be modified as well. Since multiple recipients from a single JMS queue are Competing Consumers, there is no way to predetermine which will receive a particular message. Selector expressions must be carefully constructed to ensure that no overlaps occur, otherwise unpredictable routing behavior will result.

5.6.7.2 Dynamic Selector

Building a dynamic selector requires a bit more work, but once the method is established, it can be applied as needed. Neither the JMS object, which is obtained by selecting the JMS OTD as one of the manipulation/output OTDs, nor the JMS input object, which is in fact a JMS Message object, provide access to the JMS Session object necessary to configure a selector, nor do they provide a way to find out what the selector expression is or to set one for the session. Since a JMS Session object is necessary, we will use the Java Naming and Directory Interface (JNDI) to first look up the JMS ConnectionFactory object and then the JMS Destination from which to receive messages using the dynamically constructed selector.

There is a fair bit of code involved in getting the infrastructure set up for a selective receiver with a dynamically constructed selector. The Java Collaboration shown in Listings 5-1 through 5-6 is broken into six parts to facilitate discussion.

The Collaboration uses classes from JMS and JNDI packages, so it needs to import them immediately following the package line, as in any other Java class, as shown in Listing 5-1. This code will be the same regardless of the specific selector expression used later.

LISTING 5-1: Book/MessagingInfrastructure/Selectors/DynamicSelector/jcdDynamicSelector

```
import javax.naming.Context;
import javax.naming.InitialContext;
import javax.jms.QueueConnectionFactory;
import javax.jms.QueueConnection;
import javax.jms.QueueSession;
import javax.jms.Session;
import javax.jms.Queue;
import javax.jms.QueueReceiver;
```

A number of static, final class fields, constants if you like, are used, as shown in Listing 5-2.

LISTING 5-2: Book/MessagingInfrastructure/Selectors/DynamicSelector/jcdDynamicSelector

```
static final long lTimeout = 5 * 1000;
static final String cJMS_HOST = "localhost";
static final String cJMS_PORT = "20007";
static final String cRECEIVE_FROM = "qReceiveFrom";
static final String cPROVIDER_URL
                        = "stcms://" + cJMS_HOST + ":" + cJMS_PORT;
static final String cCONNECTION_FACTORY
                        = "connectionfactories/queueconnectionfactory";
static final String cINITIAL_CONTEXT_FACTORY
                        = "com.stc.jms.jndispi.InitialContextFactory";
static final boolean cTRANSACTED = true;
```

Note that it is more appropriate to obtain values for lTimeout, cJMS_HOST, cJMS_PORT, and cRECEIVE_FROM fields at runtime than to hardcode them. The values are hardcoded here in order not to obfuscate the essential JNDI and JMS code with matters that are tangential.

Next we need to add code to obtain the value for the JMSCorrelationID to be used in constructing the selector expression; this is shown in Listing 5-3. In this case, the value is the entire content of the JMS message. In a more realistic implementation, it could be some part of the input message, whether acquired through JMS or using some other connector. It is likely that this code will change to accommodate specific application requirements. The application may require using other Message header fields and user-defined properties in constructing the selector expression.

LISTING 5-3: Book/MessagingInfrastructure/Selectors/DynamicSelector/jcdDynamicSelector

```
public void receive
    (com.stc.connectors.jms.Message input
    ,ud1.udtCorrelationIDInput1752469071.Udtcorrelationidinput vCorrIDIn
    ,com.stc.connectors.jms.JMS W_toJMS )
        throws Throwable
{
    // construct dynamic selector expression
    ;
    vCorrIDIn.unmarshalFromString( input.getTextMessage() );
    String sCorrelationID = vCorrIDIn.getCorrelationid();
    ;
    String sSelector = "JMSCorrelationID = '" + sCorrelationID + "'";
    ;
```

Next we create a timed JMS Receiver with the dynamically constructed selector expression. It is unlikely that this code will change. This is pretty much how you would address the JNDI and JMS to obtain the selective receiver required for dynamic selector use. Listing 5-4 illustrates it.

LISTING 5-4: Book/MessagingInfrastructure/Selectors/DynamicSelector/jcdDynamicSelector

```
// get a receiver for the specific Queue object
;
QueueConnection myConnection = null;
QueueSession mySession = null;
QueueReceiver myReceiver = null;
;
try {
    java.util.Hashtable env = new java.util.Hashtable();
    env.put
      ( Context.INITIAL_CONTEXT_FACTORY, cINITIAL_CONTEXT_FACTORY );
    env.put( Context.PROVIDER_URL, cPROVIDER_URL );
    InitialContext jndiContext = new InitialContext( env );
    QueueConnectionFactory QCFactory =
        (QueueConnectionFactory) jndiContext.lookup
                                    ( cCONNECTION_FACTORY );
    myConnection = QCFactory.createQueueConnection();
    Queue myQueue = (Queue) jndiContext.lookup
                                    ( "queues/" + cRECEIVE_FROM );
```

```
    mySession = myConnection.createQueueSession
            ( cTRANSACTED, Session.AUTO_ACKNOWLEDGE );
    myReceiver = mySession.createReceiver( myQueue, sSelector );
    myConnection.start();
} catch ( Exception e ) {
    e.printStackTrace();
    throw new Exception( "\n===>>> Exception from jndi processing", e );
}
;
```

Once the selective receiver is available, we can attempt to read one or more messages from the JMS queue. This part of the collaboration will likely change as required by the implementation. In this sample, we read as many messages that satisfy the selector expression as there are and append their bodies to a string. This is not particularly realistic but is simple enough for illustration of the concepts. In the example in Listing 5-5, we send the string, assembled by reading selected messages, to a "regular" JMS Destination configured through the connectivity map.

LISTING 5-5: Book/MessagingInfrastructure/Selectors/DynamicSelector/jcdDynamicSelector

```
// prepare canned text to preprend to messages
// sent out
;
String sOutText = "";
sOutText += "Using Selector Expression [" + sSelector + "]";
sOutText += "\nReceived input message with Correlation ID ";
sOutText += vCorrIDIn.getCorrelationid();
;
// is there at least one message in the correlation queue?
;
javax.jms.TextMessage m = null;
m = (javax.jms.TextMessage) myReceiver.receive( lTimeout );
if (m == null) {
    sOutText = "";
    sOutText += "\nNo candidate messages for the selector [";
    sOutText += myReceiver.getMessageSelector();
    sOutText += "] from queue [";
    sOutText += myReceiver.getQueue().getQueueName() + "]";
    mySession.rollback();
}
;
// process all related messages in the correlation queue
;
while (m != null) {
    sOutText += "\n Message Body: [";
    sOutText += m.getText();
    sOutText += "] for Message: ";
```

```
    sOutText += m.getJMSMessageID();
    m = (javax.jms.TextMessage) myReceiver.receive( lTimeout );
}
;
com.stc.connectors.jms.Message msgOut = W_toJMS.createTextMessage();
msgOut.getMessageProperties().setCorrelationID( sCorrelationID );
msgOut.setTextMessage( sOutText );
W_toJMS.send( msgOut );
```

Note that in addition to setting the body of the outgoing message, we are also setting the CorrelationID JMS header property just in case the downstream component has a need or use for it.

Finally, we dismantle the selective receiver infrastructure and finish, as shown in Listing 5-6.

LISTING 5-6: Book/MessagingInfrastructure/Selectors/DynamicSelector/jcdDynamicSelector

```
mySession.commit();
mySession.close();
myConnection.stop();
myConnection.close();
;
logger.debug( "\n===>>> sent message: " + sOutText );
```

The collaboration discussed here is triggered by a JMS message that conveys the Correlation ID to be used by the selective receiver. The JMS queue used could be the same Queue as the one in which all other messages exist or it could be a different queue. In the former case, you would expect a static selector expression to pick just the message that starts the ball rolling and to ignore messages that the collaboration is to explicitly receive. In the latter case, you would have to ensure that the JMS queue that triggers the selective receiver collaboration receives only trigger messages and no others. The sample connectivity map in Figure 5-11 uses two distinct JMS queues, one to receive trigger messages and one to receive all other messages.

While what was discussed is a practical way of implementing a selective receiver with the selector expression created dynamically at runtime, it is a fairly inefficient one as the entire process of looking up and creating appropriate JMS objects and destroying them after use is performed each time through the collaboration. A knowledgeable reader can likely improve efficiency by using statics to hold various objects and not destroying objects on exit from the collaboration.

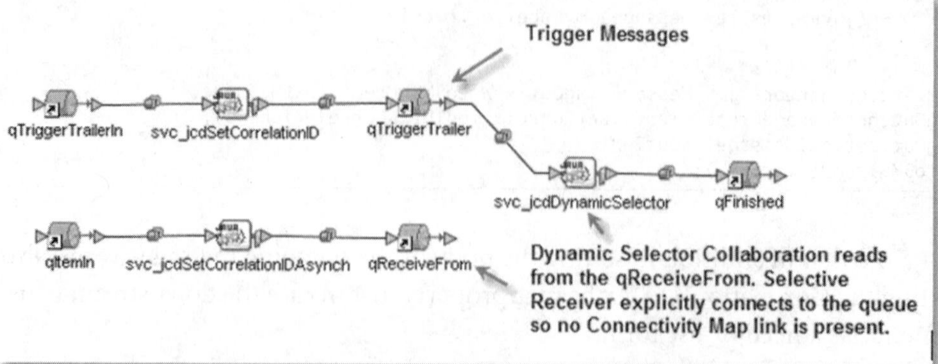

FIGURE 5-11: Book/MessagingInfrastructure/Selectors/DynamicSelector/cm_DynamicSelector

The connectivity map may or may not imply that a selective receiver is used. This depends on the site naming conventions and the designer's willingness to provide hints to others that there exist implicit relationships that the connectivity map does not show.

This discussion is illustrated with an example in Chapter 3, section 3.2.1.2, "Dynamic Selectors," in Part II.

Since the JMS Message Server URL is constructed using hardcoded values, the collaboration is not portable between Message Servers. A better way would be to configure the URL using values acquired at runtime so that changes can be externalized and made without affecting the collaboration or requiring projects that use it to be rebuilt and redeployed.

This method can be used to implement eGate-only-based correlations. Indeed, this method is used in Chapter 11, "Message Correlation," section 11.11, to re-implement one of the Message Relationship patterns implemented using eInsight.

5.6.8 FIFO Modes

Behavior of JMS Competing Consumers, using the Sun SeeBeyond JMS Message Server, with respect to message sequencing can be configured so that message order is strictly preserved, loosely preserved, or not preserved. These configuration settings are referred to as FIFO modes and are discussed at length in Chapter 4, section 4.8.2.

5.6.9 Throttling

By Saurabh Sahai

The Integration Server delivers messages to registered consumers as fast as the consumers are able to accept them. In certain situations, the number of available messages on a particular destination, or within the JMS Message Server, starts to grow faster than messages can be processed. This can occur for any number of reasons, including use of serial message processing, having a small number of concurrent consumers, consumers involving substantial processing time, or consumers having problems that are transient in nature (such as connectivity to an external system). In such cases, producers send messages to the Message Server at a faster rate than these messages can be processed.

The Sun SeeBeyond JMS Message Server provides the means to throttle message producers so that the Integration Server does not become saturated and the message consumers can catch up with the message producers. Figure 5-12 shows the Messaging Behavior Tab in the Integration Server Administration console through which these settings of the Sun SeeBeyond IQ Manager can be changed.

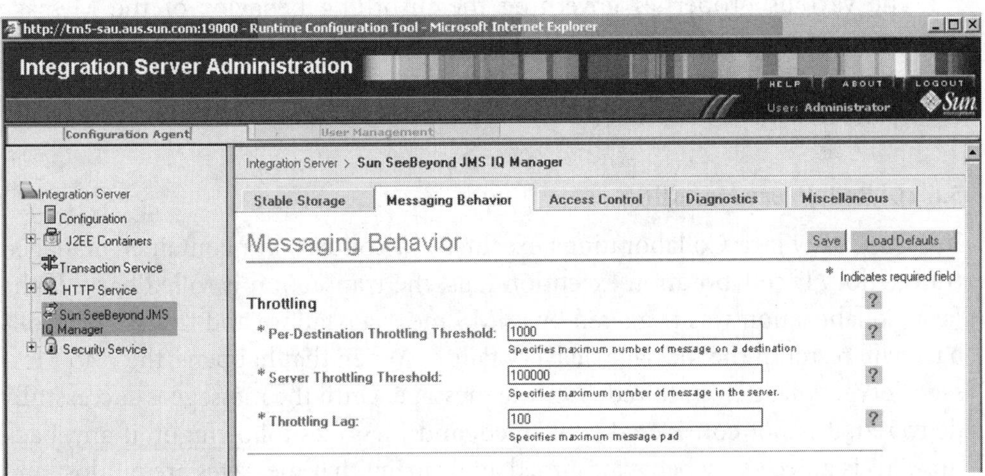

FIGURE 5-12: Throttling settings for Sun SeeBeyond IQ Manager

Within the Sun SeeBeyond JMS Message Server, throttling of a message producer is governed by the following rules:

- The JMS Message Server throttling threshold is set in the Server Throttling Threshold property. If the sum total of available messages on all the destinations within the Message Server is below this limit, throttling is not enforced.
- The default value for this property is 100,000 messages. A value of 0 for this threshold will result in no throttling being enforced.
- The Per-Destination Throttling Threshold determines the threshold at which producers for a particular destination will be throttled once the Server Throttling Threshold has been reached. When the number of messages on a given producer exceeds the Per-Destination Throttling Threshold and the Server Throttling Threshold is also reached, all producers for the destination will be throttled until one or both of the following become true:
  - The number of available messages within the JMS Message Server falls below the Server Throttling Threshold.
  - The number of available messages on the destination falls to a value less than the Per-Destination Throttling Threshold's Throttling Lag.
- The Throttling Lag denotes the number of messages that needs to be consumed from the destination before producers for that destination will be unthrottled.

The various properties governing the throttling behavior of the Message Server are set via the Integration Server Administration Console, as illustrated in Figure 5-12. Updating any of these values will require the restart of the server before the new values take effect.

5.6.10 Redelivery Handling

In Java CAPS, Java Collaborations execute in a context of a container-managed transaction. If collaboration execution fails, the transaction is rolled back. If the Java Collaboration was triggered by a JMS message, failure and transaction rollback will result in the message delivery failure. When that happens, the JMS Message Server will attempt to redeliver the message. Until the message is successfully delivered, it is not considered consumed, and messages following it, if any, back up. This is a necessary behavior aimed at ensuring that messages are not lost and are delivered in order. It is possible that the failure is transient and the message can be redelivered successfully. Once this happens, subsequent messages will be able to be delivered. This is not, however, likely. Collaboration failures usually occur because of programming errors, bad messages, resource exhaustion, or some other condition that is unlikely to be automatically resolved.

In ICAN 5.0, JMS automatic redelivery behavior would result in a redelivery loop that essentially brought the Integration Server down as redeliveries and rollbacks consumed all available resources. Since there was no means of delaying redelivery or limiting the number of delivery attempts, programmatic means of varying reliability had to be used.

Java CAPS 5.1 provides the means of delaying redelivery on failure, limiting the number of redelivery attempts, and specifying redelivery failure "I am giving up" action. Section 5.13 discusses at length the means of specifying redelivery handling in Java CAPS 5.1.x. It is worth noting at this point that the redelivery behavior, which was configured globally for each JMS Message Server in Java CAPS through release 5.1.1, changed in release 5.1.2 such that it is possible to specify different redelivery behavior for each sender/publisher.

5.6.11 Message Journaling

The Sun SeeBeyond JMS IQ Manager supports journaling of delivered messages. Journaling is enabled globally through the Integration Server Administration console or through the Enterprise Manager "Configure Integration Server" interface, shown in Figure 5-13. Figure 5-14 shows the Enable Journal checkbox checked.

Since journaling is enabled globally and journaled messages, even after expiration, are not removed from the journal storage, manual procedures must be put in place to remove messages from the journal storage to prevent it from growing indefinitely.

Once enabled, the Enterprise Manager Explorer node SeeBeyond_JMS_IQ_Manager will enable access to journaled messages. Figure 5-15 shows the toolbar button that facilitates switching between Journaled and Live views.

Perhaps unintuitively, the Journal/Live display toolbar button says "L" when the display shows journaled messages and says "J" when the display shows live

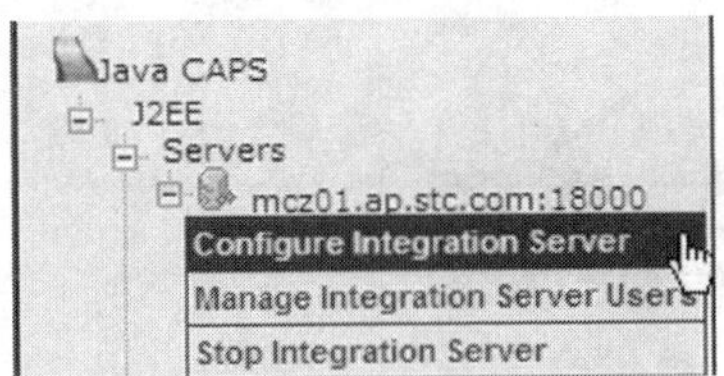

FIGURE 5-13: Accessing Integration Server Configuration from the Enterprise Manager

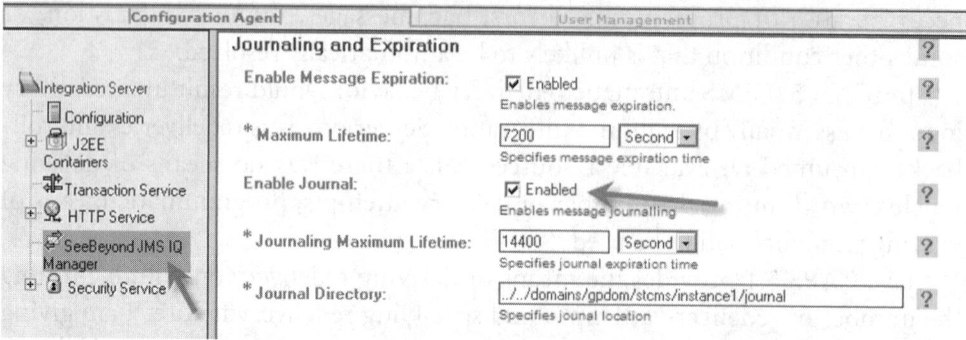

FIGURE 5-14: Enabling Sun SeeBeyond IQ Manager Journaling

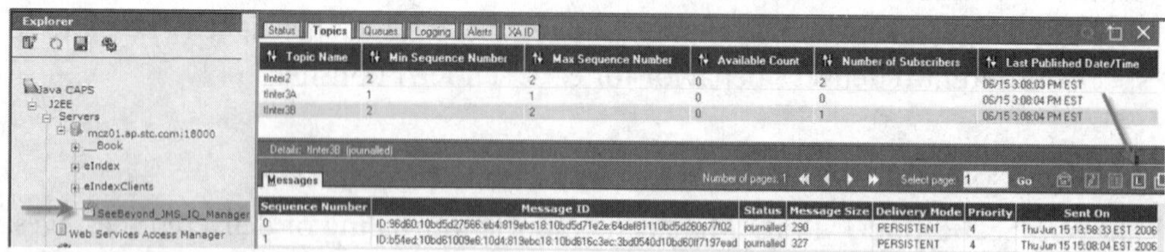

FIGURE 5-15: Accessing journaled messages

messages. To avoid confusion, look at the Status column (Figure 5-16). Journaled messages will have the status of journaled.

Alt+J will switch to Journaled and Alt+L will switch to Live.

Note

The only way to remove messages from the journal store is by using the stcmsctlutil command-line tool, described in [JMSREF, pp. 105].

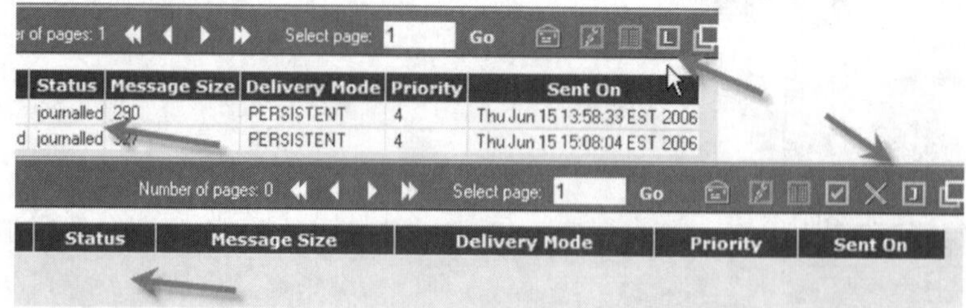

FIGURE 5-16: Switching between Journaled and Live message view

Journaling can be used as an implementation of a Message Store [EIP], a mechanism to selectively resubmit a message that has been already processed or a mechanism to resubmit a message that expired without having been consumed by a receiver or a subscriber. Some of these topics are discussed in Chapter 4, section 4.9.

5.7 Resilient JMS with JMS Grid

By Sebastian Krueger

High availability and scalability are important capabilities in an Enterprise-class messaging solution. The JMS Message Server has been one of the areas in messaging solutions where hardware-based high-availability implementations were needed to address resilience.

The Sun Java Message Service Grid (Sun JMS Grid) implementation provides a software-based high-availability implementation based on a multidaemon clustered architecture with fault tolerance and automated cluster recovery within heterogeneous networks. JMS Grid is JMS 1.1 compliant and supports dynamic destination creation, load balancing of clients across clusters, load balancing of queue messages across daemons, JMX-based management, automatic recovery of daemons, and SSL and HTTP/HTTPS Tunneling across firewalls, to name a few features.

Unlike the Sun SeeBeyond JMS Message Server, Sun JMS Grid supports wildcard destinations, allowing messages to be sent to or consumed from multiple destinations, using hierarchical notation. Sun JMS Grid also supports content-based selectors that operate on the JMS message body as well as the JMS message header, using XPath for XML messages and Beans selectors for Object messages.

JMS Grid consists of two or more cooperating JMS Message Servers, termed daemons, typically deployed to independent hardware platforms, treated as a cluster. Figure 5-17 illustrates a JMS Grid cluster with two daemons and two JMS clients, each connected to a different daemon in the cluster. Daemons in a JMS Grid cluster implement resilience by transparently replicating messages and maintaining synchronization among themselves. From the standpoint of a JMS client, the entire JMS Grid cluster, however it is configured and however many daemons it contains, is treated as a single JMS Message Server. JMS Grid clusters can be combined into JMS Grid networks.

Deploying a two-daemon JMS Grid cluster over two physical machines in a single site provides resilience in the face of single machine failure. The cluster will

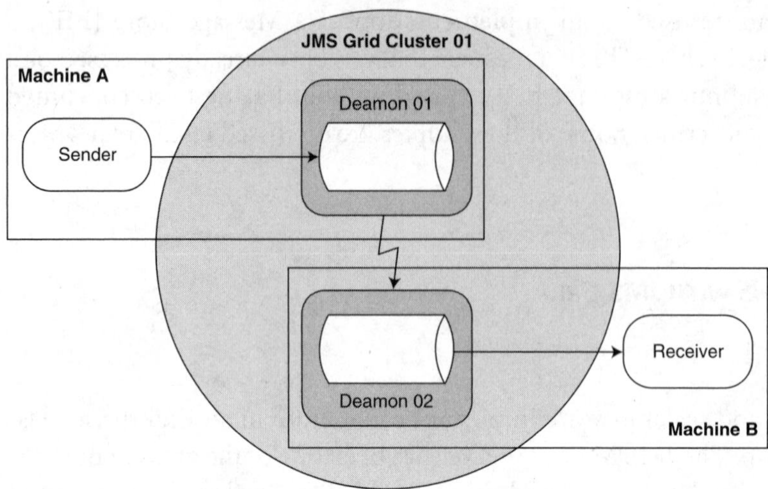

FIGURE 5-17: JMS Grid cluster

continue processing messages. All JMS clients connected to the machine that failed will be automatically reconnected to the surviving machine. Deploying a JMS Grid cluster in which participating machines are distributed over different sites, as shown in Figure 5-18, provides resilience in the face of a failure of the entire site. The cluster will continue processing messages in the surviving site. Any JMS clients connected to the JMS Grid daemon at the site that failed will be automatically reconnected to the daemon at the surviving site unless they themselves were brought down by the failure.

We would consider deploying a JMS Grid network, in which two or more JMS Grid clusters are interconnected, to create a Messaging Bridge [EIP] or to overcome latency and throughput issues that sometimes exist between components distributed over multiple sites with slow or low-bandwidth network links.

A typical JMS Grid network configuration would consist of a network of two clusters, each with two daemons. This kind of architecture provides intrasite as well as intersite redundancy.

Best Practice

Aim for a cluster size of two daemons if you use message persistence. Due to the JMS Grid's support for fully replicated clustering of message daemons, every persistent message is stored on every node in the cluster before an acknowledgment is sent back to the message producer. Thus, the more daemons in a cluster, the longer the replication process will take.

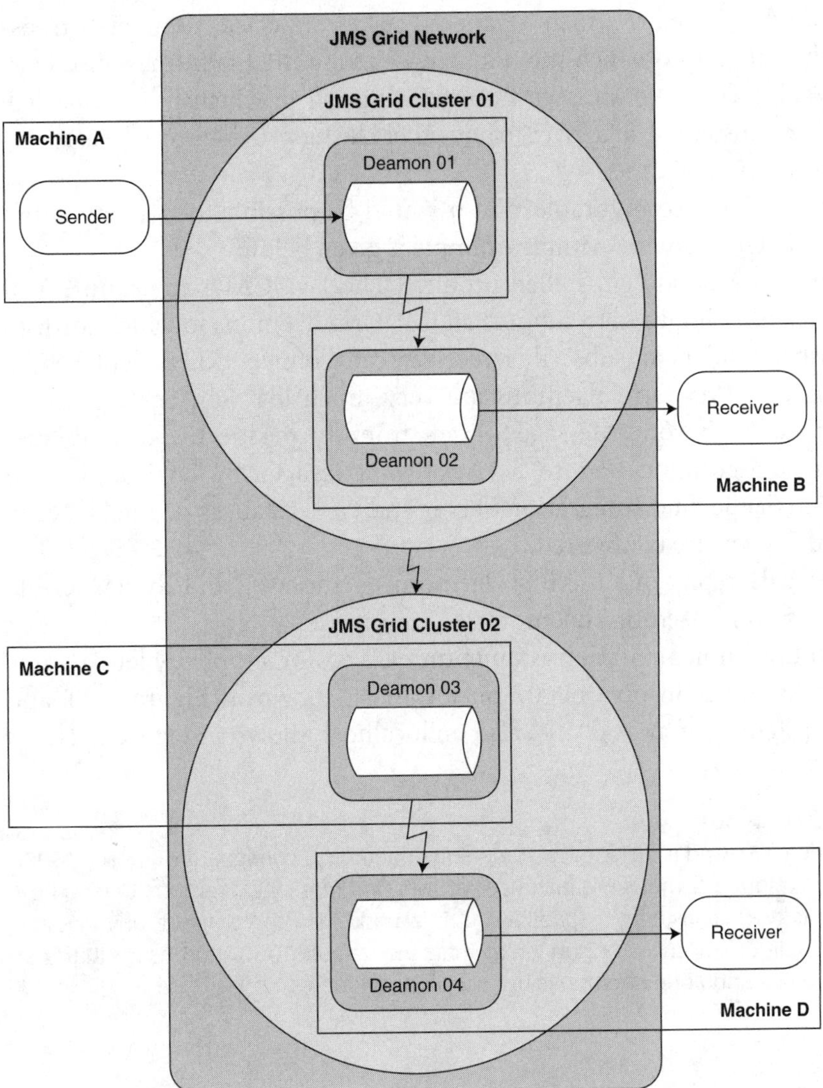

FIGURE 5-18: JMS Grid network

When a message is published by a JMS client to the JMS Grid cluster, specifically to the daemon to which the client is connected, it is transparently and synchronously replicated to all other daemons in the cluster, as well as asynchronously across the network to the other cluster in the network. The message is acknowledged to the JMS client only once it has been replicated across all daemons in the cluster. This behavior enables the message subscriber/receiver to receive the message from any daemon in the cluster, to which it happens to be connected, completely transparently. If the daemon to which the message was submitted fails, the subscriber/receiver will still receive the message from the daemon to which it is connected. Should an entire cluster fail, a failover to any other cluster provides complete recovery of all messages in real time.

JMS Grid is highly configurable, and it would be possible to write an entire book about JMS Grid alone. A simple example is given below.

JMS Grid is a separately installed product. The Java CAPS environment in eDesigner must be configured to support all JMS Grid daemons to which the JMS client, publisher/sender, or subscriber/receiver can connect when deployed to that environment. JMS Grid daemons are very much like Sun SeeBeyond IQ Managers or Sun SeeBeyond Message Servers, from the perspective of eDesigner environment configuration. Figure 5-19 shows a Java CAPS environment in which one Sun SeeBeyond Integration Server and two instances of the Sun JMS Message Grid Servers are configured.

The JMSGrid1 represents the first daemon (daemon01), and the JMSGrid2 represents the second daemon (daemon02).

Although this implementation is quite unrealistic, for simplicity let's assume daemon01 is listening on port 60607 on localhost, shown in Figure 5-20, and daemon02 is listening on port 60608, also on localhost, shown in Figure 5-21.

Best Practice

When JMS Grid is installed, a standalone daemon is configured on port 50607. Standalone daemons are instances of JMS Grid message daemons that do not contain any clustering capabilities. It is a good idea to configure any cluster-capable daemons on a port other than the default 50607 to ensure that the default standalone daemon is not accidentally addressed.

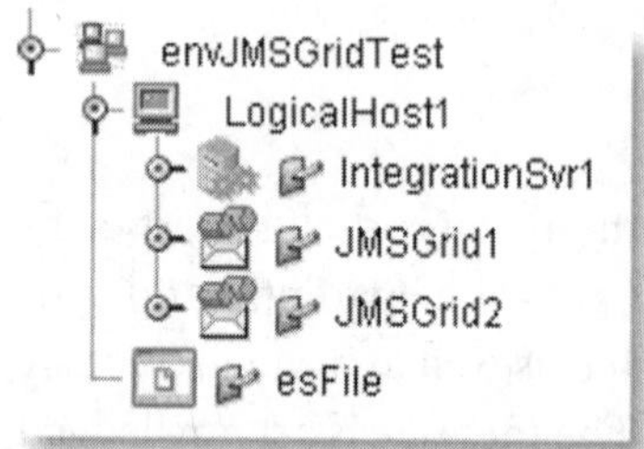

FIGURE 5-19: JMS Grid Message Servers in a Java CAPS environment

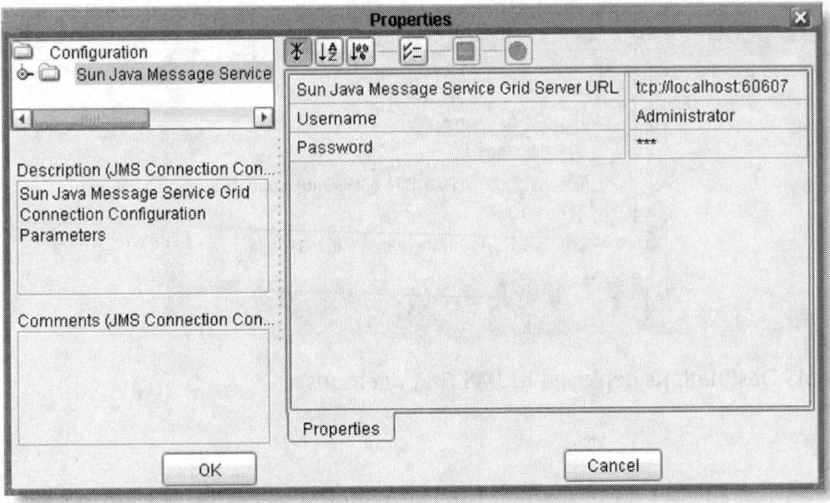

FIGURE 5-20: Daemon to listen on port 60607

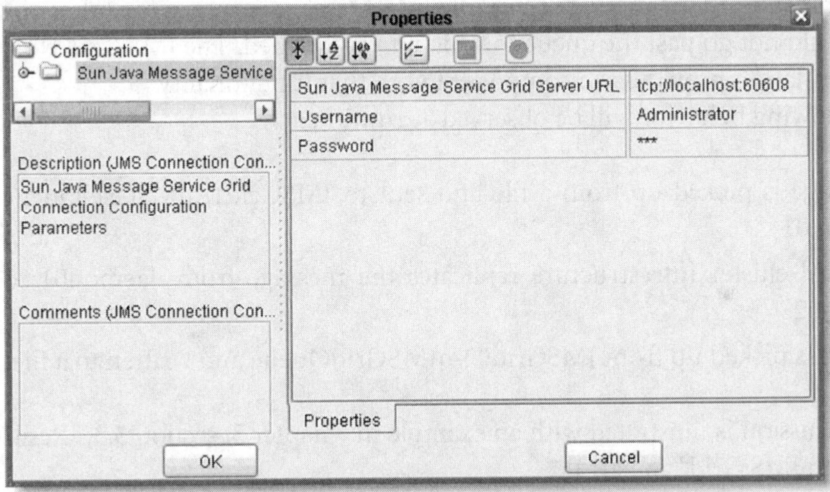

FIGURE 5-21: Daemon to listen on port 60608

Now let's create a deployment profile and deploy components, as shown in Figure 5-22. Here the sender (svc_jcdFileToJMS → 1JMSGridQueue) will connect to JMSGrid1 daemon, and the receiver (qJMSGridQueue → svc_jcdJMSToFile) will connect to JMSGrid2 daemon. The JMS Grid cluster will take care of propagating messages between daemons.

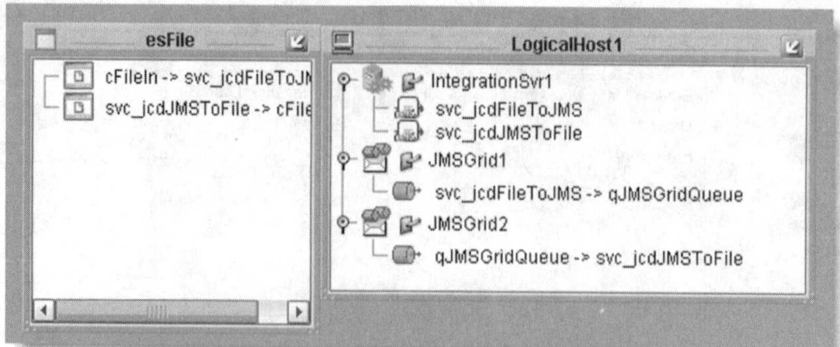

FIGURE 5-22: JMS Destinations deployed to JMS Grid daemons

If the JMS Message Servers to which the publisher/sender and the subscriber/receiver are deployed were not part of the same JMS Grid cluster, there would be a disconnect between the sender and the receiver. Unless a separate component somehow transported the message from one JMS Message Server to the other, the message would not go past the queue to which it was queued. The JMS Grid cluster implementation provides the component with that functionality.

The following behavior will be observed at runtime:

- A message is picked up from a file and sent to JMSGrid1/qJMSGridQueue (daemon01).
- JMS Grid cluster infrastructure replicates the message from daemon01 to daemon02.
- Message is picked up from JMSGrid02/qJMSGridQueue and written to a file.

This discussion is illustrated with an example in Chapter 3, section 3.3, "Resilient JMS with JMS Grid," in Part II.

Unlike the Sun SeeBeyond IQ Manager, which is "self-administering," the JMS Grid Admin Console must be used to create required networks, clusters, and daemons.

Let's create a runtime environment now.

The default installation is straightforward and well documented in [JMSGrid-UserGuide]. Once you have started the JMS Grid Admin Console, create the JMS Grid Network with one JMS Grid cluster and two JMS Grid daemons, as shown in Figure 5-23. Vary hosts and port numbers as appropriate.

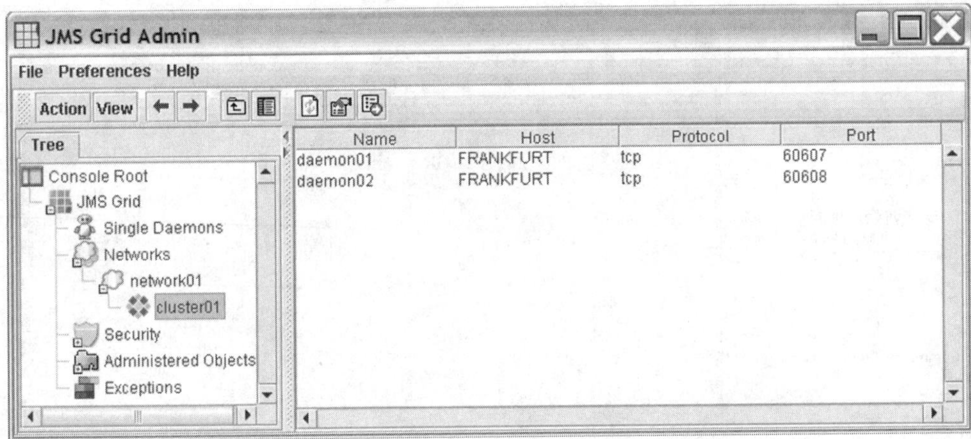

FIGURE 5-23: JMS Grid daemons in JMS Grid Admin Console

On Windows, start both daemons by executing the following commands:

```
startserver.bat /n daemon01
startserver.bat /n daemon02
```

Let's now submit the file to be picked up and observe that the message is correctly sent, and transparently replicated and received.

As mentioned, you would normally ensure that all JMS clients are aware of all daemons in the cluster in order to be able to be transparently failed over from daemon to daemon. This awareness is configured by specifying the URLs of all daemons participating in the cluster separated by a comma. Figure 5-24 shows the Sun Java Message Service Grid Server URL property whose value contains references to two daemons.

```
http://localhost:60607,http://localhost:60608
```

Note the comma between the daemon message server URLs.

The [JMSGridUserGuide] goes into the specific details of what configuration settings are recommended for maximum throughput, as well as client load balancing, client failover, and fault tolerance.

As you have seen, the actual JMS Grid specifics have absolutely no effect on the development process. Apart from specifying the JMS Grid Message URL, there was no JMS Grid–specific code anywhere. This is a great advantage, as you

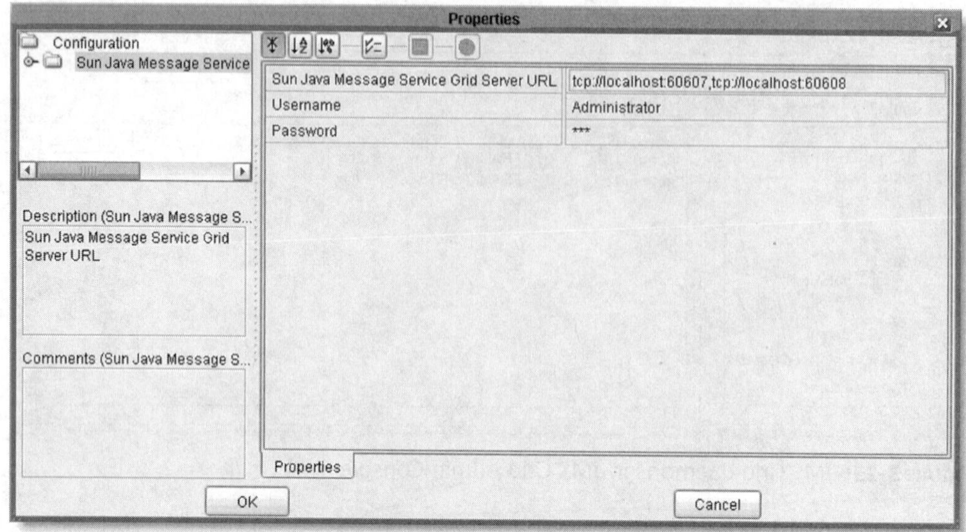

FIGURE 5-24: Configuring JMS Grid client connection configured for failover

can develop your code without having to worry about high availability, scalability, or resilience during development. Once you migrate to your production environment, you get all these for free. No refactoring of any previous development effort is required.

Best Practice
Develop your Java CAPS solutions using the Sun SeeBeyond IQ Manager that is part of the Logicalhost domain. This is the easiest option for quickly testing your projects, as you don't have to worry about starting and stopping the JMS Grid message daemons or any added JMS Grid configuration overhead. Then when you migrate to your test and production environments, you can switch to a JMS Grid setup without any extra development effort.

The JMS Grid message daemons can provide you with the required high availability and resilience that your enterprise may need. It is highly configurable and leaves a lot of room for custom tuning to your particular requirements.

5.8 Competing Consumers

Messages might be arriving at a particular Java Collaboration faster than the collaboration can process them. If the collaboration's activities do not rely on messages arriving in order, it might be useful to have multiple copies of the collaboration work concurrently, starting a new copy of the collaboration as soon as a message arrives, achieving parallel processing. Even if serial processing is required, a degree of parallelism can be achieved by configuring the appropriate FIFO Mode [JMSREF, p. 69].

5.8.1 eGate and Java Collaborations

One way to implement the Competing Consumers pattern in Java CAPS is to explicitly replicate processing services in the connectivity map. Figure 5-25 shows three instances of the service configured to receive from the same JMS queue in order to parallelize message processing.

By default, each receiver is configured with Serial mode concurrency, meaning only one copy of the receiver will be created. It will receive a message when it is ready and a message is available. Messages that cannot be delivered because the receiver is busy will be queued until it is no longer busy.

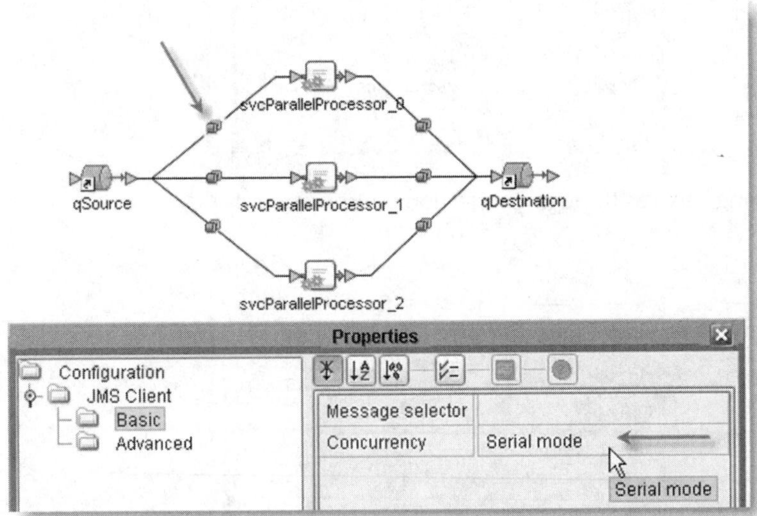

Figure 5-25: Explicitly replicated services

In the example in Figure 5-25, there are three explicit receivers. Each would be implemented using the same Java Collaboration. You would merely drag the collaboration onto the Connectivity Map Editor Canvas three times.

Another way to implement the Competing Consumers pattern is to drag a single Java Collaboration to the Connectivity Map Editor Canvas and configure the JMS Connector Basic Concurrency property to Connection Consumer mode. Figure 5-26 shows the Concurrency property of the JMS consumer configured to support Connection Consumer mode.

Figure 5-27 shows the advanced property Server Session Pool Size set to the desired maximum number of services, to execute in parallel, when the Concurrency is set to Connection Consumer mode.

Warning

There is no visual indication that the receiver operates in a Connection Consumer mode. When inspecting connectivity maps, keep an eye out for these things, as solution runtime behavior may be very different in either case.

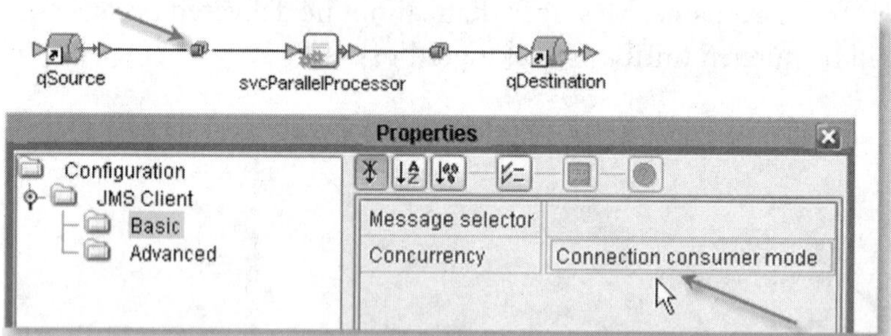

FIGURE 5-26: Replicating services through Connection Consumer mode

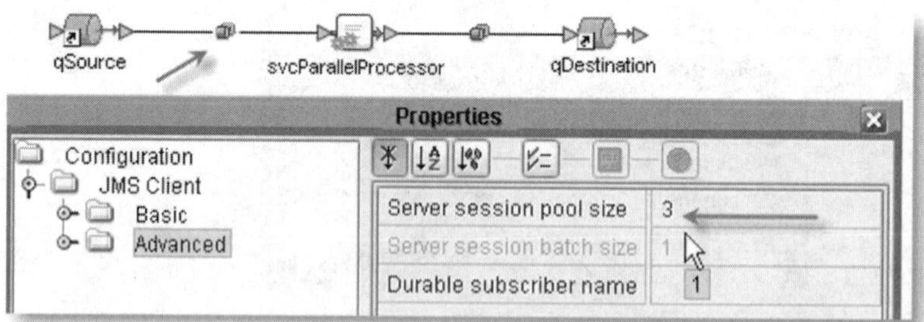

FIGURE 5-27: Specifying Server Session Pool Size property value

Warning
FIFO modes affect parallelism in Connection Consumer mode.

This works only if the service is implemented as a Java Collaboration. Java Collaborations are expected to be relatively short-lived. An implicit transaction is started when the message is delivered to the consumer and only completed when the consumer completes. The longer the consumer takes to process a message, the more likely it is that a new message will become available and a new copy of the consumer will be started to process it.

5.8.2 eInsight Business Processes

If the receiver is an eInsight Business Process, the behavior is very different. An eInsight Business Process is, effectively, a Web Services orchestration. Since Business Processes can be long-running, as in hours, days, or even months, it would normally be impossible in practice to impose on them transactional behavior like that imposed on short-lived Java Collaborations. Business Process Execution Language for Web Services (BPEL4WS), which is at the core of eInsight, relies on compensating transactions to reverse side effects produced by individual steps in the Business Process rather than on commit/rollback transactional behavior for the entire Business Process. As of Java CAPS 5.1, XA transactionality can be imposed in specific circumstances over an eInsight Business Process.

The implication for the discussion on Competing Consumers is that as soon as the JMS Receive Web Service delivers a message to the next activity in the Business Process, it sends an acknowledgment the JMS Message Server. The JMS Message Server completes the transaction and, if another message is available, delivers the next message to a new instance of the Business Process. In all likelihood, both instances will continue executing in parallel for a while.

If there is considerable message traffic, in all but the most trivial case of "do nothing" Business Process, there may be many process instances running concurrently. This is similar to the behavior observed with Java Collaboration configured for Connection Consumer mode, but there is a critical difference. The number of concurrent Business Process instances receiving messages from a JMS Destination cannot be throttled through the Server Session Pool Size. In fact, eInsight behaves, to all intents and purposes, the same way regardless of the setting of the JMS Connector Concurrency property, unless Sun SeeBeyond JMS Time Order Group is defined or the entire Business Process is subjected to XA transactional semantics.

Warning

Unchecked, this behavior could result in explosive growth in the number of Business Process instances, competing for finite machine resources and effectively bringing the whole solution to a halt.

The number of concurrently executing eInsight Business Processes can be configured on a per-eInsight-Business-Process-execution-engine basis in version 5.1.0 (Figure 5-28) and on a per-eInsight-Business-Process basis in version 5.1.1 or later (Figure 5-29), both through the Integration Server eInsight engine configuration property MaxConcurrentInstances.

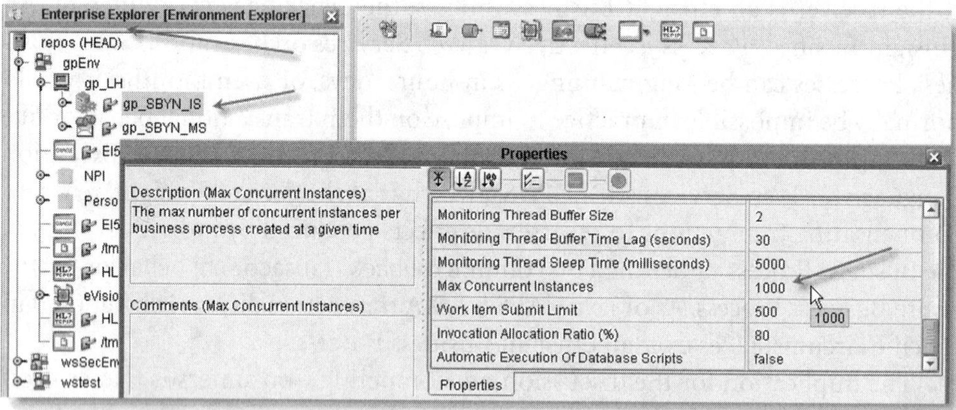

FIGURE 5-28: MaxConcurrentInstances in 5.1.0

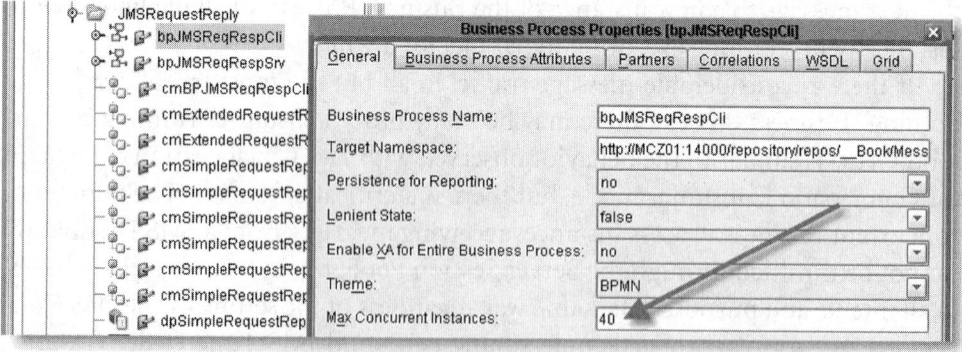

FIGURE 5-29: MaxConcurrentInstances in 5.1.1 and later

Note

As of Java CAPS 5.1, XA transactional behavior can be imposed on the entire eInsight Business Process. This effectively serializes processing, and instead of behaving like Competing Consumers, a new eInsight Business Process instance is not created to receive a message until the previous instance finishes processing a message.

This facility must be turned on with a great deal of forethought. Imposing XA transactional semantics on long-running processes that access external resources with exclusive locks may result in greatly increased contention for scarce resources and/or deadlocks.

As mentioned before, the eInsight Business Processes that are receivers behave much like Java Collaboration receivers with the JMS Connector property Concurrency configured to Connection Consumer mode. This effectively means that multiple parallel Business Process instances will be executing. Since Business Processes are likely to be long-lived, and the execution duration is largely dependent on the time it takes the various Web Services Business Processes invoked to respond, it is likely that different messages may take different amounts of time to be processed. The messages may arrive at their destination in an order different from that in which they arrived at the JMS Destination from which the Business Process picked them up, unless Sun SeeBeyond JMS Time Order Group is implemented to serialize message processing on a per-Message-Server basis.

Note

If preservation of message ordering in the presence of Business Processes as receivers is important, the solution will need to enforce serialization or implement resequencing of messages at the destinations where sequence matters.

5.9 Point-to-Point Channel

A Point-to-Point Channel ensures that only one receiver consumes a given message [EIP]. The Point-to-Point Channel is none other than a JMS queue, discussed earlier in section 5.5.

5.10 Publish-Subscribe Channel

A Publish-Subscribe Channel has a single input channel and multiple output channels, one for each subscriber [EIP]. The Publish-Subscribe Channel is none other than the JMS topic, discussed earlier in section 5.5.

5.11 Datatype Channel

A Datatype Channel [EIP] is a channel over which only one type of message is transmitted. [EIP] suggests using this approach to address the issue of a receiver not knowing what message type it is receiving without additional information, for example, a Format Indicator [EIP].

5.11.1 JMS Message Body Formats

Most receivers simply receive data and provide it to processing components as a single payload buffer, whether a byte array or a string. Some receivers are, however, "sensitive" to data representation in that they provide multiple buffers of different types, only one of which is populated, as dictated by the sender. The most obvious example of these is a JMS client. JMS clients operate in pairs: one JMS client sends/publishes a message to the JMS Message Server and another receives/subscribes to it.

JMS recognizes different message body representations, most notably TextMessage, BytesMessage, MapMessage, StreamMessage, and ObjectMessage. Java CAPS JMS client OTD provides different message buffers for different types. To interoperate, either the sender and the receiver must both agree on the form of the JMS body, or the receiver must have a way of figuring out the form of the JMS message body.

Note

Java CAPS through version 5.1.3 does not provide an ObjectMessage buffer for either sending or receiving, so, effectively, it does not support ObjectMessage type. Even if it did, the usefulness of the ObjectMessage, which by definition is supposed to carry a Java serializable object, would be questionable as non-Java receivers would have no way to deal with these kinds of messages.

Note

Since one can specify name/value pairs in JMS header user properties, the relevance of the MapMessage format is somewhat questionable.

Note

The usefulness of the StreamMessage format is somewhat questionable. StreamMessages carry Java primitive types that non-Java components may be unable to interpret.

This discussion is illustrated with detailed examples in Chapter 3, section 3.4.1, "JMS Message Body Formats," in Part II.

5.11.2 Endpoint-Dependent Datatypes

Concern with the datatype of the message implies that the receiver cares about what the datatype of the message payload is, implying in turn that the payload is structured, and it is this structure that is of specific interest.

Whether or not a Java CAPS channel is a Datatype Channel depends principally on the endpoint from which a Java CAPS component receives messages. If the endpoint is an HL7 eWay, for example, HL7 being a very common healthcare standard, the eWay will reject any messages that are not HL7 messages before they make it to a Java Collaboration or a Business Process. If configured to do so, the HL7 eWay can also reject HL7 messages that are not the correct version or do not originate from the correct source, to name a few of the available options. With an endpoint of this type, a processing component can assume that it will only deal with messages of the type it is expecting because all other kinds will not make it that far. Endpoints other than the HL7 eWay may similarly prefilter messages by datatype before delivering them to processing components—see relevant eWay documentation for specifics.

Generic endpoints, like the HTTP eWay, the TCP/IP eWay, a JMS client, or the Batch eWay, are oblivious to the type of payload data with which they are dealing (but see discussion of JMS message body formats in section 5.11.1). Such endpoints will deliver messages to processing components, which are expected to deal with messages as best they can.

5.11.3 Multiple Datatypes in Java Collaborations

Java Collaborations can have only one input message, so the [EIP] suggestion that a component receives different messages from different channels is not, strictly speaking, implementable in a Java Collaboration. Once triggered by that one message source, be it a scheduler, a JMS Message Server, an HTTP server, or some other endpoint, the Collaboration can explicitly invoke receive methods of other endpoints, polling multiple channels for messages. This is one way in which the Datatype Channel pattern can be implemented, though implementing the Format Indicator pattern using a single JMS endpoint is less complex and therefore easier and more efficient.

Assume a JMS text message arrives at a Java Collaboration. The collaboration may assume it is only dealing with one type of message, unmarshal the message, and process it. If the message is of the wrong type, the unmarshal operation will fail and throw an UnmarshalException. What happens to the message at that point very much depends on how the collaboration is designed.

If the collaboration does not handle the exception, the exception will be propagated up and will eventually cause the message to be rolled back to the JMS Destination from which it came. Unless overridden by JMS redelivery handling configuration for the JMS Destination (version 5.1.2) or globally (version 5.1.1), the message will be immediately submitted back to the collaboration, which, having not changed in the meantime, will treat it the same as before—badly.

If the collaboration handles the exception, by virtue of having a try-catch surrounding the unmarshal operation, it can ignore the message and return (message loss), it can deliver the message to an Invalid Message Channel [EIP], write it to a file, or do any number of other things depending on what the designer needs to do.

One of the ways to handle a non-unmarshalable message is to unmarshal it into another OTD to see if the message has a different structure. This brute-force approach may be valid if there is no other way to distinguish message types except by trying to unmarshal them into successive OTDs until one fits. If the volume of messages that have the structure that successfully unmarshals into the first OTD is significantly greater than the volume of messages with different structures, this approach is even fairly efficient.

Rather than using a trial-and-error approach, it might be better to use a Format Indicator [EIP], discussed in Chapter 4, section 4.10. In the case of a JMS message, the Format Indicator could be carried as a JMS message header user-defined property so it would be available for controlling execution flow even before the payload was unmarshaled.

5.11.4 Multiple Datatypes in Business Processes

Unlike a Java Collaboration, an eInsight Business Process can have multiple receive activities configured using a Business Process Execution Language (BPEL) Event-Based Decision construct. This in effect achieves for eInsight Business Processes what [EIP] suggests as an approach to implementing a Datatype Channel pattern. Event-Based Decision can be used to implement a variety of solutions, including timeouts, gathers, message-driven alternatives, and others, where message sources, message types, or timer events may vary at runtime. Examples of the use of this construct for timeouts and message type alternatives are provided in Chapter 11, "Message Correlation," section 11.10. A detailed implementation example of a multi-input Service Activator is provided in Chapter 7, section 7.5, "Multi-Input Service Activator," in Part II.

An eInsight Business Process is not inherently any more clever at detecting different datatypes than a Java Collaboration is. Using the Event-Based Decision construct to receive different messages only works if each alternate receive activity receives from a different source. Even if there is more than one JMS receive activity, each has to be related to a different JMS Destination; otherwise a randomly chosen branch of the Event-Based Decision will be used, defeating the purpose of having an Event-Based Decision.

Much as was the case with a Java Collaboration, from the standpoint of a JMS receive activity in an eInsight Business Process, all messages are the same if they are of the same JMS message body format: text, bytes, or map. Also, much as was the case with the Java Collaboration, it is not until a JMS message is unmarshaled into an OTD that the Business Process can access elements of the message if it succeeded in unmarshaling, or until it discovers that the message has the wrong datatype if not. Solutions to these issues are exactly the same as solutions to these issues in Java Collaborations: discard the message, requeue the message, or try different OTDs until successful unmarshaling occurs.

Note that unlike in the case of a Java Collaboration, an eInsight Business Process has no way of rolling back the JMS receive unless the entire Business Process is configured as subject to an XA transaction. A JMS message is deemed to have been consumed as soon as it is delivered to the Business Process and is acknowledged as such. As of version 5.1.1, the entire Business Process can be made subject to an XA transaction; therefore, an unhandled failure somewhere in the process will result in a fault being propagated and the XA transaction being rolled back. This, in turn, will result in the JMS message being rolled back and redelivered, moved, or deleted depending on the configuration of redelivery handling; see section 5.13.

5.12 Invalid Message Channel

Unlike a Dead Letter Channel [EIP], discussed in section 5.13, to which messages that cannot be delivered are sent, the Invalid Message Channel [EIP] is a channel for messages that are received but that the components cannot process for one reason or another. The discussion on handling messages of different datatypes in section 5.11 touched upon the subject of what to do with a message that is not acceptable to the component that received it.

From the Java CAPS perspective, an Invalid Message Channel is just a channel. Components that receive messages they cannot process can send these messages to any channel they are configured to use. It is the solution architecture–specific decision, rather than a Java CAPS feature or facility, that dictates whether Invalid Message Channels will be used, by which components, and in what circumstances.

5.13 Dead Letter Channel

By Andrew Walker

In most circumstances, an EAI infrastructure must guarantee message delivery. Messages must not be lost. This expected behavior would result in continuous attempts to deliver a message regardless of whether the recipient is present or able to receive the message. However well a particular integration solution may be designed, there may be circumstances when a message cannot be delivered to its intended destination. The reasons may be many and varied, including misconfiguration of a sender or removal of a receiver from the system. To prevent continuous redelivery attempts on the one hand, and undetected message loss on the other hand, the solution must make provision for finite retries and diversion of undeliverable messages to alternate destinations, typically known as a Dead Letter Queues, referred to by [EIP] as Dead Letter Channels.

It was only with the release of Java CAPS 5.1.0 that this mechanism became available in the Sun SeeBeyond JMS IQ Manager. In previous versions of the JMS Server this facility did not exist, so message redelivery continued indefinitely. In discussing this topic, we need to be mindful of the difference between a Dead Letter Channel and an Invalid Message Channel. A Dead Letter Channel is a function of the messaging system itself and not of any of the other components that interact with it, an obvious example of this being a Java Collaboration.

5.13.1 Java CAPS Releases Prior to 5.1.2

Unless specified otherwise, the following discussion applies to Java CAPS releases prior to release 5.1.2.

In the Sun SeeBeyond JMS IQ Manager, the Dead Letter Channel is implemented using the JMS Redelivery feature. It is configured globally for an individual JMS IQ Manager; thus the configuration will be applied to all messages that are processed through that JMS IQ Manager regardless of whether the messages are held in topics or queues and regardless of the message producers and/or consumers. As such, it can be seen as an "all-or-nothing" feature.

Let's take a look at how the JMS Redelivery feature can be configured to implement a Dead Letter Channel. As illustrated in Figure 5-30, configuration of redelivery handling is done through the STC Message Server URL property of the JMS IQ Manager. No changes to the connectivity map are required.

The URL has the form:

```
stcms://<jmshost>:<jmsport>?JMSJCA.redeliveryhandling=<redeliverySpecification>
```

To enable Dead Letter Channel behavior, you must use the move() option in the JMS Redelivery configuration URL. This option instructs the JMS IQ Manager to move an undeliverable message to another queue or topic. The parameters to the move option determine the destination. Examples are:

- `1:25;10:250;100:5000;200:move(queue:qDeadLetter)`
  After the message has failed 200 redelivery attempts, move the message to a JMS queue named qDeadLetter.
- `1:25;10:250;100:5000;200:move(topic:tpcDeadLetter)`
  After the message has failed 200 redelivery attempts, move the message to a JMS topic named tpcDeadLetter.
- `1:25;10:250;100:5000;1000:move(same:DLQ$)`
  After the message has failed 1,000 redelivery attempts, move the message to the same type of destination as the source message (JMS topic or JMS queue), the name of which is DLQ<original_Topic_or_Queue_name>.

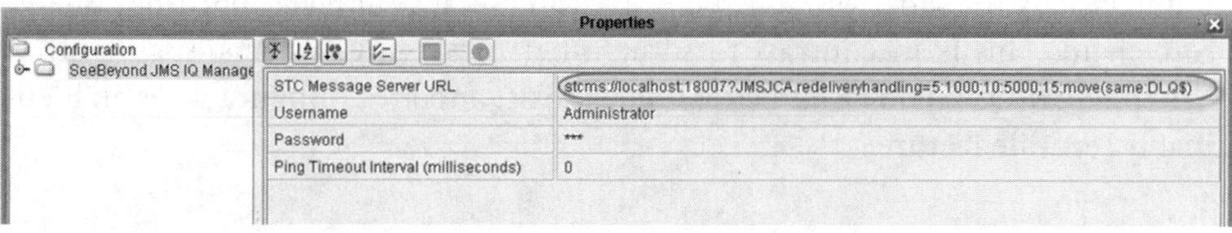

FIGURE 5-30: Configuring redelivery handling

Redelivery configuration is designed to be applied to each message individually regardless of its source or destination. Thus, when formulating the required syntax for the configuration, you must think at the message level and remember that the configuration will take effect for all messages that are processed through that particular JMS IQ Manager.

Actually, if you do not explicitly enter any configuration for JMS Redelivery, a default configuration will take effect. The default configuration is as follows:

- After 3 redeliveries, 25ms delay
- After 5 redeliveries, 50ms delay
- After 10 redeliveries, 100ms delay
- After 20 redeliveries, 1 sec delay
- After 50 redeliveries, 5 sec delay

The default behavior would be encoded as 3:25;5:50;10:100;20:1000;50:5000. However, as can be seen, the default configuration does not include the move() option, thus Dead Letter Channel is not enabled by default in the Sun SeeBeyond JMS IQ Manager; message redelivery attempts will continue indefinitely, though at increasing time intervals, until the message is delivered, expires, or is explicitly removed from the JMS Destination. Note that the delay value must not exceed 5 seconds (5,000 milliseconds).

The JMS Redelivery feature, and thus the implementation of the Dead Letter Channel, is limited to message delivery retries only. It is not intended to handle other nondelivery conditions such as message expiration. Message expiration can be handled, if required, using the Journaling feature discussed in section 5.6.11.

As can be seen from this discussion, the Dead Letter Channel facility provided in the SeeBeyond JMS IQ Manager is simply an extension of the normal JMS topic and queue infrastructure. There is nothing special about the topics or queues that are used as targets in the JMS Redelivery move() option. They function in exactly the same way as other topics and queues and are indistinguishable from them. This is in contrast to some other messaging systems, such as IBM WebSphere MQ, where Dead Letter Queues exist and are configurable as an identifiably separate feature.

5.13.2 Java CAPS Release 5.1.2

By Michael Czapski

Java CAPS release 5.1.2 extends redelivery handling implementation such that individual redelivery configurations can be specified for each sender/publisher. Configuration options are specified through JMS Sender/Publisher connector configuration properties in the connectivity map, illustrated in Figure 5-31.

Note
If Action is specified as "no final action," message redelivery attempts will continue until the message is delivered or until it is manually removed from the JMS Destination.

Note
If there is a redelivery handling specification provided at the Sun SeeBeyond JMS IQ Manager URL in the Java CAPS environment in releases 5.1.2 and 5.1.3, as shown in Figure 5-32, it will override any redelivery handling specification for individual JMS Destinations!

Note, too, that redelivery specification, wherever it is configured, is J2EE application-specific. If there is a specification at the IQ Manager level when an application is built, it will affect that application (EAR file). If it is subsequently changed, the newly built EAR files will carry the changed specification.

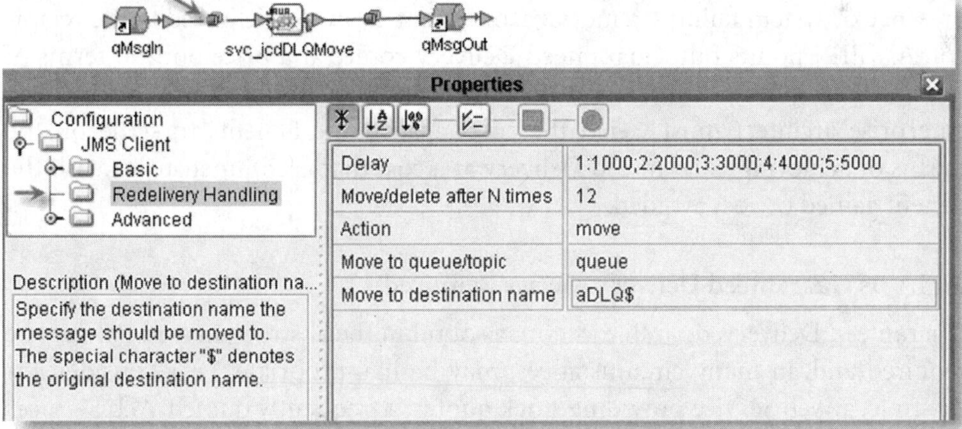

FIGURE 5-31: __Book/MessagingInfrastructure/DeadLetterChannel/DLQMove/cmDLQMove

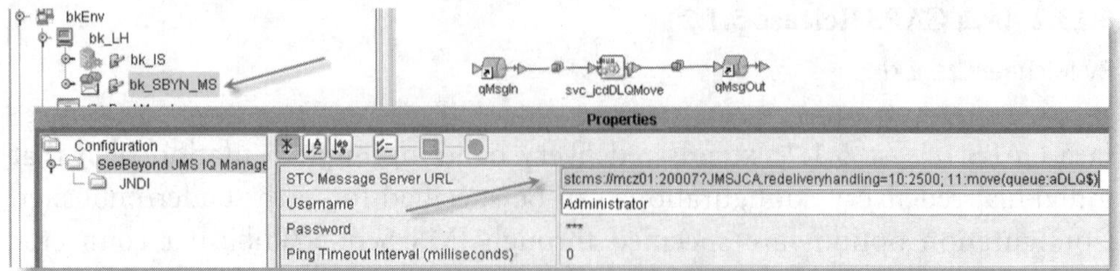

FIGURE 5-32: Sun SeeBeyond STCMS redelivery handling specification

Redelivery handling is illustrated with an example in Chapter 3, section 3.4.2, "Dead Letter Channel in 5.1.2," in Part II.

5.13.3 Documentation Note

The JMSJCA implementation, used to provide support for redelivery handling, is documented in <LogicalHostRoot>/extras/JMSJCA-readme.html. This document, and related material in the same directory, provides deep-dive technical information on the implementation of JMSJCA and its options.

5.14 GUARANTEED DELIVERY

Guaranteed Delivery is the property of the messaging system whereby, even in the presence of system failures, a message, once sent, is always delivered to the recipient. As [EIP] points out, Guaranteed Delivery comes at a price both in terms of the necessary physical infrastructure and in terms of performance impact. The enterprise architect must weigh the costs against the benefits to settle on the means of achieving Guaranteed Delivery at a cost that is commensurate with the benefit gained or cost avoided.

5.14.1 Is Guaranteed Delivery Always Required?

Guaranteed Delivery, desirable as it may sound in the abstract, may not always be required and, in many circumstances, may be inappropriate. Let's consider, for example, a Web Service providing stock quotes, a frequently quoted Web Services scenario. The Web Service invoker typically polls the stock quote service at an interval. From the invoker's perspective, if the quote response does not make it back, there is no great harm done. The response is expected to come on the next poll. The quotes are transient, they change frequently and unpredictably, so a missed quote is unlikely to have a great impact on the business application that is using the service. A delayed quote, on the other hand, depending on how long it is delayed, as not reflecting temporal reality, may have serious adverse consequences. Let's imagine our service is implemented in such a way that when it receives a quote request, it guarantees that the response is delivered to the requester regardless of failures that the infrastructure may experience. The component that provides quotes is built in such a way that it never loses quotes. Let us further imagine a failure has occurred and the component that provides quotes is not available for 30 minutes. Our service will not get, and therefore will not deliver, the response for 30 minutes. The quote that is eventually delivered is 30 minutes old and, in the absence of a catch-up mechanism, all subsequent quotes are 30 minutes old until the system is reset. Clearly, guaranteed delivery in this kind of solution is not only unnecessary but harmful.

Let's consider a twist on the scenario. Let's assume the quote requester is prepared to wait for a quote for no more than 6 seconds before assuming the response will never come and retrying the request. There are two undesirable things that will happen to the service implementation that guarantees delivery. First, it will have $10 \times 30 = 300$ outstanding requests before it can deliver a response. Second, 299 of these responses will not be deliverable, as the requester, having abandoned these requests, will no longer be there to receive the responses. The service will unnecessarily waste resources maintaining information about requests and will perform the work necessary to produce the responses that will never be delivered.

Web Services, so much in vogue these days, are typically implemented using the Request/Reply pattern. This is perhaps because one-way operation Web Services are less well understood or less well supported by development tools. The enterprise architect must seriously consider the appropriateness of using request/reply Web Services in applications in which Guaranteed Delivery is required or the appropriateness of requiring Guaranteed Delivery in request/reply scenarios with short-lived/ "impatient," stateless requesters.

5.14.2 Java CAPS Facilities for Guaranteed Delivery

Once it has been determined that Guaranteed Delivery of a particular level is required, and that the physical infrastructure to support it is available, it is time to consider which facilities of Java CAPS can be used to achieve it for the particular solution or its subset.

Guaranteed Delivery is typically achieved by storing in-flight messages in persistent, possibly redundantly configured storage until delivered; implementing a message service–level acknowledgment scheme with commit/rollback and retry functionality; implementing an application-level acknowledgment scheme with retry functionality; or implementing a multiphase commit protocol, possibly using XA to coordinate transaction processing over multiple cooperating resources. A number of these mechanisms can be used jointly to achieve increasing levels of reliability.

Java CAPS provides in-flight message persistence using JMS for in-between services Guaranteed Delivery and eInsight Persistence for Guaranteed Delivery within a Business Process.

Java CAPS solutions can take advantage of JMS Transacted Sessions, Persistent Delivery mode, and Message Acknowledgments. JMS is used to persist messages between Java Collaborations and/or Business Processes. As of Java CAPS 5.1, Java Collaborations by default operate in XA mode, so when JMS is the source of the message, if an exception occurs the message that the collaboration is operating upon will be rolled back.

For both Java Collaborations and eInsight Business Processes, what happens to a message received through a non-JMS endpoint in case of a failure depends on whether Java CAPS acknowledged message receipt and whether this makes sense for the endpoint, and whether the endpoint considers the message consumed at the time of the failure. In the case of an HTTP eWay or any other HTTP-based server endpoint like a Web Services implementation, the message will be dropped with the expectation that the HTTP client will take steps to recover, whatever that may mean in its context.

eInsight Business Processes, once a message is received by them, can optionally persist the message to the eInsight Persistence Store between individual Business Process activities. Persistence permits message recovery to the last point of persistence.

5.14.3 Persistence Notes

All forms of Guaranteed Delivery require persistent storage of messages while they are vulnerable to failure-induced loss. JMS persistence is implemented as a set of disk files with an internal structure required to support JMS messages, message expiry, message journaling, selectors, and other features a JMS implementation must support. eInsight Persistence is implemented as a set of database tables, in one of the supported relational database management systems (RDBMSs), which allow point-in-time recovery of Business Process instances in flight as well as monitoring eInsight process instances. Solutions architects may implement their own forms of persistence.

A large subset of Java CAPS solutions makes heavy use of JMS. To increase availability of JMS and to reduce or eliminate potential for message loss, Sun JMS Grid can be considered as the JMS implementation for high-availability and Guaranteed Delivery. JMS Grid, discussed in section 5.7, provides transparent JMS message replication across multiple JMS Grid cluster members and transparent JMS client failover, both of which assist in Guaranteed Delivery of JMS messages.

Failure scenarios are not restricted to the failure of Java CAPS components. The potential for hardware failures is typically the principle motivator for concern over Guaranteed Delivery. A catastrophic loss of a system to which a Java CAPS solution is deployed, through system crash for example, may result in message loss if steps are not taken to persist in-flight messages. The loss of a storage device to which messages are persisted will definitely result in data loss, potentially on a very large scale. Thus it is not enough to use persistence and other software-based means to assure Guaranteed Delivery; storage device redundancy and resilience measures, such as RAID (Redundant Arrays of Independent Disks) devices, disk replication/mirroring, and/or cluster-based redundant storage configuration will also have to be used.

The configuration of file systems at the operating system level may affect Guaranteed Delivery in the presence of persistence. Some configurations of file systems, in order to optimize disk I/O, allow the caching of disk writes. If the disk I/O cache contains unwritten data at the time of hardware failure, message loss may occur. Raw disks or write-through caches can be used. Configuration of such facilities, while potentially affecting Java CAPS–based solutions, is well beyond the scope of this book.

5.14.4 JMS-Based Guaranteed Delivery

To put the theoretical assertions about Guaranteed Delivery into perspective, let's consider some Guaranteed Delivery–related facilities a Java Message Service must provide.

JMS has the notions of Transacted and non-Transacted Sessions, Persistent and non-Persistent Delivery modes, and message timeToLive. The Sun SeeBeyond JMS

Message Server can also be configured to control caching disk writes. Configuration of all these things has an impact on whether Guaranteed Delivery can be achieved, at what cost, and what expectation the sender and the receiver can have from the messaging system in different circumstances.

5.14.4.1 Message Expiry

The Sun SeeBeyond JMS Message Server can be globally configured to expire undelivered messages after a period of time. By default, this period is set at 30 days. This topic is discussed in Chapter 4, section 4.9. Individual JMS clients, embedded in custom components such as JMS OTDs, allow setting of timeToLive properties for individual messages. Both of these configuration choices affect a solution's ability to guarantee message delivery. If a message expires before it gets delivered to a component, it effectively becomes lost, as far as the solution is concerned, thus compromising Guaranteed Delivery.

5.14.4.2 Transacted Sessions

The Sun SeeBeyond JMS Message Server supports Transacted and XA Sessions. Consumers always operate in XA Session mode. Producers can operate in Transacted or XA Session mode. Figure 5-33 illustrates the Transaction mode property value of the JMS receiver configured to support transacted sessions.

In Transacted mode, messages are committed automatically and cannot be rolled back even if an exception is thrown by the Java Collaboration.

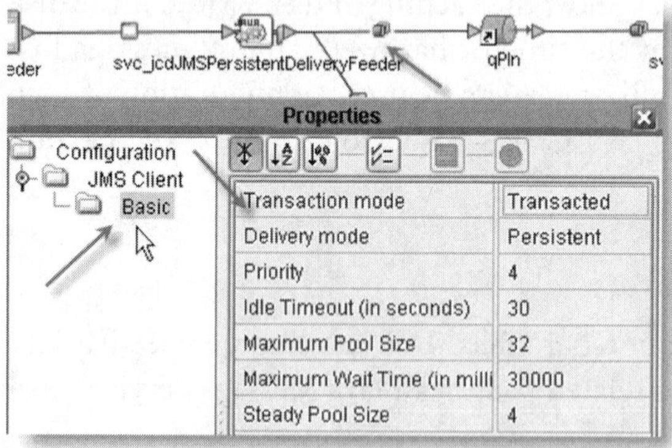

FIGURE 5-33: _Book/MessagingInfrastructure/GuaranteedDelivery/JMSGuaranteedDeliveryFile/cmJMSGuaranteedDelivery

In XA mode, a two-phase commit protocol is used, which prevents message loss and message duplication in the event of system failure.

5.14.4.3 Persistent Delivery Mode

The JMS Provider can be instructed to deliver messages using the Persistent Delivery mode. In this mode, the JMS Provider will take care that the message is not lost in transit due to JMS Provider failure. A provider in Persistent Delivery mode will deliver the message once and only once. This is in contrast with Non-Persistent Delivery mode where the provider will ensure that the message is delivered at most once. To ensure that the JMS Provider does not discard partly processed messages in case of failure, the JMS client should use Client Acknowledgment mode or Transacted Session. Only Persistent Delivery mode in conjunction with Client Acknowledgment or Transacted Session mode guarantee once-and-only-once delivery, assuming a failure that destroys the message in persistent storage does not occur.

The Java CAPS Persistent Delivery mode that applies to the JMS Destination is configured through the JMS Connector properties in the connectivity map. If it is desired to nominate Delivery mode on a per-message basis, then the Delivery Mode JMS Message property can be set programmatically within a Java Collaboration or a Business Process.

The Sun SeeBeyond Message Server global property Sync to Disk, which is disabled by default, can be enabled to force synchronization of the JMS cache with the physical device in a Unix environment. Figure 5-34 shows this setting in the Stable Storage tab of the Sun SeeBeyond IQ Manager section of the Integration Server Administrator console. Enabling this option minimizes the possibility of message loss arising out of system failure at the expense of performance and affects the "persistence" of the Persistent Delivery mode.

5.14.5 eInsight Guaranteed Delivery

An eInsight Business Process typically represents a series of distinct activities, operating on one or more messages, possibly accessing multiple external resources, potentially involving human interaction, and frequently built to take minutes, hours, or days to complete.

The long-running nature of Business Processes poses special challenges to Guaranteed Delivery.

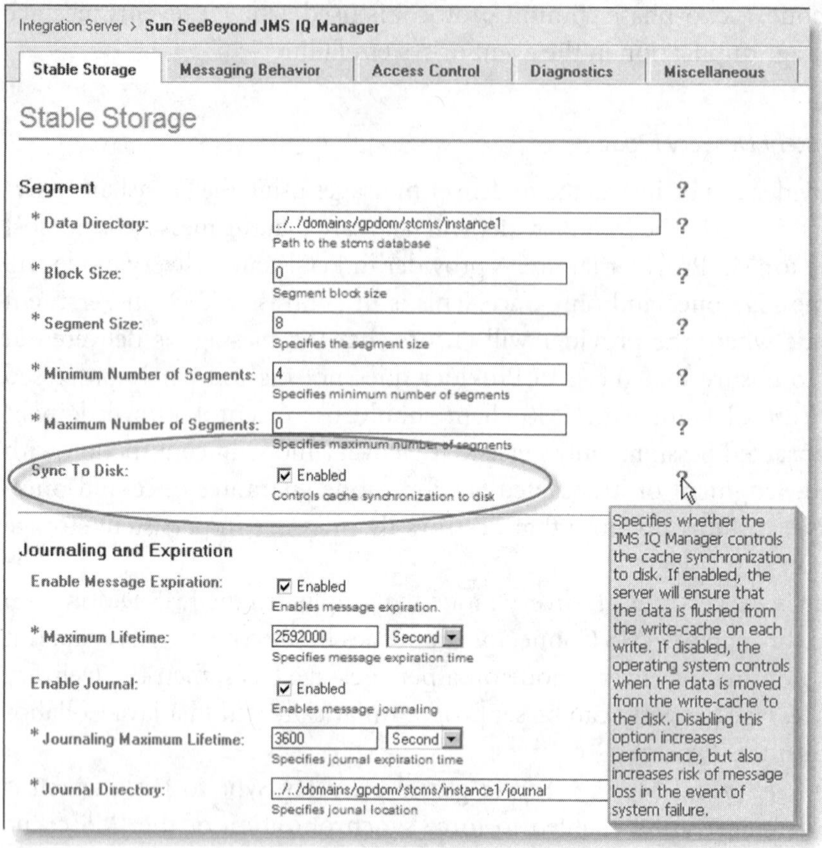

FIGURE 5-34: SyncToDisk property of Sun SeeBeyond JMS IQ Manager

5.14.5.1 eInsight XA Transactionality

XA transactionality is not, strictly speaking, related to Guaranteed Delivery. XA is, more properly, "Guaranteed Nondelivery on Failure." XA transactionality can play an important role in ensuring data consistency at persistence points in persistence-based Guaranteed Delivery solutions. If, for example, an eInsight Business Process is triggered by a JMS receive and it fails before completion, the JMS message will normally have been consumed and other activities within the Business Process may have made permanent changes to external resources such as database tables. Imposing XA transactionality on the process in these circumstances will allow the side effects to be rolled back, the JMS message to be rolled back to the JMS Destination, and the whole process retried as part of recovery processing.

XA transactional semantics can be imposed upon an eInsight Business Process such that either all activities that participate in a transaction complete or none do. This naturally applies only to activities that support XA. Some activities, such as writing to files, do not support commit/rollback, so they cannot be rolled back even if the Business Process is an XA process.

This discussion is illustrated with a detailed example in Chapter 3, section 3.5.1.1, "eInsight XA Transactionality," in Part II.

XA does not guarantee delivery. However, since it does guarantee transactional consistency, it plays a critical role in Guaranteed Delivery solutions.

5.14.5.2 eInsight Persistence

Rather than rolling back all activities that were performed prior to failure, we could configure eInsight to resume the process at the point at which it was interrupted. To achieve this functionality, we must enable process persistence, the facility where Business Process state is persisted in a database and can be used for failure recovery and process-instance state monitoring.

Before persistence can be used, appropriate database tables must be created and the eInsight engine must be configured to support persistence. See eInsight Business Process Manager User's Guide, Release 5.1.3, sections dealing with persistence for details. For the purpose of this section, we will assume that the eInsight persistence tables are created and the eInsight engine is configured. Figure 5-35 lists the persistence tables used in Java CAPS 5.1.2, and Figure 5-36 illustrates the values of the eInsight engine properties used for persistence configuration.

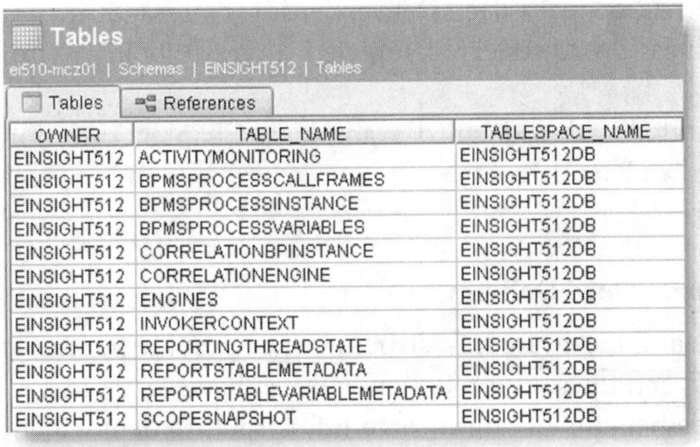

Tables

ei510-mcz01 | Schemas | EINSIGHT512 | Tables

Tables | References

OWNER	TABLE_NAME	TABLESPACE_NAME
EINSIGHT512	ACTIVITYMONITORING	EINSIGHT512DB
EINSIGHT512	BPMSPROCESSCALLFRAMES	EINSIGHT512DB
EINSIGHT512	BPMSPROCESSINSTANCE	EINSIGHT512DB
EINSIGHT512	BPMSPROCESSVARIABLES	EINSIGHT512DB
EINSIGHT512	CORRELATIONBPINSTANCE	EINSIGHT512DB
EINSIGHT512	CORRELATIONENGINE	EINSIGHT512DB
EINSIGHT512	ENGINES	EINSIGHT512DB
EINSIGHT512	INVOKERCONTEXT	EINSIGHT512DB
EINSIGHT512	REPORTINGTHREADSTATE	EINSIGHT512DB
EINSIGHT512	REPORTSTABLEMETADATA	EINSIGHT512DB
EINSIGHT512	REPORTSTABLEVARIABLEMETADATA	EINSIGHT512DB
EINSIGHT512	SCOPESNAPSHOT	EINSIGHT512DB

FIGURE 5-35: eInsight persistence tables

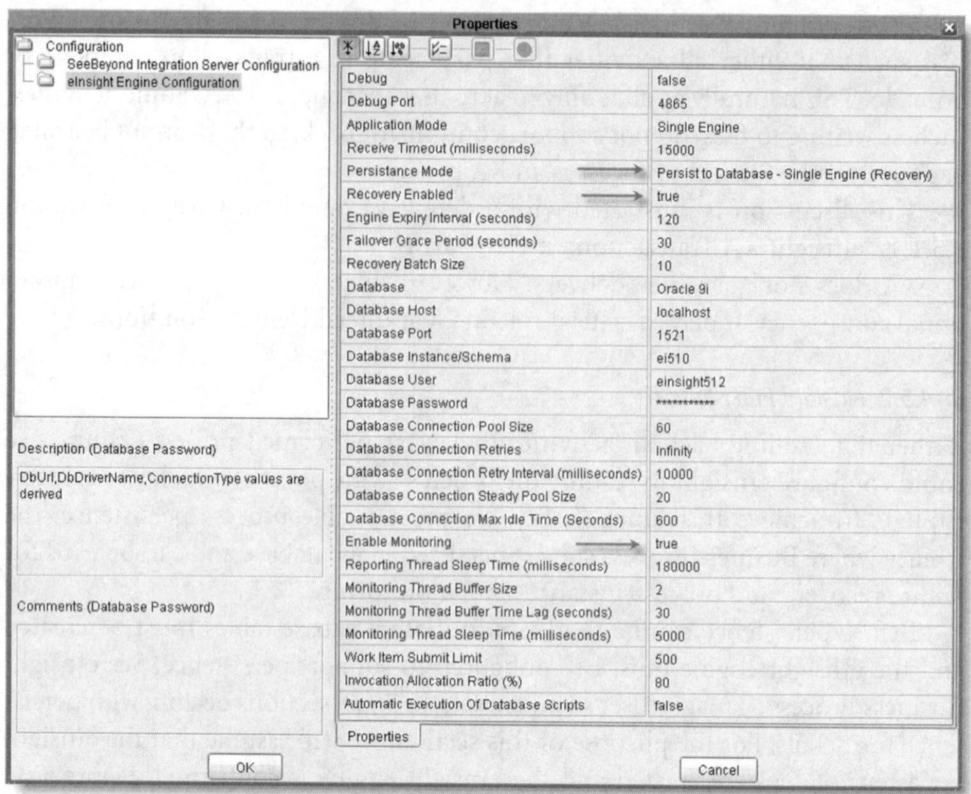

FIGURE 5-36: eInsight persistence configuration

The eInsight persistence-based Guaranteed Delivery ensures messages are not lost, and long-running Business Processes can completed successfully in spite of failures and restarts.

This discussion is illustrated with a detailed example in Chapter 3, section 3.5.1.2, "eInsight Persistence," in Part II.

5.14.6 Solution-Specific Guaranteed Delivery

However much the software and hardware infrastructure may provide by way of support for Guaranteed Delivery, the solution design will also have a part to play in enhancing or negating the benefits of appropriate infrastructure deployment and configuration.

One of the most common issues in solution design is how to deal with the unavailability of external systems on the outbound side. The message, having successfully traversed a complex integration solution, arrives at an endpoint that is supposed to deliver it to an external system. The external system is down. The endpoint infrastructure may not know that the external system is down until the message arrival requires the container to trigger it and the container attempts to validate the connection state prior to triggering the endpoint, or until a delivery to the external system is attempted by the endpoint and fails.

If the container tries to trigger an endpoint component as a result of a message arriving through JMS, it will roll the message back. The redelivery handling, if configured, may retry delivery several times before giving up and redirecting the message to a Dead Letter Queue, Invalid Message Queue, or a queue that triggers some component that simply discards it. Here Guaranteed Delivery configuration must take place outside Java Collaborations or eInsight Business Processes, since these are not invoked. The solution designer may enhance Guaranteed Delivery facilities by taking care to implement appropriate undeliverable message handling, possibly involving human intervention, or may negate the effort and resources put into implementing Guaranteed Delivery infrastructure by explicitly discarding the message or by allowing the message to be expired and discarded by JMS.

If the failure arises within a solution-specific component, such as a Java Collaboration or an eInsight Business Process, the component designer has a great deal of latitude in implementing logic that will assist or interfere with Guaranteed Delivery. Examples of how certain solutions can handle exceptions to aid or hinder Guaranteed Delivery are scattered throughout the book. Specific sections, most notably in Chapter 9, "Messaging Endpoints," section 9.4.2, and in Chapter 13, "Scalability and Resilience," sections 13.3 and 13.4, discuss specific delivery exception handling solutions, and exception and compensation handling in general.

5.14.7 Summary

A number of facilities and services must come together when designing solutions that require Guaranteed Delivery. Java CAPS can assist in implementing Guaranteed Delivery through JMS and eInsight persistence. Hardware-based resilience and recovery measures can assist in ensuring that messages are not lost as a result of hardware failures. Operating system–based resiliency and recovery measures can also assist by transparent replication and restartability.

To truly guarantee message delivery, a combination of all of these must be used where appropriate. The enterprise architect plays a critical role in determining what measures must be taken and whether the cost–benefit ratio is appropriate.

5.15 Channel Adapter

From the messaging system's perspective, the Channel Adapter [EIP] is a piece of infrastructure that intermediates between it and some application that cannot directly interact with the messaging solution. Arguably, the difference between a Channel Adapter and an endpoint is fairly subtle. For the purpose of this discussion, a Channel Adapter is an endpoint purposely built to allow communication between Java CAPS and some third-party application. Such an endpoint, in addition to providing communication services, also incorporates a greater or lesser amount of application-specific "knowledge" and frequently uses application-specific APIs to communicate with the application in a way that is facilitated and supported by the application vendor.

Java CAPS provides a number of prebuilt Channel Adapters for various common applications like SAP, PeopleSoft, Oracle applications, and others; see the list of application eWays and eWay documentation for the appropriate application to determine availability and capabilities of prebuilt Channel Adapters.

Java CAPS may not have prebuilt Channel Adapters for less common or home-grown applications. How to incorporate such applications into a messaging solution is dependent on what facilities exist to extract data from, or supply data to, these applications.

Some applications may be able to "export" data in the form of files or may be able to "import" content of files produced by others. In these cases, one of the variants of the Batch eWay, together with suitable transformation components, may be used to implement a Channel Adapter.

Some applications may be using a relational database with a well-documented schema to store application data and may even provide triggers when data in specific tables changes. Java CAPS Database or JDBC eWays, in conjunction with the appropriate transformation components, can be used to integrate such applications into messaging solutions. Whether such database-based Channel Adapters can be invoked using database triggers, or whether they must poll database tables, will depend on the application. Whether such Channel Adapters can directly modify data in the tables will also depend on the application, site requirements around data integrity, and the application vendor's attitude toward third parties directly modifying data and bypassing the vendor's application logic. All such considerations will have to be accounted for when determining whether to develop a database-based Channel Adapter and what functionality that Adapter can reasonably provide.

For applications using C, C++, or Java programming languages, as well as those capable of using Microsoft COM/DCOM, a JMS-based Channel Adapter can be developed. The Java CAPS API Kit provides APIs and related libraries for these languages. The APIs are documented, with examples, in a series of Java CAPS eGate API Kit documents.

5.16 Messaging Bridge

Organizations that have multiple messaging systems that must exchange messages may need to implement a Messaging Bridge [EIP].

Java CAPS offers a variety of means to assist in developing Messaging Bridge solutions. The Java CAPS eGate API Kit allows third-party Java-, C-, C++-, and COM/DCOM-based solutions to exchange messages directly with the Sun SeeBeyond JMS Message Server. IBM WebSphere MQ–based JMS implementation, Sun JMS Grid, and Sun Java Messaging Service JMS implementations can be transparently integrated with the Java CAPS environment, thus providing JMS-based Messaging Bridge between different JMS implementations. Endpoints, eWay Adapters, can be used to facilitate exchange of messages between Java CAPS and other messaging systems where other means are not available.

The Messaging Bridge can also be used to bridge two or more independent Java CAPS solutions, a Java CAPS solution and an ICAN 5.0.x solution, an SRE 5.0 solution, or even a TRE 5.0 solution. For those not familiar with the last three, ICAN 5.0 is a Java CAPS immediate predecessor, SRE (Schema Runtime Environment) is an ICAN-compatible and Java CAPS-compatible implementation of the original eGate 4.5.3, and TRE (Tables Runtime Environment) is an ICAN-compatible and Java CAPS-compatible implementation of the original DataGate 3.x. The SRE and TRE are not discussed here. ICAN 5.0 and Java CAPS are sufficiently similar to make the following discussion, which concentrates on Java CAPS only, directly applicable.

5.16.1 Bridging Independent Java CAPS Solutions

You will recall that, in most cases, in order for Java CAPS to subscribe to or receive from a JMS Destination, or to publish or send to a JMS Destination, you must create a connectivity map. This is where JMS Destinations are placed and connected to Java Collaborations or eInsight Business Processes that interact with these destinations.

In the Sun SeeBeyond JMS implementation, the JMS Message Server and the JMS clients, where both senders/publishers and receivers/subscribers are clients, all communicate with one another using the TCP protocol. The JMS Message Server is a part of the Java CAPS Application Server domain. Its properties, in particular the port on which it will listen for connections from JMS clients, are configured when the domain is created. These properties live in the domain-specific configuration directory in a file called stcms.default.Properties. When the JMS Message Server starts, it reads that file, among others, and starts listening for client connections on the specified port. In contrast, client connectivity properties, particularly which host and port to use to connect to the JMS Message Server, are configured through the eDesigner in the Java CAPS Environment → Logical Host → Sun SeeBeyond IQ Manager (JMS Message Server). Figure 5-37 shows the value of the STC Message Server URL pointing out the host and port values used to point the clients at the appropriate JSM Message Server instance.

Note that there is no reconciliation between the host and port values specified in eDesigner and the port number on which a JMS Messages Server listens for connections. If the JMS Message Server corresponding to the values specified in eDesigner does not exist, the deployed client will fail to start and will log exceptions in the server.log. Conversely, if there is a TCP listener, on a host specified in the eDesigner, listening on the specified port, supporting the Sun SeeBeyond JMS implementation's Wire Protocol, the client will connect to it and exchange messages regardless of whether or not that listener is running within the same Integration Server domain as the client. It is this "disconnected" nature of the implementation

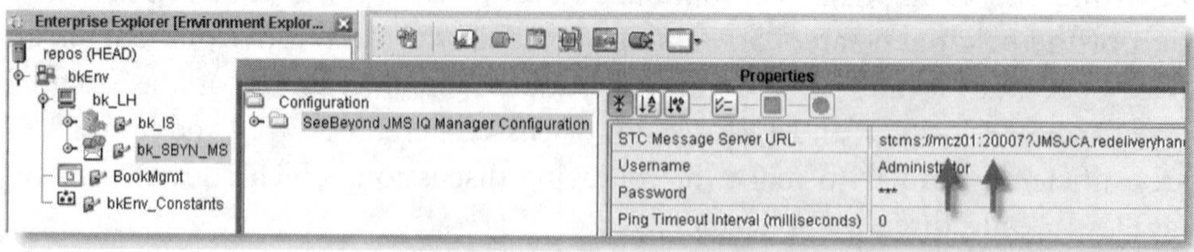

FIGURE 5-37: Sun SeeBeyond IQ Manager JMS Message Server URL property

that is exploited in bridging independent Sun SeeBeyond JMS Message Server instances, whether Java CAPS, ICAN, SRE, TRE, or a combination of these.

Every JMS Destination deployed to a specific Message Server will use the JMS Message Server communication parameters specific to that Message Server to connect and exchange messages.

A Java CAPS eDesigner environment can have multiple logical hosts, each of which can have zero or one Integration Server and/or zero or more JMS Message Servers. Even if multiple message servers are defined in the environment, the domain startup will only cause one to be started. It is possible to configure, through eDesigner, a JMS Message Server with a hostname and port number different from the JMS Message Server that is associated with the runtime domain. An expectation is that some other compatible JMS Message Server is running on the host whose name is configured in the properties and listening on the nominated port for JMS client connections.

To establish a Messaging Bridge between two independent Java CAPS installations, you would point specific JMS clients in one installation at the JMS Message Server in another installation by adding a subordinate JMS Message Server whose host name and port number were in fact those of the JMS Message Server in the other installation. This JMS Message Server would not actually correspond to its runtime counterpart in the domain corresponding to the Java CAPS installation in which it is defined. A JMS Message Server defined in this way is sometimes called a Shadow Message Server.

A two-domain environment configuration with mutual shadow JMS Message Servers might look like that shown in Figure 5-38, where JCAPS02_MS in envJCAPS01 is a shadow for a real JMS Message Server JCAPS02_MS in envJCAPS02, and the JCAPS01_MS in envJCAPS02 is a shadow for a real JMS Message Server JCAPS01_MS in envJCAPS01.

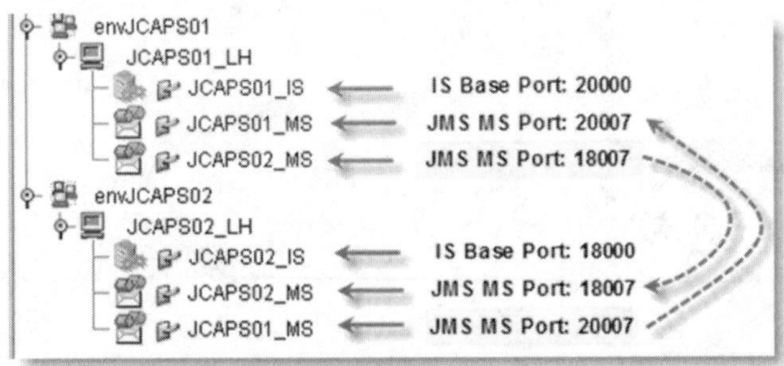

FIGURE 5-38: JMS Message Server Shadow configuration

The JMS Message Server JCAPS01_MS in environment envJCAPS01 does not specify a host or a port, as shown in Figure 5-39, thus allowing the domain-specified values to be used.

The JMS Message Server JCAPS02_MS in environment envJCAPS01 specifies the host name and port number of the JMS Message Server in the other domain, where a JMS Message Server with that host name and port number actually runs. Figure 5-40 illustrates the STC Message Server URL property where the host and port are explicitly specified.

In order to allow projects deployed to the integration server JCPAS01_IS to publish to JMS Destinations in the JMS Message Server hosted in the envJCAPS02, the envJCAPS01 must have a shadow JMS Message Server defined. If it is necessary for projects deployed to envJCAPS02 to also publish to JMS Destinations hosted in envJCAPA01, envJCAPS02 must also have a shadow JMS Message Server defined to

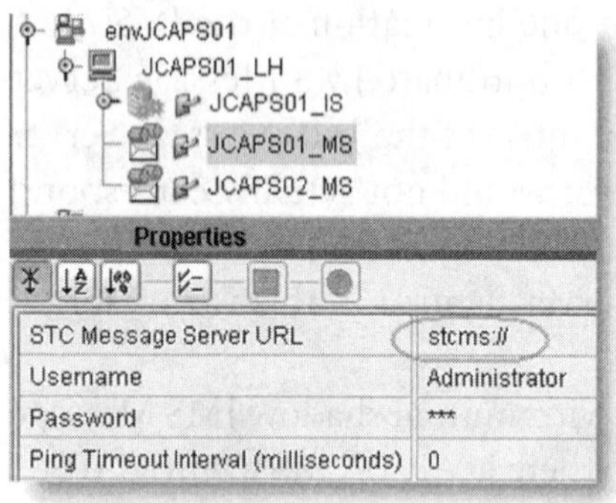

FIGURE 5-39: Default STC Message Server URL

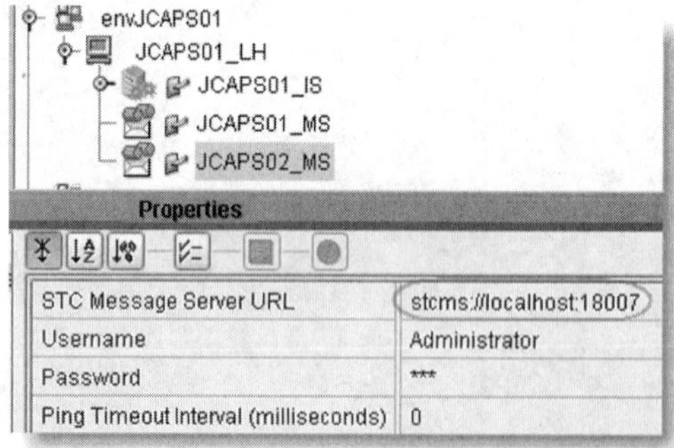

FIGURE 5-40: Actual host and port numbers for the Shadow Message Server

point to the JMS Message Server hosted in the envJCAPS01; otherwise only one shadow server is required.

Given the environments just described, and two connectivity maps as shown in Figure 5-41, you would create two deployment profiles, one each for each of the domains.

The connectivity map cmJavaCAPSBridgeSender is used in deployment profile dpJavaCAPSBridgeSender, and the components are mapped as shown in Figure 5-42. Note that publication svc_jcdJMStoJMS → qPassOn is deployed to the shadow JMS Server JCAPS02_MS running in environment envJCAPS02. This collaboration is what implements the Messaging Bridge that transfers messages between the two Java CAPS domains.

The components defined in the connectivity map cmJavaCAPSBridgeReceiver are all deployed to the Integration Server and Message Server in the environment envJCAPS02 in the usual way, as shown in Figure 5-43. This deployment is a standard deployment.

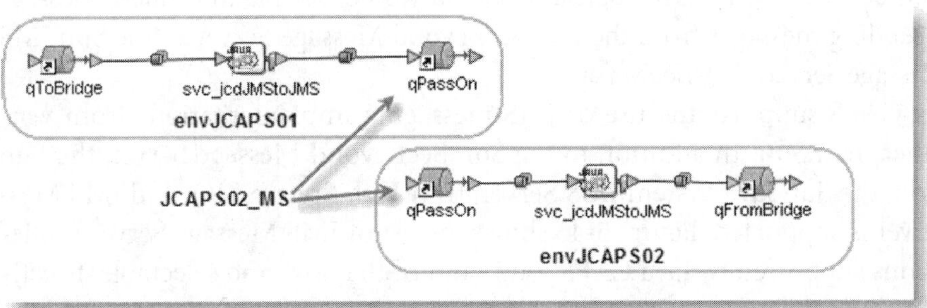

FIGURE 5-41: __Book/MessagingInfrastructure/MessageBridge/JavaCAPSBridge/cmJavaCAPSBridgeXXX

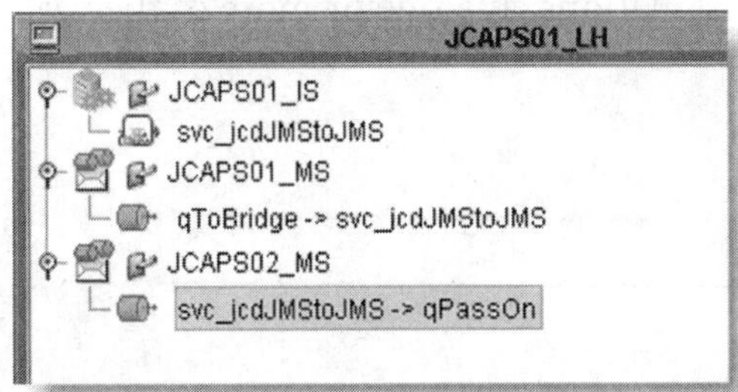

FIGURE 5-42: Components mapped in dpJavaCAPSBridgeSender

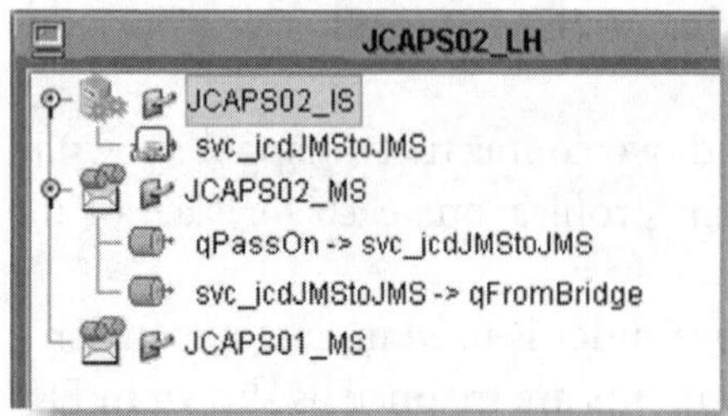

FIGURE 5-43: Components mapped in dpJavaCAPSBridgeReceiver

5.16.2 Bridging Other JMS Messaging Implementations

To create a Message Bridge between the Sun SeeBeyond JMS Message Server and the Sun JMS Grid Server, you would define both JMS Message Server objects in the environment and configure them appropriately.

Given the environment shown in Figure 5-44, with a Sun SeeBeyond Message Server, Grid01_SBYN_MS, and a Sun JMS Grid Message Server, Grid01_JMSGrid_MS, both defined in the same logical host, you would be able to create a Message Bridge sending messages from the Sun SeeBeyond Message Server to the Sun JMS Grid Message Server, and vice versa.

Java CAPS supports the use of JMS messaging implementations from vendors other than Sun. In addition to the Sun SeeBeyond Message Server, the Sun JMS Grid, the Sun Java System JMS Server, IBM Web Sphere MQ, and JMS Message Server is supported. Figure 5-45 shows the list of JMS Message Server implementations supported by Java CAPS 5.1.3, "out of the box" and selectable directly for use in configuring Java CAPS environments.

5.16.3 Other Bridging Solutions

In addition to bridging between different JMS implementations and JMS implementations in independent Java CAPS installations, any one or more of the vari-

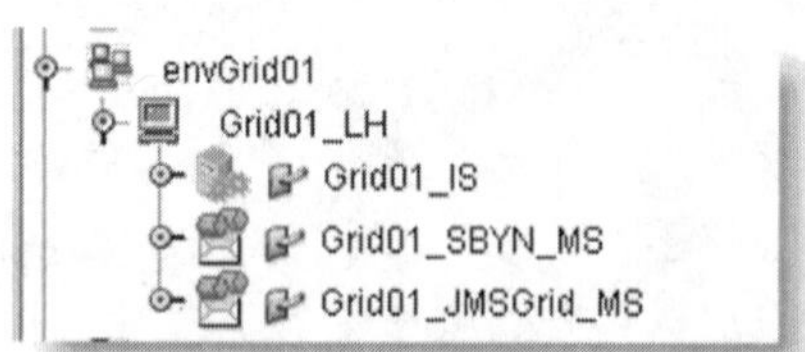

FIGURE 5-44: Environment for bridging between Sun SeeBeyond IQ Manager and JMS Grid

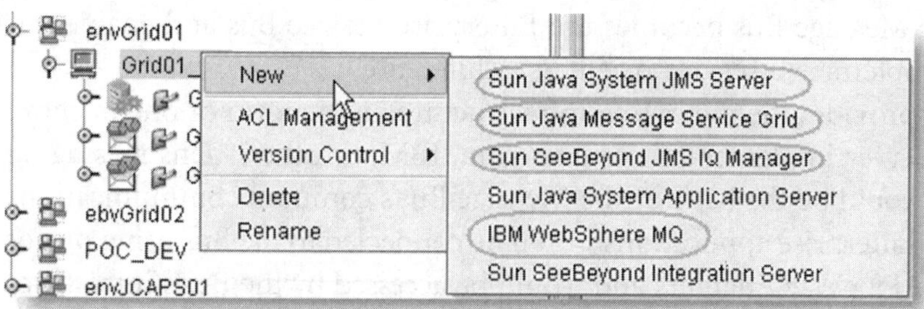

FIGURE 5-45: JMS implementations supported by Java CAPS 5.1.3

ety of eWays, Connectors, and Adapters can be used to create a Messaging Bridge between independent messaging systems. If, for example, the ability to send messages over a TCP/IP channel is the lowest common denominator for interoperability, then the TCP/IP eWay can be used to receive messages from the other messaging system or send messages to it. Similarly, the HTTP eWay or even a Batch eWay could be used to bridge the technological divide between two messaging solutions.

5.17 MESSAGE BUS

Message Bus [EIP] is an enterprise integration infrastructure used by enterprise applications as a means of interacting with other enterprise applications in a loosely coupled manner. The Message Bus implements the Canonical Data Model [EIP] and a common command structure. Enterprise applications connect to the Message Bus using appropriate adapters. These adapters convert, if necessary, between the canonical message and application-specific messages and facilitate exchange of messages between the application and the Message Bus. Since receiving applications may not know what sending application sent the messages, the Bus must implement a set of commands that all participating applications understand. These could be get, add, update, and similar commands to request the application to perform the corresponding operation in an application-specific manner. Implied in this model is the means of routing messages from intending to intended applications. By defining a set of commands that participating applications implement in an application-independent manner, you effectively create a set of services with predefined interfaces and operations. These services shelter other participants from each other's implementation and technology specifics.

Ultimately, the Message Bus becomes the Enterprise Service Bus and enables an enterprise to implement a service-oriented architecture.

Java CAPS provides the messaging infrastructure, in the form of one or more JMS Message Server implementations from Sun, IBM, or others. This messaging infrastructure would be the basis of the Message Bus's common communications infrastructure. Enterprise applications would be connected to the Bus using one of over 80 Java CAPS eWay Adapters and would be accessed by the Bus's infrastructure as Web Services endpoints, JMS request/reply endpoints, or in any other way that the enterprise architects chose as the corporate standard. The OTD framework would be used to define and implement the Canonical Data Model. While Java CAPS supplies all the technology required to implement a Message Bus, as defined by [EIP], the design of the Canonical Data Model and service interfaces and the choice of Adapters are enterprise-specific. The Message Bus for the enterprise would ultimately be designed by the enterprise's architecture and implementation teams.

When discussing the Message Bus, the [EIP] uses an example of an interactive application that uses the Bus to access data from multiple disparate systems. In effect, the example discusses a service orchestration implementation or, as Java CAPS and others call it, a Composite Application. Java CAPS, through the eVision product, goes further than just facilitating construction of a Message Bus. It also provides the means to develop an Enterprise Web Application that uses other parts of the Java CAPS suite to facilitate creation of Composite Applications using the Message Bus.

5.18 Chapter Summary

This chapter discussed details of the default Java CAPS messaging infrastructure, the Sun SeeBeyond IQ Manager, in order to provide the background necessary to understand how [EIP] patterns that employ the messaging infrastructure are implemented in this chapter and elsewhere in the book. A JMS Grid product, the high-availability JMS implementation, was mentioned, and a number of [EIP] messaging patterns were discussed.

This chapter discussed Sun SeeBeyond Java CAPS JMS specifics that have a significant bearing on implementation of EAI patterns:

- Java Messaging Service
- JMS Implementation Interoperability

- Using JMS to Integrate Non-JMS Environments
- JMS Queues and Topics
- Sun SeeBeyond IQ Manager (JMS Message Server)
- JMS Grid High-Availability JMS Implementation

This chapter also discussed specific [EIP] concepts and patterns that use the JMS or the Java CAPS infrastructure in their implementation:

- Competing Consumers
- Point-to-Point Channel
- Publish-Subscribe Channel
- Datatype Channel
- Invalid Message Channel
- Dead Letter Channel
- Guaranteed Delivery
- Channel Adapter
- Messaging Bridge
- Message Bus

Some of the patterns discussed are presented in [EIP] in Messaging Channels, some in Message Construction, and some in Messaging Endpoints.

CHAPTER SIX

Message Routing

6.1 Introduction

This chapter discusses message routing patterns. It includes discussion and application of patterns from [EIP] Messaging Systems and Message Routing. The chapter briefly discusses where a Java CAPS solution developer can make routing decisions and discusses each of the routing patterns in turn, specifically Splitter, Aggregator, Resequencer, Scatter-Gather, Routing Slip, Process Manager, and Message Broker.

6.2 Overview

A messaging-based integration solution, whether or not and however it transforms messages as they pass through, inevitably routes messages from one or more sources to one or more destinations. A Java CAPS solution can make message routing decisions in four areas: the JMS Message Server, the connectivity map, the Java Collaboration definition, and the eInsight Business Process. Typical solutions that use just the eGate infrastructure would perform routing through the JMS Message Server, the connectivity map, and possibly the Java Collaborations. Typical solutions that use eInsight Business Process Management (BPM) would perform routing predominantly within eInsight Business Processes but may also route in the connectivity map. In all but the simplest solutions, routing will likely be performed by multiple components.

Routing in the JMS Message Server is performed as a consequence of configuring nondefault redelivery handling, which can divert messages to Dead Letter Queues. This issue was discussed in Chapter 5, "Messaging Infrastructure," section 5.13.

The connectivity map, the graphical representation of how Java CAPS components are connected, is the means to both collect all integration solution components that will be deployed as part of a single enterprise application and to configure certain aspects of the message endpoints that are logical in nature, such as JMS Destination names and properties, or names and name patterns for file system objects. The simplest functional Java CAPS solution must have a minimum of two components: a message source and a service that operates on messages from that source. Unlikely as it may seem, in special circumstance, such an apparently useless solution might be valid and reasonable. What [EIP] calls the Channel Purger would be an example of a solution that receives messages from an endpoint and routes them to nowhere. Figure 6-1 shows a connectivity map for a basic Channel Purger.

This is the simplest example of message routing: Fixed Routing [EIP].

Note

A Java CAPS implementer would typically look at the connectivity map for routing information—which components publish and subscribe to which JMS Destinations and how many, and which JMS Destinations are subscribed to/published to by an eInsight Business Process. For that reason, a solution that makes explicit routing decisions in Java Collaboration Definitions (JCDs) or Business Processes will be more difficult to analyze by an implementer new to it. It will also make it harder for the original developers to recall where and how routing decisions are made. If no other considerations dictate specific choices, given a choice of explicit routing in a JCD and explicit routing in an eInsight Business Process, choose the latter, as its graphical depiction of processing logic makes it more obvious that explicit routing takes place. Multiple subscriptions and/or publications by a service on a connectivity map are a strong hint that explicit routing is taking place inside a service component.

Message Router [EIP], a specialized Filter [EIP], represents a component in an integration solution that causes messages to be passed from a source to a destination depending on a possibly empty set of criteria. Unlike connectivity map–

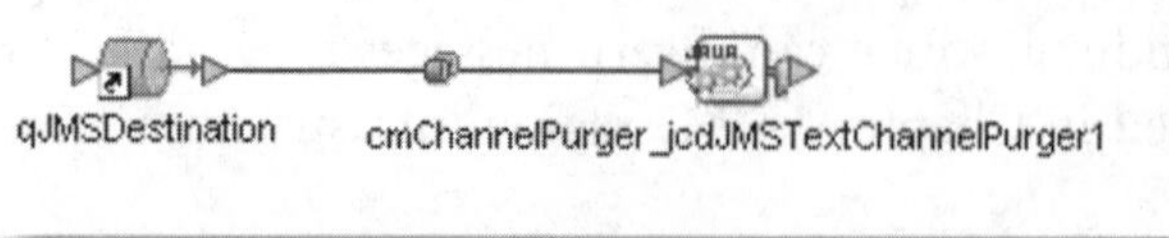

FIGURE 6-1: Channel Purger

based fixed routing, Message Router variants that make explicit routing decisions programmatically can all be implemented in a Java CAPS solution using either JCDs or eInsight Business Processes or both.

The following sections discuss implementation of most of the router patterns using Java CAPS as the infrastructure.

6.3 Fixed Router

A fixed router, one where a single channel is a source of messages and a single channel is a destination, is the most trivial form of a Message Router. You would typically configure the connectivity map source and destination to configure a fixed router. If necessary, however, a Java Collaboration or a Business Process can be constructed to explicitly choose a destination if that destination is a JMS Destination.

Given the connectivity map shown in Figure 6-2, we would expect that the Java Collaboration publishes messages to the JMS Destination (queue) qDummy-Destination.

Inspection of the collaboration source, shown in Figure 6-3, reveals that it is the JMS Destination (queue) qNewQueue that is the actual destination of messages. This destination is hardcoded in the fixed router.

The same effect could be achieved by explicit assignment of the destination queue name prior to sending the message, as shown in Figure 6-4.

Given the connectivity map shown in Figure 6-5, we would again expect the queue qDummyDestination to be the destination of messages.

Inspecting the business rules embedded in the eInsight Business Process, shown in Figure 6-6, reveals this to not be the case.

In this example, an explicit assignment of a JMS Destination name to the destination node of the JMS OTD results in messages being explicitly routed to a JMS Destination (queue) qNewJMSDestination.

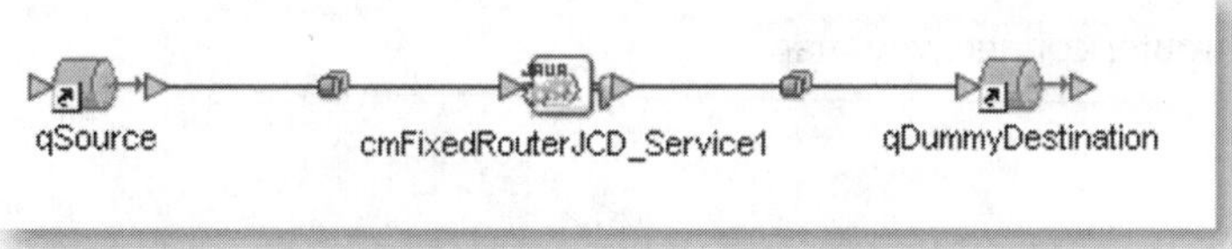

Figure 6-2: Connectivity map of an implicit fixed router

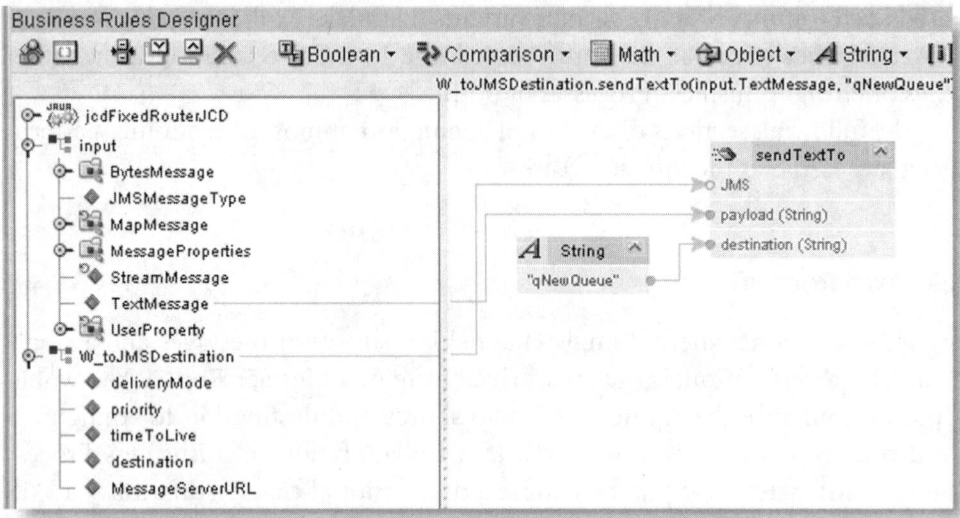

FIGURE 6-3: Hardcoded JMS queue name in a fixed router, which uses a sendTo() OTD method

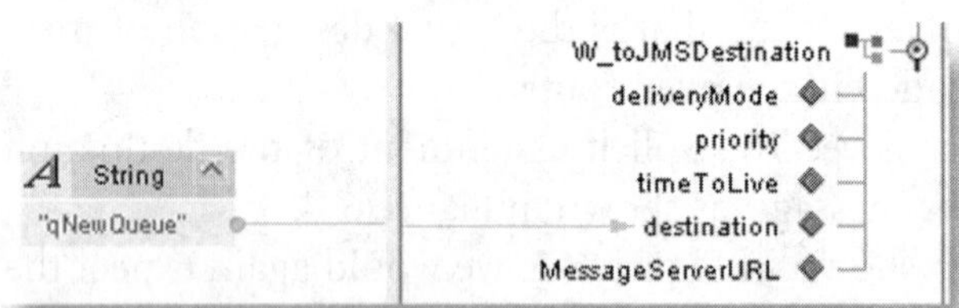

FIGURE 6-4: Hardcoded JMS queue name in a fixed router using a "destination" OTD node

FIGURE 6-5: Implicit fixed router connectivity map

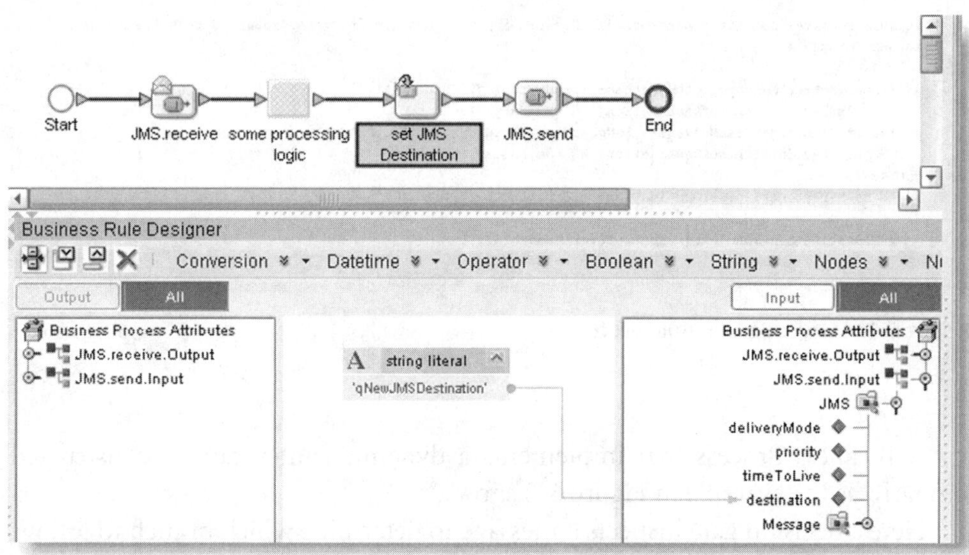

FIGURE 6-6: Explicit JMS queue assignment in a Business Process

Note

In all of the previous examples, the JMS Destination name contained the literal Dummy. This is a hint to the developer who inspects the connectivity map that the actual destination is likely different and is configured within the component that publishes to the "dummy" destination. This is a good practice suggestion, since no part of Java CAPS enforces naming conventions.

6.4 Content-Based Router

Content of the message may dictate the destination to which the message must be delivered. Content-based Router [EIP] inspects the message it receives and sends it to a destination depending on the content.

In a simple case, a Java Collaboration or a Business Process would have a set of destinations hardcoded within a switch or an if-then-else construct that operates on all or part of the message. An example in Figure 6-7 is a simple Java Collaboration that illustrates dynamic JMS Destination selection.

```
public void receive( com.stc.connectors.jms.Message input, com.stc.connectors.jms.JMS W_toJMSDestination )
    throws Throwable
{
    if (input.getTextMessage().toUpperCase().endsWith( "PRIMARY" )) {
        W_toJMSDestination.setDestination( "qToPrimary" );
    } else if (input.getTextMessage().toUpperCase().endsWith( "SECONDAR" )) {
        W_toJMSDestination.setDestination( "qToSecondary" );
    } else {
        W_toJMSDestination.setDestination( "qToCatchOther" );
    }
    W_toJMSDestination.sendText( input.getTextMessage() );
}
```

FIGURE 6-7: Hardcode dynamic router

A Business Process that implements a dynamic router can be constructed similarly, as the example in Figure 6-8 shows.

Here a decision gate inspects a message to determine which branch to follow. A Business Rules activity assigns a string literal to the JMS Destination's destination attribute, and the JMS.send activity gets the message delivered to the destination so set.

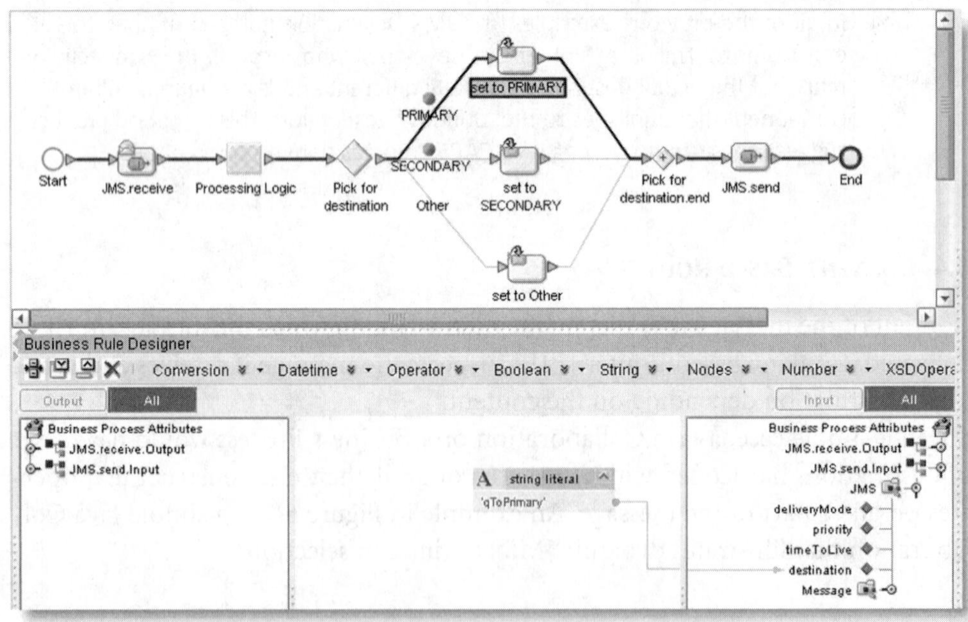

FIGURE 6-8: eInsight Business Process–based dynamic router

Whether a JCD or a Business Process is used, the connectivity map for the example will be identical to that used for the fixed router in the example in the previous section (i.e., the name of the JMS Destination will be unrelated to the actual JMS Destination to which messages will be delivered).

In the two examples shown in Figures 6-7 and 6-8, a conditional was evaluated to determine the destination of the message, which was hardcoded. If additional destinations were required, the collaboration or the process would have to be modified, and the application containing it would have to be redeployed to propagate changes to the runtime environment. This implementation of a Content-based Router is potentially a high-maintenance implementation if destinations change frequently.

In a special case, you could use the message, or the message component, as the complete name or a part of the name of the destination. You would not need to use a conditional or hardcode destination names.

The JCD in Figure 6-9 appends the first 10 characters of the input message to a literal qDest to form the name of the destination. The message is then written to the destination with the resulting name.

If the first 10 characters of messages were PRIMARY??? and SECONDARY?, where ? represents a space character, the resulting destination names would be qDestPRIMARY and qDestSECONDARY respectively. If using the Sun SeeBeyond JMS implementation, which does not require you to preconfigure JMS

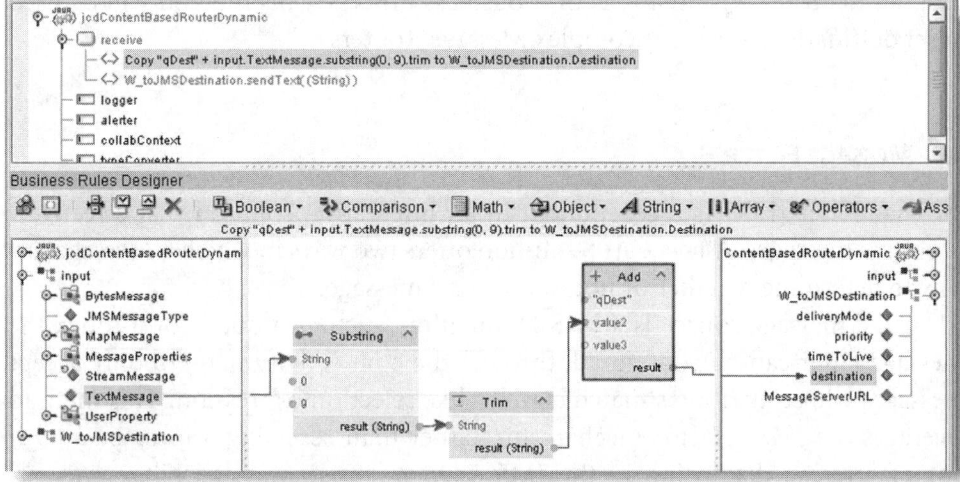

FIGURE 6-9: Dynamically generating JMS Destination names

Destinations ahead of time but rather creates JMS Destinations on first reference if they don't already exist, this could result in a completely dynamic Content-based Router. You could introduce a message whose initial characters were something other than PRIMARY??? and SECONDARY?, and the Sun SeeBeyond JMS implementation would create a new JMS Destination with that appropriate name and deliver the message there. There may not be a receiver for the message delivered to the new destination, but the Content-based Router itself would be dynamic and would not require modification. Addition of a destination would not require redeployment of the application containing such a router if no other changes were needed to take advantage of the new route. This solution does not require maintenance of the router if the number of destinations changes but makes it difficult to determine to how many destinations messages are routed, as it removes the setting of the content, upon which routing decisions are made, from the router to some other component upstream from the router or even outside the integration solution altogether.

In the previous examples, a very simple text message was used and some leading or trailing characters were extracted from the text for use in the conditional or as a part of a destination name. Messaging systems will rarely deal with such unstructured text messages. Much more likely, messages will be structured. The contents of one or more fields in the message will then be used for routing decisions or destination name derivation. For simplicity, we will continue using simple text messages wherever message structure has no bearing on the discussion.

These trivial examples demonstrate how explicit routing can be performed programmatically within a JCD or a Business Process. This method will be used to set destinations for more complex Message Routers.

6.5 Message Filter

Message Filter [EIP] is a component in an integration solution that selectively processes messages. A Java CAPS solution offers two ways in which a Message Filter can determine whether or not to process a message.

If the message source is a JMS Destination, such as a queue or a topic, the Message Filter can be configured, through the connectivity map, to only accept messages whose attributes match an SQL-like selection expression. This method leverages the JMS selector mechanism. Rather than receiving a message and, if not of interest, discarding it, the JMS selector–based Message Filter prevents delivery of messages that do not match the selector expression to the filtering receiver. This mechanism is static in that the selection expression is configured through the connectivity map and cannot be changed without redeploying the enterprise application.

Java CAPS provides the means to implement a dynamic selection solution using a Java Collaboration. This technique, discussed at length in Chapter 5, section 5.6.7, and Chapter 11, "Message Correlation," section 11.11, allows selection expression to change at runtime, thus providing the means to implement dynamic routing solutions.

6.6 Recipient List

By Saurabh Sahai

Often, it is required that a message be selectively sent to more than one recipient. The recipients that are to receive each message are determined either dynamically, based on the message content, or statically, based on external business rules. For example, an expense approval request message, pertaining to expenses below a certain amount, may get sent to the immediate manager for approval, whereas a message above the defined limit must also be sent to the business unit head for special approval.

A recipient list processor is similar to a Content-based Router; however, unlike a Content-based Router that routes the message to a specific destination based on message content, a recipient list processor sends the message to one or more designated recipients. The list of recipients can be static, hardcoded within the implementation, or dynamic, provided to the implementation from an externally maintained source. The latter approach provides greater flexibility as it allows the recipient list to be dynamically configured.

In Java CAPS, a recipient list can be implemented using either a JCD or a Business Process. In either case, once the message is received, the list of intended recipients is computed from the available recipients, and the message is forwarded as required.

The Java Collaboration shown in Figure 6-10 receives an expense report message for an amount greater than $300. Based on business rules, the collaboration looks up additional approvers that are required to approve this expense report and sends a copy of the message to these approvers in addition to the default approver. This is an example of a dynamic recipient list, where the collaboration uses information stored in an external store such as the organization's Lightweight Directory Access Protocol (LDAP) server to create the required recipient list. Exception processing has been omitted in Figure 6-10 to focus on the essentials of the example.

In the example in Figure 6-10, the additional approval threshold has been hardcoded within the Java Collaboration. In a more realistic example, externally configurable delegation of authority rules would be loaded into the collaboration using one of the techniques for dealing with dynamic runtime reconfiguration of components, discussed elsewhere in the book.

The example uses a hypothetical sendMail() method to send the expense report to a recipient for approval. The collaboration could have equally validly used multiple JMS Destinations, a single JMS Destination with target recipient indicated using JMS user properties, a Batch eWay, WebSphere MQ eWay, or any number of other endpoints, as dictated by the environment or business requirements.

```
private static final float DEF_APPROVER_EXPENSE_LIMIT = 300.0f;

public void receive( com.stc.connectors.jms.Message input, xsd.ExpenseReport516785849.ExpenseReport_ otdExpenseReport,
                     com.stc.connectors.jms.JMS otdJMS ) throws Throwable
{
    // unmarshal the incoming expense report into the ExpenseReport OTD
    String expenseReport = input.getTextMessage();
    otdExpenseReport.unmarshalFromString( expenseReport );
    // compute the expense total
    float expenseTotal = 0f;
    int numExpenseItems = otdExpenseReport.getExpenseDetails().countExpenseItem();
    for (int i = 0; i < numExpenseItems; i++) {
        expenseTotal += otdExpenseReport.getExpenseDetails().getExpenseItem( i ).getAmount();
    }
    // Determine the recipients for this expense report
    String employeeID = otdExpenseReport.getEmployeeID();
    if (expenseTotal <= DEF_APPROVER_EXPENSE_LIMIT) {
        // send the expense report to the default approver.
        // lookup the email id for the employee's default approver
        String defaultApproverEmailId = lookupApprovingManagerEmailId( employeeID );
        sendMail( defaultApproverEmailId, expenseReport );
    } else {
        // lookup email IDs for senior approvers required to approve expenses above the predefined limit
        String[] snrApproverEmailIDs = lookupSeniorApproveEmailIds( employeeID );
        for (int i = 0; i < snrApproverEmailIDs.length; i++) {
            // send expense report to each designated approver
            sendMail( snrApproverEmailIDs[i], expenseReport );
        }
    }
}
```

FIGURE 6-10: Recipient list example

6.7 SPLITTER

By Saurabh Sahai

An incoming message may encapsulate one or more submessages. It is often desired to process submessages independently as separate messages. For example, an order message may consist of multiple order line items, each of which corresponds to a unique item type and may be fulfilled by a separate inventory store.

A splitter solves the problem of processing a composite message comprising multiple submessages, each of which may be processed differently by breaking up the message into individual messages and sending each separate message for further processing by a downstream component.

A splitter can be implemented in Java CAPS in multiple ways. Java Collaborations can be used to receive the composite message, iterate over the individual submessages, and, on the basis of the message content, send each of them to a unique destination that is responsible for processing a specific type of message.

The collaboration shown in Figure 6-11 is an example of processing an incoming message consisting of multiple order items. The collaboration iterates over each order item and creates a new message, enriched with the original order item information, and sends it for processing by a specific system. The item number contained in each order item is used to determine the destination address where the enriched order item message is to be sent. Exception processing has been omitted in the example to focus on the essentials of the example.

Splitter is a component that, as the name suggests, breaks messages into component parts. How easy or difficult it is to split original messages and create component messages largely depends on the size and complexity of the message structures involved. As a general rule, it is easier to handle a composite message with more than one level of components using a Java Collaboration than to do so using an eInsight Business Process. Implementing nested loops in a Java Collaboration is easier and more compact than doing the same in Business Process Execution Language (BPEL) using the graphical environment. While loops, whether single-level or nested, are clearly visible in an eInsight Business Process graphic, making it obvious that splitting is taking place, it is necessary to reset the target OTD structure prior to its being populated in each iteration, which is neither obvious nor easily discovered by the casual observer.

```
/**
 * Receives an Order consisting of multiple order items each of which is to be processed by an
 * individual inventory system. The collaboration iterates over each of these individual
 * order items and sends an enriched message containing the order item and the original order id
 * to the appropriate inventory item for the fulfillment of the order item. For this example,
 * the queue for each inventory that will be used to fulfill the order item is determined using
 * the item number embedded in the order item message.
 */
public void receive( com.stc.connectors.jms.Message input, xsd.Order595920194.CompositeOrder otdCompositeOrder,
                     xsd.Order595920194.SubOrder otdSubOrder, com.stc.connectors.jms.JMS otdJMS )
    throws Throwable
{
    String inputOrder = input.getTextMessage();
    /*
     unmarshal the incoming composite message into the CompositeMessage OTD
     */
    otdCompositeOrder.unmarshalFromString( inputOrder );
    int numOrderItems = otdCompositeOrder.countOrderItem();
    String orderId = otdCompositeOrder.getOrderId();
    otdSubOrder.setOrderId( orderId );
    for (int i = 0; i < numOrderItems; i++) {
        String itemNumber = otdCompositeOrder.getOrderItem( i ).getItemNumber();
        int itemQty = otdCompositeOrder.getOrderItem( i ).getQuantity();
        /*
          Update the outgoing message with the itemNumber and quantity.
         */
        otdSubOrder.getOrderItem().setItemNumber( itemNumber );
        otdSubOrder.getOrderItem().setQuantity( itemQty );
        /*
          Send the individual order item to the inventory system.
          The inventory queue is identified by concatenating "q" with the item number.
         */
        String qInventorySystem = "q" + itemNumber;
        otdJMS.sendTextTo( otdSubOrder.marshalToString(), qInventorySystem );
    }
}
```

FIGURE 6-11: Dynamic content-based routing

6.8 AGGREGATOR

Aggregator [EIP] is a special Filter that collects related messages until some completeness condition has been reached, at which point it processes the related messages to obtain a single aggregated message that is then passed on to the next component.

An Aggregator must be able to correlate related messages, store related messages until ready to process, determine when the completeness condition is met, and implement the aggregation logic.

Java CAPS eInsight engine is a convenient tool to use for building Aggregators, as it inherently supports correlations and transparently stores related messages. The specific eInsight Business Process must only implement the completeness condition and the aggregation logic in order to become a specific Aggregator.

At the heart of every Aggregator is correlation logic, logic that determines which messages are related and therefore are subject to aggregation. Chapter 11 discusses at length the topic of message correlation with references to a number of specific examples presented in Part II (located on the accompanying CD-ROM). Chapter 11, section 11.10, discusses in detail a number of correlation implementations that incorporate an Aggregator.

Implementing an Aggregator without the benefit of eInsight is much harder. In addition to having to implement a completeness condition and aggregation logic, the solution designer must also do all the work related to storing and correlating messages. Chapter 11, section 11.11, discusses this topic and presents an example of how to accomplish the task of storing and correlating messages using just eGate and the Sun SeeBeyond JMS Message Server.

[EIP] discusses a number of completeness conditions an Aggregator might implement: Wait for All, Timeout, First Best, Timeout with Override, and External Event. Variants of these completeness conditions are discussed in Chapter 11, section 11.10. Implementing these conditions using eInsight with correlations is rather trivial. Implementing most of them using just eGate is much more difficult.

[EIP] also discusses a number of aggregation algorithms, including Select Best, Condense, and Collect for Later. Variants of these are also discussed in Chapter 11, section 11.10. Since aggregation will not start until all related messages are collected—that is, until the completeness condition has been satisfied—implementing aggregation logic is equally simple whether eInsight or eGate is used.

6.9 Resequencer

By Sebastian Krueger

Messages can arrive out of order for many reasons. If these messages are required to be delivered in sequence to a downstream component, the easiest solution would be to make sure that they never get out of order in the first place. Such approaches were discussed in Chapter 4, "Message Exchange Patterns," section 4.8. However, there may be times when we don't have a choice of how the upstream components are implemented; for example, we may control only the receiving side. Thus, the need to implement a component that will reorder messages may arise.

A number of implementations of a resequencer are possible. Chapter 4, section 4.2, "Resequencer," in Part II, discusses and illustrates two implementations using examples: a simple buffered resequencer and a persisted resequencer, both of which are discussed in the remainder of this section.

The simple buffered resequencer operates as follows. When the resequencer receives a message, it adds that message to an internal buffer. It then sends all consecutive messages from the buffer.

In order to send all consecutive messages, the resequencer component needs to know the current sequence number index and whether a message with this index is in the buffer. If the index is not found in the buffer, then the message has not arrived yet. The resequencer will not send out buffered messages until at least the next message arrives.

A resequencer implementation requires all messages to have a unique sequence number. Not only do these sequence numbers have to be unique, they also have to be consecutive. That is, no gaps are allowed to exist in the sequence.

If a message gets lost and never arrives, messages would be queued up and would never be sent out because the resequencer component would be waiting for a message that will never arrive. To get around this issue, the designer could implement a solution whereby the resequencer only waits a set time for a message to arrive and then moves on to the next messages, effectively ignoring the message that never arrived. However, what if the message arrives late? What if a duplicate message arrives? Strategies for dealing with these conditions would have to be considered in designing a robust resequencer. The designer could, for example, discard the message, or send it to a Dead Letter Channel for alerting and auditing purposes.

When a simple resequencer starts, it expects the first message to have a sequence number of 0. However, what if this is not the case? For example, the resequencer might restart. Unless the sequence is persisted, the resequencer would expect the message sequence to start at 0 again. There are two ways to get around this problem. An initialization message could be sent that informs the resequencer which number is the start of the sequence. Alternatively, the sequence could be persisted so that it can be recovered in appropriate circumstances.

Another point that a simple resequencer does not handle is buffer overrun. If too many messages get queued up, the HashMap, used to store messages while assembling message sequences, may get too large to fit into the JVM allocated memory.

Implementation of a robust and scalable resequencer would require a significant amount of code and would likely be domain specific. An improved resequencer is discussed next. Implementation of a perfect resequencer is beyond the scope of this book.

An improvement to the previous resequencer would be to implement the buffer as a database table. By moving the message buffer to a persistent store, we solve two problems exhibited by the previous implementation. First, we effectively have an unlimited buffer, so no buffer overflow will occur. Second, in case of a server failure, buffered messages are not lost.

There are still unresolved issues with this persisted resequencer. The initialization of sequence numbers expects the first message to always start at 0. Also, we have not accounted for messages that never arrive. We briefly touched on the some of these issues in the previous section. They are out of the scope of this chapter.

While the two resequencers discussed in this chapter are by no means perfect, they do give examples of simple resequencers and give an indication of what is required to implement a robust resequencer.

6.10 Composed Message Processor

Composed Message Processor [EIP] is a higher-order component of a messaging system that accepts a message, breaks it up into submessages that are dispatched and processed by multiple lower-order components, then reassembles submessages into a final message.

In Java CAPS, as in any messaging system, implementation of a Composed Message Processor requires the use of correlations. Superficially, Composed Message Processor pattern is no different from the Scatter-Gather pattern [EIP]. Both involve breaking a message and reassembling the pieces once they are processed by independent intermediate components.

Chapter 11 discusses correlation implementation options provided by Java CAPS and presents a number of correlation examples. Section 11.10.5 provides a Java CAPS example of a Scatter-Gather pattern and Composed Message Processor pattern implementation.

6.11 Scatter-Gather

The Scatter-Gather [EIP] pattern involves breaking up a message, or replicating a message, delivering multiple messages to multiple components, then collecting related messages back together. Implementation of a Scatter-Gather pattern requires the use of correlations. It is discussed in various sections of Chapter 11.

6.12 Routing Slip

Routing Slip [EIP] is a mechanism that can be used to dynamically route a message through a series of components such that individual components do not embed routing logic. The route the message is to take can be computed by a router that embeds the necessary logic. This route is then attached to the message as a Routing Slip, and each component through which the message passes, once it performs its processing, forwards the message onto the next component specified in the Routing Slip. [EIP] discusses at length the rationale behind a desire to implement the Routing Slip pattern. Java CAPS, and its underlying JMS Message Server implementation, lends itself to building Routing Slip–based solutions; however, eInsight Business Processes may be better, in many circumstances, as an approach to conditional component invocation and dynamic route determination.

In a fixed Routing Slip solution, the message, once it leaves the router, is passed from component to component. There is no opportunity to change the message route once it is computed. An alternative to this approach is to have the router compute the next component to which to send the message, send the message to it, and have the component return the message back to the router once it is done. Routing decisions are still centralized, making routing logic simple to maintain, and the route the message takes can be changed by the router at any time based on the outcome of message processing.

In Java CAPS, a Routing Slip, or return destination, can be attached to the message in one of two ways. It can be passed via JMS user-defined properties if the message is passed from component to component over JMS, or the message can be packaged into an Envelope Wrapper and the Routing Slip can be incorporated into the Envelope metadata.

Envelope Wrapper is discussed at length in Chapter 8, "Message Transformation," section 8.2. The route, computed by the router, could be represented in the Envelope node as a series of labels delimited by some delimiter, or an ordered, repeating collection of labels.

Chapter 4, section 4.3, "Routing Slip," in Part II, illustrates this discussion with an example implementation of a Routing Slip pattern using Java Collaborations and JMS.

We could have used an eInsight Business Process to implement the kind of functionality that the Routing Slip facilitates. Each processing component could have been implemented as a New Web Service Java Collaboration or an eInsight subprocess. The Business Process would orchestrate execution of these components according to routing logic rules it implements.

6.13 Process Manager

One of the Routing Slip solutions involves a single routing component that determines the next component to which a message must be sent and receives the message back once the component is finished with it. This central routing component directs flow of messages using routing logic it embeds. Since it always receives messages that are processed by the processing components, it can modify the route a message is to take based on the outcome of processing by a particular component. Thus, the route the message finally takes may be different from the route a fixed router, which does not use intermediate processing results for routing decisions, would have determined.

Process Manager is a component that implements conditional routing logic and orchestrates execution of other processing components. Java CAPS supports implementation of the Process Manager, with functionality as described in the opening paragraph, as a Java Collaboration using JMS, possibly in Request/Reply mode, to dispatch and receive messages to and from processing components. The disadvantage of this approach is that the routing logic is hidden away in the Java code and, depending on the size and complexity of logic involved, may be difficult to understand.

Java CAPS eInsight Business Process Manager provides a graphical Business Process modeling environment. It overcomes the understandability limitations of a Java-only implementation and offers a number of features for Business Process modeling, component orchestration, and runtime monitoring that are not available with Java-only implementations.

Using eInsight Business Process Manager, you can implement any desired routing and component orchestration solutions. eInsight examples appear in most sections of this book and illustrate all manner of solutions of varying complexity. When a dynamic routing or component orchestration is required, eInsight Business Process can be developed to satisfy the requirement.

6.14 Message Broker

Message Broker [EIP] is an EAI architectural style wherein a component of a messaging system implements centralized routing for all messages flowing through the system. [EIP] also uses the term hub-and-spoke when referring to this architectural style. SeeBeyond's DataGate 3.6 product, predecessor to eGate 4.x, ICAN 5.0, and Java CAPS 5.1, is a Message Broker–based EAI package.

Message Broker architecture allows decoupling of senders from receivers. The senders need not know where the messages are going, and receivers need not know from where the messages are coming. The Message Broker embeds all routing logic necessary to get messages from senders to receivers. This centralizes routing logic maintenance.

In Java CAPS, and ICAN before it, each connectivity map could be considered to represent a Message Broker–based solution. In effect, all collaborations and Business Processes present in a connectivity map route messages from sources to destinations. Each eInsight Business Process could also be considered a Message Broker implementation, as it, too, makes routing decisions when orchestrating a series of activities. Collections of connectivity maps sharing common channels could be considered hierarchies of Message Brokers [EIP].

While Java CAPS can certainly be used to implement centralized routing solutions in the spirit of Message Broker, doing so does not appear particularly necessary or particularly advantageous.

6.15 Chapter Summary

This chapter discussed [EIP] message routing and message routing–related patterns. It included discussion and application of patterns from [EIP] Messaging Systems and Message Routing.

The chapter briefly discussed where a Java CAPS solution developer can make routing decisions and discussed each of the routing patterns, specifically Splitter, Aggregator, Resequencer, Scatter-Gather, Routing Slip, Process Manager, and Message Broker.

CHAPTER SEVEN

Message Construction

7.1 Introduction

This chapter discusses the [EIP] concept of Message, how it is manifested in Java CAPS, and the related Java CAPS concept of Object Type Definitions (OTDs). It discusses briefly how OTDs can be built from database tables, views, and stored procedures; XML Schemas and other source formats; how to marshal (serialize) and unmarshal (deserialize) them; how to manipulate them; and how to use them for transformations and connector operations.

The [EIP] Envelope Wrapper pattern is also discussed. Diverse implementations of the pattern, intended to convey metadata with message payload, use different Java CAPS facilities ranging from a user-defined custom Envelope Wrapper OTD, to carrying unparsed XML within an XML Envelope, to ways of passing metadata using JMS message header properties.

7.2 Message

Integration solutions typically collect messages from external systems and, after due transformations and routing, deliver messages to external systems. Both the sending and receiving external systems use message formats that are specific to them. The implementation of the interface between the external system and the messaging infrastructure requires that formats of messages to be exchanged over it be agreed upon. Any unforeseen variations from the agreed message formats will likely break some part of the implementation.

While some solutions involving an integration infrastructure are designed such that an external system tells the messaging solution how to transform or route the message, such solutions do not leverage the integration infrastructure's capabilities and therefore do not obtain the benefits of using it. It is much more likely that the message payload is all that is exchanged over the "external system–integration solution" interface and that the message payload structure is all that is agreed upon.

7.3 Object Type Definitions

Java CAPS message structures, data structures that Java CAPS components manipulate, are called Object Type Definitions (OTDs, XML Schema Definition [XSD] objects, and Web Services Description Language [WSDL] objects, depending on the type).

Unlike some other tools, Java CAPS does not use a predetermined data representation, such as XML, to represent data internally. On the contrary, in general, whenever an external message uses a native standardized data representation (XML, HL7, SAP IDOC, etc.) as distinct from a Java object, data from a data source such as a database, or data from a format-agnostic endpoint, Java CAPS uses that native format until told otherwise.

To allow components to manipulate fields within messages, the Java CAPS developer would explicitly deserialize (unmarshal) data from its native format, whatever that may be, into a Java class hierarchy for Java components such as Java Collaboration Definitions (JCDs) and into XML Document Object Model (DOM) structures for XML-based components such as XSLT Collaboration Definitions and Business Process Execution Language for Web Services (BPEL4WS)-based Business Processes. Both marshal and unmarshal methods are provided as part of the OTD when the OTD is generated or built. If a component does not need to inspect or manipulate data fields, it does not need to unmarshal data into an OTD. This, depending on the design of the solution, may result in significant efficiency gains over solutions where data is always converted from a native representation into an internal representation, such as XML.

Note

In recent years, the Extensible Markup Language (XML) gained popularity as a universal data representation format. Some zealots went to the lengths of using XML to implement procedural languages (BPEL4WS), databases, and all manner of things to which XML has dubious applicability and where XML introduces considerable overheads for little or no real gain. Whenever designing integration solutions, particularly ones where message throughput and processing efficiency are important, consider very carefully the appropriateness, or otherwise, of using XML as the underlying data representation. In a recent project, where HL7 delimited messages were converted to an alternate XML-based format, message size increased an average of 19 times over 5,700 messages processed! If issues of this sort are a consideration, do not use XML.

There are two basic types of OTDs: Connector OTDs and Message OTDs. Connector OTDs are associated with specific endpoints, such as eWays or JMS connectors. In addition to representing message and metadata, these OTDs expose methods that allow developers some control over connectivity aspects of the related adapters. The JMS object, used later in the user properties discussion, is an example of the Connector OTD. It exposes the send(), the sendTo(), and similar methods that exercise specific functionality of the underlying connector. Other Connector OTDs, such as database eWay OTDs, expose other methods pertinent to the connectors they represent. Connector OTD frameworks are installed together with the corresponding eWay or as part of the JMS messaging implementation. In many cases—for example, SAP or Database eWays—OTDs will be generated as part of solution development to represent specific IDOCs or database tables.

In contrast, Message OTDs represent message structures and facilitate deserialization (unmarshaling), serialization (marshalling), and access to components of messages. Message OTDs can be constructed as user-defined OTDs or generated from external source forms. Manual construction of user-defined OTDs is covered extensively in [eDesigner]. Generation of Message OTDs from source forms is documented in a number of places in the Java CAPS document set—for example, database eWay documentation for database OTDs.

7.3.1 Generating Oracle Table OTD

To give you a feel for the process, this section walks through generation of a Message OTD for a table in an Oracle database. Assume the existence of a standard Oracle 9i installation containing the Scott schema with the EMP table. Listing 7-1 shows the Data Definition Language (DDL) for the EMP table, if you don't have the Scott schema.

LISTING 7-1: SCOTT Schema EMP table DDL

```
CREATE TABLE "SCOTT"."EMP"
 (  "EMPNO" NUMBER(4,0),
    "ENAME" VARCHAR2(10),
    "JOB" VARCHAR2(9),
    "MGR" NUMBER(4,0),
    "HIREDATE" DATE,
```

```
    "SAL" NUMBER(7,2),
    "COMM" NUMBER(7,2),
    "DEPTNO" NUMBER(2,0),
     CONSTRAINT "PK_EMP" PRIMARY KEY ("EMPNO")
USING INDEX PCTFREE 10 INITRANS 2 MAXTRANS 255
STORAGE(INITIAL 65536 NEXT 1048576 MINEXTENTS 1 MAXEXTENTS 2147483645
PCTINCREASE 0 FREELISTS 1 FREELIST GROUPS 1 BUFFER_POOL DEFAULT)
TABLESPACE "SYSTEM"  ENABLE,
     CONSTRAINT "FK_DEPTNO" FOREIGN KEY ("DEPTNO")
     REFERENCES "SCOTT"."DEPT" ("DEPTNO") ENABLE
 ) PCTFREE 10 PCTUSED 40 INITRANS 1 MAXTRANS 255 NOCOMPRESS LOGGING
STORAGE(INITIAL 65536 NEXT 1048576 MINEXTENTS 1 MAXEXTENTS 2147483645
PCTINCREASE 0 FREELISTS 1 FREELIST GROUPS 1 BUFFER_POOL DEFAULT)
TABLESPACE "SYSTEM"
```

Right-click on a project name where you need the Oracle table OTD, and choose New → Object Type Definition.

In the resulting dialog, shown in Figure 7-1, choose Oracle Database, and press Next.

Provide credentials for the database schema that contains the EMP table, as shown in Figure 7-2, and then click Next.

Note

The mechanism underlying this dialog uses a Java Database Connectivity (JDBC) driver to query database metadata.

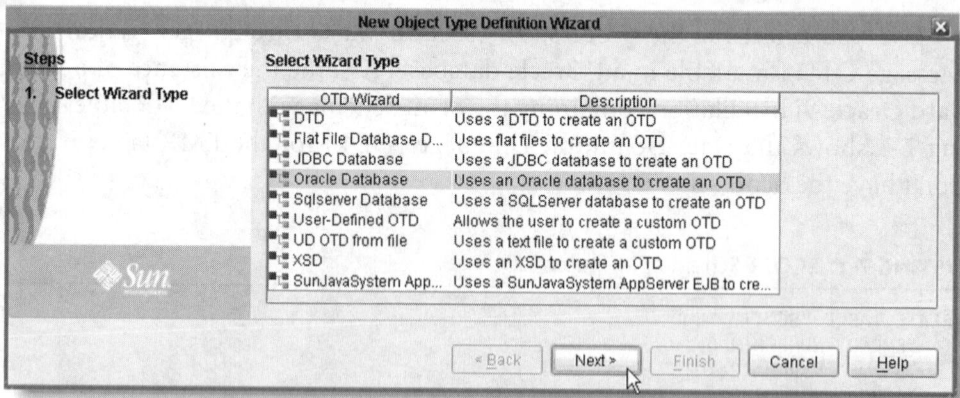

FIGURE 7-1: Starting the Oracle Database OTD Wizard

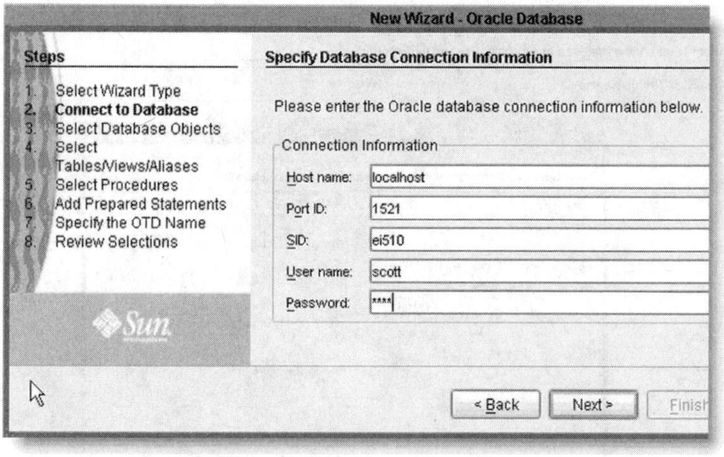

FIGURE 7-2: Provide credentials for the SCOTT schema

Check the Tables/Views/Aliases checkbox, as shown in Figure 7-3, and click Next. Note that using this dialog sequence you could also generate an OTD from a stored procedure or a prepared statement.

Click the Add button to add tables/views/aliases to the OTD that will be produced. Choose the schema, Scott in this case, and press Search. Select the EMP table, and press OK, as shown in Figures 7-4 and 7-5.

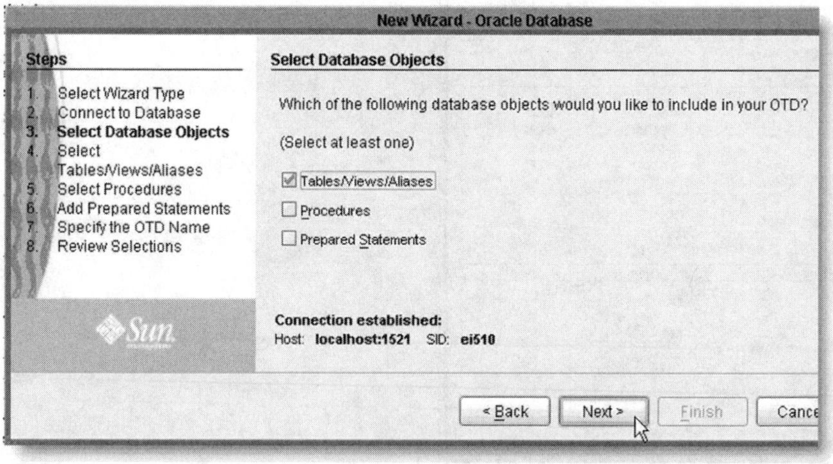

FIGURE 7-3: Choosing Oracle object types for OTD generation

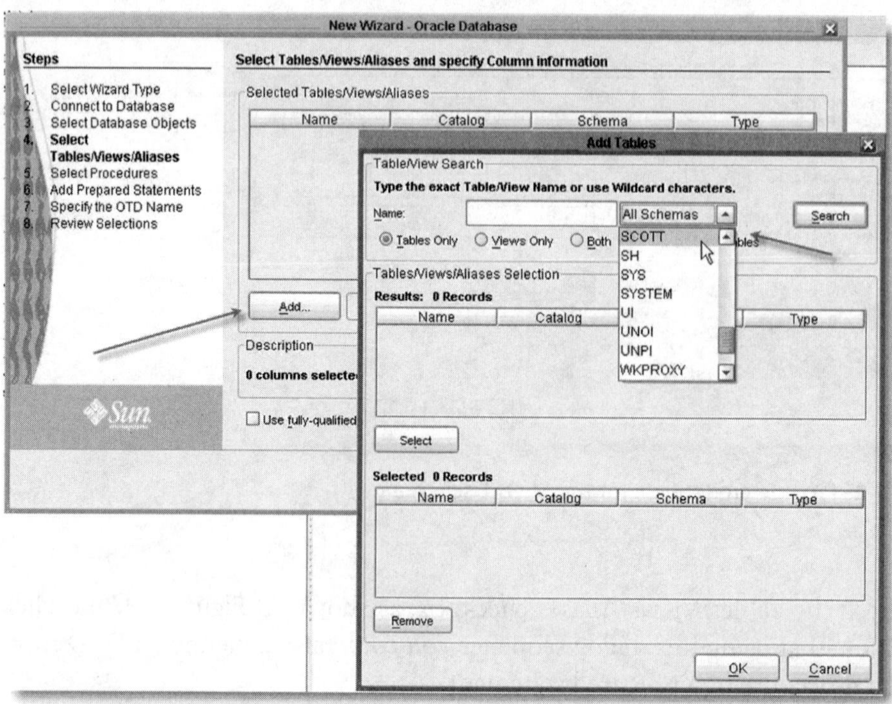

FIGURE 7-4: Selecting Oracle schema for OTD generation

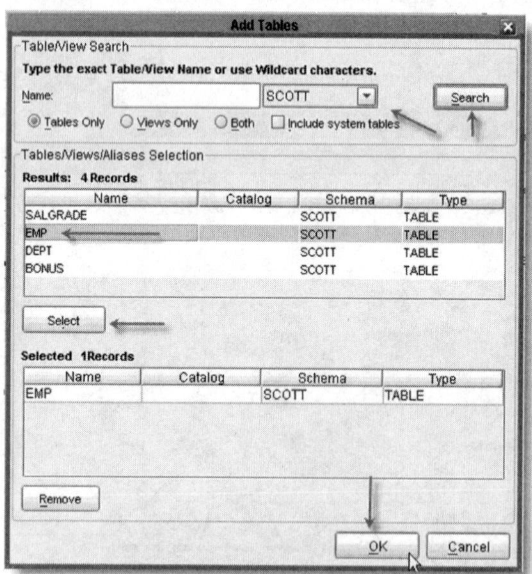

FIGURE 7-5: Selecting Oracle objects for OTD generation

Press Next, name the OTD "tblEMP," and press Next, as shown in Figure 7-6.

Review the results and complete the Wizard by pressing the Finish button, as shown in Figure 7-7.

The OTD is generated and displayed in the OTD Editor Canvas, as shown in Figure 7-8.

Notice a field for every column in the table, with the name that corresponds to the name of the underlying column. In addition, there is a series of methods, to be used in a JCD, and a series of services, to be used in a BPEL-based eInsight Business Process, for accessing and manipulating data represented by the OTD. This is pointed out in Figure 7-9.

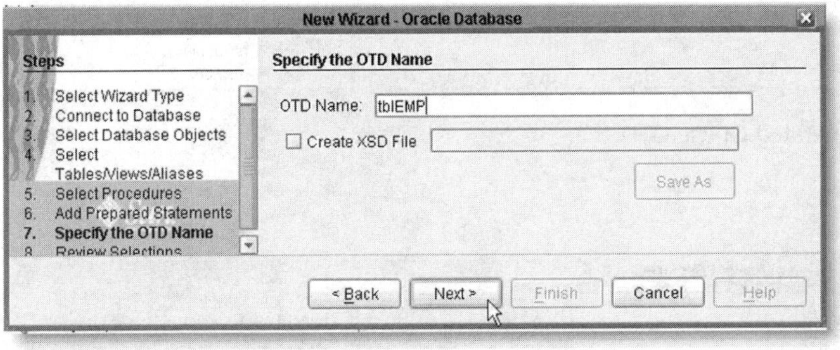

FIGURE 7-6: Naming generated Oracle OTD

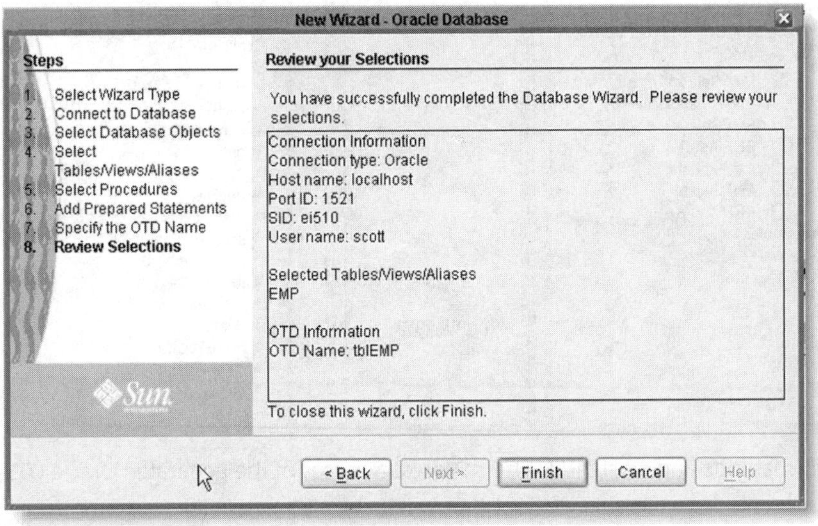

FIGURE 7-7: Naming generated Oracle OTD

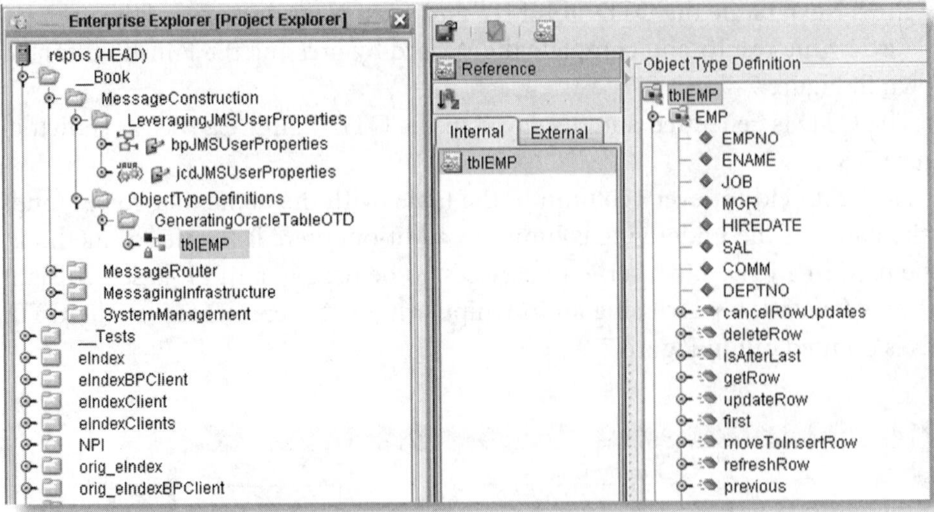

FIGURE 7-8: Generated Oracle OTD

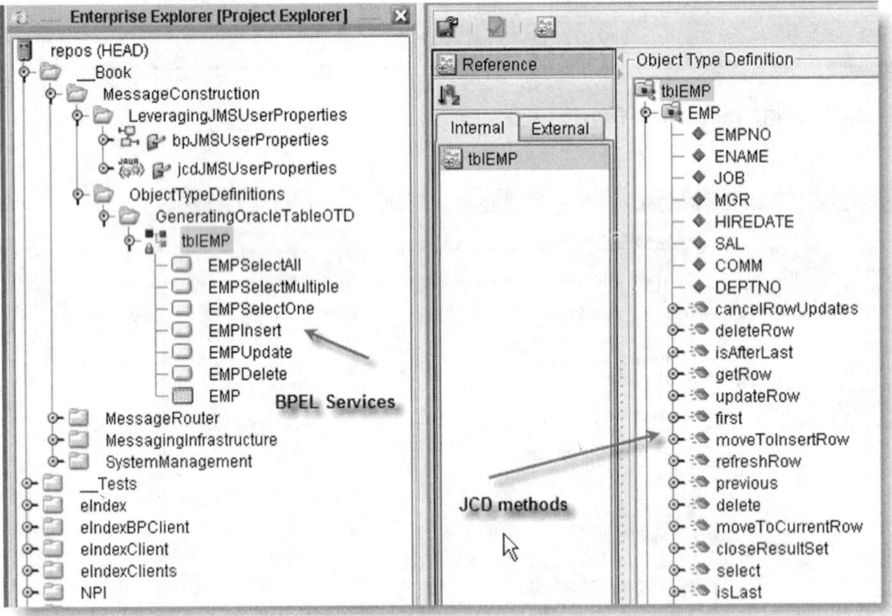

FIGURE 7-9: JCD methods and eInsight Business Process Services of the generated Oracle OTD

Note

Java methods allow much more detailed control over the operations performed through the OTD, concurrency and transactional aspects of the database connection, and the resultset manipulation, than is possible in BPEL. Since you can invoke a JCD as a service from BPEL, if fine control over the database access is required, develop a New Web Service JCD to handle database access.

Note

The OTD provides prebuilt BPEL services for most common database operations—select one row, select multiple rows, select all rows, insert, update, and delete—thus greatly simplifying the developer's work.

The OTD that represents the Oracle Scott EMP table is ready. You can now query the database and insert, update, and delete rows. Needless to say, the underlying database will reflect the changes you make through this Connector OTD.

7.3.2 Other OTD Wizards

Figure 7-10 lists some of the available OTD Wizards.

This list represents the wizards installed with the eWays and other components in the product installation used for developing examples for the book. Additional products and connectors provide additional OTD Wizards. Some notable omissions are SAP, DB2, PeopleSoft, and other specialized products available as part of the suite but not installed in the working environment.

Select Wizard Type

OTD Wizard	Description
DTD	Uses a DTD to create an OTD
Flat File Database Definition	Uses flat files to create an OTD
JDBC Database	Uses a JDBC database to create an OTD
Oracle Database	Uses an Oracle database to create an OTD
Sqlserver Database	Uses a SQLServer database to create an OTD
User-Defined OTD	Allows the user to create a custom OTD
UD OTD from file	Uses a text file to create a custom OTD
XSD	Uses an XSD to create an OTD
SunJavaSystem AppServer	Uses a SunJavaSystem AppServer EJB to create an OTD

FIGURE 7-10: Some of the OTD Wizards available in Java CAPS

7.4 Envelope Wrapper

Some systems use messages that consist of business and control data in the loosest meaning of the terms. Such messages are sometime structured to consist of a header, which contains control data, and a body, which contains business data. This header/body structure is a specialization of a general enveloped message wherein a business payload is enclosed within a message containing other, non-payload data.

Envelope Wrapper in Java CAPS is merely an OTD whose structure accommodates both the header/trailer requirements and the payload requirements. When designing an Envelope Wrapper OTD, you must consider the structure and size of the payload and the cost of marshaling and unmarshaling it. If the complexity of the header/trailer is low, and frequency of access to the header/trailer components is high, compared to the complexity of the payload and frequency of access to payload components, then the Envelope Wrapper OTD should be constructed such that the payload node in the OTD is opaque and does not get parsed when the OTD is unmarshaled. This will save the resources and time required for parsing the payload when it is not used at the cost of having to develop a payload OTD, which likely will have to be developed anyway, and the cost of explicitly unmarshaling the payload into the payload OTD when required.

Picture a payload with the structure shown in Listing 7-2.

LISTING 7-2: Purchase Order payload structure

```
PurchaseOrder
        Number
        Date
        Total
```

Picture also an Envelope Wrapper with the structure shown in Listing 7-3.

LISTING 7-3: Envelope structure

```
POEnvelope
        SourceSystem
        DestinationSystem
        SequenceNumber
        Duplicate
        Payload
```

You could construct a user-defined, delimited OTD, with two levels of delimiters, which looks like that shown in Figure 7-11, to represent the enveloped Purchase Order, where delimiters are "|" and ":", as shown in Figure 7-12.

Since the payload is simple, there would be little penalty in unmarshaling this structure every time access to the SourceSystem or DestinationSystem node was required.

A Java Collaboration would perform an unmarshal operation to get access to fields in the OTD, as shown in Figure 7-13.

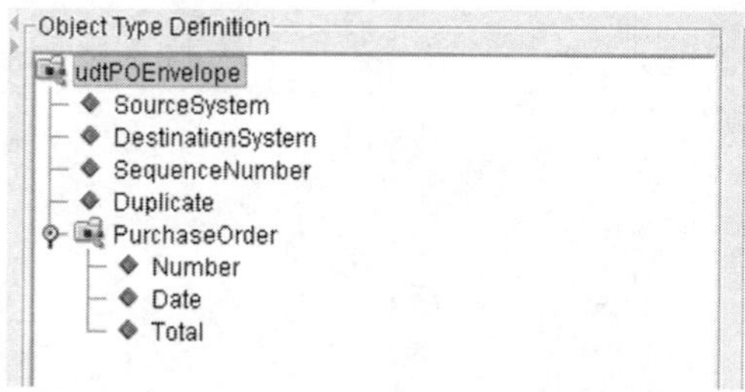

FIGURE 7-11: User-defined, delimited OTD representing the enveloped Purchase Order structure

Delimiter List Editor

Delimiter List

Level	Type	Delimit...	Preced...	Optiona...	Termina...	Offset	Length
Lev							
	normal	|	10	never	never	0	0
Lev							
	normal	:	10	never	never	0	0

FIGURE 7-12: Purchase Order OTD delimiters

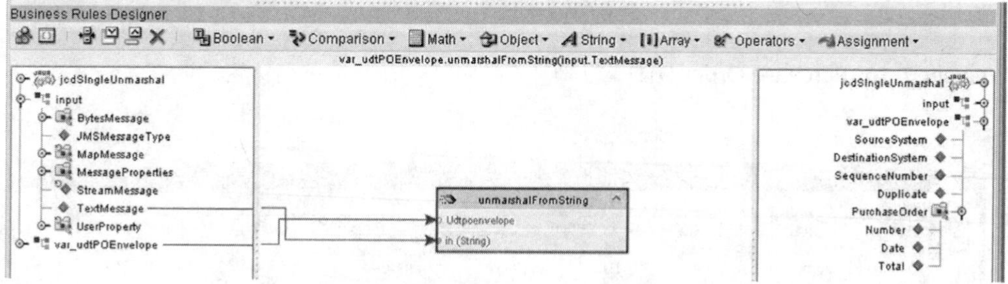

FIGURE 7-13: Unmarshaling data into the OTD

7.4.1 Delimited Envelope Wrapper

If the Purchase Order structure was more complex, perhaps containing multiple repeating items with many fields per item, unmarshaling such a structure each time access to the header fields was required, but where no access to the purchase order fields was required at all, would be a major and unnecessary overhead.

Picture two OTDs: An Envelope OTD, shown in Figure 7-14, with a single level of delimiters ("|"), shown in Figure 7-15.

Picture also a Purchase Order OTD with a single level of delimiters (":"), shown in Figures 7-16 and 7-17.

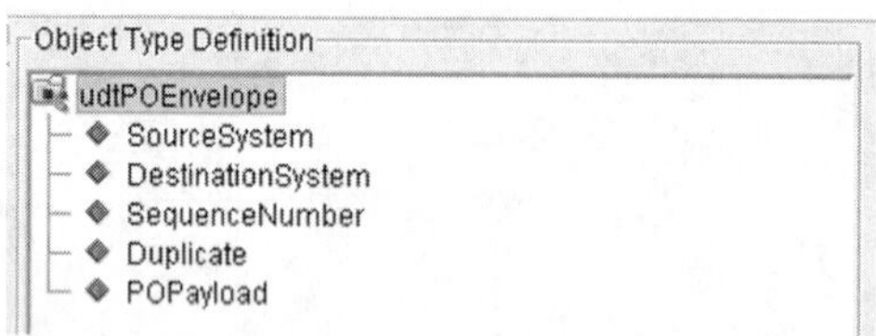

FIGURE 7-14: Purchase Order Envelope OTD

Delimiter List Editor

Delimiter List

<table>
<tr><th>Level</th><th>Type</th><th>Delimiter Byt...</th><th>Precedence</th><th>Optional Mo...</th><th>Terminator Mode</th><th>Offset</th><th>Length</th></tr>
<tr><td>Level 1</td><td></td><td></td><td></td><td></td><td></td><td></td><td></td></tr>
<tr><td>Delimiter</td><td>normal</td><td>|</td><td>10</td><td>never</td><td>never</td><td>0</td><td>0</td></tr>
</table>

FIGURE 7-15: Purchase Order Envelope delimiters

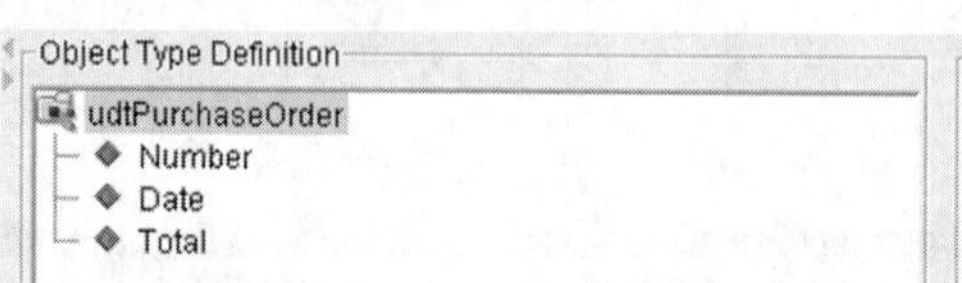

FIGURE 7-16: Purchase Order OTD

Delimiter List Editor

Delimiter List

Level	Type	Delimiter Byt...	Precedence	Optional Mo...	Terminator Mode	Offset	Length
Level 1							
Delimiter	normal	:	10	never	never	0	0

FIGURE 7-17: Purchase Order OTD delimiters

A Java Collaboration would unmarshal the input node into the udtPOEnvelope to get at the Header fields and, if needed, would unmarshal the POPayload field into the udtPurchaseOrder to get at the Purchase Order fields themselves. Figure 7-18 shows the two OTDs included in the Java Collaboration at design time.

First, enveloped input is unmarshaled into the Envelope Wrapper OTD, as shown in Figure 7-19.

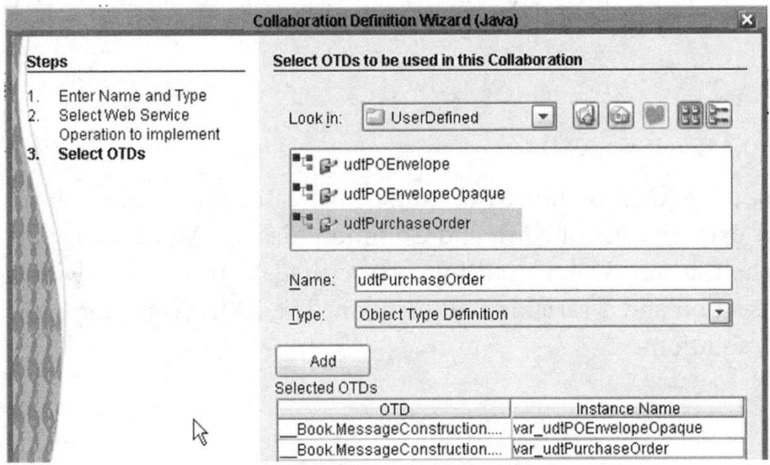

FIGURE 7-18: Selecting OTD to use in a Java Collaboration

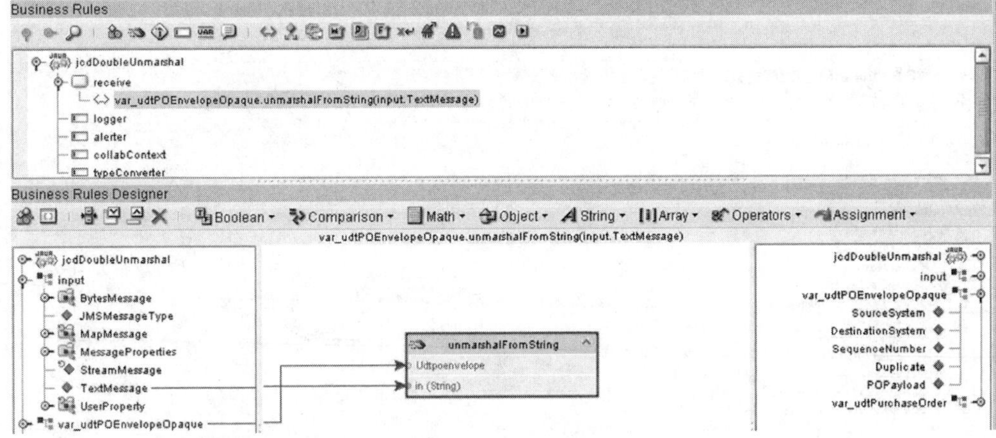

FIGURE 7-19: Unmarshaling enveloped input message into the Envelope OTD

Then payload is unmarshaled from the POPayload node of the Envelope Wrapper into the Purchase Order OTD, as shown in Figure 7-20.

Thus, if access to the Purchase Order details is not required in a particular collaboration, the second unmarshal is not performed and the cost of parsing the Purchase Order data is not incurred.

The content of the POPayload could be XML as easily as delimited. The Envelope Wrapper could also be an XML structure. If the envelope and the payload were XML structures, then the payload node in the envelope structure would have to be of type "any" in order to allow well-formed XML to be transported unparsed.

7.4.2 Enveloping XML within XML

An issue of enveloping XML within XML comes up reasonably commonly in projects that make extensive use of XML and Common Message Model concepts. Usually it is couched in terms of a need for a structured XML message with a common Header section and a variable Body section. The XML Schema specification offers a few solutions.

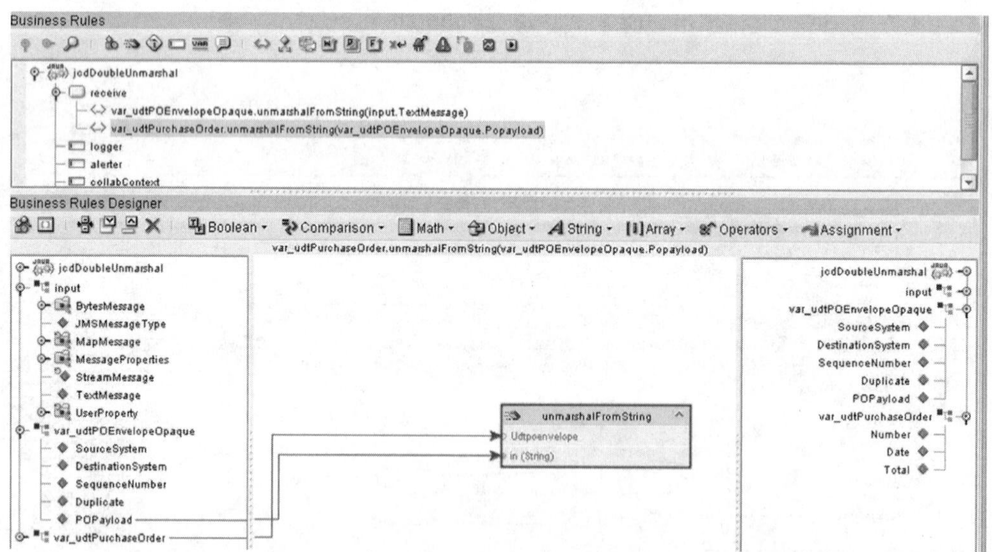

FIGURE 7-20: Unmarshaling Purchase Order data into the Purchase Order OTD

Take an XML Schema document, OpaqueXMLPayloadEnvelope.xsd, which looks like that shown in Listing 7-4.

LISTING 7-4: Opaque XML Payload Envelope XML Schema

```
<?xml version="1.0" encoding="UTF-8"?>
<xs:schema
  xmlns:xs="http://www.w3.org/2001/XMLSchema">
  <xs:element name="OpaqueXMLPayloadEnvelope">
    <xs:complexType>
      <xs:sequence>
        <xs:element name="Header">
          <xs:complexType>
            <xs:sequence>
              <xs:element name="Type" type="xs:string"/>
              <xs:element name="Hdr02" type="xs:string"/>
              <xs:element name="Hdr03" type="xs:string"/>
            </xs:sequence>
          </xs:complexType>
        </xs:element>
        <xs:element name="XMLPayload">
          <xs:complexType>
            <xs:sequence>
              <xs:any
                processContents="skip"
                minOccurs="0"
                maxOccurs="unbounded"/>
            </xs:sequence>
          </xs:complexType>
        </xs:element>
      </xs:sequence>
    </xs:complexType>
  </xs:element>
</xs:schema>
```

Note the element XMLPayload of type "any" and processContents attribute of "skip." This element can contain any well-formed XML except XML processing instructions [XMLSchema]. The XML Schema specification uses the term *wildcard*. We exploit this to create an OTD that allows arbitrary well-formed XML to be contained in a node of a structured OTD without having to define the structure of that node.

Create an XSD-based OTD, as shown in Figure 7-21.

Note an element called XMLPayload. Its optional, repeating subnode __AnyText__ will carry the well-formed XML.

Take an XML Schema document, XMLPayloadType_A.xsd, which looks like that shown in Listing 7-5.

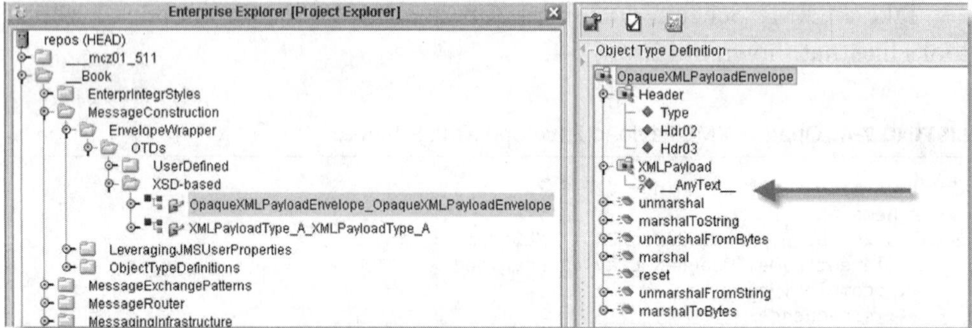

FIGURE 7-21: XSD-based OTD created from the Envelope Schema

LISTING 7-5: Payload Type A XML Schema

```
<?xml version="1.0" encoding="UTF-8"?>
<xs:schema
  xmlns:xs="http://www.w3.org/2001/XMLSchema">
    <xs:element name="XMLPayloadType_A">
    <xs:complexType>
      <xs:sequence>
        <xs:element name="PA_OrderNumber" type="xs:integer"/>
        <xs:element name="PA_OrderQuantity" type="xs:decimal"/>
        <xs:element name="PA_Description" type="xs:string"/>
      </xs:sequence>
    </xs:complexType>
  </xs:element>
</xs:schema>
```

Create an XSD-based OTD, as shown in Figure 7-22.

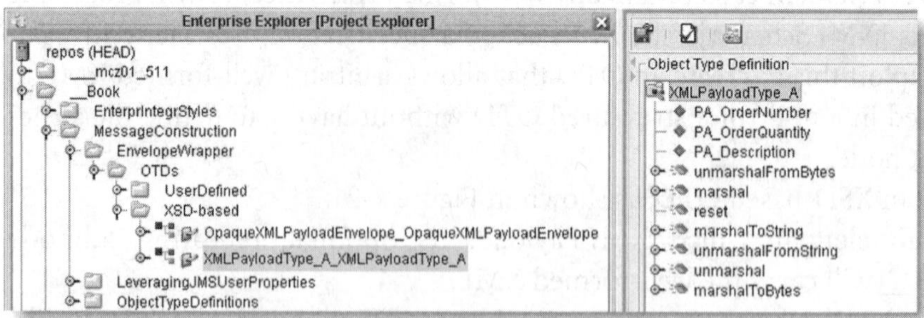

FIGURE 7-22: Purchase Order payload OTD

Take an XML Schema document, XMLPayloadType_B.xsd, which looks like that shown in Listing 7-6.

LISTING 7-6: Payload Type B XML Schema

```
<?xml version="1.0" encoding="UTF-8"?>
<xs:schema
  xmlns:xs="http://www.w3.org/2001/XMLSchema">
  <xs:element name="XMLPayloadType_B">
    <xs:complexType>
      <xs:sequence>
        <xs:element name="PB_OrderNumber" type="xs:integer"/>
        <xs:element name="PB_OrderItems" maxOccurs="unbounded">
          <xs:complexType>
            <xs:sequence>
              <xs:element name="ItemNumber" type="xs:integer"/>
              <xs:element name="ItemDescription" type="xs:string"/>
              <xs:element name="ItemQuantity" type="xs:integer"/>
            </xs:sequence>
          </xs:complexType>
        </xs:element>
      </xs:sequence>
    </xs:complexType>
  </xs:element>
</xs:schema>
```

Create an XSD-based OTD, as shown in Figure 7-23.

Test by invoking the OTD Tester, as shown in Figure 7-24, on the OpaqueXML-PayloadEnvelope OTD and making it unmarshal two files, one containing Type A XML Instance document and one containing Type B XML Instance document.

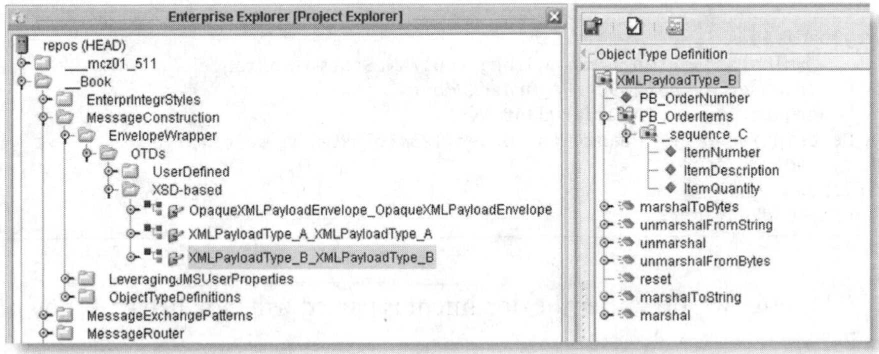

FIGURE 7-23: Payload Type B OTD

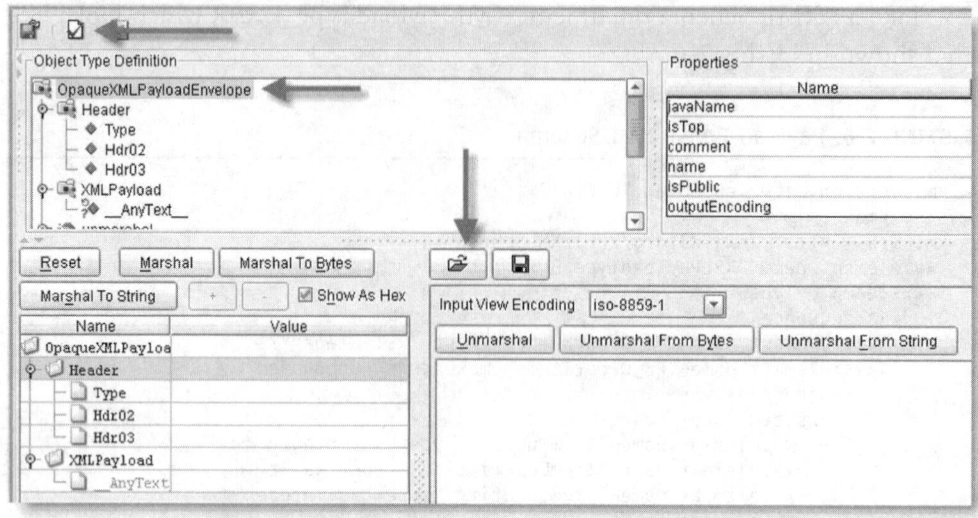

FIGURE 7-24: Testing the OTD

Listing 7-7 shows the Type A XML Instance document.

LISTING 7-7: Type A XML instance document

```
<?xml version="1.0" encoding="UTF-8"?>
<OpaqueXMLPayloadEnvelope
              xmlns:xsi="http://www.w3.org/2001/XMLSchema-instance">
  <Header>
    <Type>A</Type>
    <Hdr02>Header 02 content</Hdr02>
    <Hdr03>Header 03 content</Hdr03>
  </Header>
  <XMLPayload>
    <XMLPayloadType_A
              xmlns:xsi="http://www.w3.org/2001/XMLSchema-instance">
      <PA_OrderNumber>1234567890</PA_OrderNumber>
      <PA_OrderQuantity>5</PA_OrderQuantity>
      <PA_Description>Order Header for Order 1234567890</PA_Description>
    </XMLPayloadType_A>
  </XMLPayload>
</OpaqueXMLPayloadEnvelope>
```

The OTD Tester window after the document is parsed will look like that shown in Figure 7-25.

The Type B XML Instance document is shown in Listing 7-8.

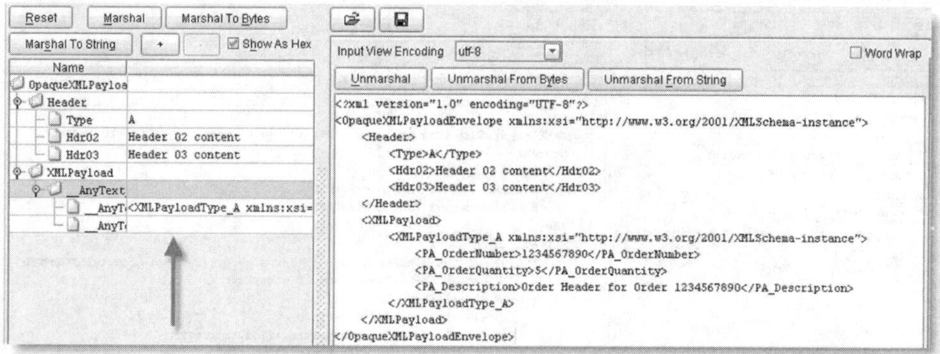

FIGURE 7-25: Parsed input document in the OTD Tester

LISTING 7-8: Type B XML Instance document

```
<?xml version="1.0" encoding="UTF-8"?>
<OpaqueXMLPayloadEnvelope
      xmlns:xsi="http://www.w3.org/2001/XMLSchema-instance">
  <Header>
    <Type>B</Type>
    <Hdr02>Header 02 content</Hdr02>
    <Hdr03>Header 03 content</Hdr03>
  </Header>
  <XMLPayload>
    <XMLPayloadType_B
           xmlns:xsi="http://www.w3.org/2001/XMLSchema-instance">
      <PB_OrderNumber>1234567890</PB_OrderNumber>
      <PB_OrderItems>
        <ItemNumber>1</ItemNumber>
        <ItemDescription>First Item</ItemDescription>
        <ItemQuantity>12</ItemQuantity>
      <PB_OrderItems>     </PB_OrderItems>
        <ItemNumber>2</ItemNumber>
        <ItemDescription>Second Item</ItemDescription>
        <ItemQuantity>7</ItemQuantity>
      </PB_OrderItems>
    </XMLPayloadType_B>
  </XMLPayload>
</OpaqueXMLPayloadEnvelope>
```

The OTD Tester window after type B document is parsed is shown in Figure 7-26.

In a Java Collaboration or an eInsight Business Process, use the OpaqueXML-PayloadEnvelope_OpaqueXMLPayloadEnvelope OTD to unmarshal the XML Instance document in order to access envelope header elements. Once you determine payload type from the value of the OpaqueXMLPayloadEnvelope/Header/Type node you can choose the appropriate payload OTD into which you would

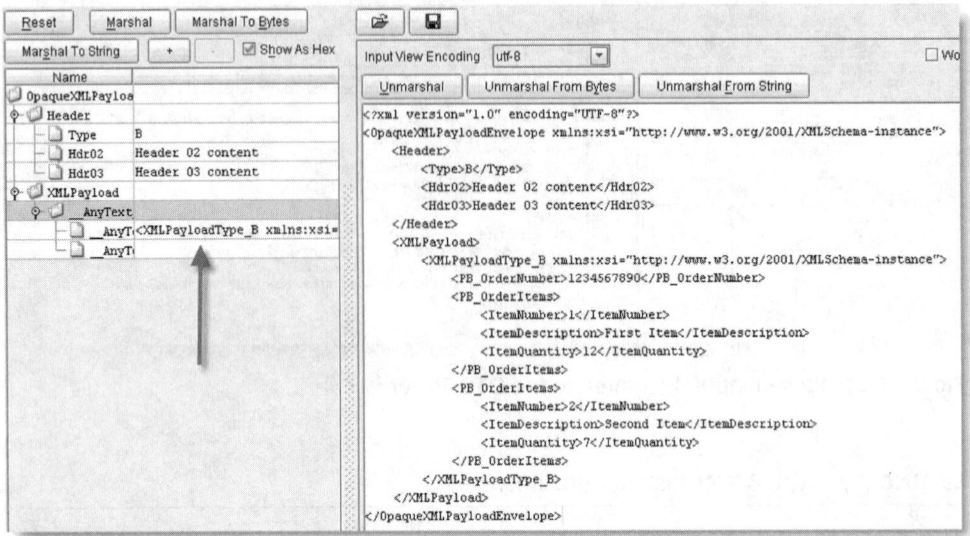

FIGURE 7-26: Parsed input document in the OTD Tester

unmarshal the opaque payload. In the previous examples, it would be either the XMLPayloadType_A or XMLPayloadType_B.

Remember that this technique allows you to envelope arbitrary well-formed XML within a node of another XML document and unmarshal the envelope without having to unmarshal the payload.

A similar technique, exploiting the XML Schema specification, can be used to create an XML Envelope that can carry both well-formed XML and non-XML data within a node.

Picture an XML Schema that looks like that shown in Listing 7-9.

LISTING 7-9: Opaque Payload Envelope sample schema

```
<?xml version="1.0" encoding="UTF-8"?>
<xs:schema
  xmlns:xs="http://www.w3.org/2001/XMLSchema">
    <xs:element name="OpaquePayloadEnvelope">
    <xs:complexType>
      <xs:sequence>
        <xs:element name="Header">
          <xs:complexType>
            <xs:sequence>
              <xs:element name="Type" type="xs:string"/>
              <xs:element name="Hdr02" type="xs:string"/>
```

```
              <xs:element name="Hdr03" type="xs:string"/>
            </xs:sequence>
          </xs:complexType>
        </xs:element>
        <xs:element name="Payload">
          <xs:complexType mixed="true">
            <xs:complexContent mixed="true">
              <xs:restriction base="xs:anyType">
                <xs:sequence>
                  <xs:any processContents="skip"
                    minOccurs="0"
                    maxOccurs="unbounded"/>
                </xs:sequence>
              </xs:restriction>
            </xs:complexContent>
          </xs:complexType>
        </xs:element>
      </xs:sequence>
    </xs:complexType>
  </xs:element>
</xs:schema>
```

When you build an OTD from a schema containing the construct italicized in Listing 7-9, the part of an XML document instance between <Payload> and </Payload> can contain any well-formed XML or non-XML text (other than XML processing instructions)—the unmarshaler will deliver the unspecified content in a node called __AnyText__.

For example, an XML document that looks like the sample in Listing 7-10 will parse, using the OTD Tester, into the OTD structure shown in Figure 7-27.

LISTING 7-10: Sample XML Instance document that carries unparsed non-XML payload data

```
<?xml version="1.0" encoding="UTF-8"?>
<OpaquePayloadEnvelope
        xmlns:xsi="http://www.w3.org/2001/XMLSchema-instance">
  <Header>
    <Type>C</Type>
    <Hdr02>Header 2</Hdr02>
    <Hdr03>Header 3</Hdr03>
  </Header>
  <Payload>
     Litwo! Ojczyzno moja! ty jestes jak zdrowie.
     Ile cie trzeba cenic, ten tylko sie dowie, Kto cie stracil.
     Dzis pieknosc twa w calej ozdobie Widze i opisuje,
     bo tesknie po tobie.
  </Payload>
</OpaquePayloadEnvelope>
```

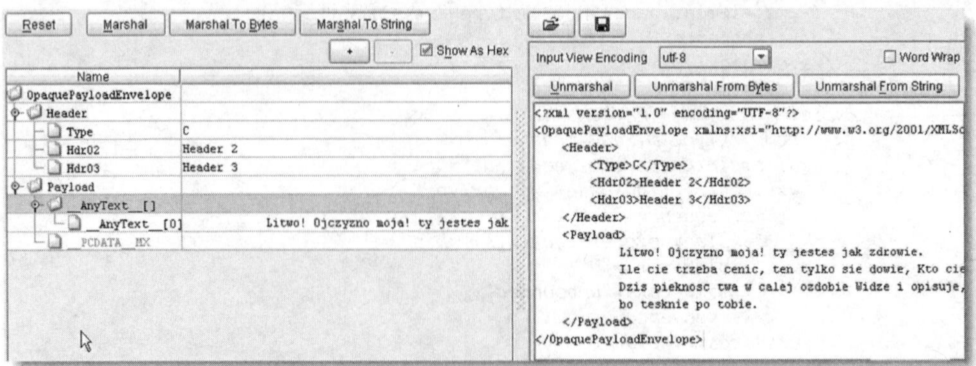

FIGURE 7-27: Sample XML Instance document in OTD Tester window

An XML document, which is presented in Listing 7-11, will also parse, using the OTD Tester, into the same OTD structure, as shown in Figure 7-28.

LISTING 7-11: Sample XML Instance document that carries unparsed XML payload data

```
<?xml version="1.0" encoding="UTF-8"?>
<OpaquePayloadEnvelope
            xmlns:xsi="http://www.w3.org/2001/XMLSchema-instance">
  <Header>
    <Type>D</Type>
    <Hdr02>Header 2</Hdr02>
    <Hdr03>Header 3</Hdr03>
  </Header>
  <Payload>
    <XMLPayloadType_A
            xmlns:xsi="http://www.w3.org/2001/XMLSchema-instance">
      <PA_OrderNumber>1234567890</PA_OrderNumber>
      <PA_OrderQuantity>5</PA_OrderQuantity>
      <PA_Description>Order Header for Order 1234567890</PA_Description>
    </XMLPayloadType_A>
  </Payload>
</OpaquePayloadEnvelope>
```

These are some of the techniques that can be used with XML-based Envelope Wrappers.

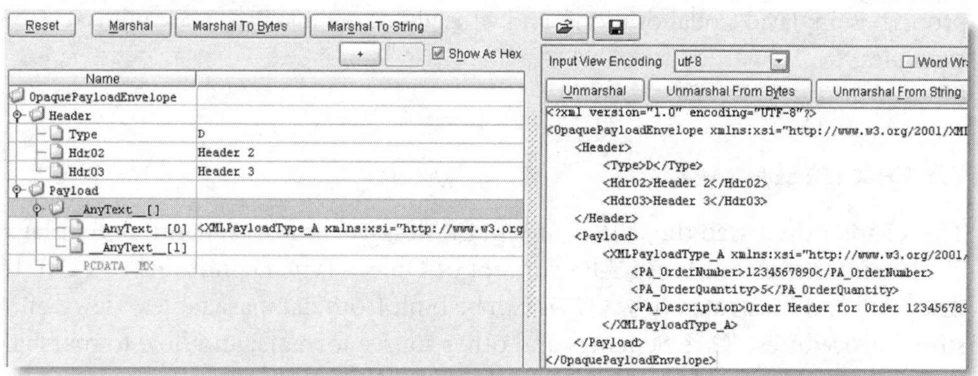

FIGURE 7-28: Parsed XML Instance document carrying unparsed XML payload

7.4.3 JMS User Properties Envelope Wrappers

A designer of the integration solution could define an enveloped message structure and marshal and unmarshal the payload into or from that structure in each component where specific access to metadata and payload was required.

In addition to the message payload and standard JMS message headers, such as JMSMessageID, JMSTimestamp, JMSCorrelationID or JMSExpiration, each JMS message can carry a collection of arbitrary properties, expressed as name/value pairs.

In solutions where messages are conveyed from component to component over JMS, which would be the majority of Java CAPS–based solution, the designer could use JMS user properties to pass between components the metadata that is not part of the payload but is required by components to do their work. In effect, a JMS message is already an envelope-wrapped [EIP] message. Unlike for a typical envelope-wrapped message, the designer does not need to define the envelope structure (JMS implementation already defines that) or marshal and unmarshal messages explicitly. Further, the Java CAPS implementation provides convenient accessors that allow arbitrary JMS user properties to be created and accessed. A solution can leverage that infrastructure to implement an implicit Envelope Wrapper and pass around metadata without modifying the payload or constructing and manipulating an enveloped message.

Chapter 5, section 5.2.1, "JMS User Properties Envelope Wrappers," in Part II (located on the accompanying CD-ROM), illustrates the use of JMS user-defined properties in Java Collaborations and eInsight Business Processes with several examples.

7.5 Chapter Summary

This chapter discussed the [EIP] concept of Message, how it is manifested in Java CAPS, and the related Java CAPS concept of Object Type Definitions (OTDs). It discussed and illustrated how OTDs can be built from database tables, views, and stored procedures; XML Schemas and other source formats; and how to marshal (serialize) and unmarshal (deserialize) them.

The [EIP] Envelope Wrapper pattern was discussed and illustrated with examples. Diverse implementations of the pattern used different Java CAPS facilities ranging from user-defined custom Envelope Wrapper OTDs, to carrying unparsed XML within an XML Envelope, to ways of passing metadata using JMS message header properties.

CHAPTER EIGHT

Message Transformation

8.1 Introduction

This chapter discusses message transformation patterns and how they can be implemented in Java CAPS.

Java CAPS toolbox provides support for message transformation within Java Collaborations, within Business Process Execution Language (BPEL)–based Business Processes and within XSLT Collaborations. Whichever method is used, the source message must be represented as an Object Type Definition (OTD) and the destination message must be represented as an OTD.

[eDesigner] discusses the use of Java Collaborations and XSLT Collaborations for message transformation in detail. [eInsight] discusses the use of business rules in a process model for transformation.

8.2 Envelope Wrapper

Envelope Wrapper and related concepts are discussed at length in Chapter 7, "Message Construction," section 7.4.

8.3 Content Enricher

Content Enricher [EIP] is a component that receives a message, enriches it by adding information not already carried in the message, and passes on the enriched message. Additional information, such as order-total calculation using item quantities and item prices carried in the message, could be computed by an algorithm implemented in the Content Enricher. Additional information, such as a timestamp, could be obtained from the environment in which the solution operates. Additional information could also be obtained from an external system—for example, item price could be looked up in an inventory system given the item number carried in the message. All three methods of obtaining additional information can be combined; for example, transforming a purchase order into an invoice could involve looking up item prices in the inventory system, calculating item totals and order total, obtaining the invoice date from the environment, and assembling an invoice message containing both the original the order information and the additional information produced by the Content Enricher. Content Enricher is a specialized Message Translator [EIP].

In Java CAPS–based solutions, Content Enricher is one of the most commonly implemented components. It can be implemented both as a Java Collaboration and as an eInsight Business Process. Facilities to obtain environment values, such as timestamps, are built right into the infrastructure through Java language facilities and BPEL functions. A plethora of eWay Adapters can be used to obtain information from external systems. Arbitrary business algorithms can be implemented using both.

Chapter 6, section 6.2, "Content Enricher," in Part II (located on the accompanying CD-ROM), illustrates this discussion with a detailed example.

8.4 Content Filter

Content Filter is another specialized Message Transformer. Unlike a Content Enricher, which adds information to messages, a Content Filter [EIP] removes information from messages before passing them on. Reasons for removing content from messages are many. They vary from the need to reduce message size for transportation, to externalizing static information to improve message system performance, to removing sensitive information before passing messages to external systems with no "need to know." Other reasons for the use of Message Filters might be the desire to "flatten" a highly structured message for ease of processing or the desire to implement a Splitter as a series of Message Filters operating on copies of an original message through a subscription mechanism. Java CAPS OTD framework can be readily used to transform messages both in Java Collaborations and eInsight Business Processes, including implementing arbitrarily complex Message Filters.

8.5 Claim Check

The Claim Check pattern [EIP] is a solution in which some information is removed from a message in a processing step, then retrieved by some subsequent processing step. Intermediate processing steps deal with a smaller message, one that does not contain "uninteresting," "irrelevant," or "sensitive" information. Claim Check, unless implemented as a Business Process, requires the use of at least three individual components and a backing store. This is why it is classified here as a solution rather then as a component. The initial step is, in essence, a Message Filter. The final step is, in essence, a Message Enricher.

In a Claim Check solution, the Message Filter transforms an incoming message into two messages: a reduced message that contains information to be passed on and a "to-be-stored" message that contains either the entire original message or those parts of the original message that are not to be passed along. In order to allow a downstream Message Enricher to gain access to information removed in this step, the removed information must be stored in a backing store. Before storing the message, the Message Filter must create a unique identifier to be associated with this information. This unique identifier is added to the reduced message for passing along. It is also associated with the stored message to facilitate later retrieval. This identifier becomes the Claim Check. Intermediate components operate on the reduced message in whatever manner is appropriate, taking care to preserve the Claim Check. Once the reduced message reaches the Message Enricher, the Claim Check is used to retrieve information from the backing store and enrich the message or reconstitute the original message.

[EIP] discusses various ways in which the unique identifier can be generated. If the message volume is low, fewer then one message per millisecond, java.utilDate().getTime() can be used to generate a timestamp-based unique identifier. If the volume may vary and may exceed one message per millisecond, this method is not appropriate. To reduce the possibility of duplicates, you could use java.rmi.server.UID, java.rmi.dgc.VMID, or some other implementation of a Globally Unique Identifier (GUID).

The backing store, necessary to this implementation, could be a Java Database Connectivity (JDBC)–compliant database, accessed via an appropriate Java CAPS database eWay Adapter, or a file in a file system, accessed through one of the Batch eWay variants. The key requirement is that both the Content Filter and the Content Enricher have access to that store.

The preceding discussion assumes that separate Java Collaborations are used as the Message Filter and the Message Enricher; consequently, an external Message Store is required.

Using Java CAPS eInsight Business Process, the Claim Check can be implemented as a single component with no external message store and no need for a unique identifier. A message, received by a Business Process Instance, can be transformed into a message expected by some intermediate component. The Process Instance can invoke this component, passing it the reduced message, and receive a response. It would then use the response and the original message, to which it still has access, to create a final message to pass on to a component downstream from it. The Message Filter is implicit in the initial message transformation. The Message Enricher is implicit in the final message transformation. The message store is internalized to the Business Process Instance, as the message continues to be accessible to the Process Instance while not being accessible to the intermediate component the instance invoked. This implementation is typical of what an eInsight Business Process would do, so attaching the name of Claim Check seems contrived. To follow [EIP] discussion of using Process Manager with Claim Check, this is what such a Business Process implements.

8.6 Normalizer

Message Normalizer [EIP] is a component that transforms messages with the same informational content, but of different formats, into a Canonical Message Format. Normalizer may be required where there are multiple systems, perhaps acquired through mergers and acquisitions, that send the same kinds of messages, perhaps purchase orders. The purchase orders receiving system can only deal with purchase orders of a specific format. Normalizers, introduced between sending systems and the receiving system, transform purchase orders from sending systems' native formats to a format that the receiving system expects or the canonical format if one is in use in the enterprise.

The Java CAPS OTD framework would be used to create OTDs corresponding to the various message formats, and Normalizers would be constructed using Java Collaborations or eInsight Business Processes to transform between formats.

8.7 Canonical Data Model

When message senders and receivers use different message formats, it is necessary to deploy message transformation components. A naïve approach would see a message transformation component built for each sender and receiver pair. Such an approach would rapidly lead to exponential growth in the number of message transformations and, ultimately, to a messaging solution that is brittle and difficult to manage. If there are a significant number of message senders and receivers that use different message formats or whose number is expected to grow over time, it can become a significant issue. Canonical Data Model [EIP] is a solution that introduces an intermediate message format. Messages arriving into the system are transformed to the canonical format and passed around in that format. Outgoing messages are transformed from the canonical format to the format expected by the external system. This introduces a degree of indirection, decouples senders from receivers, and reduces the number of transformations to the point where it will be at most as large as the number of external systems involved. As a side benefit, each external system and its corresponding message transformation can be replaced without affecting other parts of the system. A drawback of this approach, which needs to be weighed against the benefits, is that messages would need to be transformed twice on the way between the sender and the receiver, increasing resource consumption and increasing latency.

Java CAPS OTD Framework can be used to implement the message formats, and Java Collaborations and eInsight Business Processes can be used to implement transformation rules.

The Canonical Data Model need not be XML based. In traditional healthcare enterprises, for example, a specific version of the HL7 messaging standard might be chosen as the basis of the Canonical Data Model. All other HL7 version messages would be transformed to the chosen version, and other normalization, such as code table synchronization, would be applied, thus producing canonical HL7 messages. Other message structure standards, like X12 or UN/EDIFACT, used in various industries, could similarly be chosen as the basis for Canonical Data Models in appropriate environments.

8.8 Chapter Summary

This chapter discussed how Java CAPS can be used to implement common message transformation patterns. Content Enricher, Content Filter, Claim Check, Normalize, and Canonical Data Model were discussed.

CHAPTER NINE

Messaging Endpoints

9.1 Introduction

This chapter discusses a series of patterns [EIP] grouped under the Messaging Endpoints category. A number of these patterns, such as Competing Consumers and Event-Driven Consumer, were covered in earlier chapters. In many cases, a number of Java CAPS features and facilities must be used together to implement specific patterns, such as Polling Consumer and Service Activator. Examples developed to illustrate these topics, which introduce some advanced techniques, are worth studying in themselves.

9.2 Messaging Gateway

Messaging Gateway is, according to [EIP], the means of encapsulating access to the messaging system. The goal is to ensure that the application need not be aware of the intricacies of directly communicating with the messaging system via its APIs. A further goal is to expose the messaging system to the application using business-level constructs like GetCreditScore rather than "connect, send message, receive response, disconnect," or similar actions. Following the discussion of the Messaging Gateway provided in [EIP] leads to an inescapable conclusion that a Messaging Gateway is none other than a Service Façade, very much in vogue with increased interest in service-oriented architectures.

Java CAPS offers several ways in which messaging solutions can be accessed from external applications. The low-level JMS API libraries, provided by the eGate API Kit, come in Java, C/C++, and COM+ flavors. Depending on the nature of the application that needs access to the Java CAPS solution, and the technology platform it uses, one of these libraries can be used to develop a Messaging Gateway with appropriate functionality. The JMS API Kit supports both synchronous and asynchronous messaging between applications and the Sun SeeBeyond JMS Message Server implementation and, through it, Java CAPS–based messaging solutions. The use of the JMS API Kit ties the application very closely to the Sun SeeBeyond JMS Message Server. This may be considered a major drawback if a high degree of vendor independence is sought.

Further down the scale, toward looser coupling, lie the eWays that support standard messaging protocols like TCP/IP and HTTP. A Messaging Gateway constructed to exchange messages with the messaging system over a TCP/IP-based channel, for example, requires the use of generic API libraries supported by most development environments. An example of TCP/IP-based integration between an external environment and Java CAPS is shown in the TCPSender client. This client was built to submit messages to a Java CAPS solution using an external scheduler, but the same code can be used to integrate the interaction into an arbitrary Java-based application. See Figure 2-3 in Chapter 2, section 2.2.1, "External Scheduler Example," in Part II (located on the accompanying CD-ROM). The Gateway is vendor independent from the technology standpoint; however, both the gateway and the messaging solution, the access to which it encapsulates, must agree on the application messaging protocol to use. By application messaging protocol, we mean the types of messages that must be exchanged, the order of message exchange, and the meaning of various bits of information each message carries, and so on. This protocol is very likely to be proprietary, gateway/solution-specific. While such a gateway can be used with different messaging solutions, the solutions must support the proprietary application messaging protocol developed for the gateway.

Further still down the scale of coupling, the Web Services standards–based Messaging Gateway offers the greatest degree of vendor independence and the loosest coupling between the Messaging Gateway and the Java CAPS solution to which it is a Façade. Java CAPS allows Web Services Interoperability–compliant Web Services to be constructed and exposed graphically, including automatic registration of Web Services implementations in Java CAPS–provided UDDI Registry. Numerous development environments provide the means of automatic or semiautomatic generation of application code given the Web Service Definition Language (WSDL)-based interface definition. Sun NetBeans IDE is one such environment.

9.3 Transactional Client

[EIP] defines Transactional Client as an application that can begin, coordinate, and complete a transaction involving a number of resources external to it, one or more of which can be the messaging system. Java CAPS does little to assist the external application in implementing and coordinating a transaction that involves it. In general, most endpoints/eWays/Adapters are not transactional in the sense that their activities cannot be externally coordinated or even undone/rolled back. In fact, endpoints such as a Batch eWay, an HTTP eWay, or a TCP/IP eWay are nontransactional. Other endpoints, such as database eWays or JMS clients, can be used transactionally. With the exception of JMS, for which there is an API and the associated object library, eWays cannot be used outside Java CAPS, so those that can be used transactionally must be used within a Java CAPS solution. eGate JMS API Kit, the API, and the associated library can be used by a third-party application. Since JMS can be used transactionally, the JMS API Kit can be used to develop a Transactional Client that orchestrates a number of resources, one of which is the Java CAPS JMS message publisher or sender.

A Java client application could send messages directly to the Java CAPS JMS Message Server using Client Acknowledgment mode and explicit JMS Session Commit. Such a client could orchestrate a transaction involving a number of resources, including a Java CAPS JMS Message Server.

9.4 Polling Consumer

While Java CAPS is principally an event-driven messaging system, some of its components can be configured to poll external systems for messages rather than setting up listeners.

Polling Consumer [EIP] is a consumer that checks the channel at intervals to determine whether there is a message to receive. It would be implemented in situations where it is impossible or impractical for an external system to notify the messaging system that a message is available or where solution design calls for polling interaction.

9.4.1 Polling File System

Polling Consumers are most commonly used in solutions that involve reading files deposited in a file system by an independent application. The application that creates a file is not directly integrated with the messaging solution—it typically has no way of notifying the messaging system that it has finished writing the file and the file is ready for processing, nor is it even aware that the file it produces gets processed by some other system. A typical file system is not integrated with the messaging system, so it too has no way to notify the messaging system that a file is ready for processing. This also applies to solutions involving remote file systems accessed using some variant of the File Transfer Protocol (FTP).

In Java CAPS, reading files is typically performed by a Batch Local File eWay. This eWay does not have a Receive service, so it cannot be used to trigger a Java Collaboration or a Business Process. Because Java CAPS is an event-driven system, the component that checks the file system for the presence of a file must be triggered somehow. Batch Local File eWay must be used from a Java Collaboration or an eInsight Business Process. Either can be triggered by a Scheduler eWay.

Occasionally there arises a need to poll for files whose names match a pattern constructed at runtime, perhaps involving date components or sequence numbers. The Polling Consumer necessary to support this requirement is somewhat different from that discussed in the previous section. Rather than configuring the regular expression in the Batch Local File eWay connector in the connectivity map, the Java Collaboration dynamically configures the regular expression to be used for polling. Alas, unlike a statically configured regular expression, the dynamically configured regular expression is cleared by the reset() method, so it has to be configured again each time through the multiple file loop.

Unlike the File eWay, the Batch eWay and all its variants can be dynamically configured at runtime, including dynamically specifying the regular expression to use for matching file names.

In the preceding discussion, polling functionality of the Batch eWay was triggered by a Scheduler eWay. The collaboration would use the Batch Local File eWay to read a file if it existed. Unless the getIfExists() method of the Batch Local File OTD was used, a "file not found" exception would be thrown that would have to be handled. If the getIfExists() method was used, the null payload condition, indicating that the file was not found, would still have to be handled. Every time the timer fired, the collaboration would be invoked. Since we are polling for a file in the local file system anyway, it would be better to have some component directly poll the file system to a schedule and invoke the collaboration only if file was available for processing. The Batch Inbound eWay, another variant of the Batch eWay, provides just this kind of functionality. Since it made its appearance sometime in ICAN 5.0.x, it has been used instead of the Scheduler eWay or the File eWay to implement file polling solutions.

The Batch Inbound eWay polls a directory for a file with a name that is explicitly specified as a literal or that satisfies a specified regular expression. When a matching file is found, the eWay renames the file in place by prefixing a Globally

Unique ID (GUID) to the file name and invokes the collaboration or the Business Process, passing to them the original name of the file, the original directory in which file exists, and the new name of the file after it has been renamed. This approach has a number of benefits. First, if the regular expression on which to match file names is correctly specified, the Batch Inbound will not match the new name, so the component that will process the file can take its time processing the file without running the risk of the file becoming a candidate for processing again. Second, until the file becomes available, no collaboration or Business Process is triggered. Third, when invoked, the collaboration or the Business Process will have a single file to process. Any exceptions are error situations that need handling rather than being benign exceptions like "file is not found because it is not there yet."

Note

If the regular expression is badly specified, such that it will match the name of the original file as well as the name of the file after a GUID is prepended to it, recursion will occur. The renamed file will be processed again on the next poll, getting another GUID prepended to its name. Eventually, after some number of repetitions, this process will cause the Batch Inbound eWay to exceed the length of the file name acceptable to the file system and will cause an exception. The collaboration or the Business Process will not be invoked and the file will not be processed.

Note

Batch Inbound eWay does not process the file it locates except to rename it by prefixing a GUID to the original file name. The new file name, the original file name, and the path to the file/directory where the file exists are made available to the eInsight Business Process or a Java Collaboration as values in the BatchInbound OTD. It is expected that some other eWay will be used to actually read the file and process its content as required. This ensures that the same file will not be picked up on the next poll and submitted for processing again.

Note

Batch Inbound only delivers one file name per poll. To process many files in a directory as rapidly as possible, the Batch Inbound would usually be configured with a very short schedule interval. This is resource intensive and inefficient if files are deposited for processing in bursts.

Chapter 7, section 7.2.1, "Polling File System," in Part II, illustrates this discussion with several Java CAPS examples. Chapter 4, "Message Exchange Patterns," section 4.11 (in Part I) discusses data streaming using the Batch eWay.

9.4.2 Other Batch Pollers

The Batch eWay has several variants supporting file reading and writing in various protocol and security contexts. Local file systems, traditional FTP, and secure FTP (over SSL as well as using SSH-based SFTP and SCP protocols) are supported. All these variants of the Batch eWay can be implemented in a File Polling Consumer as long as the means of triggering the collaboration or the Business Process are available. For a local file system, it can be either a timer/scheduler or the Batch Local File eWay. For remote file access, it will likely be a scheduler-based trigger, though Batch Local File eWay can also be used if appropriate in the context of the solution. In such a case, a local directory will be polled for a local file in order to read a remote file—not exactly intuitive, but it might have valid applications; for example, a telephone call is received announcing that the remote file is available, so the operator can manually trigger an FTP poll.

9.4.3 Polling JMS Destination

Much less commonly there arises a requirement to periodically poll a JMS Destination instead of configuring a message listener and processing messages as soon as they are available. One scenario in which a Polling Consumer polling a JMS Destination would be appropriate is a try-wait-retry implementation. For example, a solution might receive, from JMS, a message to deposit at an FTP server. The FTP server may be unavailable. Instead of rolling the message back and having it immediately redelivered, the solution might park the message in a "retry queue" with no connected receivers. An independent collaboration might be triggered, at intervals, to poll the retry queue and resubmit any messages it finds there to the original queue, thus causing the FTP process to be retried. One reason to avoid rolling the message back to the original queue is that the next message might be for a different FTP server. Rolling back the current message will prevent delivery of the subsequent messages, clearly an undesirable situation when messages are intended for independent destinations.

The architectural schematic in Figure 9-1 shows the try-wait-retry part of a larger solution.

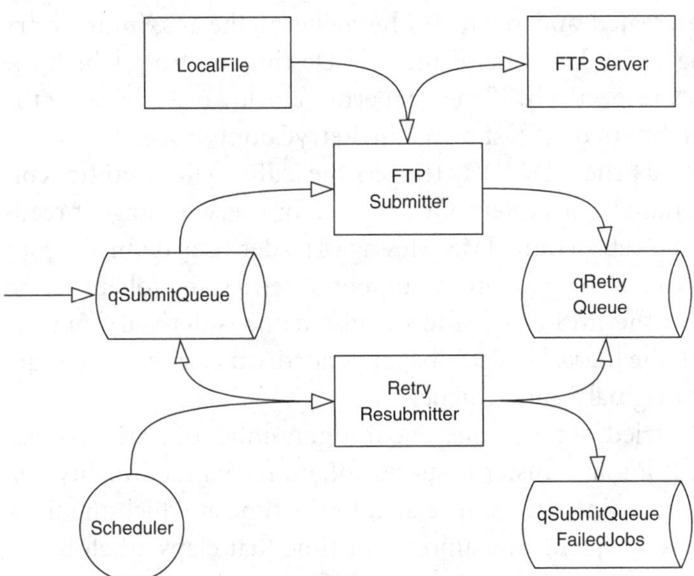

FIGURE 9-1: JMS-based try-wait-retry pattern schematic

Note

The solution in Figure 9-1 explicitly does not preserve order of message delivery. The intent is to ensure that a message that cannot be delivered to the final destination does not block later messages and prevent their delivery to other destinations that are ready to receive them. The design does not assure preservation of order of message delivery even to the same destination because a message waiting in a retry queue may not get an opportunity to get delivered until after a subsequent message for the same destination manages to get delivered.

A set of components, upstream from qSubmitQueue, construct a Job Message containing the name of the file to be submitted by FTP, the maximum number of times to retry if delivery fails, the address and credentials of the FTP server, and the directory at the FTP server to which the file must be written. Upon receipt of this message, jcdFTPSubmitter attempts to dynamically connect to the nominated FTP server, using the address and credentials provided in the Job Message. If connection succeeds, file transfer is attempted. If connection fails, the Job Message is requeued to qRetryQueue. If the message does not have JMS Message Header user-defined properties, RetryCount, MaximumRetryCount, and

SourceQueue, they are created and set to 0, the value of the maximum retry count in the Job Message, and the name of the JMS Destination from which the message originally came, respectively. If the properties already exist, because the message was already resubmitted at least once, the RetryCount property is incremented. Every *n* minutes, a Scheduler eWay triggers the jcdRetryResubmitter collaboration. This collaboration polls qRetryQueue, and for every message it reads from there, it inspects the retry count JMS Message Header user-defined property. If the retry count exceeds the maximum number of retries, the collaboration resubmits the message to the JMS Destination whose name is derived from the SourceQueue name with the literal "FailedJobs" appended; otherwise, it requeues the message back to the original SourceQueue.

Every transfer will be tried, at most, the "maximum number of retries" times, at nominated intervals. If initial transfer is successful, no retry functionality will be invoked. Because the retry interval is unrelated to the time at which the message was queued to the retry queue, the amount of time that elapses before the message is requeued to the original queue may vary from nothing to the scheduled interval.

Chapter 7, section 7.2.2, "Polling JMS Destination," in Part II, illustrates this discussion with the example Java CAPS implementation.

9.5 Event-Driven Consumer

As mentioned in the previous section, Java CAPS is essentially an event-driven messaging system. Endpoints register message listeners, which are activated as soon as a message they are to process becomes available. Occurrence of an event causes the Java Collaboration or the Business Process to begin executing. Even the Polling Consumers discussed in the previous section are Event-Driven Consumers, as each is activated by a Scheduler eWay or by a Batch Inbound eWay, triggering the component that implements polling functionality. All Java Collaborations and all eInsight Business Processes are Event-Driven Consumers.

Java CAPS offers a series of configuration properties, dependent on the endpoint in use, which allow control over whether Event-Driven Consumers can be automatically replicated to process messages concurrently and, if so, how many copies of the consumer there can be. This facility, discussed in passing in Chapter 4, section 4.8.1, allows Event-Driven Consumers to accommodate spikes in workload at the cost of increased resource use.

9.6 Competing Consumers

The Competing Consumers pattern facilitates processing multiple messages concurrently. In Java CAPS, Competing Consumers are typically JMS queue receivers. Multiple receivers from the same queue will compete for messages. As a message becomes available for processing, the JMS Message Server will randomly pick a consumer from among the consumers configured to receive from the queue and will deliver the message to it.

Java CAPS Java Collaborations are, by default, configured to receive from JMS queues in Serial mode. Only one collaboration instance will be created to receive a message. Any messages available for processing while the instance is actively processing a message will wait until the instance is finished so that the next message can be processed. Java Collaborations are not, by default, configured to operate as Competing Consumers. To implement Competing Consumers with Java Collaborations, you can explicitly drag several copies of the collaboration onto the connectivity map and make them receive from the same JMS queue; see Chapter 4, section 4.8.2, and Chapter 5, "Messaging Infrastructure," section 5.8.1, for a discussion and an example of this approach. This approach is explicit in that a casual viewer of the connectivity map will immediately see the processing model implemented in the connectivity map. A different approach to implementing Competing Consumers using Java Collaborations is to configure the JMS Receiver Concurrency property to Connection Consumer mode, specifying the maximum number of threads that can be created to process messages. This approach is discussed in Chapter 5, section 5.8.1. This approach makes it harder for a casual viewer to discern what the real processing model is without verifying JMS Receiver connector property settings.

For eInsight Business Processes, the default processing model is to have the eInsight Engine create as many Business Process instances as there are messages to process. If an instance is processing a message when another message becomes available, the eInsight Engine will create a new instance to process it. This topic is discussed at length in Chapter 5, section 5.8.2. With Java CAPS 5.1, this default behavior can be changed by making the process an XA process, effectively serializing processing for this process.

Note

Not exactly what a desirable design ought to be, it is possible to configure multiple Batch eWays to read files with overlapping name patterns from directories with the same name or overlapping name patterns. eWays configured this way would in effect be Competing Consumers, but since there is no synchronization between them, it is possible that multiple eWays might attempt to read the same file with highly undesirable consequences.

9.7 Message Dispatcher

Discussion of Message Dispatcher in [EIP] is somewhat confusing. On the one hand, Message Dispatcher is compared to a selective consumers-based solution; on the other, it is compared to a multithreaded application wherein a dispatcher invokes "performers" executing in the context of the same process. The peculiar characteristics that make this pattern a Message Dispatcher are its ability to receive messages of different types over the same channel, its ability to recognize different messages by some means, and its ability to distribute messages for processing to different channels based on these different attributes. Since Java CAPS Integration Server is, effectively, the container in which all deployments execute, and it is a single process, the "single process" distinction is irrelevant. In Java CAPS, for all intents and purposes, Message Dispatcher is no different from a dynamic router.

Implementation of a Message Dispatcher as a Java Collaboration or as an eInsight Business Process is the same as implementation of any collaboration or Business Process. Both Java Collaborations and Business Processes receive messages from a channel. Java Collaborations receive messages over only one channel, whereas Business Processes can receive messages over multiple channels. The tricky part, if any, is to decide how to implement discrimination rules so that the dispatcher, much as a dynamic router, does not become a maintenance burden.

One implementation that may be useful in specific circumstances is a message dispatcher solution consisting of Message Inspector, whether implemented as a collaboration or a Business Process, a JMS Destination, and a set of Selective Consumers, statically configured or dynamic. The Inspector will parse messages it receives, extract key information, populate the JMS Message Correlation ID property, and submit messages to a JMS Destination. Different Selective Consumers will pick up messages whose selector values match those they expect to process. The overall operation will be that of a Message Dispatcher.

9.8 Selective Consumer

Typically associated with JMS, Selective Consumers [EIP] are consumers that receive only some of the messages from their associated channel. Java CAPS supports Selective Consumers by implementing JMS Message Selectors that, when statically configured for receivers and subscribers, instruct the JMS Message Server to deliver only selected messages. A technique also exists that allows a Java Collaboration to create a selector dynamically and poll the JMS Destination for messages that satisfy the selector expression. JMS-based Selective Consumers are discussed at length in Chapter 5, section 5.6.7.

It is worth noting that, effectively, all Batch eWay variants are used to implement Selective Consumers. Much as JMS selectors instruct the Message Server to deliver messages whose properties match the selector expressions, so too the file and directory name patterns instruct the Batch eWay implementation to select only matching files.

9.9 Durable Subscriber

When dealing with JMS Destinations, we expect messages that are sent or published to be retained by the JMS Message Server until they are picked up by a receiver, are delivered to all subscribers, or expire and are removed or moved off to a Message Journal. This is generally a reasonable expectation with one exception. JMS topics, as discussed in Chapter 5, section 5.5, behave differently with respect to message consumption, depending on whether subscribers are durable or nondurable.

A durable subscriber is one that the Message Server recognizes by its client name and for which the Message Server retains messages until they expire or are consumed by that subscriber. This means that even if the subscriber is not connected, at the time a message becomes available for delivery, the message will be kept for it. All retained messages will be delivered as soon as the subscriber connects if the messages have not expired in the meantime. In contrast, a nondurable subscriber will receive messages only when it is connected. This messaging model is known as a store-and-forward messaging model.

The durability property of the JMS subscriber client is configured through the JMS client connector in the connectivity map.

Chapter 7, section 7.3, "Durable Subscriber," in Part II, provides an illustration that walks through building and exercising a simple solution that eventually leads to deployment of a durable subscriber.

9.10 Idempotent Receiver

By Andrew Walker

An Idempotent Receiver is a receiver that can safely handle the receipt of the same message more than once. In the context of this discussion, it is important to understand the definition of *idempotent* and also of *safely*, and to understand what is meant by *duplicate message.*

First, idempotent, a mathematical term that made its way into computer science, is used to describe any function that has the same effect whether executed once or multiple times; see http://en.wikipedia.org/wiki/Idempotent_(software). Applied to messaging systems, idempotent means that the effect of the receipt of a particular message is the same even if the message is received multiple times.

To define *safely*, let's first consider the focus of our discussion in this section. We are considering how to implement an Idempotent Receiver as part of a larger Java CAPS application. For simplicity, let's call this Java CAPS application the "system." A Java CAPS application normally accepts a message from an external application or the messaging system and then processes it in some fashion, often updating other external applications or data stores or triggering processing in another Java CAPS application—it causes permanent side effects. Our requirement for *safely* is based on the idea that the message will be processed within a Java CAPS solution and that the processing will cause the state of the system to change in some manner (side effects), either by updating data within the system or by causing the system to carry out further processing actions—for example, publishing another message to one or many external applications or causing the execution of other processes internal or external to Java CAPS. So *safely* requires that even if a duplicate message is received, the system will remain in the same state it was before the duplicate message arrived; that is, no data will be updated and no processing actions with undesirable side effects will be executed.

A duplicate message is one that would cause the system to repeat exactly the same processing steps, and possibly result in unintended and undesirable side effects external or internal to the system. A good example is the processing of a message that contains transaction data for a withdrawal transaction on a bank account. The system should process the same withdrawal only once. A duplicate message would contain the same transaction data, so a duplicate message, which has the same data content, would cause the withdrawal to be invalidly processed again—an undesirable side effect.

It is important to remember that some operations are inherently idempotent. Reading a database, for example, is idempotent, whereas updating the same database is not, unless the database is updated with the data that is already there (i.e., there is no change to the database content, which makes the update also idempotent in this specific case).

It is also important to consider the requirement for idempotence in the context of a wider solution. If a solution inserts records into a database table with a unique primary key, for example, and a record with such unique primary key already exists, then the solution is likely to receive a duplicate key exception. It can then alter logic flow based on the duplicate key event without special code required to guarantee idempotence if the unique primary key constraint already ensures that no undesirable side effects occur elsewhere in the solution.

In addressing the issue of idempotence in general, it is important to consider what action needs be taken by a solution when the requirement for idempotence is not met. Should the solution simply stop processing the message and discard it, or should it do something else, like alert an operator, negatively acknowledge the message, or take some action more appropriate to and dependent on the problem being solved?

All solutions to the idempotence issue rely on one or both of two properties of a message being processed. One is the ability to determine whether the message has already been processed at least once—duplicate message recognition. The other is the ability to determine from the message whether a particular action or a set of actions taken to process the message are already idempotent and therefore require no special treatment from the idempotence standpoint.

The following discussion presents one of the possible solutions to the issue of duplicate message recognition and relies on the ability of a relational database system, used in the example, to distinguish between a new record insertion and attempted insertion of a duplicate record.

Keep in mind that the source of a duplicate message is not constrained just to external applications but may also be the messaging system itself. The cause and the source of the duplication are not relevant to the design of an Idempotent Receiver. The causes of message duplication are many but generally occur due to the effects of exceptional or unforeseen circumstances, software bugs, or unreliable networks. The key point in designing an Idempotent Receiver is to not make assumptions or restrict yourself to one set of possible conditions that may cause message duplication.

To construct an Idempotent Receiver, we must create what we will refer to as a "de-duping" service—a service that, given a message, will advise whether the message is a duplicate of a message that was already processed. At the heart of a de-duping service is a method of keeping a history of all messages received so that it is possible for a receiver to determine if the currently received message has already been processed sometime in the past by examining the history. Of course, it would be very inefficient to store the entire contents of each message received, and that approach is not recommended. A much better strategy is to store some kind of Message ID or computed message digest for every message processed.

The selection of a good Message ID is critical to the success of the duplicate detection strategy. The Message ID must be unique for every unique message received. When we talk about uniqueness, we are talking about the message content being unique. A bad choice of Message ID would be any internal ID used by the messaging system, since this ID does not guarantee that any two messages have identical message data content. A much better choice of ID is one based on the business data that the message contains, such as a Product Order ID. If multiple messages may legitimately contain the same candidate IDs, then a compound ID needs to be created that includes the business ID plus extra information from the message data itself so that the message ID is unique—for example, a transaction code or transaction type, such as New, Update, Delete, or Modify. A timestamp field is another example of a bad choice of Message ID, since a timestamp usually has no bearing on how the message data is processed but simply supplies additional information about the data (i.e., at what time the data was created or entered). Having said that, it is worth pointing out that if the external sender, which creates the timestamp and other data used for Message ID, is the source of duplicate messages, and duplicate messages have the same timestamp and other ID components, then the timestamp may be a good choice as a part of a composite ID. Once an appropriate Message ID has been selected, we can move on to consider how to actually store these Message IDs in a list for the purpose of implementing a de-duping service.

On first thought, there appears to be two possible approaches to implementing an Idempotent Receiver in Java CAPS: in-memory and persisted to a backing store. It quickly becomes clear that an in-memory system, while seemingly attractive because of its obvious speed advantage, is fatally flawed for the simple reason that it is not reliable in the face of system failures. The list of Message IDs is lost once the system is shut down or restarted. A reliable Idempotent Receiver must have a persistent store of Message IDs to use for checking.

In general, it is more efficient to design the system such that the Idempotent Receiver acts as a gatekeeper to de-dupe the messages as they enter the system, as opposed to making every receiver of a particular message type in the system capable of handling duplicate messages.

To store the list of Message IDs, we need a persistent store such as a database that serializes updates to the store so that each receiver always sees an identical and consistent view of the Message ID list. Thus, even when duplicate messages of the same type are received at the same time and processed by different receivers, one of the messages is always guaranteed to be detected as a duplicate of the other.

Since the list of Message IDs is kept in a persistent store, the list will keep growing indefinitely unless some kind of cleanup is done to keep the list at a manageable size. Two obvious strategies for a cleanup process are one that uses a time condition (i.e., remove all Message IDs from the list older than a certain period of time) and one that uses a size condition of the Message ID list (i.e., keeps only the last *x* number of Message IDs received). The choice of which of these two strategies to implement will depend on the business requirements of the message handling and also, to a certain extent, on the message volume and message processing performance required of the system. When choosing a cleanup strategy, a balance needs to be achieved between the competing demands of performance and risk mitigation.

9.11 Service Activator

In pursuit of reusability integration, architects and solution designers seek to define services that implement some core functionality but can be invoked in a variety of ways. It may be that a service must be invoked synchronously by one application and asynchronously by another. It may be that a service must process payload that can be delivered as a JMS Message or as a flat file. It may be that a message to be processed must be transformed from source format to the format the service requires. To address these kinds of issues, the architect or the designer can implement one or more Service Activators [EIP], each of which invokes the same service on behalf of some other component, providing transformation services and endpoint bridging as necessary.

In general, remotely invocable Java CAPS services can use one of three interfaces: a JMS Request/Reply, an eInsight subprocess, or a Web Service. Similarly, Java CAPS Service Activators can be constructed to invoke services via one of these interfaces. With one degree of indirection, an eGate-only solution can be constructed to implement this pattern. The functionality would be implemented in a Java Collaboration, and one or more separate Java Collaborations, exposed as Web Services or JMS Listeners, for example, would receive requests and forward them to the functionality-implementing collaboration. It is also possible, however "hacky," to invoke a Java Collaboration directly from another Java Collaboration.

Chapter 12, "Reusability," sections 12.4 and 12.5, discuss how the same eInsight Business Process can used as a subprocess as well as an independent Web Service by another eInsight Business Process. In the former case, the invoking process is a Service Activator, and in the latter case, the Web Service Client is a Service Activator.

Chapter 4, section 4.5.1, contains an example of an eInsight Business Process invoking a piece of business functionality exposed as a JMS Request/Reply service using a wrapper collaboration that implements the JMS Request/Response functionality on its behalf. The wrapper collaboration is an example of a Service Activator.

While not an example of a Service Activator, the example of JMS Request/Reply Responder, discussed in Chapter 4, section 4.5.1, demonstrates how a JMS Responder can be implemented to return a response to a JMS Destination provided by the invoker, thus acting as a synchronous service, or pass it on to a connectivity map–configured JMS Destination, thus acting as an asynchronous service. This particular service can be invoked synchronously, by the client specifying the response destination via the JMSReplyTo property, or asynchronously, by the client not specifying a response destination. Both client implementations could be classified as Service Activators for the same service.

An eInsight Business Process can be used to implement a Service Activator using a Business Process Execution Language (BPEL) event-based decision construct. Chapter 7, section 7.5, "Multi-input Service Activator," in Part II, walks through the implementation of an eInsight-based multi-input Service Activator.

Note

A multi-input Service Activator can be used in a solution that is built and deployed incrementally. For example, a part of the solution may be ready to be deployed and used. Messages come from a file system because the sending system cannot deal with any other method of providing input to an integration solution. Sometime later, this system is replaced by one that can use

IMS to submit messages directly, or a Messaging Bridge that uses JMS to submit messages is developed. With a multi-input Service Activator that can accept messages using a Batch eWay and a JMS client, the solution that this Service Activator is a part of does not need to change and does not need to be redeployed to accept messages from different sources.

Multi-input Service Activators can also assist with unit testing solution components by allowing test message feeds at different points from different sources.

9.12 Chapter Summary

This chapter discussed a series of patterns [EIP] grouped under the Messaging Endpoints category. In many cases, a number of Java CAPS features and facilities are used together to implement specific patterns, such as Polling Consumer and Service Activator.

CHAPTER TEN

System Management

10.1 Introduction

This chapter reviews system management facilities provided by Java CAPS out-of-the-box and discusses how Java CAPS solution–specific system management facilities can be designed into the solution for runtime monitoring, statistics collection, testing, and configuration using [EIP] system management patterns.

Additional solution-specific [EIP] system management and monitoring patterns, Control Bus, Detour, Wire Tap, Message History, Message Store, Channel Purger, and Test Message are discussed.

10.2 Java CAPS Monitoring and Management

10.2.1 Overview

Whether strictly eGate-based, strictly eInsight-based, or mixed, each Java CAPS solution can be managed and monitored using the Java CAPS management and monitoring framework. Web-based user interface, the Enterprise Manager, provides the ability to start and stop each integration server and each message server; start, restart, and stop individual components; view message consumption statistics; manipulate messages that have not been consumed; view and resubmit processed messages that have been journaled; deploy and undeploy applications; manage users; and perform many other runtime management and control tasks.

Since Java CAPS is a J2EE-based framework, it supports the Java Management Extensions (JMX) technology. JMX tools can be used to interact with the Java CAPS environment, and the components deployed within it, at runtime. The Enterprise Manager back-end infrastructure uses JMX to interact with Java CAPS components. Java tools that use JMX can be used or developed to provide additional runtime control if necessary.

To obtain an accurate picture of the runtime characteristics of a solution, a variety of runtime metrics would prove useful. Out-of-the-box Java CAPS provides message processing counts. It does not provide other metrics like message processing times statistics or message size statistics. If required, facilities for collecting these kinds of statistics must be built into each solution as it is developed.

The following sections briefly describe management and control facilities provided with Java CAPS, and they discuss how [EIP] management and control patterns can be instrumented into Java CAPS solutions.

10.2.2 Monitoring eGate-Based Solutions

Java CAPS solutions can be purely eGate based, where all components are Java Collaborations, connecting eWays and JMS Destinations. Depending on the granularity of deployment, there may not be a single graphical representation of the solution architecture at design time. There may not be a single graphical representation of the entire solution at runtime. The design time and runtime relationships between solution components are depicted in units of connectivity maps.

Consider a project with the components shown in Figure 10-1.

The connectivity map for the project looks like that shown in Figure 10-2.

This connectivity map shows, reasonably clearly, the relationships between components of a fairly small and simple solution involving five JMS Destinations, seven Java Collaborations, and three File eWays, for a total of 23 deployable components, as seen in eDesigner's Connectivity Map Editor Canvas. It would not

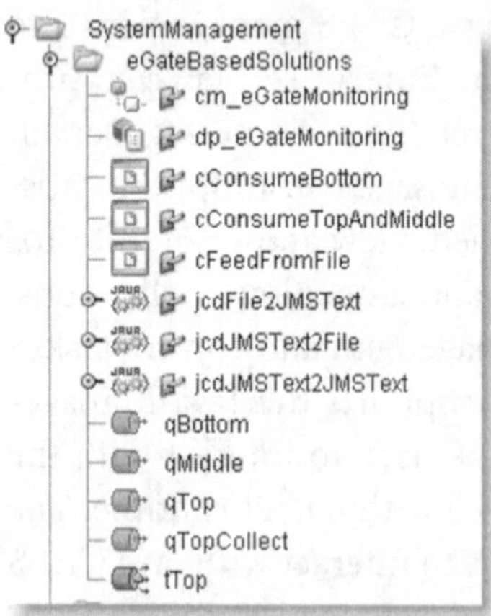

FIGURE 10-1: Sample project components

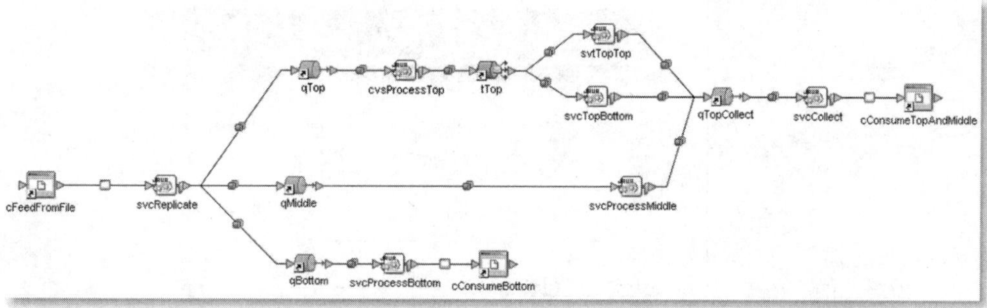

FIGURE 10-2: Sample project connectivity map

stretch the imagination to visualize a connectivity map for a larger solution to see how complex it can get and how quickly.

In eManager, the runtime components are represented similarly, as shown in Figure 10-3.

Clicking on the components in the tree displays runtime information that varies from component to component, as shown in Figure 10-4.

A Java Collaboration display will show collaboration state, message consumption, and the number of messages waiting to be processed. Collaboration can also be stopped and restarted if running, and started if stopped.

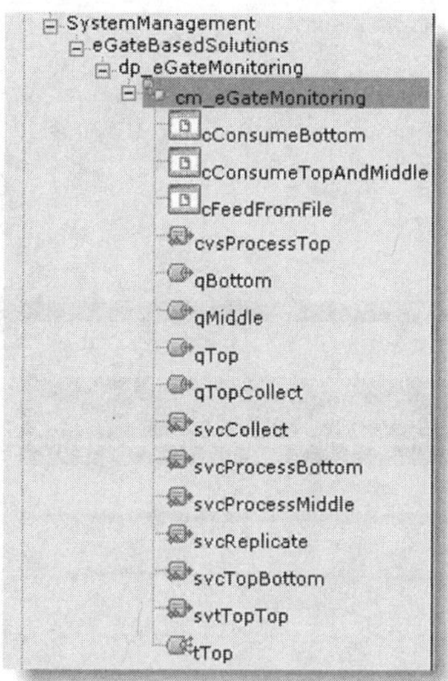

FIGURE 10-3: Project components in the Enterprise Manager Project View

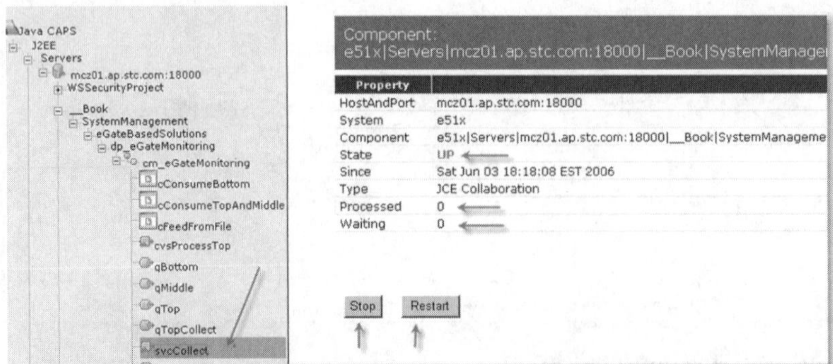

FIGURE 10-4: Component information in the Enterprise Manager

The connectivity map can be seen at runtime through the Enterprise Manager when the connectivity map node in the project tree is clicked, as shown in Figure 10-5.

Information displayed below the connectivity map varies with the component selected. Within components, different classes of information are organized using tabbed panels.

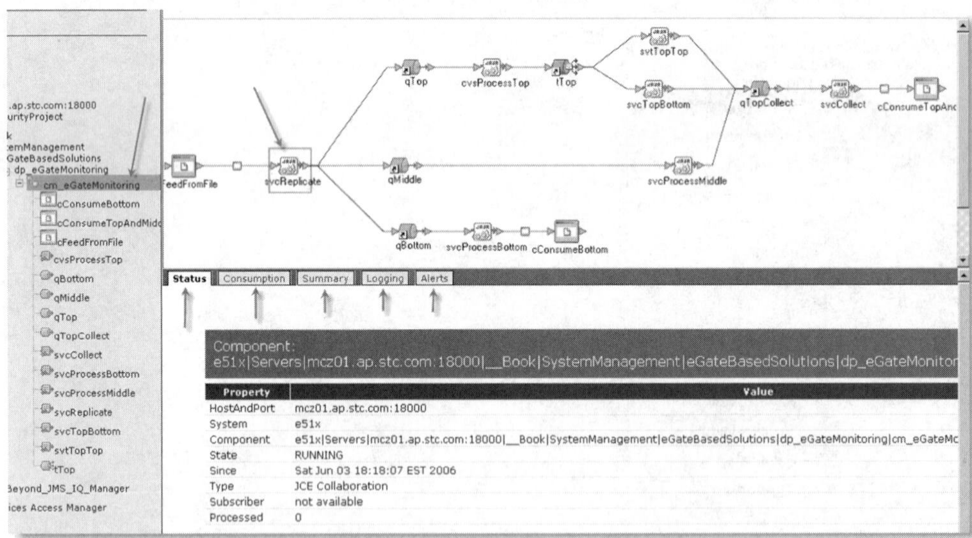

FIGURE 10-5: Connectivity map in the Enterprise Manager, with information for a selected component

Collaborations have a Status tab, as shown in Figure 10-6; a Consumption tab, as shown in Figure 10-7; a Logging tab, as shown in Figure 10-8; and an Alerts tab, as shown in Figure 10-9.

JMS Destinations show the message counters and allow messages waiting to be delivered to be edited, resubmitted, or deleted. New messages can also be injected through this interface. Figure 10-10 shows the JMS queue selected in a connectivity map and the JMS message manipulation interface in the Enterprise Manager.

See Chapter 6 of the Sun SeeBeyond eGate Integrator System Administration Guide [eGateSAG] for details of the Enterprise Manager, information it displays, and the ways it facilitates manipulation of components at runtime.

Using the Enterprise Monitor, you can review the counts of messages processed and messages waiting to be processed by each Java Collaboration. Similarly, you can

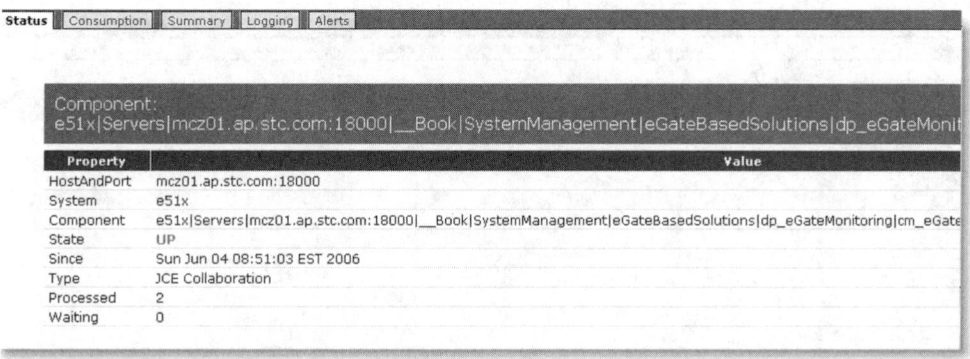

FIGURE 10-6: Status tab for a collaboration

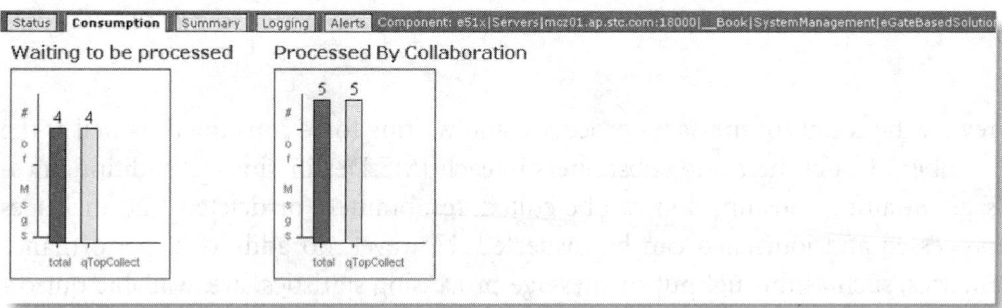

FIGURE 10-7: Consumption tab for a collaboration

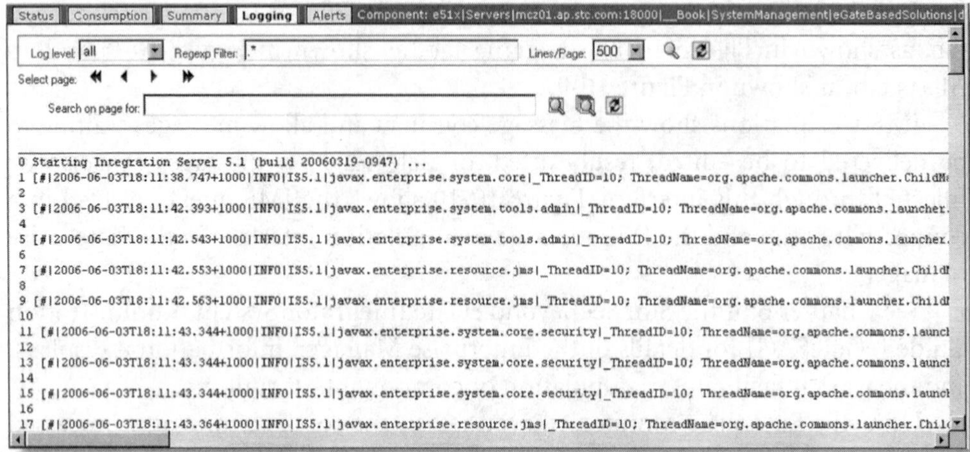

FIGURE 10-8: Logging tab for a collaboration

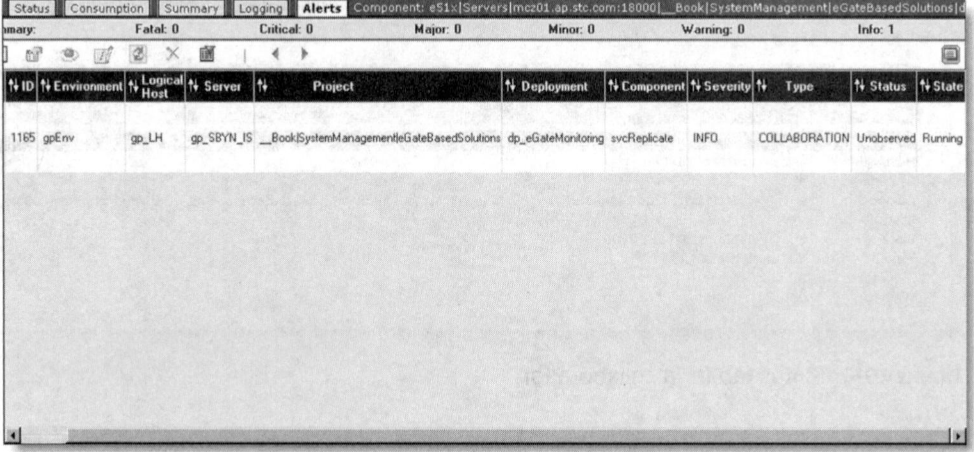

FIGURE 10-9: Alerts tab for a collaboration

review the counts of messages processed and waiting to be consumed, as well as the number of publishers and subscribers in each JMS Destination. In addition, messages awaiting consumption can be edited, resubmitted, or deleted, and messages processed and journaled can be inspected. However, no additional performance metrics, such as throughput or message processing statistics, are available out-of-the-box; these will have to be engineered into each solution as and if required.

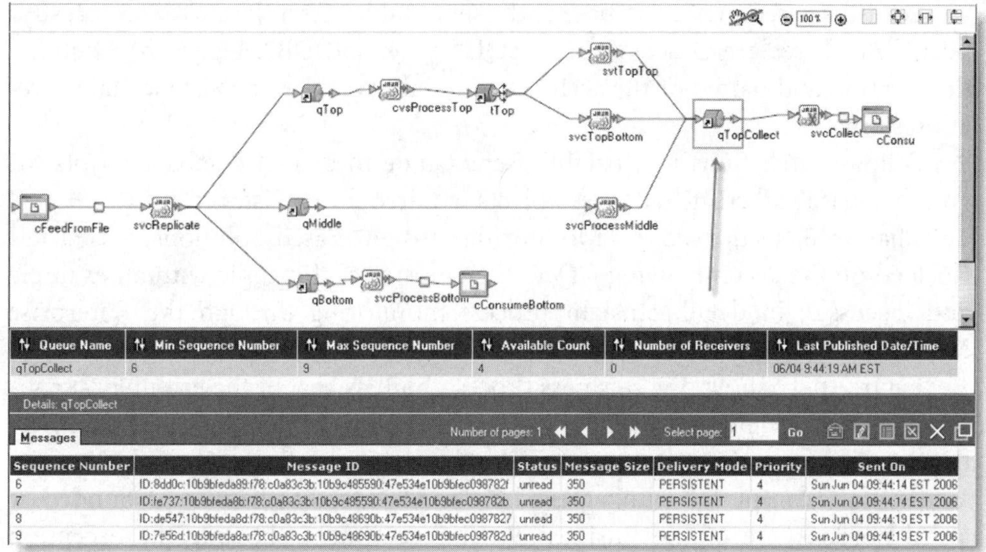

FIGURE 10-10: JMS queue and message manipulation interface in the Enterprise Manager

10.2.3 Monitoring eInsight-Based Solutions

eInsight Business Process instances can be monitored and managed, when in progress, through the Enterprise Manager Web Interface. Once completed, Business Process attributes of the instances can be inspected. Monitoring eInsight Business Processes requires that persistence be enabled in the Business Process engine configuration of the enterprise application of which the Business Process that is to be monitored is a part. By default, only the values of containers—such as inputs and outputs of the marshal/unmarshal activities, receive or send activities, or invoke activities—are persisted and accessible for monitoring. If the Business Process uses Business Process attributes internally to manipulate data or keep track of data of interest, it is necessary to enable Persistence for Reporting for the Business Process and to create an appropriate database table whose Data Definition Language (DDL) definition is generated by eDesigner. Once all these configuration activities are completed, and the Business Process is built and deployed, subsequent execution of a solution containing this Business Process will result in Business Process recovery and monitoring data being automatically collected and stored in the configured database. This data, after some delay, will be available for inspection through the Enterprise Manager.

Persistence requires a database and a set of tables. As at Java CAPS 5.1.2, supported databases are Oracle, Sybase, SQL Server, and DB2. Figure 10-11 shows the location and names of the archives containing eInsight persistence table creation scripts.

Follow instructions in eInsight User's Guide to extract database scripts for your database and create database objects required for persistence.

Chapter 8, section 8.2.1, "Monitoring eInsight-Based Solutions," in Part II (located on the accompanying CD-ROM), illustrates this topic with an example and discusses, in detail, eInsight process monitoring through the Enterprise Manager.

Figure 10-12 shows the Business Process, built as part of the example, at runtime. One of the process instances is inspected. In the illustration, the activity that invoked a Java Collaboration failed. All activities leading to the failed activity are shown as completed, with a green border. The failed activity is surrounded by a red border. One of the Business Process attributes, showing the exception received from the failed activity, is highlighted. The complete example is built and exercised in Chapter 8, section 8.2.1, in Part II.

Enabling persistence for eInsight Business Processes enables monitoring and management of process instances at runtime. Enabling and configuring persistence for reporting for individual Business Processes causes Business Process attribute values to be collected and gives access to these attributes through the Enterprise Manager. While these things are desirable, it must be borne in mind that persistence is rather expensive in terms of resource consumption, so it should be used advisedly.

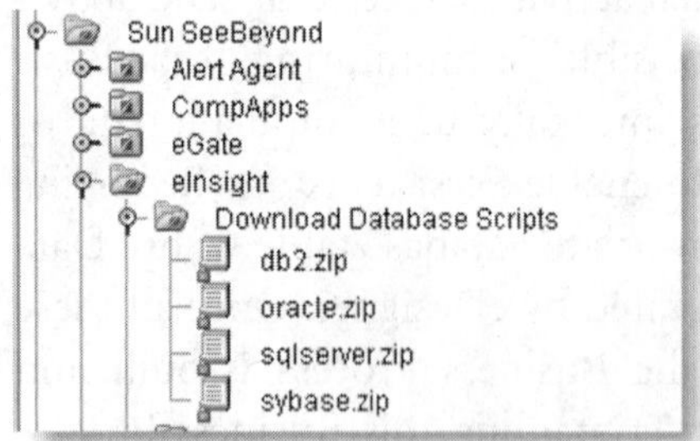

FIGURE 10-11: eInsight persistence tables create script archives

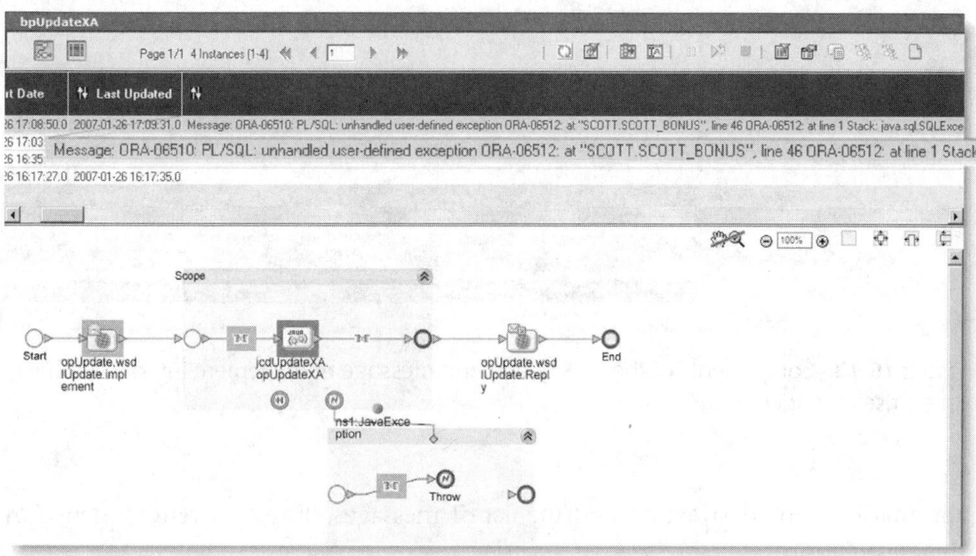

FIGURE 10-12: Persistence for monitoring an action at runtime

10.2.4 JMS Administration Tools

10.2.4.1 Sun SeeBeyond JMS IQ Manager

A graphical interface for monitoring and maintenance of Sun SeeBeyond JMS IQ Manager (Message Server), JMS Destinations, and messages is integrated into the Enterprise Manager Web User Interface. Figure 10-13 calls out components of that interface. Various aspects of the Enterprise Manager are exhibited in examples throughout both parts of the book. Specific aspects of the Enterprise Manager that can be used to manage and monitor the IQ Manager are discussed in this chapter to review and summarize available facilities.

The illustration in Figure 10-13 shows some aspects of JMS monitoring available through the Enterprise Manager. The connectivity map of each deployed enterprise application is shown in the explorer-like tree at the left. Expanding the tree from the Servers node down to the connectivity map and clicking on the connectivity map name will present the connectivity map graphic at the right. Any JMS Destinations present in the connectivity map are active components. Clicking one of the JMS Destinations in the connectivity map graphic will break the right pane into two sections, with the bottom section displaying the JMS Destination

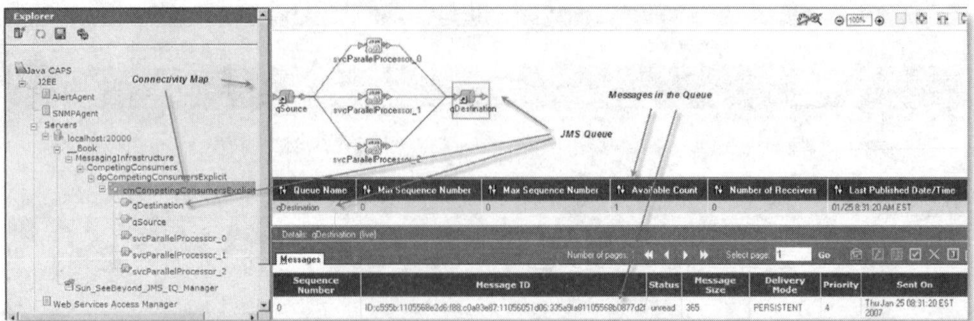

FIGURE 10-13: Components of the JMS queue and message management interface in the Enterprise Manager

summary for the destination and the list of messages, if any, currently queued in that destination.

Content of messages in the destination can be viewed if the payload type supports display of message content. Typically, text, bytes, and map messages can be viewed. Stream messages cannot be viewed. Figure 10-14 illustrates viewing the content of a text message.

Regardless of message type, message header properties can be viewed, including user-defined JMS header properties, if any, as shown in Figure 10-15.

Message content, for messages of suitable type, can be altered in place (text messages only), as illustrated in Figure 10-16.

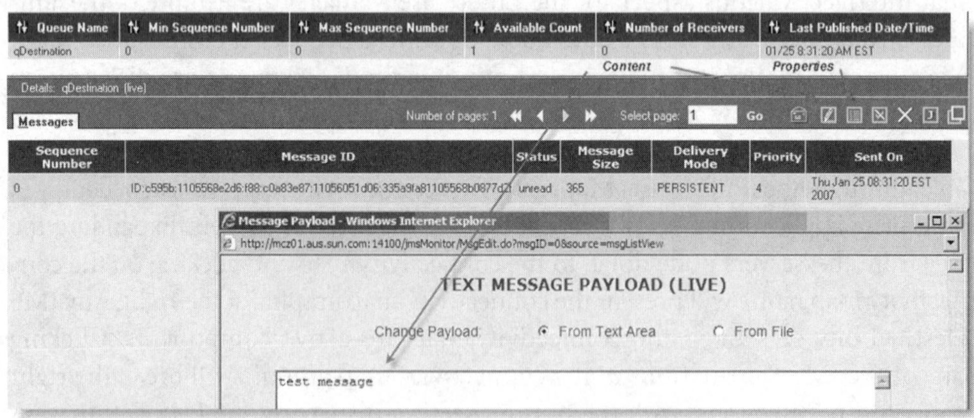

FIGURE 10-14: Content of a JMS text message

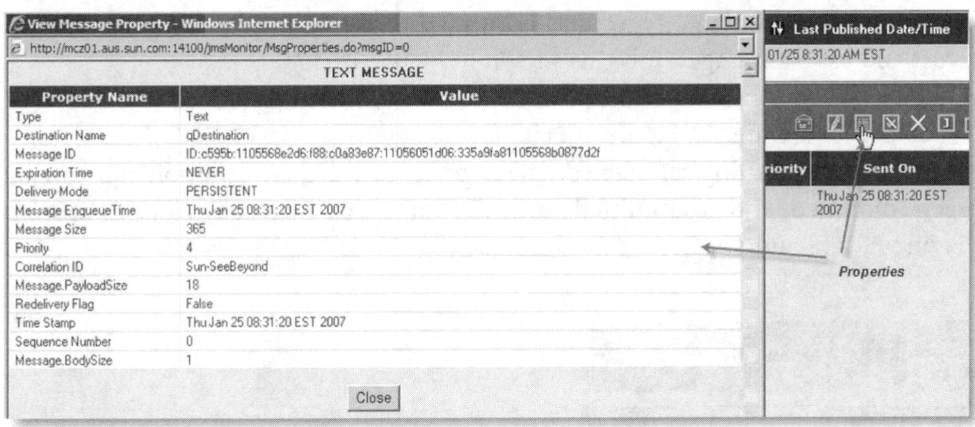

FIGURE 10-15: JMS message properties

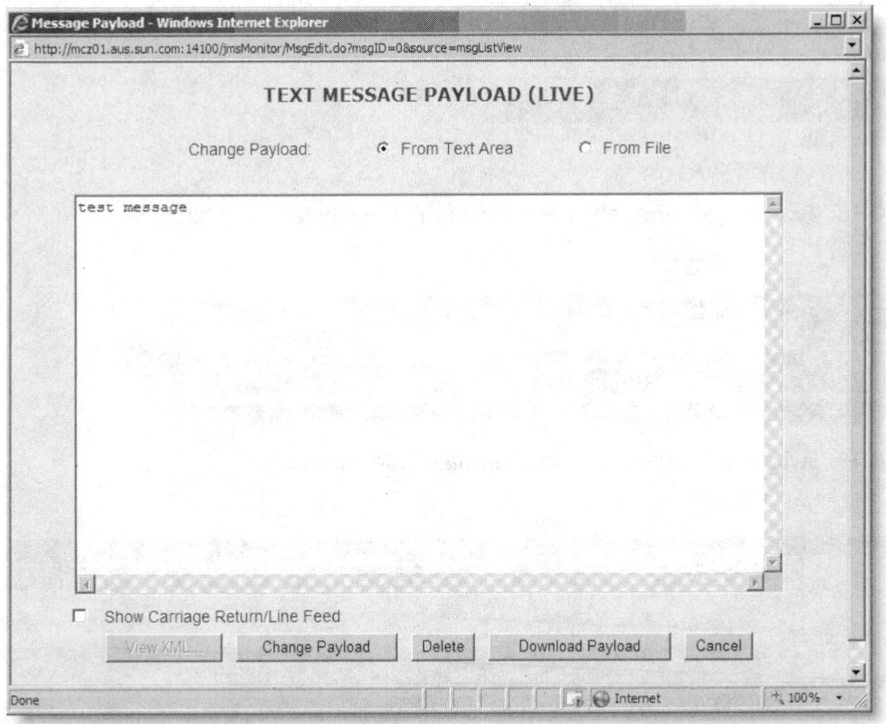

FIGURE 10-16: Modifying the content of a JMS text message using the Enterprise Manager

Messages of suitable type can be injected directly into the JMS Destination (text and bytes messages only), as shown in Figure 10-17.

Messages in the destination can be selected, individually or as a group, and deleted, as illustrated in Figure 10-18.

If JMS journaling is enabled, messages consumed by components can be seen, modified, and resubmitted from the Journaled Messages view, as seen in Figures 10-19 and 10-20.

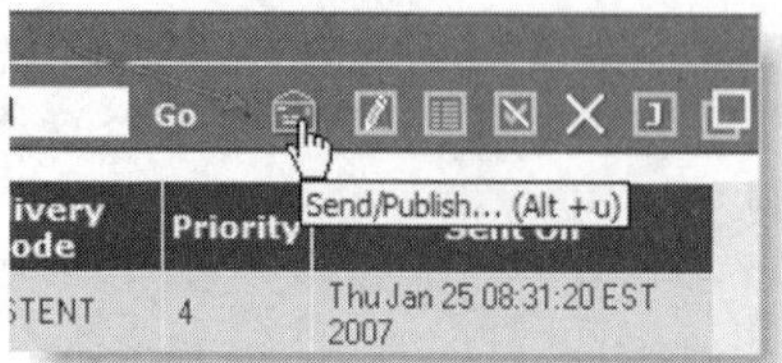

FIGURE 10-17: Injecting messages into JMS Destinations using the Enterprise Manager

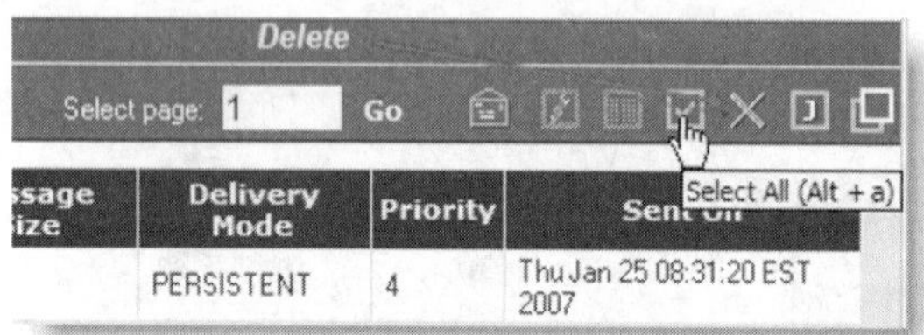

FIGURE 10-18: Tools for deleting JMS messages through the Enterprise Manager

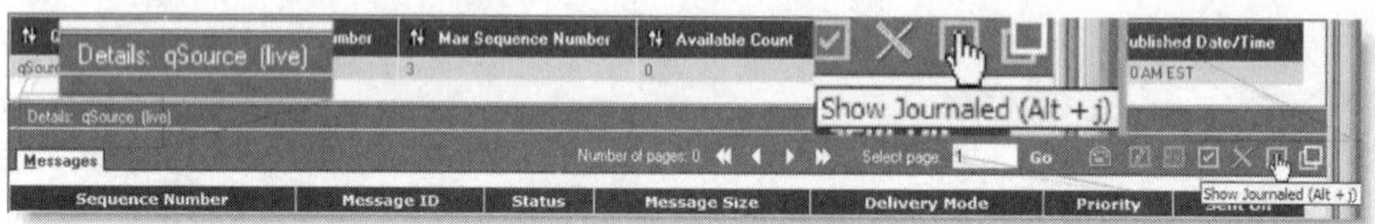

FIGURE 10-19: Switching between Live and Journaled Messages view

FIGURE 10-20: Viewing journaled messages

In addition to accessing JMS Destinations through their connectivity map representation, you can interact with JMS Destinations and subscribers through the Sun_SeeBeyond_JMS_IQ_Manager node in the explorer tree, as shown in Figure 10-21.

All queues and all topics as well as logging and alerts for the JMS Message Server can be seen and manipulated.

In Queues or Topics view, messages in a selected queue or topic can be manipulated much the same way as in the Connectivity Map view, as shown in Figure 10-22. In this view, queues and topic can also be created and deleted.

In Topics view, subscriptions to the topic can be deleted and durable subscriptions can be created, as shown in Figure 10-23.

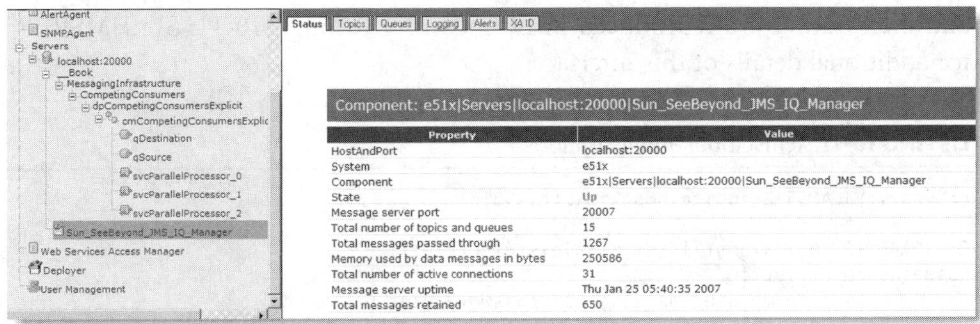

FIGURE 10-21: Selecting the Sun SeeBeyond JMS IQ Manager to manage the JMS Message Server and its queues, topics, messages, and so on

Status | Topics | **Queues** | Logging | Alerts | XA ID

Queue Name	Min Sequence Number	Max Sequence Number	Available Count	Number of Receivers	Last Published Date/Time
qDestination	3	4	2	0	01/25 10:18:25 AM EST
qC	0	0	0	0	NA
qSource	5	5	0	3	01/25 10:18:22 AM EST
qFeeder	0	0	0	0	NA
qZ	0	0	0	0	NA
qB	0	0	0	0	NA
qD	0	0	0	0	NA
qA	0	0	0	0	NA

Details: qDestination (live)

Messages — Number of pages: 1 — Select page: 1 Go

Sequence Number	Message ID	Status	Message Size	Delivery Mode	Priority	Sent On
3	ID:e8ebf:1105568e526:f88:c0a83e87:11056613422:335a9fa81105568b08778c1	unread	367	PERSISTENT	4	Thu Jan 25 10:11:55 EST 2007
4	ID:1a3d3:1105568e582:f88:c0a83e87:1105667290f:335a9fa81105568b0877823	unread	367	PERSISTENT	4	Thu Jan 25 10:18:25 EST 2007

FIGURE 10-22: Sun SeeBeyond IQ Manager Queues interface in the Enterprise Manager

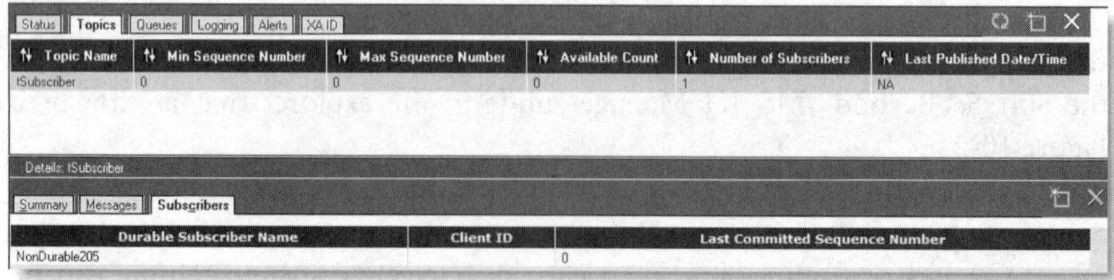

FIGURE 10-23: Sun SeeBeyond JMS IQ Manager Topics interface in the Enterprise Manager

In addition to the Web-based User Interface, Sun SeeBeyond JMS implementation provides a command-line utility, stcmsctrlutil, which can be used to manage and monitor the Sun SeeBeyond Message Server. The invocation syntax and options depend on the functionality that is required. Some sample commands and their output are reproduced in Listings 10-1 through 10-11. See [JMSREF] for additional details of this interface.

LISTING 10-1: stcmsctrlutil and its options

```
c:\>cd c:\JCAPS512\logicalhost\is\stcms\bin

C:\JCAPS512\logicalhost\is\stcms\bin>stcmsctrlutil -?
Usage: stcmsctrlutil
        [-username user name] [-userpassword user password]
        [--version] [-msversion] [-shutdown] [-status]
        [-topiclist] [-sublistall] [-sublistfortopic topic]
        [-topicstat topic] [-queuelist]
        [-recvlistforqueue queue] [-recvlistall]
        [-queuestat queue] [-host host-name]
        [-port port-number] [-offset port-offset]
        [-createtopic topic] [-deletetopic topic]
        [-createqueue queue] [-deletequeue queue]
        [-createsub topic sub client]
        [-deletesub topic sub client]
        [-qmsglist queue seqNo nmsgs]
        [-tmsglist topic seqNo nmsgs] [-qmessage queue seqNo]
        [-tmessage topic seqNo] [-deltmsg topic seqNo]
        [-delqmsg queue seqNo] [-changetmsg topic seqNo]
        [-changeqmsg queue seqNo] [-msgtype type]
        [-locktopic topic] [-unlocktopic topic]
        [-lockqueue queue] [-unlockqueue queue]
        [-tmimport topic seqNo nmsgs]
        [-qmimport queue seqNo nmsgs] [-journaler]
        [-archiver dir command] [-backup file date]
        [-timeout seconds] [-locale Unicode|locale-name]
        [-txlist] [-isjournalenabled] [--help]
```

Listing 10-2 demonstrates the command used to show the Sun SeeBeyond JMS IQ Manage status and the output of this command.

LISTING 10-2: JMS IQ Manager status

```
C:\JCAPS512\logicalhost\is\stcms\bin>stcmsctrlutil ^
    -username Administrator -userpassword STC ^
    -port 20007 -status
Up since: Thu Jan 25 05:40:35 2007
Memory used by data messages: 369.440 K(Bytes)
Total messages passed through: 1776
Total messages retained: 907
Number of message queue(s): 16
Number of connection(s): 36
Port number: 20007
Process ID: 3976
Server state: Ready and running...
```

Listing 10-3 shows the command used to list all JMS queues and its output.

LISTING 10-3: List of JMS queues

```
C:\JCAPS512\logicalhost\is\stcms\bin>stcmsctrlutil ^
        -username Administrator ^
        -userpassword STC -port 20007 -queuelist
Number Of Queue(s): 9
Queue List:
        qB
        qD
        qZ
        qA
        qFeeder
        qC
        STCMS.Alert
        qSource
        qDestination
```

Listing 10-4 shows the command used to list all receivers that receive from a particular queue and its output.

LISTING 10-4: Listing queue receivers

```
C:\JCAPS512\logicalhost\is\stcms\bin>stcmsctrlutil ^
        -username Administrator -userpassword STC ^
        -port 20007 -recvlistforqueue qSource
Number Of Receiver(s): 3
Receiver ID: 10543568
```

```
Receiver ServerID: 1432937827,374 (no name)
        Queue name: qSource
        Session ID: 1169664042339
        Committed messages: 1
        Uncommitted messages: 0
        Message selector:
Receiver ID: 10541648
Receiver ServerID: 1432937828,375 (no name)
        Queue name: qSource
        Session ID: 1169664042340
        Committed messages: 0
        Uncommitted messages: 0
        Message selector:
Receiver ID: 17186424
Receiver ServerID: 1432937829,376 (no name)
        Queue name: qSource
        Session ID: 1169664042341
        Committed messages: 0
        Uncommitted messages: 0
        Message selector:
```

Listing 10-5 shows the command used to obtain statistics for a particular queue and its output.

LISTING 10-5: Queue statistics

```
C:\JCAPS512\logicalhost\is\stcms\bin>stcmsctrlutil ^
        -username Administrator -userpassword STC ^
        -port 20007 -queuestat qSource
Queue Name: qSource
First enqueue time: 01252007:10:18:22
Last enqueue time: 01252007:10:18:22
Number of current receivers: 3
Message count: 0
Messages sent and committed: 5
Min sequence Number: 5
Max sequence Number: 5
Suspended: No
```

Listing 10-6 shows the command used to obtain a detailed list of all messages in a particular queue and its output.

LISTING 10-6: Detailed listing of messages in a queue

```
C:\JCAPS512\logicalhost\is\stcms\bin>stcmsctrlutil ^
        -username Administrator -userpassword STC ^
        -port 20007 -qmsglist qDestination 0 100
```

```
Number Of Messages(s): 2
Message[1]:
Message.SeqNo=3
Message.Size=367
Message.PayloadSize=20
Message.BodySize=1
Message.EnqueueTime=01242007:23:11:55
Message.JMSProperty.CI=Sun-SeeBeyond
Message.JMSProperty.DM=2
Message.JMSProperty.DN=qDestination
Message.JMSProperty.EX=0
Message.JMSProperty.MI=ID\:e8ebf\:1105568e526\:f88\:c0a83e87\:11056613422\:335a9fa
81105568b08778c1
Message.JMSProperty.PR=4
Message.JMSProperty.RD=False
Message.JMSProperty.TS=01242007:23:11:55
Message.JMSProperty.TY=Text

Message[2]:
Message.SeqNo=4
Message.Size=367
Message.PayloadSize=20
Message.BodySize=1
Message.EnqueueTime=01242007:23:18:25
Message.JMSProperty.CI=Sun-SeeBeyond
Message.JMSProperty.DM=2
Message.JMSProperty.DN=qDestination
Message.JMSProperty.EX=0
Message.JMSProperty.MI=ID\:1a3d3\:1105568e582\:f88\:c0a83e87\:1105667290f\:335a9fa
81105568b0877823
Message.JMSProperty.PR=4
Message.JMSProperty.RD=False
Message.JMSProperty.TS=01242007:23:18:25
Message.JMSProperty.TY=Text
```

Listing 10-7 gives an example of a command that shows content of the message with a specific sequence number in a specific queue and its output.

LISTING 10-7: List a message in a queue by sequence number

```
C:\JCAPS512\logicalhost\is\stcms\bin>stcmsctrlutil ^
       -username Administrator -userpassword STC -port 20007 ^
       -qmessage qDestination 3
test message 4
```

Listing 10-8 provides an example of a command that deletes a message with a specific sequence number from a specific queue and its output.

LISTING 10-8: Deleting a message from a queue by sequence number

```
C:\JCAPS512\logicalhost\is\stcms\bin>stcmsctrlutil ^
        -username Administrator -userpassword STC ^
        -port 20007 -delqmsg qDestination 3
Message: 3 has been deleted
```

Listing 10-9 shows an example command that can be used to determine if message journaling is enabled on the server and its output.

LISTING 10-9: Verifying whether journaling is enabled for a specific Sun SeeBeyond IQ Manager

```
C:\JCAPS512\logicalhost\is\stcms\bin>stcmsctrlutil ^
        -username Administrator -userpassword STC ^
        -port 20007 -isjournalenabled
Journal server is enabled
```

Most commands can be supplemented with the "–journaler" flag to display information about the message journal if journaling is enabled. For example, the command in Listing 10-10 displays queue statistics for the journaled queue.

LISTING 10-10: Journaled queue statistics

```
C:\JCAPS512\logicalhost\is\stcms\bin>stcmsctrlutil ^
        -username Administrator -userpassword STC ^
        -port 20007 -journaler -queuestat qSource
Queue Name: qSource
First enqueue time: 01252007:08:52:24
Last enqueue time: 01252007:10:18:22
Number of current receivers: 0
Message count: 0
Messages sent and committed: 0
Min sequence Number: 4
Max sequence Number: 4
```

Listing 10-11 shows a command used to list journaled queues and its output.

LISTING 10-11: Listing of journaled queues

```
C:\JCAPS512\logicalhost\is\stcms\bin>stcmsctrlutil ^
        -username Administrator -userpassword STC ^
        -port 20007 -journaler -queuelist
Number Of Queue(s): 7
```

```
Queue List:
        qChildOut
        qChildrenIn
        qSource
        qFeeder
        qA
        qC
        qEater
```

In addition to obtaining information about JMS Destinations and messages, creating and removing JMS Destinations and messages, modifying queued messages, and operating on journaled information, the utility allows backing up of live and journaled messages and browsing backup archives.

[JMSREF] discusses the use of the stcmsctrlutil utility with additional examples.

Sun SeeBeyond JMS Message Server can also be monitored and managed using the JMS interface, discussed later in this chapter. The following JMX MBean, under the com.sun.appserv domain, provides access to much the same functionality as the Enterprise Manager User Interface and the stcmsctrlutil:

```
type=messaging-server-admin-
mbean,jmsservertype=stcms,name=Sun_SeeBeyond_JMS_IQ_Manager
```

Which method of monitoring and managing the Sun SeeBeyond IQ Manager is the most appropriate will depend on the circumstances. The Enterprise Manager is easy to use and eminently visual. The stcmsctrlutils can be used in command scripts. The JMX interface can be used in Java-based applications or JMX-capable enterprise monitoring and management tools.

10.2.5 Event Notification with Alert Agent

As Java CAPS components are started or stopped, as components report problems, and as solutions explicitly log alerts, events occur and event messages are recorded in the Event Database. The Enterprise Manager User Interface and the Enterprise Manager Web Service Interface would be used to view, "observe," and "resolve" alerts. Both interfaces are passive in that an administrator or a programmed component must explicitly invoke an interface to access the Alert Database. This implies reactive and polling operation. For solutions that must react to events in real time, or near real time, automatic notification of events as they occur is required. Sun SeeBeyond Alert Agent (AlertAgent) is the component that provides this kind of functionality. Alert Agent receives event notifications in real time and, based on its filtering and notification configuration, delivers alert messages to external destinations using Simple Mail Transfer Protocol (SMTP), JMS, or Simple Network Management Protocol (SNMP) technologies. While Alert Agent can be used standalone to provide real-time notifications to operations and administration staff directly, it can also provide the integration of Java CAPS operational notification infrastructure with third-party enterprise-monitoring systems.

10.2.5.1 Configuring Alert Agent

When installed, Alert Agent is configured through the AlertAgent node of the Java CAPS Enterprise Manager, as shown in Figure 10-24.

Alert Agent receives all alerts as they occur. Alert Agent configuration determines what it does with alerts, if anything.

The Alert Agent Channel is the mechanism through which alerts are delivered to a destination.

Note
Unless at least one channel is defined, no notifications can be defined and therefore no alerts will be delivered.

Three types of channels can be configured: SMTP (electronic mail), JMS, and SNMP (network management).

An SNMP Channel always delivers to the SNMP Agent; therefore, there is little point in defining more than one channel of this type. This channel has no additional configuration; see Figure 10-25.

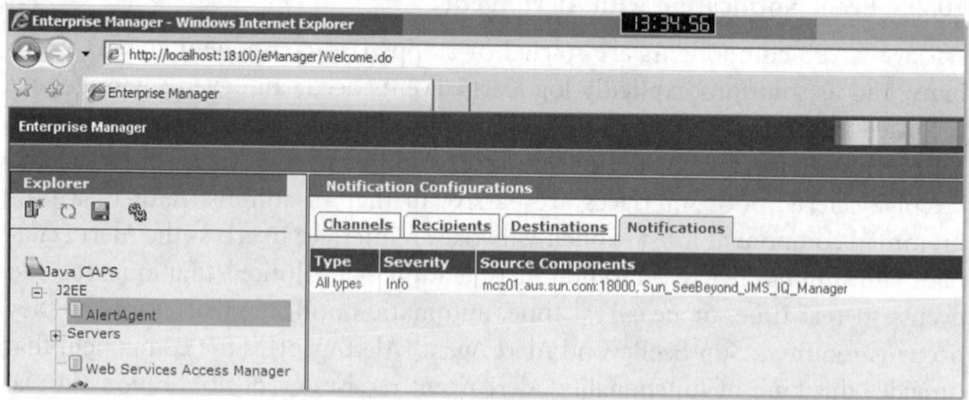

FIGURE 10-24: AlertAgent in the Enterprise Manager

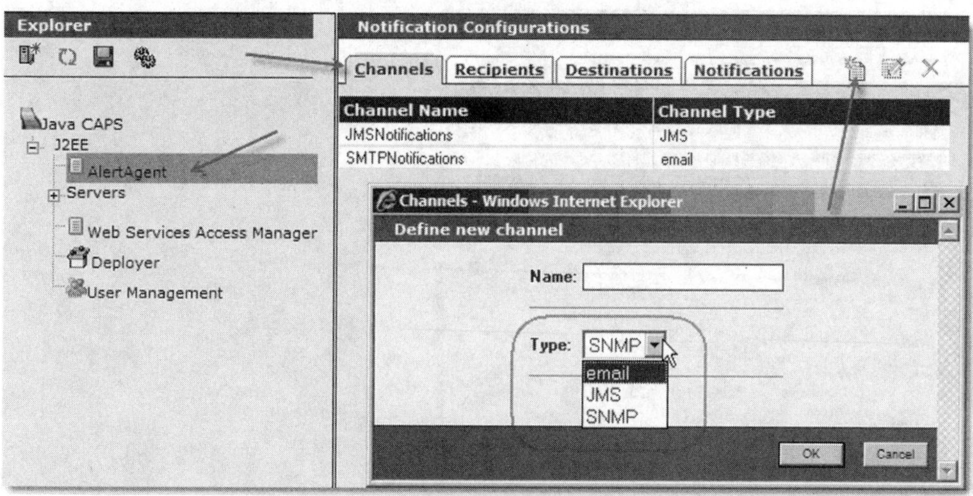

FIGURE 10-25: AlertAgent SNMP Channel configuration

Configuring an SNMP Channel allows Java CAPS Alerts to be delivered to a third-party enterprise-monitoring system that supports SNMP v2 Traps. Note that exactly one recipient that uses the SNMP Channel must be configured, and exactly one destination and one or more notifications must be configured, before alerts are delivered to the SNMP Agent. This is discussed later.

Any number of SMTP Channels can be defined. Each such channel would typically be configured to use a different mail server account. Only one SMTP Channel per mail server account is required. Any number of mail recipients can be configured as alert recipients using one mail server account. This configuration is performed using the Recipients tab, discussed later.

Each "e-mail" channel requires additional configuration. The SMTP Server's host, port, account, and password, as well as whether or not to use Secure Sockets Layer (SSL) for the transport, must be configured as necessary; see Figure 10-26. Some SMTP Servers do not require login for sending mail and therefore do not require the account to be configured.

By default, the sender of alerts is preconfigured to be JavaCAPSAlertAgent @sun.com. Sites may wish to change this to something more appropriate for them. The property senderEmailAddress is configured in the properties file:

```
<EMInstallRoot>/emanager/server/monitor/config/alertagent.properties
```

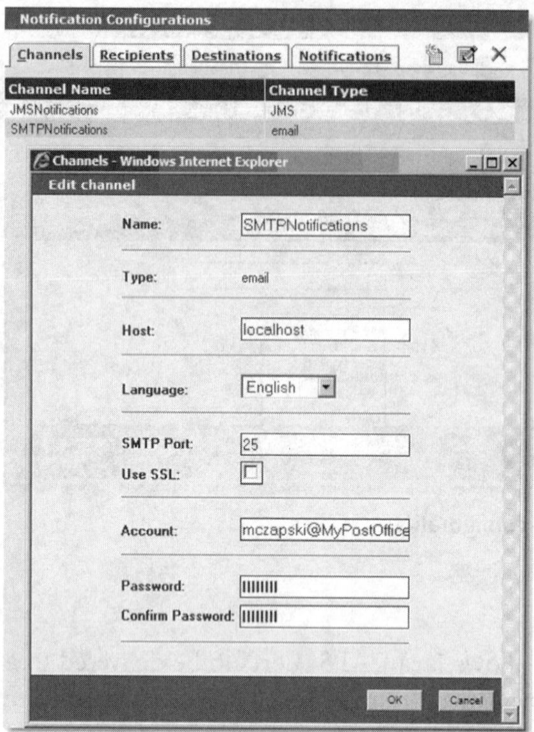

FIGURE 10-26: AlertAgent SMTP Channel configuration

Configuring one or more SMTP Channels allows Java CAPS Alerts to be delivered to electronic mail recipients. Note that one or more recipients that use the SMTP Channel must be configured, and at least one destination and notification must be configured to use the recipient, before alerts are delivered to the SMTP Server. This is discussed later.

The JMS Channel defines an association between the Alert Agent JMS Channel and the JMS Message Server to which to deliver alerts using JMS. One JMS Channel would be defined for each different JMS Message Server instance, as shown in Figure 10-27. The JMS Message Server would ideally be different from the one used by the domain being monitored.

Configuring one or more JMS Channels allows Java CAPS Alerts to be delivered to JMS-based infrastructure. Note that one or more recipients that use the JMS Channel must be configured, and at least one destination and notification must be configured to use the recipient, before alerts are delivered to the JMS Message Server. This is discussed later.

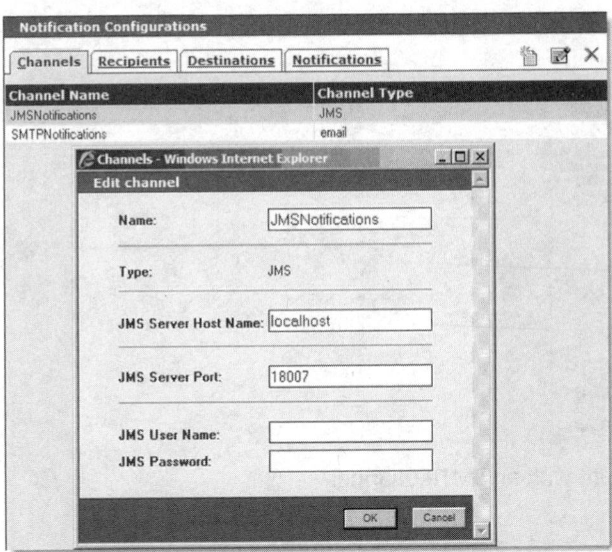

FIGURE 10-27: AlertAgent JMS Channel configuration

Once all channels are defined, they can be used to define alert recipients. Except for the SNMP Channel, which only reasonably needs one recipient, there can be one or more recipients using each of the SMTP and JMS Channels.

Each SMTP Recipient defines the association between the SMTP Channel, defined earlier, and an electronic mail address of a recipient to whom electronic mail will be sent using the mail server and account defined by the SMTP Channel. This is illustrated in Figure 10-28.

Each JMS Recipient defines the association between the JMS Channel, defined earlier, and the JMS topic to which alert messages will be sent using the JMS Message Server defined by the JMS Channel, as illustrated in Figure 10-29.

Note that the "Recipient Address" in this case is the name of the JMS topic. If the topic does not have at least one durable subscriber or at least one active non-durable subscriber, all messages delivered to the topic will be silently discarded by the JMS Message Server.

For a SNMP Channel the Recipient Address value will be the literal "SNMP."

Whereas channels and recipients together define alert delivery endpoints, an Alert Agent Destination is a logical grouping of recipients. The destination name is used in configuring notifications, discussed later. The collection of recipients defined through the destination will receive the same alerts. A destination can include any number of recipients of different types.

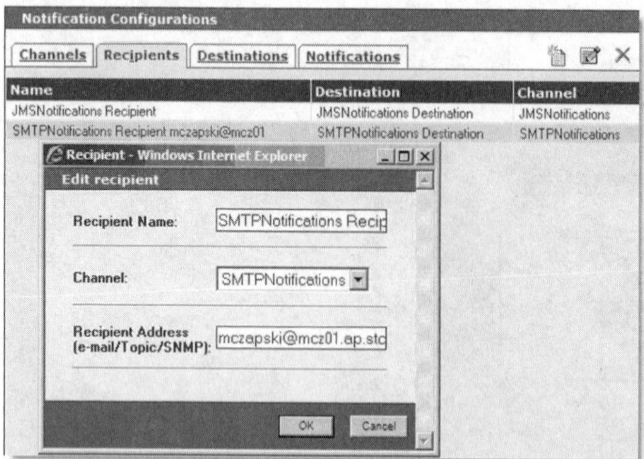

Figure 10-28: Associating a recipient with an SMTP Channel

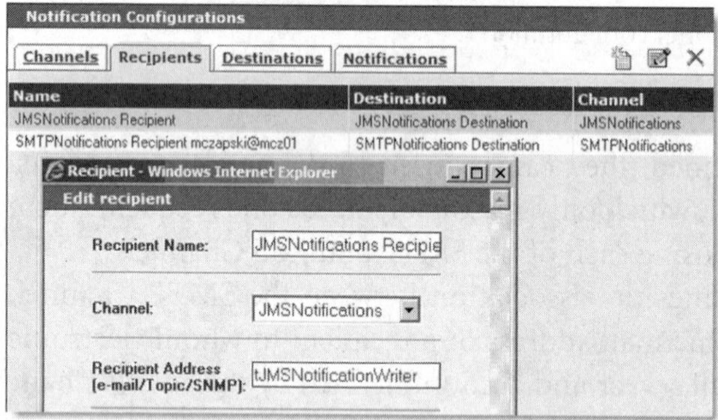

Figure 10-29: Associating a recipient with a JMS Channel

Alert Agent Notification defines an association between an alert filter and a destination to which to send alerts that satisfy the filter criteria. While Alert Agent documentation does not use the term filter, Notification is a filtering expression combined with the destination.

Notification allows filtering of alerts by type, severity, and component.

The all-encompassing type CODE-00001 denotes all alert types. Alert types are added by Java CAPS products at installation time and are stored in various property files under

```
<EMInstallRoot>/emanager/server/monitor/alertcodes
```

Note
Not all endpoints support alerts. See property files in the alertcodes directory and its subdirectories for property files corresponding to various endpoints and alert values they define.

Note
Stopping and starting a Web Services provider generates no alerts.

Note
Starting and stopping eInsight Business Processes generates no alerts.

Some of the alert types, corresponding to components in the installation used for the examples in this book, and alert message templates used by them, are enumerated in Table 10-1.

TABLE 10-1: Alert Codes for Selected Components

Alert Type	*Alert Text*
CODE-0001	All types.
BATCH-FTP-EWAY-CONFIG-FAILED	(BATCH): Batch FTP eWay configuration error, message=[{0}].
BATCH-FTP-EWAY-CONN-ACQUIRE-FAILED	(BATCH): Batch FTP eWay error when acquiring connection from pool, message=[{0}].
BATCH-FTP-EWAY-CONN-INIT-FAILED	(BATCH): Batch FTP eWay connection initialization failed, message=[{0}].
BATCH-FTP-EWAY-CONNECTION-FAILED	(BATCH): Batch FTP eWay connection failed, method=[{0}], message=[{1}].
BATCH-FTP-EWAY-ERROR	(BATCH): Batch FTP eWay error, message=[{0}].
BATCH-FTP-EWAY-OPERATION-ERROR	(BATCH): Batch FTP eWay error when doing data transfer operation in [{0}], message=[{1}].

(continues)

Table 10-1: Alert Codes for Selected Components *(continued)*

Alert Type	***Alert Text***
BATCH-INBOUND-EWAY-CONFIG-FAILED	(BATCH): Batch Inbound eWay configuration error, message=[{0}].
BATCH-INBOUND-EWAY-ERROR	(BATCH): Batch Inbound eWay error, message=[{0}].
BATCH-INBOUND-EWAY-RUNNING	(BATCH): Batch Inbound eWay is running.
BATCH-INBOUND-EWAY-STARTED	(BATCH): Batch Inbound eWay is started.
BATCH-INBOUND-EWAY-STOPPED	(BATCH): Batch Inbound eWay is stopped.
BATCH-INBOUND-EWAY-STOPPING	(BATCH): Batch Inbound eWay is being stopped.
BATCH-INBOUND-EWAY-SUSPENDED	(BATCH): Batch Inbound eWay is suspended.
BATCH-INBOUND-EWAY-SUSPENDING	(BATCH): Batch Inbound eWay is suspending.
BATCH-LOCALFILE-EWAY-CONFIG-FAILED	(BATCH): Batch Local File eWay configuration error, message=[{0}].
BATCH-LOCALFILE-EWAY-CONN-ACQUIRE-FAILED	(BATCH): Batch Local File eWay error when acquiring connection from pool, message=[{0}].
BATCH-LOCALFILE-EWAY-CONN-INIT-FAILED	(BATCH): Batch Local File eWay connection initialization failed, message=[{0}].
BATCH-LOCALFILE-EWAY-ERROR	(BATCH): Batch Local File eWay error, message=[{0}].
BATCH-LOCALFILE-EWAY-OPERATION-ERROR	(BATCH): Batch Local File eWay error when doing file operation in [{0}], message=[{1}].
BATCH-REC-EWAY-CONFIG-FAILED	(BATCH): Batch Record eWay configuration error, message=[{0}].
BATCH-REC-EWAY-CONN-ACQUIRE-FAILED	(BATCH): Batch Record eWay error when acquiring connection from pool, message=[{0}].
BATCH-REC-EWAY-CONN-INIT-FAILED	(BATCH): Batch Record eWay connection initialization failed, message=[{0}].
BATCH-REC-EWAY-ERROR	(BATCH): Batch Record eWay error, message=[{0}].

TABLE 10-1: Alert Codes for Selected Components *(continued)*

Alert Type	*Alert Text*
BATCH-REC-EWAY-OPERATION-ERROR	(BATCH): Batch Record eWay error when doing record operation in [{0}], message=[{1}].
COL-00001	(COL): Collaboration running.
COL-00002	(COL): Collaboration stopped.
COL-00003	(COL): Collaboration user-defined alert.
DBCOMMON-CANNOT-GET-ISOLATION-LEVEL	(DBCOMMON): Unable to get isolationLevel for the transaction. Reason: [{0}].
DBCOMMON-CONNECT-FAILED000001	(DBCOMMON): Failed to connect to database {0} on host {1}. Reason: The Pooled connection could not be allocated: [{2}].
DBCOMMON-CONNECT-FAILED000002	(DBCOMMON): Operation failed because of a database connection error. Reason: [{0}].
DBCOMMON-CONNECT-FAILED000003	(DBCOMMON): Connection handle not usable. Reason: [{0}].
DBCOMMON-XACONNECT-FAILED000001	(DBCOMMON): Failed to connect to database {0} on host {1}. The XA connection could not be allocated: Reason [{2}].
DBCOMMON-XAEND-FAILED000001	(DBCOMMON): XAEnd failed. Reason: [{0}].
DBCOMMON-XARESOURCE-FAILED000001	(DBCOMMON): Unable to get XAResource for the database. Reason: [{0}].
DBCOMMON-XASTART-FAILED000001	(DBCOMMON): Unable to perform XAStart for the connection. Reason: [{0}].
DEFAULT-NOTSPECIFIED	(DEFAULT): Message code is not specified.
ETL-00001	(ETL): Execution of eTL Collaboration; {collabName} is started. The CollabId is {collabId}.
ETL-00002	(ETL): Execution of eTL Collaboration {collabName} is completed. The CollabId is {collabId}.

(continues)

Table 10-1: Alert Codes for Selected Components *(continued)*

Alert Type	*Alert Text*
ETL-00003	(ETL): Critical error encountered while executing eTL Collaboration {collabName}. The CollabId is {collabId}. {exception}.
ETL-00004	(ETL): Transformation for Target table {targetTableName} started. The CollabId is {collabId}, Execution Id is {executionId}.
ETL-00005	(ETL): Transformation for Target table {targetTableName} completed. The CollabId is {collabId}, Execution Id is {executionId}.
ETL-00006	(ETL): Critical error encountered while executing transformation for Target table {targetTableName}. The CollabId is {collabId}, Execution Id is {executionId}. {exception}.
EWAY-ERROR	(EWAY): Eway error for link {0} encountered.
EWAY-RUNNING	(EWAY): Eway for link {0} now running.
EWAY-STARTED	(EWAY): Eway for link {0} started.
EWAY-STOPPED	(EWAY): Eway for link {0} stopped.
EWAY-STOPPING	(EWAY): Eway for link {0} stopping.
EWAY-SUSPENDED	(EWAY): Eway for link {0} suspended.
EWAY-SUSPENDING	(EWAY): Eway for link {0} suspending.
FILE-ASCANTCREATEINPUTDIR000004	(FILE): Unable to create input directory {0}.
FILE-ASINPUTDIRNONEXISTENT000002	(FILE): Input directory {0} does not exist. Creating the directory.
FILE-ASINPUTDIRNOTDIR000003	(FILE): Input directory {0} is not a directory.
FILE-ASRENAMEFAILED000001	(FILE): Failed attempting to rename input file {0}.
FILE-CANTWRITEOUTPUTDIR000005	(FILE): Error writing to output directory {0}.
FILE-CANTWRITEOUTPUTFILE000006	(FILE): Error writing to output file {0}.

TABLE 10-1: Alert Codes for Selected Components *(continued)*

Alert Type	*Alert Text*
FTP-SSL-EWAY-CONFIG-FAILED	(FTP): Batch FTP Over SSL eWay configuration error, message=[{0}].
FTP-SSL-EWAY-CONN-ACQUIRE-FAILED	(FTP): Batch FTP Over SSL eWay error when acquiring connection from connection pool, message=[{0}].
FTP-SSL-EWAY-CONN-INIT-FAILED	(FTP): Batch FTP Over SSL eWay connection initialization error, message=[{0}].
FTP-SSL-EWAY-CONNECTION-FAILED	(FTP): Batch FTP Over SSL eWay connection failed, method=[{0}], message=[{1}].
FTP-SSL-EWAY-ERROR	(FTP): Batch FTP Over SSL eWay error, message=[{0}].
FTP-SSL-EWAY-OPERATION-ERROR	(FTP): Batch FTP Over SSL eWay error when doing data transfer operation in [{0}], message=[{1}].
HTTPCLIENTEWAY-CONFIG-FAILED000001	(HTTPCLIENTEWAY): Configuration error encountered for HTTP Client eWay.
HTTPCLIENTEWAY-CONNECT-FAILED000002	(HTTPCLIENTEWAY): Failed to prepare the HTTP Client agent for establishing the connection to the HTTP server.
HTTPCLIENTEWAY-GET-FAILED000004	(HTTPCLIENTEWAY): Failed on HTTP GET request to URL {0}.
HTTPCLIENTEWAY-POST-FAILED000005	(HTTPCLIENTEWAY): Failed on HTTP POST request to URL {0}.
HTTPCLIENTEWAY-URL-FAILED000003	(HTTPCLIENTEWAY): Invalid URL specified {0}.
HTTPSERVEREWAY-REQUEST-FAILED000001	(HTTPSERVEREWAY): Failed to process the POST or GET request.
IS-00001	(IS): Integration Server started.
IS-00002	(IS): Integration Server stopped.

(continues)

Table 10-1: Alert Codes for Selected Components *(continued)*

Alert Type	*Alert Text*
MS-00009	(MS): Message Server has reached the throttling threshold of total number of messages.
MS-00010	(MS): Message Server has moved below the throttling threshold of total number of messages.
MS-00011	(MS): Message Server has reached the throttling threshold for message destinations.
MS-00012	(MS): Message Server has moved below the throttling threshold for message destinations.
SCP-EWAY-CONFIG-FAILED	(SCP): Batch SCP eWay configuration error, message=[{0}].
SCP-EWAY-CONN-ACQUIRE-FAILED	(SCP): Batch SCP eWay error when acquiring connection from connection pool, message=[{0}].
SCP-EWAY-CONN-INIT-FAILED	(SCP): Batch SCP eWay connection initialization error, message=[{0}].
SCP-EWAY-CONNECTION-FAILED	(SCP): Batch SCP eWay connection failed, method=[{0}], message=[{1}].
SCP-EWAY-ERROR	(SCP): Batch SCP eWay error, message=[{0}].
SCP-EWAY-OPERATION-ERROR	(SCP): Batch SCP eWay error when doing data transfer operation in [{0}], message=[{1}].
SFTP-EWAY-CONFIG-FAILED	(SFTP): Batch SFTP eWay configuration error, message=[{0}].
SFTP-EWAY-CONN-ACQUIRE-FAILED	(SFTP): Batch SFTP eWay error when acquiring connection from connection pool, message=[{0}].
SFTP-EWAY-CONN-INIT-FAILED	(SFTP): Batch SFTP eWay connection initialization error, message=[{0}].
SFTP-EWAY-CONNECTION-FAILED	(SFTP): Batch SFTP eWay connection failed, method=[{0}], message=[{1}].
SFTP-EWAY-ERROR	(SFTP): Batch SFTP eWay error, message=[{0}].

TABLE 10-1: Alert Codes for Selected Components *(continued)*

Alert Type	*Alert Text*
SFTP-EWAY-OPERATION-ERROR	(SFTP): Batch SFTP eWay error when doing data transfer operation in [{0}], message=[{1}].
SNMP-00001	(SNMP): SNMP Agent has been configured.
SNMP-00002	(SNMP): SNMP Agent has not been configured.
SNMP-00003	(SNMP): SNMP Agent is running.
SNMP-00004	(SNMP): SNMP Agent has stopped.
SNMP-00005	(SNMP): SNMP Agent is not installed.

A JMS Recipient definition associates a JMS Message Server and a JMS topic within that server. When used as part of the destination and notification definitions, the JMS topic on the specified JMS Message Server will receive alert messages. It is expected that at some point a solution that processes these alerts will be developed and deployed.

Severity filters ensure that only alerts of specific severity, and more severe, are included in notifications.

Given a project hierarchy, all of the components, or only selected components, can be included in the notification definition. Figure 10-30 illustrates component selection from the component hierarchy.

Finally, once filtering criteria are specified, one or more destinations can be specified to identify notification targets, as illustrated in Figure 10-31.

By defining multiple recipients, destinations, and notification filters, a site can develop an event notification schema of desired complexity.

Some problems, such as database connection credential issues, arise before Java Collaborations are invoked. Alert Agent can be used to provide real-time notification of the occurrence of these kinds of problems.

Chapter 8, section 8.2.2.1, "Simple Alert Processor for a JMS Channel," and section 8.2.2.2, "Catching 'Uncatchable' Exceptions," in Part II provide examples of Java CAPS solutions that handle alerts sent to a JMS Channel by the Alert Agent, and catch and process "uncatchable" exceptions, ones thrown by code that surrounds Java collaborations.

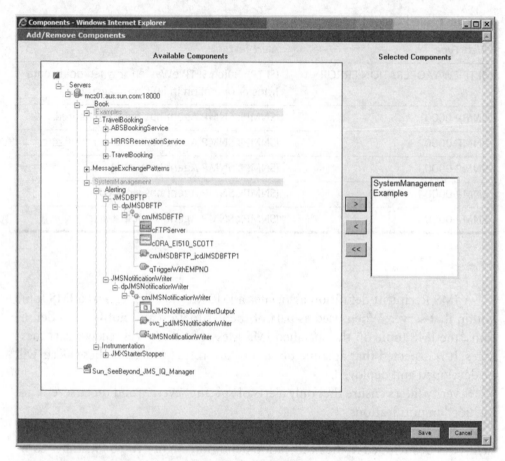

FIGURE 10-30: Selection of component from component hierarchy

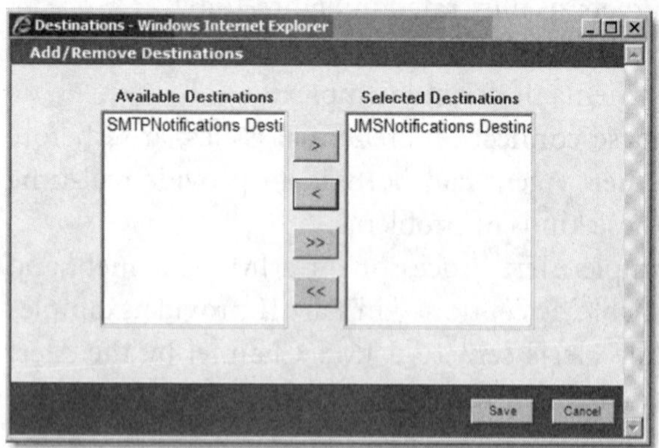

FIGURE 10-31: Selecting notification targets

10.2.5.2 Summary

Java CAPS Alert Agent can be used to forward notable events, generated by Java CAPS infrastructure and solutions, to electronic mail, JMS, and SNMP recipients in real time. By creating appropriate notification definitions, sites can establish convenient early warning systems, minimizing "time to discover" and "time to resolve" when problems occur. In case of exceptions relating to inability to establish a connection with an external resource, for container-managed connections, Alert Agent may be the only way to alert operations staff of an occurrence of a connection problem. If Alert Agent–based infrastructure is configured, components of Java CAPS solutions can explicitly generate custom alerts, to be handled in the same manner as other alerts, to notify operations and administration staff or enterprise-monitoring systems about business-level events of interest.

10.2.6 SNMP Agent

By Peter Vaneris

While Java CAPS offers a number of methods to monitor and manage its solutions, an enterprise may already have a monitoring and management solution in place, and may require that Java CAPS monitoring and management be integrated into it. Enterprise monitoring and management solutions typically provide support for SNMP. Because Java CAPS also supports SNMP, it is one of the most obvious ways to integrate Java CAPS into an enterprise management system framework.

The Java CAPS SNMP Agent provides SNMP support for Java CAPS. The SNMP Agent is an optional subcomponent of the Java CAPS Enterprise Manager, and while it has its own configuration, it depends on the Java CAPS Enterprise Manager. In addition, if you want to filter your SNMP Traps before they are sent by the Java CAPS SNMP Agent, then you need the Java CAPS Alert Agent.

Note
Alert Agent is only used if event filtering is required. The default behavior (Auto-Routing enabled) is for the SNMP Agent to send all Java CAPS Enterprise Manager Events as SNMP Traps.

The Java CAPS Alert Agent can be used for event filtering prior to SNMP Trap sending by the SNMP Agent. By default, Auto-Routing enabled, the SNMP Agent receives all alerts generated in the Java CAPS Enterprise Manager. This

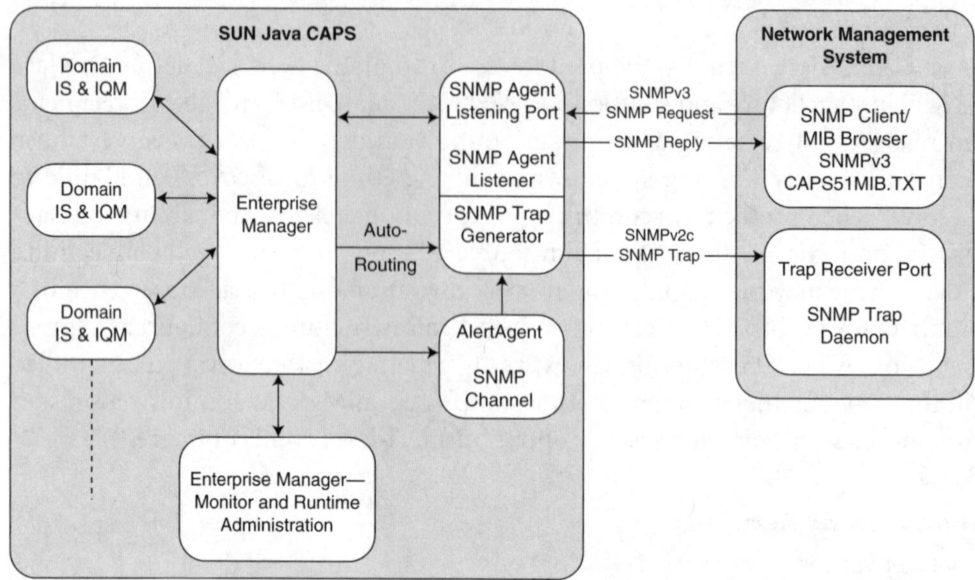

FIGURE 10-32: SNMP communication between Java CAPS and the network management system

includes all events generated by "managed" Integration Servers. To send only filtered alerts, you can use the Alert Agent by specifying which alerts are to go to the SNMP Channel and disabling Auto-Routing in the SNMP Agent configuration.

Note
SNMP Agent configuration changes require an SNMP Agent Restart. Alert Agent configuration changes are dynamic.

The diagram in Figure 10-32 shows the SNMP communications between Java CAPS SNMP Agent and a typical network management system.

The enterprise management system can proactively manage Java CAPS components by sending SNMP version 3 requests to the Java CAPS SNMP Agent Listening Port and processing SNMP replies.

Java CAPS supports passive monitoring by an enterprise management system by sending SNMP Traps to the enterprise management system's SNMP Trap daemon.

10.2.6.1 SNMP Agent Configuration

SNMP Agent is an optional component. Since it can depend on the Alert Agent, another optional component, both the SNMP Agent and optionally the Alert Agent must be installed and configured. See Chapter 3 of the SNMP Agent User's Guide and Chapter 4 of the Alert Agent User Guide for installation details.

Once installed, both the Alert Agent and the SNMP Agent nodes are added to the J2EE hierarchy in the JCAPS Enterprise Manager; see Figure 10-33. To gain access to the SNMP Agent's configuration, expand the SNMP Agent node and click on the Configuration tab.

Settings enumerated in Table 10-2 furnish additional information.

10.2.6.2 SNMP Agent Traps

Traps to be sent by the SNMP Agent are configured in the Java CAPS Enterprise Manager as per the SNMP Agent and Alert Agent documentation. The diagram in Figure 10-34 shows the flow of SNMP Trap Events.

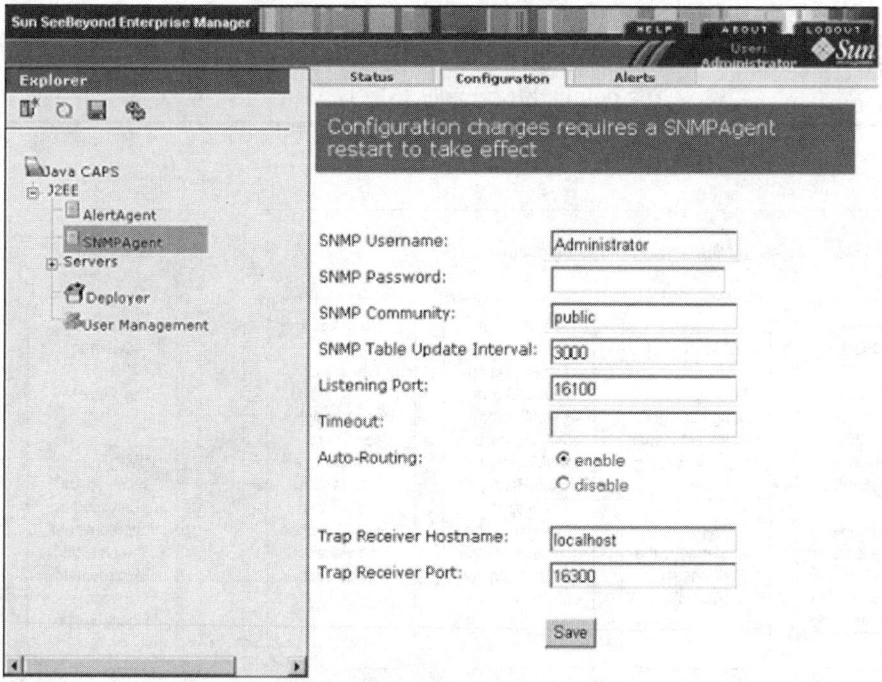

FIGURE 10-33: SNMP Agent configuration

TABLE 10-2: SNMP Agent Configuration Properties

SNMP Username	SNMPv3 name. (Note that SNMP Username and SNMP Password must match with an existing fully privileged user and password in the Enterprise Manager.)
SNMP Password	This sets both the SNMPv3 authPassword and the SNMPv3 privPassword. (Note that SNMP Username and SNMP Password must match with an existing fully privileged user and password in the Enterprise Manager.)
SNMP Community	Sets the SNMPv2 Trap Community. It also sets the SNMPv1 and SNMPv2 readCommunity and writeCommunity.
Listening Port	Listening port for SNMPAgent. Make sure this port is not already in use.
Auto-Routing	Enable: All events are sent as SNMP Traps. Disable: Only Alert Agent SNMP Channel Events are sent as SNMP Traps.
Trap Receiver Hostname	Hostname or IP address of your network management system.
Trap Receiver Port	Trap daemon port for your network management system. The default is normally 162.

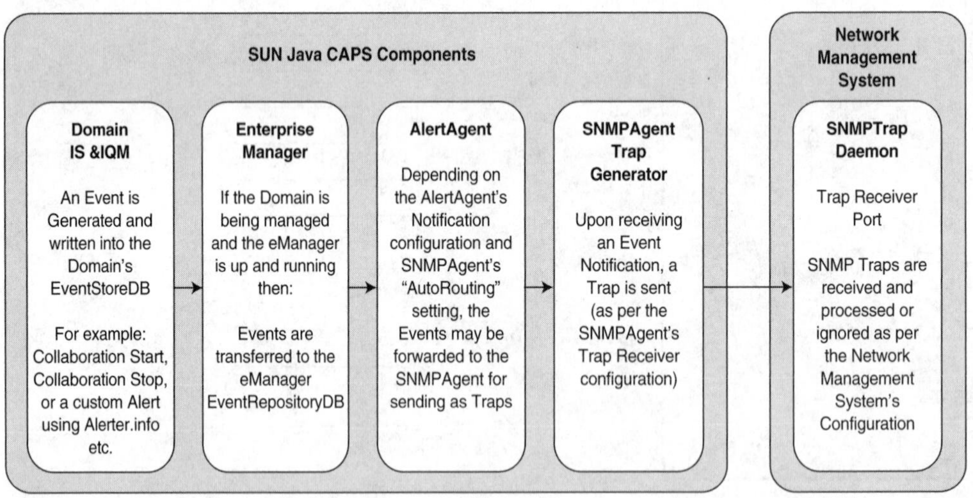

FIGURE 10-34: Flow of SNMP Trap Events

The Java CAPS SNMP Agent sends events as SNMPv2c Traps to the enterprise management system. The only major decision you need to make is where to do the filtering of events: in Java CAPS or a third-party network management system.

- The answer will probably depend on where your organization's experience is and your IT department's direction. You will need to work this out yourself.
- Depending on the direction you wish to follow, you will need to configure one of the following:
  - To filter events in Java CAPS, disable Auto-Routing and fully configure the Alert Agent.
  - To filter events in your network management system, enable Auto-Routing and disable all SNMP Channel notifications in the Alert Agent.

Note
It is possible to enable Auto-Routing and to configure the Alert Agent SNMP Channel. In this case, you will produce SNMP Traps for all events plus the Alert Agent–configured events. You will receive Alert Agent–configured events more than once.

Selecting Components in Alert Agent → Notifications → Components

If you select the Connectivity Map, only collaboration events will be matched.

If you select the Deployment Profile or above, you will match both collaboration events and eWay events.

If you select the Integration Server, then you will match collaboration, eWay, and JMS events.

Internal SNMP Events

With Auto-Routing disabled, no SNMP Agent events will be sent.

With Auto-Routing enabled, only SNMP Agent Running events will be sent.

The SNMP Alerts tab only lists SNMP Agent events—for example, SNMP Agent Running or SNMP Agent Stopped.

An example of a Java CAPS SNMP Agent Trap, captured by a packet sniffer, is shown in Figure 10-35.

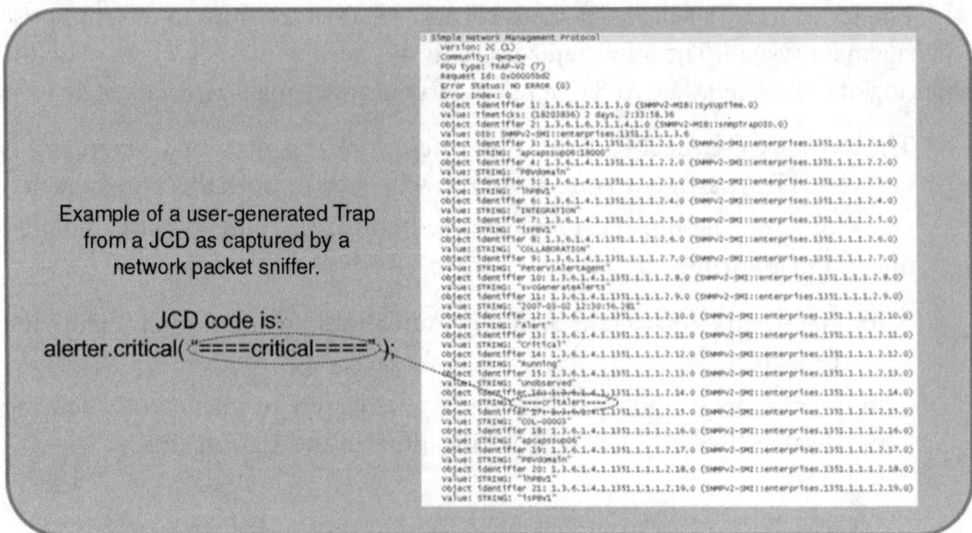

FIGURE 10-35: A SNMP Agent Trap

10.2.6.3 SNMP Agent Listener

The SNMP Agent Listener is configured in the Java CAPS Enterprise Manager as per the SNMP Agent documentation. It exposes a number of properties for management using SNMPv3 requests.

The diagram in Figure 10-36 shows the flow of SNMP management and monitoring information. Note that all requests start from the network management system.

10.2.6.4 SNMP Agent Security Configuration

Usernames, passwords, and community names must match for the SNMP Agent to work correctly with the network management system. You can choose usernames, passwords, and community names as long as the relationships shown in Figure 10-37 are maintained.

Note
Some SNMP tools enforce the SNMPv3 minimum password length of 8 characters. The Java CAPS SNMP Agent does not.

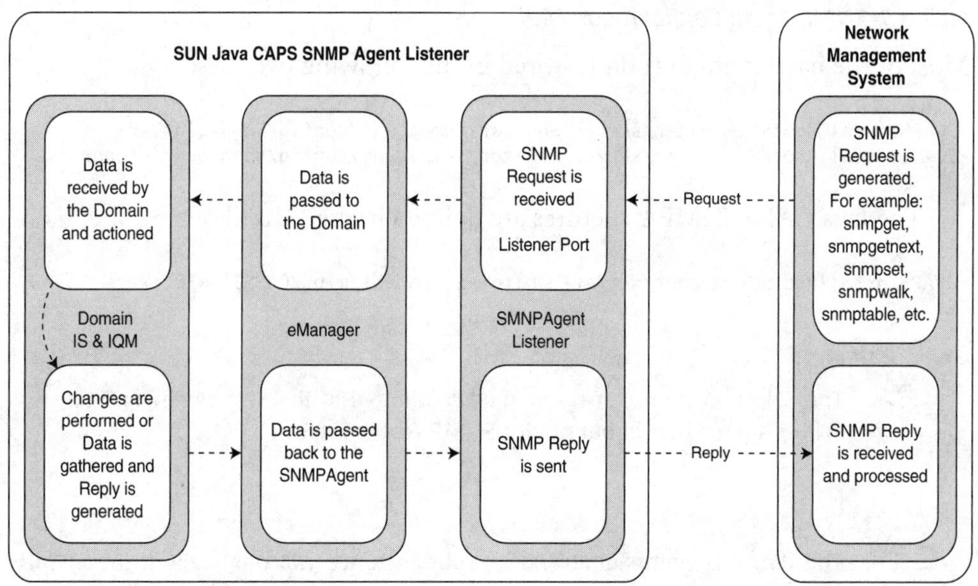

Figure 10-36: Flow of SNMP information

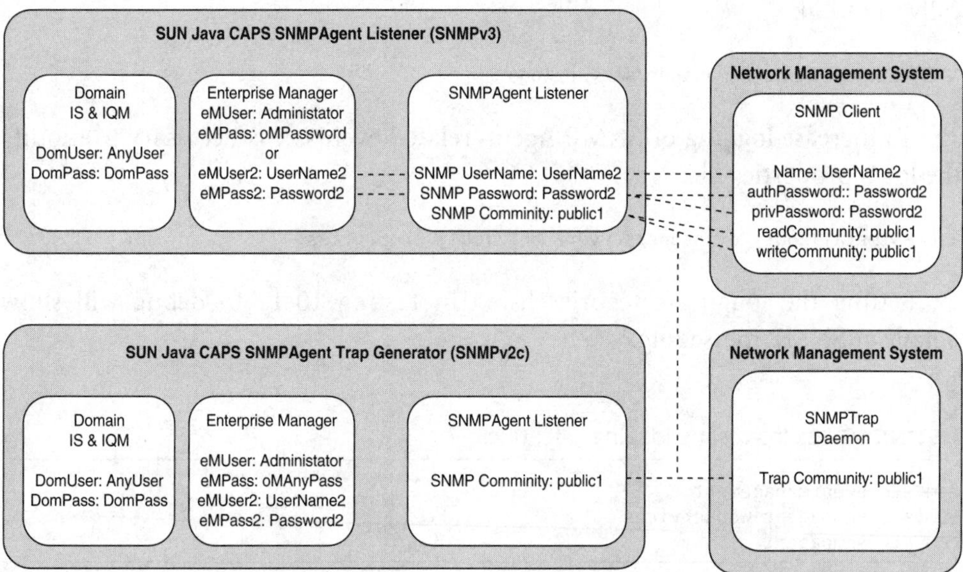

Figure 10-37: Relationships between property values in Java CAPS and SNMP components

10.2.6.5 SNMP Agent Configuration Files

Most of the base configuration is stored in the following two files:

```
<JCAPSInstallRoot>/emanager/server/monitor/snmpagent/config/SnmpAgent.xml
<JCAPSInstallRoot>/emanager/server/monitor/snmpagent/config/snmpagent.properties
```

The Java CAPS SNMP structures are defined in the MIB file:

```
<JVAPSInstallRoot>/emanager/server/monitor/snmpagent/mibs/CAPS51-MIB.txt
```

Note
The SNMP version can be manually changed in the SnmpAgent.xml file for SNMP Agent Listener but not for SNMP Agent Traps.

Note
The directory snmpagent and its subdirectories will only exist if the SNMP Agent is installed.

10.2.6.6 SNMP Agent Debug Logging

A log of SNMP-related activities is merged into the Enterprise Manager log, typically found in:

```
<JCAPSInstallRoot>/emanager/server/logs
```

To increase logging of SNMP Agent–related events, it is necessary to modify the log4j.properties file:

```
<JCAPSInstallRoot>/emanager/server/conf/log4j.properties
```

Setting the logging categories listed in Listing 10-12 to debug will show details of SNMP messaging.

LISTING 10-12: Interesting logging categories

```
com.stc.eventmanagement
com.stc.snmpagent.webservices
com.stc.snmpagent
```

10.2.7 Enterprise Manager Command-Line Tool

The Enterprise Manager Command-Line Client [eGateSAG] can be used to create command scripts for automated monitoring solutions much favored by Unix administrators. To be used, the command-line client must be downloaded from the Repository and extracted to a file system directory.

Invoking the command-line client script em-cmdline-client.[bat|sh] with no arguments generates a brief usage note, as shown in Listing 10-13.

LISTING 10-13: Em-cmdline-client usage note

```
C:\JCAPS512\em-client>echo off
Invalid value for parameter userid[null]. Parameter is required
usage: com.stc.soap.client.EMSoapClient
 -P <parameter=value>    value for a given method parameter
 -h,--help               displays basic usage
 -l,--host               host name
 -m,--method             method name
 -n,--signatures         displays signatures only
 -p,--port               port number
 -s,--service            service name
 -t,--timeout            HTTP request timeout (milliseconds)
 -u,--userid             user ID
 -v,--validate           runs with parameters validation
 -w,--password           user password
```

The Command-Line Client is documented in the [eGateSAG], so it is not discussed in detail here. To convey the flavor of the utility, the kinds of information it can provide, and the kinds of management activities it supports, a few example commands and their output are shown on the following pages. In all commands, the port number, host name, and credentials correspond to the environment in which book examples were developed. The port, 14100, is the port the Enterprise Manager Agent uses.

Obtain a list of methods supported by the runtime service. These methods apply to manipulating runtime components. Methods supported for manipulating alerts can be obtained using the alert service, AlertService51x, instead of the runtime service, RuntimeService51x, as is done in the examples shown in Listings 10-14 through 10-19.

LISTING 10-14: Usage note for manipulating the RuntimeService

```
C:\JCAPS512\em-client>em-cmdline-client -l localhost -p 14100 ^
More? -u Administrator -w STC ^
More? -s RuntimeService51x -n

C:\JCAPS512\em-client>echo off
usage: com.stc.soap.client.EMSoapClient
 -P <parameter=value>   value for a given method parameter
 -h,--help              displays basic usage
 -l,--host              host name
 -m,--method            method name
 -n,--signatures        displays signatures only
 -p,--port              port number
 -s,--service           service name
 -t,--timeout           HTTP request timeout (milliseconds)
 -u,--userid            user ID
 -v,--validate          runs with parameters validation
 -w,--password          user password
 Note: the order of the parameters is important.
 Available methods and parameters:
-m getState -Pcomponent=<component> -PcomponentType=<componentType>
-m startComponent -Pcomponent=<component> -PcomponentType=<componentType>
-m getComponentsList
-m stopComponent -Pcomponent=<component> -PcomponentType=<componentType>
-m getStatus -Pcomponent=<component> -PcomponentType=<componentType>
```

Listing 10-15 shows a command used to obtain a list of currently deployed components, and its output.

LISTING 10-15: List of currently deployed components

```
C:\JCAPS512\em-client>em-cmdline-client -l localhost -p 14100 ^
More? -u Administrator -w STC -s RuntimeService51x ^
More? -m getComponentsList

C:\JCAPS512\em-client>echo off
e51x|Servers|localhost:20000      is51x
e51x|Servers|localhost:20000|Sun_SeeBeyond_JMS_IQ_Manager      jms51x
e51x|Servers|localhost:20000|__Book|SystemManagement|Programmatic|JMSPassThrough|d
pJMSPassThrough|cmJMSPassThrough|qEater      messageService.Queue
e51x|Servers|localhost:20000|__Book|SystemManagement|Programmatic|JMSPassThrough|d
pJMSPassThrough|cmJMSPassThrough|qFeeder      messageService.Queue
e51x|Servers|localhost:20000|__Book|SystemManagement|Programmatic|JMSPassThrough|d
pJMSPassThrough|cmJMSPassThrough|qPassOn      messageService.Queue
e51x|Servers|localhost:20000|__Book|SystemManagement|Programmatic|JMSPassThrough|d
pJMSPassThrough|cmJMSPassThrough|svc_jcd_00      jce.JavaCollaborationDefinition
e51x|Servers|localhost:20000|__Book|SystemManagement|Programmatic|JMSPassThrough|d
pJMSPassThrough|cmJMSPassThrough|svc_jcd_01      jce.JavaCollaborationDefinition
```

```
e51x|Servers|localhost:20000|__Book|SystemManagement|Programmatic|ManagerHttp|dpMa
nagerHttp|cmManagerHttp|cHTTPClient      HTTPADAPTER.ExternalApplication
e51x|Servers|localhost:20000|__Book|SystemManagement|Programmatic|ManagerHttp|dpMa
nagerHttp|cmManagerHttp|cmManagerHttp_jcdGetStatus1    jce.JavaCollaborationDefinition
e51x|Servers|localhost:20000|__Book|SystemManagement|Programmatic|ManagerHttp|dpMa
nagerHttp|cmManagerHttp|cmManagerHttp_jcdGetStatus1|cmManagerHttp_jcdGetStatus
1_cHTTPClient      HTTPADAPTER.ExternalApplication.LINK
e51x|Servers|localhost:20000|__Book|SystemManagement|Programmatic|ManagerHttp|dpMa
nagerHttp|cmManagerHttp|qDummy      messageService.Queue
e51x|Servers|localhost:20000|__Book|SystemManagement|Programmatic|ManagerHttp|dpMa
nagerHttp|cmManagerHttp|qGetStatus      messageService.Queue
Leaving command line client.
```

Listing 10-16 shows a command used to obtain state and basic details of Java Collaboration service svc_jcd_00, and its output.

LISTING 10-16: Obtaining state and basic details of a service

```
C:\JCAPS512\em-client>em-cmdline-client -l localhost -p 14100 ^
More? -u Administrator -w STC -s RuntimeService51x ^
More? -m getStatus ^
More? -Pcomponent="e51x|Servers|localhost:20000|__Book|SystemManagement|Programmat
ic|JMSPassThrough|dpJMSPassThrough|cmJMSPassThrough|svc_jcd_00" ^
More? -PcomponentType=jce.JavaCollaborationDefinition

C:\JCAPS512\em-client>echo off
HostAndPort = localhost:20000
State = Up
Component = e51x|Servers|localhost:20000|__Book|SystemManagement|Programmatic|JMSP
assThrough|dpJMSPassThrough|cmJMSPassThrough|svc_jcd_00
System = e51x
Leaving command line client.
```

Listing 10-17 shows a command used to obtain status of Java Collaboration service svc_jcd_00, and its output.

LISTING 10-17: Component State

```
C:\JCAPS512\em-client>em-cmdline-client -l localhost -p 14100 ^
More? -u Administrator -w STC -s RuntimeService51x ^
More? -m getState ^
More? -Pcomponent="e51x|Servers|localhost:20000|__Book|SystemManagement|Programmat
ic|JMSPassThrough|dpJMSPassThrough|cmJMSPassThrough|svc_jcd_00" ^
More? -PcomponentType=jce.JavaCollaborationDefinition
```

```
C:\JCAPS512\em-client>echo off
Up
Leaving command line client.
```

Listing 10-18 shows the commands used to stop Java Collaboration service svc_jcd_00 and verify that it is stopped, and their output.

LISTING 10-18: Stopping components and verifying component state

```
C:\JCAPS512\em-client>em-cmdline-client -l localhost -p 14100 ^
More? -u Administrator -w STC -s RuntimeService51x ^
More? -m stopComponent ^
More? -Pcomponent="e51x|Servers|localhost:20000|__Book|SystemManagement|Programmat
ic|JMSPassThrough|dpJMSPassThrough|cmJMSPassThrough|svc_jcd_00" ^
More? -PcomponentType=jce.JavaCollaborationDefinition

C:\JCAPS512\em-client>echo off
Leaving command line client.

C:\JCAPS512\em-client>em-cmdline-client -l localhost -p 14100 ^
More? -u Administrator -w STC -s RuntimeService51x ^
More? -m getState ^
More? -Pcomponent="e51x|Servers|localhost:20000|__Book|SystemManagement|Programmat
ic|JMSPassThrough|dpJMSPassThrough|cmJMSPassThrough|svc_jcd_00" ^
More? -PcomponentType=jce.JavaCollaborationDefinition

C:\JCAPS512\em-client>echo off
Down
Leaving command line client.
```

Listing 10-19 shows commands used to start Java Collaboration service svc_jcd_00 and verify its state.

LISTING 10-19: Starting component and verifying its state

```
C:\JCAPS512\em-client>em-cmdline-client -l localhost -p 14100 ^
More? -u Administrator -w STC -s RuntimeService51x ^
More? -m startComponent ^
More? -Pcomponent="e51x|Servers|localhost:20000|__Book|SystemManagement|Programmat
ic|JMSPassThrough|dpJMSPassThrough|cmJMSPassThrough|svc_jcd_00" ^
More? -PcomponentType=jce.JavaCollaborationDefinition

C:\JCAPS512\em-client>echo off
Leaving command line client.

C:\JCAPS512\em-client>em-cmdline-client -l localhost -p 14100 ^
More? -u Administrator -w STC -s RuntimeService51x ^
```

```
More? -m getState ^
More? -Pcomponent="e51x|Servers|localhost:20000|__Book|SystemManagement|Programmat
ic|JMSPassThrough|dpJMSPassThrough|cmJMSPassThrough|svc_jcd_00" ^
More? -PcomponentType=jce.JavaCollaborationDefinition

C:\JCAPS512\em-client>echo off
Up
Leaving command line client.
```

The Enterprise Manager Command Line Client can also be used to review, observe, resolve, reset, and delete alerts. Alerts can be manipulated selectively using query filters that select alerts on which to operate. [eGateSAG] shows examples of command lines used to manipulate alerts.

Components manipulation and alert manipulation options of the Enterprise Manager Command Line Client can be used to develop unattended Integration Server maintenance and management scripts.

10.2.8 Enterprise Manager Web Service API

The Enterprise Manager API, see [eGateSAG], can be used to develop custom Web Services–based Java CAPS monitoring and management applications.

The following URLs provide access to Web Services Description Language (WSDL) interface definitions for management services exposed through the Enterprise Monitoring Agent infrastructure.

Service Manager Services:

```
http://<eManagerHost>:<eManaerPort>/EMServices/services/ServicesManager?wsdl
```

Login Services:

```
http://<eManagerHost>:<eManaerPort>/EMServices/services/Login?wsdl
```

Runtime Services:

```
http://<eManagerHost>:<eManaerPort>/EMServices/services/RuntimeService51x?wsdl
```

Alert Services:

```
http://<eManagerHost>:<eManaerPort>/EMServices/services/AlertService51x?wsdl
```

The following sections discuss the Enterprise Manager Web Services in greater detail.

10.2.8.1 Service Manager Service

The Service Manager Service returns an array of Enterprise Manager Web Service listeners, or fails. Given a SOAP Request, shown in Listing 10-20, the service returns, in the book development environment, the response shown in Listing 10-21.

LISTING 10-20: Web Service Request asking for a list of available services

```
<soapenv:Envelope
      xmlns:xsi="http://www.w3.org/2001/XMLSchema-instance"
      xmlns:xsd="http://www.w3.org/2001/XMLSchema"
      xmlns:soapenv="http://schemas.xmlsoap.org/soap/envelope/"
      xmlns:soap="http://soap.ws.services.em.egate.stc.com">
   <soapenv:Header/>
   <soapenv:Body>
      <soap:getAvailableServices
     soapenv:encodingStyle="http://schemas.xmlsoap.org/soap/encoding/"/>
   </soapenv:Body>
</soapenv:Envelope>
```

LISTING 10-21: List of available services response

```
<soapenv:Envelope
      xmlns:soapenv="http://schemas.xmlsoap.org/soap/envelope/"
      xmlns:xsd="http://www.w3.org/2001/XMLSchema"
      xmlns:xsi="http://www.w3.org/2001/XMLSchema-instance">
   <soapenv:Body>
      <ns1:getAvailableServicesResponse
       soapenv:encodingStyle="http://schemas.xmlsoap.org/soap/encoding/"
       xmlns:ns1="http://soap.ws.services.em.egate.stc.com">
         <getAvailableServicesReturn
             soapenc:arrayType="soapenc:string[2]"
             xsi:type="soapenc:Array"
             xmlns:soapenc="http://schemas.xmlsoap.org/soap/encoding/">
           <getAvailableServicesReturn
              xsi:type=
         "soapenc:string">RuntimeService51x</getAvailableServicesReturn>
           <getAvailableServicesReturn
              xsi:type=
         "soapenc:string">AlertService51x</getAvailableServicesReturn>
         </getAvailableServicesReturn>
      </ns1:getAvailableServicesResponse>
   </soapenv:Body>
</soapenv:Envelope>
```

It may or may not be worthwhile knowing that these services are running. When the Enterprise Manager Agent Server is not running, none of the Enterprise Manager Web Services will be available.

10.2.8.2 Login Service

All operations of the Runtime Service and the Alert Service require a Session ID parameter. The Login Service's only operation, openSession, requires a username and a password. Listing 10-22 shows a sample SOAP Request invoking the openSession operation with credentials.

LISTING 10-22: openSession SOAP Request

```
<soapenv:Envelope
      xmlns:xsi="http://www.w3.org/2001/XMLSchema-instance"
      xmlns:xsd="http://www.w3.org/2001/XMLSchema"
      xmlns:soapenv="http://schemas.xmlsoap.org/soap/envelope/"
      xmlns:soap="http://soap.ws.services.em.egate.stc.com">
   <soapenv:Header/>
   <soapenv:Body>
      <soap:openSession
       soapenv:encodingStyle="http://schemas.xmlsoap.org/soap/encoding/">
         <name xsi:type="soapenc:string"
               xmlns:soapenc=
        "http://schemas.xmlsoap.org/soap/encoding/">Administrator</name>
         <password xsi:type="soapenc:string"
               xmlns:soapenc=
        "http://schemas.xmlsoap.org/soap/encoding/">STC</password>
      </soap:openSession>
   </soapenv:Body>
</soapenv:Envelope>
```

In response to this request, the Login Service returns the Session ID that can be used when invoking Runtime and Alert services. Listing 10-23 shows the SOAP Response.

LISTING 10-23: openSession SOAP Response

```
<soapenv:Envelope
      xmlns:soapenv="http://schemas.xmlsoap.org/soap/envelope/"
      xmlns:xsd="http://www.w3.org/2001/XMLSchema"
      xmlns:xsi="http://www.w3.org/2001/XMLSchema-instance">
   <soapenv:Body>
      <ns1:openSessionResponse
```

```
      soapenv:encodingStyle="http://schemas.xmlsoap.org/soap/encoding/"
      xmlns:ns1="http://soap.ws.services.em.egate.stc.com">
        <openSessionReturn
           xsi:type="soapenc:string"
           xmlns:soapenc="http://schemas.xmlsoap.org/soap/encoding/">
D134E3B637D819749A8A30FDD1C3BBB5</openSessionReturn>
      </ns1:openSessionResponse>
   </soapenv:Body>
</soapenv:Envelope>
```

Regardless of whether credentials are valid, a Session Id is returned. If the credentials are invalid, the Session ID will be rejected and another SOAP Fault will be returned—for example, an insufficient privileges message when another service attempts to use it. Listing 10-24 shows a SOAP Fault returned in response to a request with invalid credentials.

LISTING 10-24: Invalid credentials SOAP Response

```
<soapenv:Envelope xmlns:soapenv="http://schemas.xmlsoap.org/soap/envelope/"
xmlns:xsd="http://www.w3.org/2001/XMLSchema"
xmlns:xsi="http://www.w3.org/2001/XMLSchema-instance">
   <soapenv:Body>
      <soapenv:Fault>
         <faultcode>soapenv:Server.userException</faultcode>
         <faultstring>
java.rmi.RemoteException: User does not have privileges for requested operation.
         </faultstring>
         <detail>
            <ns1:hostname xmlns:ns1="http://xml.apache.org/axis/">
MCZ01</ns1:hostname>
         </detail>
      </soapenv:Fault>
   </soapenv:Body>
</soapenv:Envelope>
```

Both Runtime and Alert services implement closeSession operations. One of these operations should be invoked to close and invalidate the management session opened by the invocation of the openSession operation of the Login Service.

Note that Session ID does not survive Enterprise Manager Agent Service restart. If an invalid Session ID is used, a SOAP Fault is returned, as illustrated in Listing 10-25.

LISTING 10-25: "Session Not Found" Fault

```
<soapenv:Envelope
       xmlns:soapenv="http://schemas.xmlsoap.org/soap/envelope/"
       xmlns:xsd="http://www.w3.org/2001/XMLSchema"
       xmlns:xsi="http://www.w3.org/2001/XMLSchema-instance">
   <soapenv:Body>
      <soapenv:Fault>
         <faultcode>soapenv:Server.userException</faultcode>
         <faultstring>
java.rmi.RemoteException: Session not found for:D134E3B637D819749A8A30FDD1C3BBB5
         </faultstring>
         <detail>
            <ns1:hostname xmlns:ns1=
                     "http://xml.apache.org/axis/">MCZ01</ns1:hostname>
         </detail>
      </soapenv:Fault>
   </soapenv:Body>
</soapenv:Envelope>
```

10.2.8.3 Runtime Service

At runtime the Integration Server may support many Java CAPS projects deployed and executing concurrently. Operational reasons may dictate that some components need to be stopped and started automatically. The execution state of components may need to be confirmed at intervals to satisfy the dictates of the operational monitoring policy of the site. A third-party enterprise monitoring solution may need to obtain status information for runtime components.

The Runtime Service supports such requirements by providing access to the list of components executing within the Integration Server, obtaining their state and status and starting and stopping them programmatically.

To successfully invoke any of the Alert Service Web Services operations, the invoker must have a valid Session ID. Session ID is obtained by invoking the Login Service's openSession operation; see section 10.2.8.2.

Let's invoke the service operation getComponentList to obtain the list of components visible to the Enterprise Manager. Listing 10-26 shows a sample request.

LISTING 10-26: getComponentList request

```
<soapenv:Envelope
       xmlns:xsi="http://www.w3.org/2001/XMLSchema-instance"
       xmlns:xsd="http://www.w3.org/2001/XMLSchema"
```

```
        xmlns:soapenv="http://schemas.xmlsoap.org/soap/envelope/"
        xmlns:soap="http://soap.ws.services.em.egate.stc.com">
    <soapenv:Header/>
    <soapenv:Body>
       <soap:getComponentsList
        soapenv:encodingStyle="http://schemas.xmlsoap.org/soap/encoding/">
          <sessionId
             xsi:type="soapenc:string"
             xmlns:soapenc="http://schemas.xmlsoap.org/soap/encoding/">
BB0396DF02BBB43932872B597BFDFA7A</sessionId>
       </soap:getComponentsList>
    </soapenv:Body>
</soapenv:Envelope>
```

The response looks like that shown in Listing 10-27.

LISTING 10-27: Component list response

```
<soapenv:Envelope
      xmlns:soapenv=http://schemas.xmlsoap.org/soap/envelope/
      xmlns:xsd=http://www.w3.org/2001/XMLSchema
      xmlns:xsi="http://www.w3.org/2001/XMLSchema-instance">
   <soapenv:Body>
      <ns1:getComponentsListResponse
         soapenv:encodingStyle=
                 "http://schemas.xmlsoap.org/soap/encoding/"
         xmlns:ns1=http://soap.ws.services.em.egate.stc.com>
         <getComponentsListReturn
              soapenc:arrayType="xsd:anyType[10]"
              xsi:type="soapenc:Array"
              xmlns:soapenc=
                  "http://schemas.xmlsoap.org/soap/encoding/">
            <getComponentsListReturn xsi:type="soapenc:string">
e51x|Servers|localhost:20000     is51x
            </getComponentsListReturn>
            <getComponentsListReturn xsi:type="soapenc:string">
e51x|Servers|localhost:20000|Sun_SeeBeyond_JMS_IQ_Manager     jms51x
            </getComponentsListReturn>
            <getComponentsListReturn xsi:type="soapenc:string">
e51x|Servers|localhost:20000|__Book|Examples|WSSPXA|DPs|dpWSSPXA|cmWSSPXA|cXAOra_1
ORACLEADAPTER.ExternalApplication
            </getComponentsListReturn>
            <getComponentsListReturn xsi:type="soapenc:string">
e51x|Servers|localhost:20000|__Book|Examples|WSSPXA|DPs|dpWSSPXA|cmWSSPXA|cXAOra_2
ORACLEADAPTER.ExternalApplication
            </getComponentsListReturn>
            <getComponentsListReturn xsi:type="soapenc:string">
e51x|Servers|localhost:20000|__Book|Examples|WSSPXA|DPs|dpWSSPXA|cmWSSPXA|svc_bpUp
dateXA     BPMS.BusinessProcessRepositoryObject
            </getComponentsListReturn>
            <getComponentsListReturn xsi:type="soapenc:string">
```

```
e51x|Servers|localhost:20000|__Book|Examples|WSSPXA|DPs|dpWSSPXA|cmWSSPXA|svc_jcdU
pdateXA      jce.JavaCollaborationDefinition
            </getComponentsListReturn>
            <getComponentsListReturn xsi:type="soapenc:string">
e51x|Servers|localhost:20000|__Book|Examples|WSSPXA|DPs|dpWSSPXA|cmWSSPXA|svc_jcdU
pdateXA|svc_jcdUpdateXA_cXAOra_1      ORACLEADAPTER.ExternalApplication.LINK
            </getComponentsListReturn>
            <getComponentsListReturn xsi:type="soapenc:string">
e51x|Servers|localhost:20000|__Book|Examples|WSSPXA|DPs|dpWSSPXA|cmWSSPXA|svc_jcdU
pdateXA|svc_jcdUpdateXA_cXAOra_2      ORACLEADAPTER.ExternalApplication.LINK
            </getComponentsListReturn>
            <getComponentsListReturn xsi:type="soapenc:string">
e51x|Servers|localhost:20000|__Book|Examples|WSSPXA|DPs|dpWSSPXA|cmWSSPXA|wssWebSe
rviceApplication      WSSoapHttpApplication.WSSoapHttpApplication
            </getComponentsListReturn>
            <getComponentsListReturn xsi:type="soapenc:string">
e51x|Servers|localhost:20000|__Book|Examples|WSSPXA|DPs|dpWSSPXA|cmWSSPXA|wssWebSe
rviceApplication|wssWebServiceApplication_svc_bpUpdateXA
WSSoapHttpApplication.WSSoapHttpApplication.LINK
          </getComponentsListReturn>
          </getComponentsListReturn>
      </ns1:getComponentsListResponse>
   </soapenv:Body>
</soapenv:Envelope>
```

Component paths such as the following, required to invoke other Runtime Service operations, can be obtained through the Enterprise Manager:

```
e51x|Servers|localhost:20000|__Book|Examples|WSSPXA|DPs|dpWSSPXA|cmWSSPXA|wssWebSe
rviceApplication|wssWebServiceApplication_svc_bpUpdateXA
```

The Java Collaboration service svc_jcdUpdateXA belongs to the connectivity map cmWSSPXA in deployment profile dpWSSPXA in project __Book/Examples/WSSPXA/DPs, as shown in Figure 10-38.

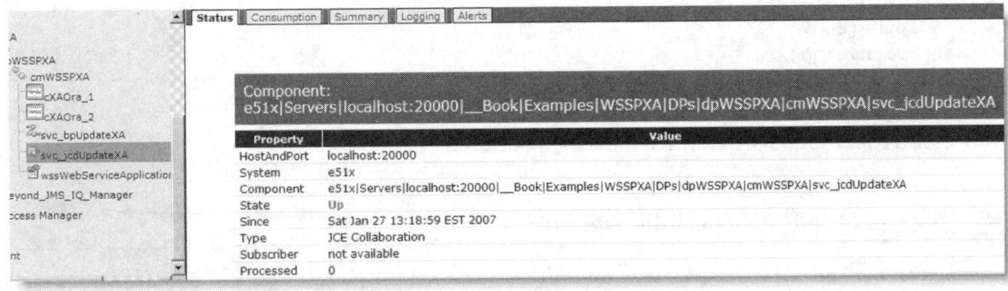

FIGURE 10-38: Component path in Enterprise Manager

Component types, also required to invoke component-specific operations, must be obtained by invoking the getComponentList operation and inspecting the result for the component in question. For example, let's query the status of component

```
e51x|Servers|localhost:20000|__Book|Examples|WSSPXA|DPs|dpWSSPXA|cmWSSPXA|svc_jcdU
pdateXA
```

of type

```
jce.JavaCollaborationDefinition
```

The request is shown in Listing 10-28.

LISTING 10-28: Component status request

```
<soapenv:Envelope
        xmlns:xsi="http://www.w3.org/2001/XMLSchema-instance"
        xmlns:xsd="http://www.w3.org/2001/XMLSchema"
        xmlns:soapenv="http://schemas.xmlsoap.org/soap/envelope/"
        xmlns:soap="http://soap.ws.services.em.egate.stc.com">
   <soapenv:Header/>
   <soapenv:Body>
    <soap:getStatus soapenv:encodingStyle=
                             "http://schemas.xmlsoap.org/soap/encoding/">
     <sessionId xsi:type="soapenc:string" xmlns:soapenc=
                             "http://schemas.xmlsoap.org/soap/encoding/">
BB0396DF02BBB43932872B597BFDFA7A
     </sessionId>
     <component xsi:type="soapenc:string"
         xmlns:soapenc="http://schemas.xmlsoap.org/soap/encoding/">
e51x|Servers|localhost:20000|__Book|Examples|WSSPXA|DPs|dpWSSPXA|cmWSSPXA|svc_jcdU
pdateXA
     </component>
     <componentType
         xsi:type="soapenc:string"
         xmlns:soapenc="http://schemas.xmlsoap.org/soap/encoding/">
jce.JavaCollaborationDefinition
     </componentType>
    </soap:getStatus>
   </soapenv:Body>
</soapenv:Envelope>
```

The response is shown in Listing 10-29.

LISTING 10-29: Component status response

```
<soapenv:Envelope
        xmlns:soapenv="http://schemas.xmlsoap.org/soap/envelope/"
        xmlns:xsd="http://www.w3.org/2001/XMLSchema"
```

```
      xmlns:xsi="http://www.w3.org/2001/XMLSchema-instance">
   <soapenv:Body>
    <ns1:getStatusResponse soapenv:encodingStyle=
                                      "http://schemas.xmlsoap.org/soap/encoding/"
                           xmlns:ns1="http://soap.ws.services.em.egate.stc.com">
     <getStatusReturn href="#id0"/>
    </ns1:getStatusResponse>
    <multiRef id="id0" soapenc:root="0" soapenv:encodingStyle=
              "http://schemas.xmlsoap.org/soap/encoding/"
          xsi:type="ns2:Map" xmlns:ns2="http://xml.apache.org/xml-soap"
          xmlns:soapenc="http://schemas.xmlsoap.org/soap/encoding/">
     <item>
      <key xsi:type="soapenc:string">HostAndPort</key>
      <value xsi:type="soapenc:string">localhost:20000</value>
     </item>
     <item>
      <key xsi:type="soapenc:string">System</key>
      <value xsi:type="soapenc:string">e51x</value>
     </item>
     <item>
      <key xsi:type="soapenc:string">Component</key>
      <value xsi:type="soapenc:string">
e51x|Servers|localhost:20000|__Book|Examples|WSSPXA|DPs|dpWSSPXA|cmWSSPXA|svc_jcdU
pdateXA
      </value>
     </item>
     <item>
      <key xsi:type="soapenc:string">State</key>
      <value xsi:type="soapenc:string">Up</value>
     </item>
    </multiRef>
   </soapenv:Body>
</soapenv:Envelope>
```

If the component is not deployed or is disabled, the SOAP Fault response will be returned. This response is quite misleading, as it states that the component type is invalid for the component rather than saying that the component does not exist, as shown in Listing 10-30.

LISTING 10-30: SOAP Fault arising out of status request for a disabled component

```
<?xml version="1.0" encoding="UTF-8"?>
<soapenv:Envelope
      xmlns:soapenv="http://schemas.xmlsoap.org/soap/envelope/"
      xmlns:xsd="http://www.w3.org/2001/XMLSchema"
      xmlns:xsi="http://www.w3.org/2001/XMLSchema-instance">
      <soapenv:Body>
              <soapenv:Fault>
                      <faultcode>soapenv:Server.userException</faultcode>
                      <faultstring>
```

```
java.rmi.RemoteException: Invalid componentType: jce.JavaCollaborationDefinition f
or component: e51x|Servers|localhost:20000|__Book|SystemManagement|Programmatic|JM
SPassThrough|dpJMSPassThrough|cmJMSPassThrough|svc_jcd_00</faultstring>
                        <detail>
                       <ns1:hostname xmlns:ns1="http://xml.apache.org/axis/">
MCZ01
                       </ns1:hostname>
                        </detail>
                </soapenv:Fault>
        </soapenv:Body>
</soapenv:Envelope>
```

Components can be stopped and started using appropriate operations. What is unclear is whether there are any limitations as to what kind of components can be managed this way. It would appear that some forms of Java Collaborations can be stopped and started, such as collaborations invoked by arrival of a JMS Message.

The ability to stop and start components programmatically could lead to solutions that automatically start and stop components to a schedule, for example, to synchronize a Java CAPS solution with an operational downtime window of external systems, or to automatically bring additional components on line to smooth out processing peaks.

Note

Enterprise Manager API WSDL interface definitions are not WS-I compliant. Neither Java CAPS nor NetBeans 5.x nor Axis 2 can cope with them. Of the generally available tools, SoapUI readily deals with the WSDL and successfully invokes all operations.

To take advantage of the interface from Java CAPS, a lowest common denominator solution, HTTP Request/Reply, can be constructed to invoke service operations. Input SOAP Request can be constructed using string operations, and SOAP Responses can be processed using substring operations. Low tech but guaranteed to work.

See project __Book/SystemManagement/Programmatic/ManagerHttp (on the accompanying CD-ROM) for an example of how to implement a lowest common denominator solution that uses the Enterprise Manager Web Services API to obtain component status. A solution that starts and stops components using the same techniques can be readily developed using this project as the basis.

10.2.8.4 Alert Service

As events occur within Java CAPS, components are started or stopped, components report problems, solutions explicitly log alerts, and alert event messages are collected in the event database. Until a user explicitly acknowledges having seen a particular alert, or having "observed" it, the alert has the "unobserved" status. An observed alert will have the observed status until a user explicitly "resolves" the alert. Marking alerts as observed and resolved is performed through the Enterprise Manager. The Alert Service provides programmatic access to Alert management and maintenance. Using this service, a solution can automate observing and resolving alerts, resetting alerts to unobserved state, and deleting alerts from the event database. Performing automated maintenance of selected routine alerts will reduce the size of the event database and the number of alerts displayed in the Enterprise Manager. Judiciously implemented, this will reduce the clutter in the Enterprise Manager alert display and focus operations personnel on alerts of importance.

Note
The Web Services interfaces are not WS-Interoperability compliant, so most of the services cannot be directly invoked from Java CAPS using built-in Web Services support frameworks.

To successfully invoke any of the Alert Service Web Services operations, the invoker must have a valid Session ID. Session ID is obtained by invoking the Login Service's openSession operation, explained in section 10.2.8.2.

Some of the Web Services operations operate on complete collections of alerts. These operations require a valid Session ID and affect all alerts. getAllAlerts, observeAllAlerts, resolveAllAlerts, deleteAllAlerts, and resetAllAlerts all fall into this category. Note that all of these operations potentially operate on a very large collection of alerts. Note, too, that the getAllAlerts potentially returns a very large SOAP Response message.

A SOAP Request for all alerts is shown in Listing 10-31.

LISTING 10-31: getAllAlerts request

```
<soapenv:Envelope
      xmlns:xsi="http://www.w3.org/2001/XMLSchema-instance"
      xmlns:xsd="http://www.w3.org/2001/XMLSchema"
      xmlns:soapenv="http://schemas.xmlsoap.org/soap/envelope/"
      xmlns:soap="http://soap.ws.services.em.egate.stc.com">
```

```
  <soapenv:Header/>
  <soapenv:Body>
    <soap:getAllAlerts
    soapenv:encodingStyle="http://schemas.xmlsoap.org/soap/encoding/">
      <sessionId
        xsi:type="soapenc:string"
        xmlns:soapenc="http://schemas.xmlsoap.org/soap/encoding/">
815C0B9F5750CDEA1D73A3349706881F</sessionId>
    </soap:getAllAlerts>
  </soapenv:Body>
</soapenv:Envelope>
```

The request will return a very large SOAP Response with a collection of all alerts and their complete details. The example response in Listing 10-32 has been edited, removing most of the repetitions for brevity.

LISTING 10-32: getAllAlerts response

```
<soapenv:Envelope
      xmlns:soapenv="http://schemas.xmlsoap.org/soap/envelope/"
      xmlns:xsd="http://www.w3.org/2001/XMLSchema"
      xmlns:xsi="http://www.w3.org/2001/XMLSchema-instance">
  <soapenv:Body>
    <ns1:getAllAlertsResponse
          soapenv:encodingStyle="http://schemas.xmlsoap.org/soap/encoding/"
          xmlns:ns1="http://soap.ws.services.em.egate.stc.com">
      <getAllAlertsReturn
            soapenc:arrayType="ns2:local[500]"
            xsi:type="soapenc:Array"
            xmlns:ns2="myNameSpace:fixIt"
            xmlns:soapenc="http://schemas.xmlsoap.org/soap/encoding/">
        <getAllAlertsReturn href="#id0"/>
...
        <getAllAlertsReturn href="#id499"/>
      </getAllAlertsReturn>
    </ns1:getAllAlertsResponse>
    <multiRef id="id54"
            soapenc:root="0"
          soapenv:encodingStyle=
                     "http://schemas.xmlsoap.org/soap/encoding/"
            xsi:type="ns3:local"
            xmlns:ns3="myNameSpace:fixIt"
            xmlns:soapenc="http://schemas.xmlsoap.org/soap/encoding/">
      <alertName xsi:nil="true" xsi:type="soapenc:string"/>
      <comment xsi:nil="true" xsi:type="soapenc:string"/>
      <component xsi:type="soapenc:string"></component>
      <componentName xsi:type="soapenc:string"></componentName>
      <componentProjectPathName
            xsi:type="soapenc:string"></componentProjectPathName>
```

```
        <componentType
               xsi:type="soapenc:string">INTEGRATION</componentType>
        <date xsi:type="xsd:dateTime">2007-01-23T10:34:00.513Z</date>
        <deploymentName xsi:type="soapenc:string"></deploymentName>
        <details
               xsi:type="soapenc:string">Application Server Started</details>
        <elementName xsi:type="soapenc:string"></elementName>
        <environmentName xsi:type="soapenc:string"></environmentName>
        <event xsi:nil="true" xsi:type="xsd:anyType"/>
        <eventName xsi:type="soapenc:string">null</eventName>
        <eventType xsi:type="soapenc:string">ALERT</eventType>
        <id xsi:type="soapenc:string">4626</id>
        <index xsi:nil="true" xsi:type="soapenc:long"/>
        <logicalHostName xsi:type="soapenc:string">MCZ01</logicalHostName>
        <message xsi:type="soapenc:string">IS-00001</message>
        <messageCode xsi:type="soapenc:string">IS-00001</messageCode>
        <name xsi:nil="true" xsi:type="soapenc:string"/>
        <observationalState
               xsi:type="soapenc:string">Unobserved</observationalState>
        <observed href="#id500"/>
        <operationalState xsi:type="soapenc:string">Started</operationalState>
        <physicalHostName
               xsi:type="soapenc:string">localhost:20000</physicalHostName>
        <reference xsi:nil="true" xsi:type="xsd:anyType"/>
        <resolved href="#id501"/>
        <serverName xsi:type="soapenc:string">MCZ01</serverName>
        <serverType xsi:type="soapenc:string">INTEGRATION</serverType>
        <severity xsi:type="soapenc:string">INFO</severity>
        <timeStamp xsi:type="soapenc:string">01/23/07 09:34:00 PM</timeStamp>
        <type xsi:type="soapenc:string">INTEGRATION</type>
     </multiRef>
...
     <multiRef id="id470"
               soapenc:root="0"
               soapenv:encodingStyle="http://schemas.xmlsoap.org/soap/encoding/"
               xsi:type="ns502:local"
               xmlns:ns502="myNameSpace:fixIt"
               xmlns:soapenc="http://schemas.xmlsoap.org/soap/encoding/">
        <alertName xsi:nil="true" xsi:type="soapenc:string"/>
        <comment xsi:nil="true" xsi:type="soapenc:string"/>
        <component xsi:type="soapenc:string">svc_jcdUPDATE_XA</component>
        <componentName xsi:type="soapenc:string">svc_jcdUPDATE_XA</componentName>
        <componentProjectPathName
            xsi:type="soapenc:string">DLI_POC2|XA|DPs</componentProjectPathName>
        <componentType xsi:type="soapenc:string">COLLABORATION</componentType>
        <date xsi:type="xsd:dateTime">2007-01-15T22:31:44.568Z</date>
        <deploymentName xsi:type="soapenc:string">dpUPDATE_XA</deploymentName>
        <details xsi:type="soapenc:string">
Collaboration svc_jcdUPDATE_XA is RUNNING
        </details>
        <elementName xsi:type="soapenc:string">svc_jcdUPDATE_XA</elementName>
        <environmentName xsi:type="soapenc:string">envDLIPOC</environmentName>
        <event xsi:nil="true" xsi:type="xsd:anyType"/>
```

```
        <eventName xsi:type="soapenc:string">null</eventName>
        <eventType xsi:type="soapenc:string">ALERT</eventType>
        <id xsi:type="soapenc:string">4208</id>
        <index xsi:nil="true" xsi:type="soapenc:long"/>
        <logicalHostName xsi:type="soapenc:string">DLIPOC_LH</logicalHostName>
        <message xsi:type="soapenc:string">COL-00001</message>
        <messageCode xsi:type="soapenc:string">COL-00001</messageCode>
        <name xsi:nil="true" xsi:type="soapenc:string"/>
        <observationalState
            xsi:type="soapenc:string">Unobserved</observationalState>
        <observed href="#id1498"/>
        <operationalState xsi:type="soapenc:string">Running</operationalState>
        <physicalHostName
            xsi:type="soapenc:string">localhost:20000</physicalHostName>
        <reference xsi:nil="true" xsi:type="xsd:anyType"/>
        <resolved href="#id1499"/>
        <serverName xsi:type="soapenc:string">DLIPOC_IS</serverName>
        <serverType xsi:type="soapenc:string">INTEGRATION</serverType>
        <severity xsi:type="soapenc:string">INFO</severity>
        <timeStamp xsi:type="soapenc:string">01/16/07 09:31:44 AM</timeStamp>
        <type xsi:type="soapenc:string">COLLABORATION</type>
    </multiRef>
    <multiRef
        id="id885"
        soapenc:root="0"
        soapenv:encodingStyle="http://schemas.xmlsoap.org/soap/encoding/"
        xsi:type="xsd:boolean"  xmlns:soapenc=
            "http://schemas.xmlsoap.org/soap/encoding/">false</multiRef>
    <multiRef
        id="id1227"
        soapenc:root="0"
          soapenv:encodingStyle="http://schemas.xmlsoap.org/soap/encoding/"
        xsi:type="xsd:boolean"
        xmlns:soapenc="http://schemas.xmlsoap.org/soap/encoding/">
false
    </multiRef>
...
    <multiRef id="id760"
        soapenc:root="0"
    soapenv:encodingStyle="http://schemas.xmlsoap.org/soap/encoding/"
        xsi:type="xsd:boolean"
    xmlns:soapenc="http://schemas.xmlsoap.org/soap/encoding/">false</multiRef>
  </soapenv:Body>
</soapenv:Envelope>
```

Let's work with the following alerts in the Enterprise Manager, as shown in Figure 10-39.

Let's "observe" all alerts (not just the ones listed but all alerts for all components) using a SOAP Request like the one shown in Listing 10-33.

FIGURE 10-39: Selected Enterprise Manager alerts

LISTING 10-33: ObserverAllAlerts request

```
<soapenv:Envelope xmlns:xsi="http://www.w3.org/2001/XMLSchema-instance"
xmlns:xsd="http://www.w3.org/2001/XMLSchema" xmlns:soapenv="http://
schemas.xmlsoap.org/soap/envelope/" xmlns:soap="http://
soap.ws.services.em.egate.stc.com">
   <soapenv:Header/>
   <soapenv:Body>
    <soap:observeAllAlerts
         soapenv:encodingStyle="http://schemas.xmlsoap.org/soap/encoding/">
     <sessionId xsi:type="soapenc:string"
         xmlns:soapenc="http://schemas.xmlsoap.org/soap/encoding/">
5DABD3370E5D3C02C41C5E334C5D40D8
     </sessionId>
    </soap:observeAllAlerts>
   </soapenv:Body>
</soapenv:Envelope>
```

Submitting this request will result in the response like the one shown in Listing 10-34.

LISTING 10-34: ObserveAllAlerts response

```
<soapenv:Envelope
        xmlns:soapenv="http://schemas.xmlsoap.org/soap/envelope/"
        xmlns:xsd="http://www.w3.org/2001/XMLSchema"
        xmlns:xsi="http://www.w3.org/2001/XMLSchema-instance">
   <soapenv:Body>
    <ns1:observeAllAlertsResponse
        soapenv:encodingStyle="http://schemas.xmlsoap.org/soap/encoding/"
        xmlns:ns1="http://soap.ws.services.em.egate.stc.com"/>
   </soapenv:Body>
</soapenv:Envelope>
```

The Enterprise Manager will show all alerts as observed (see Figure 10-40).

Let's now reset all alerts using a SOAP Request similar to that shown in Listing 10-35.

LISTING 10-35: resetAllAlerts request

```
<soapenv:Envelope
       xmlns:xsi="http://www.w3.org/2001/XMLSchema-instance"
       xmlns:xsd="http://www.w3.org/2001/XMLSchema"
       xmlns:soapenv="http://schemas.xmlsoap.org/soap/envelope/"
       xmlns:soap="http://soap.ws.services.em.egate.stc.com">
   <soapenv:Header/>
   <soapenv:Body>
    <soap:resetAllAlerts
       soapenv:encodingStyle="http://schemas.xmlsoap.org/soap/encoding/">
     <sessionId xsi:type="soapenc:string"
       xmlns:soapenc="http://schemas.xmlsoap.org/soap/encoding/">
5DABD3370E5D3C02C41C5E334C5D40D8
     </sessionId>
    </soap:resetAllAlerts>
   </soapenv:Body>
</soapenv:Envelope>
```

The Response looks like that in Listing 10-36.

LISTING 10-36: resetAllAlerts response

```
<soapenv:Envelope
       xmlns:soapenv="http://schemas.xmlsoap.org/soap/envelope/"
       xmlns:xsd="http://www.w3.org/2001/XMLSchema"
       xmlns:xsi="http://www.w3.org/2001/XMLSchema-instance">
   <soapenv:Body>
    <ns1:resetAllAlertsResponse
       soapenv:encodingStyle="http://schemas.xmlsoap.org/soap/encoding/"
       xmlns:ns1="http://soap.ws.services.em.egate.stc.com"/>
   </soapenv:Body>
</soapenv:Envelope>
```

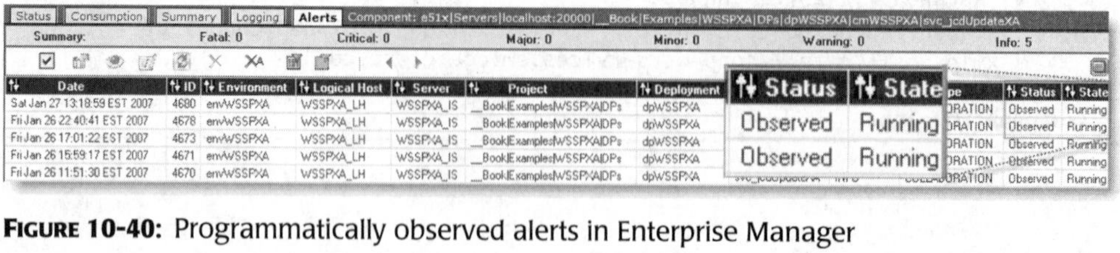

FIGURE 10-40: Programmatically observed alerts in Enterprise Manager

For each of the xxxxAllAlerts operations, there is an xxxxAlerts operation that requires a Session ID and a filter. The filter is an expression that restricts the collection of alerts to which the operation applies to these that satisfy the filter expression.

The filter expression has the following form, where semicolon is the AND operator. There may well be other operators, like the OR operator or a negation operator, but our experimentation did not uncover any:

```
fieldName=fieldValue;fieldName=fieldValue
```

fieldName can be one of the items returned by the getAlertQueryFields operation with a request like the one shown in Listing 10-37.

LISTING 10-37: getAlertQueryFields request

```
<soapenv:Envelope
      xmlns:xsi="http://www.w3.org/2001/XMLSchema-instance"
      xmlns:xsd="http://www.w3.org/2001/XMLSchema"
      xmlns:soapenv="http://schemas.xmlsoap.org/soap/envelope/"
      xmlns:soap="http://soap.ws.services.em.egate.stc.com">
  <soapenv:Header/>
  <soapenv:Body>
   <soap:getAlertQueryFields
      soapenv:encodingStyle="http://schemas.xmlsoap.org/soap/encoding/">
    <sessionId xsi:type="soapenc:string"
      xmlns:soapenc="http://schemas.xmlsoap.org/soap/encoding/">
5DABD3370E5D3C02C41C5E334C5D40D8
    </sessionId>
   </soap:getAlertQueryFields>
  </soapenv:Body>
</soapenv:Envelope>
```

The response, shown in Listing 10-38, enumerates all "Query Fields" that can be used.

LISTING 10-38: getAlertQueryFields response

```
<soapenv:Envelope
      xmlns:soapenv="http://schemas.xmlsoap.org/soap/envelope/"
      xmlns:xsd="http://www.w3.org/2001/XMLSchema"
      xmlns:xsi="http://www.w3.org/2001/XMLSchema-instance">
  <soapenv:Body>
   <ns1:getAlertQueryFieldsResponse
      soapenv:encodingStyle="http://schemas.xmlsoap.org/soap/encoding/"
      xmlns:ns1="http://soap.ws.services.em.egate.stc.com">
```

```
    <getAlertQueryFieldsReturn
       soapenc:arrayType="soapenc:string[16]" xsi:type="soapenc:Array"
       xmlns:soapenc="http://schemas.xmlsoap.org/soap/encoding/">
      <getAlertQueryFieldsReturn
        xsi:type="soapenc:string">from</getAlertQueryFieldsReturn>
      <getAlertQueryFieldsReturn
        xsi:type="soapenc:string">to</getAlertQueryFieldsReturn>
      <getAlertQueryFieldsReturn
        xsi:type="soapenc:string">id</getAlertQueryFieldsReturn>
      <getAlertQueryFieldsReturn
        xsi:type="soapenc:string">environmentName</getAlertQueryFieldsReturn>
      <getAlertQueryFieldsReturn
        xsi:type="soapenc:string">physicalHostName</getAlertQueryFieldsReturn>
      <getAlertQueryFieldsReturn
        xsi:type="soapenc:string">logicalHostName</getAlertQueryFieldsReturn>
      <getAlertQueryFieldsReturn
        xsi:type="soapenc:string">serverName</getAlertQueryFieldsReturn>
      <getAlertQueryFieldsReturn
        xsi:type="soapenc:string">
componentProjectPathName
      </getAlertQueryFieldsReturn>
      <getAlertQueryFieldsReturn
        xsi:type="soapenc:string">deploymentName</getAlertQueryFieldsReturn>
      <getAlertQueryFieldsReturn
        xsi:type="soapenc:string">componentName</getAlertQueryFieldsReturn>
      <getAlertQueryFieldsReturn
        xsi:type="soapenc:string">severity</getAlertQueryFieldsReturn>
      <getAlertQueryFieldsReturn
        xsi:type="soapenc:string">type</getAlertQueryFieldsReturn>
      <getAlertQueryFieldsReturn
        xsi:type="soapenc:string">observationalState</getAlertQueryFieldsReturn>
      <getAlertQueryFieldsReturn
        xsi:type="soapenc:string">operationalState</getAlertQueryFieldsReturn>
      <getAlertQueryFieldsReturn
        xsi:type="soapenc:string">messageCode</getAlertQueryFieldsReturn>
      <getAlertQueryFieldsReturn
        xsi:type="soapenc:string">details</getAlertQueryFieldsReturn>
     </getAlertQueryFieldsReturn>
    </ns1:getAlertQueryFieldsResponse>
   </soapenv:Body>
</soapenv:Envelope>
```

The fields are tabulated and discussed in Table 10-3.

Table 10-3: Alert Query Fields

from	Date in the format MM/DD/YYYY
to	Date in the format MM/DD/YYYY
id	Event ID from the Enterprise Manager

TABLE 10-3: Alert Query Fields *(continued)*

environmentName	Name of the eDesigner environment, for example, envWSSPXA
~ physicalHostName	Does not seem to apply
logicalHostName	Name of the logical host in the eDesigner environment
serverName	Name of the Integration Server in the eDesigner environment
componentProjectPathName	For example, __Book|Examples|WSSPXA|DPs
deploymentName	Name of a deployment profile
componentName	Name of a named component, for example, service name from the connectivity map
~ severity	Does not seem to apply
type	snmpagent51x, INTEGRATION, COLLABORATION, etc.; see Table 10-5
~ observationalState	Does not seem to apply
~ operationalState	Does not seem to apply
messageCode	See Alert Agent message codes; IS-00001 is IS Started, IS-00002 is IS Stopped, Collaboration Started is COL-00001, etc.; see Table 10.4
details	Unquoted literal content of an alert message; for example: "Collaboration svc_jcdProcessMessage_qA is RUNNING" or "Application Server has Stopped," which are system-defined detailed messages, or "Failed to do update Employee Number: 7876, BP Instance ID: 192.168.62.135:-4bebe2ad:1102aa40a61:-7ba3," which is a user-defined message. By prefixing a string with %, we obtain a query "like %xxxx%"; with no % at the beginning of the string, we get "like xxxx%" instead

Table 10-4 lists values that can be used for the messageCode.

TABLE 10-4: Message Codes

Class	*Meaning*	*messageCode*
Logical Host	EXITED	LH-00001
	RUNNING	LH-00002
	STARTED	LH-00003
	STOPPED	LH-00004
	STOPPED2	LH-00005
	KILLED	LH-00006
	NOT_RESPONDING	LH-00007
	ALREADY_RUNNING	LH-00008
Integration Server	STARTED	IS-00001
	STOPPED	IS-00002
	STARTING	IS-00003
	STOPPING	IS-00004
	KILLED	IS-00005
Message Server	EXITED	MS-00001
	RUNNING	MS-00002
	STARTED	MS-00003
	STOPPED	MS-00004
	STOPPED2	MS-00005
	KILLED	MS-00006
	NOT_RESPONDING	MS-00007
	ALREADY_RUNNING	MS-00008
	MESSAGE_LIMIT_EXCEEDED	MS-00100
Collaboration	COLLAB_IS_RUNNING	COL-00001

TABLE 10-4: Message Codes *(continued)*

Class	*Meaning*	*messageCode*
	COLLAB_IS_STOPPED	COL-00002
	COLLAB_CUSTOM_USER	COL-00003
SNMP Agent	CONFIGURED	SNMP-00001
	NOT_CONFIGURED	SNMP-00002
	RUNNING	SNMP-00003
	STOPPED	SNMP-00004
	NOT_INSTALLED	SNMP-00005

Table 10-5 lists values that can be used for type.

The following values can be used for severity. Since severity does not seem to work, however, this information is perhaps not very relevant.

```
FATAL, CRITICAL, MAJOR, MINOR, WARNING, INFO
```

The following values can be used for operationalState. Since operationalState does not seem to work, however, this information is perhaps not very relevant.

```
UNKNOWN, STARTING, SUSPENDING, SUSPENDED, STOPPING, STOPPED, RUNNING
```

TABLE 10-5: Table of types

Meaning	*type*
SERVER_TYPE_INTEGRATION	INTEGRATION
SERVER_TYPE_MESSAGE	MESSAGE
COMPONENT_TYPE_COLLABORATION	COLLABORATION
COMPONENT_TYPE_STCMS	JMS
COMPONENT_TYPE_EWAY	EWAY
COMPONENT_TYPE_BPEL	BPEL

The following values can be used for observationalState. Since observationalState does not seem to work, however, this information is perhaps not very relevant.

```
UNOBSERVED, OBSERVED, RESOLVED
```

Alerting and SNMP agent logging can be increased or decreased by configuring one or more of the logging categories listed in Listing 10-39 in the Enterprise Manager's log4j.properties.

LISTING 10-39: Alert Agent logging categories

```
com.stc.eventmanagement
com.stc.snmpagent.webservices
com.stc.snmpagent
```

Now that we discussed filtering and filter values, let's submit a request with a filter expression asking for all "Component Running" alerts for the collaboration svc_jcdUpdateXA on January 26, 2007. The filter expression will be:

```
from=01/26/2007;to=01/27/2007;componentName=svc_jcdUpdateXA;messageCode=COL-00001
```

The request in Listing 10-40 uses that filter expression to get corresponding alerts.

LISTING 10-40: getAlerts request with a filter expression

```
<soapenv:Envelope
        xmlns:xsi="http://www.w3.org/2001/XMLSchema-instance"
        xmlns:xsd="http://www.w3.org/2001/XMLSchema"
        xmlns:soapenv="http://schemas.xmlsoap.org/soap/envelope/"
        xmlns:soap="http://soap.ws.services.em.egate.stc.com">
   <soapenv:Header/>
   <soapenv:Body>
    <soap:getAlerts
        soapenv:encodingStyle="http://schemas.xmlsoap.org/soap/encoding/">
     <sessionId xsi:type="soapenc:string"
        xmlns:soapenc="http://schemas.xmlsoap.org/soap/encoding/">
5DABD3370E5D3C02C41C5E334C5D40D8
     </sessionId>
     <filter xsi:type="soapenc:string"
        xmlns:soapenc="http://schemas.xmlsoap.org/soap/encoding/">
from=01/26/2007;to=01/27/2007;componentName=svc_jcdUpdateXA;messageCode=COL-00001
     </filter>
    </soap:getAlerts>
   </soapenv:Body>
</soapenv:Envelope>
```

The (edited) response is shown in Listing 10-41.

LISTING 10-41: getAlerts with a filter response

```
<soapenv:Envelope
        xmlns:soapenv="http://schemas.xmlsoap.org/soap/envelope/"
        xmlns:xsd="http://www.w3.org/2001/XMLSchema"
        xmlns:xsi="http://www.w3.org/2001/XMLSchema-instance">
   <soapenv:Body>
    <ns1:getAlertsResponse
        soapenv:encodingStyle="http://schemas.xmlsoap.org/soap/encoding/"
        xmlns:ns1="http://soap.ws.services.em.egate.stc.com">
     <getAlertsReturn soapenc:arrayType="ns2:local[5]" xsi:type="soapenc:Array"
        xmlns:ns2="myNameSpace:fixIt"
        xmlns:soapenc="http://schemas.xmlsoap.org/soap/encoding/">
      <getAlertsReturn href="#id0"/>
...
      <getAlertsReturn href="#id4"/>
     </getAlertsReturn>
    </ns1:getAlertsResponse>
    <multiRef id="id1" soapenc:root="0"
        soapenv:encodingStyle="http://schemas.xmlsoap.org/soap/encoding/"
        xsi:type="ns3:local" xmlns:ns3="myNameSpace:fixIt"
        xmlns:soapenc="http://schemas.xmlsoap.org/soap/encoding/">
     <alertName xsi:nil="true" xsi:type="soapenc:string"/>
     <comment xsi:nil="true" xsi:type="soapenc:string"/>
     <component xsi:type="soapenc:string">svc_jcdUpdateXA</component>
     <componentName xsi:type="soapenc:string">svc_jcdUpdateXA</componentName>
     <componentProjectPathName xsi:type="soapenc:string">
__Book|Examples|WSSPXA|DPs
     </componentProjectPathName>
     <componentType xsi:type="soapenc:string">COLLABORATION</componentType>
     <date xsi:type="xsd:dateTime">2007-01-26T11:40:41.903Z</date>
     <deploymentName xsi:type="soapenc:string">dpWSSPXA</deploymentName>
     <details xsi:type="soapenc:string">
Collaboration svc_jcdUpdateXA is RUNNING
     </details>
     <elementName xsi:type="soapenc:string">svc_jcdUpdateXA</elementName>
     <environmentName xsi:type="soapenc:string">envWSSPXA</environmentName>
     <event xsi:nil="true" xsi:type="xsd:anyType"/>
     <eventName xsi:type="soapenc:string">null</eventName>
     <eventType xsi:type="soapenc:string">ALERT</eventType>
     <id xsi:type="soapenc:string">4678</id>
     <index xsi:nil="true" xsi:type="soapenc:long"/>
     <logicalHostName xsi:type="soapenc:string">WSSPXA_LH</logicalHostName>
     <message xsi:type="soapenc:string">COL-00001</message>
     <messageCode xsi:type="soapenc:string">COL-00001</messageCode>
     <name xsi:nil="true" xsi:type="soapenc:string"/>
     <observationalState xsi:type="soapenc:string">Unobserved</observationalState>
     <observed href="#id5"/>
     <operationalState xsi:type="soapenc:string">Running</operationalState>
     <physicalHostName
         xsi:type="soapenc:string">localhost:20000</physicalHostName>
     <reference xsi:nil="true" xsi:type="xsd:anyType"/>
```

```
      <resolved href="#id6"/>
      <serverName xsi:type="soapenc:string">WSSPXA_IS</serverName>
      <serverType xsi:type="soapenc:string">INTEGRATION</serverType>
      <severity xsi:type="soapenc:string">INFO</severity>
      <timeStamp xsi:type="soapenc:string">01/26/07 10:40:41 PM</timeStamp>
      <type xsi:type="soapenc:string">COLLABORATION</type>
     </multiRef>
...
     <multiRef id="id2" soapenc:root="0"
           soapenv:encodingStyle="http://schemas.xmlsoap.org/soap/encoding/"
           xsi:type="ns7:local" xmlns:ns7="myNameSpace:fixIt"
           xmlns:soapenc="http://schemas.xmlsoap.org/soap/encoding/">
      <alertName xsi:nil="true" xsi:type="soapenc:string"/>
      <comment xsi:nil="true" xsi:type="soapenc:string"/>
      <component xsi:type="soapenc:string">svc_jcdUpdateXA</component>
      <componentName xsi:type="soapenc:string">svc_jcdUpdateXA</componentName>
      <componentProjectPathName xsi:type="soapenc:string">
__Book|Examples|WSSPXA|DPs
      </componentProjectPathName>
      <componentType xsi:type="soapenc:string">COLLABORATION</componentType>
      <date xsi:type="xsd:dateTime">2007-01-26T06:01:22.358Z</date>
      <deploymentName xsi:type="soapenc:string">dpWSSPXA</deploymentName>
      <details xsi:type="soapenc:string">
Collaboration svc_jcdUpdateXA is RUNNING
      </details>
      <elementName xsi:type="soapenc:string">svc_jcdUpdateXA</elementName>
      <environmentName xsi:type="soapenc:string">envWSSPXA</environmentName>
      <event xsi:nil="true" xsi:type="xsd:anyType"/>
      <eventName xsi:type="soapenc:string">null</eventName>
      <eventType xsi:type="soapenc:string">ALERT</eventType>
      <id xsi:type="soapenc:string">4673</id>
      <index xsi:nil="true" xsi:type="soapenc:long"/>
      <logicalHostName xsi:type="soapenc:string">WSSPXA_LH</logicalHostName>
      <message xsi:type="soapenc:string">COL-00001</message>
      <messageCode xsi:type="soapenc:string">COL-00001</messageCode>
      <name xsi:nil="true" xsi:type="soapenc:string"/>
      <observationalState xsi:type="soapenc:string">Observed</observationalState>
      <observed href="#id13"/>
      <operationalState xsi:type="soapenc:string">Running</operationalState>
      <physicalHostName
           xsi:type="soapenc:string">localhost:20000</physicalHostName>
      <reference xsi:nil="true" xsi:type="xsd:anyType"/>
      <resolved href="#id14"/>
      <serverName xsi:type="soapenc:string">WSSPXA_IS</serverName>
      <serverType xsi:type="soapenc:string">INTEGRATION</serverType>
      <severity xsi:type="soapenc:string">INFO</severity>
      <timeStamp xsi:type="soapenc:string">01/26/07 05:01:22 PM</timeStamp>
      <type xsi:type="soapenc:string">COLLABORATION</type>
     </multiRef>
     <multiRef id="id14" soapenc:root="0"
           soapenv:encodingStyle="http://schemas.xmlsoap.org/soap/encoding/"
           xsi:type="xsd:boolean"
           xmlns:soapenc="http://schemas.xmlsoap.org/soap/encoding/">
false
```

```
    </multiRef>
...
    <multiRef id="id10" soapenc:root="0"
          soapenv:encodingStyle="http://schemas.xmlsoap.org/soap/encoding/"
          xsi:type="xsd:boolean"
          xmlns:soapenc="http://schemas.xmlsoap.org/soap/encoding/">
false
    </multiRef>
   </soapenv:Body>
</soapenv:Envelope>
```

The query field content and operation comments in Table 10-3 are a result of empirical study. There is no documentation, to which the author has access, that describes any of this.

Following are some example filters that work.

Select alert messages generated between January 26, 2007, and January 26, 2007 (single day):

```
from=01/26/2007;to=01/26/2007
```

Select alert messages, generated on January 26, 2007, for all collaborations:

```
type=COLLABORATION;from=01/26/2007;to=01/26/2007
```

Select alert with event ID of 4677:

```
id=4677
```

Select alert messages, generated on January 26, 2007, for all components hosted in the specified logical host:

```
from=01/26/2007;to=01/26/2007;logicalHostName=MCZ01.aus.sun.com
```

Select all "Start the Integration Server" (IS-00001) alerts, generated on January 26, 2007, for the Integration Server within the specified logical host:

```
from=01/26/2007;to=01/26/2007;logicalHostName=MCZ01.aus.sun.com;messageCode=
IS-00001
```

Select all alerts for the specific connectivity map service, generated on January 26, 2007:

```
from=01/26/2007;to=01/27/2007;componentName=svc_jcdUpdateXA
```

Other filters may well work as well. The experiments were conducted using SoapUI, which is a quick and easy way to invoke Web Services for experimentation.

Filterable operations for which filters are required are deleteAlerts, getAlerts, observeAlerts, resolveAlerts, and resetAlerts.

Finally, the Alert Service supports the closeSession operation, which allows the session established with the Login Service to be closed and the Session ID to be invalidated.

Attempting to perform an operation using a Session ID for which the session has been closed results in a SOAP Fault similar to the one shown in Listing 10-42.

LISTING 10-42: Session Not Found SOAP Fault

```
<soapenv:Envelope
        xmlns:soapenv="http://schemas.xmlsoap.org/soap/envelope/"
        xmlns:xsd="http://www.w3.org/2001/XMLSchema"
        xmlns:xsi="http://www.w3.org/2001/XMLSchema-instance">
   <soapenv:Body>
    <soapenv:Fault>
     <faultcode>soapenv:Server.userException</faultcode>
     <faultstring>
java.rmi.RemoteException: Session not found for:5DABD3370E5D3C02C41C5E334C5D40D8
     </faultstring>
     <detail>
      <ns1:hostname xmlns:ns1="http://xml.apache.org/axis/">MCZ01</ns1:hostname>
     </detail>
    </soapenv:Fault>
   </soapenv:Body>
</soapenv:Envelope>
```

While it is unfortunate that most of the Alert operations cannot be invoked from a Java CAPS solution directly, it is possible to incorporate them into an operational system by building standalone components, using Sun's Net Beans IDE, and deploying them to the Sun Application Server. These components could use one of the techniques discussed in Chapter 5, "Messaging Infrastructure," section 5.15, to support integration into a Java CAPS solution.

10.2.9 Java Management Extensions (JMX)

Since Java CAPS is a J2EE-based toolset, the JMX technology can be used to manage the container and the components. Discussion of JMX is beyond the scope of this text. Refer to online sources for further information.

JMX instrumentation can be used to inspect component attributes and change component states, including stopping and starting components that are capable of being stopped and started. The following section discusses the JMX Console Web Application, provided with the Java CAPS distribution; the J2SDK 1.5's JConsole application and its use with Java CAPS; and briefly discusses the MC4J JMX Console. Chapter 8, section 8.2.3.1, "Programmatic Management," in Part II, implements an example project that programmatically manipulates Java CAPS components using JMX.

10.2.9.1 Java CAPS JMX Console Web Application

[eGateSAG] mentions the use of the Java CAPS JMX Console. To invoke the JMX Console, use the URL that points to the host and port for the Application Server domain to be monitored, with the literal "jmx-console" as the servlet context. For example:

```
http://localhost:20000/jmx-console
```

where 20000 is the _base port_ for the domain as distinct from the port of the default Web Container in the domain.

Once logged in with administrator credentials, you will see a page similar to the one shown in Figure 10-41, where the number of links will vary with the number of enterprise applications deployed to the domain.

Enterprise Manager information, obtained by clicking the Enterprise Manager link, will look similar to that shown in Figure 10-42, with host names, port numbers, and other site-specific information different from that in the illustration.

Those familiar with the internals of the Sun Application Server 8.0 can use the Management Beans (MBeans) to obtain information about various aspects of the Java CAPS integration server and JMS implementation, and modify modifiable properties and attributes.

Just how useful this information may be will vary. Since documentation is scarce, and the System Administration Guide names only one MBean as supported, what you see may vary from release to release.

As an example, let's look at com.sun.appserv domain's name=logmanager, category=runtime link, as shown in Figure 10-43.

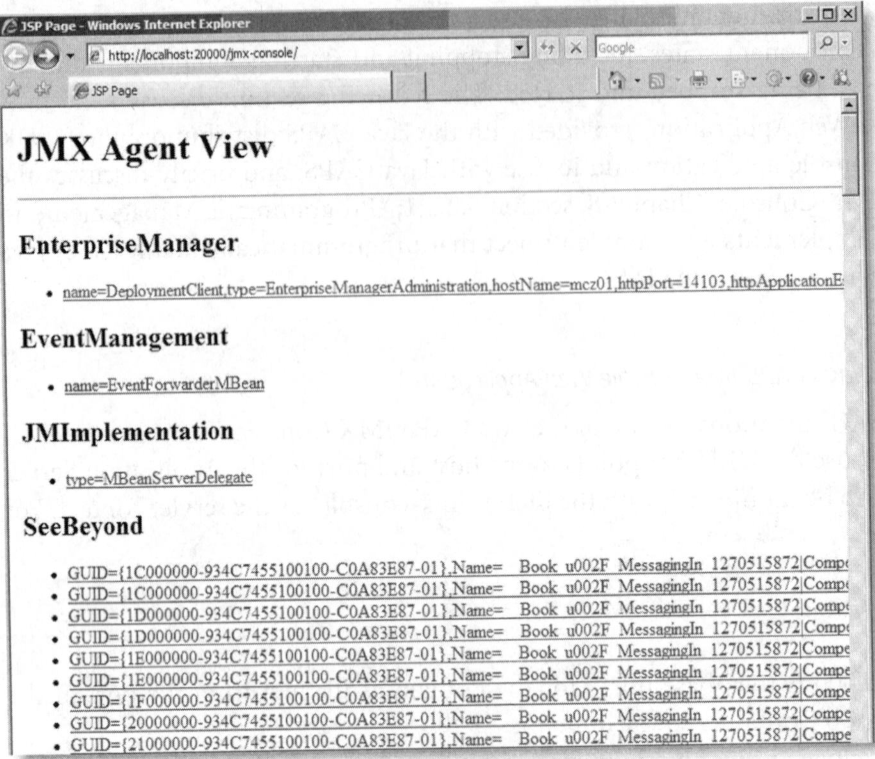

FIGURE 10-41: Java CAPS jmx-console servlet display

The MBean supports a number of operations. Invoking its getLogDump operation, as shown in Figure 10-44, produces some insightful information about the logging categories and their dependency hierarchy (Figure 10-45). The list is long.

Executing the getLoggerNamesUnder() operation specifying category com.stc .bpms produces a list of names for which log levels can be specified, as shown in Figure 10-46.

Figure 10-47 shows the list, which is longish and unformatted.

Copying the list, pasting into a text editor, and reformatting yields a list of "interesting" logging categories (see Listing 10-43) that can be specified for logging various aspects of the eInsight execution environment.

FIGURE 10-42: Results of clicking on the Enterprise Manager link

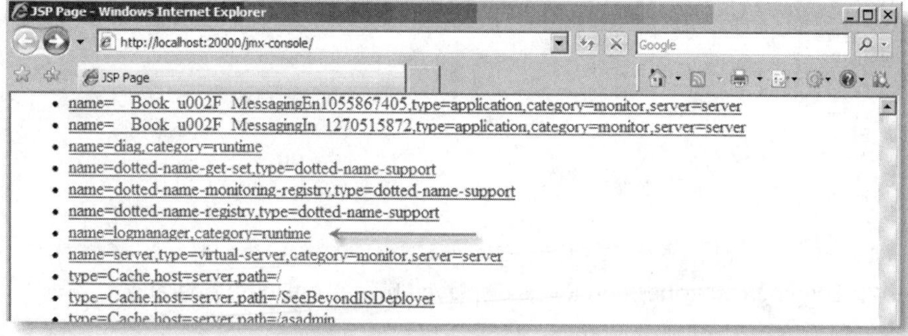

FIGURE 10-43: Runtime logmanager link

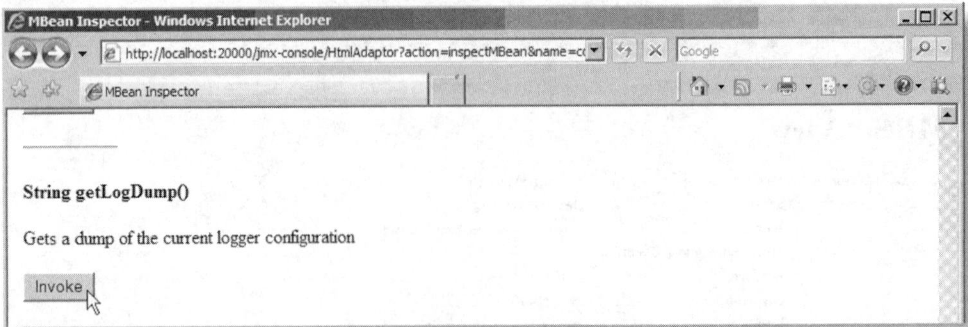

FIGURE 10-44: getLogDump operation button

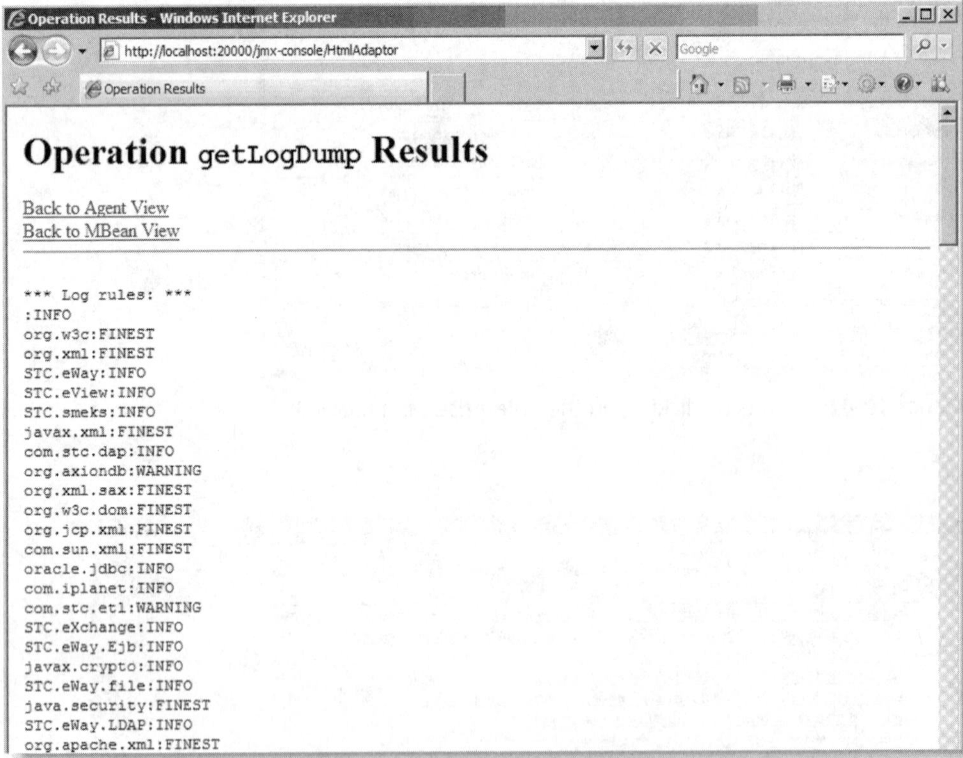

FIGURE 10-45: Logging categories and levels displayed by getLogDump operation

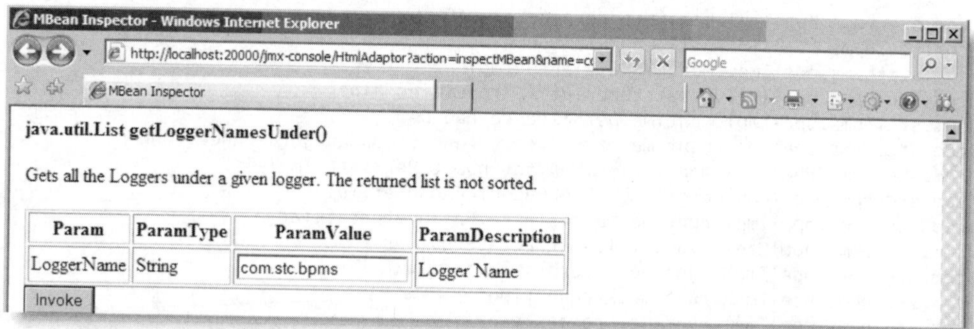

FIGURE 10-46: Asking for a list of loggers under the com.stc.bpms category

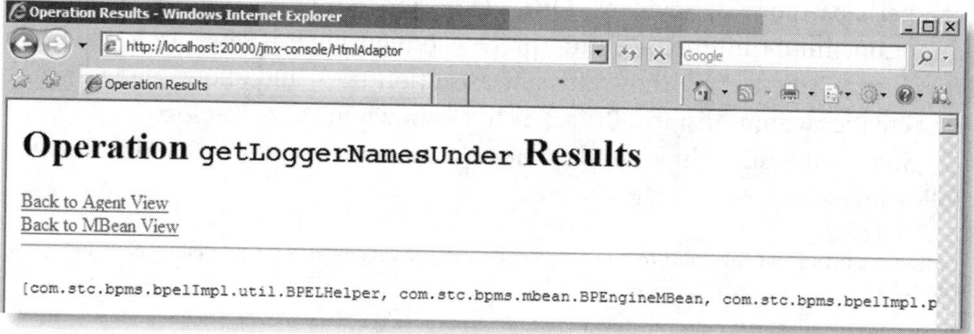

FIGURE 10-47: List of loggers under com.stc.bpms

LISTING 10-43: Logging categories under the com.stc.bpms logging category

```
com.stc.bpms.bpelImpl.util.BPELHelper
com.stc.bpms.mbean.BPEngineMBean
com.stc.bpms.bpelImpl.persistence.adapter.impl.DBAdapter
com.stc.bpms.bpelConnector.ConnectionFactoryImpl
com.stc.bpms.bpelConnector.impl.WorkListenerImpl
com.stc.bpms.bpelImpl.runtime.ExtendedAssignerImpl
com.stc.bpms.bpelImpl.persistence.reporting.ReportsTableDataPersister
com.stc.bpms.bpelImpl.runtime.BPELInterpreter
com.stc.bpms.bpelImpl.runtime.persistence.connectionManager.ConnectionMgr
com.stc.bpms.bpelConnector.impl.ExecutorImpl
com.stc.bpms.bpelConnector.impl.EndPointFactoryRegistryInfoImpl
com.stc.bpms.bpelImpl.runtime.AbstractEventHandler
```

```
com.stc.bpms.bpelImpl.persistence.adapter.DAO
com.stc.bpms.bpelImpl.util.CorrelationHelper
com.stc.bpms.bpelImpl.model.BPELAlerterImpl
com.stc.bpms.bpelImpl.persistence.util.PropertiesHelper
com.stc.bpms.bpelImpl.runtime.persistence.dao.DAO
com.stc.bpms.bpelImpl.runtime.persistence.connectionManager.ConnectionPool
com.stc.bpms.bpelImpl.monitoring.MonitoringDataPersisterImpl
com.stc.bpms.bpelConnector.impl.BPELResourceAdapterImpl
com.stc.bpms.bpelImpl.runtime.persistence.FailoverPersister
com.stc.bpms.bpelConnector.impl.AbstractWSProvider
com.stc.bpms.bpelImpl.runtime.Interpreter
com.stc.bpms.bpelImpl.runtime.RecoveryImpl
com.stc.bpms.bpelImpl.runtime.ProcessType
com.stc.bpms.bpelImpl.runtime.persistence.connectionManager.ConnectionImpl
```

What some of these categories are likely to log can only be guessed at. Others are perhaps more self-evident. One of the more useful categories is com.stc.bpms.bpelImpl.runtime.BPELInterpreter. Configuring this category to Fine, or a more verbose level, will show eInsight execution trace and allow debug logging on activities within Business Processes to be shown in the server.log.

Some interesting links under the com.sun.appserv domain might be the following:

```
type=messaging-server-config-mbean,jmsservertype=stcms,name=Sun_SeeBeyond_JMS_IQ_Manager

type=messaging-server-admin-mbean,jmsservertype=stcms,name=Sun_SeeBeyond_JMS_IQ_Manager

type=jvm,category=monitor,server=server (provides information on JVM's heap size and heap utilization)

j2eeType=JVM,name=MCZ01_1169686101366,J2EEServer=server,category=runtime (where the name, here shown as MCZ01_xxx, will be different)

j2eeType=J2EEServer,name=server,category=runtime
```

You may find, under the SeeBeyond domain, references to Business Process engines, like the following:

```
EARId=__Book_u002F_MessageExch1329550651,type=BPEngineMBean
```

You could, with some effort, use this link to manage eInsight Business Processes using the JMX interface.

Under the com.stc.Logging domain, there are other, potentially interesting links:

```
name=LogConfigurator,type=AppServerLogConfigurator

name=LogReader,type=AppServerLogReader,logger=jms

name=LogReader,type=AppServerLogReader,logger=server
```

There are a number of other links, in the JMX Console page, that provide access to information and operations of greater or lesser value, depending on your familiarity with the solutions and application server internals.

10.2.9.2 J2SDK 1.5 JConsole

By default in Java CAPS 5.1.3, JMX instrumentation support required to use JConsole and similar JMX console applications is not enabled, so JConsole cannot be used. To enable interaction with the JConsole, the Integration Server must be started with one or more additional Java Virtual Machine (JVM) options. See [JMXNote] and [JMXNote2] for discussions of the topic.

In brief, setting one or more JVM options for the Integration Server, and restarting the Integration Server, will enable JConsole's local and/or remote access to the application. Note that depending on the options and how they are set, you may end up with an insecure connection.

To enable the JMX agent for local access, add the following JVM property:

```
-Dcom.sun.management.jmxremote
```

Setting this property registers the JVM instrumentation MBeans and publishes the Remote Method Invocation (RMI) connector via a private interface to allow JMX client applications to monitor a local Java platform, that is, a JVM running on the same machine. When you start the JConsole application, it presents a display similar to that shown in Figure 10-48.

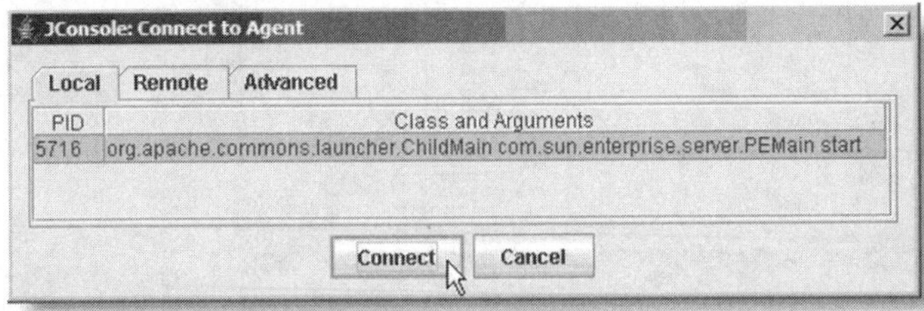

FIGURE 10-48: Connecting JConsole to a JVM running on a local machine

Pressing Connect will cause JConsole to connect and will provide access to the console's functionality. [JConsole] has a nice discussion of JConsole and its capabilities. Here are some examples.

The Heap graph is shown in Figure 10-49.

The Threads graph is shown in Figure 10-50.

Attributes of a selected MBean for a component of the solution deployed to the Integration Server are shown in Figure 10-51, and operations are shown in Figure 10-52. For additional information and specific examples, see Chapter 8, section 8.2.3.1, "Programmatic Management," in Part II.

Some of the virtual machine and environment information is shown in Figure 10-53.

All of the above can be accessed with JConsole as long as JConsole and the monitored application reside on the same physical machine. To enable remote monitoring, a couple of other JVM options, shown in Listing 10-44, need to be set.

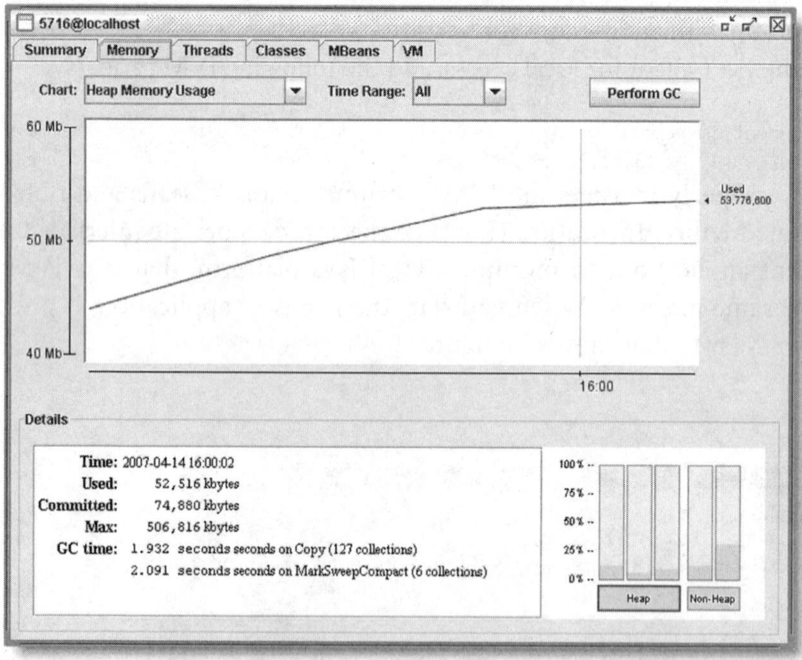

FIGURE 10-49: Heap Graph

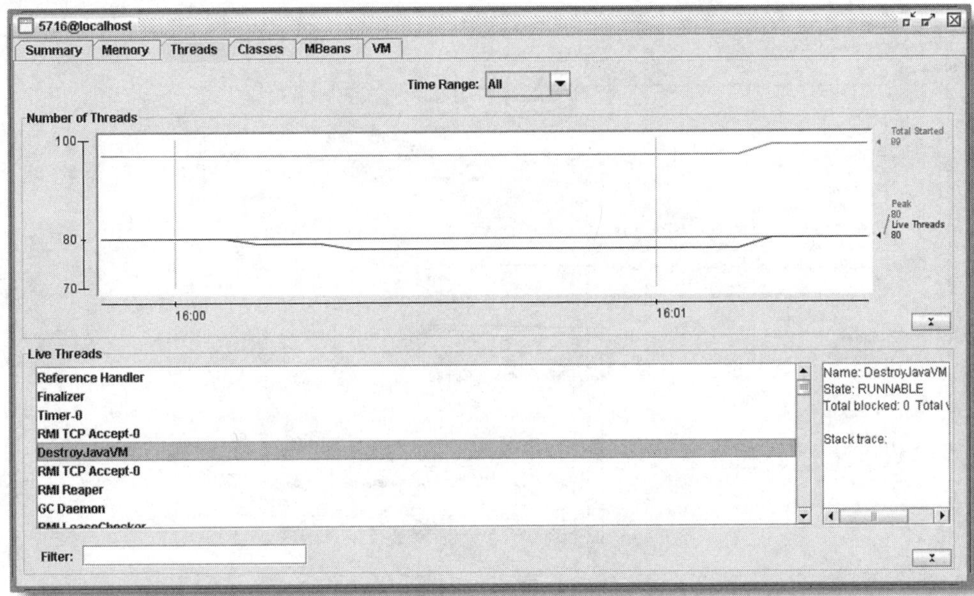

FIGURE 10-50: Threads graph

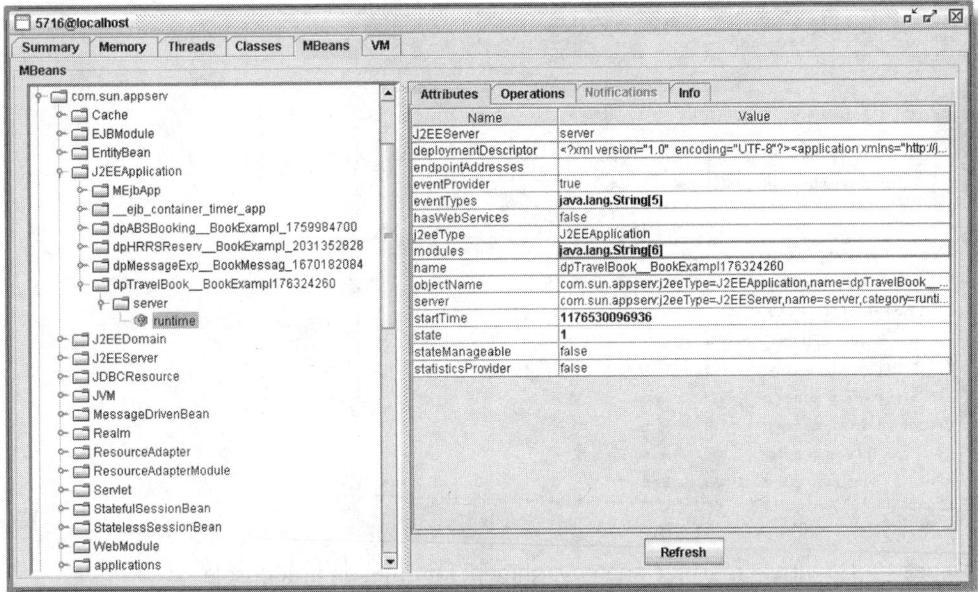

FIGURE 10-51: MBean for a selected enterprise application

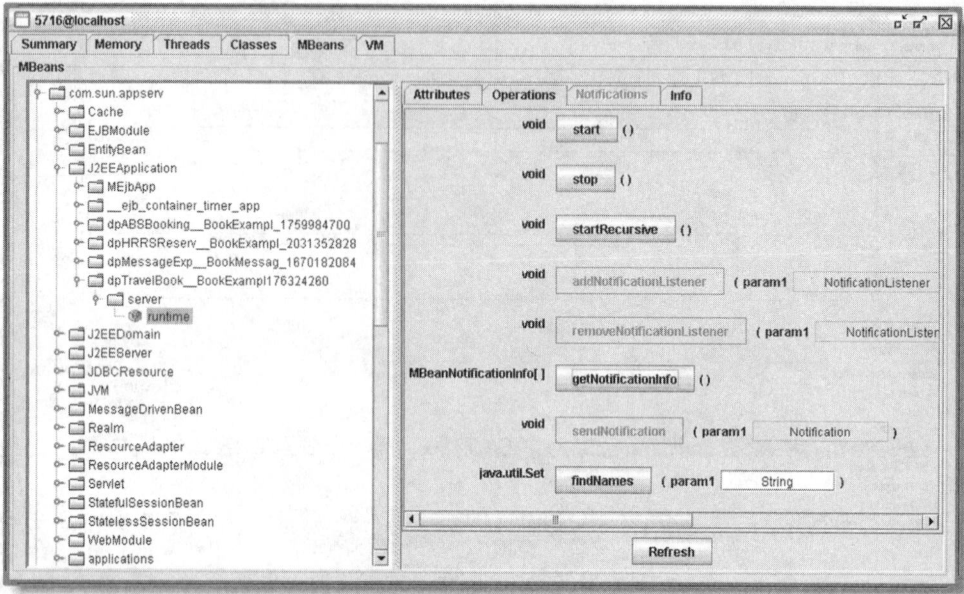

FIGURE 10-52: MBean operations

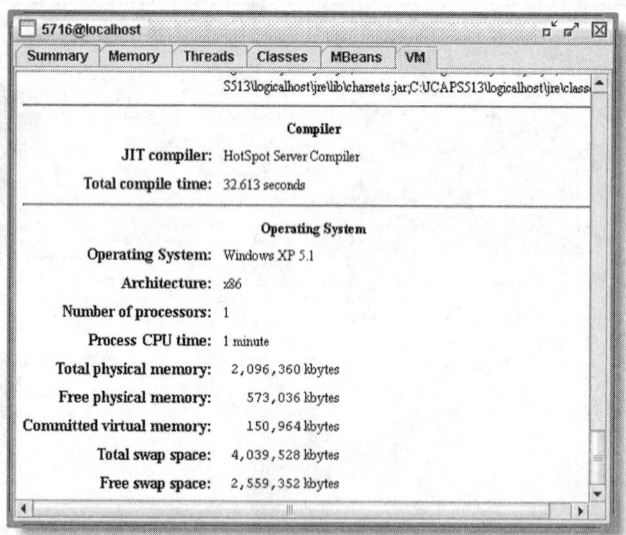

FIGURE 10-53: Virtual machine and environment information in JConsole

LISTING 10-44: JVM Options required to enable remote monitoring with JConsole

```
-Dcom.sun.management.jmxremote.port=portNum
-Dcom.sun.management.jmxremote.ssl=false
-Dcom.sun.management.jmxremote.authenticate=false
```

This will allow a remote JConsole to connect to the Integration Server without authentication and over an insecure connection, as shown in Figure 10-54. Remote monitoring and management may be desirable, as JConsole is fairly heavy on resources. Running it on the host already heavily utilized will skew some results.

See [JMXNote2] for a discussion of how to enable authentication and channel security for remote JMX management.

10.2.9.3 MC4J JMX Console

The URL for programmatic access to the managed resource, given port number of 9999 and the application running on localhost, is:

```
service:jmx:rmi:///jndi/rmi://localhost:9999/jmxrmi
```

Figure 10-55 shows the dialog box where this value must be entered.

The URL in Figure 10-55 is what you would specify to the MC4J [MC4J], another JXM Console application that some people might prefer and perhaps find more friendly, to permit it to connect to the Java CAPS Integration Server.

Figure 10-56 shows MC4J connection properties that allow MC4J to connect to the Java CAPS environment.

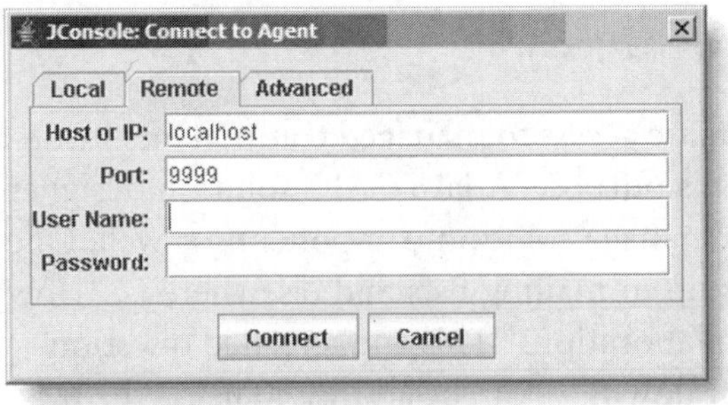

FIGURE 10-54: JConsole properties used to connect to the remote JVM

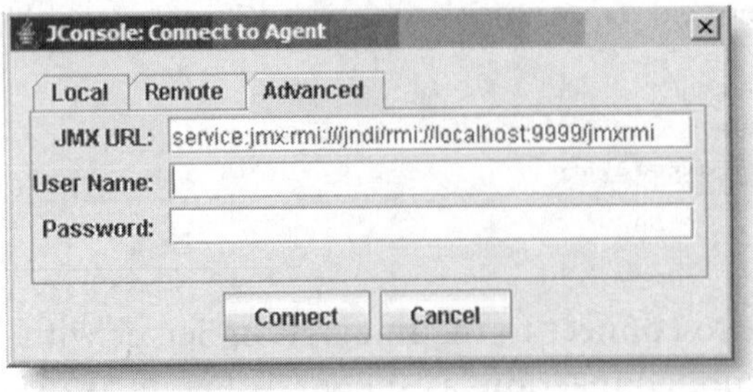

JConsole: Connect to Agent

Local | Remote | Advanced

JMX URL: service:jmx:rmi:///jndi/rmi://localhost:9999/jmxrmi

User Name:

Password:

Connect | Cancel

FIGURE 10-55: JMX URL for remote monitoring

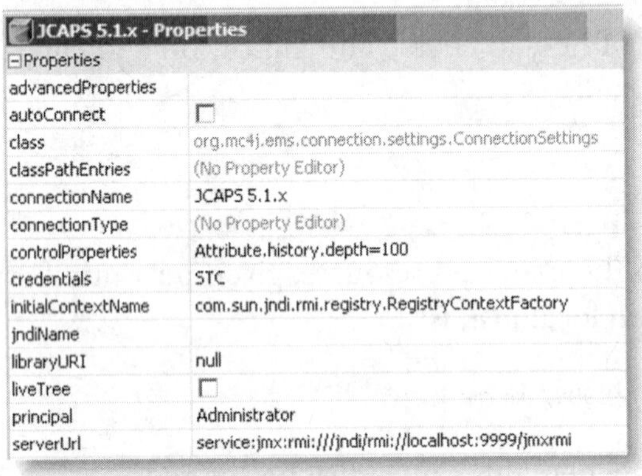

JCAPS 5.1.x - Properties

Properties	
advancedProperties	
autoConnect	☐
class	org.mc4j.ems.connection.settings.ConnectionSettings
classPathEntries	(No Property Editor)
connectionName	JCAPS 5.1.x
connectionType	(No Property Editor)
controlProperties	Attribute.history.depth=100
credentials	STC
initialContextName	com.sun.jndi.rmi.registry.RegistryContextFactory
jndiName	
libraryURI	null
liveTree	☐
principal	Administrator
serverUrl	service:jmx:rmi:///jndi/rmi://localhost:9999/jmxrmi

FIGURE 10-56: MC4J properties needed to monitor a Java CAPS solution

10.2.9.4 Programmatic Management

The URL for programmatic access to the managed resource, given port number of 9999 and the application running on localhost, is:

```
service:jmx:rmi:///jndi/rmi://localhost:9999/jmxrmi
```

JMX technology allows programmatic access to managed components. JConsole and MC4J use the JMX API for this purpose. A Java CAPS solution designer can use the API to programmatically manage solution components as well. One of the questions that frequently pops up in mailing lists and elsewhere is, "How can I programmatically stop a Java Collaboration?" This and a related question—"How can I tell if a component is up or down?"—can be addressed using the JMX API. This section discusses an example Java Collaboration that can be used to execute JMX management actions on other Java CAPS components, including stop, start, getStatus, and others. Which actions can be executed depends on the component. The example itself is developed in Chapter 8, section 8.2.3.1, "Programmatic Management," in Part II.

Knowing the name of the MBean associated with a particular Java CAPS component allows you to manage it. Both the name of the MBean and the management actions supported by a component can be discovered using JConsole or MC4J. Let's take the example from project __Book/MessageExchangePatterns/MessageExpiration developed for this book, with the project hierarchy shown in Figure 10-57.

The connectivity map in Figure 10-58 shows the following components: qIn, qOut, qPark, svc_jcdExpireMessageEarly, and svcJMS2JMSShowExpiration.

The deployment profile is named dpMessageExpiration.

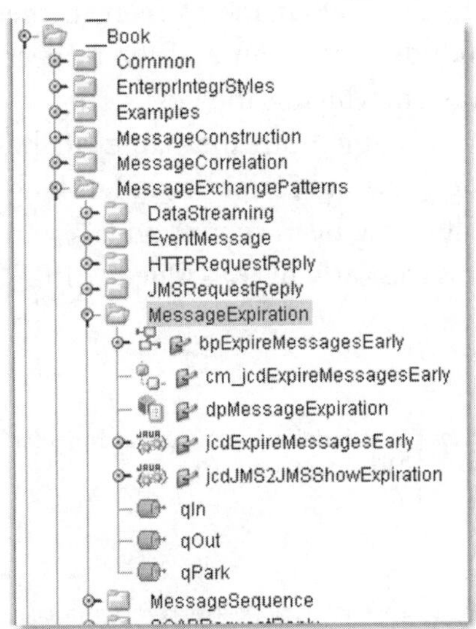

FIGURE 10-57: MessageExpiration project hierarchy

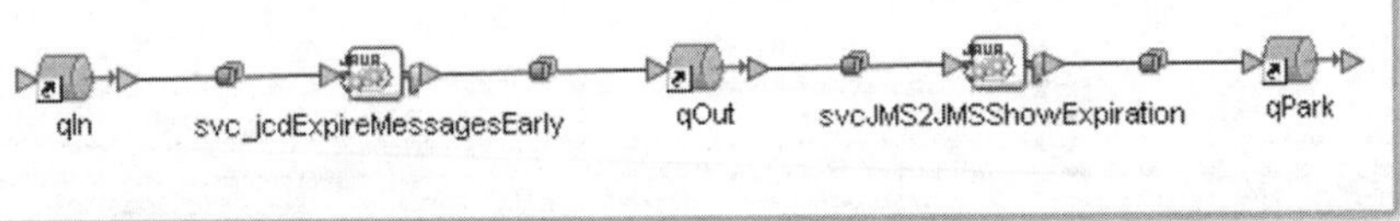

FIGURE 10-58: Connectivity map for project MessageExpiration

The deployed project appears in the Enterprise Manager's Deployer, as shown in Figure 10-59.

MC4J, under the domain named SeeBeyond, lists all the MBeans created for the components in this project, as shown in Figure 10-60.

The text in Figure 10-60 is unreadable, so let's reformat the list so it is decipherable. Listing 10-45 shows the reference to the MBean, which is discussed in subsequent paragraphs, where all components are in reality on a single line.

LISTING 10-45: Management Bean reference

```
Name=dpMessageExp__BookMessag_1670182084
    |MessageExpiration
    |dpMessageExpiration
    |qIn_svc_jcdExpireMessagesEarly
    ,GUID={8E010000-48F444ED110100-C0A83C02-01}
```

The string following Name= corresponds to the EAR name as seen in the Deployer. The string MessageExpiration corresponds to the name of the project containing deployment profile, dpMessageExpiration, which is the next string.

The string qIn_svc_jcdExpireMessagesEarly contains both the name of the JMS queue and the name of the Java Collaboration that subscribes to it. Looking back to the connectivity map, we will surmise that this MBean corresponds to the subscription of the CM service svc_jcdExpireMessagesEarly to JMS Queue qIn.

The GUID is not particularly interesting.

Here are the remaining components.

```
Name=dpMessageExp__BookMessag_1670182084|MessageExpiration|dpMessageExpiration|qOu
t_svcJMS2JMSShowExpiration, GUID={8F010000-48F444ED110100-C0A83C02-01}
```

dpMessageExp__BookMessag_1670182084 | __Book|MessageExchangePatterns|MessageExpirationdpMessageExpiration

FIGURE 10-59: Project represented by deployment profile dpMessageExpiration in Deployer

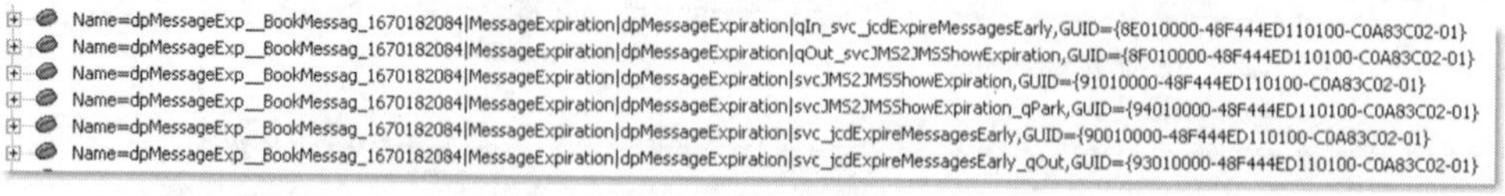

```
Name=dpMessageExp__BookMessag_1670182084|MessageExpiration|dpMessageExpiration|qIn_svc_jcdExpireMessagesEarly,GUID={8E010000-48F444ED110100-C0A83C02-01}
Name=dpMessageExp__BookMessag_1670182084|MessageExpiration|dpMessageExpiration|qOut_svcJMS2JMSShowExpiration,GUID={8F010000-48F444ED110100-C0A83C02-01}
Name=dpMessageExp__BookMessag_1670182084|MessageExpiration|dpMessageExpiration|svcJMS2JMSShowExpiration,GUID={91010000-48F444ED110100-C0A83C02-01}
Name=dpMessageExp__BookMessag_1670182084|MessageExpiration|dpMessageExpiration|svcJMS2JMSShowExpiration_qPark,GUID={94010000-48F444ED110100-C0A83C02-01}
Name=dpMessageExp__BookMessag_1670182084|MessageExpiration|dpMessageExpiration|svc_jcdExpireMessagesEarly,GUID={90010000-48F444ED110100-C0A83C02-01}
Name=dpMessageExp__BookMessag_1670182084|MessageExpiration|dpMessageExpiration|svc_jcdExpireMessagesEarly_qOut,GUID={93010000-48F444ED110100-C0A83C02-01}
```

FIGURE 10-60: MBeans under the SeeBeyond domain

qOut_svcJMS2JMSShowExpiration is the subscription of svcJMS2JMSShowExpiration to qOut.

```
Name=dpMessageExp__BookMessag_1670182084|MessageExpiration|dpMessageExpiration|svc
JMS2JMSShowExpiration, GUID={8F010000-48F444ED110100-C0A83C02-01}
```

svcJMS2JMSShowExpiration is the Java Collaboration service.

```
Name=dpMessageExp__BookMessag_1670182084|MessageExpiration|dpMessageExpiration|svc
JMS2JMSShowExpiration_qPark, GUID={8F010000-48F444ED110100-C0A83C02-01}
```

svcJMS2JMSShowExpiration_qPark is the publication of svcJMS2JMSShowExpiration to JMS Destination qPark.

```
Name=dpMessageExp__BookMessag_1670182084|MessageExpiration|dpMessageExpiration|svc
_jcdExpireMessagesEarly, GUID={8F010000-48F444ED110100-C0A83C02-01}
```

svc_jcdExpireMessagesEarly is the Java Collaboration service.

```
Name=dpMessageExp__BookMessag_1670182084|MessageExpiration|dpMessageExpiration|svc
_jcdExpireMessagesEarly_qOut, GUID={8F010000-48F444ED110100-C0A83C02-01}
```

svc_jcdExpireMessagesEarly_qOut is the publication of svc_jcdExpireMessagesEarly to JMS queue qOut.

Any one of these MBeans can be used to inspect the attributes of the corresponding component. Some MBeans will allow their managed object to be started, stopped, or queried. Which actions or operations are supported will vary from object to object. JMS queue subscription or a Java Collaboration service, for example, can be started and stopped. Publication to a JMS queue cannot be started or stopped.

Let's use the MC4J JMX Console to look at the subscription qIn_svc_jcdExpireMessagesEarly, as shown in Figure 10-61.

Some of the more interesting operations are getStatus, isStoppable, isStartable, Stop, and Start. Executing some of these operations produces results that vary with operation. Figures 10-62 through 10-64 illustrate execution of getStatus and isRestartable operations.

The same can be achieved from a standalone Java application or from a Java Collaboration.

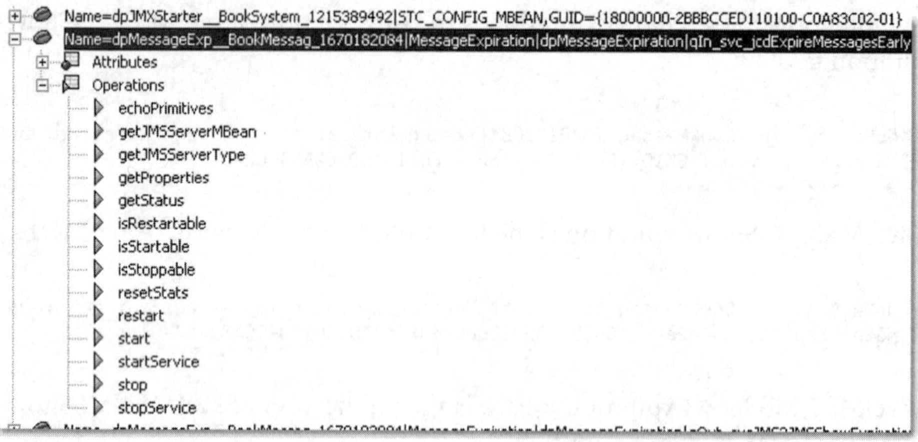

FIGURE 10-61: Operations under subscription qIn_svc_jcdExpireMessagesEarly

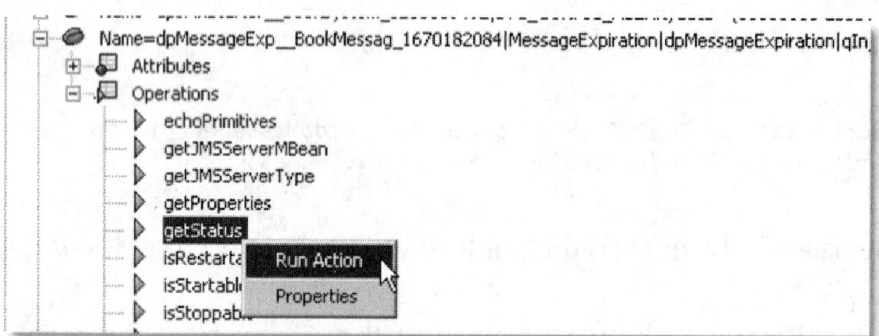

FIGURE 10-62: Execute getStatus operation

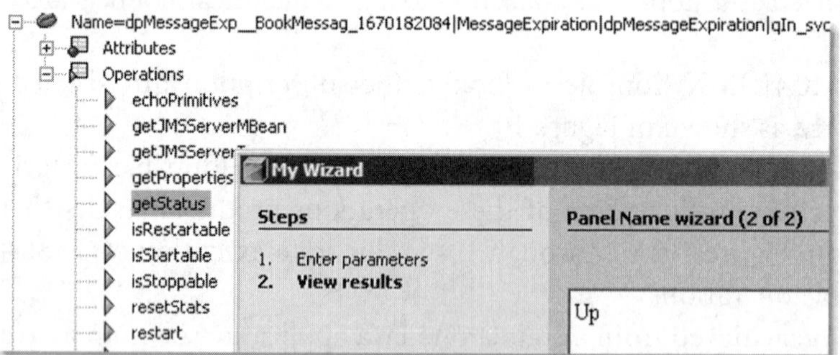

FIGURE 10-63: Result of execution of the getStatus operation

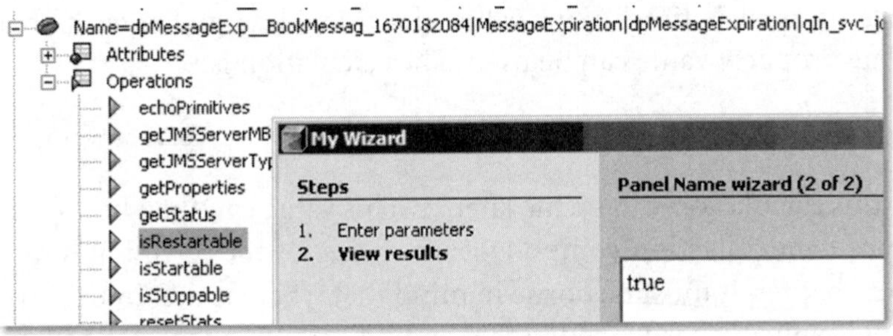

FIGURE 10-64: Results of execution of the isRestartable operation

10.2.10 Instrumenting Performance Data Collection

10.2.10.1 JMS Latency

In a solution that takes advantage of the JMS Message Server infrastructure to pass messages from component to component, latency, the amount of time it takes for the message to travel from the sending component to the next receiving component downstream, may be of interest. Regardless of the characteristics of the platform and of the workload, there will always be some minimum latency. Latency is affected by the workload and by solution design. The design involving serial receivers is more likely to experience increased latency with increased workload than the design involving concurrent consumers.

Measurement of latency can be accomplished by taking advantage of the timeToLive parameter to most JMS send() methods in senders and the JMS Message Server–calculated message Expiration property value of messages at the receivers.

For the explicitly set timeToLive value, the calculation is:

```
timeToLivesender - (Expirationreceiver - CurrentTimeMillisecondsreceiver)
```

The result of this calculation will be the latency. This value can be passed to the performance data collection component using one of the techniques discussed later in this chapter. It must be borne in mind that performing latency calculation based on timeToLive value introduces interdependency between the sender, which sets the timeToLive value, and the receiver, which uses it to calculate latency, as both components must agree on the value and both hardcode it. Needless to say, the calculation itself introduces some overhead unrelated to the primary purpose of the component in which it occurs.

In the absence of explicit timeToLive value, the JMS Message Server global Maximum Lifetime property value can be used. The calculation is:

```
Maximum Lifetimeglobal - (Expirationreceiver - CurrentTimeMillisecondsreceiver)
```

The result of this calculation will be the latency. This value can then be passed to the performance data collection component using one of the techniques discussed later in this chapter. It must be borne in mind that whereas the timeToLive value is presumably explicitly hardcoded in the sending component and therefore will not readily change, the Maximum Lifetime value is configurable through the Integration Server Administration interface and can be readily changed, affecting results of all latency calculations that are based on this property. Furthermore, the receiver that calculates latency must hardcode the Maximum Lifetime value to perform the calculation. This value will become incorrect if the global JMS Message Server property value changes.

Instead of hardcoding timeToLive or Maximum Lifetime values, you could read these values from a database or a properties file. This would make the solution more adaptable to change but in itself introduces additional complexity and overheads that require careful consideration.

For the purpose of calculating latency, it is immaterial whether the sender is a Java Collaboration or an eInsight Business Process. It is the receiver that performs the calculation. A receiver Java Collaboration could use code similar to that shown in Listing 10-46 to calculate latency.

LISTING 10-46: __Book/SystemManagement/Instrumentation/JMSLatency/jcdJMS2JMSShowExpiration

```
public void receive
    (com.stc.connectors.jms.Message input
    ,com.stc.connectors.jms.JMS W_toJMS )
        throws Throwable
{
    long lExpiration = input.getMessageProperties().getExpiration();
    long lNow = System.currentTimeMillis();
    long lTimeToLive = 60000;
    ;
    long lLatency = lTimeToLive - (lExpiration - lNow);
    ;
    logger.debug( "\nLatency: " + lLatency );
    ;
    W_toJMS.send( input );
}
```

A receiver eInsight Business Process has no built-in access to the value of the current time in milliseconds; therefore a helper Java Collaboration is required. This collaboration would be invoked as an activity and would return a long time value needed for the latency calculation.

Chapter 8, section 8.2.4.1, "JMS Latency," in Part II, provides an example of both the helper collaboration and the solution that calculates JMS latency using eInsight Business Process.

10.2.10.2 Instrumenting Collection of Runtime Data

Whereas JMS latency can be readily calculated from information already carried in messages during normal processing, it can only be calculated on a hop-by-hop basis and "inlined" in the processing components themselves.

If there are multiple components in a solution and message processing statistics like latency and throughput are to be calculated on a global basis, standard JMS Header properties cannot be used to collect the necessary data.

Recall that JMS topics with no durable subscribers act as Channel Purgers [EIP]. Any message placed in such a topic is discarded by the JMS Message Server. This property can be exploited to introduce Wire Taps [EIP] into solutions at the time business functionality is developed, without the need to concurrently develop statistics collection and processing components.

Let's imagine that a Wire Tap is added as the first activity in the first component of a solution and as the last activity in the last component of a solution. As each message passes through the set of components, it is replicated to both JMS topics, which are the Wire Taps, in full or in part, and its message identification is propagated as a Correlation ID property or a user-defined property in the JMS Message Header. The solution is completed, tested, and deployed in production. The cost of the overhead of replicating messages, only to have them discarded by the JMS Message Server, will vary with the size of messages, how much information is sent to Wire Taps, and the message volume.

Some time later, when the organization decided in what statistics it might be interested, a messaging system management and information processing solution, or two, or three, can be developed and deployed. The existing production solution will be unaffected by deployment of the solution that processes messages placed in Wire Taps.

Just correlating messages from the initial and the final Wire Taps leads to a number of useful statistics:

- Calculating the difference between enqueue times to the final and to the initial Wire Tap provides message processing latency of each message.
- Message latency, collected over time, leads to minimum, maximum, and average latency statistics.
- Continuously incrementing a single global counter each time a message is received from the initial Wire Tap and decrementing it each time a corresponding/correlated message is received from the final Wire Tap leads to a continuously updated "number of messages in progress" statistic.
- Message size statistics, such as minimum size, maximum size, and average size, can be collected.
- Message volume statistics, collected hourly or at some other interval, can be used to discern processing peaks.

All these statistics can be obtained with no disruption and minimum overhead to the business solution and without even looking at what the messages themselves are. Because Wire Taps are implemented as JMS topics, a number of independent statistics processing solutions can be built and deployed over time to operate concurrently. If the overhead of processing statistics becomes excessive, statistics processing solutions can be deployed to a separate, independent Application Server.

Once you start looking at the messages themselves, other useful statistics can be obtained, including the following:

- Processing peaks by message type
- Message size statistics by message type
- Message processing latencies by message type

With the aid of judiciously placed Wire Taps, both new and existing solutions can be readily instrumented to feed management and monitoring solutions with information about messages being processed. Information gleaned from message traffic can be collected and manipulated to provide useful statistics on the state and performance of the messaging systems. Using tools like Business Activity Monitor—for example, Sun eBAM—runtime statistics can be displayed, alerts can be raised, and solution components can be reconfigured based on real-time feedback.

10.2.11 Summary

Java CAPS provides a number of facilities for runtime monitoring and management. Some, like the JMS Destination management and eInsight Business Process monitoring, have prebuilt user interfaces integrated into the Enterprise Manager Web-based User Interface. Others, like JMX support and Web Services–based Enterprise Manager API, provide APIs and built-in frameworks that allow integration of monitoring and management of Java CAPS solutions into enterprise monitoring infrastructures already in place.

Generic monitoring and management facilities may not fulfill all of a site's requirement. As Java CAPS–based solutions are built, they can be instrumented to provide additional performance data, such as latency and throughput, for specific components or critical integration paths. This data can be collected as a side effect of processing ordinary workload. As an example of such solution-specific monitoring, a method of calculating JMS latency was discussed.

10.3 Solution-Specific Management

10.3.1 Overview

Each solution can be instrumented to supplement Java CAPS-provided monitoring and management facilities with its own management, monitoring, and performance data gathering facilities.

In a solution that includes a Control Bus [EIP], components could collect timing data, such as how long it took to process a message and how large the message was, and forward that data, through the Control Bus, to a statistics collection and analysis component. An eVision-based statistics display solution could be constructed to show performance metrics collected from the running system.

Instrumentation, included in a solution at design time, could include management and monitoring components such as a Detour, a Wire Tap, a Message History collector, a Message Store, a Smart Proxy, a Channel Purger, or a Test Message generator and consumer. All these [EIP] patterns should be implemented at design time, though some can be readily added to an existing solution if necessary. The amount of effort involved in reengineering an existing solution will vary with the pattern to be implemented and the number of components affected.

10.3.2 Control Bus

[EIP] suggests that management and control of a distributed messaging system requires the use of a Control Bus. Control Bus, according to [EIP], uses messaging systems' infrastructure to collect information about component states and message traffic. The channels used for the bus are different from the channels used for regular message traffic. Information about components and messaging traffic is collected and displayed through a Central Console [EIP]. The Console can also be used for starting and stopping components and similar management functions.

Java CAPS, a J2EE-based messaging system, is instrumented using the JMX API to facilitate monitoring and management of components and messaging infrastructure. Chapter 10, "System Management," section 10.2, discusses a variety of means Java CAPS provides for displaying state information and managing components at runtime. These include the Enterprise Manager Web-based Graphical User Interfaces, the Alert Agent, the SNMP Agent, the JMX Console, and a number of specific command-line utilities and application programming interfaces including a Web Services-based management interface.

With the variety of means of runtime information gathering that Java CAPS provides, construction of the Control Bus should not be required. Furthermore, the use of JMX for management and information gathering eliminates the need to use messaging systems channels for data gathering, thus minimizing management overhead and resource consumption. Java CAPS Enterprise Manager is the principle Live Console [EIP] used to display runtime information and manage components.

10.3.3 Detour

In an eGate-based solution, or a solution in which components exchange messages via the JMS infrastructure, introducing a detour by JMS Destination diversion is almost trivial. Recall that JMS Destinations are identified by names and that these names are global within the JMS Message Server instance. Unless they use explicit JMS Destination names to deliver messages to specific destinations, which is not a good practice, logical project components that publish and subscribe to JMS Destinations are ignorant of the name of the JMS Destination with which they are associated. Figure 10-65 shows a connectivity map with explicitly named JMS Destinations and an explicit publication and subscription relationships.

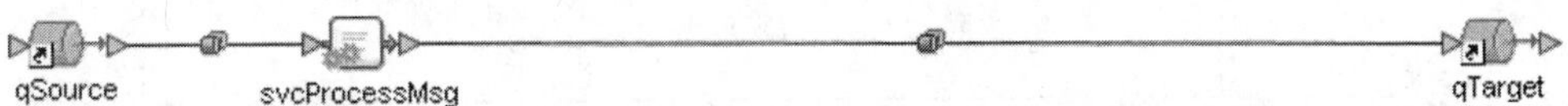

FIGURE 10-65: JMS Destinations in an explicit publication and subscription relationship to a service

Both types and names of JMS Destinations are set in connectivity maps; thus it is easy to introduce a Detour by changing, in a connectivity map, the name of the JMS Destination to which a component is publishing messages. Figure 10-66 illustrates this.

This will divert messages to a different queue, for example, one to which the first component in a Detour is subscribing. The final component in a Detour will publish to the original target destination.

Both the original components and the Detour may be configured in a single connectivity map or in multiple connectivity maps. In fact, the same part of the solution may have multiple connectivity maps, one with the original destination and one with the Detour destination. By deploying the application using the appropriate connectivity map, you can readily add or remove a Detour without changing either collaborations or Business Processes.

Unlike a Detour introduced via JMS Destination diversion in the connectivity map, introducing a Detour into an eInsight Business Process requires the process to be modified, the connectivity map that includes the Business Process to be modified, and the application to be redeployed and retested.

10.3.4 Wire Tap

Wire Tap is effectively a form of Detour; as such, introducing a Wire Tap at the JMS Destination is trivially easy. Figure 10-67 shows a connectivity map for the original solution.

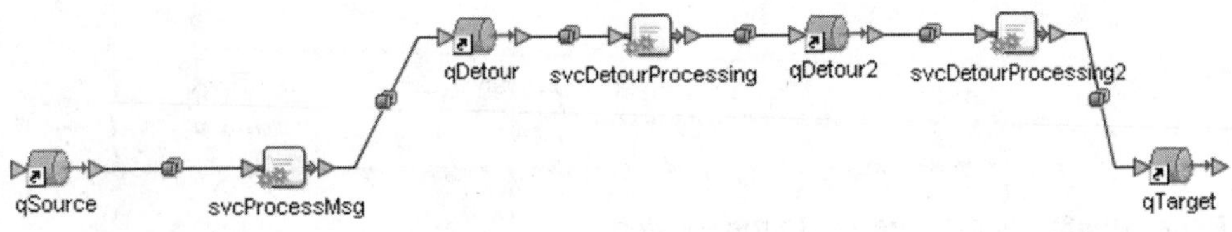

FIGURE 10-66: Introducing a Detour

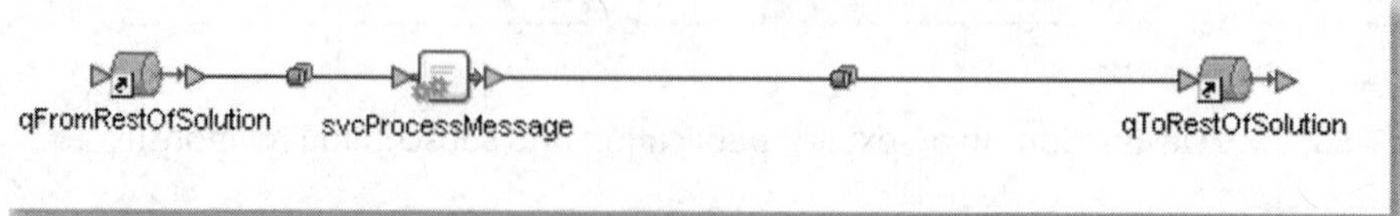

FIGURE 10-67: Original solution before the Wire Tap is introduced

With the solution shown in Figure 10-67, a Wire Tap requires addition of two JMS Destinations and a collaboration that forwards messages to both the original destination and the new destination. This is shown in Figure 10-68.

The Wire Tap collaboration itself only needs two lines of Java code, as shown in Figure 10-69.

If addition of two JMS Destinations and a Java Collaboration is an issue, perhaps because there are already many JMS Destinations and collaborations in a solution and the resources are scarce, an existing Java Collaboration can be modified by addition of a single line of Java code and a JMS Destination for the Wire Tap itself. This naturally requires that the modified component be retested and redeployed and, if the Wire Tap is no longer required, that the change be reversed.

Introducing a Wire Tap at a JMS topic is even easier. Since all active subscribers to a JMS topic will receive a copy of each message, it is only necessary to build a Java Collaboration or a Business Process to process each message and have them subscribe to the topic.

Clearly, some component must be prepared to process messages that are delivered through the Wire Tap; otherwise messages will be queued indefinitely if the Wire Tap destination is a JMS queue or a JMS topic with a durable subscriber, or it will be discarded if the destination is a JMS topic and no subscribers are registered as durable or currently subscribed.

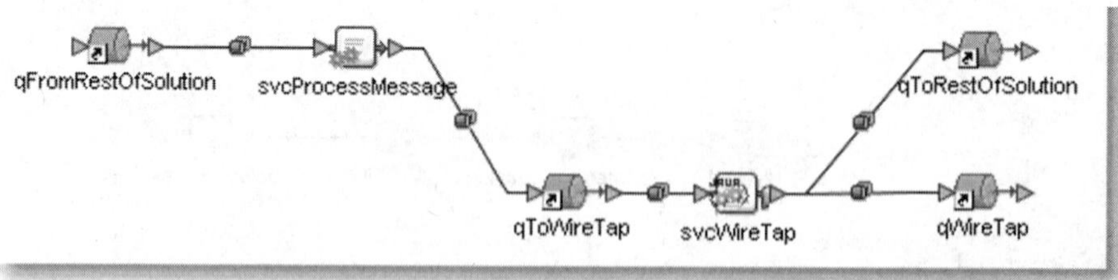

FIGURE 10-68: Adding Wire Tap to the solution

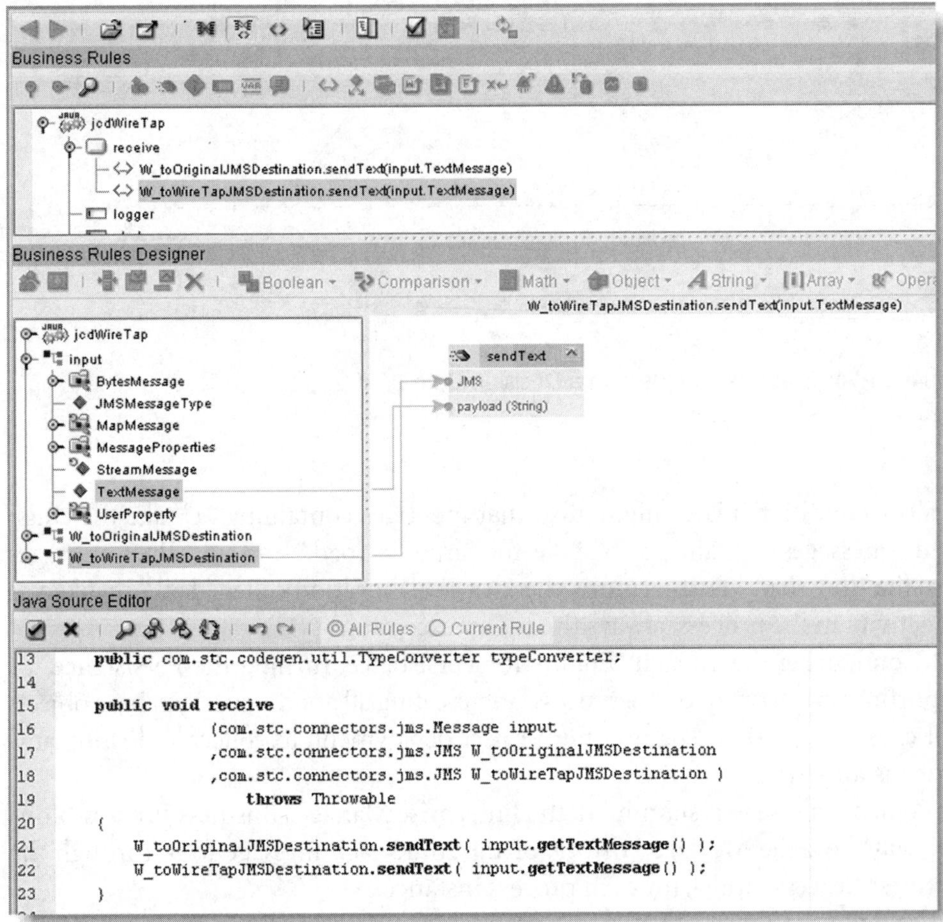

FIGURE 10-69: The Wire Tap collaboration

10.3.5 Message (Route) History

The eInsight Business Process Manager facilitates configuration of process monitoring and recovery through the Persistence feature. If configured, the path that each message takes through the Business Process model will be highlighted, and access to the Business Process attribute values at each activity in the process will be available for inspection. Completed activities will be highlighted in a different color from those that are in progress, that failed, or that were not performed.

Let's consider a Business Process model shown in Figure 10-70.

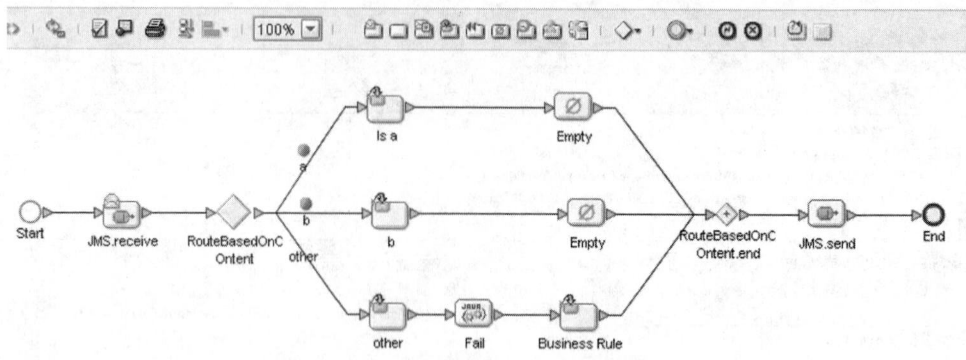

FIGURE 10-70: Business process with a Decision Gate

The conditional is configured so that messages containing "a" take the "high road," messages containing "b" take the "middle road," and all other messages take the "low road." Furthermore, the Java Collaboration called "Fail," invoked as an activity in the process, always throws an exception.

Configuring the eInsight Engine for Persistence, turning the Persistence for Reporting property on for the process, and creating all appropriate database objects will cause the eInsight engine, after project deployment, to collect and store runtime instance data.

When a message is submitted, the Enterprise Manager Business Process Monitor will show the Message History, or the route each message took through the Business Process model, for each process instance.

When a message with the content of "a" is submitted, the process instance flow following the high path will be displayed for the corresponding Business Process Instance, as seen in Figure 10-71.

The message was processed successfully, as indicated by the status of COMPLETE, and took the high road, as indicated by the activities with green borders.

When a message with the content of anything other than "a" or "b" is submitted, the process flow graph shown in Figure 10-72 will be displayed for the corresponding Business Process instance.

Here the low road was taken and the "Fail" Java Collaboration threw an exception, as indicated by the red border around the Fail activity. Since the exception was not handled, the eInsight Engine terminated the process, as indicated by the status of TERMINATED.

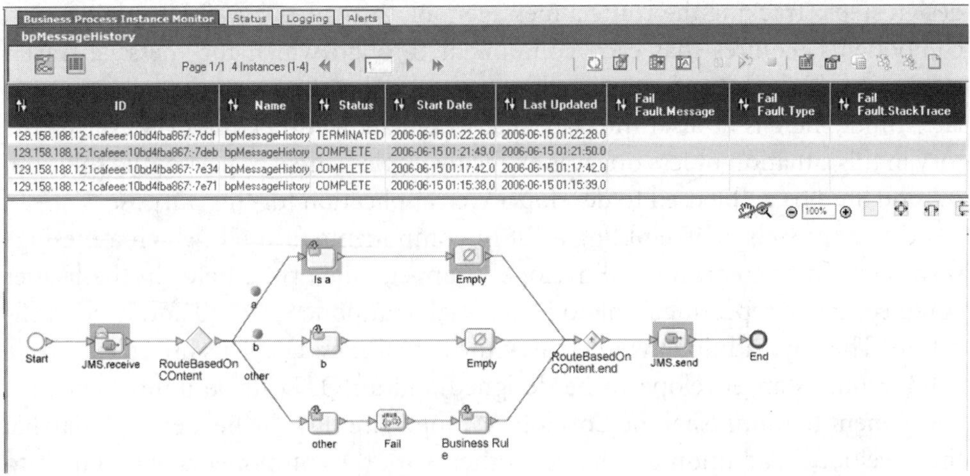

FIGURE 10-71: Process instance following the "high" path.

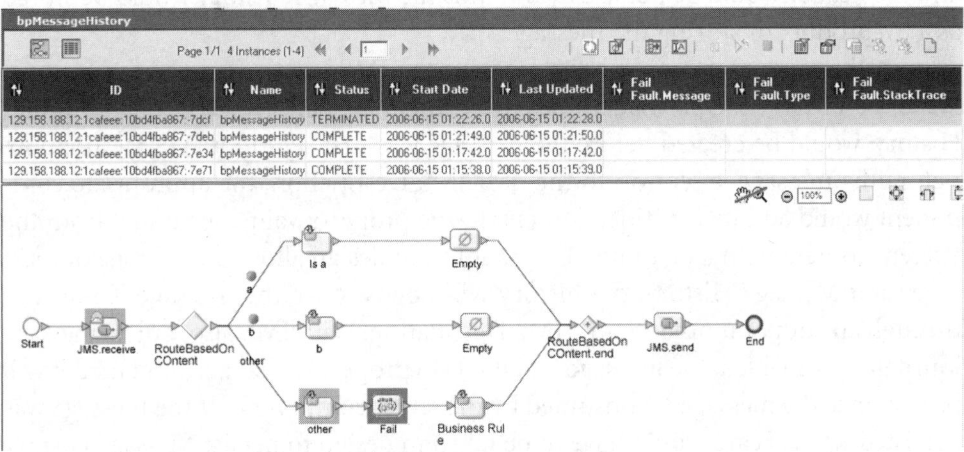

FIGURE 10-72: Process instance following the "low" path

The process models can be arbitrarily complex, representing perhaps the entire integration solution, so Message History can be implemented as a by-product of enabling persistence for recovery and monitoring.

If a solution consists of several components connected via JMS Destinations, implementing Message History becomes more complex and requires explicit design steps. Tracking the route a message took through a set of destinations and components requires that each component through which the message travels somehow adds its identification to the message so that the list can be inspected at a later time. There is no user interface that would allow inspection of Message History in this situation unless one was explicitly implemented as part of the solution. eVision Studio can be used to develop a Web application for this purpose.

One approach to assembling a list of components through which a message travels would be to create an Envelope Wrapper. One of the fields in the header could contain a repeating node to which each component would add its identification. The payload node would carry the actual message. This approach, while valid, requires an envelope to be designed and an OTD to be built, then each component to unmarshal the Envelope Wrapper, modify the header, and marshal the envelope, in addition to whatever other work the components would have to perform to achieve their regular business objectives. The advantage of the approach is that if the message is persisted in a Message Store, both the payload and the header would be persisted, and thus the Message History would be stored as a by-product of storing the message.

Another approach would be to leverage the JMS user properties for Message History and carry the payload as message content. A user property, such as RouteHistory, would be created before the message was first sent to a JMS Destination. Before the message is sent on to the next JMS Destination, the appropriate component would add its identification text to the property value, separated from the current content with a delimiter. Unless solution design allows for storage of messages and Message History, the history will be lost once the message is sent out through an endpoint other than a JMS Destination. With JMS also, unless message journaling is enabled, the message and the JMS properties that accompanied it will be lost once the message is consumed by the target component. If the message was persisted, special care would have to be taken in design to persist Message History as well as the payload, if required.

Consider a solution in which each component adds its connectivity map name, and a separator, to a JMS user property called MessageRoute. Figure 10-73 presents a connectivity map for such a solution.

Code similar to that presented in Figure 10-74 could be used for this purpose.

A message sent through the solution, in the absence of a receiver for the JMS queue qEnd, will be queued at the qEnd. Inspecting message properties for a message in that queue will show the user property MessageRoute and its value. In the example shown in Figure 10-75, it is svcSourceToInter1|svcInter1|svcInter2B|svc-

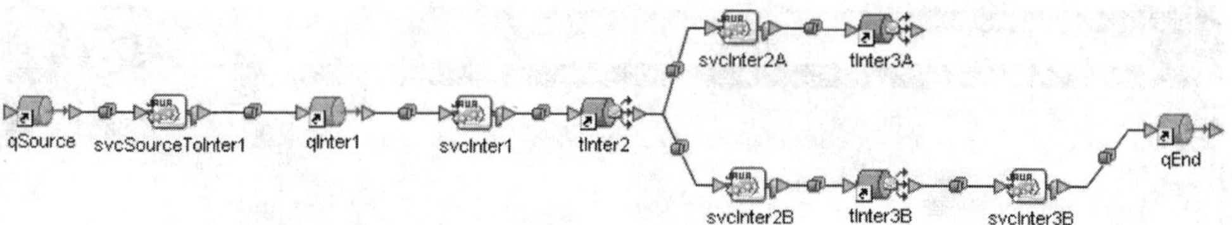

FIGURE 10-73: Connectivity map for a Message History solution

```
public void receive( com.stc.connectors.jms.Message input, com.stc.connectors.jms.JMS W_toJMS )
    throws Throwable
{
    // CollaborationName is the name assigned to the service in the connectivity map. Since all services
    // on a single connectivity map must have unique names this guarantees that each service will be distinct
    // as long as it is in the same connectivity map even if it uses the same Java Collaboration code
    ;
    String sSelfID = collabContext.getCollaborationName();
    String sRouteSoFar = "";
    for (int i = 0; i < input.countUserProperty(); i++) {
        if (input.getUserProperty( i ).getName().equalsIgnoreCase( "MessageRoute" )) {
            sRouteSoFar = (String) input.getUserProperty( i ).getValue();
            continue;
        }
    }
    sRouteSoFar += (sRouteSoFar.length() == 0 ? "" : "|") + sSelfID;
    input.storeUserProperty( "MessageRoute", sRouteSoFar );
    W_toJMS.send( input );
}
```

FIGURE 10-74: Adding connectivity map service name as a JMS property to record the message route history

Inter3B, identifying the services that processed the message in the order in which the message traversed them.

A consumer can retrieve the property value, break it up at the delimiters, and process service names as required.

10.3.6 Message Store

Java CAPS JMS, the underlying store-and-forward infrastructure used to pass messages from component to component, typically persists messages until they are consumed by some component or another. Once consumed, messages are no longer accessible through any Java CAPS built-in user tools, unless journaled, and are candidates for being deleted from the persistence stores by the JMS cleanup

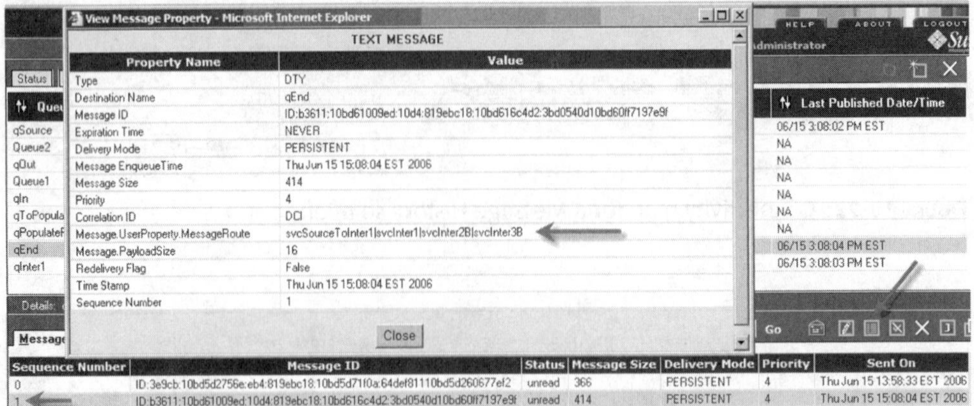

FIGURE 10-75: Message Route property showing the route message traversed thus far

process. If JMS user properties are used for management and control purposes, for example, to implement Message (Route) History, the properties disappear together with the message.

Message Store can be created to record messages during and after processing by the integration solution. Since Java CAPS has JCA Adapter support for all major relational database products, including those from Oracle, Sybase, and Microsoft, as well as any other Java Database Connectivity (JDBC)-compliant database products, it is relatively easy to implement a Message Store at the appropriate points in the solution. In addition, Java CAPS JMS-provided journaling facility, normally not enabled, can be enabled to provide a transparent Message Store for the entire integration solution.

Implementing a Message Store through JCA Adapters and third-party relational databases has its advantages and disadvantages. The chief advantage is that the architect has total control over where in the solution Message Stores are deployed and what data is stored. The chief disadvantages are the need to source, install, and maintain a third-party relational database, possibly at considerable expense; the need to define table structures to accommodate data to be stored; the need to develop specific code to collect and store message data; and the need to develop some means of inspecting and maintaining the content of the Message Store. All these requirements add complexity to the architecture and add time to the development schedule.

Using Sun SeeBeyond JMS Message Server journaling to provide the Message Store also has advantages and disadvantages. Enabling JMS journaling requires a once-only change to the JMS Message Server configuration and Message Server restart. Journaling is performed by the JMS Message Server transparently—there is no need to implement Message Store support in the solution itself. Java CAPS provides Enterprise Manager and command-line tools support for inspection, replay, and maintenance of journaled messages. The chief disadvantage of using JMS journaling is that enabling journaling causes all messages to be journaled, regardless of the JMS Destination. The solution cannot selectively enable journaling for specific JMS destinations and not for others.

10.3.7 Test Message

[EIP] sees the Test Message as the means through which a component can perform self-diagnosis. Specifically, a test message with known data, when processed by a component, will produce a message with a known result. This result can be compared to a stored result to verify that processing logic executes as intended.

The validity of this approach to confirming that a component operates as intended is debatable. Components should be thoroughly tested before being put into production use. With any but the simplest components thoroughly testing logic during production operation, just to see that the component still does what it was designed to do, will introduce considerable overhead. This overhead, arising out of the need to generate test data or submit pre-prepared test data, process test data through the component, then compare results with expected results, will be proportional to the complexity of the components. Additional components will have to be added to the solution to generate or submit test data and to verify results. Ultimately, for every component that processes producing messages, there are likely to be at least two additional components that are involved in testing. This leads us to ask the ancient question, *Quis custodiet ipsos custodes?*—loosely translated as "Who watches the watchers?" Will the additional components need test message and the test message infrastructure to confirm that they themselves perform as designed?

A bigger issue with the concept of the Test Message is that it does not, in general, work for components with side effects or collections of related components, some with side effects. For example, if a component updates a database as part of its processing logic, and some of the logic depends on the results of the update, a Test Message will need to cause database update in order to verify component logic. Setting up the infrastructure to support this kind of operation without adversely affecting other components or applications may require additional logic in the component itself, in other components, and in other applications. The overhead increases and spreads well beyond the boundaries of the component whose logic integrity is to be tested, with little or no real benefit.

While it is expected that components are thoroughly tested before they are put into production use, logic errors frequently are not discovered until components are in operation for some time. The principle reason for that is that test data used in testing may not have been complete and may not have exercised all logic paths. By definition, if complete test data collection cannot be assembled for unit and integration testing, it cannot be assembled or generated to perform runtime integrity testing.

Assuming that components are thoroughly tested before production use, expecting that a component will develop an unexpected problem where the problem did not exist at deployment to production time is to expect that the code will somehow deteriorate through use. If such deterioration occurs on electronic devices, then no amount of additional code can be trusted to correctly detect this condition.

Regardless of a designer's attitude to the concept of Test Message, Java CAPS can assist in implementing infrastructure to support it.

If components are connected to one another through JMS Destinations, a test message can be injected at any JMS Destination and be delivered to a component that receives from/subscribes to that destination.

A message typically arrives to a component as a binary object that has to be parsed/unmarshaled before its constituent parts can be used. The test message may have a completely different structure from the regular message. Unmarshaling a test message using regular message's OTD will result in unmarshal exception, which can be caught and handled. The exception handler may well recognize the test message and change processing logic based on this knowledge. By handling unmarshal exception rather than testing incoming messages for being a test message or a regular message, the amount of code executed for routine messages is minimized.

JMS messages carry JMS Header properties. Test messages may carry a user-defined property indicating their nature. Components may interrogate JMS Header properties to determine if a message is a test message and change logic flow accordingly.

Ultimately, whether to use test messages and how to handle test messages at runtime requires specific solution design. Java CAPS features and facilities can assist in building a solution that includes test message handling infrastructure, but it does not come with such infrastructure prebuilt.

10.3.8 Channel Purger

In the most simplistic case, a Channel Purger picks up messages from the channel and discards them. If this is all that is required, implementing a Channel Purger is simplicity itself. Take a File eWay as an example. Figure 10-76 shows the connectivity map and a Java Collaboration for a Channel Purger that discards messages from a File eWay.

Figure 10-77 presents a Channel Purger for a JMS Destination. As in the previous example, the Java Collaboration does nothing at all.

The difference between the File eWay purger and a JMS Destination purger is the input Connector OTD that is configured. There will be a different JCD required for each kind of a Channel Purger.

Channel Purgers like the ones mentioned above are unlikely to be used in production environments. The only reasonable use for such simplistic "discard all" components would be an integration need where an external system must be configured and deployed in production before the receiving solution is ready to be deployed.

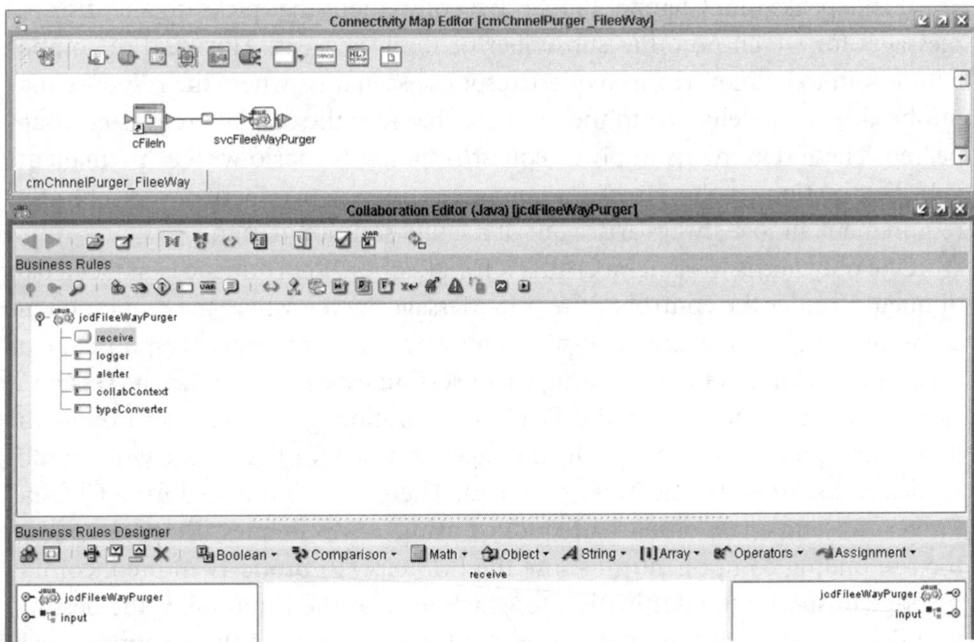

FIGURE 10-76: File eWay and JCD-based Channel Purger

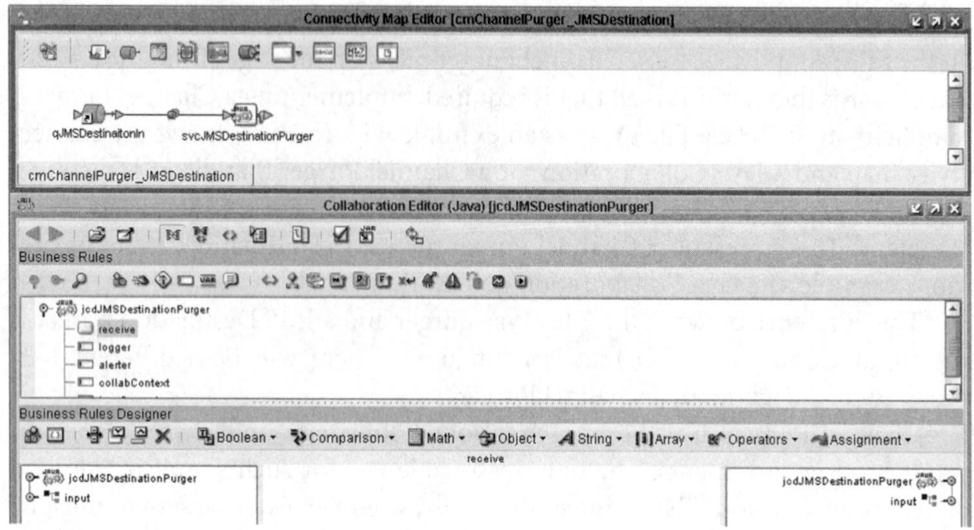

FIGURE 10-77: JMS Channel Purger

[EIP] speaks of a Channel Purger as a component that picks up and discards messages for which no other subscriber or receiver exists. This kind of component is said to be required in request/response scenarios where the response may not be able to be delivered to the requester because the original requester disappeared. These statements imply a request/response scenario with a "permanent" JMS Destination as the target for responses. In practice, with Java CAPS, this requirement almost always arises out of a faulty solution design.

One only needs to remember that a JMS Request/Reply queue is in fact a pair of queues, under the control of the JMS Message Server, where the request queue is "permanent," visible, and accessible, and where a "temporary" response queue exists only as long as the requesting client session exists. As soon as the session is closed—for example, when the Java Collaboration completes executing—the temporary queue is destroyed. Any messages destined for that queue will be automatically discarded by the Message Server. There will be no need for a Channel Purger. To send a response to a requestor using a JMS Request/Response queue, the responding component must use the JMSReplyTo property in the incoming message to specify the destination to which to send the response. If the destination does not exist at the time the responder needs to send the response, it will receive an exception and the response will not be sent.

In the same spirit, if it is necessary to deploy a solution where messages are sent to a JMS Destination but the component that will eventually process these messages is not yet developed, a JMS topic with no durable subscribers will effectively provide a Channel Purger. Recall that any message that is sent to a JMS topic that has no active subscribers and no durable subscribers will be discarded by the Message Server. If it turns out later that a JMS queue is required, a minor correction to the connectivity map will address the issue without the sending component being aware of the change.

10.4 Chapter Summary

This chapter reviewed system management facilities provided by Java CAPS out-of-the-box and discussed how Java CAPS solution–specific system management facilities can be designed into the solution for runtime monitoring, statistics collection, testing, and configuration using [EIP] system management patterns.

Solution-specific [EIP] system management and monitoring patterns, Control Bus, Detour, Wire Tap, Message History, Message Store, Channel Purger, and Test Message were also discussed.

SECTION III

Specialized Java CAPS Topics

CHAPTER ELEVEN

Message Correlation

11.1 Introduction

This chapter focuses on Java CAPS facilities that can be used to implement solutions involving message correlation. Rather than discussing the details of correlation and implementation for each [EIP] pattern individually, this chapter presents the Java CAPS material necessary to understand how [EIP] patterns that call for correlation are implemented in Java CAPS.

Message correlation in Java CAPS, the facilities and techniques used to accomplish message correlation, correlation concepts, eInsight Business Process Execution Language (BPEL) Correlation services, and how correlation can be accomplished when eInsight is not available are discussed. Chapter 9, "Message Correlation," in Part II (located on the accompanying CD-ROM), provides a number of detailed examples illustrating these topics.

Because configuration of BPEL Correlation is rather nonintuitive, this chapter walks you through discussion of various correlation scenarios starting with an incorrect, naïve implementation and progressing through correct, increasingly more complex implementations.

The chapter also introduces common Message Relationship patterns, implementation of which requires correlation. Specifically, the following Message Relationship patterns are discussed:

- Header-Items-Trailer
- Any Order Two Items
- Any Order Two Items with Timeout
- Items-Trailer
- Header-Counted-Items
- Counted and Timed Items
- Scatter-Gather

Part II provides implementation examples of each Message Relationship pattern.

In the absence of an eInsight correlation service, correlation in Java CAPS can still be accomplished using other techniques. One such technique, using JMS with dynamic selectors, is introduced with illustration provided in Part II. The technique, which uses JMS API to manipulate JMS objects and which is discussed in detail in this chapter, is applied elsewhere to implement JMS Polling.

Along the way, discussion touches upon related [EIP] patterns like Scatter-Gather and Aggregator, which are discussed in Chapter 6, "Message Routing."

11.2 Overview

The word *correlation*, used in statistics and similar sciences, denotes a degree of relationship between two or more variables. To the extent that it implies a continuous relationship between variables, it is totally inappropriate for describing that variables are, or are not, related, which is a strictly binary relationship. Be that as it may, Java CAPS has a number of features that can be used to implement correlation-based message processing. This chapter discusses both the technologies available in Java CAPS for message correlation and Java CAPS–based implementation of the common Message Relationship patterns.

Correlation is a process of collecting related messages, using specific values known as Correlation Identifiers within messages, in order to process them together.

In messaging systems, correlation is complex. It can be implemented in the messaging system itself, in the processing components, or in both. The parts of the integration solutions that perform message correlation are called *correlation processors.*

Correlation of multiple related messages implies that there is some "initial" message used to establish the Correlation Identifier value, and there are "subsequent" messages whose Correlation Identifier values will be the same as that of the initial message.

The relationship between the initial message and subsequent messages may be simple. The initial message happens to arrive before subsequent messages. Or it can be more complex. The initial message is somehow "special" among all messages with the same Correlation Identifier value. Processing of messages with the same Correlation Identifier value before receipt of the initial message is different from processing after it is received. These relationships could be described as Message Relationship patterns.

11.3 JMSCorrelationID

The JMS Message Service Specification [JMSSpec] provides for a number of predefined JMS Header fields, which are transmitted to JMS clients together with each message. Some of these fields are assigned by the sending client, others are assigned by the provider, and still others are assigned by the application that uses the JMS client.

JMSCorrelationID is one of the predefined JMS Message Header fields. Its value is essentially application-specific. The JMS Message Server will not assign a useful value to this field. In Java CAPS this field will carry the literal string "SunSeeBeyond" assigned to it by the JMS client code unless it is explicitly assigned a value by the application.

Despite the name given to this required JMS Message Header field, the JMS Specification [JMSSpec] does not describe any mechanism within a JMS provider that will implement correlation and does not require the use of the JMSCorrelationID field for anything. It is up to the application to assign a useful value to this field and implement a correlation mechanism.

The Sun SeeBeyond JMS Message Server does not implement a proprietary message correlation service.

Note
For all intents and purposes, the JMS Correlation Identifier is simply another JMS Message Header field that can be used by the application. A user-defined JMS Message property can be used for message correlation just as readily as the JMSCorrelationID field.

11.4 eInsight Correlations

Business Process Execution Language for Web Services (BPEL4WS), implemented in Java CAPS eInsight, supports message correlation—the ability of a single Business Process instance to process multiple related messages based on the value of some user-defined message component(s), called correlation keys.

> Message correlation is the BPEL4WS mechanism which allows processes to participate in stateful conversations. It can be used, for example, to match returning or known customers to long-running business processes. When a message arrives for a Web service which has been implemented using BPEL, that message

must be delivered somewhere—either to a new or an existing instance of the process. The task of determining to which conversation a message belongs, in BPEL's case the task of locating/instantiating the instance, is what message correlation is all about. [BPEL4WS06]

Subsequent sections discuss in more detail how eInsight Correlation facilities can be used to implement a variety of solutions that involve Message Relationship patterns.

Note
As of Java CAPS 5.1, eInsight Business Processes can be deployed in multiple-engine configurations for Business Process instance failover.

This does not apply to Business Processes that use the eInsight Correlation feature. In multiple-engine deployments, correlations will not work when the instance is failed over to another engine.

11.5 eInsight Correlation Processor: First Cut

An eInsight Business Process is triggered by receipt of a message at the endpoint that, wrapped as a Receive Service, is the initial receive activity in the process. The eInsight engine takes care of creating an instance of the Business Process and delivery of the message to the initial receive activity. From that point on, the process will continue invoking Web Services defined within it until it completes or is terminated. The initial receive activity has the special property Create Instance set to yes. At least one receive activity within a process must have this property set to yes in order to deploy a solution that contains the process.

A typical eInsight Business Process will have one initial receive activity that will cause instance creation. Figure 11-1 illustrates the receive activity property that determines whether instance creation will take place.

Note
When using the Event-Based Decision construct, illustrated in Figure 11-2, the initial receive activity may be one of many alternative receive activities, but only one of them will cause instance creation, and other receive activities will be ignored for the process instance.

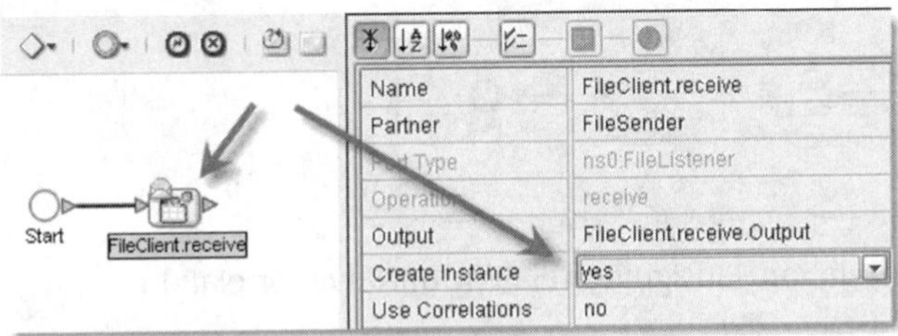

FIGURE 11-1: Create Instance property

The reason for the foregoing discussion is to introduce a "subsequent" receive activity and matters related thereto.

Picture a process where two different messages are to be received, combined, and sent out. Assume JMS Destinations are the sources and destinations of the messages involved, though it does not really matter because most of the following discussion is applicable regardless the types of sources and destinations. Both messages must be received before the process can do its work.

Note that the example being discussed will result in a solution in which correlation *does not work.* This example is intended to walk you through a naïve implementation to introduce concepts that will be used later to construct correlation solutions that do work as intended.

A naïve designer might design a Business Process in which there are two receive activities, one after the other, as illustrated in Figure 11-3.

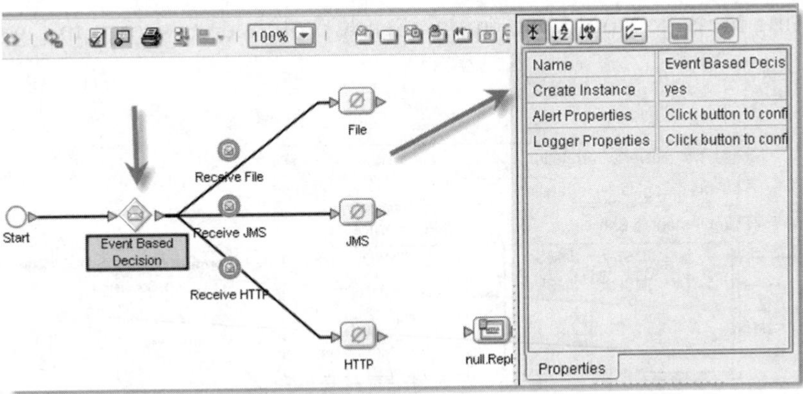

FIGURE 11-2: Create Instance property in the Event-Based Decision

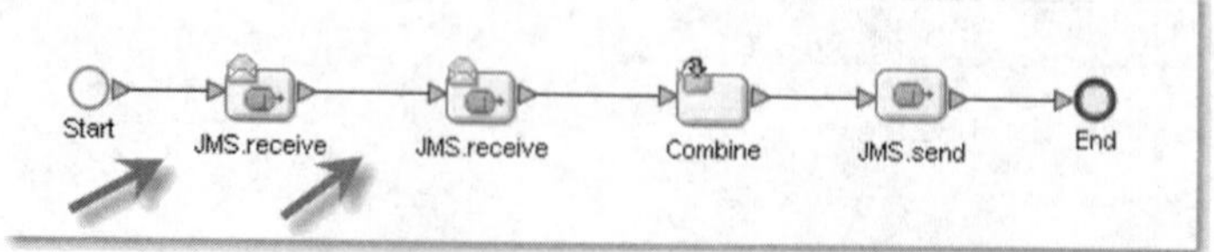

FIGURE 11-3: _Book/MessageCorrelation/EInsightCorrelation/bpNaiveCorrelation

Each receive activity would be connected in a connectivity map to a different JMS queue, as shown in Figure 11-4. At runtime, a message in the first queue would cause the Business Process instance to be created and the message delivered to it. The process would then wait at the second receive activity and, when a message was put there and delivered to the process, it would combine both messages and send the combined message on its way.

Let's concatenate text messages from both JMS receive activities and send the combined message out, as shown in Figure 11-5.

The complete example is presented in Chapter 9, section 9.2, "eInsight Correlation Processor: First Cut," in Part II.

If you were to manually submit a message to the qReceive_1 using the Enterprise Manager, the eInsight engine would create a Business Process instance and hand it the message, as shown in Figure 11-6.

The first receive activity would complete and the second receive activity would be invoked. It would block waiting for a message to be delivered to the qReceive_2.

Manually submitting a message to the qReceive_2 would cause the eInsight engine to unblock the process, deliver the message to the second receive activity, and allow the process to continue.

The resulting message would end up in qSendCombined, as shown in Figure 11-7.

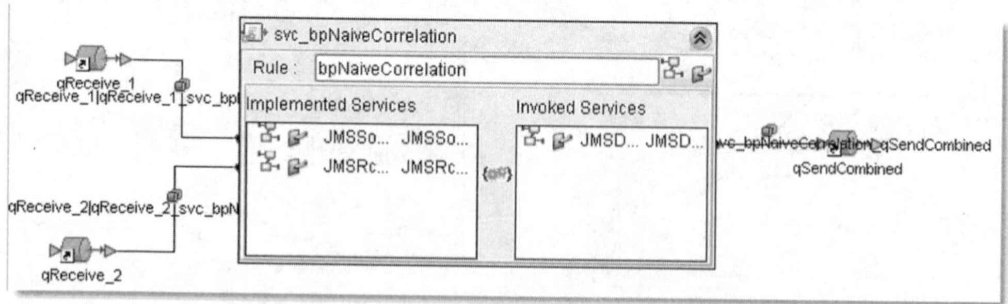

FIGURE 11-4: Two different JMS queues provide input to a process

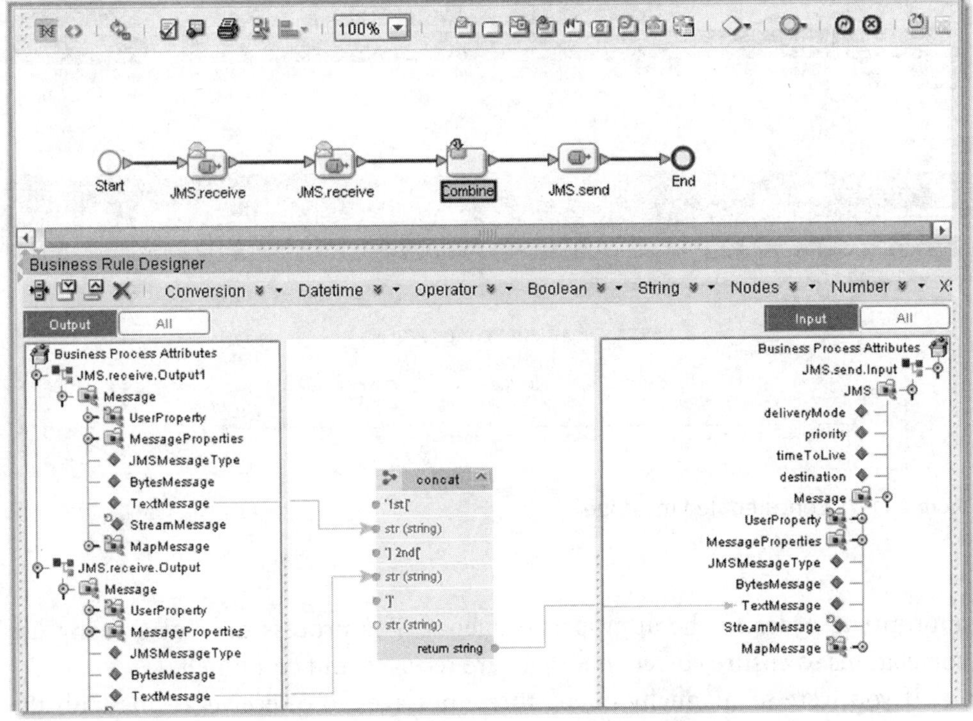

FIGURE 11-5: Business Rule concatenating outputs of the two receive activities

Status | Topics | Queues | Logging | Alerts | XA ID

Queue Name	Min Sequence Number	Max Sequence Number	Available Count	Number of Receivers	Last Published Date/Time
qFeeder	2	2	0	0	09/10 12:00:33 PM EST
qReceive_1	1	1	0	1	09/10 2:59:31 PM EST
qEater	2	2	0	0	09/10 12:00:34 PM EST
qReceive_2	0	0	0	1	NA

Details: qReceive_1

Number of pages: 0 Select page: 1 Go

Messages

Sequence Number	Message ID	Status	Message Size	Delivery Mode	Priority	Sent On

FIGURE 11-6: Submit initial message

Each receive activity received a message in turn. The process combined the two messages into a result message and delivered the result message to the outgoing queue.

Superficially all is well. In reality, the fact that the two messages were correctly received and combined is merely a function of the messages being queued in an

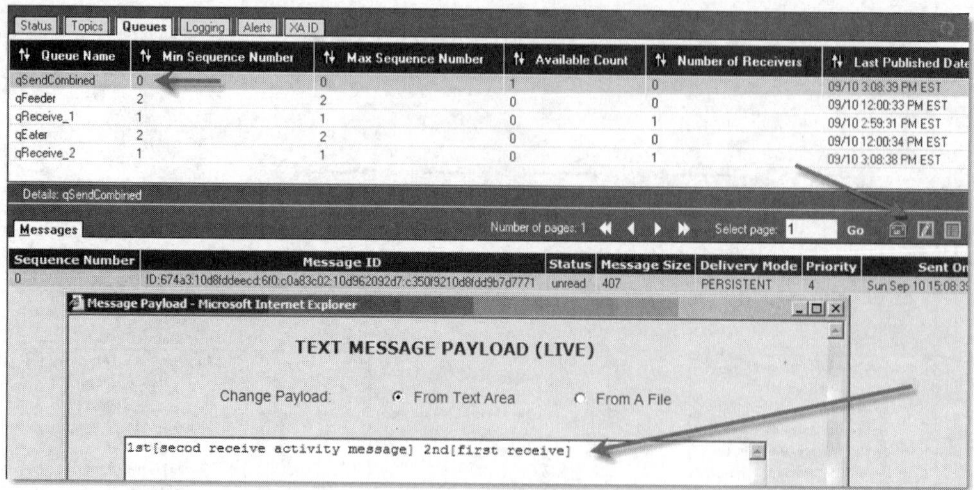

FIGURE 11-7: Concatenated message

appropriate order to the appropriate queues. The process did not actually use correlations to ensure correct messages are received and combined.

If you were to manually queue three messages to qReceive_1, one with the content of a, one with the content of b, and one with the content of c, then manually queue three messages to qReceive_2, one with the content of b, one with the content of c, and one with the content of a, the resulting combined messages in qSendCombined would be combinations of messages with content of a, b, and c, where no message contained both a's, both b's, or both c's. Rather, the messages would have been a+b, b+c, and c+a. Messages from qReceive_2 would have been combined with messages from qReceive_1 in the order they were submitted, regardless of their content.

This is an example of combining messages from two queues by brute force, which may be valid in certain circumstances. As a general proposition, however, this approach is not likely to meet the requirements.

There are a few issues with this approach:

1. Any two messages, one from qReceive_1 and one from qReceive_2, will be combined, whether or not they are in any way related. Neither the eInsight engine nor the Business Process care whether the two messages in fact can be meaningfully combined.

2. If there are multiple instances of the process waiting for a message to show up in qReceive_2, there is no way to tell to which instance it will be delivered. For all intents and purposes, the eInsight engine will choose one at random.
3. If a message for the first receives activity arrives, and the Business Process instance is created, but a message for the second receive activity never arrives, the Business Process instance will wait. The wait will end when the Integration Server is shut down, the enterprise application of which it is a part is undeployed, or the instance is explicitly deleted, whichever comes first.
4. If a message for the second activity arrives but there is no Business Process instance waiting for it, attempts to deliver it will continue according to the JMS Message Server global redelivery policy and Message Time-to-Live value, whether explicit or JMS Message Server global. If a File eWay, which should not be used for serious work, is used instead of JMS receiver, and the Resend on Error property is set to true, the eWay will continue attempts to redeliver the file indefinitely; otherwise it will try once and give up. Behavior of other eWays may vary—see eWay documentation for redelivery behavior, if any. This behavior is different from what might be used in ICAN 5.0.5, where the message that cannot be matched to a process instance would be unceremoniously dumped, and it applies only to JMS receivers.

Issues 3 and 4 must be addressed by appropriate solution design, incorporating message expiry, process instance timeout, and endpoint redelivery behavior configuration. These issues are common to all Message Relationship patterns and are discussed later.

Issues 1 and 2 can be addressed with the aid of Message Correlation facilities that the Java CAPS eInsight engine provides. Before we address these issues, the notion of Correlation Identifier is discussed in general, and more specifically how it is used in eInsight to ensure related messages are delivered to the same eInsight Business Process instance.

11.6 Correlation Identifier

Correlation Identifier is that part of a message that allows the integration solution to associate a message with another message that has the Correlation Identifier containing the same value.

Correlation Identifier may be derived from a simple value—a value of a field or a contiguous part of a message—or it can be complex—values of multiple message fields or multiple noncontiguous message parts.

For purpose-built Correlation Processors, whether implemented as Java Collaboration–based components or as eInsight Business Processes, the Collaboration Identifier can be any value that is directly present within a message or that can be derived from data within a message. A purpose-built Correlation Processor in this case is a component that receives all messages of interest, isolates or derives the Correlation Identifier in each, and causes related messages to be processed together, however that is implemented. This is distinct from the eInsight engine built-in correlation facilities, discussed next.

11.7 eInsight Correlation Processor: Second Cut

The eInsight Business Process Management (BPM) engine offers automatic correlation facilities. These facilities allow process designers to identify the parts of initial and subsequent messages whose values are to be used for correlation. The correlation process itself is delegated to the eInsight engine. It will ensure that subsequent messages are delivered to the Business Process instance created to process the corresponding initial message.

The eInsight engine is a BPEL4WS processor. Every activity within a Business Process is a Web Service invocation, whether implemented as an explicit SOAP Request/Reply invocation or using more efficient internal mechanisms. This implies that each activity has an input message and an output message. Each of these Web Service messages has some, more or less complex, structure.

In order for the eInsight engine to correlate messages on behalf of a Business Process, it must be configured to recognize Correlation Identifier values in messages that cause new Business Process instance creation. This allows the engine to identify Correlation Identifier values in messages that are to be delivered to existing Business Process instances and therefore to identify process instances to which to deliver these messages.

A Business Process, bpSimpleCorrelation, shown in Figure 11-8, illustrates the concepts.

So far, this process is identical to the naïve implementation presented earlier. Now we need to enable correlations and identify the Correlation Identifiers to use.

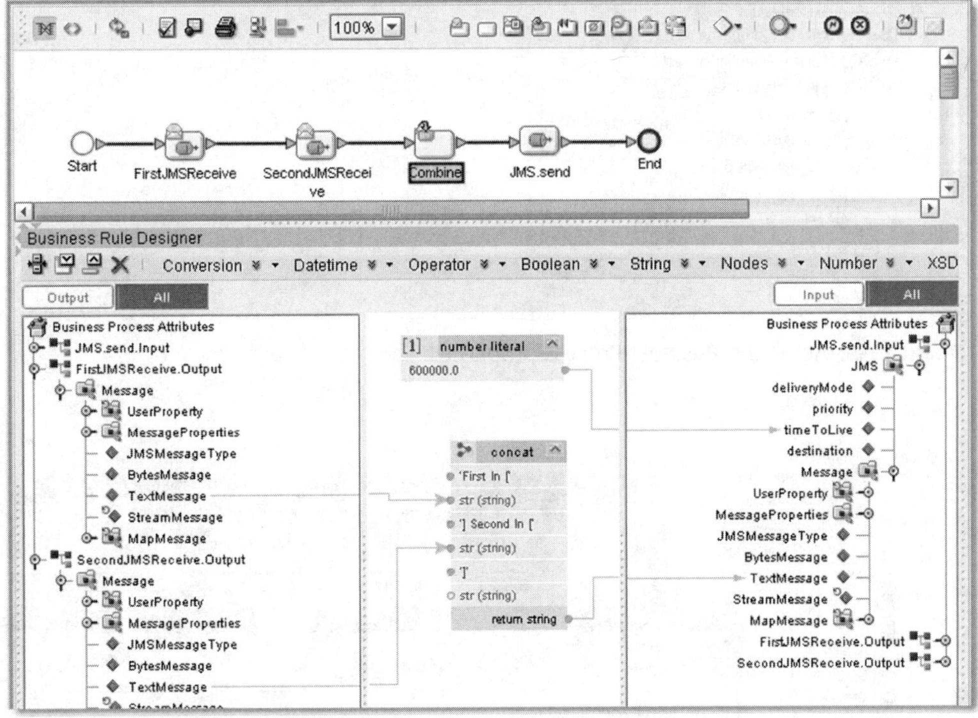

FIGURE 11-8: _Book/MessageCorrelation/EInsightCorrelation/bpSimpleCorrelation

Figure 11-9 illustrates access to Business Process properties, some of which govern the use of correlations.

Correlations are enabled by creation of Correlation Keys and Correlation Sets through Business Process properties for the appropriate Business Process, and assignment of Correlation Sets to appropriate activities. The process is described in detail in the eInsight User Guide [eInsightUG].

In this example, we wish to use the entire message as the Correlation Identifier. To do so, it is necessary to add a Correlation Key and a Correlation Set naming the JMS message's entire Text Message node as the Correlation Identifier, using a series of dialogue boxes, as shown in Figures 11-10 and 11-11.

First, JMS receive activity's Use Correlations property must be configured to use the Correlation Set defined previously. The Initialize Set value must be set to Yes, as shown in Figure 11-12.

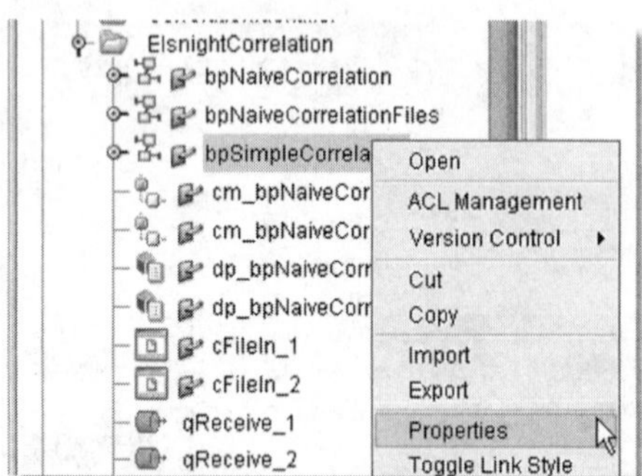

FIGURE 11-9: Accessing Business Process properties

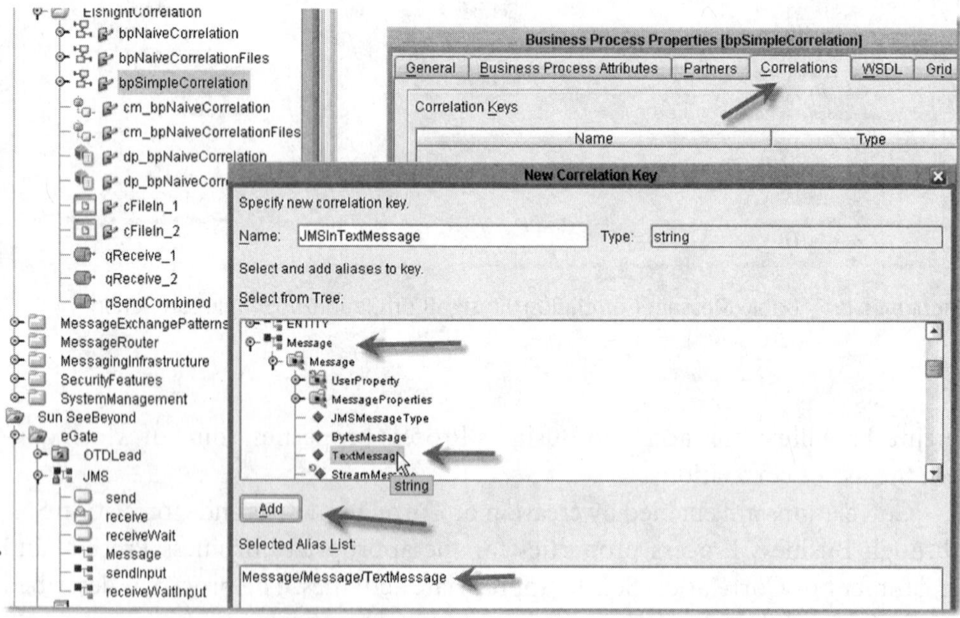

FIGURE 11-10: Defining the Correlation Key

The second JMS receive activity's Use Correlations property must be configured to use the Correlation Set defined previously. The Initialize Set property must be set to No, as illustrated in Figure 11-13.

The complete example is presented in Chapter 9, section 9.4, "eInsight Correlation Processor: Second Cut," in Part II.

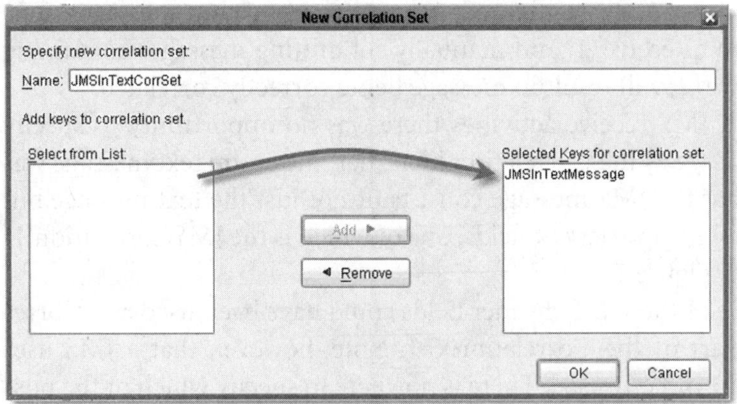

FIGURE 11-11: Defining the Correlation Set

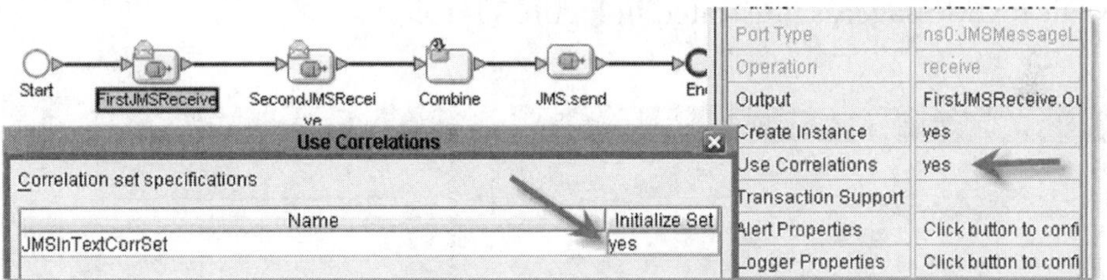

FIGURE 11-12: Configuring correlation for the initial receive activity

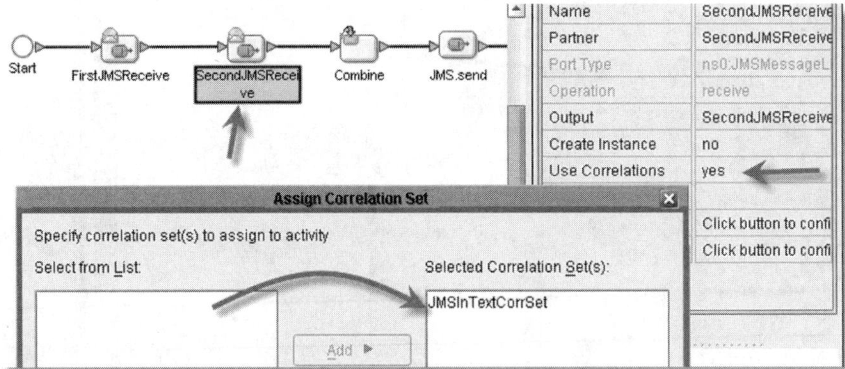

FIGURE 11-13: Configuring correlation on the second receive activity

With correlation properly configured, manually submitting messages containing a, b, and c to qReceive_1, and manually submitting messages containing b, c, and a to qReceive_2, will result in message being correctly correlated.

Notice that with JMS receive activities there was no opportunity to specify parts of the text message as the Correlation Identifier: the entire text message was used. Notice, too, that the JMS message consists of not just the text message but also the JMS header with a variety of fields, one of which is the JMSCorrelationID field, as illustrated in Figure 11-14.

Any one or more of these JMS header fields could have been used as a Correlation Key and as part of the Correlation Set. Note, however, that a JMS user property could not be directly used. There is nowhere to specify which of the possibly many user properties will carry the value to use.

Consider a receive activity in the bpNaiveCorrelationFiles process. Expand the Business Process properties, select the Correlations tab, and click the Create button to open the New Correlation Key dialogue box. Scroll to the entry that reads FileTextMessage, as illustrated in Figure 11-15.

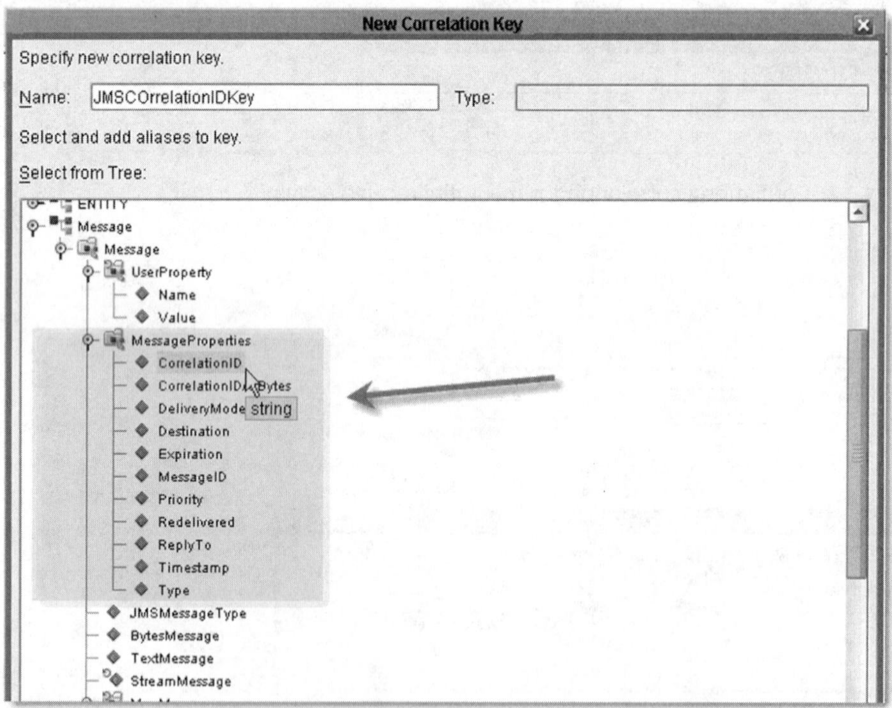

FIGURE 11-14: JMS message properties that can be selected for use in correlations

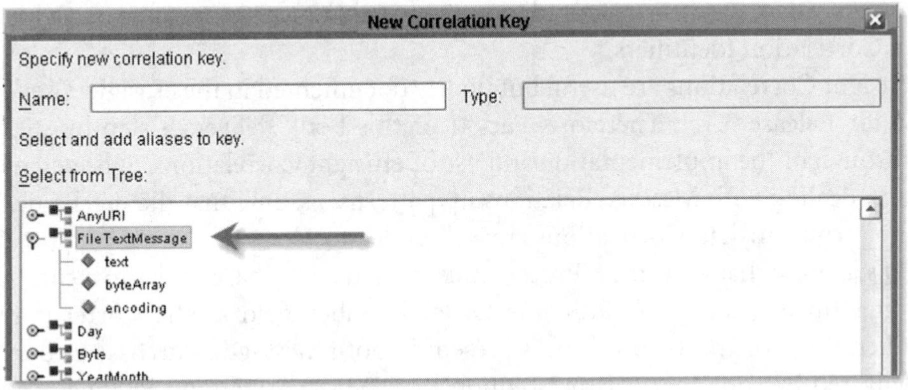

FIGURE 11-15: _Book/MessageCorrelation/EInsightCorrelation/bpNaiveCorrelationFiles

Notice that for the File eWay, there are only two alternatives for the Correlation identifier: the entire text node or the entire byteArray node. If we wished to specify only a fragment of the message as the Correlation Identifier, we could not do so when using the JMS message, other than JMS header fields, or the file message, or for that matter any endpoint message where discrete fields are not defined.

This issue and the issue of how to use specific parts of JMS messages or other eWay messages as parts of Correlation Sets are discussed in the next section.

11.8 Derived Correlation Identifiers

Regardless of which endpoint delivers a message to the business process, only directly accessible fields of the message can be used as part of the Correlation Identifier. The eInsight engine can only access those parts of incoming messages that are identifiable using internally defined XPath expressions—remember that all that eInsight works with are Web Services with XML input and output messages. The New Correlation Key dialogue box provides no means of directly specifying the XPath expression. It formulates XPath expressions on the basis of which fields of which messages the developer chooses in the node tree. If access to subcomponents of a message is required, then a new Web Service must be created and a new, properly structured message must be defined for it to return.

The following discussion concentrates on receiving a structured message from JMS and using message structure to derive the appropriate Correlation Identifier. The same technique applies to any receive activity where the endpoint returns a payload as an unstructured message and that message must be parsed to obtain Correlation Identifiers.

eInsight Correlations are useful but poorly documented in the eInsight User's Guide for Release 5.1.x. Therefore, Part II of this book delivers a step-by-step walkthrough of the implementation and use of eInsight Correlations. Subsequent sections, dealing with Message Relationship patterns, assume that the mechanics of configuring eInsight Correlations are well understood.

Let's assume that a Business Process must match a Purchase Order to a corresponding Invoice using the Purchase Order Number field as the Correlation Identifier. Data for this component is present in both messages. Purchase Orders are delivered by some part of the solution to a JMS Destination qPOQueue as JMS text messages. Invoices are delivered to a JMS Destination qInvQueue as JMS text messages.

The issue lies in supplying the content of the JMS text message, containing the Purchase Order or the Invoice, to the eInsight engine in such a way that it can address the Purchase Order Number field using an XPath expression.

The Purchase Order and the Invoice XML Schemas will be used to construct OTDs used to receive Purchase Orders from qPOQueue and Invoices from qInvQueue.

The XML Schema documents are shown in Listings 11-1 and 11-2.

SOAPRequestReply_PO.xsd is shown in Listing 11-1.

LISTING 11-1: Purchase Order XML Schema document

```
<?xml version="1.0" encoding="UTF-8"?>
<xsd:schema
    xmlns:xsd="http://www.w3.org/2001/XMLSchema"
    xmlns:tns="http://MCZ01:14000//SOAPRequestReply"
    targetNamespace="http://MCZ01:14000//SOAPRequestReply"
    >
    <xsd:element name="PO">
        <xsd:complexType>
            <xsd:sequence>
                <xsd:element name="PONumber" type="xsd:string"/>
                <xsd:element name="PODate" type="xsd:string"/>
                <xsd:element name="Items" maxOccurs="unbounded">
                    <xsd:complexType>
                        <xsd:sequence>
                            <xsd:element name="ItemNumber"
                                         type="xsd:string"/>
                            <xsd:element name="ItemQuantity"
                                         type="xsd:integer"/>
                        </xsd:sequence>
                    </xsd:complexType>
```

```
            </xsd:element>
        </xsd:sequence>
    </xsd:complexType>
</xsd:element>
</xsd:schema>
```

SOAPRequestReply_Inv.xsd is shown in Listing 11-2.

LISTING 11-2: Invoice XML Schema document

```
<?xml version="1.0" encoding="UTF-8"?>
<xsd:schema
    xmlns:xsd="http://www.w3.org/2001/XMLSchema"
    xmlns:tns="http://MCZ01:14000//SOAPRequestReply"
    targetNamespace="http://MCZ01:14000//SOAPRequestReply"
    >
    <xsd:element name="Inv">
        <xsd:complexType>
            <xsd:sequence>
                <xsd:element name="PONumber" type="xsd:string"/>
                <xsd:element name="Items" maxOccurs="unbounded">
                    <xsd:complexType>
                        <xsd:sequence>
                            <xsd:element name="ItemNumber"
                                         type="xsd:string"/>
                            <xsd:element name="ItemQuantity"
                                         type="xsd:integer"/>
                            <xsd:element name="TotalPrice"
                                         type="xsd:double"/>
                        </xsd:sequence>
                    </xsd:complexType>
                </xsd:element>
                <xsd:element name="InvoiceTotal" type="xsd:double"/>
            </xsd:sequence>
        </xsd:complexType>
    </xsd:element>
</xsd:schema>
```

By itself, the JMS receive activity will return a text message or a bytes message, and a series of JMS Message Header properties. To allow the eInsight engine access to the structure of the body of the message, we must create a receive activity that returns the body as a structured message. One way to facilitate this is to wrap the JMS receive activity into a "notify"-style subprocess that returns the necessary XML structure. This subprocess will be used in place of the JMS receive activity in the main Business Process that processes correlated messages. This is illustrated in detail in Chapter 9, section 9.5, "Derived Correlation Identifiers," in Part II.

The basic process, bpCorrelatePOandInvoice, receives a Purchase Order and an Invoice, concatenates them, and sends the result to a JMS Destination, as shown in Figure 11-16. A real process would do something more useful with the Purchase Orders and Invoices.

It is necessary to identify the parts of the Purchase Order and the Invoice messages that are to be used for correlation and to configure the receive activities so that the eInsight engine can actually correlate messages.

We identified the PONumber fields in both the Purchase Order and the Invoice as the field that will contain values to match on. eInsight, implementing BPEL4WS techniques, requires us to define the Correlation Key and the Correlation Set.

In Business Process Properties, right-clicking on the name of the process bpCorrelatePOandInvoice and selecting the Correlations tab gives access to correlation properties.

You would create a new Correlation Key, ckPONumber message reqPO, expand the entry until PONumber node is seen, select it, and add it to the Correlation Key, as illustrated in Figure 11-17.

The process is repeated for resInv, as illustrated in Figure 11-18.

The reqPO is the structure returned by the sbpReceivePO. The resInv is the structure returned by the sbpReceiveInv. The Correlation Key defines which field values, in different messages, will be matched to determine if the messages are related. The names of the fields do not have to be the same. The datatypes and

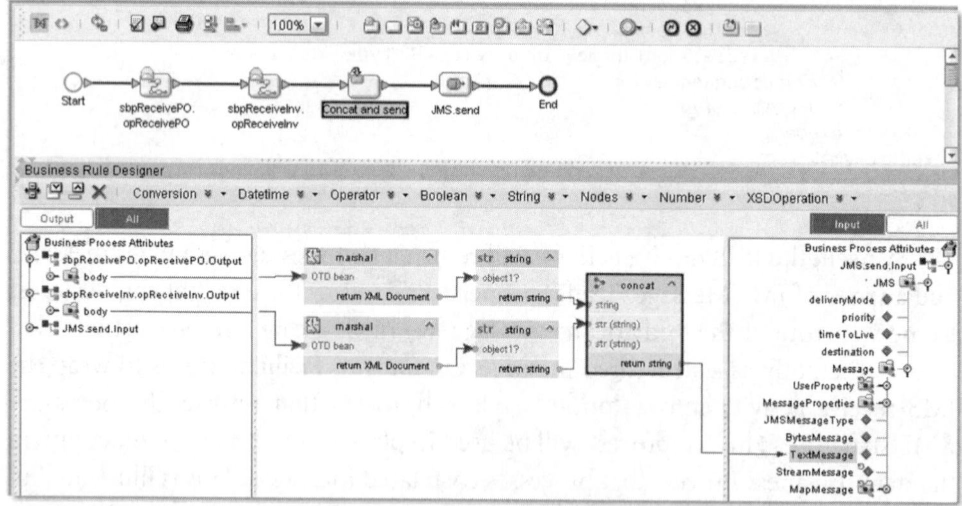

FIGURE 11-16: Constructing a result message from two input messages

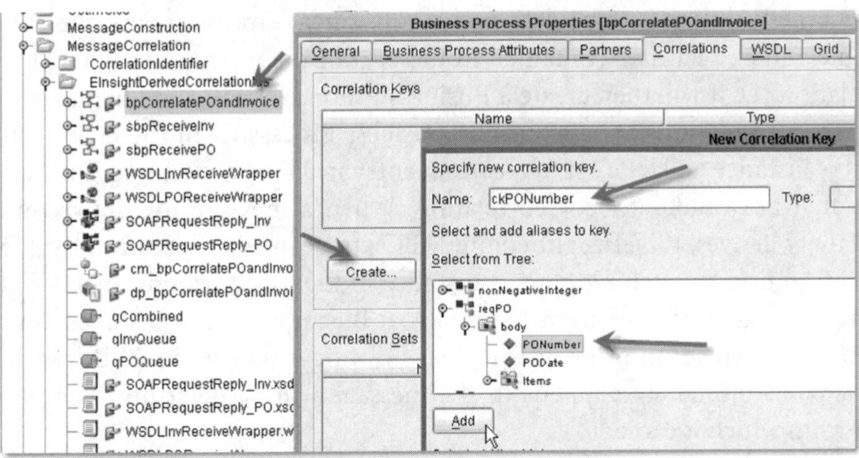

FIGURE 11-17: Selecting Correlation Key field from the Purchase Order message

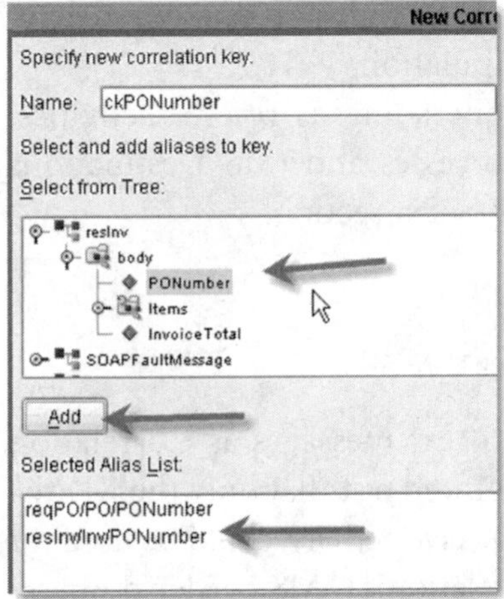

FIGURE 11-18: Selecting Correlation Key field from the Invoice message

sizes must be the same because it is expected that values in these fields in different messages will be identical.

Having defined the Correlation Key, you would define the Correlation Set that references the Correlation Key, then configure Use Correlation properties of the appropriate receive activities.

The entire process is presented in a step-by-step fashion in Chapter 9, section 9.5, "Derived Correlation Identifiers," in Part II.

When a message that is to be delivered to a Business Process arrives, the eInsight engine will extract data contained in the part of the message designated as the Correlation ID. It will then create a Business Process instance and hand it the message. The Correlation ID data and the Business Process ID of the new Business Process instance will be used to create an entry in a list of executing Business Processes that are candidates for correlation. When a message for the second receive activity arrives, the eInsight engine will extract the Correlation ID value and attempt to find a matching process instance in the list. If it finds one, it will deliver the message to the receive activity of that Business Process instance, thus completing the correlation process. If it does not find a match, it will throw an exception. What ultimately happens to the message will be determined by the endpoint from which it came.

Although we used JMS Destinations as sources of messages for the subprocesses, the method discussed above is a generic method; it can be used to wrap arbitrary endpoints. The point in all this is to allow the eInsight engine to locate the parts of messages it needs for correlation even if the endpoint does not deliver messages in a form that lends itself to XPath manipulation.

What we achieved, using subprocesses masquerading as receive activities, could have been achieved using independent processes and JMS Destinations with JMSCorrelationID properties, discussed in the next section.

11.9 Derived Correlation Identifiers: Alternative

Correlation using JMS receive activities and JMS text messages as Correlation Identifiers was discussed in section 11.7. It was pointed out that only the XPath-accessible fields, within messages returned by the receive activity, could be used for correlation. It was also observed that the JMSCorrelationID JMS header property by default will carry a literal string "Sun-SeeBeyond." The JMS header properties are accessible using XPath expressions; therefore, we can use the JMSCorrelationID JMS header field to carry a Correlation Identifier value of our choosing. The trick to using JMS receive activities directly, without having to wrap them up in subprocesses, is to make sure to set correct values in JMSCorrelationID fields, of messages to be correlated, and mark these fields for correlation.

In the previous section, we were receiving messages from endpoints in a subprocess, unmarshaling them, and returning the structured payload as the output message. Rather than doing that, we could preprocess messages in separate components to obtain and set Correlation Identifiers. We would receive messages from endpoints, unmarshal them in specialized components, extract the values to be used for correlation, set the JMSCorrelationID values in JMS messages, and finally send the JMS messages to the appropriate JMS Destinations. The main process would then deal with JMS receive activities, as described earlier, and the eInsight engine would use JMSCorrelationID values in JMS messages to determine which messages belong to which Business Process instances. There would be no need to create subprocesses as wrappers, thus making the solution simpler and more efficient.

To illustrate this notion, Figure 11-19 shows a connectivity map containing all relevant components.

Either an eInsight Business Process or a Java Collaboration can receive the message, unmarshal it, configure the JMSCorrelationID and JMS Payload, and send the message on its way. For clarity and brevity, Java Collaboration sources are shown in Listings 11-3 and 11-4.

LISTING 11-3: Book/MessageCorrelation/EInsightDerivedCorrelationIds/jcdSetCorrelationID_PO

```
public void receive
    (com.stc.connectors.jms.Message input
    ,com.stc.connectors.jms.JMS W_toJMS
    ,stcgen.fcxotd.http___MCZ01_14000__SOAPRequestReply.PODocument vPO )
        throws Throwable
{
    vPO.unmarshalFromString( input.getTextMessage() );
    com.stc.connectors.jms.Message msgOut = W_toJMS.createTextMessage();
    msgOut.getMessageProperties().setCorrelationID
                                        ( vPO.getPO().getPONumber() );
    msgOut.setTextMessage( input.getTextMessage() );
    W_toJMS.send(msgOut);
}
```

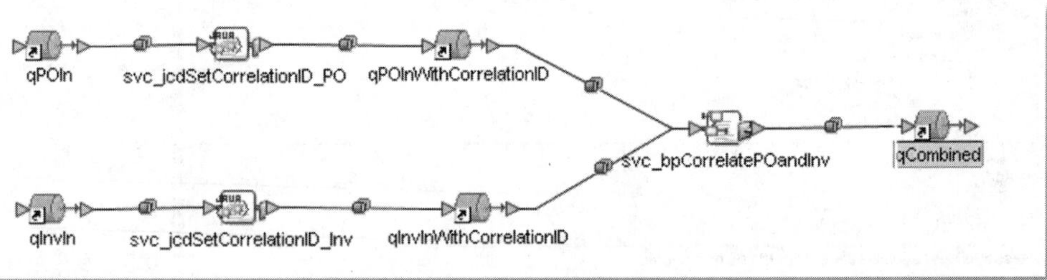

FIGURE 11-19: __Book/MessageCorrelation/EInsightDerivedCorrelationIds/cm_EInsightDerivedCorrelationIdsAlt

LISTING 11-4: Book/MessageCorrelation/EInsightDerivedCorrelationIds/jcdSetCorrelationID_Inv

```
public void receive
    (com.stc.connectors.jms.Message input
    ,com.stc.connectors.jms.JMS W_toJMS
    ,stcgen.fcxotd.http___MCZ01_14000__SOAPRequestReply.InvDocument vInv )
        throws Throwable
{
    vInv.unmarshalFromString( input.getTextMessage() );
    com.stc.connectors.jms.Message msgOut = W_toJMS.createTextMessage();
    msgOut.getMessageProperties().setCorrelationID
                                        ( vInv.getInv().getPONumber() );
    msgOut.setTextMessage( input.getTextMessage() );
    W_toJMS.send(msgOut);
}
```

Copy eInsight Business Process bpSimpleCorrelation from the eInsightCorrelation project and modify its Correlation properties or create an equivalent new Business Process. Define the Correlation Key and the Correlation Set to use the JMSCorrelationID property of the JMS message, as shown in Figure 11-20.

Make sure the Use Correlations properties on both JMS receive activities are set as appropriate—refer to section 11.7 for details.

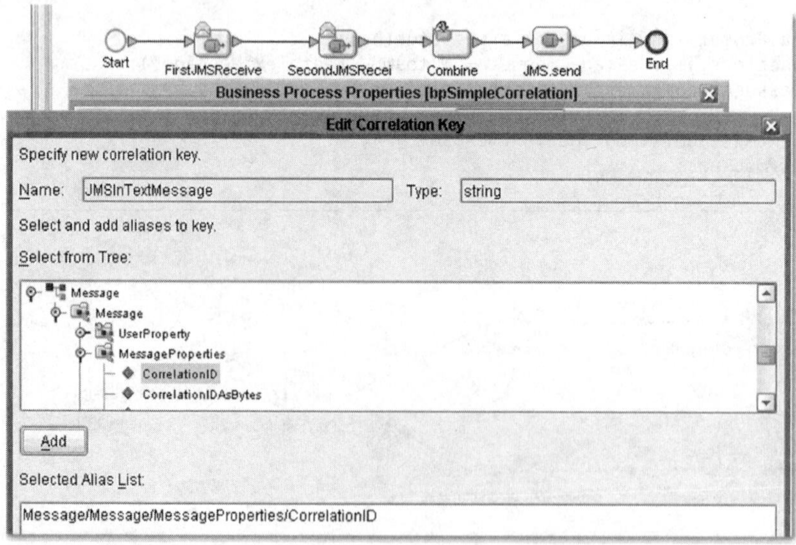

FIGURE 11-20: _Book/MessageCorrelation/EInsightDerivedCorrelationIds/bpSimpleCorrelation

The advantage of this approach is that Web Services Description Language (WSDL) interface definitions are not required, since no subprocesses are required. The disadvantage is that two additional JMS queues are required and that messages must be unmarshaled again in the main process, even though they were already unmarshaled in the Java Collaborations. This was done in order to obtain values for the JMSCorrelationID properties. To minimize the number of queues, you could venture to configure static JMS selectors, discussed in Chapter 5, so that only one additional JMS queue would be required. Ultimately, it is up to the implementer to determine the best way to address this issue.

11.10 Message Relationship Patterns

Correlation can be used to process messages that follow several distinct Message Relationship patterns. In the earlier versions of SeeBeyond products, this feature was called Event Linking and Sequencing.

11.10.1 Header-Items-Trailer Correlation

The Header-Items-Trailer Message Relationship pattern is one where a particular kind of a message, called the Header Message, causes the correlation process for a series of messages to start. Subsequent messages with the same Correlation Identifier, called Items, are collected until another special message, with the same Correlation Identifier, called the Trailer, is received. This causes collection of related messages to stop. Collected messages are then processed together.

In previous sections dealing with correlations, the relationship between correlated messages was very simple: the Purchase Order was expected to arrive first and the Invoice was expected to follow. The relationship between the Purchase Order Message and the Invoice Message could be considered to be a special case of a Header-Items-Trailer Message Relationship pattern. The Purchase Order is the Header, a Message that initiates the correlation process, and the Invoice is the Trailer, a Message that causes the correlation process to finish. Here the Items messages were not present. While this may be a valid relationship, the simplistic processes that were implemented did not consider some runtime issues that might arise. The first and foremost was that if the Invoice arrived before the corresponding Purchase Order, the Invoice would be lost. There would be no existing eInsight Business Process instance to which to deliver it. Subsequent arrival of the Purchase Order would result in creation of a new eInsight Business Process instance for which the Invoice would never arrive. What would happen to that instance would depend on whether persistence was turned on for the process or not. In the former case, the instance would exist until explicitly deleted. In the latter case, it would be eliminated upon Integration Server shutdown.

What is required is that the two documents are correlated. In this case, it does not matter which arrives first. A more reasonable solution that would not lose an Invoice document if it arrived before the Purchase Order document would be to allow the documents to arrive in any order. To do so, rather than place the receive activities one after the other, you would use an Event-Based Decision.

This discussion is illustrated with a detailed example in Chapter 9, section 9.7.1, "Header-Items-Trailer Correlation," in Part II.

Whichever the order of submission, the messages will be correlated correctly.

Rather then being restricted to correlating two messages, the process can be extended to any number of messages coming in from distinct endpoints.

In the initial implementation, messages were required to arrive in a predefined order, and issues would arise if they did not. In this implementation, messages can arrive in any order, so this issue was avoided.

Another issue arises if an initial message arrives but a subsequent message does not. This will result in a process instance hanging around indefinitely, if persistence was enabled for it, or until the Integration Server is shut down if not. This is wasteful of resources. Furthermore, if persistence is not turned on, there is no way to see or operate on such in-flight instances. Without persistence, the Enterprise Manager will not display eInsight process instances and will not offer the "terminate" option to terminate them.

To work around this issue, a process instance must be able to time out receive activities on which it is blocked for an excessive amount of time.

The third variant of the process adds a Timer Event as an additional receive activity. When the timer expires, the Business Process will terminate regardless of whether all expected messages were received. Any messages that were received up to that point will be sent to an exception queue.

11.10.2 Any Order Two Items Correlation

We are required to match Purchase Orders and Invoices, one of each, in any order. It matters not whether the Invoice arrives first or the Purchase Order arrives first.

To implement this pattern, we need two sets of receive activities, one set that causes the Correlation Set to be initialized and one that does not. The process is shown in Figure 11-21. Since either the Purchase Order or the Invoice can arrive

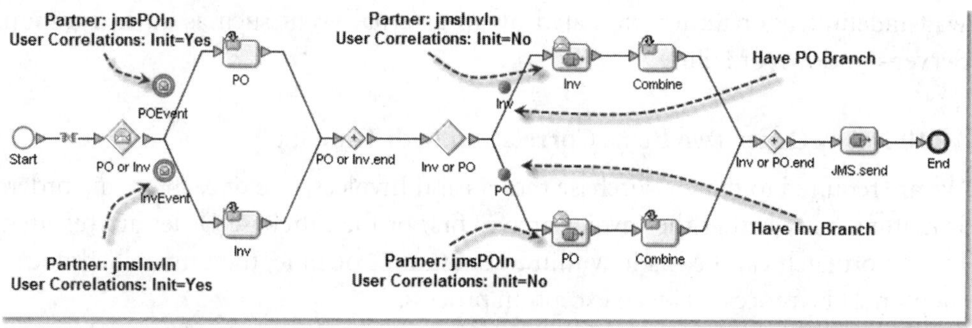

FIGURE 11-21: Any Order Two Items correlation process

first, the initial set of receive activities will use the Event-Based Decision. Once we have one of the required messages, we will branch to the appropriate receive activity to receive the other.

The connectivity map uses two inbound and one outbound JMS queues, as shown in Figure 11-22.

Project __Book/MessageCorrelation/EInsightCorrelations/AnyOrder implements this example. The complete example is reproduced in Chapter 9, section 9.7.2, "Any Order Two Items Correlation," in Part II.

This implementation will accept the two messages in any order: it will not lose messages and wait if messages arrive out of order, as the simplistic solution shown previously would.

The issue from which this solution suffers, as the simple solution shown before also did, is that if the subsequent message never arrives, the process instance will

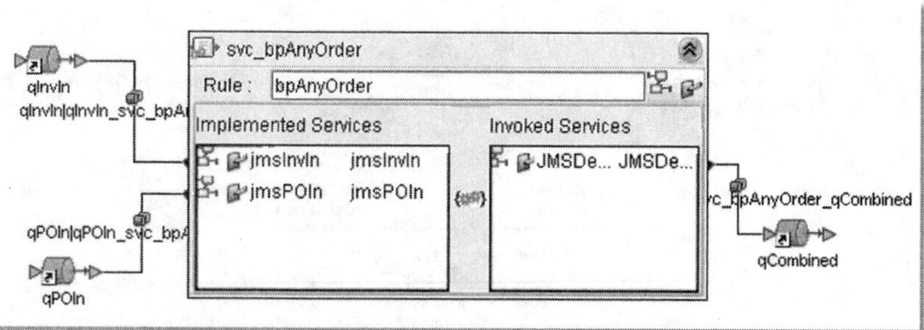

FIGURE 11-22: Connectivity map for the Any Order Two Items correlation

wait indefinitely or until terminated by an external event such as an Integration Server shutdown or failure.

11.10.3 Any Order Two Items Correlation with Timeout

We are required to match Purchase Orders and Invoices, one of each, in any order. It matters not whether the Invoice arrives first or the Purchase Order arrives first, but if no match can be made within a set amount of time, the unmatched document must be processed by an exception process.

The implementation of this pattern is very similar to the Any Order Two Items Correlation pattern discussed previously. It is illustrated in Figure 11-23. The difference is the addition of two Event-Based Decisions, with a receive activity and a timer event activity each, to replace the two plain receive activities.

Timer Event timeout value can be static or dynamic, set to a Duration Literal or a Business Process Attribute value, which also must be a Duration Literal.

Some might ask why a timeout is associated with the second receive activity and not with the first. This is because until a message destined for the first receive activity arrives, the Business Process instance does not exist, so there is no process to time out.

11.10.4 Items-Trailer Correlation

We are required to collect related messages until a "special" trailer message, indicating that a batch of messages is finished, arrives. When it does, we are to process

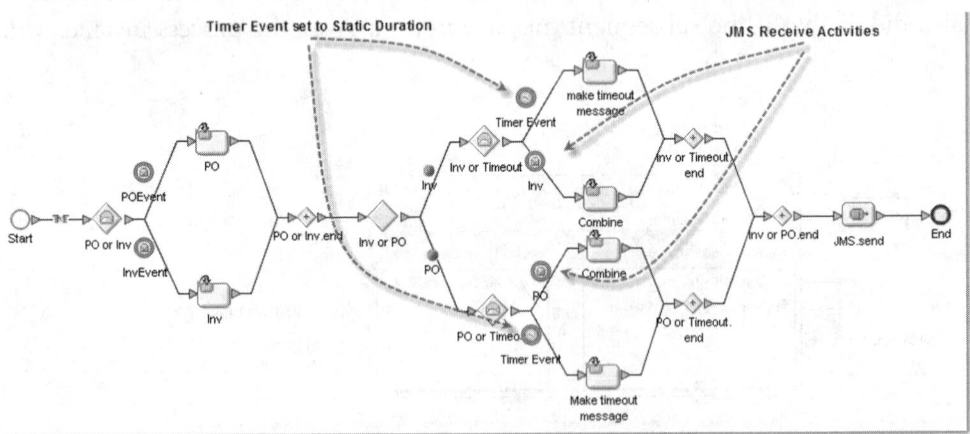

FIGURE 11-23: Any Order Two Items correlation with Timeout process

all messages collected so far and release them for further processing by the next component.

Let as assume that each ordinary message carries a Purchase Order Number, an Item Number, and a Quantity to be delivered. The trailer message carries the same Purchase Order Number, a dummy Item Number, and a count of items for cross-check. The messages are to be assembled into a Purchase Order with the Purchase Order Number and a repeating group of Item Number and Quantity. Ordinary messages will come from a JMS Destination qItemsIn. The trailer message will come from another JMS Destination, qTrailerIn. This is a contrived example. With the items-trailer, you would perhaps be better off using a single queue and a trailer message with a sentinel value in one of the fields, perhaps an ItemNumber value of TRAILER or similar.

Since the item messages are structured and only one field of each, the Purchase Order Number, will be used for correlation, it is necessary to preprocess messages as they arrive. We use JMS to receive messages, so we unmarshal them in a Java Collaboration and set the JMSCorrelationID JMS header property to the value of the Purchase Order Number so that the correlation logic can associate related messages. Depending on preferences, wrapper subprocesses could have been used instead.

The Business Process starts with a single receive activity with Use Correlations configured, and the Correlation Set Initialized property set to Yes, to receive the initial item. This is followed by a loop containing an Event-Based Decision with two receive activities, one for the remaining items and one for the trailer message. As items are processed, they will be counted and their item numbers and quantities will be set in the Purchase Order structure.

If a trailer arrives that cannot be matched to an existing set of items, it will not be delivered and will be processed according to the global JMS Server retry policy.

Since this solution does not use timers to restrict the amount of time given for the correlation to complete, it suffers from the same issue as other solutions that do not use timers. If the trailer message never arrives, the correlation will never complete. If no persistence is used and the Integration Server goes down, messages accumulated by the process instance will be lost. A simple modification that adds a timed branch would address this issue.

While this modified solution does address the issue of the trailer not arriving within a reasonable amount of time, it does so in a fairly simplistic manner. A more reasonable solution would be to have the partially completed Purchase Order sent to an alternate destination, perhaps an exception destination tied into a human workflow.

The Items-Trailer Message Relationship pattern described in this section could be looked at as a Gather component implementation in a Scatter-Gather pattern.

This discussion is illustrated with a complete example in Chapter 9, section 9.7.4, "Items-Trailer Correlation," in Part II.

11.10.5 Header-Counted-Items Correlation

We are processing Purchase Orders to generate Invoices. Each Item in the Purchase Order is sent as a separate message to the ProvideItemPrice service, which has the smarts to work out volume discounts and, given the Item Number and Quantity, will return the Price for that Quantity of that Item. We need to then collect all the responses from the service, using the Purchase Order Number as a Correlation Key, assemble the Invoice message, and send it for further processing.

This narrative describes an implementation of a final part of a Scatter-Gather or a Composed Message Processor pattern. The Header-Counted-Items correlation implements the Gather part of the Scatter-Gather pattern or the Aggregator part of the Composed Message Processor pattern.

Assume that the Scatter part of the Scatter-Gather implementation breaks up the Purchase Order message into as many Item messages as there are items. Since the Scatter implementation knows how many items there are in each order, it will also assemble a header message, PricedItemsHeader, containing the PONumber and the number of items in the ItemCount.

A Business Process will do the Gather work. It needs a receive activity to receive the CostedItemsHeader message and a receive activity in a while loop to receive the CostedItems messages. Figure 11-24 illustrates this process. The loop is controlled

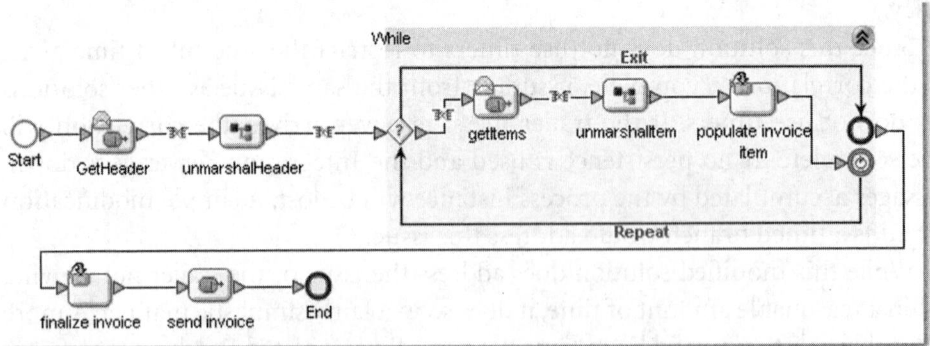

FIGURE 11-24: Header-Counted-Items correlation process

by the loop counter, which is incremented for every item received until it reaches the value of the count of items to receive, which is set from the ItemCount field in the header message. Item cost and invoice total are calculated as the loop executes.

This solution could potentially benefit from a timeout on the second receive activity to abort processing if not all messages arrived within a reasonable time. The complete example is presented in Chapter 9, section 9.7.5, "Header-Counted-Items Correlation," in Part II.

11.10.6 Counted and Timed Items Correlation

We are running a Shoe Warehouse serving all states in the country. Shoes ship in boxes of the same size. For cost-efficiency, we only ship to a particular state if there are enough orders to fill a carton of 125 boxes, all going to the one state. As orders come, in we identify the State, the Order Number, and the Item Number and send a message to the warehousing system. When enough orders are available, the warehousing system prints the list of items to be assembled for shipment to a particular state so the carton can be filled and dispatched. We have a service level agreement with the states requiring us to deliver the goods within, at most, 3 days. If there are not enough boxes to fill a carton within 3 days, we make and ship a partial shipment.

The narrative above describes a Counted-Items Message Relationship pattern. All messages are the same and consist of the State, OrderNumber, and ItemNumber.

The State field will be used for correlation. The first message for which there is no Business Process instance will start the correlation process. Orders from the particular state will be collected until there are 5 or the timer of 5 minutes expires, whichever is sooner, at which point the list of items will be sent for picking. This process is illustrated in Figure 11-25.

The complete example is presented in Chapter 9, section 9.7.6, "Counted and Timed Items Correlation," in Part II.

11.10.7 Timed Items Correlation

We batch like items for a period of time. When the time expires, we send the batch on regardless of how many items were accumulated.

Whatever the narrative excuse for a Timed Items Correlation, the Business Process that implements this pattern will be identical, with one exception, to the Counted and Timed Items pattern discussed previously. The sole difference will be the while loop conditional. Rather than counting items as they are received,

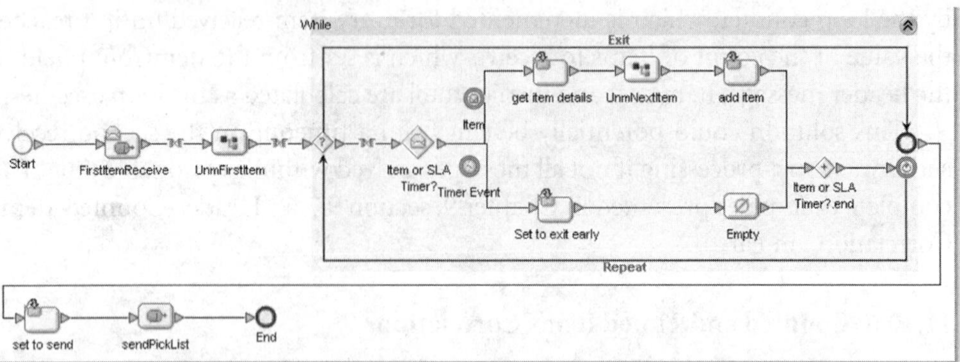

FIGURE 11-25: Counted and Timed Items correlation

the loop will accumulate items until the timer expires. At this point, the loop conditional will be reset to false so the loop can exit and the batch can be sent.

Here, too, a preprocess collaboration or a subprocess wrapper will be used to ensure the correlation key value is available to the eInsight engine in the appropriate XPath-addressable structure.

11.10.8 Scatter-Gather Correlation

We order goods from suppliers. A Purchase Order (PO) is submitted to a supplier. Some time later, an Advanced Shipping Notice (ASN) is received, followed later still by the Delivery Notice (DN) indicating the goods were received. The process that tracks purchases and deliveries must collect all of these documents together for processing by the finance department. If the ASN is not received within a fixed period of time, an alert must be sent to the purchasing department to initiate a followup action. If goods are not received within a fixed period of time, an alert must be sent to the receiving department to initiate a follow-up action.

The narrative describes a Scatter-Gather pattern. A component sends one or more messages, then waits for one or more asynchronous response messages that are related to the messages sent.

The eInsight Business Process needs to be triggered by some event, let's say an arrival of a Purchase Order. The Purchase Order Number is extracted from the Purchase Order message and used to initialize the Correlation Set. The Purchase Order message is then sent to a JMS queue. The receiving Business Process parses the PO, constructs the ASN and sends it to the ASN queue, then constructs a DN and sends it to the DN queue. In a more realistic implementation, the event that results in a DN message being generated would happen some time after the event that resulted in generation of the ASN message, so in all likelihood a separate process would handle the DN and deliver it for correlation.

The process that handles sending of the PO and correlation of the ASN and the DN might look like that shown in Figure 11-26.

Note that we have four send activities and three receive activities, each associated with a distinct JMS queue.

The complete step-by-step implementation of this example is included in Chapter 9, section 9.7.8, "Scatter-Gather Correlation," in Part II.

This is one of the possible implementations of the Scatter-Gather pattern. Another implementation, using asynchronous subprocess, is presented in Chapter 12, "Reusability," section 12.4.2.

11.10.9 Message Relationship Patterns Summary

Message Relationship patterns discussed in the preceding sections represent basic relationships that exist between messages in messaging solutions. Other, more complex patterns can be broken down into these basic patterns. All of the Message Relationship patterns, which would be implemented using eInsight, rely on the eInsight engine's ability to identify key data values in messages and use that key data to associate messages with Business Processes and, in particular, Business Process instances that are collecting related messages. To be effectively employed in integration solutions, all implementations must have a notion of when to stop waiting for related messages and to processes messages that are already collected. Common indicators are timeout expiration, collection of a predefined number of

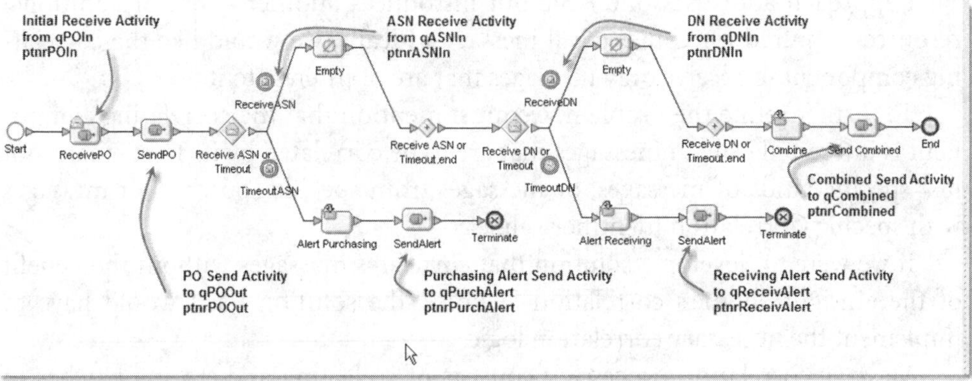

FIGURE 11-26: Scatter-Gather correlation process

messages, or arrival of a sentinel message that indicates end of collection. The basic examples discussed in this section are common to all implementations of a type and can be used as the basis for extended implementations. Custom logic will need to reflect processing requirements of assembled collections of messages, such as selections of a lowest price or a highest bid, rather than how the collection is performed or when collection ends and processing begins.

11.11 eGate Correlation with Dynamic Selectors

eInsight-based correlation takes advantage of the eInsight engine's correlation facilities. The eInsight engine ensures that processing components receive only messages they require. Without eInsight, correlation must be implemented differently.

As a general proposition, a correlating component would receive all messages, determine which are of interest, and discard or return to sender those that are not. It would then pass the messages of interest to the processing component or would process them itself. The major issue with this approach is that the correlating component receives all messages even if only a small proportion of them are of interest to it. This is an overhead in terms of resources required to receive all messages and increased latency while the component determines whether or not it is required to process each message and return it to the sender. The component could rapidly become a bottleneck. Resubmitting messages to the sender could result in the same messages being continually redelivered to the correlating component only to be continually returned to the sender. This issue could be addressed by having the correlating component subscribe to a JMS topic so that it receives copies of all messages and can safely discard those that are not of interest. That approach addresses one issue but introduces another—that of additional resources required for copies of all messages. Ideally, we would like the correlating component to receive only messages that are of interest to it.

To further refine the problem, we must mention that the correlating component is interested only in messages that are to be correlated by it. That means not just specific kinds of messages, or messages from specific sources, but messages with specific Correlation Identifier values.

If we were to develop a solution that correlates massages without the benefit of the eInsight engine's correlation facilities, the solution itself would have to implement the necessary correlation logic.

Message correlation processing consists of collecting and storing batches of related messages until batch completion criteria are met and submission of completed batches to the processing components for processing. With eInsight-based correlation, all of the logic necessary to determine if a message is related to any other message(s) is performed by the eInsight engine. All of the logic necessary to collect, store, determine completion criteria state, and process the batch of messages is implemented by eInsight Engine and eInsight Business Processes.

The fundamental piece of functionality would be that which determines if a current message is related to any other message already known or isolating and making available the pieces of data necessary for some component to make that determination.

Another fundamental piece of functionality necessary for correlation would be the storage of batches of related messages, as they are being assembled, prior to invocation of the completed batch processing component.

Yet another fundamental piece would be the functionality that determines batch completion and delivers related messages for processing.

The final piece of functionality would be that which processes batches of related messages.

Short of developing a sophisticated and, most likely, large Java Collaboration that implements all of the required functionality, there is no real way to develop a generic Java Collaboration Definition (JCD)–based correlation processor. Not all is lost, however. We will discuss a re-implementation of one of the Message Relationship patterns using just the JMS Message Server and JCDs.

Bear in mind that it still is much easier to implement correlations using eInsight than it is to do so without it.

11.11.1 Items-Trailer Correlation

Let's re-implement the Items-Trailer Message Relationship pattern without the use of eInsight and eInsight correlation functionality.

Recapping the scenario, we are required to collect related messages until a "special" trailer message, indicating that a batch of messages is finished, arrives. When it does, we are to process all messages collected so far and release them for further processing by the next component.

Let as assume that each ordinary message carries a Purchase Order Number, an Item Number, and a Quantity to be delivered. The trailer message carries the same Purchase Order Number, a dummy Item Number, and a count of items for cross-check. The messages are to be assembled into a Purchase Order with the Purchase Order Number and a repeating group of Item number and Quantity. Ordinary messages will come from a JMS Destination, qItemsIn. The trailer message will come from another JMS Destination, qTrailerIn. This is a contrived example. With the items-trailer, we would perhaps be better off using a single queue and a trailer message with a sentinel value in one of the fields, perhaps an ItemNumber value of "TRAILER" or similar.

With just the eGate and the JMS Message Server, we need to figure a way of collecting related items and triggering processing of related items once the trailer is received.

One way to implement storage of items is to use a JMS Destination with no current receiver/subscriber—all messages sent there will remain until expired or until explicitly received by some component, whichever is the sooner. One way to implement collection of related items, such that they can be retrieved as a collection of related messages, is to use JMS Correlation ID property to store the Correlation ID of related items and to use the JMS selector mechanism to retrieve items related by the common Correlation ID. One way to trigger processing of related items is to create a Java Collaboration that will be triggered by a trailer message containing the Correlation ID to use and that will retrieve and process related items from the JMS queue using a dynamically constructed selector expression that contains the Correlation ID.

Of the required infrastructure, only dynamic selectors are not available out-of-the-box. Review material presented in Chapter 5, section 5.6.7.2, before continuing with this discussion.

The implementation schematic in Figure 11-27 shows the major user-developed components involved in the solution.

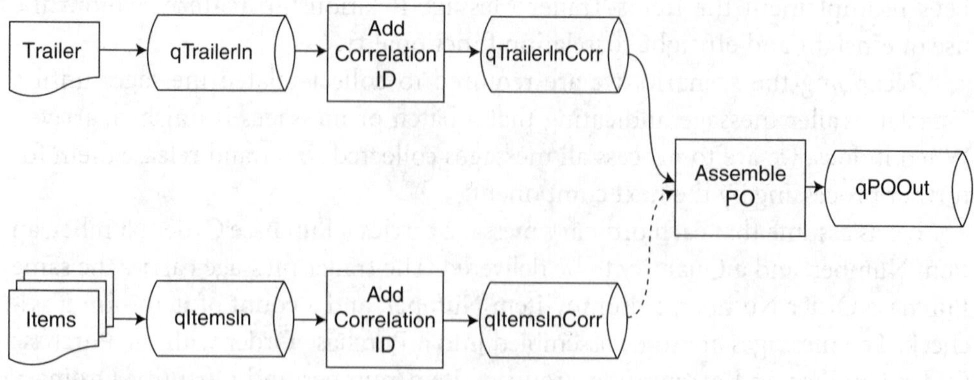

FIGURE 11-27: eGate-based Items-Trailer correlation schematic

Any items or trailer messages submitted to qItemsIn and qTrailerIn will be passed to the Add Correlation ID collaboration, where the Purchase Order value will be extracted and assigned to the JMS header property Correlation ID. The Assemble PO collaboration will be invoked by the arrival of the trailer message. Using the Correlation ID in the trailer message, it will construct a dynamic selector expression, create a selective receiver, receive all messages with the matching Correlation ID from qItemsInCorr, combine them, and finally send the combined message to qPOOut.

Here the JMS Message Server is the means of storing messages while they are being correlated and retrieving related messages.

The Assemble PO collaboration receives all messages using the selective receiver and constructs the PO message. This is the business part of the correlation infrastructure—the rules that govern what is to be done with the related messages. In this case, the PO message is assembled. In other cases, item costs could be summed up and a summary message could be sent out. In still other cases, each message would be inspected to choose the highest bid, the lowest price, or whatever business requirement is being met by message correlation implementation.

The complete example is presented in Chapter 9, section 9.8.1, "Items-Trailer Correlation," in Part II.

This implementation of the Items-Trailer Message Relationship pattern takes advantage of the JMS Message Server to support storage and selective retrieval of related messages. If configured for discrete timeout, which could be done when messages are queued by the jcdAddCorrelationID, messages for which there is no trailer would be discarded by the JMS Message Server when expired.

11.12 Chapter Summary

This chapter discussed message correlation in Java CAPS, the facilities and techniques used to accomplish message correlation, correlation concepts, eInsight BPEL Correlation services, and how correlation can be accomplished when eInsight is not available.

The chapter also discussed common Message Relationship patterns, implementation of which requires correlation. Specifically, the following Message Relationship patterns were discussed:

- Header-Items-Trailer
- Any Order Two Items

- Any Order Two Items with Timeout
- Items-Trailer
- Header-Counted-Items
- Counted and Timed Items
- Scatter-Gather

An eGate-only correlation implementation technique, using JMS with dynamic selectors, was introduced. This technique, which uses JMS API to manipulate JMS objects, is applied elsewhere to implement JMS Polling.

CHAPTER TWELVE

Reusability

12.1 Introduction

In any complex developments, similar patterns and problem solutions occur repeatedly. Judiciously abstracting and packaging such patterns and solutions can give developers a library of reusable components and, ultimately, save development and testing time. This chapter deals with engineering Java CAPS solutions for reusability, packaging of functionality as services, and implementation of technologies that can be used for service interfaces. In particular, reusing Java CAPS components through the JMS Request/Reply, HTTP Request/Reply, eInsight subprocesses, and eInsight-based Web Services is discussed. Both Request/Reply, Notification, and OneWay WSDL-based subprocesses and Web Services are discussed.

12.2 Using JMS Request/Reply

In Chapter 4, "Message Exchange Patterns," section 4.5.1, the use of JMS for implementation of the Request/Reply pattern was discussed. It was noted that a JMS responder could be constructed as a reusable component, able to be invoked from various parts of the overall solution using the JMS requestResponse() method. This is one way in which loose coupling could be achieved. The trick is to ensure that the functionality embedded in such a component is generic enough to be reusable.

It was pointed out that a Business Process cannot directly invoke a JMS Request/Response component, since the JMS object lacks the appropriate service. A Wrapper Java Collaboration that allows the Business Process to invoke the requestReply() method was shown. This collaboration accepts an opaque string message and, after performing a JMS Request/Response operation, returns the response as an opaque string. This is an example of a generic, reusable component. This wrapper collaboration can be used in numerous places, since the only thing that must be varied is the JMS request queue name, and that name is set in the connectivity map. The result is a universal JMS Request/Reply wrapper for use in any eInsight Business Process!

12.3 Using New Web Service Collaborations

It may be observed that an HTTP Client eWay would typically submit a body of data to an HTTP Server identified by a URL dynamically set by the eWay itself or statically configured in the HTTP Client External System container. The HTTP Request/Response interaction using the HTTP eWay always involves a number of steps, which somewhat vary depending on whether HTTP GET or HTTP POST operations are implemented, whether HTTP headers are sent or received, whether cookies are used, and what the payload type is. All in all, a minimum of several lines of Java code or several BPEL mappings are required.

By defining appropriate input and output messages, we could construct a New Web Service collaboration that would wrap the HTTP request and response interaction into a reusable component. This component could then be used from any eInsight Business Process that needs to invoke HTTP Request/Reply functionality with minimum fuss and no knowledge of HTTP interaction details. The input message could consist of two fields: a possibly empty URL and a request body text. The output message could consist of two or three fields: a status (success/failure) field, an optional status text field, and a response body field.

Other kinds of reusable functionality can be similarly wrapped into New Web Service Java Collaborations and used in multiple eInsight Business Processes. One kind that springs to mind is a large and complex Object Type Definition (OTD)-based transformation, such as HL7 2.3 to HL7 2.4 mapping, where the number of OTD nodes to be mapped exceed about 20 or so and where subtree mapping is repeated a number of times.

Chapter 10, section 10.2, "Using New Web Service Collaborations," in Part II (located on the accompanying CD-ROM), implements and exercises an example reusable HTTP Request/Response collaboration.

A reusable Java Collaboration component can be used equally readily from any number of eInsight Business Processes. The processing logic it implements can be arbitrarily complex; for example, it can be built to cope with HTTP Response codes in the 300 to 399 range, HTTP redirects, or it can accept a list of URLs and try each in turn until successful.

Other reusable components can be built in this manner to encapsulate arbitrary reusable logic to be invoked by multiple eInsight Business Processes.

12.4 Using eInsight Subprocesses for Reusability

A Business Process–based integration solution can be implemented as a series of eInsight Business Processes, possibly related in a hierarchical manner, to achieve desired granularity of design and monitoring. This section deals with constructing eInsight subprocesses, which can be invoked as activities in other eInsight processes, their types and their implementation details.

Note that most of this discussion applies to eInsight Business Processes exposed or consumed as Web Services, using the HTTP Binding, from activities in eInsight Business Processes. Where relevant, the differences will be noted. The principle difference is that subprocesses, using an internal transport, must be deployed to the same Integration Server as the processes that invoke them. Web Services, on the other hand, can be deployed to different Integration Servers without restrictions. For logical partitioning of an eInsight-based solution, subprocesses are appropriate; for physical partitioning, Web Services or endpoint-based partitioning are required.

eInsight, based as it is on Business Process Execution Language for Web Services (BPEL4WS), treats all activities as Web Service invocations. As a consequence, creation of an eInsight subprocess begins with the creation of a Web Services Description Language (WSDL) interface contract document—a WSDL definition. This can be achieved using Java CAPS's built-in WSDL Editor or using a third-party tool and importing the WSDL. Bear in mind that Java CAPS expects WSDL definitions to be WS-I compliant. If the WSDL you have is not WS-I compliant, there is a distinct possibility that it will not be accepted at all, that it will not parse correctly, or that the resulting service will fail at runtime.

A typical WSDL 1.1 definition consists of a series of related sections in two groups: the service interface definition and the service implementation definition, illustrated in Listing 12-1. WSDL 1.2 changed terminology—the portType is an interface, and the two groups are called abstract and concrete respectively.

LISTING 12-1: WSDL 1.1 definition skeleton

```
<definitions xmlns:xsd="..." ... >

  <types>
    ...
  </types>

  <message name="...">
    ...
  </message>
  <message name="...">
    ...
  </message>

  <portType name="...">
    <operation name="...">
      <input name="..." message="..."/>
      <output name="..." message="..."/>
...
    </operation>
  </portType>
...
</definitions>
```

The types section, using the XML Schema conventions, defines data elements and types that can be used in message sections to define the structure of messages that will be used by the Web Service. Instead of, or in addition to, defining types directly within the WSDL document, you can import existing XML Schema documents.

The message sections define messages, based on types defined or imported previously, that can be used by the Web Service as input, output, or both.

The PortType section defines the Web Services operations and associates messages with these operations. PortType is a rough equivalent of a class or a module. Operations are rough equivalents of methods or functions within that class or module.

Additional sections, not used when creating eInsight subprocesses, are the binding section and the service section, which belong to the interface implementation definition or concrete section.

WSDL 1.1 specification has a notion of four types of Web Services, classified according to how they interact with the invokers. The most common and most widely supported is the Request/Response Web Service. Much rarer are OneWay-Operation Web Services, where a SOAP Message is sent without an expectation of a response, and Notification Web Services, where a SOAP Message is received without an expectation of having to provide a response. Finally, a Solicit/Response is a service where a SOAP Message sent to a service causes a service to send an asynchronous notification SOAP Message that is correlated with the original solicit message.

eInsight directly supports Request/Response and OneWayOperation services. It, with some cheating, supports notification services as well. Solicit/Response is not supported, or I have not found a way to make it work with WSDL and the built-in Web Services implementation framework.

Given the support for different types of Web Services, you can implement three kinds of main process/subprocess relationships as well as Web Service invoker/provider relationships.

An ordinary request/response relationship is one where a main process invokes a subprocess, passing it an input message, blocking until the subprocess performs its work, and receiving an output message from it. The main process can invoke any number of subprocesses—this is the basis for Business Process orchestration and construction of composite applications.

A OneWayOperation relationship is one where a main process invokes a subprocess with an input message and continues while the subprocess is started and proceeds independently of the main process. In effect, a OneWayOperation subprocess executes in parallel with the main processes from the point at which it was invoked. This relationship is a OneWayOperation as viewed from the main process's perspective.

A notification relationship is one where a subprocess submits an output message to a main process waiting at a receive activity and both proceed in parallel from that point onward. This relationship is a notification relationship as viewed from the main process' perspective.

If the receive activity in the main process of the notification relationship is the first receive activity, or the receive activity of a subprocess in the OneWayOperation relationship is the first receive activity, the implementation is the same. The difference is a logical classification of processes into main and subprocesses.

WSDL 1.1 Specification is readily available. This section does not elaborate on the subject any more than is necessary to create basic WSDL definitions for use in development of eInsight subprocesses; the practical manner in which the WSDL definitions are created here may depart somewhat from the dogma.

12.4.1 Request/Response Subprocess

A Request/Response subprocess is one that accepts an input message, performs some work, and returns a response message. While the subprocess is busy, the invoker waits.

All messages in WSDL, both input and output messages, are defined using the XML Schema semantics within the types section of the WSDL or within the XML Schema document imported into the WSDL.

The WSDL document, defining the subprocess interface, specifies only the service interface definition, or abstract section. eInsight takes care of the implementation details. This is one of the major differences between creating WSDL definitions for subprocesses and creating WSDL definitions for Web Services.

Chapter 10, section 10.3.1, "Request/Response Subprocess," in Part II, contains a complete example implementing a Request/Response subprocess solution.

The amount of functionality encapsulated within the subprocess is arbitrary, dictated by the requirements of the solution under construction. The subprocess can be invoked by any number of other Business Processes located in arbitrary project hierarchies, not necessarily the same as the subprocess itself. The connectivity map makes the association between the subprocess and the process that calls it; therefore, since the components on the connectivity map can come from any number of arbitrarily organized projects, a library of common reusable subprocesses can be constructed.

12.4.2 OneWayOperation Subprocess

Unlike in a Request/Response relationship, where the invoker blocks until the subprocess returns the response, in a OneWayOperation relationship, the main process submits the input message to the subprocess and continues without waiting for the subprocess to complete. In fact, the main process and the subprocess execute in parallel from the point of invocation, and the invoking process may complete before the subprocess does.

Chapter 10, section 10.3.2, "OneWayOperation Subprocess," in Part II, illustrates a OneWayOperation Subprocess with a complete Java CAPS implementation example.

OneWayOperation subprocess can be used in a variety of integration solutions. The main process and the subprocess must appear in the same connectivity map and will therefore be deployed to the same Integration Server. You can encapsulate an arbitrary amount of postprocessing business logic in a OneWayOperation subprocess for reuse where required.

12.4.3 Notification Subprocess

As mentioned before, a notification relationship is one where a subprocess submits a message to a main process whose instance does not exist, causing a process instance to be created, or to an existing instance of a process waiting at a receive activity. Both proceed in parallel from that point onward. This relationship is a notification relationship as viewed from the main process's perspective. eInsight does not directly support the use of notification WSDL, like the WSDL shown in Listing 12-2.

LISTING 12-2: Notification subprocess WSDL

```
<definitions
  xmlns:xsd="http://www.w3.org/2001/XMLSchema"
  xmlns="http://schemas.xmlsoap.org/wsdl/"
  xmlns:soap="http://schemas.xmlsoap.org/wsdl/soap/"
  xmlns:cust="http://seebeyond/Notification"
  xmlns:tns="http://seebeyond/wsdlNotification"
     targetNamespace="http://seebeyond/wsdlNotification"
  >
  <types>
    <xsd:schema xmlns:xsd="http://www.w3.org/2001/XMLSchema">
      <xsd:import
            namespace="http://seebeyond/Notification"
            schemaLocation="Notification.xsd"/>
    </xsd:schema>
  </types>

  <message name="msgNotification">
    <part
      name="msgNotification"
      element="cust:NotificationMsg"/>
  </message>

  <portType name="prtNotification">
    <operation name="opNotification">
      <output
        name="msgNotification"
        message="tns:msgNotification"/>
    </operation>
  </portType>
</definitions>
```

Despite what some tools might say, this WSDL is perfectly valid. eInsight will happily import and validate it. However, dragging the Web Service operation from the WSDL object to the eInsight Business Process Editor canvas will produce an error dialogue box, illustrated in Figure 12-1.

To implement a notification relationship using eInsight, some cheating is called for. The technique is discussed and illustrated with an example in Chapter 10, section 10.3.3, "Notification Subprocess," in Part II.

FIGURE 12-1: Error creating a Notification Web Service

The business excuse for using notifications, much as Request/Response and OneWayOperation subprocesses, is that the main process deals with business objects at a fairly high level. It orchestrates services, each of which implements a considerable amount of business logic, but it does not do detailed business processing itself. A fair amount of processing must be done to input messages before they are ready to be submitted to the main process for on-passing to other components. This is one way of refactoring large processes into a hierarchy of subprocesses orchestrated by an overseer process. The subprocess must be able to kick-start the main process via a receive activity, which is the only way to cause instance creation; therefore it must be representable as a receive activity. The notification subprocess, as built following the technique presented here, is such a subprocess.

As before, an arbitrary amount of business logic can be implemented as a subprocess. This subprocess can then be reused by the solution wherever required, as a single activity in a main process.

12.5 Using eInsight Web Services for Reusability

12.5.1 Request/Response Web Service

Recall discussion of the Request/Response subprocess where it was said that until the connectivity map is constructed, there is no difference between implementing a subprocess and implementing a Web Service with the same abstract interface, or service interface definition, as WSDL 1.1 has it. Rather than connecting a main process and subprocess directly, we introduce a Web Services external application between the two, as illustrated in Figure 12-2.

This is where the relationship that was formerly a main process/subprocess relationship becomes a Web Services invocation/provision relationship. Rather than using some internal mechanism, as was done in the subprocess's case, the

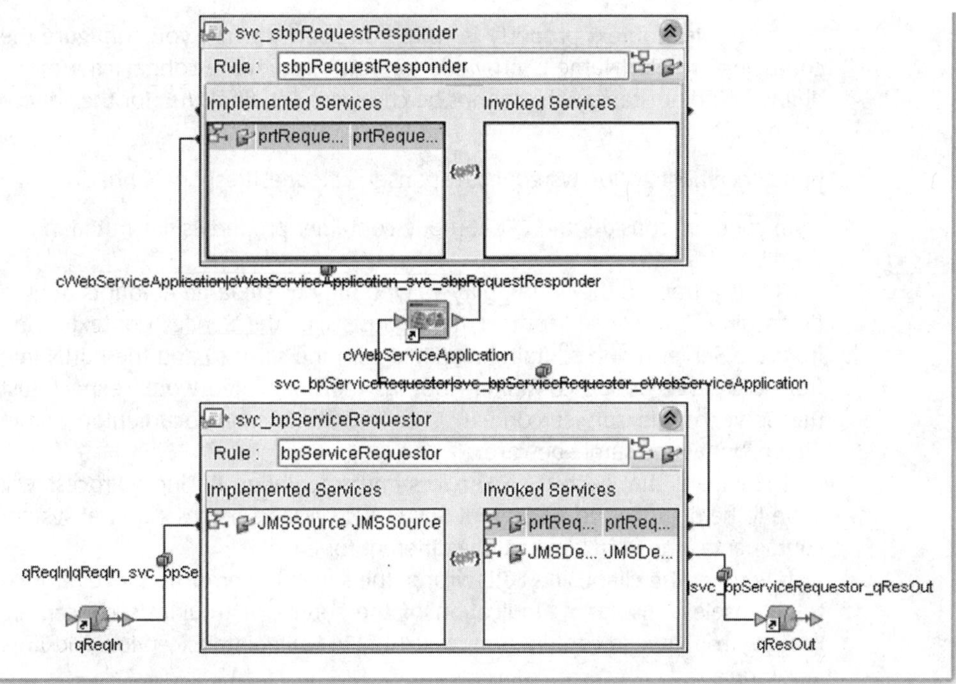

FIGURE 12-2: Converting subprocess to Web Service invocation through the connectivity map

deployment will explicitly use a SOAP over HTTP mechanism for communication between the invoker and the invoked. Note that when connecting the process to the Web Services external application object, we implicitly created the binding section of the concrete implementation or, as WSDL 1.1 would have it, the service implementation definition. We did not specify the service part of the concrete implementation. The service configuration is done via the properties of the Web Services external system containers in the Java CAPS environment.

Note

When on the subject of service configuration, please note that the "servlet context" that is specified in the SOAP/HTTP Web Services external system container in the environment is different in Server mode from the one specified in the Client mode even for the same service.

Consider the Server mode container properties shown in Figure 12-3.

The servlet context property is what you specify when you configure the container. The PortName is provided for you through the connectivity map–defined binding stanza and cannot be changed. The final URL for the service will be:

http://localhost:20001/wsrequestresponse/prtRequestResponseBndPort

In contrast, consider the Client mode container properties illustrated in Figure 12-4.

This is a trap for the young players who may waste large amounts of time diagnosing. The servlet context here consists of the Servlet Context string from the Server mode container suffixed with the slash (/) and the PortName from the Server mode container—not, as the uninitiated would expect, just the Server mode servlet context. This is undoubtedly documented somewhere, but all the same, beware.

This means that each Web Services implementation Business Process will have to be deployed to a different SOAP/HTTP Web Services external system container, as the PortName will be different for each!

If you get the client-side URL wrong, the server.log error messages will be totally useless insofar as indication of the source of trouble is concerned, ranging from Invalid content-type: text/html to NullPointerException and Java stack trace.

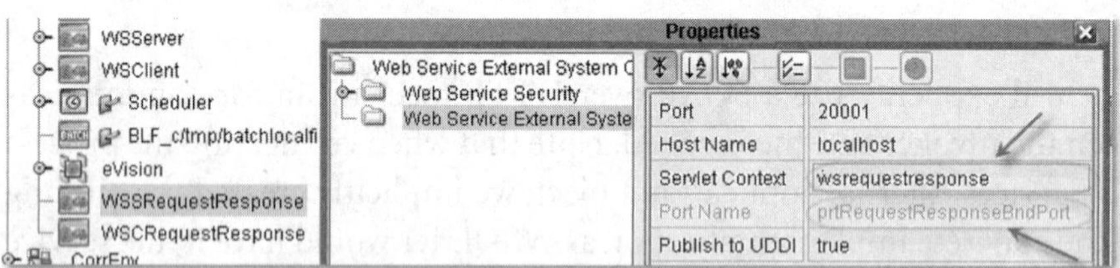

FIGURE 12-3: Web Services Server container properties affecting servlet context

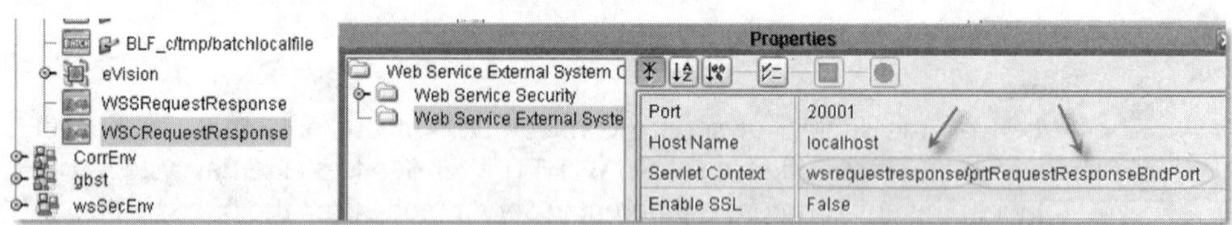

FIGURE 12-4: Web Services client container servlet context property

This discussion is illustrated with an example in Chapter 10, section 10.4.1, "Request/Response Web Service," in Part II.

For continuity of argument, we reused the single connectivity map. This causes both the invoker and the invoked to be deployed to the same Integration Server. Rather that restricting ourselves to that, we could have broken the connectivity map into two: the service implementation, containing the Web Services Server external application and the sbpRequestResponder process, and the service invocation, containing the bpServiceRequestor process, the JMS Destinations, and the Web Services client external application. This way, each of the now independent components could be deployed to a different Integration Server on the same or on different hardware platforms. Even though the original connectivity map contained both the invoking and the invoked (provider) services, the provider was advertised through the UDDI Registry upon build and could be invoked independently of the invoker.

12.5.2 OneWayOperation Web Service

Much as the Request/Response subprocess–based implementation was made loosely coupled and distributable by changing it into a Request/Response Web Services–based implementation, so too can the OneWayOperation subprocess–based implementation be changed into a Web Services–based one, applying exactly the same technique as was applied to the Request/Response service. Here too the single connectivity map could be broken into two, the requester and the responder, and both applications could be deployed to different Integration Servers.

12.5.3 Notification Web Service

Much as the Request/Response and OneWayOperation subprocess–based implementations that were made loosely coupled and distributable by changing them into Request/Response and OneWayOperation Web Services-based implementations, so too the Notification subprocess–based implementation can be changed into a Web Services–based one.

Chapter 10, section 10.4.2, "Notification Web Service," in Part II, reimplements the Notification subprocess example as a Web Service.

12.6 eInsight Service Process Reusability Note

You will have undoubtedly noticed that whether in the case of the Request/Response, OneWayOperation, or Notification implemented using a subprocess, or in the case of the Request/Response, OneWayOperation, or Notification implemented using a Web Services invocation, the eInsight processes involved were identical. No changes whatsoever were made to the processes to deploy them as Web Services rather than as main process/subprocess. You will also have observed by now that regardless of where within the project/subproject hierarchy a component, such as a Business Process, exists, it can be included in a connectivity map defined in a totally different place in the process/subprocess hierarchy. This was demonstrated in the previous section. It should then come as no surprise that an eInsight Business Process, implemented as a service, can be deployed both as a subprocess and as a Web Services provider in different, or even in the same, connectivity maps. This in turn leads to the notion of service process libraries, implementing specific functionality, that are used to compose higher order solutions in a tightly coupled (subprocess invocation) or loosely coupled (Web Services invocation) manner as needs dictate.

12.7 Chapter Summary

This chapter dealt with facilities that help an enterprise architect engineer Java CAPS solutions for reusability and package functionality as services and implementation technologies that can be used for service interfaces. In particular, reusing Java CAPS components through the JMS Request/Reply, HTTP Request/Reply, eInsight subprocesses, and eInsight-based Web Services was discussed. Request/Reply, Notification, and OneWay WSDL–based subprocesses and Web Services were discussed.

Scalability and Resilience

13.1 Introduction

Some inherent scalability and resilience features are present in the Java EE platform, the Application Servers, the JMS Message Servers, and in the hardware platforms. To take advantage of these inherent features, and add explicit features where they are lacking, scalability and resilience of the solution must be architected into it from inception.

Java CAPS solution components can be distributed over available infrastructure to facilitate scaling. The approach to distribution will vary depending on the extent to which eInsight Business Processes are involved. Business Processes may need to be refactored to support component distribution for scalability. This is discussed in section 13.2.

Resilience, the ability of a solution to withstand disruptions caused by expected or unexpected exceptions, is greatly influenced by solution design. Exception interception and handling properties of the tools greatly influence the designer's ability to construct resilient solutions. Some solutions require exception handling that spans multiple components at the business level rather than technical level. These issues are discussed in sections 13.3 and 13.4.

Constructing highly available solutions that take advantage of hardware and infrastructure software is discussed in section 13.5.

13.2 Distributing Components

Scalability and resilience can be achieved by carefully factoring the overall solution into smaller components that can be replicated and deployed to multiple physical devices.

Java CAPS solution factoring is dependent on the nature of the solution. Strictly eGate-based solutions typically would be broken up at JMS Destinations, which are the logical break points. Strictly eInsight-based solutions may not use many JMS Destinations, so large Business Processes may need to be broken up into multiple smaller processes to address resilience and scalability requirements. Layered architectures, typically found in service-oriented architecture (SOA) environments, can be broken up at the interlayer interfaces, typically Web Services invocations.

13.2.1 eGate Component Distribution

JMS Destinations give the architect a considerable degree of flexibility in factoring large solutions into multiple solution fragments for replication and distribution. This flexibility, however, makes it more difficult to understand the runtime environment and to monitor and manage the solution. In the presence of multiple JMS Message Servers in the runtime environment, maintainers of the solution must ensure that JMS Destinations are deployed to the correct Message Servers to avoid unintentional solution fragmentation.

Figure 13-1 shows an exclusively eGate-based solution that involves several services. Each service performs some processing on an incoming message before forwarding it to the next component using a JMS Destination. What the components actually do is immaterial. In this case, each component is a Java Collaboration that adds the name of the connectivity map service, to which it is assigned, to a Route JMS user property, to record the route the message takes; see Chapter 10, "System Management," section 10.3.5.

The Java CAPS environment to which this solution will be deployed consists of three logical hosts—LH01, LH02, and LH03—each with one Integration Server—IS01, IS02, and IS03 respectively—and each with one Message Server—MS01, MS02, and MS03 respectively. The Java CAPS environment is depicted in Figure 13-2.

The single deployment profile assigns components to containers, as shown in Figure 13-3.

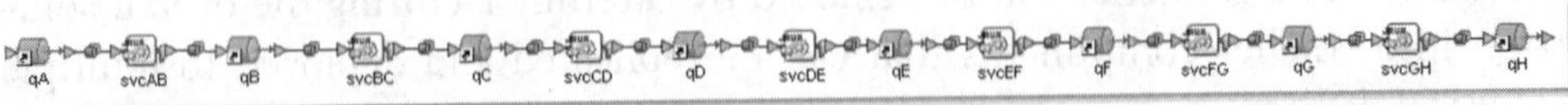

FIGURE 13-1: JMS-based message routing solution

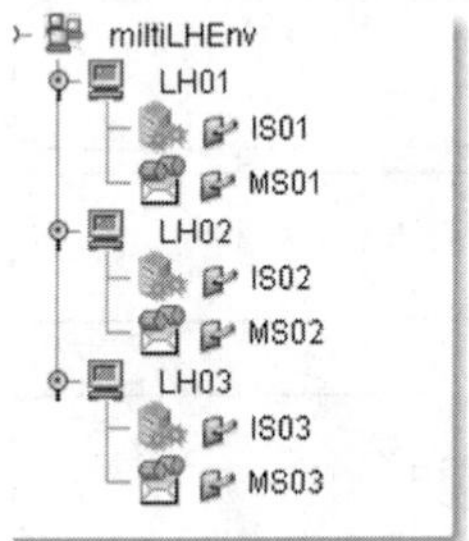

FIGURE 13-2: Java CAPS environment

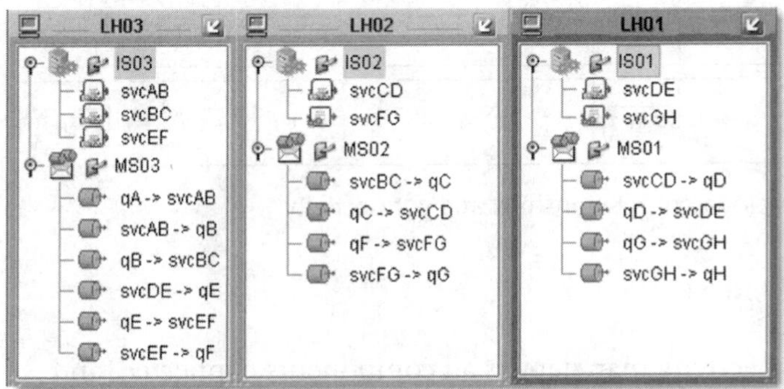

FIGURE 13-3: Component deployment

Note that most JMS queues have two objects that are deployed, a sending client—for example, qB → svcBC—and a receiving client—for example, qA → svcAB. The receiving client corresponds to a subscription by the service to a JMS Destination. The sending client corresponds to a publication by the service to a JMS Destination.

A JMS Destination, configured in a connectivity map with a particular name, is global within the JMS Message Server instance. The publication and the subscription, deployed to the same JMS Message Server, will operate on the same JMS Destination. If the publication and subscription are deployed to different JMS Message Servers, as is the case with qF and qG, the JMS Destinations are different.

Figure 13-4 depicts deployment of the components assigned in the deployment profile, as shown in Figure 13-3.

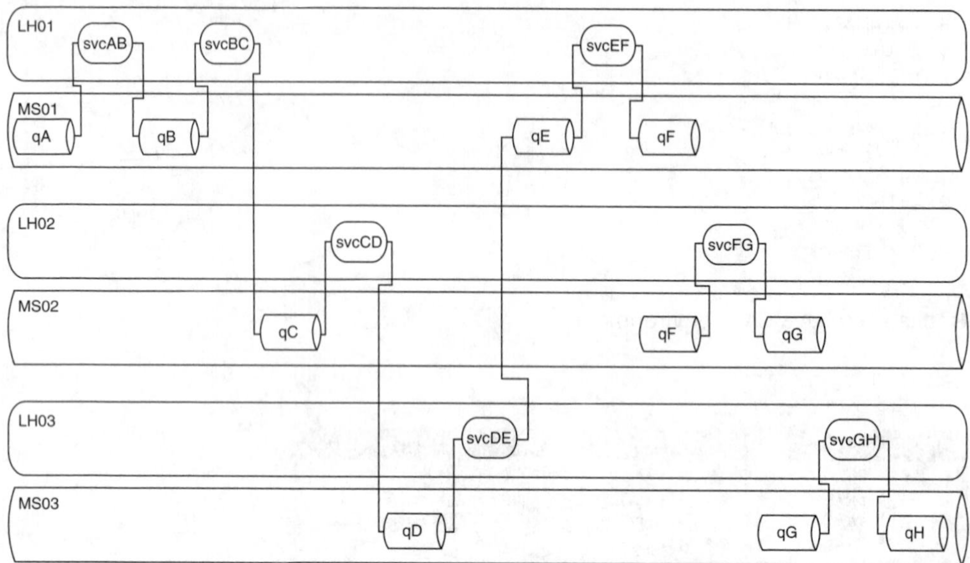

FIGURE 13-4: Component deployment relationships and connectivity

Even though the connectivity map depicts all components connected, and we would expect the message picked up from qA to end up in qH, submitting a message to qA will cause the message to end up in qF and go no further. Similarly, submitting a message to qF deployed in MS02 will cause the message to end up in qG in the same JMS Message Server and go no further. This is because qF in MS01 is different from qF in MS02 and qG in MS02 is different from qG in MS03. In the presence of multiple logical hosts in the environment, care must be taken to ensure publications and subscriptions are deployed where expected.

Components from one or more connectivity maps can be deployed together through one deployment profile or they can be deployed through multiple deployment profiles. Components in each deployment profile can be assigned to one or more logical hosts. Needless to say, components in different deployment profiles can be assigned to different logical hosts as well. Java CAPS allows the designer and the architect to distribute components in a number of ways. The solution architecture can leverage this ability to create a runtime environment with the desired scalability and resiliency properties.

13.2.2 eInsight Component Distribution

When faced with building integration solutions in Java CAPS, there is a temptation to either use multiple Java Collaborations or build a single large eInsight Business Process to accomplish the same thing. There are a couple of major reasons people choose to design an eInsight Business Process to solve an integration problem.

The first and foremost is that by turning on eInsight Persistence, you will immediately obtain the benefits of Message (Route) History. Each Business Process instance will be able to be inspected to determine the route each message took, whether it succeeded or where it failed, and whether it completed or is still in flight. Advantages of runtime monitoring are quite obvious. This kind of functionality is simply not available using just Java Collaborations unless it is explicitly built into the solution. The second is that all the logic of the solution is explicit and visible in a single canvas. The drawback of the approach is that the Business Process is monolithic and its components cannot be distributed. A further disadvantage is that persisting process states and attribute contents to a backing store imposes a significant overhead in terms of performance and storage.

To obtain the advantages of a single process, but to also support component distribution for resilience and scalability, we could take a layered Business Process approach. A main Business Process would contain coarse-grained activities and high-level logic. Each activity would be implemented as a subprocess, or a separate process, or a Java Collaboration, and loosely coupled with the main process using remote invocation technologies like Web Services, TCP Sockets, or JMS. The overall process logic would still be visible, but the moving parts would be able to be distributed over multiple platforms.

An eInsight Business Process can invoke a subprocess or a Java Collaboration as an activity. While this kind of invocation is advertised as a Web Services invocation, it requires that the caller and the called be part of the same deployment and be assigned to the same Integration Server. With this tight coupling, components cannot be distributed, so the major advantage of factoring is not obtainable.

An eInsight Business Process can be exposed as a Web Service. This ability can be exploited to break up a large process into a series of subprocesses, exposed as Web Services, and orchestrated using a main process. By decoupling subprocesses from the main process using remote invocation technologies, an architect can achieve not merely a service-oriented design but also a distributed, scalable design.

13.3 Exception Handling

While all integration solutions are supposed to be designed to work, work well, and work all the time, the reality is somewhat different. Most messages follow the "happy path." Unforeseen circumstances may cause exceptions to occur. A resilient solution must account for exceptions and handle them in a way that is compatible with the objectives of the solution. Solution developers must be aware of the inherent capabilities and limitations of the platform to design exception handling strategies that take advantage of the platform's capabilities and transcend its limitations. The "unhappy path" must be designed and implemented.

13.3.1 Exceptions in Java Collaborations

13.3.1.1 JMS-Triggered Java Collaborations

JMS-triggered Java Collaborations are special in Java CAPS in that there exists a prebuilt exception and retry handling infrastructure, provided by the JMS Message Server implementation, that will handle exceptions not explicitly handled by such collaborations. In ordinary circumstances, an unhandled exception in a JMS-triggered Java Collaboration will cause a transaction rollback to occur. The JMS Message Server will attempt to redeliver the message to the same collaboration. By default, if the condition that caused the exception persists, redelivery will continue indefinitely, preventing subsequent messages from being delivered and processed. With redelivery handling explicitly configured to change the default behavior, redelivery attempts may stop after some number of retries. Messages that could not be delivered will be discarded or diverted to another JMS Destination, depending on the explicitly configured redelivery handling behavior. Chapter 5, "Messaging Infrastructure," section 5.13, discusses JMS redelivery handling at length. Solution designers can take advantage of this infrastructure to handle exceptions. Troublesome messages can be diverted to another destination to be handled by a different component. If the condition is transient, the designer can rely on the JMS Message Server to redeliver the message once the exception condition is cleared.

On exception, all transactional resources invoked by the collaboration prior to the exception will be rolled back. Conversely, nontransactional resources will not be rolled back. Side effects caused by such resource invocation will have to be carefully considered and accounted for in exception handling design. To be more specific, database insert or update operations that occur before an exception will be rolled back, but a file write or an HTTP POST will not be rolled back, since the resources involved are nontransactional.

This discussion is illustrated with a detailed example in Chapter 11, section 11.2.1.1, "JMS-Triggered Java Collaborations," in Part II (located on the accompanying CD-ROM).

A solution designer can take advantage of the JMS redelivery handling to handle exceptions at a Java Collaboration component level. The built-in JMS redelivery mechanism can be utilized to overcome transient exception-causing conditions, such as temporary database unavailability, without requiring explicit logic in Java Collaborations. The designer must, however, consider side effects arising out of access to nontransactional resources, to minimize the adverse impact of retry attempts on these resources.

If the collaboration does not throw an exception, the message that triggered it will be consumed and the transaction that spans the collaboration will complete. If the collaboration handles exceptions that arise during its execution and does not rethrow any, the message that triggered it will also be consumed.

13.3.1.2 Other Java Collaborations

A JMS-triggered Java Collaboration does not "consume" a message if it throws an exception. The message can be redelivered, as discussed in the previous section. A collaboration triggered by other means generally consumes a message regardless of the outcome of its execution. How applicable this statement is depends on the eWay used to trigger the collaboration.

A Batch Inbound eWay, for example, might be invoked at intervals. It will scan the configured directory, and if it finds a file that matches the file name pattern, it will rename the file and deliver the new name and other details to the Java Collaboration. Once this is done, the file will not be renamed back even if the collaboration throws an exception. Effectively, the trigger will be lost and the file will not be processed. This behavior is illustrated in detail by an example in Chapter 11, section 11.2.1.2, "Other Java Collaborations," in Part II.

Transactionality of the triggering endpoint determines whether the triggering message can be rolled back and retried. In general, the only common triggering endpoint with transactional capability is the JMS client. Just about all other endpoints are nontransactional, so their messages are not automatically rolled back and retried. If a collaboration receives a message from a nontransactional endpoint, experiences an exception, and does not handle it, the message will be lost. For messaging solutions that require guaranteed delivery, it is very important that collaborations are designed to handle exceptions so as not to cause message loss. One of the simplest ways of doing so is to ensure that the message is handled by two consecutive collaborations connected by a JMS Destination. The initial collaboration, triggered by a nontransactional endpoint, performs as little work as absolutely essential and passes the message via JMS to the subsequent component. This subsequent component can implement whatever additional logic might be required. If it experiences an exception, JMS redelivery handling can be used to work around transient exceptions and to divert unprocessable messages to dead letter queues.

Within Java Collaborations, exceptions that need handling can be handled using standard Java techniques.

Because a Java Collaboration is invoked from a Stateless Session Bean or a Message-Driven Bean, hosted inside a Java EE container, there exists a class of exceptions that a Java Collaboration cannot handle. One of the things the container does, for example, is manage connections to external resources. The container establishes connections on behalf of objects that need them. If a connectivity issue arises, an exception may be thrown before the collaboration code can execute. The collaboration will not execute and will have no opportunity to intercept and handle the exception. Since these kinds of issue are outside collaborations' control, collaborations cannot be written to deal with them directly. Some eWays, subject to this behavior, will generate one or more alerts. The optional Alert Agent product can be used to intercept such alerts and provide operator notification or trigger Java CAPS or external components to implement alternate processing logic. The use of Alert Agent and JMX-based Java CAPS component control are discussed in Chapter 10, sections 10.2.5 and 10.2.9.4.

13.3.2 Faults in Business Processes

13.3.2.1 JMS-Triggered Business Processes

Chapter 4, "Message Exchange Patterns," section 4.8.3, and Chapter 5, section 5.14.5.1, discuss eInsight capabilities for guaranteed delivery in the context of distributed transactions. A JMS-triggered eInsight Business Process, enrolled with a JMS Message Server–based distributed transaction, behaves differently from an ordinary eInsight Business Process. Applying XA to the entire Business Process, and marking suitable activities as "participating," makes it behave in much the same way as a Java Collaboration. Unhandled exceptions will cause a JMS message to be rolled back and redelivered according to the JMS redelivery handling configuration.

Section 13.3.1.1 described the behavior of transactional and nontransactional resources in the context of a transaction. The same behavior applies to Business

Processes under JMS-triggered XA. When a Business Process under XA experiences a fault that it does not handle, all transactional resources it invoked to that point will be rolled back, and all nontransactional resources will not be rolled back. Chapter 11, section 11.2.2.1, "JMS-Triggered Business Processes," in Part II, walks step-by-step through a solution that illustrates this behavior.

Imposing distributed transaction semantics onto an eInsight Business Process changes its behavior with respect to XA-capable and non-XA-capable resources it orchestrates. In the presence of unhandled faults, XA-capable resources are rolled back and non-XA-capable resources are not, as is to be expected.

As at release 5.1.3, only Business Processes triggered by JMS message delivery can be configured to operate as distributed transactions. While the XA property can be enabled for Business Processes triggered by other means, this will have no effect on the behavior, as no other resource that can trigger instance creation is XA-capable.

Because the XA Business Process is triggered by a JMS message, imposing distributed transaction semantics on that process effectively serializes it with respect to the JMS Destination. The process will behave the same way as a Java Collaboration receiving from a JMS Destination with Concurrency mode set to Serial in the receiver/subscriber connector on the connectivity map. Because the XA Business Process is serialized, its property Max Concurrent Instances value will be ignored and will have the effective value of 1.

In constructing XA Business Processes, care must be taken to ensure that lockable resources do not remain locked longer then necessary, as this can lead to resource contention and possibly to deadlocks. In particular, this means that XA should not be imposed on Business Processes that use correlations or user activities. Care must also be taken to appropriately design the handling of non-XA-capable resources with side effects, possibly using eInsight Compensation.

Note
XA transactionality in BPEL 1.0 Business Processes is nonstandard.

The foregoing discussion applies to eInsight Business Processes that explicitly or implicitly delegate fault handling to the eInsight invocation framework. Business Processes that explicitly handle faults behave much the same way whether they are XA-enabled or not, since only an unhandled fault triggers JMS rollback that affects XA-capable activities.

13.3.2.2 Fault Handlers

Exception and error events may occur during execution of business processes. In BPEL 1.0, these are named faults and can be handled by the Business Process or can be ignored. [BPEL4WS06] has a good introductory discussion of this topic. Java CAPS eInsight engine implements BPEL 1.0; therefore, it implements standard fault handling. Fault handlers for a set of activities are declared by enclosing relevant activities in a scope and associating a fault handler with that scope. A fault arising in any activity within the scope will be handled by the associated fault handler. This is similar to the try-catch scope in Java. There can be a number of fault handlers associated with a single scope, one of which can be a catch-all handler. Others must handle specific named faults. Since scopes can be nested, there may be a hierarchy of fault handlers in place. Fault handlers deeper in the hierarchy may rethrow faults to be handled by enclosing the scope's fault handlers, if any. A Last Chance fault handler can be associated with a Business Process. Its implicit scope is the entire process. If present, this handler will handle all faults not handled by handlers associated with specific scopes or rethrown by them.

Since BPEL orchestrates Web Services invocations, exceptions arising in invoked resources are really SOAP faults.

eInsight User's Guide release 5.1.3, Chapter 8, "Catching Exceptions within Business Processes," briefly discusses configuring exception handlers both at the scope and at the process level.

A fault handler, associated with a scope, may terminate the process instance as part of fault handling flow. If this is not the case, upon completion of the fault handler flow, the process will resume at the point following the end of the applicable scope. It is critical to remember this, as unexpected and difficult-to-diagnose side effects can arise if this point is missed. This point is illustrated in detail in Chapter 11, section 11.2.2.2, "Fault Handlers," in Part II.

When designing fault handling, care must be taken to ensure that activities are correctly scoped and that fault handlers explicitly terminate process instances if they are not to resume execution with the activity following the scope.

Scopes can be nested. Each scope can have zero or more named fault handlers and zero or one catch-all fault handlers.

Throwing a fault within a scope, handling it in an attached fault handler, and having the fault handling flow not invoke explicit terminate activity is equivalent to unconditional "jump to the first activity following the scope." This may or may not be a valid design technique, depending on your outlook on life.

Potentially every activity in a Business Process can result in a fault being thrown. An unhandled fault will be rethrown to the eInsight execution framework. This will result in process instance termination. A "detached" fault handler that will handle all faults not otherwise handled can be implemented. This handler, behaving as though associated with an implicit scope encompassing the entire process, can handle some faults and rethrow others as may be required.

Web Services invocations, Java Collaboration invocations, subprocess invocations, eWay invocations, and OTD marshals and unmarshals can all cause a fault. Handling of exceptions thrown by a Java Collaboration is shown in Chapter 13, section 13.2.9, "Create a Business Process," in Part II. Fault handlers for handling faults from other activities can be implemented in similar manner.

13.3.3 Higher-Level Exception Handling

Exception handling may involve not just using the Java- or BPEL-provided exception interception and handling constructs but also higher-order solution components that are involved in exception handling and alternate processing logic.

Chapter 9, "Messaging Endpoints," section 9.4.2, discussed how exceptions arising out of an inability to deliver a payload to an FTP server can be handled. The associated example shows how a failed transfer attempt can be retried, at intervals, until successful, or until a set number of retry attempts has been exceeded. Some of the exceptions, which the example handles, are temporary unavailability of the FTP server, invalid credentials, and other issues that prevent the Batch FTP eWay from connecting to the host. It is an example of a generic try-wait-retry exception handling pattern. jcdRetryResubmitter Java Collaboration, featured in the example, is an implementation of a generic JMS-based resubmission handler. At intervals, it polls a JMS queue containing messages to be resubmitted to another queue, inspects metadata carried as JMS message header user-defined properties, and, based on their values, resubmits the message to the queue to which they are supposed to be resubmitted. If the count of retry attempts exceeds the maximum retry attempt limit, it queues the message to the retries failed queue, thus ending the retry cycle.

Chapter 13, section 13.2, "Web Service, Stored Procedures, and XA," in Part II, contains an example of handling exceptions from New Web Services Java Collaborations, invoked from a Business Process. The process catches the exception, extracts the exception message, formats a SOAP Fault, and passes it onto the Web Services invoker.

13.4 Compensation

eInsight User's Guide [eInsight] for Java CAPS release 5.1.3 briefly discusses the topic of compensation. [BPEL4WS06] elaborates more on the topic of compensation in BPEL4WS. Neither source is particularly illuminating.

For those familiar with transaction-oriented systems, it may come as a surprise that BPEL 1.0's concept of a transaction is not the same as that to which they are accustomed. See an interesting discussion of BPEL4WS by Jean-Jacques Dubray [BPELDisc], including discussion of the Long Running Transactions (LRTs), which are "undoable" or "compensable." In compliance with BPEL4WS 1.0, eInsight supports compensation.

eInsight 5.1 implements distributed transaction support, in the XA sense, for Business Processes initiated by a JMS receive activity that use XA-capable resources such as databases. This is discussed, in the context of implementing different patterns, in Chapter 4, section 4.8.3; Chapter 5, section 5.14.5.1; and in this chapter, section 13.3.2.1. For circumstances where a Business Process is short-lived, is triggered by JMS, and orchestrates XA-capable resources, XA may be appropriate. In all other circumstances, it may be necessary to implement compensating activities to handle reversal of side effects when a process is aborted before completion.

It is critical to appreciate that a compensating activity is an independent activity that permanently modifies a resource much as the original activity, which is being compensated, permanently modified the resource in the first place. There is no notion of a transaction with Atomicity, Consistency, Isolation, and Durability (ACID) properties. As soon as an activity modifies the resource, the modification is visible to all other accessors. A lot can happen to the resource between the time it is modified and the time the modification may need to be compensated. This severely limits the kinds of modifications that can be reasonably undone through compensation or greatly increases complexity of the process that may need to perform compensation. Let's consider a couple of examples to illustrate the point.

Let's imagine a travel reservation process that orchestrates a number of Web Services to book an airline ticket, book a room in a hotel, or rent a car. Each of these services is binary in effect. The car is reserved or it is not. A seat is booked or it is not. A room is booked or it is not. If our process instance causes a room to be booked, no other process instance, or indeed no other accessor, can book the same room. If the process causes room booking first, and fails to book an airline seat, then to compensate for the failure it simply needs to invoke a cancel room service. Once the booking is cancelled through compensation, the room is as it was, unbooked. Any other accessor can book it from that point. The compensation activity "knows" in what state the resource was and restores it to its original state.

To contrast this, let's imagine a process that causes funds transfer between accounts. The first activity credits the target account with the sum to be transferred. The second activity debits the source account with the sum to be transferred. If the source account does not have the funds, debit operation fails and credit operation must be undone. To undo the credit, you would debit the same amount from the target account. Because the credit and debit activities are not part of an atomic transaction, it is possible that funds were withdrawn from the target account, by some other application, before the debit from the source account was actioned. If the compensating activity simply restores the target account's state to that before the credit, then the withdrawal by another application will be incorrectly overwritten. Someone will have gotten some money out of thin air. If the compensating activity debits the target account to reduce the balance by the amount originally credited, then the account could become overdrawn. Not a desirable state either. The long and the short of this discussion is that you must carefully consider the kinds of resources to which to apply compensation, and the implications and possible side effects of compensation on these resources.

Travel reservation is perhaps the most often quoted example of use of Web Services. It might be argued that BPEL was invented for these kinds of application. Funds transfer, on the other hand, would be a singularly inappropriate application of BPEL. Chapter 13, section 13.3, "Example Travel Reservation," in Part II, provides an extensive example of Web Services orchestration, including compensation, based on the simplified travel booking service.

13.5 High-Availability Architecture

By Brendan Marry

The Java CAPS high-availability architecture is intended to accommodate requirements of several applications. As different applications have different availability, load, and scalability requirements, the architecture discussed here is general in nature, and it must be reviewed and adapted for specific applications and workload characteristics.

The high-availability solution discussed here is required to implement intrasite high-availability and failover and intersite failover for disaster recovery. It discusses a logical architecture and outlines one of the possible hardware architectures that satisfy named requirements.

13.5.1 Introduction

A number of factors must be considered when architecting highly available, fault-tolerant, and resilient systems:

- What is connecting externally and internally to the integration layer?
- What are the system availability requirements?
- Can multiple hardware and software configurations be used for fault-tolerance, failover, and disaster recovery (intrasite)?
- Can multiple sites to be used for fault-tolerance, failover, and disaster recovery (intersite)?
- What are security zoning requirements, if any?
- What inherent resilience can be expected from each of the components?
- What are the hardware, CPU (threads), RAM, and shared storage requirements?

This section discusses Java CAPS component properties relevant to the discussion, resilience options, and fault-tolerance properties of different component distribution and replication strategies.

13.5.2 Java CAPS Platform Components

Let's consider components of the Java CAPS environment, design, management, and runtime; their resiliency requirements; and their ability to participate in resilient solutions.

13.5.2.1 Repository

The Java CAPS development environment uses a proprietary Repository to store design-time solution artifacts in hierarchical project structures. The application build process combines solution artifacts into Enterprise Archives that can be deployed to runtime environments hosted in Java EE-compliant Application Servers. As of Java CAPS release 5.1, runtime execution and management infrastructure do not depend on development infrastructure; consequently, the requirement to host the Repository on a highly available platform is eliminated.

13.5.2.2 Enterprise Manager

The Enterprise Manager, used for runtime management and monitoring of Java CAPS solution components, consists of the Enterprise Manager Server and a Web-based user interface. The execution environment does not depend on the Enterprise Manager Server; consequently, it is not necessary to host it on a highly available platform. Should the cluster node on which an instance of the Enterprise Manager is running fail, another instance can be readily started on the surviving node.

13.5.2.3 UDDI Registry

As Java CAPS–exposed Web Services are built, they are registered in the Java CAPS Universal Directory, Discovery, and Integration (UDDI) Registry. If the UDDI Registry is not available, WSDL definitions can be exported to the file system instead. In Java CAPS, by default, UDDI Registry is only used at build time. Through version 5.1.3, there are no runtime service discovery facilities in Java CAPS that use the UDDI Registry. The Java CAPS UDDI Registry does not need to be hosted on a highly available platform unless non-Java CAPS–based frameworks need to use it for dynamic runtime service discovery.

13.5.2.4 Integration Server

The Integration Server, or one of the supported Application Servers, provides the runtime environment for enterprise applications, whose components may include Java Collaboration, XSLT Collaboration, BPEL engines, and other application services and components. The ability of enterprise applications to withstand Integration Server failures is highly dependent on how they are designed. The design must incorporate provisions for high availability or must account for the possibility of application failure on one node and resumption on another node. Stateless applications and applications that do not rely on the order of messages are good candidates for load-balancing deployments. They are very much more likely to gracefully survive failures and node switch than applications that rely on preservation of context or message order. Applications exposed for external consumption, such as Web Services, are examples of stateless applications. Applications that implement message correlation are examples of context-dependent applications. The former can be load balanced, can run in Active/Active clusters, and can be switched between nodes in failover situations. The latter generally cannot be load balanced, run in Active/Active configurations, or be failed over without potential data loss.

eInsight Business Processes are expected to be long-running and therefore are more likely to be affected by platform failures. As of release 5.1, Java CAPS eInsight Business Process Manager is cluster-aware. An executing Business Process instance can be failed over from node to node in a cluster, as long as the Business Process does not use BPEL correlations and does not implement User Activities. To support instance failover, processes must use a single database that must be accessible to all instances of the BPEL engine. Furthermore, if processes access external resources such as databases or file system objects, the storage devices hosting these objects must be accessible to all nodes in the cluster.

Java Collaborations are expected to be short-lived. They operate within container-managed transactions. If the collaboration is invoked to process a JMS message and a node failure occurs, the JMS message will be rolled back. The message will become a candidate for processing on another node in the cluster. This will occur only if the JMS Message Server itself does not fail at the same time. If a collaboration is invoked by a non-XA-capable resource, such as HTTP GET or POST, the message that triggered it will be consumed and will not be available to be processed on another node. Message loss will occur.

It should be clear by now that the ability to build resilient, highly available, and scalable solutions is totally dependent on the nature and architecture of the applications.

13.5.2.5 Sun SeeBeyond JMS IQ Manager

The Java CAPS product suite comes bundled with a JMS Message Server, the Sun SeeBeyond IQ Manager. This Message Server is an implementation of the JMS 1.1 specification. The Sun SeeBeyond JMS IQ Manager is not cluster-aware; therefore, solutions that require high availability and fault tolerance will need to employ shared storage for JMS persistence and will have to operate in Active/Passive configurations.

13.5.2.6 Sun JMS Grid

The Sun JMS Grid, designed specifically for high availability and fault tolerance, is an alternative JMS 1.1 implementation available from Sun. It can be used standalone or in conjunction with the other Java CAPS products to provide reliable asynchronous communication between components in a distributed computing environment. An example Java CAPS solution using JMS Grid is discussed and illustrated in Chapter 5, section 5.7.

A JMS Grid system consists of one or more JMS Grid clusters, each with one or more JMS Servers (daemons), and one or more JMS Grid clients. Each JMS Grid daemon is expected to operate on an independent hardware configuration. Each JMS Grid daemon is responsible for managing client connections, delivery of messages to its clients, and replication of messages to other daemons in the cluster.

Each client is connected to a specific daemon with a socket connection. Messages are routed from the sending client, through one or more daemon processes, to one or more receiving clients. Message routing is managed by the JMS Grid cluster and is automatic. A sender client does not know or care to which daemon the recipient client is connected.

- JMS Grid cluster is a tightly coupled collection of daemon processes where all daemons are interconnected. Client connections are spread across the available daemons, and all message data is replicated to provide fault tolerance. This also gives greater scalability than the JMS IQ Manager, as several JMS message daemons are servicing client requests.
- JMS Grid network is a loosely coupled collection of JMS Grid clusters. Clusters in the network are typically located at different sites and are connected over a wide area network. Specific daemons are connected between clusters in the network and forward eligible messages between clusters. Only messages required to be delivered to a client on the remote cluster are sent between clusters. Clusters and networks of clusters together provide scalability and fault-tolerance.

Figure 13-5 depicts a JMS Grid cluster with three daemons.

The diagram in Figure 13-6 shows a cluster of three daemons in a failure scenario. If one of these daemons fails, then any clients connected to that daemon are automatically and transparently failed over and reconnected to another daemon in the cluster.

JMS Grid clusters add resilience, fault tolerance, and scalability to the JMS messaging infrastructure.

JMS Grid ensures guaranteed delivery of persistent messages between clients. This is achieved using a synchronous acknowledgment mechanism between clients and daemons. When a message is sent, the sending client waits for an acknowledgment from the daemon. The acknowledgment indicates the message has been persisted in the message store and is safe from system failure. At this point the client discards the message from its in-memory cache.

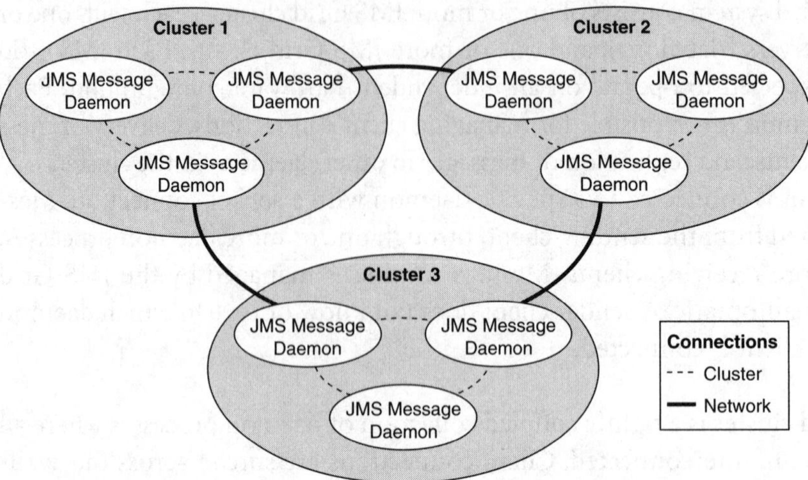

FIGURE 13-5: JMS Grid cluster with three daemons

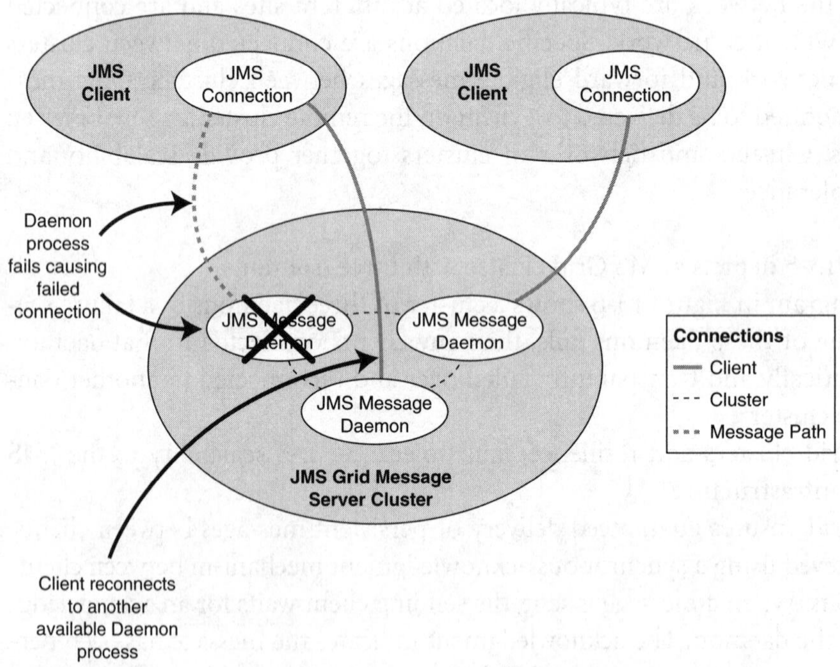

FIGURE 13-6: Automatic client failover on daemon failure

During the acknowledgment cycle, the daemon persists the message in its recoverable message store and sends replicas out to all other daemons in the cluster. It then waits for all the other daemons to send back acknowledgments that they have received and persisted each message replica. The daemon then sends an acknowledgment back to the receiving client. The process is depicted in Figure 13-7.

13.5.3 Application Connectivity

Let us consider a solution in which applications and interfaces will be deployed to a Java CAPS cluster with two or more nodes and which does not use JMS Grid. This configuration is depicted in Figure 13-8 and discussed here.

- Each application will connect to a database that stores application data.
- The JMS Message Service, which applications use, will persist messages using shared storage (SAN).

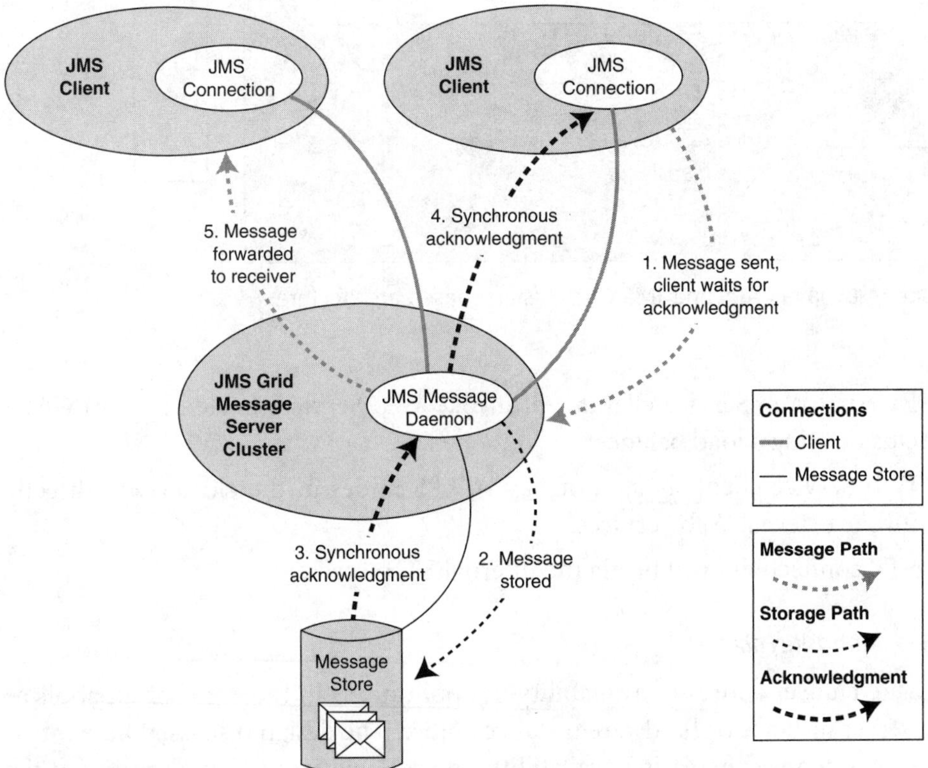

FIGURE 13-7: Guaranteed delivery with persistence process

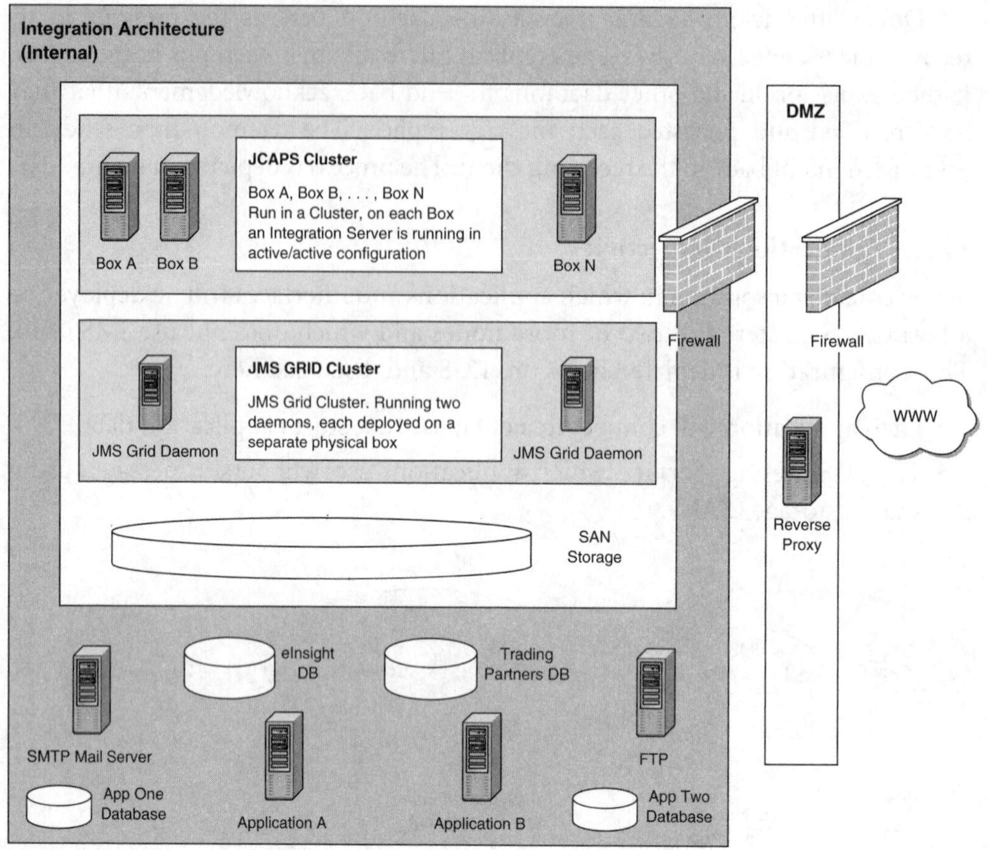

FIGURE 13-8: Java CAPS and JMS Grid clusters–based architecture

- External Web Service clients will invoke Web Services hosted by Java CAPS cluster using a load balancer.
- Web Service clients hosted on Java CAPS nodes in the cluster will directly invoke external Web Services.
- FTP connectivity will be via the internal FTP server.

13.5.3.1 Intrasite Failover

Intrasite failover addresses availability of applications in the event of an application server instance or hardware instance failure. The design discussed here introduces redundancy, increasing availability, and scalability of the applications at the single site.

An operating system cluster solution will increase horizontal scalability and provide application resilience. As the load on the cluster increases, additional nodes may be added. The cluster will monitor running instances of Java CAPS components. It will restart failed instances, if any, or will start instances on surviving cluster nodes if a node fails.

Note
JMS Grid could be used to address JMS Queue Manager resiliency without the need for shared storage.

If the Sun SeeBeyond IQ Manager process running on a node fails or the node on which the Queue Manager is running becomes unavailable, the cluster will start the IQ Manager on one of the surviving nodes. It will use the same IP address and port number. The use of SAN disks for storage of JMS persistence data introduces redundancy and protects against disk failure. Data stored on SAN disks is accessible from any node in the cluster that is currently running the IQ Manager. This is an example of an Active/Passive automatic failover configuration.

Integration Servers will be arranged in an Active/Active configuration with the same set of applications deployed on both cluster nodes. This will maximize throughput and increase scalability, as both nodes are running applications and therefore twice as many threads are executing application code. Having the same set of services running on each node in the cluster simplifies horizontal scalability and reduces complexity of the integration layer.

The load balancer is configured to deliver HTTP and TCP/IP requests to each of the running applications. Should one of the Integration Servers go down, the load balancer will deliver requests to the remaining Integration Servers. This configuration is depicted in Figure 13-9.

13.5.4 Intersite Failover Architecture

Intersite failover configuration improves availability of applications in the case of a site failure. The two sites (primary) Site A and (secondary) Site B are deployed. In the event of a disaster, the secondary site's Application Server is activated and begins receiving Web Services, HTTP, and TCP/IP request traffic from the load balancer.

A JMS Grid network or JMS persistence data replication using SAN storage replication would be implemented to ensure JMS messages are available to both

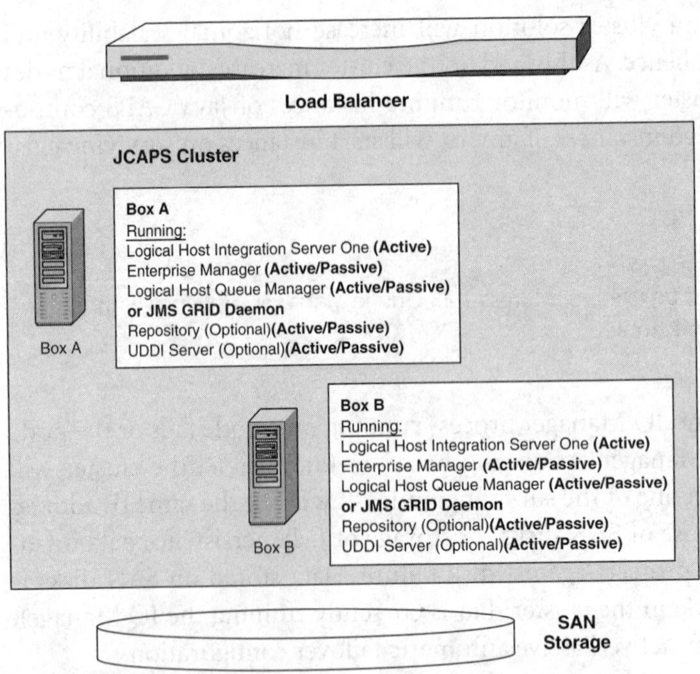

FIGURE 13-9: High-availability single-site configuration with HTTP and TCP load balancer

sites. If we assume that, after a failover, JMS Destinations are in the same state as they were on the failed site before the failure, processing of transactions will continue uninterrupted. However, implementation of this level of synchronization between sites incurs an unavoidable performance penalty. This configuration is depicted in Figure 13-10.

13.5.4.1 Queue Failover Options

As discussed, JMS Destination failover can be implemented using the JMS Grid or the JMS IQ Manager Persistence Store replication. The preferred option for a distributed architecture is JMS Grid because of its distributed capabilities.

JMS Grid clusters and networks can be used to implement guaranteed message delivery, replication, and fault tolerance of messages across both Site A and Site B.

JMS Grid network connections can withstand the connection going down for a period of time, as is sometimes the case with a WAN. In such situations, messages are simply stored on the sending cluster, ready to be forwarded when the connection is reestablished.

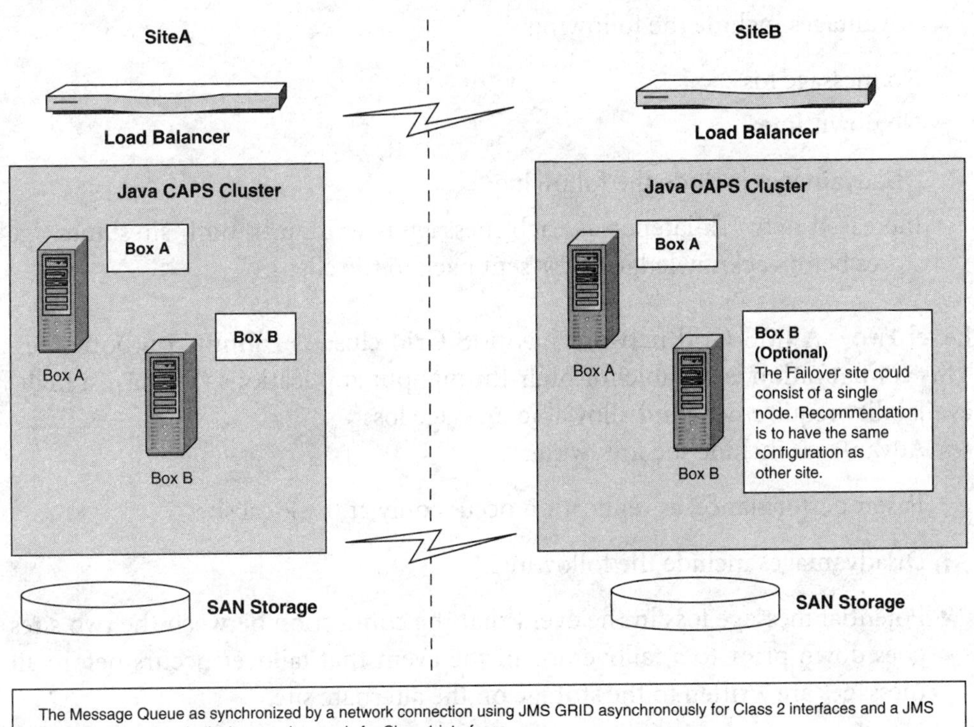

FIGURE 13-10: High-availability dual-site configuration with HTTP and TCP load balancers

This configuration gives the best for performance but has the disadvantage that messages may be lost. In the event that the connection between the sites goes down prior to a failover, or in the case where failover occurs before all messages are written to the storage on the Disaster Recovery (DR) site, messages not propagated to the alternate site become inaccessible or become lost.

13.5.4.3 JMS Grid-Based Replication

The preferred option for implementation for a distributed architecture is to implement two levels of replication. This is to give us options.

Level One A JMS Grid cluster is distributed between sites connected using a high-speed network. This configuration is appropriate for mission-critical applications that will tolerate no message loss and that require high availability.

Advantages include the following:

- No message loss.
- No downtime.

Disadvantages include the following:

- Increased network latency as each message is written to both sites' message stores before acknowledgment is sent back to the client.

Level Two A JMS Grid network has JMS Grid clusters running on both sites. This configuration is suitable for high-throughput applications that have a high-availability requirement and allowable message loss.

Advantages include the following:

- Faster performance, as replication occurs only at the local site.

Disadvantages include the following:

- Potential message loss in the event that the connection between the two sites goes down prior to a failover, or in the event that failover occurs before all messages are written to the storage on the alternate site.

13.5.4.3 Queue Manager Disk-Based Replication

This option relies on disk replication of the queue data from the primary Site A to the secondary Site B. This is the least preferred option and requires additional resources to be implemented.

13.5.5 Summary

For a highly available Java CAPS solution, in situations where costs are not a concern and the availability and fault tolerance of the integration environment are of the highest priority, consider the following suggestions:

- Java CAPS domains should be deployed in an Active/Active configuration managed by clustering software that will dynamically and horizontally scale the integration layer's processes.
- A JMS Grid cluster should be deployed to resiliently store and guarantee delivery of JMS messages among the Java CAPS domains.

- A load-balancing switch should be deployed to manage requests to the integration layer.
- A SAN storage configuration should be used for queue data and software component binaries.

To facilitate continuity of operation, it is suggested that the JMS Grid cluster be deployed over both the primary and secondary sites. In the case where availability and performance are the main concerns, it is suggested that a JMS Grid network consisting of two JMS Grid clusters, one on each site, be deployed.

As each environment and suite of applications/services may have different requirements, so too the high-availability architecture that is appropriate in different circumstances may vary.

13.6 Chapter Summary

Scalability and resilience are important in business solutions. These properties enable smooth operation as workload fluctuates and exceptional circumstances occur.

For scalability, Java CAPS solution components can be distributed over available infrastructure. This chapter discussed some approaches to distribution that varied depending on whether and to what extent eInsight Business Processes were involved. Business Processes refactoring in support of component distribution as well as distribution of eGate components were discussed.

Resilience, the ability of a solution to withstand disruptions caused by expected or unexpected exceptions, is greatly influenced by solution design. Exception interception and handling properties of the tools greatly influence the designer's ability to construct resilient solutions. Some solutions require exception handling that spans multiple components at the business level rather than the technical level. This chapter discussed exception and fault handling features of Java Collaborations and eInsight Business Processes as well as component spanning exception handling. Constructing highly available solutions that take advantage of hardware and infrastructure software was also discussed.

Together, all the features and options can be used by an enterprise architect to design and implement solutions that have the desired degree of resilience and scalability.

CHAPTER FOURTEEN

Security Features

14.1 Introduction

This chapter discusses standard security features available to solutions developed using Java CAPS or hosted in the Java CAPS Integration Server. In particular, HTTP Basic Authentication, Secure Sockets Layer (SSL), Secure batch eWay variants, and configuration of Hypertext Transfer Protocol (HTTP) and Hypertext Transfer Protocol over SSL (HTTPS) Proxy are discussed.

14.2 HTTP Proxy Server Configuration

By Peter Vaneris

A Web Proxy is an infrastructure component that mediates HTTP protocol exchanges between internal clients and external servers. In some circumstances, you may be required to connect to an external HTTP Server, whether a Web Server or a Web Service provider, via an HTTP Proxy Server. All Java CAPS components are hosted, at runtime, by the Integration Server. Configuration of HTTP and HTTPS Proxy will vary from Application Server to Application Server. For the Sun SeeBeyond Integration Server and the Sun Java System Application Server 8.x, you need to configure appropriate Java Virtual Machine (JVM) properties. Available proxy configuration options are discussed below.

To require all clients using the HTTP or the HTTPS protocol to use a Proxy Server, the following JVM properties can be set, indicating the host name/address and the port number of the proxy:

```
-DproxyHost=<ProxyServer.domain.com>
-DproxyPort=<ProxyServerPort>
```

To require all clients using the HTTP protocol, as distinct from the HTTPS protocol, to use a Proxy Server, the following JVM properties can be set, indicating the host name/address and the port number of the proxy:

```
-Dhttp.proxyHost==<ProxyServer.domain.com>
-Dhttp.proxyPort=<ProxyServerPort>
```

To require all clients using the HTTPS protocol, as distinct from the HTTP protocol, to use a Proxy Server, the following JVM properties can be set, indicating the host name/address and the port number of the proxy:

```
-Dhttps.proxyHost==<ProxyServer.domain.com>
-Dhttps.proxyPort=<ProxyServerPort>
```

To provide an exclusion list, the list of hosts for which the proxy is not to be used when HTTP protocol is used, the following JVM property can be set, listing fully qualified or wildcarded names of hosts, separated by a pipe character ("|").

```
-Dhttp.nonProxyHosts=edesigner*|emanager*|localhost
```

Note

The Enterprise Manager is referenced by both short host name and fully qualified domain name during a single session, so the hostname* covers both.

Similarly, -Dhttps.nonProxyHosts can be set to exclude hosts when the HTTPS protocol is used.

The diagram in Figure 14-1 shows HTTP communications between a Java CAPS domain and other typical components in an environment when a Proxy Server is used.

14.3 HTTP Basic Authentication

This section assumes familiarity with the theory behind the HTTP Basic Authentication mechanism. See RFC 2616 for a detailed explanation of HTTP, HTTP Basic Authentication, and related matters [HTTP].

HTTP Basic Authentication in Java CAPS is configured independently for the HTTP Client and the HTTP Server. The HTTP Client supplies credentials that

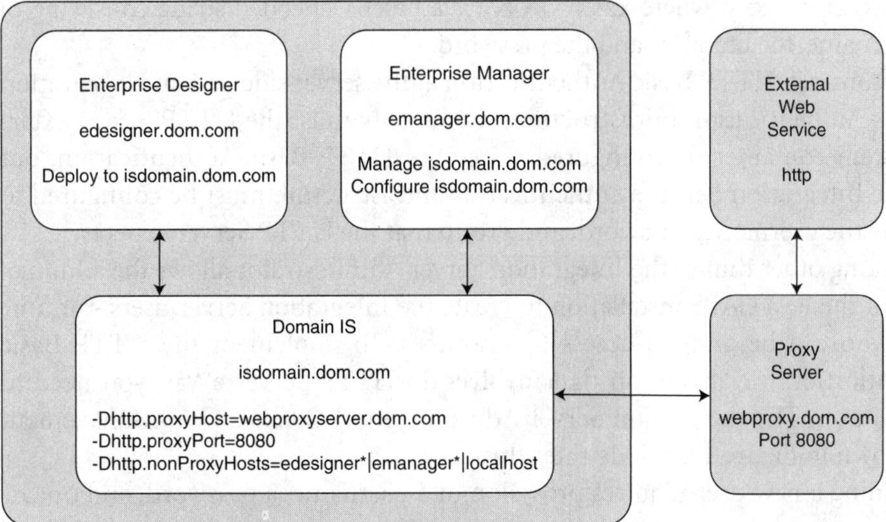

Figure 14-1: Communication in a Java CAPS environment with an HTTP Proxy

are validated against some server's authentication infrastructure. Any authentication infrastructure that might exist at the client does not get used.

You supply HTTP Basic Authentication credentials for the HTTP Client eWay through the HTTP Client external system container in the eDesigner Environment Explorer, as shown in Figure 14-2.

Needless to say if a different username/password is required for different deployments, each variation requires its own HTTP Client external system container. The runtime effect is to supply an Authentication HTTP header with the value of

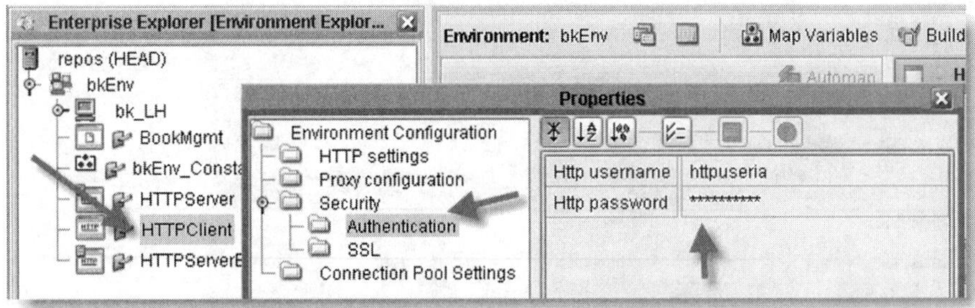

Figure 14-2: HTTP Client properties for HTTP Basic Authentication credentials

BASIC xxxxxxxxxxx, where xxxxxxxxxxx is a base64-encoded string consisting of the username, the literal ":" and the password.

In contrast, HTTP Basic Authentication at the server side uses the Integration Server's Authentication infrastructure, so not only must the HTTP Server external system container be configured to require HTTP Basic Authentication, but also the Integration Server's authentication infrastructure must be configured to support the username, password, and group that the HTTP Server expects.

Among other things, the Integration Server Administrator allows the administrator of the Java CAPS installation to create the Integration Server users–runtime users who can be granted access to resources. To implement the HTTP Basic Authentication for a solution that involves an HTTP Server eWay, you need to create a user. The Integration Server Administration Console User Management tab, shown in Figure 14-3, illustrates this.

Adding a new user requires provision of a username, a password, and one or more group names, as shown in Figure 14-4. These group names are not defined elsewhere, but one is required to configure HTTP Basic Authentication in the HTTP Server external system container.

To force HTTP Clients to use HTTP Basic Authentication, the HTTP Server external system container must be configured to require HTTP Basic Authentication. This is illustrated in Figure 14-5.

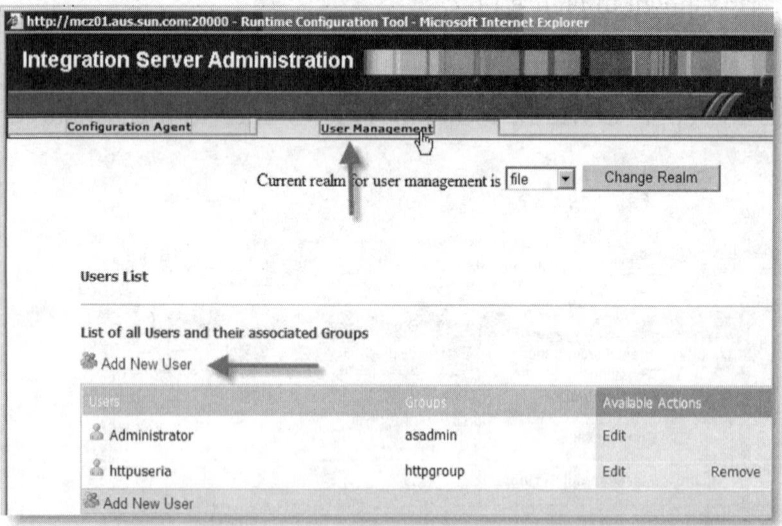

FIGURE 14-3: Adding Integration Server users

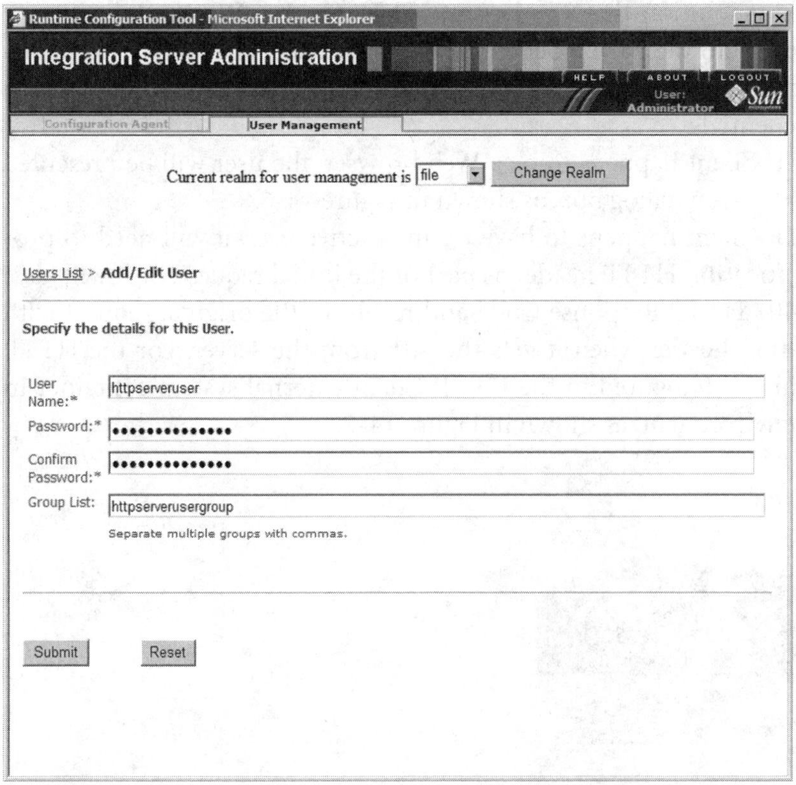

FIGURE 14-4: Providing user credentials and group membership

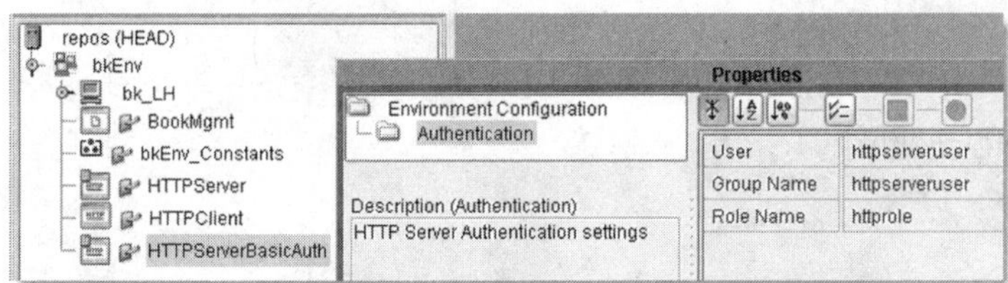

FIGURE 14-5: Requiring HTTP Basic Authentication credentials at the server side

Note the Group Name and Role Name properties. Values for these properties must be supplied; otherwise the HTTP Basic Authentication will not be enabled, but, at least through version 5.1.3, they are not used. Note also the group and role J2EE Web Container concepts. HTTP Basic Authentication has no concept of groups and roles; therefore it does not carry this information.

If you build a solution that involves an HTTP Server eWay and deploy the HTTP Server eWay to the HTTP Server container whose HTTP Basic Authentication is configured, at runtime the HTTP Client will be required to provide appropriate credentials.

If the HTTP Client happens to be a Web browser, the user will be presented with an Authentication dialog box, as shown in Figure 14-6.

If the HTTP Client happens to have no interactive user, it will need to provide the Authentication HTTP header as part of the initial request, or it will have to handle the 401 HTTP Response Code and resubmit the original request with the Authentication header when it gets the 401 from the server. For the HTTP Client eWay, this is configured in the HTTP Client external system container in the eDesigner environment, as shown in Figure 14-7.

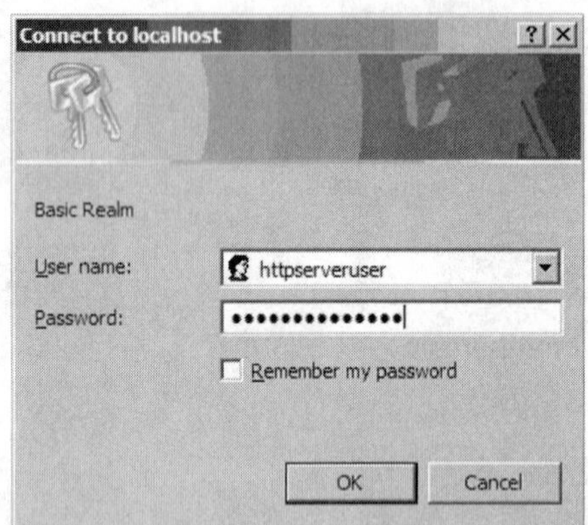

FIGURE 14-6: Authentication dialog box

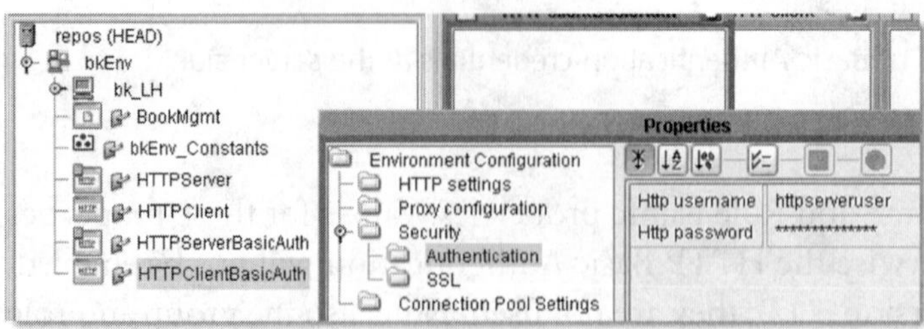

FIGURE 14-7: Supplying credentials at the Client side

At runtime, the HTTP Client eWay will use these values to create the required Authentication HTTP header that will be sent as part of the HTTP GET or POST request.

Note that if the HTTP Server eWay is deployed to an HTTP Server external system container in which HTTP Basic Authentication is not enabled, or in which it is misconfigured, no HTTP Basic Authentication will be required of the client. To prevent this from allowing unauthorized access to resources, a Java Collaboration would contain a conditional expression evaluating an authentication type header and returning a 401 Unauthorized status if not present or incorrect.

The code fragment in Listing 14-1, which assumes that the input to the collaboration is an HTTP Server eWay connector, will do the trick.

LISTING 14-1: Programmatically require HTTP Basic Authentication

```
if (input.getRequest().getAuthType() == null
|| !input.getRequest().getAuthType().equalsIgnoreCase( "BASIC" )) {
    input.getResponse().setErrorStatusCode( 401 );
    input.getResponse().setErrorStatusMsg
        ( "Invalid Request - Expected BASIC Authentication" );
    input.sendResponse();
    return;
}
```

14.4 Secure Sockets Layer (SSL, TLS)

With the advent of electronic commerce over the Internet, "secure" Web sites were typically required to provide security for submission of credit card details so that the details did not get disclosed to third parties. Transmission Control Protocol (TCP)-based HTTP protocol does not inherently provide confidentiality features necessary to prevent malicious parties from obtaining credit card details by snooping on the wire. Early in the life of the World Wide Web, two competing solutions were proposed: Secure HTTP [S-HTTP][RFC2660] and Secure Sockets Layer [SSL], subsequently standardized as Transport Layer Security (TLS) [TLS]. As history demonstrated, the SSL and its Internet Engineering Task Force (IETF) standardized reincarnation, TLS, became widely deployed for use in both the World Wide Web deployments and other applications layered over HTTP, most notably Web Services. Since TLS version 1 .0 is effectively an IETF officially blessed SSL version 3.0, the acronym SSL is used henceforth to also mean TLS. SSL implementations provide communications privacy for applications using the Internet. The protocol allows client/server applications to communicate in a way that is designed to prevent eavesdropping, tampering, or message forgery.

The need for SSL arose out of the need to ensure that submission of credit card information to an eCommerce Web site is confidential and that the Web site to which credit card information is being submitted is indeed the Web site to which the browser user intended to submit that information. This calls for confidentiality and Web Server Authentication. Confidentiality is obtained by encrypting the channel between the browser and the server. Server Authentication is obtained by requiring that the server sends its X.509 Certificate to the browser. The (human) browser is expected to verify that the X.509 Certificate is indeed the certificate of the Web Server to which the (human) browser is prepared to disclose credit card information. The technical details of how encryption and certificate conveyance are carried out are documented in the Requests for Comments and elsewhere.

There are a few important points to note about the SSL protocol:

1. SSL protocol has a notion of a session that is established between the client and the server when the SSL handshake has been successfully completed.
2. When the SSL handshake is in progress, the client and the server negotiate which cryptographic algorithm to use, among other things.
3. SSL has a notion of anonymous key exchange method; when this method is used no certificates are used for key exchange.
4. The negotiated cryptographic algorithm may not be the strongest that either the client or the server is capable of supporting.
5. Outside North America, SSL implementations by default use the "export" cipher suites, which are considered weak.
6. To use "strong" algorithms, Java-based implementations may require download of unlimited strength cryptographic policy file and reconfiguration of the runtime environment to support these algorithms.
7. Authentication of server to client, client to server, or mutual authentication are all optional. If anonymous key exchange is used, the server is considered anonymous: it does not send its certificate to the client. Whether the server is anonymous or not depends on its SSL configuration.

Note

The X.509 Certificate does not convey any meaning apart from the fact that some Certification Authority, which issued the certificate, is prepared to vouch that the public key embedded in the certificate is associated with the identity (person or organization) also specified in the certificate.

Note

Possessing a public key that you are sure belongs to Joe allows you to encrypt information with confidence that it can only be read by Joe. This confidence is provided by your trust in Bob's assertion of the relationship between Joe and Joe's Public Key and your confidence that the asymmetric cryptographic algorithm you use is strong enough to protect what information you wish to send to Joe in confidence. None of this has any relevance to SSL/TLS, since:

- SSL/TLS uses symmetric cryptography for encrypting data on the wire.
- A secure channel is established between the client software implementation and the server software implementation, not between you and Joe.
- Any data can be carried over an encrypted channel. There is no association between the channel and the data it carries; therefore authenticity of the sender or receiver is not carried over to the data that travels over the channel.
- The data that enters the secure channel can come from anywhere and can go anywhere after it leaves—a secure channel does not guarantee data security before it enters the channel or after it exits.
- Once data leaves the secure channel, any authenticity implied by it having come out of the channel is no longer valid.

Note

To make it plain: Bob, whom you may or may not know, and whom you may or may not trust, tells you that the public key with Joe's name on it belongs to Joe. You must decide whether you trust what Bob tells you and whether Joe is the Joe with whom you wish to communicate. Bob does not tell you that Joe is a good and trustworthy person, and even if he did, that is a piece of information that neither the public key nor the certificate has anything to do with.

The SSL allows the server to send its certificate to the client. So that the client does not need to obtain and install beforehand certificates of all possible parties with whom it may communicate, the client accepts this certificate if it is signed by a trusted Certification Authority. The client keeps certificates of trusted certification authorities in a truststore. Effectively, any server whose certificate is signed by a Certification Authority, whose certificate is in the client's truststore, is trusted.

In normal interaction with a secure eCommerce site, the client is the party that needs assurances as to the identity of the server. The server does not require the client to authenticate as it gets customer's credit card information, which is enough for payment to be obtained from the customer. Authenticity of the client (customer's browser) is irrelevant and not sought. This is termed *server-side authentication.*

In other circumstances the server may require the client to authenticate before service is provided. The SSL supports this by allowing the server to be configured such that after it sends its certificate to the client, it requires the client to send the client's certificate back as part of the SSL handshake. This is termed *mutual authentication.*

The identity of the party with whom the Public Key is associated through the X.509 Certificate is expressed using a number of attributes. One of these attributes may be a hostname when the subject of the certificate is a TCP host. SSL implementations can be configured to expect that the hostname attribute embedded in the certificate, which the server sends to the client, matches the hostname that the TCP implementation reports as the hostname of the host with which the client is communicating. Requiring hostname match is intended to prevent rogue sites from masquerading as legitimate sites. If the implementation is configured this way, and the hostname changes, the certificate has to be reissued. This causes expense or inconvenience or both. How to deal with such issues is a site decision.

In summary, endpoints in a secure channel can be configured to support server-side authentication or mutual authentication and can be configured to require or ignore hostname validation.

In Java CAPS, the HTTP eWay and the Web Services communications infrastructure support channel security using SSL. The rest of this chapter discusses how channel security can be configured for HTTP eWay–based applications.

Chapter 12, section 12.2, "Secure Sockets Layer (SSL, TLS)," and its subsections in Part II (located on the accompanying CD-ROM), illustrate the following discussion with complete implementation examples, including log exhibits with SSL handshake interaction traces. Server-side authentication and mutual authentication for the HTTP infrastructure as well as server-side and mutual authentication for eInsight Web Services infrastructure are covered with detailed implementation steps and execution traces.

The HTTP eWay in the Client mode can be configured to attempt to establish an SSL session with the HTTP Server, validate the Server's X.509 Certificate, and optionally validate the server's hostname against the Distinguished Name of the host for which the X.509 Certificate has been issued. The eWay can also be configured to respond to the server's request for mutual authentication with the appropriate X.509 Certificate.

14.4.1 HTTP eWay Client and Server Projects

14.4.1.1 HTTP Server/Responder

The HTTP Server external container in the environment does not have any properties that pertain to SSL.

14.4.1.2 HTTP Listener Port Assignments

By default, port basePort+1 is the plain, clear-text HTTP listener port. The server-side authentication secure channel uses port basePort+4, which is already configured when the domain is created. The mutual authentication channel will need to be created to listen on a port of its own. Default port assignments for an Integration Server start at BasePort+0 and go through basePort+8. Let's assume we have basePort+9 available and will use it to configure the SSL listener for mutual authentication. Figure 14-8 illustrates typical port assignments.

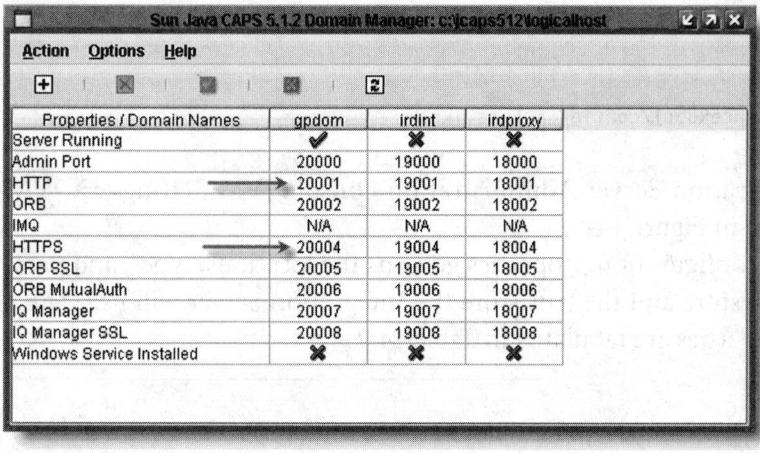

Properties / Domain Names	gpdom	irdint	irdproxy
Server Running	✔	✖	✖
Admin Port	20000	19000	18000
HTTP	20001	19001	18001
ORB	20002	19002	18002
IMQ	N/A	N/A	N/A
HTTPS	20004	19004	18004
ORB SSL	20005	19005	18005
ORB MutualAuth	20006	19006	18006
IQ Manager	20007	19007	18007
IQ Manager SSL	20008	19008	18008
Windows Service Installed	✖	✖	✖

FIGURE 14-8: Typical domain port assignments

14.4.2 HTTP eWay Clear Text Channel

14.4.2.1 Configuring the Server

There is no need to configure the Web container to support a clear-text HTTP channel. The listener on port basePort+1 was created at domain creation time and is ready to use.

Note that whether we are using the clear-text or the secure channel, the responder implementation is identical. SSL handshake and channel encryption operate at the transport layer. The responder implementation does have a way of knowing what kind of channel was used.

14.4.3 HTTP eWay Server-side Authentication

14.4.3.1 Configuring the Server

The Sun SeeBeyond Integration Server in a domain is configured at domain creation time to support clear-text HTTP channel on port basePort+1 and an SSL channel on an alternate port using an alternate listener. By default, the SSL listener is configured on port basePort+4, it is enabled, it has "access control" turned on, it supports SSL and TLS, and it does not require client authentication. This is the kind of listener that is required for SSL server-side authentication.

When the domain is created, the name and location of the keystore and the truststore, which the SSL listener will use, are defaulted to:

```
${com.sun.aas.instanceRoot}/config/keystore.jks
```

and

```
${com.sun.aas.instanceRoot}/config/cacerts.jks
```

through the Integration Server Administration console JVM Settings → JVM Options, as shown in Figure 14-9.

A set of JVM configuration properties governs the locations, types, and passphrases for the keystore and the truststore the Integration Server will use. These configuration properties are tabulated in Table 14-1.

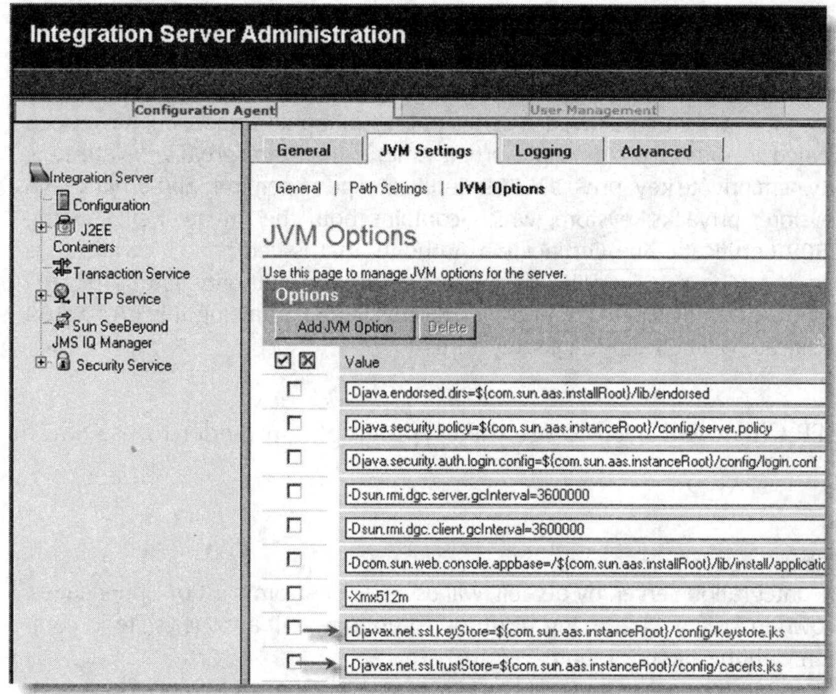

FIGURE 14-9: Providing SSL-related JVM options

TABLE 14-1: SSL-Related JVM Configuration Properties

javax.net.ssl.keyStore	Specifies the location of the keystore containing the server's Private Key. There is no default location.
javax.net.ssl.keyStoreType	Specifies the KeyStore file type. The default is the default KeyStore type: e.g., KeyStore.getDefaultType().
javax.net.ssl.keyStorePassword	Specifies the password to be used with this KeyStore.
javax.net.ssl.trustStore	Specifies the location of the TrustStore. If specified, this overrides jssecacerts and cacerts.
javax.net.ssl.trustStoreType	Specifies the KeyStore file type. The default is the default KeyStore type: e.g., KeyStore.getDefaultType().
javax.net.ssl.trustStorePassword	Specifies the password to be used with this KeyStore.

Note
Chapter 15, "Cryptographic Objects", in Part II, walks through the process of obtaining an End Use X.509 Certificate for the test party whose alias is "prtya." When the steps are followed, a series of cryptographic objects will have been created in directory c:\tmp\pki\prtya. Among them are prtya's Private Key, prty.pem.private.key; prtya's X.509 Certificate, prtya.pem.cer; and prtya's Java Keystore, prtya.jks.keystore, which contains both the Private Key and the X.509 Certificate. The Certification Authority that issued prtya's certificate is DemoCA. The X.509 Certificate of the Certification Authority, c:\tmp\pki\ca\DemoCA\DemoCA.pem.crt, and the JKS truststore containing this CA's X.509 Certificate will be DemoCA.jks.keystore.

The HTTP Client will need to use the cryptographic provider to use SSL or TLS.

Note
The Integration Server, by default, will use a cipher from a list of cipher suites, shown in Listing 14-2, trying from top to bottom until a cipher suite in common with the client is found.

LISTING 14-2: Default cipher suites

```
SSL_RSA_WITH_RC4_128_MD5
SSL_RSA_WITH_RC4_128_SHA
TLS_RSA_WITH_AES_128_CBC_SHA
TLS_DHE_RSA_WITH_AES_128_CBC_SHA
TLS_DHE_DSS_WITH_AES_128_CBC_SHA
SSL_RSA_WITH_3DES_EDE_CBC_SHA
SSL_DHE_RSA_WITH_3DES_EDE_CBC_SHA
SSL_DHE_DSS_WITH_3DES_EDE_CBC_SHA
SSL_RSA_WITH_DES_CBC_SHA
SSL_DHE_RSA_WITH_DES_CBC_SHA
SSL_DHE_DSS_WITH_DES_CBC_SHA
SSL_RSA_EXPORT_WITH_RC4_40_MD5
SSL_RSA_EXPORT_WITH_DES40_CBC_SHA
SSL_DHE_RSA_EXPORT_WITH_DES40_CBC_SHA
SSL_DHE_DSS_EXPORT_WITH_DES40_CBC_SHA
```

14.4.3.2 Configuring the Client

Unlike the HTTP Server connector in the connectivity map and the external system in the environment, which do not have properties relating to SSL support, the HTTP Client external system in the environment has properties that need to be configured to enable SSL. Figure 14-10 shows a connectivity map with an HTTP Client connector.

The HTTP Client external system in the environment must also be created and its properties configured to support SSL, as shown in Figure 14-11. Table 14-2 enumerates the properties used to configure SSL at the client side and the values used in the example implementation.

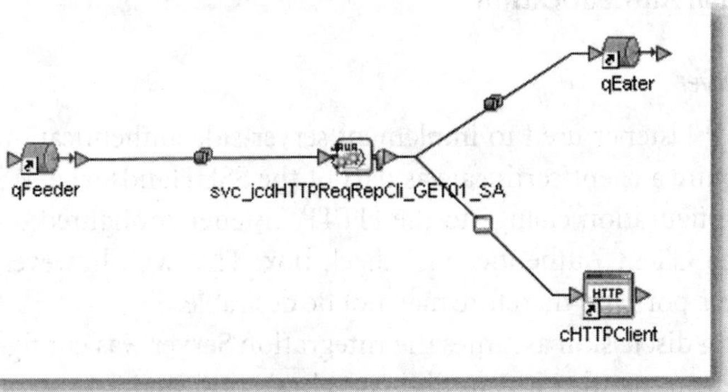

FIGURE 14-10: _Book/SecurityFeatures/SSL_HTTP/cm_jcdHTTPReqRepCli_GET01_SA

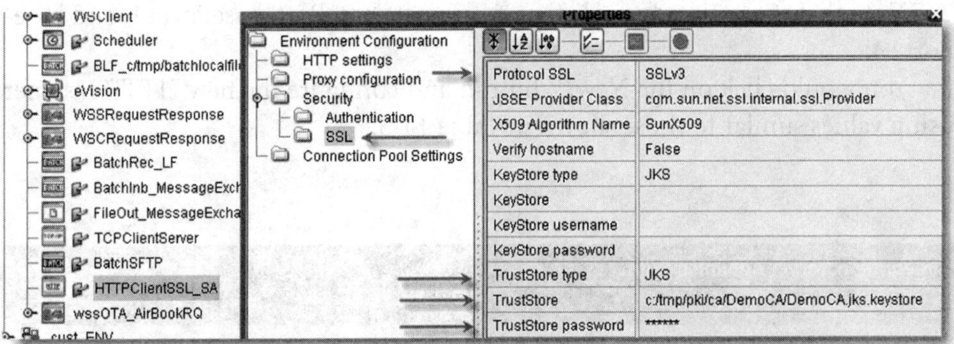

FIGURE 14-11: SSL properties of the HTTP Client connector

TABLE 14-2: HTTP Client SSL Configuration Properties

javax.net.ssl.trustStore	c:\tmp\pki\ca\DemoCA\DemoCA.jks.keystore
javax.net.ssl.trustStoreType	JKS
javax.net.ssl.trustStorePassword	democaexport

Note that because the secure channel is using Server-Side Authentication mode, meaning the client does not need to provide its certificate to the server, the keystore parameters are not configured. Note, too, that the external system is configured to use SSL version 3 protocol, as distinct from TLS version 1, or SSL version 2, all of which are supported by the eWay.

14.4.4 HTTP eWay Mutual Authentication

14.4.4.1 Configuring the Server

The Web Container/HTTP Listener used to implement server-side authentication was not configured to require a client certificate as part of the SSL Handshake. We could make the trivial configuration change to the HTTP Listener configured on basePort+4 and check the Client Authentication check box. This will, however, affect all connections to this port and therefore may not be desirable.

Note that the following discussion assumes the Integration Server was configured to support server-side authentication, as discussed in section 14.4.3.1.

To support mutual authentication, you must create and configure a completely independent HTTP Listener using port basePort+9, assumed to be available. HTTP Listeners available by default are shown in Figure 14-12.

Note that there already are listeners on ports basePort, basePort+1, and basePort+4.

You would click on the New... button and configure the new HTTP Listener using values similar to those shown in Table 14-3.

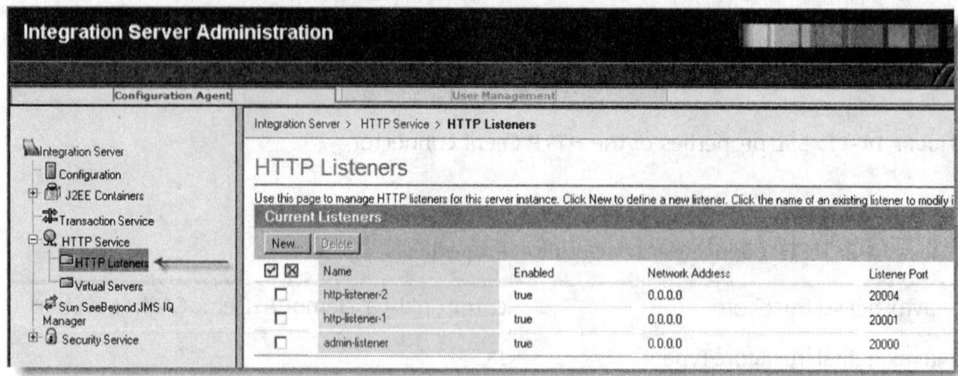

FIGURE 14-12: HTTP Listeners in a domain

fication Authority that signed the client's certificate. It so happens that both prtya's and prtyb's X.509 Certificates were issued by DemoCA, and DemoCA's certificate is in the truststore used by both the client and the server. Table 14-4 enumerates properties that must be configured and their values used for the HTTP Client in the example. Figure 14-14 shows these properties and their values in eDesigner.

Notice that we are still not requiring hostname verification and that the truststore configuration is the same as that used for an HTTP Client in server-side authentication mode.

Configuring the keystore allows the HTTP eWay to find the X.509 Certificate it is required to return to the server when requested.

14.4.4.3 Exercising the Channel

Even with the mutual authentication configured, the HTTP Requester collaboration is unaware that a secure channel was used to submit the HTTP Request and

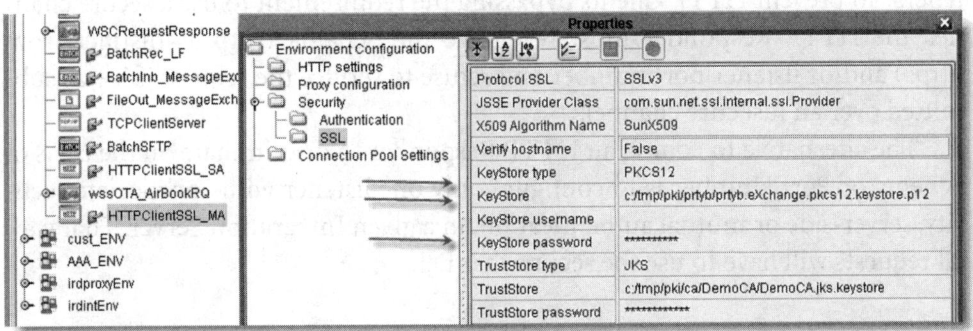

FIGURE 14-14: HTTP Client properties used to configure SSL with mutual authentication

TABLE 14-4: HTTP Client Configuration Properties Used for SSL with Mutual Authentication

javax.net.ssl.keyStore	c:\tmp\pki\prtyb\prtyb.eXchange.pkcs12.keystore.p12
javax.net.ssl.keyStoreType	PKCS12
javax.net.ssl.keyStorePassword	prtybprtyb
javax.net.ssl.trustStore	c:\tmp\pki\ca\DemoCA\DemoCA.jks.keystore
javax.net.ssl.trustStoreType	JKS
javax.net.ssl.trustStorePassword	democaexport

return the HTTP Response. It can work this out through the schema property value, https, but it is not provided with any indication of what the requester identity was. Mutual authentication happens at the transport level. If authentication fails, the responder collaboration is never invoked.

14.4.5 SSL in Java CAPS HTTP eWay Use Notes

Java CAPS does not provide the means of conveying a requester's identity—for example, the Distinguished Name embedded in the X.509 Certificate submitted to the HTTP Responder by the client on request from the server. The HTTP Responder, not knowing requester's identity, cannot perform further Authentication or Authorization. The only conclusion the responder can draw from the request is that it came from a party whose X.509 Certificate was acceptable to the Integration Server.

With three HTTP Listeners configured in the Integration Server, an HTTP Client can communicate with the same HTTP Responder using either of the listeners. To prevent HTTP Clients bypassing the requirement to use a secure channel, the HTTP Responder must recognize the Schema (http as distinct from https) and/or listener port number and refuse to service the request if it was submitted over an insecure channel.

The alternative to coding an HTTP Responder to discriminate on the basis of Schema or Port Number is to configure only one listener with appropriate security, server-side or mutual authentication, in a given Integration Server. That way, all requests will have to use the secure channel.

14.4.6 Strong Cipher Suites

To enable strong cipher support outside North America, you may need to download and install Java Cryptography Extension (JCE) Unlimited Strength Policy Files for J2SE 5 (Java CAPS's Integration Server uses Sun JDK 5). J2SE 5 site is http://java.sun.com/javase/downloads/index_jdk5.jsp. To install Unlimited Strength Policy files, unzip the downloaded archive, jce_policy-1_5_0.zip, and copy the four files it contains to the following directory, then restart the Integration Server.

```
<JCAPSInstallRoot>\logicalhost\jre\lib\security
```

Once the server is restarted, the cipher suites in Listing 14-4 become available for use, with additional 256-bit cipher suites, enabled by installation of the Unlimited Strength Policy files marked with *.

LISTING 14-4: Cipher suites added by the Unlimited Strength Policy installation

```
SSL_RSA_WITH_RC4_128_MD5
SSL_RSA_WITH_RC4_128_SHA
TLS_RSA_WITH_AES_128_CBC_SHA
TLS_RSA_WITH_AES_256_CBC_SHA *
TLS_DHE_RSA_WITH_AES_128_CBC_SHA
TLS_DHE_RSA_WITH_AES_256_CBC_SHA *
TLS_DHE_DSS_WITH_AES_128_CBC_SHA
TLS_DHE_DSS_WITH_AES_256_CBC_SHA *
SSL_RSA_WITH_3DES_EDE_CBC_SHA
SSL_DHE_RSA_WITH_3DES_EDE_CBC_SHA
SSL_DHE_DSS_WITH_3DES_EDE_CBC_SHA
SSL_RSA_WITH_DES_CBC_SHA
SSL_DHE_RSA_WITH_DES_CBC_SHA
SSL_DHE_DSS_WITH_DES_CBC_SHA
SSL_RSA_EXPORT_WITH_RC4_40_MD5
SSL_RSA_EXPORT_WITH_DES40_CBC_SHA
SSL_DHE_RSA_EXPORT_WITH_DES40_CBC_SHA
SSL_DHE_DSS_EXPORT_WITH_DES40_CBC_SHA
```

None of the new cipher suites, nor a number of other cipher suites, show up as choices in the Integration Server Administration console, as illustrated in Figure 14-15.

To force the Integration Server or the HTTP Client to use specific cipher suites, you must add a JVM Option, https.CipherSuites, as discussed in section 14.4.3.1.

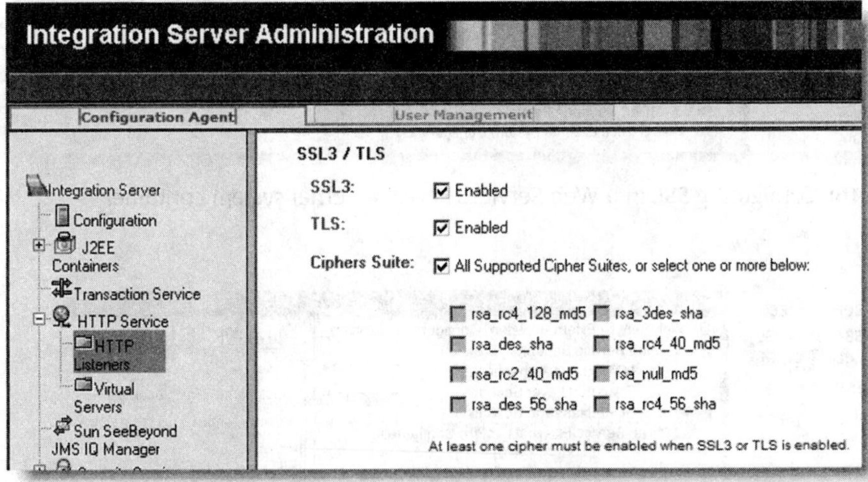

FIGURE 14-15: Cipher suites available for configuration through the Integration Server Administration console

14.4.7 Web Services and SSL

Configuration of the Integration Server, required to support Web Services over SSL channel with server-side and mutual authentication, is the same as required to support HTTP eWay–based solutions using server-side or mutual authentication (see sections 14.4.3.1 and 14.4.4.1). Let's assume that the HTTP Listener on port basePort+4 is configured to support server-side authentication and the HTTP Listener on port basePort+9 is configured to support mutual authentication; now let's create, configure, and deploy a Web Services Server and Web Services Clients.

14.4.7.1 Server-side Authentication Channel

In section 14.4.3.1, configuration of the secure channel HTTP Listener, on port basePort+4, was reviewed and modified to support server-side authentication. Server-side authentication for Web Services will use the same HTTP Listener.

Properties of the external system container must reflect our intention here—use SSL (Transport Guarantee CONFIDENTIAL), as shown in Figure 14-16.

The service container configuration, from the port, host, and servlet context perspective, must agree between the client and the server containers. Configuration of the server container is illustrated in Figure 14-17.

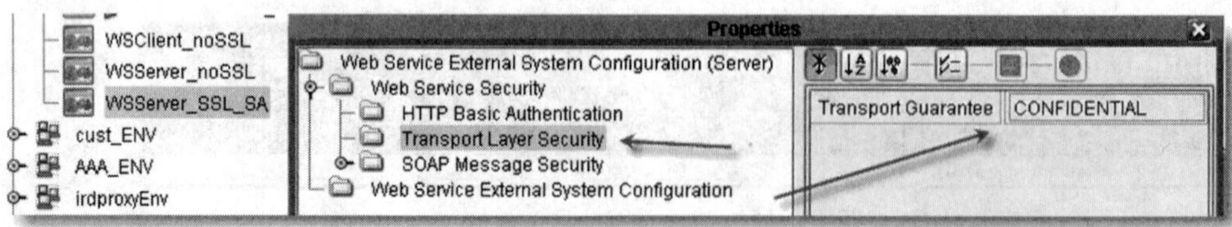

FIGURE 14-16: Configuring SSL in a Web Services Server external system container

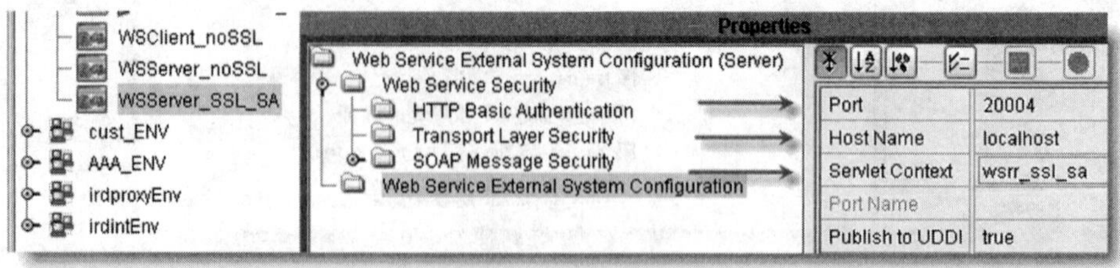

FIGURE 14-17: HTTP-related configuration properties in the Web Services server container

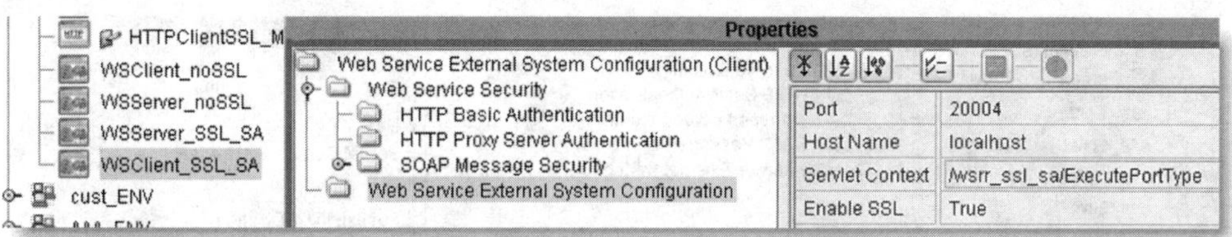

FIGURE 14-18: HTTP-related configuration properties in the Web Server Client container

Properties of the external system container must reflect our intention—SSL and the servlet context used by the Web Services implementation, as illustrated in Figure 14-18, for the Web Server Client container.

In Figure 14-18, port 20001 is our basePort+4, server-side authentication HTTP Listener, and the servlet context is the context from the WSDL published to the UDDI Registry.

14.4.7.2 Mutual Authentication Channel

In section 14.4.4.1, configuration of the secure channel HTTP Listener, on port basePort+4, was reviewed and modified to support server-side authentication. Server-side authentication for Web Services will use the same HTTP Listener.

Properties of the external system container must reflect our intention here—use SSL (Transport Guarantee CONFIDENTIAL), as shown in Figures 14-19 and 14-20.

Properties of the client external system container must reflect our intention—SSL and the servlet context used by the Web Services implementation, as shown in Figure 14-21.

In Figure 14-21, port 20009 is our basePort+9, mutual authentication HTTP Listener, and the servlet context is the context from the WSDL published to the UDDI Registry.

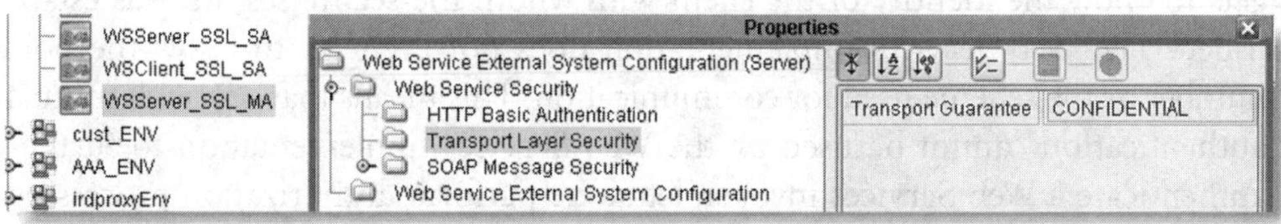

FIGURE 14-19: Enabling SSL for the Web Services Server external system container

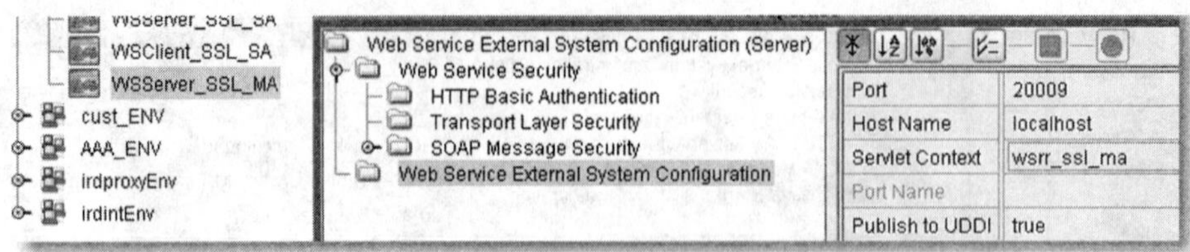

FIGURE 14-20: Web Services Server container's HTTP-related properties

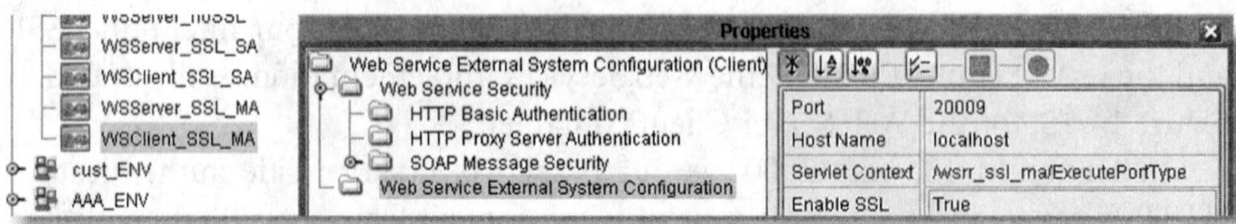

FIGURE 14-21: HTTP-related configuration properties in the Web Services Client container

Unlike in the case of the HTTP Client eWay, when configuring Web Services for SSL with mutual authentication, the Web Service external system container provides no properties to configure the path, type, and passphrase of the keystore from which to send the client's certificate. The Web Services external system container uses the keystore configured for the Integration Server to which the project, of which it is a part, is deployed.

14.4.7.3 SSL in Java CAPS Web Services Notes

Unlike in the case of the HTTP eWay, there is no property to configure to enable or disable Host Name Verification. Web Services Client infrastructure does not verify hostname.

The Web Services implementation in SSL with mutual authentication never gets to know the identity of the client with whom the secure session was established. The Web Services implementation does not even get to know the port number or the scheme used for communication. This means that SSL with mutual authentication cannot be used by the Web Services implementation to further authenticate a Web Services invoker, let alone perform authorization processing of any kind.

14.5 Secure Batch FTP Variants

Organizations needing to exchange large volumes of data over the Internet seek to protect both their internal systems and the data they are exchanging from malicious individuals. They place firewalls between the Internet and their internal networks to minimize the exposure of internal resources and minimize vulnerability of software exposed to the Internet. If confidentiality is of importance, they seek to secure data transfers by encrypting the channel over which data travels or encrypting the data itself. Interposing a firewall between a client and a server introduces complexities and, depending on the protocol in use for data transfers, prevents data exchange. Requiring data encryption necessitates the use of client and server software with interoperable support for data encryption.

Discussion on setting up the infrastructure necessary to develop and test specific examples of secure variants of the Batch eWay is well beyond the scope of this section. The rest of the section briefly discusses the variants, giving their provenance and major restrictions.

Over the years a number of methods of facilitating firewall traversal and securing data transfers were developed and standardized. Java CAPS Batch eWay includes file transfer variants that support the most common, standardized methods. It supports the plain old FTP protocol, the "firewall-friendly" variant with passive transfers, Socks-based Firewall traversal, and other "secure" variants of file transfer.

The original FTP protocol (RFC 959) suffers from the design flaw that makes it unfriendly to firewalls. It uses two independent channels for transferring "command" messages and "data" messages. The command channel, typically using TCP Port 21, is opened by the client with the server as the destination. The data channel, typically using TCP Port 22, is opened by the server with the client as the destination. This requires that the firewall, if present, allows inbound connections from the Internet to the internal network it is protecting. This is generally a very bad thing from the security perspective. Note that FTP protocol does not include any features that provide confidentiality and integrity for data transfers.

To overcome the security issue of inbound connections for the data channel, a "passive FTP" extension (RFC 1579) was adopted. Rather then attempting to connect to the client for data transfer, the FTP server creates a data channel listener and passes the TCP port the listener uses to the client in the response message. The client uses that port number to establish connection to the server and allow data transfer to commence. Although firewall-friendly, passive FTP still does not provide data integrity and confidentiality protection. In this sense, data transfers are still not secure.

At about the same time, a method was proposed to allow TCP- and User Datagram Protocol (UDP)-based applications to traverse firewalls using modified library implementations and firewall-hosted packet forwarding servers. Socks (RFC 1928) allows an application that does not have direct access to the Internet to reach out through the firewall and connect to an external service. It does so by replacing a standard connectivity library with a "socksified" version. When the application makes a "connect" or a "send" call, the library transparently redirects the call to the "Socks Server" residing at the firewall. The Socks Server makes the connection or performs the send on behalf of the application and thereafter intermediates in the message exchange process for the rest of the session or message exchange. Hopefully, the Socks Server implementation is written in such a way that an attacker cannot exploit vulnerabilities in its code to gain access to internal resources. This security feature still does not provide data integrity and confidentiality protection. Data traverses the firewall but is not encrypted or secured in any other way.

FTP over SSL (RFC 2228, RFC 4217) is implemented in the FTPOverSSL Batch eWay variant. See the RFCs for protocol details. FTP over SSL allows the channels over which data is transferred to be encrypted. Data is secured when in transit. Both Implicit and Explicit modes are supported.

SSH Tunneling support in the Batch eWay allows encryption of the command channel on the premise that user credential must be secured. Since the data channel is not encrypted, the transfer still cannot be considered secure.

Secure file transfer with the Batch SFTP [SecSHFileXfer] and Batch SCP eWay variants uses corresponding features of the Secure Shell (SSH) (RFC 425, 4251, 4252, 4253, 4254) implemented in these eWay variants. Secure FTP (SFTP), a subprotocol of the SSH, is designed to facilitate transfer of files between hosts. Since the SSH channel is encrypted, all data traversing it is encrypted. SFTP is not a derivative of the original FTP but rather is a redefinition of the file transfer protocol leveraging the SSH. Secure Copy Protocol (SCP) is also a subprotocol of SSH. Both SFTP and SCP facilitate transfer of files over an encrypted channel.

Which "secure" file transfer method, if any, to use in specific circumstances will heavily depend on which protocol the remote party supports and what security qualities are required. FTP over SSL requires the use of certificates with considerations similar to these for HTTP over SSL. The use of SSH-based file transfers requires an operating system account on the remote server. SSH Tunneling only secures the command channel but not data exchange. The use of Socks requires a Socks Server. None of the secure file transfer methods protect data before it is transferred or after it is transferred.

14.6 Chapter Summary

This chapter discussed standard security features available to solutions developed using Java CAPS or hosted in the Java CAPS Integration Server. In particular, HTTP Basic Authentication, SSL, Secure batch eWay variants, and configuration of HTTP and HTTPS Proxy were discussed.

Bibliography

[AlertAgent]
Sun SeeBeyond Alert Agent User's Guide, Release 5.1.3, Sun Microsystems, Inc., 2007.

[Batch_eWay]
Sun SeeBeyond eWay Batch Adapter User's Guide, Release 5.1.3, Sun Microsystems, Inc., 2007.

This manual provides details of installing, configuring, and using the Batch eWay Adapter.

[BPEL4WS]
"Business Process Execution Language for Web Services, Version 1.1," BEA, IBM, Microsoft, SAP AG, Siebel Systems, May 2003. Available: http://download.boulder .ibm.com/ibmdl/pub/software/dw/specs/ws-bpel/ws-bpel.pdf (accessed April 2007).

[BPEL4WS01]
"Business Process with BPEL4WS: Understanding BPEL4WS, Part 1," Sanjiva Weerawarana and Francisco Curbera, IBM TJ Watson Research Center, August 1, 2002. Available: http://www-128.ibm.com/developerworks/webservices/library/ ws-bpelcol1/ (accessed September 2006).

[BPEL4WS06]
"Business Process with BPEL4WS: Learning BPEL4WS, Part 6," Rania Khalaf and William Nagy, IBM TJ Watson Research Center, March 1, 2003. Available: http:// www-128.ibm.com/developerworks/webservices/library/ws-bpelcol6/ (accessed September 2006).

[BPELDisc]
BPEL4WS, Jean-Jacques Dubray. Available: http://www.ebpml.org/bpel4ws.htm (accessed March 2007).

[Cookie]

"HTTP State Management Mechanism," RFC 2109, D. Kristol and L. Montulli, February 1997. Available: http://www.cse.ohio-state.edu/cgi-bin/rfc/rfc2109.html (accessed August 2006).

[cXML]

cXML/1.0, Ariba, Inc., August 1999. Available: http://www.cxml.org/files/cxml.pdf (accessed April 2007).

[ebXMLMS]

Message Service Specification, Version 2.0, OASIS ebXML Messaging Services Technical Committee, 1 April 2002, Organization for the Advancement of Structured Information Standards (OASIS), April 2002. Available: http://www.oasis-open.org/committees/ebxml-msg/documents/ebMS_v2_0.pdf#search=%22ebxml%20message%20service%20oasis%22 (accessed September 2006).

[eDesigner]

Sun SeeBeyond eGate Integrator User's Guide, Release 5.1.3, Sun Microsystems, Inc., 2007.

This manual introduces the eGate Integrator platform and discusses the features and facilities provided in the Enterprise Designer IDE.

[eGateSAG]

Sun SeeBeyond eGate Integrator System Administration Guide, Release 5.1.3, Sun Microsystems, Inc., 2007.

This manual covers all aspects of Java CAPS system administration, including monitoring, configuration, LDAP integration, JMX interfaces, security, and Web Services deployment.

[eInsight]

Sun SeeBeyond eInsight Business Process Manager User's Guide, Release 5.1.3, Sun Microsystems, Inc., 2007.

This manual covers all aspects of the eInsight Business Process Manager, both design and runtime.

[EIP]

Enterprise Integration Patterns: Developing, Building, and Deploying Messaging Solutions, Gregor Hohpe and Bobby Woolfe, Addison-Wesley 2005, ISBN 0321200683.

This book provides the theoretical framework that describes the patterns used in real-life enterprise integration solutions.

[File_eWay]

Sun SeeBeyond eWay File Adapter User's Guide, Release 5.1.3, Sun Microsystems, Inc., 2007.

This manual provides details of installing, configuring, and using the File eWay Adapter.

[HTML401]

"HTML 4.01 Specification," World Wide Web Consortium, Recommendation REC-html401-19991224, Dave Raggett, Arnaud Le Hors, and Ian Jacobs, December 1999. Available: http://www.w3.org/TR/1999/REC-html401-19991224/ (accessed September 2006).

[HTTP]

"Hypertext Transfer Protocol—HTTP/1.1," RFC 2616, R. Fielding, J. Gettys, J. Mogul, H. Frysyk, L. Masinter, P. Leach, and T. Berners-Lee, June 1999. Available: http://www.faqs.org/rfcs/rfc2616.html (accessed August 2006).

[ISO8601]

ISO 8601, "Data elements and interchange formats—Information interchange—Representation of dates and times." Available: http://en.wikipedia.org/wiki/ISO_8601 (accessed March 2007).

[ISP8601Ref]

ISO 8601, From Wikipedia, the free encyclopedia. Available: http://en.wikipedia.org/wiki/ISO_8601 (accessed September 2006).

[Java CAPS Documentation]

As at July 2007, Java CAPS 5.1.x documentation is available on the main Sun Microsystems' Documentation Site, http://docs.sun.com/app/docs/prod/sj.caps#hic, under Software → Enterprise Computing → Sun Java Systems Suites → Sun Java Composite Application Platform Suite (Java CAPS).

[JConsole]

Mandy Chung, "Using JConsole to Monitor Applications," December 2004. Available: http://java.sun.com/developer/technicalArticles/J2SE/jconsole.html (accessed April 2007).

[JMSAPIC]

Sun SeeBeyond eGate API Kit for JMS IQ Manager (C/C++ Edition), Release 5.1.3, Sun Microsystems, Inc., 2006.

This manual discusses all aspects of the C- and C++-based API to the Sun SeeBeyond JMS Message Server implementation.

[JMSAPICOM]

Sun SeeBeyond eGate API Kit for JMS IQ Manager (COM+ Edition), Release 5.1.3, Sun Microsystems, Inc., 2006.

This manual discusses all aspects of the Microsoft COM+-based API to the Sun SeeBeyond JMS Message Server implementation.

[JMSAPIJ]

Sun SeeBeyond eGate API Kit for JMS IQ Manager (Java Edition), Release 5.1.3, Sun Microsystems, Inc., 2007.

This manual discusses all aspects of the Java-based API to the Sun SeeBeyond JMS Message Server implementation.

[JMSGridUserGuide]

Sun Java Message Service Grid User's Guide, Release 5.1.3, Sun Microsystems, Inc., 2007.

[JMSREF]

Sun SeeBeyond eGate Integrator JMS Reference Guide, Release 5.1.3, Sun Microsystems, Inc., 2007.

This manual discusses all aspects of the Sun SeeBeyond JMS Message Server implementation.

[JMSSpec]

Java Message Service, Version 1.1, Sun Microsystems, Inc., April 2002. Available: http://java.sun.com/products/jms/docs.html (accessed June 10, 2006).

This document specifies the Java Message Service API.

[JMXNote]

"Monitoring Local and Remote Applications Using JMX 1.2 and JConsole," Russell Miles, September 2004. Available: http://www.onjava.com/pub/a/onjava/2004/09/29/tigerjmx.html?page=1 (accessed April 2007).

[JMXNote2]

"Monitoring and Management Using JMX," Sun Microsystems, Inc. Available: http://java.sun.com/j2se/1.5.0/docs/guide/management/agent.html (accessed April 2007).

[MC4J]

"MC4J Management Console." Available: http://mc4j.org (accessed April 2007).

[OMG]

The Object Management Group (OMG). Available: http://www.omg.org (accessed April 2007).

[PBPEI]

Patterns and Best Practices for Enterprise Integration, Gregor Hohpe. Available: http://www.enterpriseintegrationpatterns.com (accessed May 8, 2006).

[RFC822]
"Standard for the Format of ARPA-Internet Text Messages," STD 11, RFC 822, UDEL, D. Crocker, August 1982. Available: http://www.sendmail.org/rfc/0822.html (accessed September 2006).

[RFC2660]
"Request for Comments: 2660, The Secure HyperText Transfer Protocol," E. Rescorla and A. Schiffman, Network Working Group, IETF, August 1999. Available: http://www.javvin.com/protocol/rfc2660.pdf (accessed December 2006).

[SecSHFileXfer]
"SSH File Transfer Protocol, draft-ietf-secsh-filexfer-13.txt," J. Galbraith and O. Saarenmaa, Secure Shell Working Group, Internet-Draft, July 10, 2006. Available: http://tools.ietf.org/wg/secsh/draft-ietf-secsh-filexfer/draft-ietf-secsh-filexfer-13.txt (accessed February 2007).

[S-HTTP]
"An Overview of S-HTTP," Adam Shostack, May 1995. Available: http://www.homeport.org/~adam/shttp.html (accessed December 2006).

[SOAP1.1]
W3C Note "Simple Object Access Protocol (SOAP) 1.1," Don Box, David Ehnebuske, Gopal Kakivaya, Andrew Layman, Noah Mendelsohn, Henrik Nielsen, Satish Thatte, and Dave Winer, May 8, 2000. Available: http://www.w3.org/TR/2000/NOTE-SOAP-20000508/ (accessed September 2006).

[SOAP1.2]
W3C Recommendation, "SOAP Version 1.2 Part 1: Messaging Framework," Martin Gudgin, Marc Hadley, Noah Mendelsohn, Jean-Jacques Moreau, and Henrik Frystyk Nielsen, June 24, 2003. Available: http://www.w3.org/TR/soap12-part1/ (accessed September 2006).

[SSL3]
"The SSL 3.0 Protocol," A. Frier, P. Karlton, and P. Kocher, Netscape Communications Corp., November 18, 1996. Available: http://wp.netscape.com/eng/ssl3/draft302.txt (accessed December 2006).

[TLS]

"Request for Comments: 2246, The TLS Protocol, Version 1.0," T. Dierks and C. Allen, Network Working Group, IETF, January 1999. Available: http://www.ietf.org/rfc/rfc2246.txt (accessed December 2006).

[Tutorial]

Sun SeeBeyond Integrator Tutorial, Release 5.1.3, Sun Microsystems, Inc., 2007.

This document introduces major components of the eGate Integrator and walks through the implementation of three sample projects.

[UBL]

"Universal Business Language 1.0," OASIS Committee Draft, September 2004. Available: http://docs.oasis-open.org/ubl/cd-UBL-1.0/ (accessed April 2007).

[UDDI]

UDDI Specifications, Best Practices and Technical Notes. Available: http://www.uddi.org/specification.html (accessed April 2007).

[WSDL]

"Web Services Description Language (WSDL) 1.1," W3C Note 15, Erik Christensen, Francisco Curbera, Greg Meredith, and Sanjiva Weerawarana, March 2001, Copyright © 2001 Ariba, International Business Machines Corporation, Microsoft. Available: http://www.w3.org/TR/2001/NOTE-wsdl-20010315 (accessed April 2007).

[XMLSchema]

XML Schema Part 1: Structures, Second Edition, W3C Recommendation, October 28, 2004. Available: http://www.w3.org/TR/xmlschema-1 (accessed August 2006).

Index

D

E

F

J

N

T

CD-ROM Warranty

Prentice Hall warrants the enclosed CD-ROM to be free of defects in materials and faulty workmanship under normal use for a period of ninety days after purchase (when purchased new). If a defect is discovered in the CD-ROM during this warranty period, a replacement CD-ROM can be obtained at no charge by sending the defective CD-ROM, postage prepaid, with proof of purchase to:

Disc Exchange
Prentice Hall
Pearson Technology Group
75 Arlington Street, Suite 300
Boston, MA 02116
Email: AWPro@aw.com

Prentice Hall makes no warranty or representation, either expressed or implied, with respect to this software, its quality, performance, merchantability, or fitness for a particular purpose. In no event will Prentice Hall, its distributors, or dealers be liable for direct, indirect, special, incidental, or consequential damages arising out of the use or inability to use the software. The exclusion of implied warranties is not permitted in some states. Therefore, the above exclusion may not apply to you. This warranty provides you with specific legal rights. There may be other rights that you may have that vary from state to state. The contents of this CD-ROM are intended for personal use only.

More information and updates are available at: informit.com/ph